CADOGANguides

MW00526795

BARCELONA & CATALONIA

'These are people who bottle their own bubbly – cava from the Penedès – and like to have a glass with their tapas in the early afternoon. A few of them drink it for breakfast.'

Dana Facaros & Michael Pauls

About the Guide

The full-colour introduction gives the authors' overview of the region, together with suggested itineraries and a regional 'where to go' map and feature to help you plan your trip.

Illuminating and entertaining cultural chapters on local history, art, architecture, food, wine and culture give you a rich flavour of the region.

Planning Your Trip starts with the basics of when to go, getting there and getting around, coupled with other useful information, including a section for disabled travellers. The Practical A–Z deals with all the essential information and contact details that you may need while you are away.

The regional chapters are arranged in a loose touring order, with plenty of public transport and driving information. The author's top 'Don't Miss' ⭐ sights are highlighted at the start of each chapter.

A language and pronunciation guide and a comprehensive index can be found at the end of the book.

Although everything we list in this guide is personally recommended, our authors inevitably have their own favourite places to eat and stay. Whenever you see this Author's Choice ⭐ icon beside a listing, you will know that it is a little bit out of the ordinary.

Hotel Price Guide (*see also* p.55)

Luxury	€€€€€	over €250
Very expensive	€€€€	€160–250
Expensive	€€€	€100–160
Moderate	€€	€70–100
Inexpensive	€	under €70

Restaurant Price Guide (*see also* p.59)

Very expensive	€€€€	over €60
Expensive	€€€	€30–60
Moderate	€€	€20–30
Inexpensive	€	under €20

About the Authors

Dana Facaros and Michael Pauls have written over 40 guides for Cadogan. They live just outside Greater Catalonia in Southwest France, but visit as often as possible.

1st edition published 2009

A Frenzy of Festivals

The question in Catalonia is not only where to go, but when. The Catalans know how to throw a party. A hardly exhaustive sampling of the best would include:

1 *Calçotada* in Valls, slurping barbecued green onions by the bushel in January.

2 Carnival in Sitges and Barcelona, in February.

3 *Sant Anastasi* in Lleida, with the world's biggest snail-eating festival, in May.

4 *La Patum* in Berga, madness and devilry during Corpus Christi.

5 *Nit de Sant Joan* (St John's Night), midsummer festival with bonfires, fireworks, and dancing throughout the region in June.

Top: Santa Tecla
Above: Nit de
Sant Joan

6 *L'Aplec de la Sardana*, Olot's big Catalan music and dance festival, in July.

7 *Aquelarre* in Cervera, with witches, dragons and monsters, in August.

8 *Festa de la Mercè*, a huge party in Barcelona, with over 600 events, in September.

9 *Santa Tecla* in Tarragona, in October.

10 *Fires de Sant Narcís*, Girona, in late October.

Above, left: castellars (human castles)

Above, right: gegants (giants)

Catalan Eccentricities

The Catalans, as you'll soon notice, do things differently, and since 2004 they have found a new symbol to express their difference: *el ruc català*, the big-headed Catalan donkey (*equus asinus var. catalana*). As only 400 or so donkeys still exist, a couple of young conservation-minded Barcelonins created a bumper sticker to attract attention to its cause, partly as a joke. It instantly filled a hunger for a national symbol: an ass to stand up to the bull of Spain. Often it will be masked ('it reminds us of Zorro', as one of them explains it). But you don't have to scratch too hard to find other Catalan eccentricities:

1   Dalí and Gaudí: two world-class oddball geniuses.

2   Eating chocolate flies in Girona.

3   The habit of stacking themselves into human towers (the *castellers*).

4   A mania for choral music, perfected in the Palau de la Música Catalana.

5   An insatiable lust for snails, pig's trotters and charred green onions.

6   Combining cookery with chemistry in the laboratory of Ferran Adrià.

7   *Caganers* (poopers) in the Christmas crib and the *Tío* log, that 'excretes' sweets on Christmas Day.

8   A fiendish obsession with the great god Design.

9   Museums dedicated to anchovies and salt (L'Escala), shoes (Barcelona), clogs (Meranges), and cork (Palafrugell).

10 A fondness for *Cap Grossos* and *Gegants* ('fat heads' and 'giants') who march in every traditional procession.

An Edifice Complex

No one can doubt that the Catalans have a way with bricks and mortar. The Modernista revolution in the late 19th century was based on skills passed down since the Middle Ages, especially in the construction of arches and vaults. Completing Gaudí's Sagrada Família in Barcelona – the biggest, most protracted and most expensive building project in Europe – demonstrates they still have their old world record-breaking spirit. Some other wonders include:

1 The works of the Catalans' teachers, the Romans, at Tarragona, including a great aqueduct, p.249, and amphitheatre, p.248, and the dome at Centcelles, p.250

2 The Saló de Tinell, with the widest masonry arches ever built, next to the skyscraper-like Mirador of King Martí, both part of the Palau Reial in Barcelona, p.84

3 The Cathedral of Girona, p.206, with the widest nave outside of St Peter's in Rome; Santa Maria del Mar in Barcelona is nearly as good, p.96

4 The shallow vaulting in the crypt of La Seu (cathedral), p.86 and under the choir of Santa Maria del Pi, both in Barcelona, p.92

5 A hundred medieval stone bridges: the one at Besalú has a distinctive dogleg, p.215

6 Figueres's 18th-century Castell Sant Ferran, above and below ground, p.198

7 Gaudí's Crypt at the Colonia Güell, Santa Coloma de Cervelló, p.158

8 Unique village churches by Jujols in the Camp de Tarragona, p.257

9 Domènech i Montaner's Hospital de la Santa Creu i Sant Pau, Barcelona, p.119

10 Modernista wine bodegas by Cesar Martinell (the best are in Gandesa, p.279, and El Pinell de Brai, p.280) and Codorníu in Sant Sadurní by Puig i Cadafalch, p.162

Right: Domènech i Montaner's Hospital de Santa Creu i Sant Pau, Barcelona

By the Sea

Catalonia's coast is one of its glories, with huge stretches of sand and massive beach resorts, but it also has some seriously beautiful nooks to seek out.

1 Stunning Cadaqués, Portlligat and Cap de Creus National Park, and the strange rocks that inspired Dalí, p.191

2 The coastal path from Calella de Palafrugell to the beaches below Begur, p.180

3 L'Estartit's Illes Medes, a protected marine park, with all kinds of aquatic flora and fauna, p.182

4 Tossa de Mar, the only walled medieval town right on the sea, with a breathtaking corniche road, p.174

5 Barceloneta, Barcelona's old seaside quarter, with city-centre beaches and seafood restaurants, p.104

6 The seaside gardens at Blanes and Lloret de Mar, p.173

7 Canet del Mar, with the home of Domènech i Montaner, p.147

8 Pretty, fun-filled Sitges, for decadent days on the beach, p.164

9 The lovely cove of Garraf, with its pretty whitewashed bathing huts, p.164

10 The Ebro Delta, with its wild beaches full of driftwood and clouds of pink flamingoes, p.274

Above: Cadaqués
Left: Illes Medes
Right: Cap de Creus

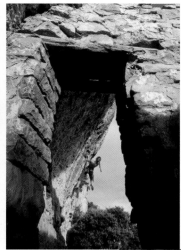

Climb Every Mountain

The Pyrenees are the most famous, but they don't have a monopoly on stunning mountain scenery. Even when you're in the middle of Barcelona, you can escape by public transport into the Collserola hills and forget you're in the big city altogether.

1 The Parc Nacional de Aigüestortes, p.322, and the Vall de Boí, in the high Pyrenees, p.319
2 Parc Natural de la Zona Volcànica de La Garrotxa, dotted with green volcanic cones, p.214
3 Twin-peaked Pedraforca, favourite of hikers and rock climbers, in the Serra del Cadí, p.231
4 Uncanny, jaggedy Montserrat, p.155
5 The stupendous bluffs of Collsacabra Natural Park east of Vic, p.222

Top: Prades
Right: Sant Miquel de Fai

6 Taking the rack railway (*cremallera*) up from Ribes de Freser to Núria, p.225
7 The lush Montseny mountains, an hour's drive from Barcelona, p.217
8 The vertiginous Prades mountains overlooking Reus and the coast, p.264
9 Sant Miquel de Fai, in a beautiful setting in a cliff-side cave, p.219
10 The pale crags of the Garraf, overlooking the sea, p.164

Itinerary 1: A Week In and Around Barcelona

Perfecting dynamic, dazzling, dizzying Barcelona is an ongoing Catalan project, and one suspects that once the Sagrada Família is finished, they'll start something else even grander.

Day 1: Take the obligatory stroll along the Rambla and visit Barcelona's medieval heart: the Cathedral, the Museu d'Història de la Ciutat, Santa Maria del Mar and the Gothic mansions of La Ribera.

Day 2: Change pace and spend a day with the Modernistas – walk up the Passeig de Gràcia to see the 'Block of Discord' by Gaudí, Domènech i Montaner and Puig i Cadafalch, and Gaudí's extraordinary La Pedrera; in the afternoon take the metro over to the Sagrada Família and Domènech i Montaner's magical Hospital de Santa Creu i Sant Pau. In the evening attend a concert at the Palau de la Música Catalana.

Day 3: For a day trip, take the train and cableway up to Montserrat for a visit to the monastery and a walk among the peaks.

Day 4: For an intermission, take the train down to Sitges to laze on the beach and take in its two excellent museums, Maricel and Can Ferrat.

Day 5: A day on Montjuïc, starting with the marvels of the Museu Nacional d'Art de Catalunya; after lunch wander through the gardens and visit the Fundació Miró, then take the aerial cableway over to Barceloneta for a seafood dinner.

Day 6: Go out to Santa Coloma de Cervelló to see Gaudí's sublime Colonia Güell crypt, and spend the evening with cocktails overlooking Barcelona from the top of Tibidabo.

Day 7: Get up early to visit the Picasso Museum and spend a last lazy afternoon with Gaudí in the wonderland of the Park Güell.

Above: La Pedrera (Casa Milà)
Right: Park Güell

01 Introduction | Itinerary

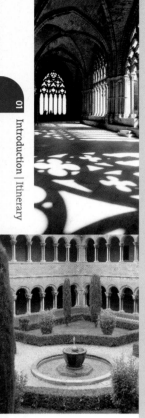

Top: La Seu Vella
Above: Ripoll

Itinerary 2: Beyond Barcelona – The Best of Catalonia in Two Weeks

Day 1–2: Head down to Tarragona and visit the great Cathedral, its Roman buildings and museum, the beautiful Pont del Diable aqueduct and Villa de Centcelles. Take a swim on one of the Costa Daurada's big beaches and, if you've brought the kids, you may have to slot in a day for Port Aventura.

Day 3: Spend a morning exploring the vineyards of El Priorat, then over to Montblanc to see the Cistercian sisters: Santes Creus, Poblet and Vallbona, then spend the night in Cervera.

Day 4: Visit the lovely town of Cervera, then drive west to Lleida to see La Seu Vella and the museum.

Day 5: Time to make for the Pyrenees: take the scenic route up to Tremp and then follow the Vall de Noguera Ribagorçana up to the remote Vall de Boí to spend a day with its lovely Romanesque churches; sleep in Vielha.

Day 6: Take a gorgeous ride in the mountains through the Vall d'Aran and Vall d'Àneu to Sort and La Seu d'Urgell.

Day 7: Visit La Seu d'Urgell's cathedral and Museu Diocesà then meander south to visit the beautiful small cities of Solsona and salty Cardona; stay in the Parador if you can.

Day 8: Make your way east to Vic to see Josep Maria Sert's astonishing murals and the Museu Episcopal, then drive north to Ripoll to see the famous portal and cloister; spend the night in Ribes de Freser.

Day 9: Take the ride up the Cremellera to Núria, and in the afternoon head to Olot.

Day 10: Spend a day among the volcanoes in the pretty Garrotxa; visit Besalú in the afternoon, then drive to Figueres.

Day 11: Visit the Dalí Museum in the morning, then make for the coast; visit spectacularly set Sant Pere de Rodes, Cadaqués and Dalí's house in Portlligat (be sure to book in advance). Overnight in Cadaqués.

Day 12: Have a look at Castelló d'Empúries and the ancient Greek and Roman site of Empúries; eat anchovies for lunch in L'Escala and drive over to Girona to visit the Cathedral and its treasure.

Day 13: See the rest of Girona and one or two of the pretty medieval towns nearby (Pals, Peratallada, Torroella de Montgrí), then go for a swim by one of the stunning beaches around Cap de Begur. Spend the night in Palafrugell.

Day 14: Visit Palamós and Sant Feliu de Guíxols, then take the beautiful corniche road to Tossa de Mar. Explore the old town and carry on to Lloret de Mar to visit the Jardí Santa Clothilde, then back to Barcelona.

CONTENTS

History
and Art

02

History

1,000,000 BC–AD 711
Catalonia Before There Were Any Catalans

As nations go, Catalonia is practically a newborn, a precocious little love child hatched in the confusions of the Dark Ages. Salvador Dalí probably would have said that through the ages the world was just waiting for it. In any case, the first million years on the southern slopes of the Pyrenees were pretty much a non-event. That is the approximate age of the earliest human remains found here, in the Vallparadís park in the industrial city of Terrassa.

It's all a blank from there to roughly 6000 BC, when **Palaeolithic** people were painting game animals and ladies in flouncy skirts in caves around the Ebro valley. Where they went, nobody knows, and no one else comes to occupy the stage until the Neolithic era. Catalonia lay far on the rustic fringes of the first great European civilization, the one that built Stonehenge, Newgrange and Carnac, leaving only a crop of **dolmens** (c. 2500–1700 BC), mostly in the Empordà, to testify to their presence.

By 800 BC, the Mediterranean shores of Spain were occupied by the tribes that would come to be known as the **Iberians**. They were warriors and farmers, economically primitive compared to peoples further east, and they were about to get a rude shock. The big dogs of the day were moving in, bringing new ideas, new technologies and plenty of a recent invention called money. First came the Carthaginians, who colonized parts of Andalusia and Ibiza. The Greek settlers came later, establishing themselves at Emporion and Rode (now Roses) c. 575 BC.

Between them, the fiercely antagonistic Greeks and Carthaginians had opened up Spain to the emerging Classical world. The bewildered Iberians had to adjust: they got assimilated into a money economy, and learned to turn ore into iron. In the 3rd century BC, **Rome** replaced the Greeks as the Carthaginians' nemesis. **Carthage** now assumed direct control where it could, making eastern Spain the heart of its empire, and in the Second Punic War Hannibal marched his elephants through Catalonia on their way to Italy. But, while Hannibal was fighting inconclusive battles on that peninsula, the Romans opened a second front. They landed at Emporion in 218 BC, and in 15 years won control of Catalonia and all Spain.

The Iberians weren't overjoyed to see them. But a massive revolt in 197 BC was brutally put down, and the Romans got down to Romanizing their new conquest. An Iberian village became the new metropolis: **Tarraco**, now Tarragona, has more Roman ruins today than any town west of Italy itself. The Romans built roads and aqueducts, founded new cities, such as **Colonia Faventia Julia Augusta Paterna Barcino** – Barcelona – and integrated Hispania into the Mediterranean world.

As the western Roman Empire fell apart in the Germanic invasions of the 5th century AD, Catalonia became one of the barbarians' first prizes. The **Visigoths** (the lusty crew that sacked Rome in 410), soon learned that pickings in impoverished Italy were slim, and they headed their wagons back over the Alps into Gaul and Hispania. Here they founded an out-of-the-way, low-rent kingdom that – at least south of the Pyrenees – would survive until the coming of the **Moors**.

711–985

With a Little Help from Wilfred the Hairy, a Nation is Born

That Visigothic Kingdom of Spain, after a promising start, went to pieces amidst the ambitions of its barons, religious bloody-mindedness and economic disarray. The Franks might well have eventually gobbled it up, had not a fiercer foe come out of nowhere to beat them to the job. This foe was the Arab-led army of Islam, which had rolled over all the Middle East and North Africa in less than a century after the death of Mohammed. Their invasion of Spain began in 711; two years later the Moors destroyed Tarraco. Barcelona took note and surrendered without a fight.

The Arabs pushed halfway up through Gaul before they were stopped by **Charles Martel** at Poitiers in 732. Martel's son and grandson, **Pepin the Short** and **Charlemagne**, would revive the Frankish Kingdom under their new **Carolingian** dynasty, while the Arabs consolidated their gains in the new **Emirate of al-Andalus** (a Caliphate after 756), occupying most of the Iberian peninsula. For some of the lands in between, however, the new dispensation meant confusion. That, as history likes to remind us, can be a blessing. In this case, it allowed the Christian Visigothic nobles in the remote northern mountains to organize new power centres, the seeds of what would one day become Castile, Navarre, Aragon and Catalonia.

Catalonia? No one is recorded using that name before the 12th century, the same time that Catalan first appears as a written language. Its origins are shadowy: some say it was originally 'Gothalanda', while another guess has it 'Castle-onia', like Castile. All through the later Dark Ages, in the safety of the Pyrenees, a population that included many refugees from the Moorish conquest was developing a distinct language and cultural identity. They were becoming a new nation, the Catalans.

In 801, the **Franks** conquered northern 'Gothalanda', but after Charlemagne's death their empire rapidly fell into decay, and the Catalans were increasingly left to their own devices. Local lords took the title of count from the Franks, and organized the Catalan lands into a number of counties, of which the **County of Barcelona** soon became the most powerful. In 870, the Franks installed an energetic Count of Barcelona named **Guifré el Pilós**, or '**Wilfred the Hairy**'. According to the chroniclers this Wilfred was hairy indeed, down to the very soles of his feet. Legends about him are numerous, for later Catalans made him into a nearly mythological founding hero. Guifré took control of three other counties, while he resettled abandoned lands and endowed Barcelona and the region with churches and monasteries.

After Guifré's death, his sons took over the counties – not as Frankish fiefs, but in their own right. Barcelona's counts grew ever more confident, and in 985, when their city was sacked by the great caliph **al-Mansur** of Córdoba and the Franks failed to respond to requests for aid, Count Borrell II declared his county's sovereign independence. The Franks could do nothing about it.

985–1213

Awash in Wool and Iron, the Catalans Make a Precocious and Slightly Eccentric Start

When things finally settled down, the Moorish-Christian boundary ran through the massif of Montsec in the west, and then down the valley of the Llobregat.

Tortosa, Lleida and Balaguer grew into prosperous Muslim cities, sharing in the golden age of the Caliphate of al-Andalus. When the Caliphate broke up in 1010, Lleida and Balaguer briefly became the capitals of kingdoms (*taifas*) of their own.

On the Christian side, some remarkable things were happening. People were spilling down from the overpopulated Pyrenees onto the foothills' border zone, living like frontiersmen and building odd round towers for protection; many of these would grow up into castles. Catalonia was growing wealthy too, far in advance of most of its neighbours. It was blessed with three of the most useful gifts a medieval economy could ask for: iron, wool and a free port.

Barcelona was probably the key. Recovering nicely from the assault of al-Mansur, the city managed to develop one of the first real urban economies in Christian Europe. The town became a centre of cloth manufacture, while in the Pyrenees the Catalans found a little iron ore and invented an advanced technique for smelting it. By the 1030s Barcelona had the first stable gold currency in western Europe.

The business interests of the city and the ambitions of the counts found a happy symbiosis and, as both grew in power, trade and the flag went hand in hand. At the same time, the balance of power between Christians and Moors was shifting decisively. Under **Ramon Berenguer I** (1035–76), Barcelona extended its control as far as Carcassonne and Montpellier in Languedoc, while at the same time the Counties of Barcelona and Urgell expanded westwards at the expense of the Moorish *taifas*.

After Ramon Berenguer I, with typical Catalan peculiarity, rule was shared by twin brothers named **Ramon Berenguer II** (1076–82) and **Berenguer Ramon II** (1076–97); the first was called 'the Towhead' and the second was nicknamed the 'Fratricide', for which crime he was eventually forced into exile.

The twins and their successors continued to direct their efforts at expansion towards the north. To the west and south lay Zaragoza and Valencia, defended by El Cid, and they couldn't beat him; the Cid in fact captured Berenguer Ramon twice. Berenguer Ramon was succeeded by his twin's son **Ramon Berenguer III** (1097–1131), who added new lands over the Pyrenees in what is now French Catalonia, or Roussillon. He and his son **Ramon Berenguer IV** (1131–1162) presided over the conquest of '**New Catalonia**', over a few decades nearly doubling the nation's size ('Old Catalonia' was mainly the counties of Barcelona and Urgell). Tarragona fell in 1118. Tortosa's turn came in 1148, with the biggest prize, Lleida, following a year later. The last Moorish redoubts in what is now Catalonia succumbed in 1153.

As the Catalan Reconquista neared completion, the new nation transformed itself from a collection of counties into a kingdom. The marriage in 1137 between Ramon Berenguer IV, Count of Barcelona, and the heiress of **Aragon**, **Petronila**, brought the city the crown of Aragon and all the prestige and patronage of royalty. Now the counts were '**count-kings**', and rulers of the second most powerful kingdom on the peninsula. The unusual title is a hint of just how important Barcelona continued to be in the new state; it also reflects the Catalans' ancient tradition of rights and privileges, codified as the *usatges* in the time of Ramon Berenguer I. Their count-king ruled not by divine right, but on a down-to-earth contractual basis, evident in the people's **oath of allegiance**: 'We who are as good as you, swear to you, who are no better than we, to accept you as our king and sovereign lord, provided you observe all our liberties and laws; but if not, not.'

That famous oath, in fact, tells only part of the story. The 'we' who are swearing it were an increasingly grasping nobility. The Catalonia of Wilfred the Hairy's time, if not really egalitarian, had at least been a place where the average man could get ahead. Now, with their increasing wealth and power, the bosses were putting on the screws. In the 12th century, wealthy merchants in Barcelona coalesced as a political force and immediately started claiming privileges that shut out the smaller operators. Even before Catalonia reached its medieval heyday, we can see signs of the social strife that would eventually bring its downfall.

Meanwhile, though, the new state continued to rack up successes. **Alfons I** (Alfonso II of Aragon, 1162–96) absorbed the rest of Roussillon. **Pere I** (Pedro II of Aragon, 1196–1213) took part in the greatest victory of the Reconquista, the 1212 **Battle of Las Navas de Tolosa** that resulted in the fall of all of al-Andalus, save only the kingdom of Granada, to Castile.

1213–1355
Catalonia Rules the Waves

Jaume I the Conqueror (1213–76) led Catalonia into its Golden Age, beginning its new maritime empire with the acquisition of Valencia and the Balearics. Jaume's descendants, by way of conquest, treaties and marriage, expanded this empire across the Mediterranean. In some ways, it was a remarkably advanced and progressive state. Barcelona's trade was regulated by a maritime code, the *Llibre del Consolat de Mar*, written under Jaume I in 1259. The same king gave Catalonia a parliament, the **Corts**, in 1249 (only 34 years after England's Magna Carta) and a permanent governing body, the **Generalitat**.

Jaume I's will divided his kingdom into two parts: **Pere II** (Pedro III of Aragon, 1276–85) got Aragon, including Catalonia and Valencia, while his younger brother Jaume ruled the trans-Pyrenean possessions and Mallorca as his vassal. As long as these two were alive the arrangement worked out well. Later Mallorcan and Aragonese rulers, though cousins, often had a hard time getting along. Occasional tiffs did little harm – they were out building an empire in the Mediterranean.

Under **Alfons II** (Alfonso III of Aragon, 1285–91), **Jaume II the Just** (1291–1327), **Alfons III** (IV of Aragon, 1327–36) and **Pere III the Ceremonious** (Pedro IV of Aragon, 1336–87), Catalan culture was at its height. It was the time of such notable figures as the philosopher and mystic **Ramon Llull** (d. 1311) and **Abraham Cresques** (d. 1387), the first scientific map-maker. Catalan painters and architects created works the equal of any in Europe, as Barcelona embellished itself with splendid Gothic monuments. For what had been a nation of farmers and shepherds only a few centuries before, the Catalans had come a long way.

1355–1479
In Which Great Ambitions Lead to a Great Fall

For all Catalonia's wealth and exploits overseas, things were not always going well at home. Barcelona in the midst of its opulence became a discontented and dangerous place, plagued by unemployment, poverty and crime. Big merchants fought against workers, while churchmen stirred up violence against the city's Jews. Despite royal protection, the first wave of **pogroms** occurred in 1391.

Overextension, and competition in trade from Genoa, brought hard times, and thanks to a string of bad harvests the city's poor even knew recurrent famines. Epidemics were also common. The Black Death arrived in 1348, killing off a third of the population. As oppression at home made peasant life unattractive, the new empire gave young men who could get out plenty of opportunities overseas.

In 1410, when **Martí I** died without an heir, the **Compromise of Caspe** gave the throne to a member of the ruling house of **Castile**, the **Trastámara**. The first of the Trastámara kings, **Ferran I** (1412–16) and **Alfons IV** (Alfonso V of Aragon, 1416–58), showed a greater interest in Castilian affairs than in Aragon's. This broke the final tie of mutual interest that had held Catalonia-Aragon's delicately balanced system together. Popular revolts in Barcelona in 1436 and 1437 were only the prelude to worse struggles to come; the real troubles began in 1462 with the **Remença Revolt** (named for a new tax). This was the curtain-raiser for the ten-year **Catalan Civil War**, which ended with the surrender of a city under siege by its own king, the notoriously brutal **Joan II** (1397–1479). Barcelona was ruined.

For the last act of the tragedy, the villain would be the son of Joan II. He was Ferran II to the Catalans, but he would have preferred to call himself by his Castilian name, **Fernando El Católico**. He had been married to **Isabel of Castile** in the middle of the wars and, when his father died and he assumed the throne in 1479, Castile and Aragon were effectively united. Spain was one, and Catalonia was suddenly a small corner of a very large kingdom; its capital was an exhausted, bankrupt metropolis that had no prospects and no friends.

1479–1830
Life in Spain's 'Golden Age': Impoverishment, Oppression and Despair

Historians tend to give Fernando and Isabel much better reviews than they deserve. This grasping, brutal and bigoted couple were interested only in squeezing all they could out of Catalonia to finance their own ambitions; their only gift to the region was the **Inquisition**, which arrived in 1487. The new rulers even took steps to ensure Catalonia would have no share in new opportunities: a codicil in Isabel's will specifically prohibited Catalan merchants from trading with the New World.

For Spain in its 'Golden Age', power and decadence went hand in hand, as the **Habsburg** successors to Fernando and Isabel strove to extend their power over three continents, while condemning the nation to exhaustion and poverty at home. They drove the Castilian heartland bust, too, but Catalonia, its old ways of making a living torn away, was reduced to despair.

The region had the added burden of being on the front lines of the long wars between Spain and France. The government quartered troops on the populace, and the soldiers distinguished themselves more in pillage and robbery than fighting the French. That, along with Madrid's continued assaults on Catalan liberties and institutions, sparked off a revolt in 1640 that Catalans call the **Reapers' War**, the *Guerra dels Segadors*, as it began with a riot by a mob of labourers who were gathered in Barcelona looking for employment on the harvest. The Generalitat, under Pau Claris, raised an army, which with French help defeated the Castilians in a battle underneath Montjuïc, but the affair was hardly settled. The Catalan leaders managed it badly, and their region lapsed into anarchy through 12 years of inconclusive struggles before the French finally betrayed them. Barcelona, left on its own, was besieged and starved into submission in 1652. In the final treaties France got to keep northern Catalonia, or the province of **Roussillon**.

In the decades that followed, Spain pursued a more conciliatory policy towards Catalonia. Nevertheless, the Catalans chose to revolt again the next chance they had, in the pan-European commotion called the **War of the Spanish Succession** (1701–14). When they backed the Austrian Archduke Charles's claim to the throne against the French Bourbon Philip V, it was a costly bet on the wrong horse. In the end, the Catalans were alone again and Barcelona came under siege once more. After 15 months of desperate resistance the city fell in November 1714, and down with it, this time, went Catalunya's *usatges*, its institutions and the last vestiges of its autonomy. From now on, Madrid treated Catalonia as just another colony, and ruled it through a viceroy. In an effort to kill off whatever remained of Catalan spirit, the publication of books in Catalan was forbidden, and the universities were closed.

But once the Catalans had been suitably punished, the Bourbon dynasty tried to earn Catalan loyalty by giving them a chance to make a living again, and through the 1700s business started to pick up. The results were dramatic. The old instincts had never died, and, like some capitalist Sleeping Beauty, the mercantile élite magically popped up from its 200-year slumber, ready to make some deals.

The Catalans found two very profitable new businesses. Depressed farmers replaced subsistence crops with vines, and Barcelona distilled their grapes into cheap brandy (*aiguardent*) and shipped it off to thirsty Latin America. After about 1730, Barcelona specialized in the manufacture of printed cotton cloth; the empty spaces outside the city walls became the *prats d'indianes*, 'fields of calico', where the cloth was hung out to dry. In 1778, Madrid finally removed the last restrictions on trading with the colonies, and the build-up turned into a boom. By 1780, when the population stood at 110,000 (it had more than doubled since 1714), the first industrial cotton mill was founded. Factory production soon replaced the medieval guilds, as Barcelona began its career as the 'Mediterranean Manchester'.

The **Napoleonic Wars** were a rude interruption. Britain's blockade stopped the American trade cold. Catalonia went into a deep depression while Napoleon's men raided and looted its churches and monasteries. As much as they hated Madrid, the Catalans learned from experience that the French were even worse.

1830–88

As Bombs and Bullets Fly, Catalonia Makes its Unexpected Comeback

After the big Napoleonic shake-up, the powers of Europe thanked Spain for its heroic resistance by throwing away its new constitution and propping the reactionary king **Fernando VII** (1814–33) back on his throne. When a coup in 1820 installed a liberal regime, they sent in 100,000 French troops to crush it. Spain was hopping mad, and no corner of it more so than Catalonia, which by now had once again become the most modern and forward-looking part of the country.

When Fernando finally died in 1833, and the infant **Isabel II** became Queen, Catalans hoped for better things. Instead, what they got was a wild rollercoaster ride of conflict, progress and setbacks that made Spain seem the very image of the banana republics that were just winning their independence from her in Latin America. Barcelona was enlivened by regular riots, rebellions, strikes, factory burnings and assassinations over the next two decades.

Out in the countryside, the trouble was coming from the opposite end of the political spectrum. Supporters of the pretender **Don Carlos**, Fernando VII's brother, launched three major rebellions, the three **Carlist Wars** (1833–36, 1846–49 and 1872–76), and Catalonia was at the centre of all of them. All Carlists wanted was to turn the clock back a few centuries, and that included restoring the Catalan *usatges*, as these mostly increased the power of the landowning nobility and the Church. Rural Catalonia, still deeply traditional and pious, found Carlism entirely to its liking, and local peasants supplied many of the recruits in the Carlist armies.

Quite amazingly, for all the troubles, Catalonia was making tremendous progress, pushed through and paid for by industry. Barcelona's businessmen dragged Spain kicking and screaming into the **Industrial Revolution**. The nation's first steam engine appeared in 1833, the first Catalan-built steamship only three years later; the first railroad opened in 1848. Barcelona filled up with factories, or *vapors* ('steamers'), and spawned a whole constellation of burgeoning industrial towns: Reus, Mataró, Badalona, Terrassa, Sabadell, Manresa. In textiles and iron, Catalonia became one of the first places in Europe to steal markets from industrial Britain.

For the second time in its history, Catalonia astounded the world, and its metropolis Barcelona enjoyed a second blossoming. The modern city, with its enormous expansion and glittering cosmopolitanism, evoked comparisons with the medieval golden age, and fostered a new pride in things Catalan. The **Renaixença**, or Renaissance, began with a movement to redeem and re-establish the Catalan language, long submerged by the forced Castilianization of Madrid. The medieval poetry competitions, the **Jocs Florals**, were revived in 1859, and the literary crusade was carried on by Catalonia's finest 19th-century poets, **Jacint Verdaguer** (1843–1902) and **Joan Maragall** (1860–1911), who led the way in bridging the historic Catalan spoken by the troubadours with the everyday language still spoken by the people. From there, the Renaixença grew into a fervent nationalist cultural movement in all the arts, from music to architecture. In this heady climate, Barcelona put on its first World's Fair, the **Universal Exhibition** in 1888; it showed the world, in the mayor's words, that the Catalans were the 'Yankees of Europe'.

1888–1939
A Most Dangerous, Most Brilliant Half-Century Ends in Disaster

By the end of the 19th century, Barcelona had one of the most developed economies of Europe, based on iron, textiles and trade – just as it had been in the Middle Ages. But, just as in those times, the new generation of the business élite proved just a little too piggish to share any of the prosperity. For a while, boom times papered over the growing discontent, but in the 1870s the city was ready to explode once more – this time, with the heat of a new ideology, known as

Anarchism. The movement grew rapidly in Barcelona, and took a violent turn after it was driven underground in 1874. While violence increased, Barcelona was paradoxically enjoying a most creative era. In the 1890s, Catalan culture flowered impressively, with the painters **Ramon Casas** and **Santiago Rusinyol** and their circle. The city's converging artistic style soon acquired a name, **Modernisme**. Its painting and poetry would not make much of an impression outside Catalonia, but in architecture the Modernistas were about to astound the world. **Antoni Gaudí**, the greatest among them, began work on the Sagrada Família in 1883.

The **Spanish-American War** of 1898 was an earthquake for all of Spain. The loss of Spain's last important colonies closed off trade opportunities, and, in the decade that followed, hard times increased popular discontent. Anarchist violence culminated in 1909 with the **Setmana Trágica**, the 'Tragic Week' of riots in Barcelona, when 116 died and Anarchist leaders were executed by the army.

Spain's neutrality in the **First World War** brought more boom times, as exports to the belligerents soared. The end of the war brought a wave of strikes and agitation, and in 1921 the Captain General of Barcelona, **Miguel Primo de Rivera**, declared a **military dictatorship** with the approval of King Alfons XIII.

The dictatorship of Primo de Rivera was proof, if the Catalans needed any, that nothing had really changed since the time of Fernando and Isabel. But after he retired, Spain voted a left-wing landslide in the 1931 municipal elections, a dramatic renunciation of the old order that lead to the abdication of Alfonso XIII and the birth of the **Second Republic**. In Catalonia, the big winner was the popular old ex-colonel **Francesc Macià**, head of the left-wing Republicans (Esquerra Republicana), who declared the 'Republic of Catalonia', although three days later he agreed for the sake of the young Spanish Republic to limit this to autonomy under the rule of a revived Generalitat. The patricians and their Lliga de Catalunya did not lose gracefully. Barcelona had always been theirs, and, when the elections of 1934 brought in a right-wing national government, they incited an insurrection that resulted in the jailing of both leftist and Catalan nationalist leaders, including **Lluís Companys**, the liberal trade union lawyer who succeeded Macià as head of the Esquerra Republicana, and ran the Generalitat until 1939.

The 1936 national elections brought the leftists back to power, but extremists on both sides seemed determined to settle the quarrel in the streets. A few months of shocking violence set the stage for **Francisco Franco**'s coup and the outbreak of the **Spanish Civil War**. The ascendant left easily won control of Catalonia and used the opportunity to make a revolution. For ten months, Barcelona made history as the only city ever to have been governed by millennial Anarchists; shops and cafés became collectives, while wearing a tie on the streets was considered a provocation. As Franco's army made major gains across Spain in 1937, Barcelona became the theatre of a left-wing war-within-a-war, which was emphatically won by the Republican Army and the Communists.

By 1938 the Republican zone was largely limited to Catalonia, Madrid and Valencia. As refugees flooded into Barcelona and other cities, Franco and his German and Italian allies bombed them to terrorize the populations. When the Nationalists reached the sea and cut the Republican zone in two, the Republicans staked the outcome on one big offensive. The **Battle of the Ebro** (*see* p.281), the bloodiest fight of the Civil War, ran for three months, and, when the Nationalists began their counter-offensive in October, the contest was effectively over. Half a million Republicans fled towards France in January 1939 as Barcelona surrendered. Franco took particular delight in humiliating the Catalans. Lluís Companys, caught by the Nazis in France, was sent back to Franco and executed. The new regime returned Catalonia to direct rule from Madrid, and banned all things Catalan; through the 1940s, even speaking Catalan in the street was risking jail.

1939–75
Four Stultifying Decades with Francisco Franco and, This Time, a Happy Ending

The next two sad and impoverished decades saw food, electricity and everything else in short supply; in 1947 Catalan cities came very close to famine. Other parts of Spain were suffering too, and Franco did everything to encourage the unemployed to move to Catalonia, hoping a tidal wave of poor Andalucians would dilute Catalanism into a harmless eccentricity. The Catalans called Franco *Paco Rana*, 'Frank the Frog'. It was clear that he was never going to win their hearts and minds, and he never tried. By the 1950s, however, the dictator gave up on overt repression, as part of a new image he was trying to project for his new friends in Washington. In 1952, the Catalan language was tentatively decriminalized.

By 1960, Franco had given up his attempt at economic self-sufficiency too, and a new generation of economists and technocrats was tooling up the country for its impressive industrial take-off of the next two decades, while the invention of the Costa Brava launched Spain's profitable new-found vocation for mass tourism. The 1960s were a strange decade; many Catalans look back on it with a shudder: the philistine tastlessness of a new bourgeoisie interested only in 'peseta pragmatism', caught between *seny*, the famous Catalan common sense, and the urge to protest, between forgetting and remembering. Still, shoots of new life were poking up through the cracks of the Castilian concrete. In 1960, future Catalan president Jordi Pujol was arrested and imprisoned for two years after devising a protest at the Palau de la Música – singing the *Song of the Catalan Flag* at a concert while a delegation of Franco's ministers was in the audience. Cultural resistance, too, was slowly being reborn. In the last decade of Francoism, while both the regime and the dictator were losing their faculties, a half-hearted machine of repression was increasingly unable to contain the critical culture that was emerging in the streets.

When Franco finally died, on 20 November 1975, every single bottle of *cava* in Barcelona was emptied. The morning after, like the rest of Spain, the Catalans started wondering what would happen next. As it became clear that their new king, **Juan Carlos**, was moving them towards democracy with a steady hand, the Catalans kept their cool and did nothing to make it more difficult for him.

When the king's appointed prime minister, **Adolfo Suárez**, won the first elections in 1977, he invited **Josep Tarradellas**, Catalunya's long-time president-in-exile, to return and restore the Generalitat. The gesture was an example, one among many, of just how mature and progressive Spaniards had become while waiting for *Paco Rana* to croak. The ideal of a monolithic Spain died with the same tick of the clock that took Franco; even in Madrid, they saw that the new Spain was going to be liberal and federal, and they welcomed it. The first regional elections in 1980 gave the presidency of the new Generalitat to **Jordi Pujol** and his Catalan nationalist CiU (Convergènicia i Unió) party. Pujol would hold it for 23 years. Barcelona, in contrast, was locally governed by the Socialists from the start, and it still is today.

The spectacular 1992 **Barcelona Olympics** was a coming-out party for the city and for the new Catalonia, a place to show off their accomplishments to the world. By any measure, those accomplishments have been remarkable. The creative channelling of 40 years of pent-up energy and Catalan quirkiness have made Barcelona the most dynamic city on the Mediterranean. It likes to see itself as the southernmost city of northern Europe and the northernmost city of the south, with a hard Protestant nose for making money, sweetened by Mediterranean colour and spontaneity. Currently, the population is over four million; by 2020 it is projected to reach seven million. Not the least of the Catalans' achievements has been defusing the little time bomb Paco Rana left for them: the hundreds of thousands of poor immigrants from southern Spain. This they managed with an effort towards good faith and fairness, and by compromising their nationalism enough to define a Catalan as anyone who wanted to be one (and who learned the language). Their non-racial inclusiveness could be a blueprint for other nationalities struggling to keep heart and soul intact in a multicultural world.

Even in an economy modernizing as formidably as Spain's has been, Catalonia has managed to stay in the lead. Both political factions hope to make the region a high-tech paradise. As soon as you leave Barcelona and have a look at the suburbs, you'll see just how important industry remains here.

In 2003, after Jordi Pujol's retirement from politics, a coalition of the three left-wing parties led by the Socialists took control of the Generalitat for the first time. A referendum in 2006 gave the Catalans even more autonomy and, more importantly, a chance to keep more of their tax money. The Generalitat now runs its own police force, the Mossos d'Esquadra, who in 2009 completed their takeover of all local policing. For the moment, politics are a little workaday and dull. Many people miss the constant buzz and excitement of the 1980s and '90s, though the region as a whole is grateful for the stability and prosperity it has achieved. Although complete independence remains the goal of many Catalan intellectuals, in recent polls only a small minority of Catalans say they want it. Nationalists now cautiously turn their sights on northern Catalonia, the French department of Roussillon, where a Catalan separatist movement is already contesting elections.

Catalan Art and Architecture

The Earliest Art

The first art in Catalonia goes back to *c.* 6000 BC, in the caves in Ulldecona and Cogul, and the first monumental buildings are the walled Iberian oppida – the biggest of which is just off the Costa Brava in **Ullastret**. Not by accident, Ullastret is only a few miles from the the the first of Catalonia's ancient Greek colonies, **Emporion** (Empúries) and **Rode** (Roses). The Romans left substantially more – the spectacular ruins in and around **Tarragona**, but also walls and towers, the Temple of Augustus and the streets under the Museu d'Història de la Ciutat in **Barcelona**.

The Middle Ages

In one sense, Catalonia's great achievement in medieval art is unique. The buildings remain, but for most of the painting and sculpture that once embellished them you'll have to visit the great Museu Nacional d'Art de Catalunya in Barcelona and some of the smaller local museums, especially those of Girona, Vic, La Seu d'Urgell and Solsona. The 11th and 12th centuries are marked by sturdy **Romanesque churches** in 'Old Catalonia' around the Pyrenees. Many of these were built or influenced by the Lombard masons of northern Italy, as shown in their tall bell towers and trademark blind arcading. Some were decorated with lively sculpture and painting, influenced by the artists of Occitan France. The painters' eccentric style and use of bold, flat colours later exerted a powerful influence on Joan Miró.

Among the most notable Romanesque churches are the great cathedral of La Seu d' Urgell, Ripoll's magnificent portal and cloister, the atmospheric Sant Joan de les Abadesses, Sant Cugat del Vallés, little Santa María at Porqueres, Sant Pere de Rodes high over the Costa Brava, Santa Maria de l'Estany's cloister, and Sant Vicenç at Cardona. Scores of charming Romanesque churches survive in the remote valleys of the Pyrenees. Those of the Vall de Boí are internationally famous for their highly stylized paintings, but there are many others, particularly in the Vall d'Aran.

The arrival of Gothic architecture in the late 12th century coincided with the conquest of New Catalonia and the tremendous upsurge of Catalan culture and political power. **Catalan Gothic** developed into a true national style in the late 13th century. Instead of the dizzying heights, pointed arches and flying buttresses that characterized the original Gothic of the Île-de-France, Catalan Gothic is restrained, practical and solid. What fascinated the Catalans was width and mass, and in their conquest of horizontal space they were as daring as the masters of Chartres. Among the earliest works are the three great **Cistercian monasteries** around Montblanc, at Poblet, Vallbona and Santes Creus. Nowhere is the style more striking than in **Girona cathedral**, the second widest in Christendom, or more beautiful than in Barcelona's **Santa Maria del Mar**. Barcelona's medieval core is full of secular wonders as well: the merchants' palaces, the Drassanes (now the Museu Marítim), the Antic Hospital de la Santa Creu, the Llotja, and, perhaps most remarkable of all, the **Saló de Tinell**, with the widest masonry arches ever built in Europe. Later cathedrals of New Catalonia deserve a mention too, impressive works at Tarragona and Lleida that were begun after reconquest from the Moors.

While following international trends, Catalan painters too developed a national style, with a naturalism of expression and gesture. **Ferrer Bassa**'s frescoes (1346) at Pedralbes are among the finest works of the century. Brothers **Jaume** and **Pere Serra** (active 1357–1405; Manresa cathedral, Sant Cugat) created the first large-scale altarpieces, or retables, of lavish colour and detail. They fell out of favour when International Gothic became the vogue; **Lluís Borrassá** (d. 1424), known for his elegant gestures, was the Catalan pioneer in the new style, followed by the very courtly **Bernat Martorell** (active 1427–52). His student **Jaume Huguet** (1412–92) was the leading Catalan artist of the 15th century. Gothic Catalonia also produced some excellent sculptors, notably **Jaume Cascalls** (d. 1378), who is considered the greatest of the **'School of Lleida'** sculptors (works also at Tarragona, Poblet, Ripoll).

As Catalonia decayed in the 16th and 17th centuries, so did its art, both in quantity and quality. There is very little of art or architecture from the Renaissance, Baroque and neoclassical eras, and even less that is distinctly Catalan.

Modernisme (1880–1910)

Things changed when Barcelona burst outside its walls into the Eixample in 1860. Now that they had money and room to build, how should they build? In the spirit of the Renaixença, Catalan architects studied Viollet-le-Duc; they agreed with Ruskin that 'ornament [was] the origin of architecture', and adored a book called *Der Stil* (1861–3) by German architect **Gottfried Semper**, one of the first to describe how a building should express its function. To mimic historical styles was repulsive. It was essential to be modern, and **Modernisme**, as the new style came to be known, would be based on Semper's dictum that 'originality is a return to origins'.

Catalonia's Modernista architects responded to Semper in surprisingly diverse ways. What they had in common, however, was their nationalism, a trait they shared with Catalonia's newly assertive bourgeoisie. Although part of the late 19th-century Arts and Crafts movement, Modernista architecture has no *fin-de-siècle tristesse*; it is vigorous, bold, colourful and playful. The first great Modernista, **Lluís Domènech i Montaner** (1849–1923), took Semper's 'return to origins' as a return to traditional Catalan brick and iron. His use of the latest technologies saved the bacon of Barcelona's 1888 Universal Exhibition, when he orchestrated the building of a massive hotel in only 59 days. His masterpieces, the Palau de la Música Catalana, the Casa Lleó Morera and the Hospital de Sant Pau, are remarkable for their complete integration of decoration. **Josep Puig i Cadafalch** (1857–1956) was more historically minded; for him, Semper meant an imaginative reinterpretation of Catalan Gothic. He left Barcelona some highly individualistic works: Casa Amatller, Els Quatre Gats, Casa de les Punxes, and the Fábrica Casaramona (now the CaixaForum exhibition space). He later adapted his style to fit **Noucentista** currents (*see* p.32); his last buildings, for the 1929 Exhibition, are almost Baroque.

By far the greatest genius of the whole international Art Nouveau movement, **Antoni Gaudí i Cornet** (1852–1926) went deep into uncharted territory; his 'return to origins' was a return to the forms and structure of nature herself. The son of a coppersmith in Reus, he had grown up watching his father make cauldrons from flat sheets of metal, a hands-on creating of volumes. Gaudí would approach architecture in the same way. He was more a sculptor and poet than an architect, and improvised as he went along. 'He didn't make plans,' said Miró. 'He made gestures.' Gaudí's life and career (*see* pp.37–8) are a remarkable study in paradox and contrariness. He hated being being called a Modernista, because as a good Catholic he didn't believe in modernity. He was a reactionary, yet he went far beyond any architect of his time into the realms of pure imagination; while others drew on Gothic, his goal was to take it to a higher stage of evolution. Convinced that 'the straight line is man's creation; the curved line, God's', he studied Moorish and Hindu designs that he would later combine with Gothic, natural forms and his own imagination, and changed the face of Barcelona.

Beyond these Modernista Big Three are some delightful talents. Gaudí's sometime collaborator **Josep Maria Jujols i Gibert** (1879–1949) was 'one of the most subtle, original, unprejudiced and provocative personalities of contemporary art', as Carlos Flores called him. His created the serpentine bench at the Park Güell, the balconies of La Pedrera, the roof of the Casa Batlló – but he also left some of his most imaginative works in villages around Tarragona. **Joan Rubió i Bellvé** (1871–1952), from Reus, created some of Barcelona's imaginative brickwork.

Modernista painters never rose to the level of the architects, but at the start of the 20th century they nurtured a young Andalucian genius named **Picasso. Ramon Casas** (1866–1932), the 'Catalan Toulouse-Lautrec' painted a handful of bold, almost photographic, political paintings, but later turned to churning out society portraits and advertisements. **Santiago Rusinyol** (1861–1931), painted landscapes, gardens and genre scenes; his legendary Modernista festivals at Sitges flirted with Symbolism. **Isidre Nonell** (1873–1911), painted poor gypsy women, inspiring Picasso's Blue Period. Rodin was the strongest influence on Modernista sculptors such as **Miquel Blay** and the delightful **Eusebi Arnau**. The most Rodin-like was **Josep Llimona** (1864–1934), whose masterpiece is Barcelona's *Monument to Dr Robert*.

Post-Modernisme (1910–present)

A reaction to the eccentricities of Modernisme expressed itself in **Noucentisme**, 'nineteen-hundredism', which sought balance and order in a return to Mediterranean roots. In art, the Noucentista reaction is represented by a Cézanne-inspired search for structure, in the paintings by **Joaquim Sunyer** of Sitges (1874–1956) and sculpture of **Josep Clarà**. Two of the more original figures of the time were **Juli González** (1876–1942) and the muralist **Josep Maria Sert** (1874–1945).

Even while Noucentisme held forth in the 1920s, change was in the air. Picasso and the **Cubists** were first exhibited at Barcelona's Dalmau Galleries in 1912. During the First World War the city became a refuge for artists: André Breton's Surrealist manifestos were signed by the two great Catalan painters of the 20th century, **Joan Miró** (1893–1983; for more *see* p.128) and **Salvador Dalí** (1904–89; *see* p.199).

Under Franco, architectural creativity ground to a halt, but **Antoni Tàpies** (b. 1923), who used found objects as a means of expression, emerged in the 1950s doldrums as one of the leading artists in Spain. One bright spot was Barcelona's luminous white Fundació Joan Miró by **Josep Lluís Sert** (nephew of Josep Maria Sert), who went into exile after the Civil War and returned to design his best building in 1972.

Barcelona's post-Franco rulers have been Socialists, but they were also solid bourgeois and wanted to make their mark on the city. Being awarded the 1992 Olympics fitted right in with their plans for revitalizing old neighbourhoods on a dazzling scale. They haven't stopped yet, although the 'vicious circle of design' – the parade of trendy architects constantly upstaging each other to be the boldest, the newest – has been at best a mixed blessing, resulting more often than not in a force-fed architecture that looks the way hothouse tomatoes taste; the 2004 Fòrum is a glowing example. Rare exceptions include the Torre de Telefònica (1992) on Montjuïc, by engineer-architect Santiago Calatrava of Valencia, and striking works by outsiders: Arata Isozaki's Palau Sant Jordi (1990), Norman Foster's Torre de Collserola (1992), and the Museu d'Art Contemporani (1995) by Richard Meier.

Topics

03

Hairy Wilfred and the Four Bars

It may sound like a yarn from Daniel Boone, but it's Catalonia's foundation myth. The Count of Barcelona, Guifré el Pilós (Wilfred the Hairy), is heroically defending Barcelona from the Moors led by Lobo ibn Mohammed, in around 898. He is mortally wounded, and, when the Frankish king Charles the Bald comes to his hirsute hero's tent, Guifré confesses that his one regret is that he is dying without having earned a coat of arms for his golden shield. The king responds by dipping his fingers in Guifré's blood and running them down the shield. Hence the *quatre barres* (those four blood-red stripes you see on the Catalan flag) are born. It's a good story, even if even the most ardent nationalists have to admit that Charles the Bald died 20 years before Guifré. Even so, Catalonia's flag is one the oldest national flags in the world, first documented on the royal seal of Alfons II of Aragon in 1159.

St Jordi and the Dragon

The bull – that passionate, earthy archetype of fertility and death – may be the totem beast of Iberia, but he has little place in Catalonia. No, the creature the Catalans hold to their hearts is more fiery, more dangerous and quirkier. Ever since 1229, when Count-King Jaume I had a vision of Sant Jordi (St George) lending a hand at the siege of Mallorca, this most chivalrous of saints has been the patron of Catalonia.

The legend of Jordi and his dragon was seamlessly grafted on to Catalonia's favourite 9th-century dragon saga. It seems that the Moors, realizing they couldn't defeat the counts of Barcelona, decided to play dirty and brought a baby dragon over from North Africa, setting it loose at Montblanc near Tarragona. When it began to grow fat on the surrounding peasants and the boldest knights, the father of Wilfred the Hairy had the Christian derring-do to slay it at last. It was skinned and displayed on feast days, the grandad of the dragons who come out to play during Catalan *festes*, spewing fireworks in the pandemonium of the *correfoc*, or fire-running.

In 1456, the Generalitat made St George's Day (23 April) the Festival of the Rose, when men give their love a rose, just as George gave his princess the rose that sprang from the dragon's blood. Since 1926 women have given their men a book, in honour of Cervantes and Shakespeare, who both died on 23 April 1616. These days, it's less proscribed: women give roses, men give books, and many give both.

The *Sardana*

As with so much that the Catalans do, they go about their national dance, the *sardana*, with a workaday seriousness. Coats and bags are placed in a pile in the centre, hands are joined to form a ring, and everyone steps intricately to the right, then to the left – slowly or vigorously, depending on the music. The feeling that this is a communal rite is always there, an affirmation of Catalan identity and unity, of Catalan feet gently awakening Catalan earth – it's as far from the wild, pounding, passionate goblin of flamenco as you can get. The dance is harder than it looks but, if you want to give it a go, don't goof about: 'To dance the *sardana* imperfectly is to commit a sin against art; it is to insult Catalonia,' according to Aureli Capmany. Franco, needless to say, banned it.

The Catalans learned the *ballo sardo* during their unwelcome occupation of Sardinia and, as the Sards claim their circle dances are Neolithic in origin, the *sardana's* roots are very deep indeed. So what comes as a surprise, seeing the serious faces, is the music, which is nothing like any folk tune you've ever heard, but rather in the vein of boulevard tunes; nearly all *sardanes* were composed in the mid-19th century by one Pep Ventura. There's an occasional melancholy strain, but it never lasts long; sometimes the tempo picks up, and the younger dancers in the inner circles even work up a bit of a sweat.

The Jocs Florals

A *mestre en gay saber*, or 'master of joyous knowledge', was a troubadour, and, if it seems peculiar that they were still running around Catalonia in the mid-19th century, it's because of the overwhelmingly nostalgic nature of the Catalan cultural reawakening, the Renaixença. The first Jocs Florals, or Floral Games, a poetry competition between troubadours, took place in Toulouse in May 1324. In 1388, Queen Violante de Bar brought the games to Barcelona, where the third prize was a silver violet, the second a golden rose and the first prize a real rose, because, like the greatest poetry, a rose can never be imitated.

Medieval Catalan verse is powerful, pithy stuff. In 1490 the genre kicked off with a bang with Joanot Martorell's *Tirant lo Blanc*, Europe's first prose novel, a mix of chivalry and satire. The heroics may well have been based on the 'White Knight', the Romanian-Hungarian Turk-crushing hero John Hunyadi, but the bawdy, ribald bits are pure Catalan. It was one of Cervantes' favourite books.

After dying out in the 15th century, the Jocs Florals were revived by Barcelona's Ajuntament in May 1859 as a way to promote Catalan verse, which had all but died out. 'Fatherland, Faith and Love' were the mottoes. A jury selected the winner, and the first prize once again was a real rose. A poet who earned three roses was deemed a modern *mestre en gay saber*. The Jocs even produced some good verse: Joan Maragall and Jacint Verdaguer, other *mestres*, are still read today. In the other arts, the Jocs Florals and their twee quaintness were perhaps most important for the reaction they provoked in the 1890s: Modernisme.

The Catalan Crapper

While attending Mass one day in Barcelona in 1959, Luís de Galinsoga, the pro-Franco director of the newspaper *La Vanguardia* couldn't stand it any longer. He stood up in church and shouted: ¡Todos los catalanes son una mierda! (All Catalans are shit!). Enough protests were raised for Franco to sack the newspaperman personally. Catalans didn't have much to laugh about that year, but Galinsoga's fate must have evoked at least a few smiles. They probably weren't even that miffed.

Medieval Barcelona grew up between two torrents, the Cagallel and the Merdança: 'turd-taker' and 'shit-stream'. Both were buried centuries ago, under what are now the Rambla and the Rec Comtal, only to become chthonic scatological streams of consciousness. The *caganer*, or Christmas crapper, a figurine with bare buttocks suspended over a lovingly carved pyramid of poo, has been an essential figure in Catalonia's Christmas cribs since the 1500s, placed just downwind from the main event in the manger. Not even Christmas-crib-mad Italy has anything like a *caganer*: plates of spaghetti, elephants, camels and Turks, yes; crappers, no. Catalonia squats alone. Ethno-psychoanalysts wonder: is the *caganer* the fertility symbol of an obsessive anal-retentive race? An expression of down-to-earth reality – the Messiah may have come, but the duodenum pushes on? The embodiment of Catalan opposition to central authority, even divine authority? Most *caganers* wear traditional costume, but there are variations for collectors – yes, you can even buy an Obama *caganer* (it's a compliment). All wear beatific smiles.

The value of a good crap is brought home in another tradition, the *tió*, or Christmas log, which the children beat with sticks, shouting, '*Caga, Tió, caga!*' (Shit, Log, shit!) until *tió* excretes sweets. After all, as cookbook writer Josep Canill de Bosch wrote in *La Cuyna Catalana* (1907): 'Regular body functions make nations strong. Strong nations lead the pack, and eventually become masters of the world.'

The Rose of Fire, or *Rauxa* vs. *Seny*

Within every Catalan there is an Anarchist.
                              Joan Maragall

Catalans consider *seny*, 'common sense' or 'practical wisdom', as their principal virtue. It makes them rich and sets them apart from the rest of Spain, or at least from old romantic Spain and its haughty nobility that regarded work and commerce with disdain.

Seny, however, has a Catalan counterpart: *rauxa*, or 'uncontrolled passion'. While the bosses sought Utopia in Modernista culture, their workers looked for theirs in Anarchism. The bourgeoisie sublimated their *rauxa* in Wagner, architectural excess and exotic sex (at least judging by the bills of fare at Barcelona's bordellos), while the Anarchists expressed it by erecting barricades. But there was *seny* on the Anarchist side as well. The one thing that the Anarchists and bourgeoisie shared was a resentment of central authority. For the bourgeoisie, this meant Madrid, especially after the government lost Cuba and the Philippines, both Catalan cash cows, in 1898. For the Anarchists, of course, 'authority" was anyone who lorded it over the brotherhood of man, be it Church, government or capital, all of whom made man evil by assuming he was so.

The history of the class struggle in Spain began in Barcelona's Bonoplata factory, one of the country's first steam-powered plants; in 1835, during the first spate of church burnings, Luddite saboteurs set it on fire, too. Things became serious in 1855, when the government banned trade unions and Barcelona responded with Spain's first general strike. This happened at a time when a family of four living in the city needed a minimum of 4,000 *reales* a year to live; an unskilled labourer made less than 2,500. And no matter who was in charge – 19th-century Spain was a Banana Republic without the bananas – nothing changed. Like Pirandello's characters in search of a play, Barcelona's frustrated workers were in search of a belief.

It arrived by train in October 1868 in the person of Giuseppe Fanelli, an apostle of Bakunin, the famous Russian theorist of Anarchism. Fanelli spoke only Italian and French, but he had some newspaper clippings of Bakunin's speeches and pamphlets, and they were enough. In that same year, the Anarchist paper *Solidaritat Obrera* was founded, and gave meaning to the sporadic uprisings of Catalan farm labourers and workers. The Anarchists staged strikes and inevitably lost; which only made them more radical. Die-hards drifted into political terrorism.

After the troubles reached a crescendo in the Setmana Tràgica of 1909, Anarchists dubbed Barcelona *La Rosa de Foc*, the Rose of Fire. Two years later, the Anarchist trade union CNT was founded, and 80 per cent of Barcelona's workers joined. Between 1910 and 1923, 800 strikes rocked Barcelona. The Civil War would be their finest hour, and their last. Anarchist military units worked effectively under elected officers, without hierarchies or salutes. In the areas they controlled, including much of Barcelona and its industrial belt, their collectivized economy ran efficiently and did more than its bit for the Republican war effort. Though Anarchists had their doubts about collaboration with any government, one of their leaders, Federica Montseny, became the Republic's Minister of Health – the first woman cabinet minister in Europe – and radically advanced women's rights while creating a first-rate public health system.

The end came in the middle of that war, not at the hands of Franco but of the Anarchists' allies in the Republic. Communist propagandists such as La Pasionaria called them traitors in the pay of Franco, and, when the two factions came to blows (absurdly enough in a fight over the Barcelona telephone company building), the Republican army intervened on the side of the Communists. After the war, Anarchist leaders who didn't escape to Mexico or France mostly died in Franco's gulags, and, when democracy returned, the Catalan workers would be listening to calmer voices who never mentioned utopias at all.

Genius and Crank

Antoni Gaudí i Cornet (1852–1926) was one of the most innovative architects of any era. Although Gaudí was regarded as an eccentric or even a hippy architect in the architectural Ice Age of the 1960s, you don't have to be in Barcelona long to realize that his reputation has since been polished and used to fuel an industry of its own. You can take an all-Gaudí tour or purchase models of his benches in Park Güell; the opera *Gaudí*, by Joan Guinjoan and Gaudí scholar Josep M. Carandell, premiered at the Liceu in 2000.

Although classed as a Modernista, Gaudí's creation of new forms and textures, and his vision of decoration as being as integral to the structure as its walls or roof, went far beyond anything built by his colleagues. No architect ever studied nature more intently; in his buildings, stone became organic, sensuous, dripping; iron was wrought into whiplash ribbons, trailing leaves and spiders' webs; the old Muslim art of covering surfaces with broken tiles (*trencadis* in Catalan) was given a new vibrant, abstract meaning, reaching an epiphany in the Park Güell. Gaudí ingeniously reinvented the parabolic arch, last seen with the ancient Hittites. Much of the mathematical work he and his colleagues had to do in those pre-computer days is astonishing.

Gaudí, however, might not have become world-famous had he not caught the eye of Eusebi Güell. Güell's father Joan was an *Americano* who made a fortune in Cuba, and Eusebi had a privileged son's knack for spending, and fancied himself the Lorenzo de' Medici of Barcelona. Perhaps he and Gaudí were destined to meet, but the actual conjunction occurred at the Paris Exhibition of 1878, when the 31-year-old Güell saw an extraordinary 10ft-tall glass, iron and mahogany display case for a glove company. It was love at first sight. Güell tracked down its 26-year-old designer. Gaudí at the time was something of a dandy and man about town, ripe to be patronized, and Güell's first commission was for the gate, lodge and stables for the **Finca Güell** in 1884. Güell was so pleased that two years later he asked Gaudí to build him a mansion, with money no object. The result, the **Palau Güell**, was fit for a Renaissance prince.

So it tends to come as a surprise to learn that Gaudí, whose very name in Catalan means 'delight', was the last man you'd want to invite over for dinner (to begin with, he was probably the only Catalan vegan ever). Gaudí was always proud to be the son of a craftsman, but in the circle of Güell he became increasingly anti-democratic and authoritarian, and the worst sort of neo-medieval religious crank. Obsessive, morbidly pious, he told friends that he saw himself as God's humble servant in a world made of punishment and pain. Yet the crankier he got, the more wonderfully he built. For his next project, the church for the **Colonia Güell** in Santa Coloma del Cervelló, he cut loose completely from historical eclecticism and soared into the realms of pure imagination. Only the crypt was ever finished, but it stands as a revolutionary architectural sculpture, a cave held together by mathematics and Catalan craftsmanship.

Güell and Gaudí's last collaboration was the **Park Güell**, ostensibly a residential colony for the rich but incidentally a secret garden of their beliefs on Catholicism and Masonry. Crankier and crankier, Gaudí reached his pinnacle of fame in 1910, with **La Pedrera (Casa Milà)** – which he designed as a pedestal for a 40ft-high statue of the Virgin Mary and a pair of angels, an idea his client prudently vetoed after the 1909 *Setmana Tràgica*, when Barcelona was still smoking from another of bout of church-burning. It never seemed to occur to the pious Gaudí that the industrialists who hired him made their bundles by keeping Barcelona's workers so downtrodden that Anarchism seemed to be their only hope. Gaudí just didn't get it. After La Pedrera, he became increasingly reclusive, devoting the rest of his life trying to expiate the church-torching sins of his fellow citizens by building the **Sagrada Família**.

The Association for the Beatification of Antoni Gaudí was founded in 1992, and in 2000 the Vatican announced that it would open the case. His followers are now busy trying to prove that he performed non-architectural miracles too.

Food and Drink

04

Restaurant Generalities

Catalans dine late: restaurants open at around 8 or 8.30pm and stay open until midnight – some, such as Barcelona's latest lounge bar-cum-restaurants that turn into nightclubs, will stay open much later. As a general rule, book for the more expensive restaurants. In the cities, many places close down in August: ring ahead.

Bars, Cafés and Tapas

Although there are places that specialize in coffee or cocktails or tapas, most serve all three, along with a selection of sandwiches (*entrepans*). Tapas (*tapes*) are not as essential to Catalan eating habits as elsewhere in Spain, but are regarded as warm-ups to the main event. If you're a big fan, however, you'll find a handful of places in the cities, usually Basque or Gallego, that specialize in delicious titbits.

Coffee-drinkers will find their brew everywhere, but tea-drinkers will despair. Traditional breakfast coffee with milk (*cafè amb llet*) comes in a cup big enough for dunking. If you order a plain *cafè*, you'll get an espresso; for a tiny splash of milk, ask for a *tallat*. If you prefer your coffee more diluted, ask for a *cafè americano*.

Catalan Cuisine

Pecat de gola Déu el perdona (God forgives the sin of gluttony).
old Catalan proverb

Catalonia's Renaixença saw a renewal of many arts, but the most ephemeral, the one in the pot, had to wait a century – until the late 1960s, to be precise, when **Josep Mercader**, chef-owner of Figueres' Hotel Empordà, the 'father of New Catalan Cuisine', started tweaking traditional recipes. What followed since is an explosion of creativity that's been heard around the world. In 1994, the path first trodden by Mercader received its international culinary kudos when **Santi Santimaria** of Can Fabes became the first Catalan chef to be awarded three Michelin stars.

Catalan Specialities

The approaches may be new, but the roots are ancient: many features go back to the Romans, especially the Catalan propensity for mixing the savoury with the sweet (salt cod with honey is a classic). The materials at hand are astonishing, as any visitor to Barcelona's La Boqueria market on the Rambla knows – a larder of Mediterranean and mountain delights that led to iconic *mar i muntanya* ('sea and mountain') dishes that can combine lobster, chicken and bitter chocolate.

In his classic book *Catalan Cuisine*, Colman Andrews describes how four concoctions underpin most dishes: *all-i-oli* (garlic pounded with olive oil); *sofregit* (usually onions, olive oil and tomatoes fried until they melt together); *picada* (almonds, hazelnuts, fried bread, garlic, parsley and sometimes saffron or chocolate, thrown into a dish at the last minute); and *samfaina* (like ratatouille, but cooked down to a thick paste). The province of Tarragona adds a fifth: *romesco*, a sauce of red peppers, tomatoes, garlic, almonds and hazelnuts.

The favourite Catalan accompaniment is *pa amb tomàquet* (thickly sliced country bread, rubbed with tomato and garlic and drizzled with olive oil). Its cousin is the

coca (plural *coques*), the Catalan pizza, with tomatoes and
anchovies, or aubergines and courgettes, or sausage.

Catalans love their *amanides*, or salads. *Amanida Catal*
salad; *esqueixada* is made with salt cod, tomatoes, oni
that is *xató*, an obsession in lands between Sitges an
village has its own recipe for it (usually, they'll inclu
tuna, olives and raw salt cod, with *romesco* sauce on
grilled aubergines, peppers, onions garlic and herbs) is ano
local *embutits* (*charcuterie*) is excellent. Try the ham from the Cerd
bewilderingly large variety of sausages all called *botifarra*; cured sausage
fuet, spicy *llonganissa*, and *xoriç* (chorizo). In early spring, especially in Tarragona
province, you might come upon another fond obsession: the *calçotada* is a meal
which centres on barbecued green onions called *calçots* (*see* p.258).

Two things Catalans take very seriously are olives and anchovies. Olives appear
everywhere; the variety called *arbequina* (originally from Arbeca, near Lleida) is
particularly prized. Catalan anchovies (*see* p.187) are arguably the best in the world,
and they'll be a revelation if you've only tasted the ones in the little tins back home.

Like everyone else in Spain, the Catalans are crazy about seafood; the variety and
quality of fish and shellfish on offer in the markets is astounding. Seafood and rice
in various forms is a favourite, with *arròs negre* ('black' rice tinted with cuttlefish
ink) perhaps the favourite of favourites (bring a friend, since most restaurants will
only make it for two). Everything you can do with rice can also be done with *fideus*
(thin noodles). *Bacallà* (salt cod) is always a treat, and there are at least a dozen
traditional ways of preparing it . You'll also see *sarsuela* (an elaborate seafood
casserole), but more often *suquet de peix*, usually made from hake (*lluç*) and
monkfish (*rap*) boiled in a thick broth with *sofregit*, garnished with mussels. Try
graellada de peix i marisc (a platter of grilled fish and shellfish), or *cim-i-tomba* – a
Costa Brava fisherman's fish and potato dish with *all-i-oli*.

Inland, the pig holds pride of place; if you find a restaurant in the Pyrenees that
doesn't serve trotters, let us know. The list of local sausages includes 17 officially
recognized types, but the most important is *botifarra*, similar to a mild Italian
sausage, which is the star of the mainstay *botifarra amb mongetes* (with beans).
Other dishes include *escudella*, a pork, chicken and vegetable stew with a million
recipes, including a celebratory version, *escudella i carn d'olla*, that includes (wait for
it): veal, bacon, beef, chicken, pig's ear and trotters, pork, *botifarra*, chickpeas, beans,
potatoes, cauliflower, egg, turnip, carrot, garlic, pepper, cinnamon *and* parsley.

In autumn, Catalonia goes mad for wild mushrooms and truffles, and many
people head for the forest to find their own (particularly around Berga and Olot).
The closer you get to the mountains, the more game dishes appear on the menu.

Catalonia isn't really a cheesy region, though: the one kind it takes pride in is
mató, a ricotta-type white cheese (Montserrat's is famous) served as a dessert with
honey. Catalans generally don't devote a lot of thought to desserts; *crema catalana*,
similar to *crème brûlée*, is the inevitable classic.

In his book Colman Andrews issued a warning about Catalan cuisine: 'Like much
traditional cooking around the world it tends to be monochromatic, murky-looking
brown. It is food made to be eaten, not admired from a few steps back.' This is

ot true of the newest New Catalan cuisine, which is often stunning to
goes under several names – 'conceptual', 'molecular', 'techno-gastro-
nal' – and its originator and high priest, El Bulli's **Ferran Adrià** (*see* p.189) is
stantly voted the Best Chef in the World. If Santimaria is a Modernista, Adrià
often been called the 'Dalí of the Kitchen' – like Birtain's Heston Blumenthal, a
erious researcher into the chemical essences of each ingredient, ready to modify
and combine foods no one ever imagined possible. Though many dismiss his over-
the-top approach as decadent gimmickry, Adrià's disciples in Catalonia are legion. It
will be interesting to see how many of their restaurants survive the 2009 recession.
There was already dissent in the air in 2007, led by Santimaria. As *Time* magazine
reported from the Madrid Fusion conference in 2007, Santimaria was given a
standing ovation when he stated, like a true Catalan: 'The only truth that matters is
the product that comes out of the earth, passes through the ovens to the mouth of
the eater, and is then defecated.'

If all this sounds too excitingly mouth-watering, we'll close with a caveat. Some
restaurants here serve up cooking as good as anything you'll find around the Med.
Plenty of others do not. As everywhere in Spain, the food revolution of the post-
Franco decades has been an uneven process. Lots of cooks haven't got the message
yet, and lots of restaurants that look inviting will disappoint you with bland,
indifferent food. We think we've ferreted out many of the good ones; let us know.

Wines, *Cava* and other Drinks

Ever since the ancient Greeks planted the first vines, Catalan wines have had an
up-and-down history. In the Middle Ages, the peasants tended vineyards under an
agreement known as *rabassa mort* – which meant they could keep them for as long
as the vines were alive. They became very good at keeping them alive – and the
monasteries became very good at helping them turn the grapes into wine.

Everything changed in the late 18th century, when Madrid finally let Catalonia
trade with the New World. The Americas, the Catalans quickly discovered, were
thirsty. The wine was made into a brandy called *aiguardent*, which took up less
room in the ships. Business boomed – until phylloxera killed off every last vine.

Today the region has eleven DOs (*Denominació d'Origen*), nearly all to the west
and south of Barcelona. The most famous of these is bubbly *cava* (*see* p.162),
produced since the 1860s around Sant Sadurní d'Anoia. Pre-phylloxera, most of
Catalonia's grapes were red, but when the vineyards were replanted, the rising
popularity of *cava* reversed the proportions: today 70 per cent are white. The fruity,
non-fizzy Penedès whites are a perfect match with the region's tasty seafood.

Catalonia's red minority, however, is noteworthy, especially El Priorat (*see* p.266),
the only one to achieve *Denominació d'Origen Qualificada* (DOQ, or DOC in Spanish)
stature along with La Rioja. There are good rosés too, mostly from Empordà-Costa
Brava, which also does some good dessert wines.

The national cocktail is the *barreja*, two parts chilled Moscatell wine, one part
Anís del Mono *anisette*. In the Pyrenees, people pride themselves on their
homemade *ratafia*, a grappa-based, sweet liquor with a pungent mix of *anisette*,
nuts, coffee, herbs, and spices, all left to brew outdoors for a fortnight.

Catalan Menu Reader

Amanides, Entremesos, Sopes (Salads, Starters, Soups)

avocat avocado
amanida catalana chef's salad
brou broth
bunyols fritters
carns fredes cold meats
escalivada salad of roast peppers, aubergines and onions
esqueixada shredded salt cod salad
pernil dolç cooked ham
pernil serrà or *salat* cured ham
sopa soup
xató salad with salt cod and *romesco* sauce

Peix i Marisc (Fish and Shellfish)

anguiles eels
anxoves anchovies
bacallà salt cod
brandada salt cod purée
calamars squid
cloïsses clams
cranc crab
escabetxos cooked and marinated fish
gambes prawns
garotes sea urchins
llagosta spiny lobster
llamàntol lobster
llagostins giant prawns
llenguado sole
llobarro sea bass
lluç hake
lluçet whiting
marisc shellfish
mero perch
moll or *roger* mullet
musclos mussels
navalles razor-clams
nero grouper
orada gilthead sea bream
ostres oysters
palaia plaice
peix espasa swordfish
percebes barnacles
pop octopus
rap monkfish
salmó (fumat) salmon (smoked)
sarsuela fish stew
seitons fresh anchovies
suquet Catalan fish stew
tonyina tuna
truita trout
vieires scallops

Carn (Meat)

ànec duck
anyell spring lamb
be, xai, corder lamb
bistec steak
botifarra sausage
bou beef
broquetes kebabs
cabrit kid
caça game
colomi pigeon
conill rabbit
costelles chops
cua de brau bull's tail
cuixa leg
embotits charcuterie
entrecot sirloin
escudella i carn d'olla soup with boiled meats and vegetables
estofat stew
faisà pheasant
fricandó fricassé
gall d'indi turkey
garri porcell suckling pig
graellada mixed grill
guatlla quail
llebre hare
llom pork loin
llonganissa cured sausage
mandonguilles meatballs
oca goose
perdiu partridge
pintada guinea fowl
pollastre chicken
porc pork
porc senglar wild boar
rostit escalivat roast
salsitxa sausage
vedella veal
xoriç spiced sausage (chorizo)
vísceres offal
cap-i-pota stewed calf's head and foot
cervell brains
fetge liver
llengua tongue
peus de porc pig's trotters
ronyons kidneys
tripa tripe

Verdura (Vegetables)

albergínies aubergine (eggplant)
all garlic
amanida salad
bledes swiss chard
bolets wild mushrooms

ring onions
pumpkin
fes artichokes
a onion
cigrons chickpeas
ciurenys cep mushrooms
col cabbage
col-i-flor cauliflower
cogombre cucumber
enciam lettuce
endívies endives
espàrrecs asparagus
espinacs spinach
faves broad beans
fesols white beans
fredolics wood blewits (wild mushrooms)
julivert parsley
llenties lentils
menta mint
mongetes (tendres) beans (French)
naps turnips
olives olives
pastanagues carrots
patates (fregides) potatoes (fried)
pebrot pepper
pèsols peas
porros leeks
remolatxa beetroot
rabassols morels
rossinyol girolle mushroom
rovellons wild mushroom
tòfones truffles
tomàquets tomatoes
tombet vegetable casserole
xampinyons button mushrooms

Fruita (Fruit)
albercocs apricots
cireres cherries
figues figs
gerds raspberries
maduixes strawberries
magrana pomegranate
meló melon
panses raisins
pera pear
pinya pineapple
poma apple
préssec peach

raïm grape
taronja orange
síndria watermelon

Dolços (Desserts)
arròs amb llet rice pudding
crema catalana crème brûlée
galetes biscuits (cookies)
gelat ice cream
menjar blanc almond milk pudding
mel i mató soft cheese (with honey)
panellets marzipan cakes with pine nuts
pastissos pastries
tortell tart
turró almond nougat
xocolata chocolate

Drinks
aigua mineral (amb gas, sense gas) water
  (mineral, sparkling/still)
cervesa beer
suc juice
vi (negre, rosat, blanc) wine (red, rosé, white)

Miscellaneous
amanida salad
ametlles almonds
arròs rice
avellanes hazelnuts
cargols snails
coca (coques) Catalan pizza
espaguetis spaghetti
farcit stuffed
fideus noodles
formatges cheese
iogurt yogurt
llet milk
mantega butter
mel honey
oli oil
vinagre vinegar
ous eggs
pa bread
pastís cake or pie
pinyons pine nuts
sal salt
pebre pepper
sucre sugar
truita omelette

Planning
Your Trip

05

When to Go

Climate

For general touring Catalonia is a year-round destination, especially Barcelona. The climate is Mediterranean, fairly temperate but often quite humid: **July** and **August** are the hottest months, but the sea breeze often comes to the rescue to keep it from being stiflingly so. Northern parts of the region, influenced by the wild *tramuntana* wind off the Pyrenees, are most variable.

No matter where you go in **winter** you'll want a nice warm coat. You may need an umbrella any time up to **June; spring** in particular tends to be changeable. **January** can be surprisingly sunny; **February** is great for walking. In **August** many shops and restaurants close altogether.

If you can pick and choose and want to do more than sit on a beach, February to May or September and October are usually the most delicious months, and September has the added attraction of great festivals, while early October is the peak time for wild mushrooms.

Festivals

Catalans take festivals seriously; they love to swan around in medieval costumes or don their *barretinas* (floppy red hats) and set off as many firecrackers as possible. Traditional events, especially the **Festes Majors**, are

Average Maximum Temperatures in °C (°F)

	Jan	April	July	Oct
Barcelona	17 (63)	25 (77)	33 (91)	24 (75)
Andorra	6 (42)	14 (57)	26 (78)	16 (60)

occasions for a very specialized battery of Catalan folklore and traditional music. You'll find processions of *gegants* (12ft figures of wood and papier-mâché, supported by a man in the skirts) and *cap grossos* (demonically grinning 'fat heads', made of the same materials), dragons and other creatures. There are the daring human towers, supported by *castellers* who climb on each other's shoulders to the eerie music of the *grolla*, attaining eight or even nine levels. Common dances include the national circle dance, the *sardana*, the *Ball de Gitanes* (Gypsy Dance), and the *Ball de Bastons* (Stick Dance). At night, the big event is the *correfoc*, or 'fire-running', when terrifying dragons (made up of teams under canvas and wood) spit fireworks into the crowds, chased by devils brandishing fireworks; sometimes the devils have the show to themselves.

Note that dates for most festivals tend to be fluid, flowing towards the nearest weekend; if the actual date falls on a Thursday or a Tuesday, Catalans 'bridge' the date with the weekend to create a four-day whoopee. Ask at the tourist office in advance.

For national holidays, *see* p.60.

Calendar of Events

January

1 The **new year** is brought in with big parties and the custom of gulping down a grape for each bell-chime at midnight, for luck
5 The Three Kings arrive in Barcelona by sea and join a parade through the streets, tossing sweets to the children
End of month *Calçotada*, feast of spring onions, held everywhere, particularly in Valls.

February

2 *Candelaria, Festa Major* in L'Ametlla del Mar
Variable *Carnestoltes* (carnival) is celebrated throughout Catalonia. Ten days of costumes, dancing and parades in Barcelona and many cities, plus a gay carnival in Sitges. Solsona has

a carnival with the explosive 'marriage of the mad giant' and the ascent of a donkey (now an effigy) up the church tower
Lent Passion Play. Performances every year at Olesa de Montserrat, Cervera and Esparreguera

March

Throughout month Jazz Festival, Terrassa
Early Sant Medir, patron saint of broad beans, in Gràcia, Barcelona
Late Mar-early April International Dixieland Festival, Tarragona
Setmana Santa solemn religious processions
Holy Thursday *Verges*, Dance of Death

April

2nd week *Setmana Medieval*, Montblanc

23 *St Jordi*, exchange of books and roses, Barcelona, *see* p.34

Mid April–mid June Barcelona Guitar Festival

Last week–first week of May Andalucian fun at the April Fair at the Fòrum, Barcelona

May

Early *Trobada Gegantera* (festival of *gegants*), Montblanc

10–11 May Festival, with the burning of the devil, Badalona

11 *Sant Anastasí*, the *Festa Major* of Lleida, with parades featuring the oldest *gegants* in Catalonia; includes the *Aplec dels Caragols*, world's biggest snail festival, where 584 cooks serve snails to 300,000 people

Mid month *Temps de Flors*, Girona

17 Wool and country wedding festival, Ripoll

Corpus Christi (end of May or early June) *La Patum*, Berga (*see* p.231); Sitges (where the streets are covered with flower carpets); *L'Ou com Balla*, Ritual of the 'dancing egg', in fountains all around Barcelona's Barri Gòtic; giants and dragons parade, Solsona

June

Variable *Trobada Castellera*, a grand meeting of *castellers* in Plaça Catalunya, Barcelona

23 *Nit del Foc*, 'Night of Fire'. St John's Night is the maddest night of the year in Catalonia. Celebrations, bonfires and fireworks, followed by dancing everywhere, notably the *Falles* in Isil and the Vall de Boí.

End of month to early August Barcelona Festival Grec, the city's biggest cultural festival, see *www.barcelonafestival.com*

Late June *Habaneres* Song Festival, Calella de Palafrugell

29 *Festa de Sant Pere*, with *tronada* (explosions) and *castellers*, Reus

29–30 *Festa de Sant Pere*, L'Ametlla del Mar; *Festa Major*, Terrassa

July

Throughout month Pallaresa Rally, Noguera; international kayak and canoe competitions, Sort

Variable European Balloon Festival, Igualada; Doctor Loft Festival, massive 24-hour dance party, Empuriabrava; International World Music Festival, Vilanova i la Geltrú

July–Aug Peralada Festival, a huge variety of concerts (*www.festivalperalada.com*)

First week International Fireworks Festival, Tarragona; on the first weekend, *Festa del Transsegre*, a mock naval battle between the neighbourhoods of Balaguer; *Els Raiers*, Pobla de Segur, river raft races, music and food

12 Harvest Festival, Avià

2nd Sunday *Aplec de la Sardana*, big Catalan dance and music festival, Olot

16 *Festa del Carmen* with boat parade, Cambrils, L'Ampolla, Sant Carles de la Ràpita

Mid July Roman Sun Festival of Guissona (with gladiators)

3rd Sat *Festa del Cava*, Prades; *cava* flows from the town fountain all night

Mid-July–Aug Cadaqués Music Festival; Torroella de Montgrí International Music Festival

24 *Santa Cristina*, maritime processions, etc., Lloret de Mar

Last week Vendrell Festival, with *castellers*, dances, etc.; *Festa Major*, L'Espluga de Francolí

August

First week *Firagost*, August farmer's market and fair, Valls; *Festa Major*, Vilanova

12 Fire Festival, Maçanet, with lots of *correfocs*

9–15 *Festa Major* with big fireworks, Salou

15–22 *Festa Major de Gràcia*, Barcelona, an exuberant street festival

19 *Sant Magi*, Tarragona

Last week *Festa Major*, Sitges; *Aquelarre*, Cervera, parades of witches, dragons and monsters; *Festa Major*, Manresa

24 *Festa Major*, Roda de Barà

29 *Festa Major*, Mora d'Ebre

30 *Festa Major*, Vilafranca del Penedès, with fiery devils' dances

Last Sun Catalan sheepdog trials, Castellar de N'Hug

September

Early Schubertiada Chamber Music Festival, Vilabertran

First weekend Medieval Festival, Besalú; *Festa de Rey Jaume*, Salou; *Festa Major*, Tortosa, Gandesa

4 *Festa Major*, Torredembarra

8 Virgin's birthday, ceremonies at Montserrat, Cambrils, Montblanc; *Festa Major* in Solsona, Benifallet

9 *Corre de Bou* (bull-running) and Barrel Bull Dance, Cardona

11 *Diada Català*, Catalan National Day; *Terra del Troubadors* medieval festival, Castelló d'Empúries

Mid-month *Festa de la Sal*, anchovy-salting festival, L'Escala

16 Misericordia Festival, Reus

24 *Festa de La Mercè*. Barcelona says farewell to summer with a week-long event featuring 600 events and an alternative music festival BAM, all culminating in a frenzied *correfoc*

Fourth Sun *Festa Major*, Cervera

23 *Santa Tecla*, huge 12-day festival, Tarragona

23 La Minerva Festival, Calella, with lots of *sardana* dancing

Late Sept–early Oct Girona Jazz Festival

October

Throughout month *Festival Internacional Enric Granados*, classical music, Lleida

First week Berga mushroom festival; Cinema Festival, Sitges

2nd Sun *Festa Major* with bullfights, Ulldecona

15 *Fira de Santa Teresa*; traditional livestock fair (since 1163) with food, crafts and festivities, Esterri d'Aneu

21 *Santa Ursula*, major *casteller* action in Valls

Late Girona film festival and the *Fires* of *Sant Narcis*

November

9 *Festa Major*, Balaguer

11 *Festa Major*, Altafulla

December

Early Medieval Christmas market, Vic

First Sunday Ratafia festival, Besalú

8–24 *Fira de Santa Llúcia*, Barcelona, Christmas market in front of the cathedral, with a huge selection of *caganers*

Tourist Information

After receiving millions of tourists each year for the last four decades, no country has more information offices, or more helpful ones, or more intelligent brochures and detailed maps. Every city will have an office, and you will usually find someone who speaks English except in rural areas. Sometimes they'll be less helpful in the big cities in the summer. More often, though, you'll be surprised at how well they know the details of accommodation and transport. Many large cities also maintain municipal tourist offices. **Opening hours** for most tourist offices are Monday to Friday, 9.30–1.30 and 4–7.

Nearly every town and city in Catalonia has its own website for everything you might want to see and do whilst there; some are more informative than others. For more information, ring the following: in Catalonia **t** 012; outside Catalonia in Spain, **t** 90 240 00 12; from abroad **t** 34 90 240 00 12, *www.turismedecatalunya.com*.

Spanish National Tourist Offices

UK: 22–23 Manchester Square, London W1V 3PX, **t** (020) 7486 8077, *www.tourspain.co.uk*. Also see the **Catalan Tourist Board**, 17 Fleet Street, 3rd Floor, EC4Y 1AA, **t** (020) 7583 88 55, *www.catalunyatourism.com*.

USA: Water Tower Place, Suite 915 East, 845 North Michigan Avenue, Chicago, Illinois

60611, **t** (312) 642 1992; 8383 Wilshire Blvd, Suite 960, Beverly Hills, California 90211, **t** (323) 658 7188; 666 Fifth Avenue, New York, NY 10103, **t** (212) 265 8822; 1221 Brickell Avenue, Suite 1850, Miami, Florida 33131, **t** (305) 358 1992; **Barcelona Convention and Visitors Bureau**, Marketing Challenges Intl, Inc., 10 East 21st Street, Suite 600, New York NY 10010, **t** (212) 529 8484, *www.catalunya tourism.com*.

Canada: 2 Bloor St West, Suite 3402, Toronto, Ontario, M4W 3E2, **t** (416) 961 3131, *www. tourspain.toronto.on.ca*.

Japan: Daini Toranomon Denki Building, 6F, 3-1-10 Toranomon, Minato Ku, Tokyo 105-0001, **t** + 81 (3) 3432 6141, *www.spaintour.com*. Provides information for Australian and New Zealand nationals.

Embassies and Consulates

Foreign Embassies in Spain

UK: Avda Diagonal 477–13°, Barcelona, **t** 93 366 6200, *http://ukinspain.fco.gov.uk*.

Ireland: Paseo de la Castellana, 46–4°, Madrid, **t** 91 436 40 93.

USA: Consulate: Pg Elisenda Montcada 23, Barcelona, **t** 93 280 22 27, *http://barcelona. usconsulate.gov*.

Canada: Plaça Catalunya 9, 1st floor, Barcelona, **t** 93 412 72 36, *www.dfait-maeci. gc.ca*.

Australia: Plaza Descubridor Diego de Ordás 3, Madrid, **t** 91 353 66 00, *www.spain.embassy.gov.au*.

Spanish Embassies Abroad

UK: 20 Draycott Place, London SW3 2RZ, **t** (020) 7589 8989; 1a Brook House, 70 Spring Gardens, Manchester, **t** (0161) 236 1262; 63 North Castle Street, Edinburgh, **t** (0131) 220 1843, *http://spain.embassyhomepage.com*.

Ireland: 17a Merlyn Park, Ballsbridge, Dublin 4, **t** (01) 269 1640.

USA: 31 St James Avenue, Suite 905, Boston, MA 02116, **t** (617) 536 2506; 180 North Michigan Avenue, Chicago, IL 60601, **t** (312) 782 4588; 2655 Le Jeune Road, 203 Coral Gables, Florida, **t** (305) 446 5511; 5055 Wilshire Blvd, Suite 960 Los Angeles, CA 90036, **t** (323) 938 0158; 150 East 58th Street, New York, NY 10155, **t** (212) 355 4080; 1405 Sutter St, San Francisco, CA 94109, **t** (415) 922 2995/96; 1800 Bering Dr., Suite 660, Houston, TX 77057, **t** (713) 783 6200; 2375 Pennyslvania Avenue NW, Washington, DC 20009, **t** (202) 728 2330, *www.maec.es*.

Canada: 4 Stanley Avenue, Ottawa, Ontario, K1M 1P4, **t** (613) 747 2252; 2 Bloor Street East, Suite 1201; Toronto, Ontario M4W 1A8, **t** (416) 977 1661; 1 West Mount Square, Montreal H3Z 2P9, **t** (514) 935 5235; *http://spain.embassyincanada.com*.

Australia: Level 24, St. Martin's Tower, 31 Market Street, Sydney, **t** 02 9261 2433; 9th Floor, 5 Mill Street, 6000, Perth, **t** 08 9322 6812; 16 Stanton Road, 4878, Smithfield, Queensland, **t** 7 4038 2324; 146 Elgin Street, 3053 Carlton, Victoria, **t** 03 9347 1966.

Entry Formalities

Passports and Visas

Holders of EU, US, Canadian, Australian and New Zealand passports do not need a visa to enter Spain for stays of up to three months; most other nationals do.

If you intend staying longer in Spain, you should report to the Foreign Nationals Office (*oficina de extranjeros*) at the local police station and apply for a community resident's card (*tarjeta de residente comunitario*). EU citizens are no longer required to obtain a resident's card, although it can be useful.

Non-EU citizens had best apply for an extended visa at home, a complicated procedure requiring proof of income, etc.

Customs

Duty-free allowances have been abolished within the EU. EU nationals over the age of 17 can now import a limitless amount of goods for their personal use. For travellers coming from outside the EU, the duty-free limits are one litre of spirits or two litres of liquors (port, sherry or champagne), plus two litres of wine and 200 cigarettes.

Residents of the USA may each take home US$400-worth of foreign goods without attracting duty, including the tobacco and alcohol allowance. Canadians can bring home $300 worth of goods in a year, plus their tobacco and alcohol allowances.

UK Customs, **t** 0845 010 9000, *www.hmrc.gov.uk*.

US Customs, **t** (202) 354 1000, *www.customs.gov*.

Canadian Customs, *www.cbsa.gc.ca*.

Disabled Travellers

Eurotunnel is a good way to travel to northern Spain by car from the UK, since passengers are allowed to stay in their vehicles. By train, Eurostar gives wheelchair passengers first-class travel for second-class fares. Most ferry companies will offer special facilities if contacted beforehand. Vehicles fitted to accommodate disabled people pay reduced tolls on *autoroutes* through France.

Once you arrive, the facilities for disabled travellers are limited outside Barcelona, which has ramps everywhere. All city buses take wheelchairs, although so far only the two newest metro lines (L2 and L11) have lifts in all stations. The rail operator RENFE usually provides wheelchairs at main city stations, and many trains are slowly being upgraded to provide services for the disabled (lift access to platforms, etc.). Check accessibility of hotels when booking, or reserve through **Accessible Barcelona**, which provides a wide range of services for disabled travellers, *www.accessiblebarcelona.com*. For wheelchair-accessible beaches, see *www.esplaya.com*. To hire an electric scooter or power chair, see *www.cosmoscooter.com*.

Disability Organizations

In Spain

ECOM, Gran Vía de les Corts Catalanes Principal 562, Barcelona, t 93 451 55 50, www.ecom.cat. A federation of private Spanish organizations which offer services for disabled people.

Institut Municipal de Disminuïts, Avda Diagonal, 233, Barcelona, t 93 413 27 75. Municipal office with accessibility info for Barcelona. Open Mon–Fri 8.30–2.30.

ONCE, C/José Ortega y Gasset 18, Madrid, t 91 577 37 56, www.once.es. Association for the blind.

In the UK and Ireland

Access Travel, 6 The Hillock, Astley, Lancashire M29 7GW, t (01942) 88 88 44, www.access-travel.co.uk. Travel agent for disabled people.

Holiday Care Service, Enham Place, Enham Alamein, Andover SP11 6JS, t 0845 124 9971, www.holidaycare.org.uk. Information on accommodation, transport, equipment hire, services, tour operators and contacts.

Irish Wheelchair Association, Blackheath Drive, Clontarf, Dublin 3, t (01) 818 6400, www.iwa.ie. Provides travel advice and information.

RADAR (Royal Association for Disability and Rehabilitation), 12 City Forum, 250 City Rd, London EC1V 8AF, t (020) 7250 3222, www.radar.org.uk. Provides information and books.

RNIB (Royal National Institute of Blind People), 105 Judd St, London WC1H 9NE, t (020) 7388 2525, www.rnib.org.uk. The mobility unit has a 'Plane Easy' audio-tape with advice for visually impaired flyers, and also advises on finding accommodation.

Tourism for All, Hawkins Suite, Enham Place, Enham Alamein, Andover, Hants SP11 6JS, t 0845 124 9971, www.holidaycare.org.uk.

In the USA and Canada

American Foundation for the Blind, 11 Penn Plaza, Suite 300, New York, NY 10001, t (212) 502 7600, www.afb.org. Provides information for visually impaired travellers.

Fedcap, 211 West 14th St, New York, NY 10011, t (212) 727 4200. Summer tours for members.

SATH (Society for Accessible Travel and Hospitality), 347 5th Ave, Suite 605, New York, NY 10016, t (212) 447 7284, www.sath.org. Travel and access information. The website has good links and a list of online publications.

In Australia

National Disability Services, 33 Thesiger Court, Deakin, ACT 2600, Australia, t 02 6283 3200, www.nds.org.au.

Internet Sites

Access-Able Travel Source, www.access-able.com. Information for older and disabled travellers.

Access Ability, www.access-ability.org/travel.html. Information on travel agencies.

Emerging Horizons, www.emerginghorizons.com. An online newsletter for disabled travellers.

Accessible Barcelona, www.accessiblebarcelona.com. See p.49.

Insurance and EHIC Cards

Citizens of the EU are entitled to a certain amount of free medical care in EU countries if they have a free European Health Insurance Card or EHIC (available online at www.dh.gov.uk/travellers, or www.ehic.org.uk, or by calling t 0845 606 2030, or by post using the forms available from post offices). You will need a card for every family member. Because some doctors and hospitals are private, be sure to enquire in advance whether they will accept your EHIC card.

Canadians, US citizens and those of other nations should check their individual health policies. As an alternative, consider a travel insurance policy covering theft and losses and offering 100 per cent medical refund; check to see if it covers extra expenses, in case you get stranded by an airport or train strike. Beware that accidents resulting from sports are rarely covered by ordinary insurance. Save all doctor's and pharmacy receipts, plus police reports for thefts.

Maps

Cartography has been an art in Spain since the 12th-century Catalans charted their Mediterranean Empire in Europe's first great school of map-making. The tourist offices give out detailed maps of every town. Topographical maps for hikers and mountaineers can be obtained from **CNIG** (Centro Nacional de Información Geográfica), part of the Instituto Geográfico Nacional (IGN). There are shops in all provincial capitals, and their maps are usually available in larger bookshops. You can buy maps and travel books online from the Spanish travel bookshop **Altaïr**, *www.altair.es*.

If in the UK, visit **Stanfords** at 12 Long Acre, London WC2, for the biggest selection, or see *www.stanfords.co.uk*.

Money and Banks

The **currency** of Spain is the euro. Coins are issued in denominations of 1, 2, 5, 10, 20 and 50 cents, and 1 and 2 euros. Notes are issued in denominations of 5, 10, 20, 50, 100, 200 and 500 euros. For the latest **exchange rates**, check out *www.xe.com/ucc*.

Major international **credit cards** are widely used, although American Express and Diners' Club cards may not be accepted. For credit card purchases, you will have to show some photo ID (a passport or driver's licence). Smaller hotels, *pensiones*, restaurants, bars and cafés, particularly in rural areas, won't accept credit cards. Museums and sights almost never have credit card facilities.

Cash withdrawals in euros can be made from **automatic cash machines** (ATMs) using your PIN; the specific cards accepted are marked on each machine, and all give instructions in English. In cities, some of these are locked at night. Banks often charge a fee for withdrawals, although some have special partnerships with Spanish banks. It's also best to let your bank know that you're travelling.

Getting There

By Air

Catalonia has international airports in **Barcelona**, **Girona** and **Reus** and an astounding variety of flight options, especially from the UK. Trawl the internet: sometimes national airlines British Airways and Iberia offer special deals equal to those offered by the low cost carriers. There are direct flights to Barcelona from North America, or consider flying via London.

Airline Carriers

UK and Ireland (Direct)

bmibaby, (UK) t 0905 8 28 28 28, (Ireland) t (01) 890 340 122. To Barcelona from Birmingham.

British Airways, (UK) t 0844 493 0787, (Ireland) t 1890 626 747, *www.ba.com*. To Barcelona from Aberdeen, Durham-Tees Valley, Edinburgh, Glasgow, Inverness, Leeds-Bradford, Liverpool, London Gatwick, London Heathrow, Manchester and Newcastle. Code-sharing with Iberia, Spain's national airline.

easyJet, t 0905 821 0905, *www.easyjet.com*. To Barcelona from London Gatwick, London Stansted, London Luton, Liverpool, Belfast, Newcastle, East Midlands and Bristol.

FlyGlobespan, t 0871 271 9000, *www.flyglobespan.com*. To Barcelona from Aberdeen, Edinburgh and Glasgow.

Iberia, t 08706 090 500, *www.iberia.com*. The same routes as BA, above.

Jet 2, t 0906 302 0660, *www.jet2.com*. To Barcelona from Belfast and Leeds-Bradford.

KLM, t 0871 222 7474., *www.klm.com*. To Barcelona from Cardiff, Leeds-Bradford and Newcastle.

Monarch Airlines t 08700 40 50 40, *www.monarch.co.uk*. To Barcelona from Manchester.

Ryanair, (UK) t 0871 246 0000, (Ireland) t 0818 303030, *www.ryanair.com*. To Girona from London Stansted, London Luton, Liverpool, Newcastle, East Midlands. Manchester, Glasgow, Leeds, Durham-Tees Valley, Blackpool, Birmingham, Bristol, Bournemouth, Doncaster, Newquay, Shannon and Dublin. To Reus from Dublin, Glasgow, LIverpool, Birmingham, London Luton and London Stansted.

USA and Canada (Direct)

Air Transat, t 1-866 847 1112, *www.airtransat.ca*. Flights from Montreal, Toronto and Vancouver.

American Airlines, t 1-800 433 7300, *www.aa.com*. Flies directly from New York.

Continental Airlines, t 1-800 231 0856, *www.continental.com*. Direct from Newark.

Delta, t 1-800 221 1212, *www.delta.com*. Flights from Atlanta and New York.

Iberia, t 1-800 772 4642, *www.iberia.com*. Flights from Boston, New York, Chicago, Miami and Washington D.C.

US Airways, t 1-800 622 1015, *www.usairways .com*. Flights from Philadelphia.

Discounts and Youth Fares

UK and Ireland

Budget Travel, 134 Lower Baggot St, Dublin 2, t (01) 631 1111, *www.budgettravel.ie*.

Trailfinders, 194 Kensington High St, London W8 7RG, t (020) 7938 3939; 4–5 Dawson St, Dublin 2, t (01) 677 7888, plus branches in other major UK cities; www.trailfinders.co.uk.

United Travel, 12 Clonkeen Rd, Deansgrange, Blackrock, Co. Dublin, t (01) 219 0600, www.unitedtravel.ie.

STA, 52 Grosvenor Gardens, Victoria, London SW1W 0AG, t 0871 468 0649, www.statravel.co.uk. There are several other branches in London, and many in other major UK towns and cities.

USIT Now, 19–21 Aston Quay, Dublin 2, t (01) 602 1906, www.usitnow.ie. Ireland's no. 1 specialist student travel agent, with other branches around the country.

USA and Canada

Airhitch, 481 Eighth Ave, Suite 1771, New York, NY 10001-1820, t (212) 247 4482 or t 877 AIRHITCH, www.airhitch.org.

STA, t 800 781 4040, www.statravel.com. There are branches at most universities and at 30 Third Avenue, New York, NY 10003, t (212) 473 6100, and 920 Westwood Boulevard, Los Angeles, CA 90024, t (310) 824 1574.

TFI Tours, 1270 Broadway Suite 409, New York, NY 10001, t (212) 736 1140 or t 800 745 8000, www.tfitours.com.

Travel Cuts, 187 College St, Toronto, Ontario M5T 1P7, t 1 866 246 9762, www.travelcuts.com. Canada's largest student agency, with branches in most provinces.

Websites

www.cheapflights.co.uk
www.ebookers.com
www.expedia.com
www.flightcentre.com
www.flights.com
www.flydeals.co.uk
www.lastminute.com
www.opodo.com
www.orbitz.com
www.smartertravel.com
www.traveldiscounts.com

By Train

Travelling by high-speed train makes an attractive alternative to flying from the UK. **Eurostar** departs from London St Pancras with direct connections to Paris (Gare du Nord; 2hrs 15mins) and Lille (1hr 40mins). Fares are cheaper if booked in advance and/or include a Saturday night away. You must check in at least 30mins before departure or you will not be allowed on the train. Prices range from £59 return (more than 21 days in advance) to £300 for a standard return.

Once you reach Paris or Lille, France's high-speed **TGVs** (trains à grande vitesse) shoot along at an average of 180mph, when they're not breaking world records. From London to Barcelona it's a full day's trip, changing trains in Paris and at Port Bou/La Tour de Carol, Montpellier or Toulouse – although by 2012 you should be able to travel straight through to Barcelona and beyond. Also look at the increasingly popular and comfortable overnight **Trenhotel** from Paris (also Milan and Zurich) to Barcelona at www.elipsos.com.

If you plan to take some long train journeys, it may be worth investing in a rail pass. The good-value **Inter-Rail pass**, www.interrail. net (for European residents of at least six months) offers 16 days', 22 days' or one month's unlimited travel in Europe, plus discounts on trains to cross -Channel ferry terminals, and returns on Eurostar. Inter-Rail cards are not valid on UK trains. You can also get an Inter-Rail One Country Pass for three or eight days. Children under 12 are eligible for half price tickets; those aged 12–25 also get a discount.

Non-European residents have a wide choice of passes, including Eurailpass and France 'n' Spain Pass. See www.eurail.com.

For long-distance train travel, bicycles need to be transported separately and must be registered and insured (unless you can fold or dismantle them). They can be delivered to your destination, though this may take several days. On Eurostar you need to check in your bike at least 24 hours before you travel, or wait 24 hours at the other end. The cost is £20. For details, call t 08705 850 850.

Rail Europe handles bookings for all services, including Eurostar and **Motorail** (trains can transport your car from Calais as far as Narbonne in France, 123km from the Spanish border). They also sell Interrail passes.

Rail Europe, 1 Lower Regent St, London, t 08448 484 064, www.raileurope.co.uk.

Rail Europe (for travellers from outside Europe), www.raileurope.com.

Eurostar, t 08705 186 186, *www.eurostar.com*.

Spanish Rail, Regent House Business Centre. 24–25 Nutford Place, London, t (020) 7725 7063, *www.spanish-rail.co.uk*. RENFE's official UK agents.

By Coach

Eurolines offers departures several times a week in the summer (once a week out of season) from London to Barcelona via Lyon in 29 hours. Single fares at the time of writing are £75. There are discounts for anyone under 26, senior citizens and children under 12.

Eurolines, t 08717 818181, *www.eurolines.co.uk*.

By Car

From the UK via France the fastest route to Catalonia is via Paris to Perpignan, crossing the border on the Mediterranean side of the Pyrenees. Count on average 1½ days' steady driving (or see left for the Motorail option).

For a slower, more scenic drive, opt for one of the classic routes over the Pyrenees, through Puigcerdà, Andorra or Vall d'Aran.

To bring a GB-registered car into Spain, you need a vehicle registration document, full driving licence and insurance papers (a Green Card is not necessary), which must be carried at all times when driving, along with your passport. If your driving licence is of the old-fashioned sort without a photograph you are strongly recommended to apply for an international driving permit (available from the AA or RAC). Non-EU citizens should preferably have an international driving licence, which has a Spanish translation incorporated. Your vehicle should display a nationality plate indicating its country of registration. Before travelling, check

Drivers' Clubs

For more information on driving through France and Spain, including international driving permits, breakdown insurance and motorway tolls, contact the AA, RAC, or, in the USA, the AAA:

AA, General enquiries, t 0870 600 0371, *www.theaa.com*.

RAC, General enquiries, t 0870 572 2722, *www.rac.co.uk*.

AAA (USA), t 800 222 4357, *www.aaa.com*.

everything is in perfect order. Two red hazard triangles, reflective jacket, headlight converters and a spare set of bulbs and tools to change them are obligatory; if you wear corrective glasses you need to carry a spare pair. it's also recommended that you carry a first-aid kit and a fire extinguisher.

Getting Around

By Train

The Spanish national railway, **RENFE**, runs trains that are almost always clean and comfortable, and do their best to keep to the schedules – but the network remains weirdly complex and getting information out of it can be exasperating.

The hierarchy of trains begins with the new high-speed **AVE**; one runs from Barcelona to Madrid at 210 mph, stopping at Tarragona and Lleida. There are main **inter-city** lines up the coast to France and Valencia, a few smaller regional lines, and a network of **commuter trains** (cercanías in Spanish, rodalies in Catalan) emanating from Barcelona that will take you as far as Manresa or Sitges.

In addition, the Generalitat de Catalunya runs a separate line, the **FGC**, which operates some of the Barcelona suburban services, and an old **narrow gauge** line from Lleida to La Pobla de Segur that makes a pleasant tourist excursion. By 2012 FGC will run all local Barcelona services.

Every variety of train has different services and a different price – yet the system is efficient, albeit confusing for the visitor. There are discounts for children (aged 4–14, under-4s travel free), large families, senior citizens and regular travellers. If you buy a single ticket, hang on to it, because if you decide to return you are still eligible for a discount. There is a discount pass for under-26s, the *carnet joven*.

Every city has a RENFE travel office in the centre, and you can make good use of these for information and tickets. Always buy tickets in advance if you can; one of RENFE's little tricks is to close station ticket-windows 10 minutes before your train arrives, and if you show up at the last minute you could be out of luck. You can also book tickets online, or by telephone, where you'll be given a reference number called a *localizador*, good for boarding. If you miss your train, watch out; the return trip reservation will be cancelled.

RENFE, t 902 24 02 02, *www.renfe.es* (website has timetables, types of ticket available and fares, also in English). For international trains, visit *www.elipsos.com*.

By Bus

A number of companies provide bus services across Catalonia. Large towns will have a central station; otherwise tourist offices are the best sources of information. Like the trains, buses are cheap by northern European standards, but not dirt cheap. Small towns and villages are generally linked by bus to their provincial capitals but not each other. There aren't enough of them to make bus travel a good option for rural touring, and most of the scanty services available to villages are timed to be useful for working people and schoolkids.

By Car

This is the most convenient way of getting from town to town – and the worst way of getting around within one. First-time visitors to Spain are always amazed how dense and intense even small towns and villages can be. Traffic generally moves tolerably well, but finding **parking** is always difficult, and at times nearly impossible. One tip: space which appears to be private – e.g. underground car parks of apartment blocks and offices – is often public, and rates are usually modest. Catalonia's **road network** is fine, in good repair and sometimes impressive.

Petrol prices are regulated by the government (unleaded: *sense plom*; diesel: *dièsel*); it's about two-thirds cheaper in Spain than in the UK (about twice the US price).

To drive in Spain you'll need registration and insurance documents, and a driving licence (*see* 'Getting There By Car', p.53). The **speed limit** is 100km (62 miles) per hour on national highways, unless otherwise marked, and 120km (75 miles) per hour on *autopistes* (toll motorways).

Car Hire Companies

Auto Europe, (UK) **t** 0800 223 5555, (USA) **t** 1-800 223 5555, *www.autoeurope.com*.

Avis, (UK) **t** 0844 581 0147, (Spain) **t** 94 427 57 60, *www.avis.com*.

Budget, (UK) **t** 08701 56 56 56, (USA) **t** 800 527 0700, *www.budget.com*.

Europcar, (UK) **t** 08706 075 000, (USA) **t** 877 940 6900, (Spain) **t** 91 343 45 12, *www.europcar.com*.

Hertz, (UK) **t** 08708 44 88 44, (Spain) **t** 91 749 90 69, *www.hertz.com*.

Holiday Autos, (UK) **t** 0870 400 4461, (Spain) **t** 90 244 84 49, *www.holidayautos.com*.

National/ATESA, (Spain) **t** 90 210 01 01, *www.atesa.es*.

Car Hire

Car hire is slightly cheaper in Spain than elsewhere in Europe. To hire a car, you need to be at least 21 (some agencies require you to be 23 or 25) and to have held a licence for at least a year. The internet almost always delivers the best deals.

By Taxi

Taxis are cheap enough for Spaniards to use them regularly. The **average fare** for a ride in a city will be €6–10. Taxis are metered, and they are entitled to surcharges (for luggage, night-time trips, or to the airport) and, if you cross the city limits, they can charge double the fare shown. You can hail a cab from the street, and there are always a few around stations or call the information number **t** 11811 for the number of a **radio taxi**. In Barcelona, call **t** 933 033 033.

Where to Stay

Hotels in Spain are no longer the bargains they once were. However, overall rates are still pretty reasonable, and bargains can still be found. For those travelling on a tight budget, there are plenty of *hostales* (generally one- or two-star places), rooms over bars, and rooms in private homes. Prices must be posted in hotel lobbies and in rooms, and if there's a problem you can ask for the complaints book, or *llibre de reclamacions*.

Prices for single rooms will average about 60 per cent of a double, while triples or an extra bed are around 35 per cent more. Within the price ranges, the most expensive are likely to be in the big cities, while the cheapest places are in provincial towns.

If you're touring, a good investment would be the Generalitat's *Guía d'Hotels de Catalunya*, listing every classified hotel and hostal in the region, available in many bookshops (€6). Local tourist offices have complete accommodation lists.

Paradores

The government, in its plan to develop tourism in the 1928, started this nationwide chain of classy hotels to draw attention to little-visited areas. They restored old palaces, castles and monasteries for the purpose, furnished them with antiques and installed fine restaurants featuring local specialities. Not all are historic landmarks; in resort areas, they are as likely to be cleanly designed modern buildings. In most cases both the rooms and the restaurant will be the most expensive in town, though most offer substantial off-season discounts. There are also discounts for the over-55s and those aged 20-35 (but these must be booked in advance, see *www.parador.es*).

Catalonia has seven *paradores*: at Vic, Tortosa, Cardona, La Seu d'Urgell, Vielha, Artíes and Aiguablava on the Costa Brava.

Hoteles

Hoteles (H) are rated from one to five stars, according to the services they offer. These are the most expensive places, and even a one-star hotel will be a comfortable, middle-range establishment. Many of the more expensive hotels have rooms available cheaper than the rack rate (ask), and many offer internet bargains. You can often get discounts in the off season but will be charged higher rates during festivals, large trade fairs (in Barcelona) and in many cases at weekends and during Easter.

Hostales, Pensiones and Fondas

Hostales (Hs) and *pensiones* (P) are rated from one to three stars. These are usually more modest places, often a floor in an apartment block; a two-star *hostal* is

Hotel Price Ranges

Categories are based on a standard double room (en suite where available) in high season.

luxury	€€€€€	over €250
very expensive	€€€€	€160–250
expensive	€€€	€100–160
moderate	€€	€70–100
inexpensive	€	under €70

roughly equivalent to a one-star hotel, but not always.

The bottom of the scale used to be the *fonda* (F), little different from a one-star *hostal*. Today though, some rather stylish new hotel-restaurants have taken to calling themselves *fondas*. In Catalonia they've banded together in an association: you can get a complete list at *www.casafonda.com*.

Youth Hostels

Youth hostels are often a good bargain in Catalonia; we've put some in the text.

You can get a complete list from the **Youth Hostel Network of Catalonia** at *www. xanascat.cat* (also in English).

Camping

Campsites are rated from one to three stars, depending on their facilities, and Catalonia has some excellent ones, listed by province at *www.camping-spain.net*. Facilities in most first-class sites include shops, restaurants, bars, laundries, hot showers, first aid, pools, and, occasionally, a tennis court.

Cases Rurals/Turisme Rural

With the rise in hotel prices, staying in private homes has become an increasingly popular in Catalonia. *Cases rurals* (or *turisme rural*, or *agroturisme*), rural accommodation in farms or country houses (*masies*) has become extremely popular. Some are rented whole, while others offer B&B accommodation, and some offer self-catering facilities, activites and even cooking classes.

For listings see these websites:
www.toprural.com
www.casesrurals.com
www.turismerural.com
www.agroturisme.com
www.ruralcatalunya.com

Specialist Tour Operators

In the UK

Activities Abroad, Suite 2, Netherton Park, Stannington, Northumberland, t (01670) 789 991, *www.activitiesabroad.com*. Family adventures in the Catalan Pyrenees.

Alternative Travel Group, 274 Banbury Road, Oxford, t (01865) 315 678, *www.atg-oxford.co.uk*. Walking tours near Girona.

Andante Travel, The Old Barn, Old Road, Alderbury, Salisbury, Wiltshire, t (01722) 713 800, *www.andantetravels.co.uk*. Cultural tours including the Ebro Delta, and Rock Art.

Catalonia Walks, Jasmine Cottage, Wetheral, Carlisle, Cumbria, t (01228) 561990, *www.cataloniawalks.com*. Walking tours.

Exodus Travel, Grange Hills, Weir Road, London SW12 0NE, t (020) 8675 5550, *www.exodus.co.uk*. Walking, cycling, snowshoeing and mountaineering holidays.

Explore Worldwide Ltd, Nelson House, 55 Victoria Rd, Farnborough, Hants, t 0870 333 4001, *www.explore.co.uk*. Barcelona, Girona, La Garrotxa, and Pyrenees; cycling tours.

Inntravel, Nr. Castle Howard, York, t (01653) 617 946, *www.inntravel.co.uk*. Cycling and walking throughout Catalonia.

Page & Moy Ltd, Compass House, Rockingham Road, Market Harborough, Leics, t 08708 334 012, *www.page-moy.com*. Cultural guided tours in Barcelona and Girona, and hill-walking.

Plantagenet Tours, 85 The Grove, Moordown, Bournemouth, t (01202) 521 895, *www.plantagenettours.com*. Historical tours.

Ramblers Holidays, Lemsford Hill, Lemsford, Welwyn Garden City, t (01707) 331 133, *www.ramblersholidays.co.uk*. Walking tours along the coast, in the Pyrenees and Barcelona.

Sherpa Expeditions, 131a Heston Road, Hounslow, t (020) 8577 2717, *www.sherpa-walking-holidays.co.uk*. Cycle tours.

Unicorn Trails, 17, Acorn Centre, Chestnut Ave, Biggleswade, Bedfordshire, t (01767) 600606, *www.unicorntrails.com*. Riding holidays.

In the USA

Alta Tours, 1801 Skycrest Drive 7, Walnut Creek, CA 94595, t 800 338 4191,*www.altatours.com*. Tours, hotels, fly-drive holidays.

Cyclomondo, t (212) 504 8368, *www.cyclomundo.com*. Cycling tours around Girona.

Heritage Tours, 121 West 27 Street, Suite 1201, New York, NY 10001 t 800 378 4555, *www.heritagetoursonline.com*. Customized cultural tours, including concerts at the Palau de la Música, dinners with Ferran Adrià.

Kesher Kosher Tours, 347 Fifth Avenue, Suite 706, New York, NY 10016, t (toll-free) 800 847 0700, *www.keshertours.com*. Kosher tours to Barcelona, Girona and around.

Olé Spain Cultural Walking Tours, 22 Davis Street, Seekonk, MA 02771, t 888 869 7156, *www.olespain.com*. Essential Catalonia tour.

Wilderness Travel, 1102 9th Street, Berkeley, CA 94710, t 1 800 368 2794, *www.wildernesstravel.com*. Hiking in the Pyrenees.

In Spain

Catalan Bird Tours, C/Roses, 12 (Buzón 179), Vora Sitges, Canyelles,Barcelona, t (+34) 93 818 82 72, *www.catalanbirdtours.com*. Organized and bespoke birdwatching tours.

Cicloturisme i Medi Ambient, C/Impressors Oliva 4, Local A, Girona, t (+34) 97 222 10 47, *www.cicloturisme.com*. Cycling in Girona.

Costa Brava Rambles, t (+34) 62 047 90 77 *www.costabravarambles.co.uk*. Walking tours on the northern Costa Brava.

Iberian Adventures, Urb. La Avellaneda 15, Arenas de San Pedro, 05400 Ávila, Spain, t (+34) 92 037 25 44, *www.iberianadventures.com*. Activity, history, nature, gourmet holidays.

Madrid & Beyond, Specialists in Spain, Gran Via 59-8-D, 28013 Madrid, t (+34) 91 758 00 63, *www.madridandbeyond.com*. Bespoke itineraries in Barcelona and Catalonia.

Totally Spain, Barrio Zoña 36, Bajo Izquierda, Castillo, Cantabria, t 07092 001637 (UK), t (561) 828 0238 (USA), *www.totallyspain.com*. Seven- and ten-day tours of Catalonia.

Villa Holidays

Barcelona Home, Viladomat 89-95 Entlo.3, t (+34) 93 423 12 70, *www.barcelona-home.com*. Flats, and apartments in and around Barcelona.

Catalan Holidays, Santa Victoria 11, Sant Pol de Mar-Barcelona, t (+34) 93 760 06 55, *www.catalanholidays.com*. Holiday homes on Catalonia's *costas*.

North Spain Villas, t 0800 316 0244 (UK), t (+34) 93 452 13 15, *www.northspainvillas.com*. Villas across Catalonia and the Pyrenees.

Haven on Earth, 107 High Street, Hampton, t (020) 8941 1700, *www.havenonearth.co.uk*. Villas along the Costa Brava.

Individual Travellers, Spring Mill, Earby, Barnoldswick, Lancashire, t 0845 604 3877, *www.individualtravellers.com*. Village and rural accommodation.

Secret Destinations, Ulanor Hill, The Square, Grassington, N. Yorks, t 0845 612 9000, *www.secretdestinations.com*. Self-catering flats, villas and hotels throughout the region.

Practical A–Z

06

Conversions: Imperial–Metric

Length (multiply by)
Inches to centimetres: 2.54
Centimetres to inches: 0.39
Feet to metres: 0.3
Metres to feet: 3.28
Yards to metres: 0.91
Metres to yards: 1.09
Miles to kilometres: 1.61
Kilometres to miles: 0.62

Area (multiply by)
Inches square to centimetres square: 6.45
Centimetres square to inches square: 0.15
Feet square to metres square: 0.09
Metres square to feet square: 10.76
Miles square to kilometres square: 2.59
Kilometres square to miles square: 0.39
Acres to hectares: 0.40
Hectares to acres: 2.47

Weight (multiply by)
Ounces to grams: 28.35
Grammes to ounces: 0.035
Pounds to kilograms: 0.45
Kilograms to pounds: 2.2
Stones to kilograms: 6.35
Kilograms to stones: 0.16
Tons (UK) to kilograms: 1,016
Kilograms to tons (UK): 0.0009
1 UK ton (2,240lbs) = 1.12 US tonnes (2,000lbs)

Volume (multiply by)
Pints (UK) to litres: 0.57
Litres to pints (UK): 1.76
Quarts (UK) to litres: 1.13
Litres to quarts (UK): 0.88
Gallons (UK) to litres: 4.55
Litres to gallons (UK): 0.22
1 UK pint/quart/gallon = 1.2 US pints/quarts/gallons

Temperature
Celsius to Fahrenheit: multiply by 1.8 then add 32

Fahrenheit to Celsius: subtract 32 then multiply by 0.55

°C	°F
40	104
35	95
30	86
25	77
20	68
15	59
10	50
5	41
-0	32
-5	23
-10	14
-15	5

Spain Information

Time Differences
Spain: + 1hr GMT; + 6hrs EST
Daylight saving from last weekend in March to end of October

Dialling Codes
Spain country code 34
To Spain from: UK, Ireland, New Zealand dial 00; from USA, Canada 011, from Australia 0011; then dial 34 and the full number
From Spain to: UK 00 44; Ireland 00 353; USA, Canada 001; Australia 00 61; New Zealand 00 64; then the number without the initial zero
Directory enquiries: 11822
International directory enquiries: 11825

Emergency Numbers
General EU emergency number: 112
Police: 112
Ambulance: 112 or 061
Fire: 112 or 080

Embassy Numbers in Spain
UK 93 366 62 00 (Barcelona); **Ireland** 91 436 40 93 (Madrid); **USA** 93 280 22 27 (Barcelona); **Canada** 93 412 72 36 (Barcelona); **Australia** 93 490 90 13 (Barcelona); **New Zealand** 91 523 02 26 (Madrid)

Shoe Sizes
Europe	UK	USA
35	2½ / 3	4
36	3 / 3½	4½ / 5
37	4	5½ / 6
38	5	6½
39	5½ / 6	7 / 7½
40	6 / 6½	8 / 8½
41	7	9 / 9½
42	8	9½ / 10
43	9	10½
44	9½ / 10	11
45	10½	12
46	11	12½ / 13

Women's Clothing
Europe	UK	USA
34	6	2
36	8	4
38	10	6
40	12	8
42	14	10
44	16	12

Crime and the Police

General emergency number t 112

Crime is not really a big problem in Catalonia, but do keep an eye out. Barcelona and the other big cities have perhaps more than their share of street crime. Pickpocketing and bag-snatching are very common. Robbing parked cars is another popular pastime, and one current ploy is to puncture someone's tyre at a traffic light, then rob it while the driver is fixing the flat.

Note that in Spain possession of marijuana for private consumption is legal, although buying or selling it is illegal. Catalonia was the first autonomous region to legalize medical marijauna.

The Spanish **Policía Nacional** and **Guardia Civil** are still present in Catalonia, but their jobs are largely limited to border control, anti-terrorism and organized crime. Almost all normal police and traffic matters are now in the hands of the Catalan police force, the **Mossos d'Esquadra**. If you're the victim of a crime, they're the ones to contact. You can now report thefts (but not assaults), in English, in their virtual office: *www. policiadecatalunya.net*. After making your report, you'll be asked to select a police station to sign and pick up the report within 72 hours. If your passport is stolen, contact both the Mossos and your consulate for emergency travel documents.

The Mossos also patrol the highways. On-the-spot fines of up to €300 can be imposed for traffic violations or not having the requisite safety equipment on board (*see* p.53); if you don't have the money they may impound your car until you do, although usually they will escort you to the nearest ATM.

The **Guardia Urbana** are the street cops of most Spanish big cities,but their duties in Barcelona are now shared with the Mossos.

Eating Out

Catalans are late diners. In the morning it's a coffee and a roll grabbed at aa bar, followed by a huge meal at around 2 or 3pm, then after work at 7 or 8pm a few tapas at the bar to hold them over until supper at 9 or 10pm. On the coast, restaurants tend to open earlier to accommodate foreigners.

Restaurant Price Categories

Price categories in the 'Eating Out' sections throughout this book indicate the cost of the set menus, per person, without wine. It's safe to double the price for an *à la carte* meal.

very expensive	€€€€	over €60
expensive	€€€	€30–60
moderate	€€	€20–30
inexpensive	€	under €20

In non-touristy areas, restaurants are inconspicuous and few. Ask. If you dine where the locals do, you'll be assured of a good deal if not necessarily a good meal. Almost every restaurant offers a *menú* at lunchtime, featuring an appetizer, a main course, dessert, bread and drink at a set price, generally €10–15. Cheaper places may offer *plats combinats*, an all-on-one-plate quick meal. Locals rarely **tip**, although restaurant and bar staff may hope for a little something from foreigners.

Since a 2006 extension to the ban on **smoking** in public spaces, larger restaurants are required to offer a non-smoking section. Smaller restaurants and bars were allowed to choose whether to become smoking or non-smoking establishments, and almost all chose the former option. Those that allow it have signs posted by the door.

A wide array of snacking establishments will help fill in the gaps in your day. **Bars and cafés** are wonderful institutions, where you can eat breakfast or linger over a glass of beer until four in the morning. Some have music, some have great tapas (*tapes* in Catalan), some specialize in cocktails. Some are designer cutting-edge, while others are resolutely proletarian. Some are totally invisible in the day, exploding into blue-light noise palaces punctually at midnight until 6am.

For further information about eating and drinking in Catalonia, including local specialities and wines, and a menu decoder, *see* the **Food and Drink** chapter, pp.39–44.

Electricity

The current is **225 AC/220V**, the same as most of Europe. North Americans will need converters, and the British will need the usual two-pin adaptors for the different plugs. Adaptors and converters are sold in department stores and electrical shops.

Health and Emergencies

General emergency number t 112

Citizens of the EU are entitled to a certain amount of free medical care in EU countries if they have a European Health Insurance Card (EHIC). *See* **Planning Your Trip**, p.50.

In an emergency ask to be taken to the nearest *hospital de la seguritat social*.

Tourist offices can supply lists of English-speaking doctors, but if it's not an emergency, go to a pharmacy. Catalan pharmacists are highly skilled, and in Spain many drugs that require a prescription elsewhere are available freely. Look in local papers or in pharmacy windows for the rota of pharmacies that stay open at night and on holidays.

The **tap water** in Catalonia is safe to drink (though its famously awful in Barcelona), but at the slightest twinge of queasiness, switch to the bottled stuff.

Internet

Getting online is easy and cheap. Most big hotels now offer either wi-fi or some kind of Internet access, and every city of any size has an Internet café, often combined with a *locutori* (with metered phones for long-distance calls). The average cost to go on line costs from €2.50 per hour, rising to €4.

Opening Hours, Museums and National Holidays

Shops usually open at 10am, boutiques an hour or so later. Except in cities, most shops close for 2–3 hours in the afternoon and stay open until 8 or 9pm.

Most **banks** are open Mon–Fri 9–2. A few open on Sat (mainly in winter), 9–1.

Officially, main **post office** opening hours are Mon–Fri 8.30–8.30, Sat 9.30–1. This isn't necessarily the case outside the big cities. Many post offices close early in summer.

Museums and **historical sites** tend to follow shop hours, though they are shorter in winter. Nearly all close on Mondays. Many have explanations only in Catalan; if that's

National Holidays

1 January New Year's Day
6 January Epiphany
Holy Thursday (March/April)
Good Friday (March/April)
Easter Sunday (March/April)
1 May Labour Day
Corpus Christi (May/June)
24 June St John's Day
11 September Catalan National Day
15 August Assumption
12 October Columbus Day
1 November All Saints' Day
6 December Constitution Day
8 December Immaculate Conception
25 December Christmas Day
26 December St Stephen's Day

the case, ask if they have a leaflet with English translations. Note that many stop admitting visitors half an hour before the official closing time. Most museums close on national holidays (*see* above) and give discounts if you have a student ID card, or are an EU citizen under 18 or over 65 years old. In many places you'll see *Centres d'Interpretació* – part museum, part tourist office, with exhibitions on what there is to see in an area. Beware that there are quite a few 'museums' set up by artists to promote and sell their work; unless they're really worth seeing, we've left them out.

Smaller **churches** are often closed. If you're determined to visit one, it will never be hard to find the caretaker. Usually they live close by and will be glad to show you around for a tip. Don't be surprised if cathedrals and famous churches charge for admission – just consider the cost of upkeep.

Post Offices

Every city in Spain, regardless of size, seems to have one **post office** (*correus*) and no more. Unless you have packages to send you may never need visit one: most tobacconists sell **stamps** and they'll usually know the correct postage for whatever you're sending.

Post boxes are bright yellow.

Sports and Activities

Catalonia offers a dazzling array of sports, but one it doesn't have is **bullfighting**. It is so unpopular that in 1989 Tossa de Mar became the first place to declare itself 'an anti-bull-fighting city'. Many municipalities followed suit, including Barcelona in 2004; at the time of writing the Generalitat is trying to ban it altogether. Cardona has one of the last bull-orientated festivities – but, instead of *matadors* the bull gets to toss about a man hiding in a barrel.

Air Sports and Ballooning

There are quite a few opportunities to look down on Catalonia. The updraughts at the Noguera make it perfect for **paragliding**, with several firms based at Àger.

Empuriabrava has a popular **sky-diving** school (*www.skydiveempuriabrava.com*).

Several firms across the region offer **hot air balloon** rides (some of the most popular are in La Garrotxa, so you can look down on the volcanoes).

Igualada, 35km west of Barcelona, has a **gliding** club (*www.volavela.com*).

Cycling

Cycling is taken extremely seriously in Catalonia, both as a hobby and sport – especially in Girona province, where Lance Armstrong used to train. The region has four *Vías Verdes* – long distance walking and bike routes along former rail lines, (*www.viasverdes.com/GreenWays*). Otherwise many of the rural roads get very little traffic, but the hills aren't for sissies.

Fifteen marked mountain bike (*BTT* in Catalan) areas have been laid out in the Natural Parks by the Generalitat (*www.gencat.cat/turisme/btt*), covering 3,300 kilometres. The main towns and holiday centres have at least one shop that hires out bikes; tourist offices have lists. Be prepared to pay a hefty deposit on a good bike.

Fishing and Hunting

Fishing and hunting are long-standing Spanish obsessions, and you'll need to get a licence for both. **Recreational** (both sea and inland) **fishing permits** (*licencia de pesca*),

underwater fishing permits and **hunting permits** are all issued by the Generalitat; you can apply on line at *www.cat365.net*, or download the application in English and apply in person. Sea-fishing along the Costa Brava is popular, but many fishermen prefer to try their luck on the Rivers Ter, Onyar and Segre, and Lake Banyoles.

You may bring **sporting guns** to Spain, but you must declare them on arrival and present a valid **firearms certificate** with a Spanish translation bearing a consulate stamp. Boar and deer are the big game, with quail, hare, partridges and pigeons, and ducks and geese hunted along the coasts in the winter.

Golf

There are no less than 42 golf courses in Catalonia, including some of the best on the continent: nine are concentrated along the Costa Brava, including the Stadium and Tour courses of PGA Golf Catalunya in Caldes de Malavella (in a recent poll it ranked number three in Europe). The sunny, warm winters, combined with greens of international tournament standard, attract golfing enthusiasts from all over the world throughout the year. Most courses hire out clubs. Many hotels cater specifically for the golfer and there are numerous golf-package tour operators.

Federació Catalana de Golf, C/Tuset 32, 08006 Barcelona, **t** 93 414 52 62, *www.catgolf.com*.

Hiking

The Centre Excursionista is in the very heart of the Barri Gòtic in Barcelona, symbolizing hiking's importance in a country where walk-abouts seem to be part of the DNA: all the great figures of the Renaixança from Gaudí to Verdaguer were constantly going off on expeditions to explore Catalonia's natural beauty. Today the coast and mountains are crisscrossed with beautiful paths: long-distance (over 50km) *Senders de Gran Recorregut* (GR), waymarked in red and white; short distance (between 10–50km) *Senders de Petit Recorregut* (PR) waymarked in yellow and white; and *Senders Locals*, under 10km.

The **Associació Catalana de Senderisme** has an excellent website in English (*www.euro-senders.com*) with information on trails, including thematic walks such as the Route of the Cathars; they sell GR guides (including a couple in English); the website also has detailed information on Catalan refuges. In summer it's advisable to book at guarded *refugis* (mountain huts) to make sure you have a bed. *See* p.56 for tour operators who organize walking holidays.

Horses

Catalonia has scores of riding stables, many connected with rural accommodation. There are some wonderful long-distance trails as well; try Eitravel in Palafrugell (**t** *972 30 21 32, www.eitravel.com*), which organizes 6-day rides in the mountains and along the coast.

Mountain Sports

Outside of the Alps, Catalonia's Pyrenees have some of the best venues in Europe for high altitude sports: distinctive twin-peaked Pedraforca (*see* p.232) is a favourite of both mountain- and rock-climbers. Barcelona is the seat of the Spanish Mountain Sports Federation (*see* below). Or try (in English) *www.epyrenees.com* with detailed information on climbing and other mountain sports such as **canyoning**, **white-water rafting**, and **hydrospeeding** down the Noguera Pallaresa.

Federación Espanola de Deportes de Montana y Escalada, C/Floridablanca 75, 08015 Barcelona, **t** 93 426 42 67, *www.fedme.es* (Spanish only)

Tennis

Tennis is growing in Catalonia as the young are inspired by world number one Rafael Nadal – from the ex-Catalan island of Mallorca. Every resort hotel has its own courts; municipal ones tend to be rare. Get a list of clubs and courts from the federation.

Federació Catalana de Tennis, **t** 93 428 53 53, *www.fctennis.cat.*

Water Sports

L'Estartit on the Costa Brava is the diving capital of Catalonia, with the Natural Park of the Medes islets, teeming with marine life, waiting to be explored. But there are diving centres in most resorts, and sea kayaks for exploring the secret coves of the coast.

Winter Sports

Spain has 36 **ski stations**, and Catalonia has 17 of those, with 612km of ski slopes served by 130 ski lifts; when you add in the little Catalan duty-free mountain principality of Andorra you have the best skiing in Europe outside of the Alps – both downhill runs and cross-country (*esquí nordic*). Many have other features as well: snow parks for free-style **snowboarding**, **toboggan runs**, and more. Again, check *www.epyrenees.com* for complete lists and packages. Puigcerdà is the cradle of **hockey** in Spain, and has an ice palace that hosts **figure skating** as well.

Telephones

Calls within Spain are expensive (25–80 cents for a short local call), and overseas calls from Spain are among the most expensive in Europe. Public **phone booths** have instructions in English and accept **phonecards**, available from news stands, tobacconists and post offices. Most **tobacconists** sell PIN-phonecards that make international phone calls much cheaper. Expect to pay a surcharge if you make any calls from your hotel.

For **directory enquiries** and **dialling codes** *see* p.58.

A North American **mobile phone** won't work in Catalonia unless it's GSM/GPRS compatible (for instance, AT&T and T-Mobile cell phones) with a SIM card. A UK mobile will probably work, but beware the roaming charges. If necessary, mobile phone shops provide unlocking services for around €20, so that you can put in a Spanish payg SIM card.

Time

Spain is one hour ahead of UK time and six hours ahead of North American Eastern Standard Time, nine hours ahead of Pacific Coast Time. Spanish summertime runs from the last Sunday in March to the last Sunday in October.

Toilets

Apart from bus and train stations, public facilities are rare in Spain. On the other hand, every bar on every corner has a toilet; just ask for *serveis*.

Barcelona

Barcelona, the capital of the Catalans, is a city that goes about its business and pleasure with such ballistic intensity that you can't tell whether it's insanely serious or seriously insane or both. In 1975, three million Barcelonins danced in the streets like drunken banshees when they heard of Franco's death; the next day they rolled up their sleeves and channelled their crazed energy into making up for 40 stale, flat years.

They've done it: modern Barcelona fizzes and sizzles like a bottle of Catalan cava spiked with a red pepper.

07

Don't miss

⭐ Gaudí's over-
the-top cathedral
Sagrada Família p.116

⭐ A Catalan
Gothic beauty
**Santa Maria del Mar
p.96**

⭐ A treasure-
filled museum
MNAC p.124

⭐ Vertiginous
cable-car rides
Barceloneta p.105

⭐ Irrepressible
architectural
delight
Park Güell p.131

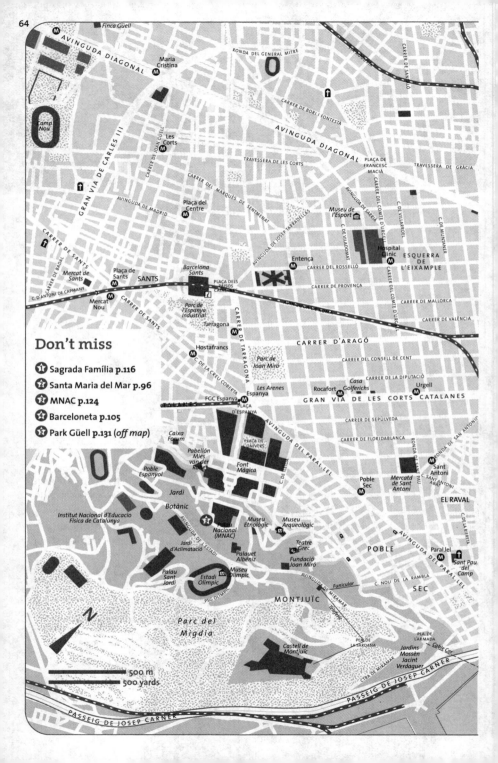

64

Don't miss

⭐ Sagrada Família p.116
⭐ Santa Maria del Mar p.96
⭐ MNAC p.124
⭐ Barceloneta p.105
⭐ Park Güell p.131 (off map)

Finca Güell

AVINGUDA DIAGONAL

Maria
Cristina

Camp
Nou

RONDA DEL GENERAL MITRE

CARRER DE SARRIÓ

CARRER DE BORI I FONTESTÀ

AVINGUDA DIAGONAL

PLAÇA DE
FRANCESC
MACIÀ

TRAVESSERA DE GRÀCIA

Les
Corts

TRAVESSERA DE LES CORTS

GRAN VIA DE CARLES III

CARRER DE JOAN GÜELL

CARRER DEL MARQUÈS DE SENTMENAT

CARRER DEL COMTE D'URGELL

AVINGUDA DE SARRIÁ

C. DE VILLARROEL

C. DE MUNTANER

AVINGUDA DE MADRID

Plaça del
Centre

AVINGUDA DE JOSEP TARRADELLAS

Museu de
l'Esport

ESQUERRA
DE
L'EIXAMPLE

CARRER DE SANTS

CARRER DE BADAL

Mercat de
Sants

Plaça de
Sants

SANTS

Barcelona
Sants

PLAÇA DELS
PAÏSOS
CATALANS

C. DE VILADOMAT

Entença

Hospital
Clínic

CARRER DEL ROSSELLÓ

CARRER DEL COMTE D'URGELL

C. D'ANTONI DE CAPMANY

Mercat
Nou

CARRER DE SANTS

Parc de
l'Espanya
Industrial

Tarragona

CARRER DE PROVENÇA

CARRER DE MALLORCA

CARRER DE VALÈNCIA

Hostafrancs

CARRER DE TARRAGONA

C. DE LA CREU COBERTA

Parc de
Joan Miró

CARRER D'ARAGÓ

CARRER DEL CONSELL DE CENT

CARRER DE LA DIPUTACIÓ

Les Arenes
Espanya

FGC Espanya

PLAÇA
D'ESPANYA

Rocafort

Casa
Golferichs

Urgell

GRAN VIA DE LES CORTS CATALANES

CARRER DE SEPÚLVEDA

Caixa
Forum

PLAÇA DE
CONIVERS

AVINGUDA DEL PARAL·LEL

CARRER DE FLORIDABLANCA

RONDA DE SANT PAU

RONDA DE SANT ANTONI

Pabellón
Mies
van der
Rohe

Font
Màgica

Sant
Antoni

C. SANT ANTONI ABAT

P
Poble
Espanyol

Jardí
Botànic

Poble
Sec

Mercat d
de Sant
Antoni

EL RAVAL

Institut Nacional d'Educació
Física de Catalunya

Museu
Etnològic

Museu
Arqueològic

POBLE

AVINGUDA DEL PARAL·LEL

Palau
Nacional
(MNAC)

Teatre
Grec

Jardí
d'Aclimatació

Palauet
Albéniz

Fundació
Joan Miró

Paral·lel

Sant Pau
del
Camp

Palau
Sant
Jordi

Estadi
Olímpic

Museu
Olímpic

SEC

AVINGUDA DE MIRAMAR

Funicular

C. NOU DE LA RAMBLA

PSG OLÍMPIC

MONTJUÏC

Parc del
Migdia

Castell de
Montjuïc

PLAÇA DE
LA SARDANA

Jardins
Mossèn
Jacint
Verdaguer

PLA DE
L'ARMADA

N

CTRA DE MIRAMAR

PASSEIG DE JOSEP CARNER

PASSEIG DE JOSEP CARNER

500 m
500 yards

Lesseps

TRAVESSERA DE DALT

CARRER DE SANT SALVADOR

CARRER DE BALCELLS

RONDA DEL GUINARDÓ

Alfons X

Guinardó

RONDA DEL GUINARDÓ

CARRER DE L'OR

CARRER DE L'ENCARNACIÓ

Fontana

FGC Gracia

Mercat de la Llibertat

GRÀCIA

Joanic

Hospital de la Santa Creu i de Sant Pau

TRAVESSERA DE GRÀCIA

CARRER DE SANT ANTONI MARIA CLARET

SAGRADA FAMILIA

CARRER DE LA INDÚSTRIA

Hospital Sant Pau

PLAÇA DE JOAN CARLES I

Casa Comalat

CARRER DE CÓRSEGA

CARRER DE CÓRSEGA

AVINGUDA DIAGONAL

C. DEL ROSSELLÓ

Sagrada Familia

L'EIXAMPLE

Diagonal

Casa Asia

Verdaguer

La Pedrera

Casa Montaner

Casa Thomas

CARRER DE PROVENÇA

CARRER DE PROVENÇA

PLAÇA DE LA SAGRADA FAMÍLIA

Sagrada Família

DRETA DE L'EIXAMPLE

CARRER DE MALLORCA

PLAÇA DE MOSSÈN JACINT VERDAGUER

PLAÇA DE GAUDÍ

CARRER DE VALÈNCIA

Museu Egipci

Fundació Tàpies

CARRER D'ARAGÓ

C. DELS ENAMORATS

Casa Batlló

Casa Amatller

Casa Lleo Morera

Passeig de Gràcia

CARRER DEL CONSELL DE CENT

AVINGUDA DIAGONAL

Fundació Francesco Godia

Museu del Parfum

CARRER DE LA DIPUTACIÓ

Girona

Els Encants

PLAÇA DE LES GLÒRIES CATALANES

Universitat Central

Tetuan

Museu Tauri Monumental

FGC Estació Glories

GRAN VIA DE LES CORTS CATALANES

GRAN VIA DE LES CORTS CATALANES

Universitat

PLAÇA DE TETUAN

FGC Catalunya

Teatre Tivoli

CARRER DE CASP

Museu de la Música

Teatre Nacional de Catalunya

CCCB

El Triangle

PLAÇA CATALUNYA

CARRER D'AUSIAS MARC

Auditori

MACBA

Catalunya

URQUINAONA

Urquinaona

FGC Arc de Triomf

Arc de Triomf

Marina

BARRI GOTIC

C. SANT PERE ALT

Sant Pere de les Puelles

Estació d'Autobuses del Nord

C. DEL PEU DE LA CREU

VIA LAIETANA

C. SANT PERE BAIX

Museu de la Xocolata

Palau de Justicia

CARRER DELS ALMOGÀVERS

CARRER DELS ALMOGÀVERS

Hospital Santa Creu

Museu Barbier-Mueller d'Art Precolumbi

CARRER DE BUENAVENTURA MUÑOZ

Bogatell

C. DE HOSPITAL

Santa Maria del Pi

Museu Picasso

Sant Agusti

Liceu

Cathedral

Gallery Maeght

PASSEIG DE PUJADES

C. DE SANT PAU

PLAÇA DE SANT JAUME

Jaume II

Museu de Zoologia

Parc de la Ciutadella

LAS RAMBLAS

C. DE FERRAN

Museu de Geologia

Parlament de Catalunya

Santa Maria del Mar

Mercat del Born

Golondrina

Museu de Cera

Basilica de la Mercè

Santa Maria del Mar

Estació de França

Parc Zoologic

Drassanes

AV. DEL MARQUÈS DE L'ARGENTERA

Museu Marítim

Centre d'Art Santa Monica

RONDA DEL LITORAL

Barceloneta

Museu d'Història de Catalunya

Ciutadella Vila Olímpica

VILA OLÍMPICA

Monument a Colom

RONDA DEL LITORAL

B10

Estació Marítima

Moll de la Fusta

IMAX

Marina

BARCELONETA

Cable-Car

Maremagnum

Aquarium

Moll d'Espanya

Mercat Barceloneta

Parc de la Barceloneta

Port Olimpic

Port Vell

World Trade Centre

Aerial Cableway

PASSEIG MARÍTIM

Platja Barceloneta

Barcelona, the treasure house of courtesy, the refuge of strangers... although the adventures that befell me there occasioned me no great pleasure, but rather much grief, I bore them the better for having seen that city.
Cervantes,
Don Quixote, Part II

With its superb legacy of Gothic and Modernista architecture, its business acumen and ambitious immigrants, its taste for the avant-garde and manic obsession with design, Barcelona is a little New York – and in many ways the only really successful modern city in old Europe.

Nor is it shy about saying so. A compulsive exhibitionist, Barcelona held two great international fairs, in 1888 and 1929, and staged one hell of a show for the 1992 Olympics. We are all the better for having seen it.

History

In later years, when this prancing peacock of a city felt the lack of a foundation myth, Barcelona's *literati* would summon up no less a personage than Hercules to play the role of city father. Hercules would have passed this way on his tenth Labour, while driving the cattle of Geryon back to Greece. He had already founded Cádiz and built the Pillars of Hercules, and the Barcelonins thought they could sneak their town on to the list, too. A different story, based on the similarity of the names, credited with the founding a leader of Carthage's most prominent and powerful family – Hamilcar Barca, Hannibal's father.

As far as anyone can tell, the first real Barcelonins were the Celto-Iberian Laietanos, who lived in scattered villages on the rich plain, with a citadel or religious centre on Montjuïc. In 15 BC, in the reign of Augustus, the Romans founded Colonia Faventia Julia Augusta Paterna Barcino on a low hill between two small streams, just north of Montjuïc. Although surrounded by fertile land, Barcino lacked a good harbour, and it never became half as important as Roman Tarraco (Tarragona). Roman Barcino, a typical walled, rectangular *castrum* of the sort found all over the Empire, covered what is now the core of the Barri Gòtic; an impressive patch of Roman foundations, still intact under the medieval city, can be visited under the Museu d'Història de la Ciutat (*see* p.84).

In AD 262, Barcino suffered a sacking at the hands of the Franks, in a raid that was a prelude to the Germanic invasions that would overwhelm the western Empire a century and a half later. The Franks did far more damage to Tarraco, and, after the Roman legions regained control of the situation, Barcino seems to have gradually supplanted it as top town in the region. The newly strengthened walls failed to keep out the Visigoths in 415 but, rather than rape and pillage, they moved in and briefly made Barcelona the seat of their court.

When a new foe, the Arab-led army of Islam, destroyed Tarraco in 713, Barcelona took note and surrendered without a fight. The Barcelonins couldn't know it, but the Arabs had just made their fortune. From now on Barcelona, and not Tarragona, would be the

Getting to and away from Barcelona

By Air

Barcelona's international airport is **El Prat de Llobregat**, 12km to the south. There are three terminals – **A, B** and **C** – and another, **Terminal 1** (T1), is due to open in late 2009 and will serve the One World group which includes Iberia and BA. Terminal B is the largest, with lockers, cash machines, a pharmacy, banks, a post office and a tourist office, **t** 932 98 38 38 (*open daily 9am–9pm*). Flight information and customer service: **t** 902 404 704, *www.aena.es*; lost property, **t** 93 298 33 49; police station **t** 93 297 12 19.

Getting to and from Aeroport del Prat

Trains, **t** 902 24 02 02, link the airport to three of the city's train stations: Sants, Passeig de Gràcia and Estació de França (6.08am–10.29pm, every 30mins). The A1 **Aerobús**, **t** 93 415 60 20, connects terminals with Plaça Catalunya (Mon–Fri 5.30am–11.15pm every 15mins, Sat and Sun 6am–11.20pm every 30mins, tickets €4.70, €8 return). **Bus** N17 makes the same journey every 20mins from 10.30pm to 5am. Bus 46 links terminals B and C to the Plaça d'Espanya every 30mins from 5.30am to 12.45am (€1.35).

Taxis to the city centre take 20–30 minutes and cost around €25.

By Sea

Trasmediterránea, Estació Marítim, Moll de Barcelona, **t** 90 245 46 45, *www.trasmediterranea.es*, runs ferry links with Livorno and Civitavecchia in Italy, as well as with the Balearic islands. There is also a ferry three times a week to Genoa with **Grandi Navi Veloci, t** (+ 39) 010 209 4591, *www.gnv.it*.

By Train

A **high-speed railway** linking Barcelona to France's TGV network is due to be completed in 2012; in Spanish high-speed trains are called **AVE**, in Catalan **TAV** (*Tren d'alta velocitat*). For information, contact **RENFE, t** 90 224 02 02 (information): **t** 90 224 34 02 (international trains), or see *www.renfe.es/ingles*.

Estació Sants on the south side of town is Barcelona's main station, although many trains also stop at the more central **Passeig de Gràcia**. Sants is the hub for the Madrid–Barcelona AVE high-speed line that eats the distance between the two cities in 2hrs 38mins. It is also the hub for: the regional AVE network, Avant, to Tarragona and Lleida; the Catalunya Express to Granollers, Girona, Figueres, Portbou and Cervera de la Marenda (Cerbère in French); and RENFE's *cercanías/rodalíes* trains to nearby towns such as Sitges.

The **Estació de França** on Av. Marquès de l'Argentera is now served by Alvia trains to Madrid, Arco trains to Valencia, and several international services – such as the Trenhotel to Paris, Zurich and Milan (*see* **Planning Your Trip**, p.52). Also Catalunya Express trains on the following routes: Sant Andreu Comtal, Tarragona, Tortosa and Valencia; Tarragona, Reus, Móra la Nova, Flix, Riba-Roja d'Ebre and Caspe; and Sant Andreu Comtal, Tarragona, Valls , La Plana-Picamoixons, Lleida and Pirineus.

Under construction at the time of writing, **Estació de la Sagrera**, partly designed by Frank Gehry in the northern part of the city, will become a major transport hub for AVE high-speed rail as well as regular international, regional and commuter *rodalíes* trains. A tunnel will link it to Sants.

Ferrocarrils de la Generalitat de Catalunya (FGC) has lines passing through Barcelona to the suburbs and beyond, departing from under Plaça de Catalunya (for Sant Cugat and Terrassa, at least one every hour) and from under the Plaça d'Espanya (to Montserrat). **FGC: t** 93 205 15 15, *www.fgc.net*.

---

leading city of northern Iberia. In the meantime, Barcelona would merely be an outpost of the new state of al-Andalus.

In 801, Charlemagne's son Louis the Pious reconquered northern 'Gothalanda'. Barcelona was an important walled fortress, and in 874 – a year of clashing coiffures – the Frankish King Charles the Bald made the local baron Guifré el Pilós, or 'Wilfred the Hairy', its first count. Guifré brought much of what is now Catalonia under his control, and he endowed Barcelona and the region with churches and monasteries. As Frankish power decayed after Charlemagne's death, Barcelona was increasingly on its own. In 985, when it was attacked by the great al-Mansur of Córdoba, the

Franks failed to respond to its requests for aid. Count Borrell II declared his county's sovereign independence, and the Franks could not stop him.

Barcelona faced the new millennium with a population of probably little more than a thousand. Over the next two centuries, however, this insignificant town would quite suddenly and startlingly grow fat and rich. It isn't entirely clear how they managed it. Its main economic assets were the two most useful gifts a medieval town could ask for: iron and wool. Yet more profit came from the produce of the surrounding farmland, and from the booty acquired by Barcelona's counts in the wars of the Reconquista against the Moors. The pennies were piling up and the city invested some of its surplus wisely, building ships and developing maritime links across the Mediterranean. By the 1030s Barcelona had the first stable gold currency in western Europe.

The business interests of the city and the ambitions of the counts found a happy symbiosis and, as both grew in power, trade and the flag went hand in hand. The marriage in 1137 between Barcelona's Count Ramon Berenguer IV and the heiress of Aragon, Queen Petronila, brought the city the Crown of Aragon and all the prestige of royalty. Now the counts were 'count-kings', the unusual name proof of the continuing importance of Barcelona.

As it acquired a new maritime empire, Barcelona's trade, and nearly everyone else's in medieval Europe, was regulated by a maritime code, the *Llibre del Consolat de Mar*, written under Jaume I in 1259. In Barcelona, Jaume organized the merchants into a kind of guild which functioned practically as a city within the city. To govern everything else, the same king instituted the Consell de Cent made up of a hundred citizens, in which even the smaller merchants were represented.

By 1300, after its string of spectacular exploits overseas (*see* p.23) Barcelona's population was up to 50,000, making it by far the largest and richest city in northern Spain. Under Jaume I the Conqueror the city was forced to begin an extensive (and expensive) new circuit of walls to fit them all in. Under Jaume II the Just (1291–1327), Alfons III (Alfonso IV of Aragon, 1327–36) and Pere IV the Ceremonious (Pedro III of Aragon, 1336–87), the Gothic city's most important and splendid monuments appeared. For all its wealth, however, things were not necessarily going well. While the great merchants prospered from a large area of relatively free trade, smaller ones and manufacturers became increasingly beset by competition.

Like a modern American city, Barcelona, despite the splendid monuments, had became a miserable place for the city's increasingly desperate poor. They suffered recurrent famines, and the Black Death arrived in 1348, killing off a third of the population.

Along with hard times came increasing factional strife and the first pogroms against the economically important Jewish population. Gang warfare seems to have been common throughout the 14th and 15th centuries, and social disorder was expressed on a slightly more elevated level in the bitter struggles of the city's two political factions, the Biga and the Busca – the 'Beam' and the 'Splinter'. The solid, conservative Biga was the party of the biggest merchants; it believed in free trade, sound money and the continuance of the great disparities of wealth that made life in Barcelona so interesting. The Busca, though not really a popular party, was interested in tariffs to save the smaller firms and manufacturers who were being damaged by the Biga's precocious medieval version of economic globalization.

The Biga usually had the better of the fight, even after its economic vision started to fall apart in the 1380s, but by the early 1400s it was clear that Barcelona's strangely modern experiment in capitalism was running out of steam. With the plagues, the hinterland was in a bad way, no longer able to feed the capital or supply it with resources. The booming city itself had already sucked away most of its life and population and, now that the boom was over, the streets of Barcelona offered little employment.

After 1400 Barcelona's population started to decline, so much so that it was surpassed in size by its arch-rival Valencia. To make matters worse, it was losing its bread-and-butter trade in the Mediterranean to the Genoese; Genoa captured the trade of Christian Seville and Moorish Granada, which gave it an opening into North Africa. The Atlantic coastal trade was growing, but this was monopolized by the Portuguese and the Basques.

If Barcelona was sinking, however, it was not apparent to the city's leaders. All through the troubles of the 14th and early 15th centuries, they continued to embellish the city as if they were on top of the world. Some of the great church-building projects went on even during the plague years, and even after 1400 new palaces were built, while the Catalan school of painting reached its height. Meanwhile, the city's fortunes continued to decline along with its political cohesion. In 1410, when Martí I the Humane died without an heir, the influential future saint of Valencia, Vincent Ferrer, helped give the throne to a Castilian house, the Trastámara.

These new rulers broke the final tie of mutual interest that had held Catalonia-Aragon's delicately balanced system together. Popular revolts in Barcelona in 1436 and 1437 were only the prelude to worse struggles to come. The great revolt that began in 1462 was essentially a struggle between Barcelona's ruling class and King Joan II. Ten years of civil war followed, finally ending with the surrender of a city under siege by its own king. Barcelona was

07 Barcelona | History

ruined. Joan's son was Ferran II to the Catalans, but he would have preferred to call himself by his Castilian name, Fernando. He had been married to Isabel of Castile in the middle of the wars and, when his father died and he assumed the throne in 1479, Castile and Aragon were effectively united. Barcelona was an exhausted, bankrupt metropolis that had no prospects and no friends.

1479–1830: A Provincial City in Spain

At first, Barcelona entertained some wan hopes that Aragon's union with powerful Castile would supply a much-needed transfusion of money and vitality. What happened was quite different. Fernando and Isabel ensured it would have no share in the new opportunities; a codicil in Isabel's will specifically prohibited Catalan merchants from trading with the New World. A lesser city than Barcelona might have disintegrated altogether, but the city's merchants showed remarkable resilience. In spite of everything, they endured decreased trade and then a series of rebellion and wars with and against France. Finally they chose the wrong side in the War of the Spanish Succession (1701–14). After 15 months of resistance the city fell to the Bourbon faction in November 1714, and down with it went Catalonia's *usatges*, its institutions and the last vestiges of its autonomy. The city's leaders were drawn and quartered, and a large number of die-hard resisters were buried in a mass grave near Santa Maria del Mar.

The old capital of the count-kings became just another provincial city of Spain, and Felipe V punished it with the construction of the Ciutadella, a huge pentagonal fort intended to protect the city from its own people. The Barcelonins were forced to pay for it themselves, and its building meant the demolition of half of a neighbourhood, La Ribera, in a city that was already suffocatingly overcrowded. To make matters worse, Madrid decreed that no one would be allowed to live outside the walls. The city began to consume itself, expanding at the expense of patios and gardens; the current maze of dark canyons in the old city is the result. For the next century and a half, Barcelona acquired taller and taller buildings, and the conditions in which its people lived became increasingly unhealthy. The new quarter of Barceloneta, built on reclaimed land around the harbour, appeared in 1753. Originally planned to house the families displaced for the Ciutadella, it came – with typical Bourbon efficiency – some 40 years too late.

At least Barcelonins were working again. Once the Catalans had been punished, Bourbon policy was never quite as black-hearted as Fernando and Isabel's. The new dynasty hoped it could eventually earn the Catalans' loyalty by giving them a chance to make a living again. The results were dramatic. Like some capitalist Sleeping

Beauty, the city's mercantile élite popped up from its 200-year slumber, full of entrepreneurial fizz. The city found two very profitable new businesses: the manufacture of cotton cloth, and cheap brandy which was shipped off to thirsty Latin America.

In 1778, Madrid finally removed the last restrictions on trading with the colonies, and the long build-up turned into a boom. By 1780, Barcelona's population had more than doubled since 1714, to 110,000. The first industrial cotton mill was founded the same year, and factory production soon replaced the old medieval guilds, as Barcelona began its career as the 'Manchester of the Mediterranean'. The merchants returned to their exchange, the Llotja, and new palaces rose along the new promenade, the Rambla. Barcelona was back in business.

The Napoleonic Wars were a rude interruption. Britain's blockade stopped the American trade cold, and the city went into a deep depression while Napoleon's men raided and looted its churches and monasteries. As much as they hated Madrid, the Catalans had learned from experience that the French were even worse. They remained steadfastly loyal to Spain this time, but, even after the French were chased out in 1814, recovery was slow. Epidemics of yellow fever and cholera hit the overcrowded city in 1821 – only the worst of many. The wheels of Barcelona industry didn't get back to full speed until the 1830s.

1830–1923: Violent Birth of the Modern City

One habit that the new Barcelona had in common with its medieval counterpart was treating its workers like dirt. Barcelona's industrialists, Spain's politicians and the Church connived to squeeze them to the limit; working conditions were appalling, especially for the women and children, who generally worked 15 hours a day. They lived in slums so unhealthy that epidemics raged and mortality rates were among the highest in Europe. Dissent or attempts at organization were ruthlessly suppressed. Anger was not limited to the workers. Barcelona's progressive middle classes had complaints of their own about the reactionary regime that King Fernando VII (1814–33) brought in after Napoleon's defeat. Between the two, the city became a hotbed of radical ideas, and it boiled over in increasingly violent revolts.

The first outbreak, in July 1835, brought the burning of most of Barcelona's monasteries and convents. Regular riots and Luddite attacks on factory machinery enlivened the next two decades. The biggest riot, in 1842, was called the Jamància, in which the rebels took control of the city but were bombarded into submission by the cannons of Montjuïc castle. To the industrialists, these were relatively minor irritations. They kept making money. In 1848, they built Spain's first railway, from Barcelona to Mataró.

Bursting at the seams, Barcelona finally got permission from Madrid in the late 1850s to demolish its walls and expand. The great grid of the Eixample, designed by Ildefons Cerdà, was one of the most ambitious planning schemes of 19th-century Europe, and nearly quintupled the size of the city. Later, two wide new streets, Passeig de Colom and Vía Laietana, were driven through the old town, following the example of Baron Haussmann's trans-formation of Paris. The modern city, with its impressive expansion and cosmopolitanism, evoked comparisons with Barcelona's medieval golden age, and fostered a new pride in things Catalan, leading to a flowering in the arts that would be called the Catalan Renaixença.

In this heady climate, under dynamic mayor Francesc de Paula Rius i Taulet, the city put on the Universal Exhibition in 1888; it showed the world, in the mayor's words, that the Catalans 'were the Yankees of Europe', and it saw the beginnings of Barcelona's distinctive Modernista architecture.

By the end of the 19th century, Barcelona had one of the most developed economies of Europe. Prosperity, however, brought little improvement in the conditions of working people, and the issues that caused all the trouble in the 1830s were still unsettled. For a while, boom times papered over the growing discontent, but in the 1870s the city was ready to explode once more – this time, with the heat of a new ideology, known as Anarchism. Even after it was driven underground in 1874, this movement gave an ideological home to those workers – increasingly, a majority of them – who were willing to meet the violence of the army and the employers' gangs of thugs with violence of their own.

The two sides battled through the streets intermittently for the next three decades, while Barcelona became the bomb capital of Europe: in 1893, Anarchist bombs killed 20; the next year, one exploded into the expensive seats at the Liceu; and, in 1896, they blew up the religious procession of Corpus Christi.

While bombs and bullets flew, Barcelona was paradoxically enjoying its most creative era. In the 1890s, Catalan culture flowered, with the painters Ramon Casas and Santiago Rusinyol and their circle – which included the young Picasso – at the café Els Quatre Gats. The city's converging artistic style soon acquired a name, Modernisme. Its painting and poetry would not make much of an impression outside Catalonia, but in architecture the Modernistas were about to astound the world. Antoni Gaudí, the greatest among them, began work on the Sagrada Família in 1883, and built La Pedrera on the Passeig de Gràcia in 1905. The

Modernistas' buildings set the tone for the rapidly developing Eixample, giving the city a new look, almost a new identity, while back in the old centre Barcelona's bohemians were perfecting the louche *demi-monde* life of the Barri Gòtic.

The Spanish-American War of 1898 was an earthquake for all of Spain. Many among Barcelona's élite had started by amassing fortunes in the colonies in tobacco, shipping or slaves; they were called *indianos* or *americanos*. The loss of Spain's last important colonies closed off considerable trade opportunities, and the end of the war filled the city with disgusted ex-soldiers with little chance of employment. By 1909 the city was a tense, dry tinderbox. The conscription of young Catalans for an unpopular imperialist war in Morocco led to a general strike on 26 July. The strike turned into a revolt, and a leaderless mob took over the city. Though discouraged by lack of support from the rest of Spain, Barcelona turned the revolt into a head-on collision with the army. At the end of what was called the Setmana Trágica, or Tragic Week, 116 people were dead and 80 buildings torched, 70 of them churches or monasteries. Barcelona had confirmed its role as the most radical city in Europe, Anarchism's 'rose of fire', and its workers gained considerable sympathy afterwards, as the army's execution in the fortress of Montjuïc of even moderate leaders shocked Europe.

Spain's neutrality in the First World War brought more boom times, as exports to the belligerents soared and the city's industrialists diversified and modernized to meet demand. Rural Catalans, impoverished by wartime inflation and seeking jobs, moved into the city; the population doubled between 1910 and 1930 as Barcelona became the largest city in Spain. In the same period the city was rocked with over 800 strikes. Workers' conditions only grew worse; by 1919, the Anarchist workers' union of Catalonia (the CNT) had over 50,000 members in Barcelona alone, but remained unrecognized by the employers even after a devastating, two-month general strike. The violence escalated, as employers hired thugs to kill unionists and the workers lashed back in kind. The chaos and the rising body count gave Spain's rightists the excuse to close down parliamentary democracy. The Captain General of Barcelona, Miguel Primo de Rivera, declared a military dictatorship and the 'abolition of the class struggle', with the approval of King Alfonso XIII.

1923–75: Dictatorship, Civil War and Franco

The dictatorship of Primo de Rivera was proof, if the Catalans needed any, that nothing had really changed since the time of Fernando and Isabel. Spain still looked on Barcelona with a mixture of contempt and fear, and was prepared to do anything to suppress it. The dictator banned the CNT, and attempted to do the same to the Catalan language and its nationalist symbols, but he did promote Barcelona's International Exhibition of 1929 to show his version of Spain to the world. This initiated another building boom, one that included the city's first metro line. It also gave it its first great wave of immigrants from other corners of Spain, especially from Andalucía, Murcia and Galicia.

The old dictator retired the next year, and a left-wing landslide in the 1931 municipal elections provided a dramatic renunciation of the old order, leading to the abdication of Alfonso XIII and the birth of the Spanish Republic. In Catalonia, the big winner was the popular old ex-colonel Francesc Macià, head of the left-wing Republicans (Esquerra Republicana), who declared the 'Republic of Catalonia', although three days later he agreed to limit this to Catalan autonomy under the rule of a revived Generalitat, and was later succeeded by liberal trade union lawyer Lluís Companys.

The other patricians and their Lliga de Catalunya were not about to support Macià's mix of Republican leftists, CNT Anarchists, professors and trade unionists. When the right won the 1934 national elections, many of the Catalan leftists got thrown in jail. When the left came back with the Popular Front in 1936, the stage was set for Francisco Franco's coup and the outbreak of the Civil War. In Barcelona, the success of the workers and loyal Republican troops in defeating the rightists revolutionized the city; churches were set alight and Falangist supporters rooted out and summarily shot, while the anguished Companys tried desperately to contain the mobs and control the situation to avoid state intervention.

The CNT remained in control for the remainder of 1936 and part of 1937, making Barcelona unique in Europe as the only city ever to have been governed by Anarchists. Shops and cafés became collectives; progressive schools were established; women's rights and healthcare were seriously addressed for the first time in Spain; servile and ceremonial forms of speech were abolished; buildings seized by workers were given rent-free to the poor. Many workers were as naïve as they were idealistic, and they ignored the darker side of organized Anarchism, the *patrullas de control*, with its old scores to settle. Many who had volunteered to be *patrullas* left in disgust at the massacres of clergy, who were especially singled out for the Church's long-standing support of the propertied classes.

As Franco made gains across Spain in 1937, Barcelona became the theatre of a left-wing war-within-a-war. Typically, the CNT lost its hold in chaotic circumstances – George Orwell, who was there, was hardly the only one to be confused. On 3 May 1937, Companys, at the time president of Catalonia only in name, but supported by the Communists, ordered a takeover of the telephone company from the CNT. The Anarchists rose one last time; supported reluctantly by the Trotskyist POUM, they built barricades and won the streets, but true to their name they didn't follow through and take political control. It was suicide, as the defeated Communists leapt forward to fill the void. In three days at least 1,500 people were killed in the fighting, until the Anarchists and POUM laid down their arms for the sake of the Republic; the next day, the Republican Army and the Communists started to round them up, saving Franco the trouble later. Anarchists and Trotskyites who weren't shot often found themselves imprisoned in the same cells as Falangists.

Near the end of the war over 200,000 refugees filled the city, while hundreds of civilians died in the indiscriminate bombings ordered by Franco and his German friends; the historic centre and Barceloneta suffered the most. In January 1939, half a million Republicans fled towards France as Barcelona surrendered. In the confusion, the Generalitat left behind enough incriminating documents for Franco's reprisal squads to have little trouble finishing off the thousands of Republicans who stayed behind.

Franco took particular delight in humiliating the city. All things Catalan were banned; even speaking Catalan in the street was risking jail. The next two sad and impoverished decades saw food, electricity and everything else in short supply; in 1947 the city came very close to famine. Other parts of Spain were suffering too; immigrants flocked to the city, and Franco did everything to encourage them, hoping a tidal wave of poor Andalucians would dilute Catalanism into a harmless eccentricity. Unlike earlier immigrants, the new arrivals didn't integrate but lived together in their shanty towns and ghettos; the banning of Catalan meant they never learned the language.

But Franco could never hope to get Spain back on its feet without Barcelona's industry. By 1960, he had given up his attempt at national self-sufficiency, and a new generation of economists was tooling up the country for its impressive industrial take-off.

Barcelona's appointed mayor, José María de Porcioles, presided over a building boom of soulless, high-rise housing projects and factories on the outskirts, and disfigured old Barcelona with massive car parks and roads. Still, shoots of new life were poking up through the cracks of the Castilian concrete. In 1960, future Catalan president Jordi Pujol was arrested and imprisoned for two years after devising a protest at the Palau de la Música – singing the *Song of the Catalan Flag* at a concert while Franco's ministers were in the audience. Not long afterwards, Barcelonins formed their first neighourhood groups. These were the seeds of a new participatory democracy, and they became very active by the mid-1970s, leading most of the protests of the period, demanding basic services and better public transport, and complaining against exploitation and the siting of factories.

1975 to the Present: Becoming the City of Cool

When Franco died, on 20 November 1975, every single bottle of *cava* in Barcelona was emptied. The morning after, like the rest of Spain, they wondered what would happen next. When the first city elections were held in 1978, the Socialists under Narcís Serra won control of the city government, the Ajuntament, and they have kept it ever since. From 1982 to 1997 the mayor was the popular Pasqual Maragall, grandson of the poet Joan Maragall, tireless improver and promoter of his city.

By any measure, the accomplishments of Maragall, Pujol and company have been remarkable; their creative channelling of 40 years of pent-up energy and Catalan quirkiness have made Barcelona the most dynamic city on the Mediterranean (it likes to see itself as the southernmost city of northern Europe and the northernmost city of the south), with a hard nose for making money, sweetened by Mediterranean colour and spontaneity. Currently, the population of the sprawling urban region is around four million; by 2020 it is projected to reach seven million. Not the least of the Catalans' achievements has been defusing the little time bomb Franco left for them: the hundreds of thousands of poor immigrants from southern Spain. This they managed with an effort towards good faith and fairness, and by compromising their nationalism enough to define a Catalan as anyone who wanted to be one (and who learned the language). Their non-racial inclusiveness could be a blueprint for other nationalities struggling to keep heart and soul intact in a multicultural world. The continuation of Gaudí's Sagrada Família, a project so big and eccentric and so essentially Catalan, is the symbol of the city's cultural *continuitat*.

All the designer tinsel of Barcelona's obsessive hipness is only the shop-window-dressing of a city that works hard for its living, and knows how to sell itself. The real Barcelona runs on metals and machine industries, textiles and chemicals and publishing (more in Spanish than Catalan). There is a busy stock exchange and countless trade fairs in complexes on Montjuïc and the Gran Via.

For all that, it has been the tinsel that gets the world's attention. Mayor Maragall, with a bit of help from Olympics czar Joan Antoni Samaranch, a Catalan, secured the 1992 Olympics and used it as a vehicle to push through a huge building programme, which radically transformed the city. It gave it a fresh orientation towards the sea, restored its monuments, cleaned up its seedier quarters and gentrified others, making it the model for any up-and-at-'em metropolis wanting to break into the ranks of the 'world cities'.

The Olympics are long over, but the city-perfecting momentum shows no sign of stopping. In 2002, the city celebrated the 150th anniversary of Gaudí's birth, and in 2004 hosted a $2.3 billion

A Little Orientation

Barcelona is situated on a plain gently descending to the sea, wrapped in an amphitheatre of hills and mountains. At the south end of the harbour rises its oldest landmark, the smooth-humped mountain of **Montjuïc**, once key to the city's defence and now its pleasure dome and Olympic 'ring'; on the landward side, the highest peak in the Sierra de Collserola is **Tibidabo**, with its amusements and priceless views.

Old Catalans may have bewailed their eclipse during the days of Imperial Spain, but moderns may be thankful that the lack of prosperity has left intact the historic centre or **Barri Gòtic**, the greatest concentration of medieval architecture in Europe. This is bounded on the southwest by **La Rambla**, Barcelona's showcase promenade; south of the Rambla and north of Av. Paral.lel, **El Raval** remains the most piquant, with a few last remnants of the once notorious red-light district, the **Barri Xinès**.

The part of the map that looks as if it were stamped by a giant waffle iron is the **Eixample**, the 19th-century extension that quadrupled the size of Barcelona, and coincided with the careers of the modernista architects, whose colourful buildings brighten its monotonous chamfered blocks.

West of the Eixample the city has digested once independent towns like **Gràcia** and **Sarrià** and spread as far up the hills as gravity permits. Meanwhile, Barcelona has turned its attention to its long neglected seafront: just south of **Barceloneta**, a planned popular neighbourhood from the 18th century, the **Port Vell** (old port), has been transformed into an urban playground, while to the north of Barceloneta the **Vila Olímpica**, founded to house Olympic athletes, has become a swanky address while the **Diagonal Mar** district to the north is a new focus for redevelopment.

dollar, three-month extravaganza known as the Universal Forum of Cultures, dedicated to 21st-century ideals of peace, sustainable development, and respect for diversity. It also provided an excuse to rebuild the shoreline at the end of Avinguda Diagonal (in spite of the lingering pong of the local sewage works).

Blame for the Forum's resounding lack of success in Barcelona, however, fell on the shoulders of Maragall's successor, Joan Clos (1997–2006), whose popularity suffered another blow when several apartment blocks in the Carmel district collapsed during the extension of the L5 metro line. In the wake of that, current plans to build high-speed train tunnels across the Eixample have engendered considerable opposition – but are nevertheless being pushed through under current mayor, Jordi Hereu i Boher, as part of the city's dream of becoming an international rail node. Another project is the world's longest metro line, the 43km-long L9, which will link the suburb of Badalona to the north to the airport, where a new terminal by Ricardo Bofill is nearing completion.

At the time of writing, no one knows how the economic tailspin of 2009 will affect Barcelona's astonishing array of other projects, including the new Diagonal Mar high-tech business zone, District 22@, with 50 new towers, including a startling 11-storey Spiralling Tower by British-Iraqi architect Zaha Hadid. The old Poblenou industrial quarter around Plaça de les Gloriès Catalanes is slated for a total revamp to become the new city centre. New Gaudí-inspired pavillions by Korean architect Toyo Ito will make the trade fair on the Gran Via the largest in Europe; and even Camp Nou is getting a makeover by Sir Norman Foster.

Getting around Barcelona

By Bus

Barcelona's public transport authority, **TMB**, is efficient, cheap and user-friendly. Its buses run until around 11pm. The 17 main lines also have after-hours **'Nitbuses'** (night, not lice), and routes and timetables are clearly posted at all stops. Timetables and fare information at TMB: t 93 318 70 74, *www.tmb.cat*.

By Metro (Ⓜ)

The city also has six metro lines, with Muzak pumped into the stations. As stylish as Barcelona is, its metro is not, but it is fast and cheap: trains run until 11pm, and all night on Saturday nights (€1.35 single). Metro **tickets** can be purchased from ticket windows or machines. **Passes**, valid for the metro, FGC (*see* p.67), buses, tram and RENFE trains (Zone 1 area), are available:

T-10: Ten single rides in Zone 1 (€7.70). The most convenient, and can be shared.

T-50/30: Fifty single rides within 30 days (€31.50); can also be shared.

T-Dia: Unlimited travel for one person for one day (€5.80).

By Tram and Funicular

TMB also operates the vintage **Tramvia Blau**, founded in 1901, running from Plaça Kennedy/Avinguda Tibidabo to Plaça Dr Andreu (*summer daily 9am–9.35pm; winter Sat and Sun only 9am–9.35pm*), where it links up to the Tibidabo **funicular**, which runs when the amusement park is open (*see* p.134). A funicular also goes from Ⓜ Paral.lel to Montjuïc, which in turn links up the **Telefèric de Montjuïc** to the Castell de Montjuïc (*open June–mid-Sept Mon–Fri 11.15–8, Sat–Sun 11.15–9; mid-Sept–Oct daily 11.30–2.45 and 4–7.30; Nov–May Sat and Sun only*).

Sleek new **trams**, t 90 219 32 75, *www.trambcn.com*, are located mainly in the suburbs, although the line linking Ⓜ Gloriès to the Fòrum, for concerts and other big events, may be of interest.

By Tourist Bus

TMB operates the **Bus Turístic**, which stops at 44 of the city's best known sites. It has three loops: a red one through the Eixample, a blue one on Montjuïc and along the sea, and a summer-only green one going along the beaches out to the Fòrum. These buses run every 20–30mins, allowing you to get off and on at will, on any route. A one-day ticket (buy it on the bus or online *www.tmb.cat*) is €21; two days (consecutive) €27; and children age 4–12 cost €17 a day. You get an impressive number of other discounts with the ticket.

By Taxi

Barcelona yellow-and-black taxis are ubiquitous and reasonable. If you want to book one in advance, try **Radio Taxi**, t 93 303 30 33, *www.radiotaxi033.com*. Taxis cabs with **disabled access**, t 93 322 22 22.

By Cable Car

Built over the harbour in 1929, the **Transbordador Aeri del Port** operates from Barceloneta to Montjuïc, with a stop at the World Trade Center. Tickets cost €12.50 return, €9 one way; call t 93 430 47 16 (*open mid-June–mid-Sept daily 11–8; Mar–mid-June and mid-Sept–mid-Oct daily 10.45–7; mid-Oct–Feb daily 10–6*).

Hiring a Car

Save money before you leave by booking on the internet or with your flight, then save on pricey parking fees by having the car delivered to your hotel when you're ready to use it.

Hiring a Bicycle

Un Cotxe Menys, C/Esparteria 3, t 93 268 21 05, *www.bicicletabarcelona.com* (Ⓜ Barceloneta).

...al punt de la trobada, C/Badajoz 24, t 93 225 05 85 (Ⓜ Barceloneta). They have tandems, too, in case you want to recreate Ramon Casas' famous painting in Els Quatre Gats.

Los Filicletos, Psg de Picasso 38, t 93 319 78 11. Near the Ciutadella.

Biciclot, Passeig Marítim de la Barceloneta, t 93 221 97 78, *www.bikinginbarcelona.net* (Ⓜ Barceloneta).

Guided Tours

Book ahead with the tourist office in Plaça de Catalunya (t 93 285 38 32, *www.barcelonaturisme.com*) for the popular walking tours in English on four themes: the Barri Gòtic (daily at 10am); Modernisme (Fri and Sat at 4pm, 6pm in summer); Gourmet (Fri and Sat at 11am); and Picasso (Tues–Sun 10.30am).

Barcelona's Showcase Promenade: La Rambla

It's the first place everyone heads for, the 'most beautiful street in the world', according to Lorca. It is also one of the busiest: day and night the Rambla is crowded with natives and visitors from every continent. Kiosks sell newspapers in every language; cafés, hotels, burger-stands and magically tacky souvenir shops line its length. Catalan Elvis impersonators, unicyclists, puppeteers, flamenco dancers, buskers and 'human statues' use it as a stage. If not the real Barcelona, the Rambla has a big share of Barcelona's extrovert soul. (La Rambla is, properly speaking, Les Rambles, because it consists of five connected streets, and locals use both terms.)

Rambla means 'sand' in Arabic, and long ago this is what it was: a sandy gully of the river that drained the Collserola mountains, and eventually carried so many less pleasant effluents that it became known as the *Cagallel*, the turd-taker. In the 13th century, when Jaume I built the first set of medieval walls, they used the *Cagallel* as a moat. By 1366 the torrent was paved over, and, at the end of the 18th century, it was decided to make the Rambla a park lane. In 1859 the first of the plane trees was planted, and thrived so well that when something prospers the Barcelonins say 'it grows like a tree in the Rambla'.

La Rambla de Santa Mònica

Like much of Barcelona, the street was tidied up for the Olympics, to the detriment of all the seedy sexy shops that once dominated the lowest Rambla, La Rambla de Santa Mònica. From the 15th to 18th century the area was a major producer of artillery, most notably of a colossal cannon named 'Santa Eulàlia' cast in 1463, which blew up into smithereens when fired for the first time. The bleakly modern **Centre d'Art Santa Mònica** or C'ASM was created by Albert Viaplana and Helio Piñón from the cloisters of the 17th-century monastery of Santa Mònica. Though eclipsed by the sleek Museu d'Art Contemporani (*see* p.109), the centre can still pack a few surprises. Just off Rambla Santa Mònica, a stately 19th-century neoclassical mansion houses the **Museu de Cera**, where everyone is an imposter. This was the brainchild of the city executioner, Nicomedes Méndez, a quiet bachelor who lived with his pet rabbit. Noting the crowds that gathered to watch famous Anarchists meet the *garrot vil*, Méndez had the idea of prolonging the thrill by displaying waxworks of its victims. The city vetoed this, although it found nothing wrong with displaying other cities' famous criminals. These days the criminals have been replaced by the likes of Princesses Leia and Diana, Salvador Dalí, and Frankenstein.

Centre d'Art Santa Mònica
La Rambla 7, t 93 316 28 10, www. centredartsantamonica. net; Ⓜ Drassanes; open Tues–Sat 11–8, Sun 11–3; adm free

Museu de Cera
Passatge de la Banca 7, t 93 317 26 49, www. museocerabcn.com; Ⓜ Drassanes; open summer daily 10am–10pm; winter Mon–Fri 10–1.30 and 4–7.30, Sat, Sun and hols 11–2 and 4.30–8.30; adm exp

Rambla dels Caputxins and the Plaça Reial

The next Rambla, Rambla dels Caputxins, defines the heart of Barcelona's old theatre district. The first wooden playhouse was built in 1579 by the Hospital de la Santa Creu (*see* p.109) after Felipe II granted it a monopoly on dramatic spectacles to raise revenue; the site today is occupied by the **Teatre Principal** (1850).

The Capuchins who lent their name to this Rambla had a convent here that had the dubious distinction of being the first to be burned in the first church-burning fury in 1835. When the rubble was cleared, the land was auctioned off, and in 1848 Francesc Daniel Molina won the competition to design the **Plaça Reial**, modelled after Madrid's Plaza Mayor. Molina enclosed it in harmonious neoclassical residences with ground-floor shops and cafés. After hitting rock bottom as a playground for muggers, addicts and prostitutes, Plaça Reial was given a face lift in the early 1980s and planted with palms. On Sunday mornings it hosts a stamp and coin market.

The palms chaperone the late 19th-century iron **Font de les Tres Gràcies** splashing in the centre and two flamboyant **Modernista lamp-posts**. These are Gaudí's earliest known works (1878), designed in his student days and covered with emblems of Hermes, the god of commerce. In the Plaça's northeastern corner, the Café-Restaurant Taxidermista was once filled with stuffed animals; Dalí, who once ordered 200,000 ants and a rhinoceros, was one of its best customers.

At the head of the Rambla dels Caputxins, on the edge of the theatre district, stood an institution that Barcelona is especially proud of: the **Gran Teatre del Liceu**, inaugurated in 1847 in place of a Trinitarian convent burned in 1835. Gutted by fire in 1861, it was rebuilt by Josep Oriol Mestres on an even grander scale, with 4,000 seats (second only to Milan's La Scala). As a symbol of the élite, the Liceu was the target of a notorious Anarchist attack, on 7 November 1893, when two bombs were hurled from the gallery, killing 22 people. In 1994, the Liceu burned to the ground during last-minute work on the set for *Turandot*. A campaign to replace it began immediately, and, by late 1999 the prima donnas were back again, tickling the ears of opera mavens.

Gran Teatre del Liceu
La Rambla 51–9,
t 93 485 99 00,
www.liceubarcelona.
com; ⓜ *Liceu; open for*
guided visits daily at
10am; express unguided
tours daily 11.30, 12,
12.30, 1; info Mon–Fri
2–8.30; adm

The new theatre is a clone of Oriol Mestres' much-loved old building, only updated. The lobby has the opulent grandeur of yore and a wide marble staircase leading up to the dazzling Salon of Mirrors. The auditorium, one of the largest in Europe, is a great whirl of gilt and red velvet; the theatre's signature red velvet chairs reappear in the fantastical ceiling paintings by Perejaume.

Back on the Rambla, the **Pla Boqueria**, with its colourful ceramic mosaic by Miró (1976), marks the medieval gate of Santa Eulàlia, where fairs and markets took place. Matching Miró's mosaic for exuberance is the **Casa Bruno Quadros** (1896), a former umbrella-maker's, defended by a swirling dragon holding a brolly, designed by Josep Vilaseca. Opposite, at No.77, is Enric Sagnier's narrow **Casa Doctor Genové**, with its mosaic-framed clock (1911), and the lavish **Antiga Casa Figueras** (1902), selling luscious Escribà cakes.

Rambla de les Flors

Pla Bouqería marks the beginning of the Rambla de Sant Josep, known as Rambla de les Flors ever since the first flower stalls sprang up during the Corpus Christi celebrations in 1853. The flower girls were once as much of an attraction as their wares: the Modernista painter Ramon Casas was surely not the first or last to have fallen in love with, and married, one.

On the left, a large Modernista neo-Gothic arch beckons you into the lively century-old Mercat de Sant Josep, better known as **La Boqueria**. Founded in 1830 on the ruins of yet another burned monastery, La Boquería had the first permanent stalls in the city and was roofed over in 1914. It is still the place to find the greatest choice of food in Barcelona. Skip past the front stalls and delve into the interior, where prices haven't taken on tourist dimensions. Just up from the market, the ivory-coloured neoclassical **Palau de la Virreina** was built in 1778 by the Viceroy Manuel Amat of Peru with loot skimmed off the fabulous silver mines of Potosí. He laid on the marriage of the century then promptly died in 1782, leaving it all to his 19-year-old widow. Now it houses the **Centre de la Imatge**, featuring exhibits dedicated to contemporary art and culture, often photography and often linked somehow to the city.

La Boqueria
open Mon–Sat 8–5; some stands open until 8.30

Palau de la Virreina
La Rambla 99, t 93 316 10 00; www.bcn.cat/ virreinacentrede laimatge; Ⓜ Liceu; opening hours vary according to exhibition

Rambla dels Estudis

The next Rambla, the Rambla dels Estudis, was named after the Estudi General, or University, founded by Martí the Humane and suppressed by Felipe V; nowadays the promenade is full of the tweets and chirps of its **bird market**. The pride of its 18th-century Jesuit church, the **Església de Betlem**, is a fancy Churrigueresque portal, but its once equally lavish Baroque interior was incinerated in 1936. Next to it, the old Jesuit College was replaced in 1880 with the **Philippines Tobacco Company** (No.109), which was run, like much else in Barcelona, by Eusebi Güell, and supplied most of Spain's cheap smokes. It's now a swish hotel. Opposite, the arcaded **Palau de Moja** was once the home of poet Jacint Verdaguer.

Rambla de les Canaletes

The last segment, the Rambla de les Canaletes, is named after the magical **Font de les Canaletes** that promises that all who drink of it will stay in or return to Barcelona. Barça fans come here to celebrate after a victory.

Plaça Catalunya

At the top of the Rambla extends the Plaça Catalunya, once an open prairie beyond the walls. The present square, as designed by Francesc Nebot, was inaugurated in 1927. During the Civil War, one building, the former Hotel Colón, was the PSUC headquarters and draped with enormous portraits of Lenin, Marx and Stalin. When Franco's troops took the city in 1939, the offending portraits were stripped away and the square was renamed Plaza del Ejército, or Army Square. Thirty-eight years later, on 11 September 1977, it was the focus of the first official post-Franco Catalan National Day celebration, attended by 250,000 souls.

The Plaça Catalunya is Barcelona's hub of human and pigeon life. Transport lines converge here, and department stores occupy the fringes: **El Corte Inglés**, a cross between a ferry boat and a radiator; and the dull **Triangle mall** (redeemed by a huge FNAC). In the hodgepodge of art, the upside-down stair on a pedestal is Subirachs' monument to Francesc Macià, Republican president of the Generalitat in 1931, a Piranesiesque hulk that looks ready to crush *The Goddess*, an older, wistful sculpture by Josep Clará.

The Barri Gòtic

On the map, you can see it at once: the 'egg yolk' from which Barcelona sprang as Roman Faventia Julia Augusta Paterna Barcino, in the loop between the curving C/Banys Nous, C/Avinyó and Via Laietana. Its lofty walls may have failed to keep out the Visigoths in 415, but for the next 1,000 years they held tight to Barcelona's heart. Gentle Mons Tàber was the acropolis, and here the institutions of medieval Barcelona took root over their Roman predecessors. When the city burst out of its girdle of walls into the Eixample in 1870, it left behind a 14th-century time capsule, the most extensive Gothic city centre in the world, remarkably intact and sunny-side up.

Roman Barcino:
Plaça Àngel to the Plaça del Rei

The best introduction to the area is **Plaça Àngel** (Ⓜ Jaume I), just outside the Portal Major or main gate. Originally this was the Plaça del Blat, or 'wheat square', where the city's grain was bought and sold. In the 9th century it witnessed a miracle: as Santa Eulàlia's relics were being ceremoniously moved from Santa Maria del Mar to the cathedral, the body, when it reached the square, became too heavy to carry. An angel appeared and pointed accusingly at an

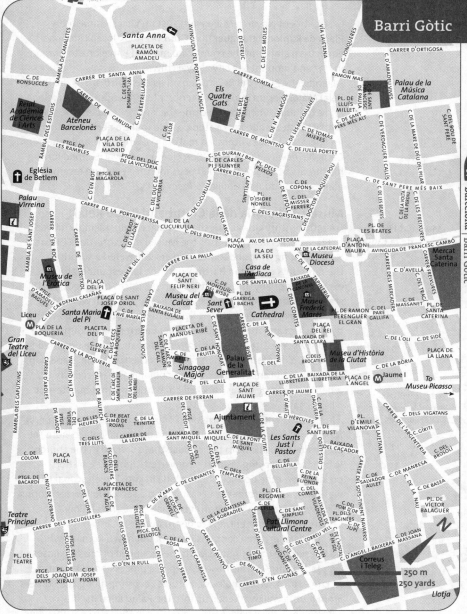

official, who confessed that he had pocketed Eulàlia's toe. He replaced it and the procession continued.

The streets around Plaça de l'Àngel have Barcino's best-preserved **Roman walls**, with towers as high as 46ft, making cameo appearances in a mesh of medieval building, especially along

C/Sots-tinent Navarro. More walls, just up Vía Laietana in the
Plaça de Ramon Berenguer III el Gran, overlook Josep Llimona's
equestrian statue of the count who married Barcelona to Aragon
in 1137 and brought the city a royal crown.

Handsome **Plaça del Rei** started off as the courtyard of the **Palau
Reial Major**, begun in the 10th century for the counts of Barcelona
and expanded when they became the kings of Aragon. The square,
with its picturesque fan of steps, would make a perfect setting for
an opera, and once witnessed real drama, when Fernando the
Catholic (never a favourite in Barcelona) narrowly escaped having
his throat cut by a disgruntled peasant. The sculpture resembling a
giant safe is Eduardo Chillida's *Topos* (1985).

Museu d'Història de la Ciutat and Palau Reial

**Museu d'Història
de la Ciutat**
*Plaça del Rei,
t 93 265 21 22,
www.museuhistoria.
bcn.es;
Ⓜ Jaume I;
open Oct–Mar
Tues–Sat 10–2 and 4–7,
Sun 10–8; April–Sept
Tues–Sun 10–8; adm,
free Sun 3–8
(admission ticket
includes entrance to the
adjacent Palau Reial
Major, Museu-Monestir
de Pedralbes, Centre
d'Interpretació del
Park Güell and Museu-
Casa Verdaguer)*

A 15th-century Gothic merchant's palace, painstakingly moved
to Plaça del Rei in 1931, houses the Museu d'Història de la Ciutat.
While digging its foundations, workers uncovered a surprise:
the remnants of **Roman Barcino**, now the largest underground
excavations of any ancient city in Europe. Traces of indigo dye still
stain the stone vats of the dyeing workshops, which were later
incorporated into the baths, fully and luxuriously equipped with a
gymnasium and massage rooms. There are remnants of the
factory where salted fish and *garum* (fish sauce) were prepared for
export. Circular fermentation vats are pocked with the grape skins
and pips of Laitania, a cheap wine popular in the 1st century BC,
when the average Gaius knocked back around three-quarters of
a litre a day.

In the 4th century, a prestigious Roman family donated property
for the city's first Christian basilica and episcopal palace; note the
pretty floor mosaic from their house that survived in the church.
When the occupying Visigoths converted, Ugnes, the bishop,
presided over the Council of Barcelona in 599. The episcopal palace
was given a facelift for the occasion, and a secret hollow for storing
relics was hidden in the altar; even back then, one's fellow
Christians were not entirely to be trusted.

A small gallery area contains busts of unknown Romans who
now resemble prize fighters with their chipped or missing noses.
Two faded early Gothic frescoes depict a procession of knights
(*c.* 1265–1300), with fabulous creatures cavorting along the borders.
From here, a walkway leads up into the **Palau Reial** itself.

Barcelona's royal palace was renovated in the 14th century, when
its great hall, the magnificent **Saló de Tinell**, was added. Begun in
1359 by Guillem Carbonell, architect to Pere the Ceremonious, its
six huge rainbow arches cross a span of 56ft, with wooden beams
filling in the ceiling between; when viewed from the corner of the

hall, the arches appear magically to radiate from a single point. Banquets, funerals and even parliaments were held in the Saló de Tinell; in 1493 Fernando and Isabel received Columbus here after his first voyage, and later the Inquisition held its trials here, so dreaded that the stones in the walls were said to move if a suspect told a lie. After 1714, the room was baroqued over as a church, and everyone presumed the Saló de Tinell was lost for ever, until someone dug under the plaster in 1934 and *voilà*.

The hall is linked to the narrow **Capella Palatina de Santa Àgata**. Begun in 1302 by Jaume II and his queen Blanche of Anjou, the chapel was re-dedicated to St Agatha by papal bull in 1601, thanks to a precious relic: the stone where the breasts of St Agatha were laid after Roman soldiers snipped them off in Catania, Sicily. The chapel's glory is the golden, lavish *Retaule del Condestable* (1466), the masterpiece of Jaume Huguet. The vestry holds a bell-tower clock, made in 1575 said to be the largest of its kind in the world.

A narrow, almost hidden, staircase leads out to the curious skyscraper which rises over the square – five storeys of galleries built by Antoni Carbonell in 1557 and anachronistically named the **Mirador del Rei Martí** (*currently closed for renovation*) after the popular humane king, to hide the unpleasant truth that it was really a spy tower for the hated viceroy, or Lloctinent, a position set up by Fernando the Catholic. To the left of the Palau Reial is the **Palau del Lloctinent**, also by Carbonell, and beautifully restored in 2008. It contains the Archives of the Crown of Aragon, one of the world's greatest collections of medieval documents. Peek into the fine courtyard to see the magnificent coffered ceiling over the stair.

Museu Frederic Marès

Museu
Frederic Marès
Plaça de Sant Iu 5,
t 93 256 35 00,
www.museumares.
bcn.cat; ⓜ *Jaume I;*
open Tues–Sat 10–7,
Sun 10–8; adm,
free Sun 3–8

Fernando the Catholic donated part of the royal palace to another of his great gifts to Barcelona, the Spanish Inquisition. Now it's home to the sublime and ridiculously amassed collection of sculptor and hoarder extraordinaire Frederic Marès (1893–1991). On the ground floor, you'll find armies of tiny Iberian ex-votos, followed by Roman, Greek and Iberian busts, coins and tombs. Then comes the largest collection of sculpture in Spain: an astonishing array of 12th–14th-century polychrome wood sculptures of sweet-faced Virgins and stylized crucifixes. The basement has more, plus an impressive 13th-century portal, capitals and columns, and tombs, including that of a 14th-century knight bearing a lovingly sculpted hawk on his left hand.

There is more gore on the first floor, with flayed and bleeding medieval saints punctured with arrows (although note one of the best pieces here, a 12th-century relief of the Vocation of St Peter).

Nineteenth-century Baby Jesuses have real hair and dolly faces, intermingling with Catalan iron, Montserrat memorabilia and colourful plaques of the Dance of Death, showing the Grim Reaper reeling with ladies, monks and peasants. In the cool, vaulted courtyard by the entrance, orange trees overlook a charming outdoor café, perfect for dizzy museum victims.

Plaça Nova and Around

The Cathedral: La Seu

La Seu
Plaça de la Seu,
t 93 310 71 95,
www.catedralbcn.org;
open daily 8–1.15 and
4.30–7.30; choir open
Mon–Fri 9–1 and
4.30–7, Sun 9–1;
***museum** open daily*
10–12.15 and 5.15–7; Sun
10–12 and 5.15–7; adm
to choir, lift to roof
and museum

C/de les Comtes leads to Barcelona's huge Gothic cathedral, which, with its fat apse, octagonal towers and spires, is hard to miss. This is the third church to stand here; the first was flattened in al-Mansur's raid in 985; of the second, a Romanesque one built by Count Ramon Berenguer I, only two doorways remain. The earliest bit of the current model is the right transept, built in 1298 by Jaume II; its Portal of Sant Iu (St Ives) has carvings of St George and Barcelona's first count, Wilfred the Hairy, fighting a dragon and griffon respectively. The main façade, based on the 1408 plans by a French master named Carli, was only begun in 1882.

Catalan Gothic is famous for its conquest of space: although La Seu has only three aisles, the architects made it look like five, part of a rich and atmospheric interior that was one of the very few to escape the attentions of Barcelona's Anarchists. The first chapel on the right, the star-vaulted **sala capitular**, contains the lucky crucifix borne by Don Juan on the mast of his flagship at the Battle of Lepanto in 1571; the S-shaped twist in Christ's body came about, they say, when it dodged a Turkish cannonball. The adjacent **baptistry** has a plaque that records the baptism here of the first six native Americans, brought over by Columbus, in 1493; its beautiful stained-glass scene of the *Noli me Tangere* is based on drawings by Bartolomé Bermejo.

The **choir** is enclosed in the middle of the nave behind a fine Renaissance screen by Bartolomé Ordóñez. The richly sculpted stalls of the 14th to 15th centuries were given fancy canopies and painted in 1514 with the arms of the kings of France, Portugal, Poland, Hungary, Denmark and England, when Emperor Charles V summoned them as Knights of the Golden Fleece to Barcelona, a proto-session of the United Nations before all were plunged into war; Henry VIII's seat is directly on the emperor's right. The fanciest carving of all, by Pere Sanglada, is on the pulpit (1403).

The choir faces the elegant, daringly low-vaulted **crypt** with an enormous keystone, designed by the Mallorcan Jaume Fabre, who was in charge of the cathedral works from 1317 to 1339. It holds the relics of the co-patroness of Barcelona, Santa Eulàlia, who lies in a beautiful 14th-century alabaster sarcophagus. Eulàlia, the daughter of a merchant of Sarrià, threw dirt on the altar of Augustus and refused to worship Rome's gods, and the scenes on her tomb show the 13 grisly trials designed to change her mind, including being thrown naked into a vat of starving fleas and a seduction attempt by the handsome son of the Roman commander. Nothing could sway her, and her martyrdom ended when her torturers lopped off her breasts and crucified her. Her original 9th-century sarcophagus is set in the back of the crypt.

After the virtuoso crypt, the **altar** is an anticlimax, supported on two Visigothic capitals, with a bland bronze Crucifix by Frederic Marès behind. To the right of this, the founders of the Romanesque cathedral, Ramon Berenguer I and his wife Almodis, lie in the velvet-covered wooden sarcophagi against the wall. The door here leads into the sacristy and the **treasury**; holding pride of place is a late 14th-century gem-encrusted monstrance, and a silver-plated processional cross by Francesc Villardel, of 1383. Of the chapels radiating from the ambulatory, the fourth one on the right, dedicated to Sant Joan Baptista i Sant Josep, has the best art: the minutely detailed altarpiece of the Transfiguration by Bernat Martorell (1450). On the far left side of the ambulatory you'll find the lift to the roof with grand views over Barcelona.

What people tend to remember most fondly about the cathedral is the charming green oasis of the **cloister**, begun in 1385. Its iron-grilled chapels were once dedicated to the patron saints of Barcelona's guilds ('Our Lady of Electricity' is still going strong) and many leading guild masters are buried in the floor. A pretty pavilion holds the **Font de Sant Jordi**, with a figure of St George rising from a mossy green blob. At Corpus Christi, flowers are wound around the fountain and a hollow egg is set to dance in the jet of water (*l'ou com balla*). The egg placers don't have to look far for one, because 13 white geese natter away next to the fountain. They have been there since anyone can remember, symbols of Santa Eulàlia's virginity or a memory of the geese that saved Rome, or (most likely) just because. Also note the Romanesque doorway into the church, the only surviving bit of Ramon Berenguer I's cathedral, cobbled together out of Roman stones and capitals.

A chapel in the cloister houses the tiny **Cathedral Museum**, with its retired retables and reliquaries. The *Pietà* (1490) by Bartolomé Bermejo is his masterpiece and one of the first Spanish oil paintings; there's a beautiful altarpiece by Jaume Huguet, painted for the guild of the *esparto* grass workers, and the organ cabinet door paintings (1560) by the Greek Pere Serafí, named 'Peter of the Seven Ps' for his 'Peter Piper' slogan '*Pere Pau pinta portes per poc preu*' ('Peter Pau paints doors for bargain prices').

Museu Diocesà

Museu Diocesà
*Plaça de la Seu,
t 93 315 22 13;
Ⓜ Jaume I; open
Tues–Sat 10–2 and 5–8,
Sun 11–2; adm*

Other works of sacred art from the diocese have been pensioned off in this excellent but often overlooked museum in the Pia Almoina, headquarters of a charitable foundation founded in 1009, although the current building, incorporating part of a Roman tower and its prophylactic head of Medusa, dates from 1423. Among the treasures are the striking Sienese-inspired *Taula de Sant Jaume*, by Arnau and Ferrer Bassa; a reliquary of Sant Cugat (1312); a tormented Crucifixion from the 13th century; and Romanesque frescoes of the Apocalypse from the apse of Sant Salvador de Polinyà (1122), a precursor of Picasso's *Guernica*. The *Custodia de Santa Maria del Pi* (1587) by Llàtzer de la Castanya is a masterpiece of the goldsmith's art, and there are retables by Bernat Martorell and the Portuguese Pere Nunyes. A startling 15th-century anonymous *Retaule de Sant Bartomeu* is a candidate for the goriest in Barcelona (although it has plenty of competition). Upstairs are alabaster Virgins, including one by Pere Joan, and Gil de Medina's huge *St Christopher* (1545).

Plaça Nova

On Thursdays, a flea market takes place in front of the cathedral in Plaça Nova, which also hosts the Christmas market, where discriminating shoppers can find a fine array of *caganers* (*see* pp.35–6). Plaça Nova's **Col.legi d'Arquitectes** (1962) is a poor ad for the architectural trade, but its façade is decorated by a sketchy frieze of popular celebrations by Picasso – he sent the designs from France for his only piece of public art in Barcelona. Opposite are two **Roman towers**, renovated in the 12th century, along with an arch of the Roman aqueduct reconstructed in 1958. Huge iron letters, erected by the poet Joan Brossa in 1994, spell out 'Barcino'. Just here, at 1 C/Santa Llúcia, is the 12th–14th-century **Casa de l'Ardiaca** (of the Archdeacon), now home to an archive of newspapers. In 1902, when the building was owned by the lawyers' college, Domènech i Montaner was called upon to install a postal slot. The swallow and tortoise expressed his opinion of lawyers – the swallows with wings to soar into the realms of truth, the tortoise plodding at the pace of court procedures. He also created a charming tiled courtyard, with a lofty palm and pretty Gothic fountain; it is also used for Corpus Christi Day egg-dancing.

Opposite is the Romanesque **Capella de Santa Llúcia** (1268), founded by Bishop Arnau de Gurb, whose tomb is within. Long, straight C/Bisbe separates the Casa de l'Ardiaca from the medieval **Palau Episcopal**, the bishops' palace, built on the Roman wall.

Just down C/Bisbe, **Plaça Garriga i Bachs** is dedicated to five heroes of 1809, who attempted to take Montjuïc Castle from the Napoleonic occupiers; three hid in the cathedral organ for three

Sant Sever
open Thurs 5–7.30pm;
adm free

days before they were caught and hanged or garrotted. The church here is Sant Sever; like the cathedral, this church was protected by armed guards during the Civil War, and is one of the few to preserve its frothy Baroque interior, with an altar in a *trompe l'œil* setting.

The lane next to the Palau Episcopal, C/Montjuïc del Bisbe, leads back to the pretty, nearly enclosed **Plaça Sant Felip Neri**, its melancholy air perhaps derived from its former role as the burial ground of the executed, whether prisoners or heroes. Its components are simple: one fountain, two trees and a church of **Sant Felip Neri** (1751), with a severe façade and a big Baroque altar inside. During the Civil War a bomb went off here (you can still see scars on the church), and in the 1940s, when the square was rebuilt, two handsome buildings were relocated here: the Renaissance **Casa del Gremi de Calderers**, once headquarters of the coppersmiths' guild, and the **Casa del Gremi dels Sabaters**, the shoemakers' guild, founded in 1202 under the sign of their patron St Mark. It now contains the Museu del Calçat, a delightful journey into the history of shoes, from reproductions of Roman sandals to 17th-century toe-pinchers and brogues made for the statue of Columbus for his wedding to New York's Statue of Liberty.

Museu del Calçat
Plaça de Sant Felip Neri, t 93 301 45 33;
Ⓜ *Jaume I; open Tues–Sun 11–2; adm*

Around Plaça Sant Jaume

The Plaça Sant Jaume, originally the Roman forum, has always been the heart of civic Barcelona. It was recarved out of a warren of streets in the 1840s along with C/Ferran, opening up an ongoing, face-to-face dialogue between the Catalan government (the Generalitat) and Barcelona's City Hall (the Ajuntament).

Palau de la Generalitat

Created by Jaume I in 1249, the Generalitat was made up of representatives of the three Estates of the Catalan Corts (Church, military, and civilian), and in 1359 it assumed fiscal responsibility for the realm, making it Spain's first real parliament since Roman times. The Palau de la Generalitat was begun in the 15th century to give it a permanent seat. When Felipe V abolished the Generalitat in 1714, the palace was occupied by the Reial Audiencia, which rubberstamped Madrid's policies. But such is the Catalan virtue of *continuitat* that it resumed its function in 1977 – not something many secular medieval buildings get to do.

Palau de la Generalitat
Plaça de Sant Jaume, t 93 402 46 00;
Ⓜ *Jaume I; open for guided tours only, second and fourth Sundays of each month, in English at 11am; adm free but bring photo ID and arrive early to sign up*

The façade on C/Bisbe, designed in 1416 by Marc Safont, has some of the best gargoyles and modillions in Barcelona, topped by a superb rondel of St George by Pere Joan – a work that so pleased the Generalitat that they paid the sculptor double the agreed price. C/Bisbe passes under a picturesque **Bridge of Sighs**, a much maligned pseudo-Gothic touch added in 1928. What sighs, if any, are exhaled on the bridge are by the president as he leaves his official residence, the 16th-century **Casa dels Canonges** (the former canons' house), on his way to work.

The Gothic **courtyard** of the Generalitat is especially lovely: a carved exterior stair ascends on a daring stone arch to a gallery colonnaded with the slimmest of columns. The whole is crowned with pinnacles and gargoyles that resemble medieval Barcelonins. The **chapel** is entered by way of Marc Safont's **Gothic portal** (1436), flamboyant, vertical and ornate in a town that prefers its Gothic unadorned and broad in the beam. This, of course, is dedicated to Catalonia's patron, Sant Jordi, or George (*see* p.34).

When the Generalitat was enlarged in 1526, it added the orange-tree courtyard, the **Pati dels Tarrongers**, and beyond that the ceremonial **Golden Room**, with a 16th-century gilt ceiling. Here Flemish tapestries on the triumphs of Petrarch replace the Noucentista frescoes by Torres Garcia, which fell out of favour under Primo de Rivera (his detached works are now in another room). The president and his ministers meet in the **Sala Antoni Tàpies**, with the eponymous master's painting based on the four medieval chronicles of Catalonia. The Generalitat is proud of its 40-bell carillon, which sounds every hour between 8am and 8pm.

Ajuntament

Ajuntament
Plaça de Sant Jaume,
t 93 402 70 00,
www.bcn.es; Ⓜ *Jaume I;*
open Sun 10–1.30; adm
free, bring photo ID

Jaume I sowed the seeds for the Ajuntament (city council) at the same time as the Generalitat, when he appointed a committee of 20 peers in 1249; by 1272 this had evolved into the annually selected Consell de Cent (Council of a Hundred), who ruled the city until 1714. It proved to be one Europe's most successful representative governments, partly through its unusual flexibility: tradesmen as well as patricians served, and the number 100 was not set in stone, but varied as circumstances saw fit.

The Ajuntament's neoclassical façade, added in the 1840s, is cold potatoes, but like the Generalitat it preserves a Gothic façade, on C/Ciutat, watched over by Santa Eulàlia. The oldest part of the Ajuntament, the **Saló de Cent** by Pere Llobet (1372), has round ribs reminiscent of the Saló de Tinell; it was restored by Domènech i Montaner in the 1880s, and Gothic bits were added in 1914. The **Saló de las Cròniques** is lined with bravura golden murals on the glories of Catalan history, by Josep Maria Sert (1928).

From the Plaça Sant Jaume, narrow C/Paradís leads to the summit of **Mons Tàber**, marked by an ancient millstone in the pavement. Here, just inside the Gothic courtyard of the **Centre Excursionista de Catalunya**, are four impressive Corinthian columns and part of the podium from the 1st-century AD Roman **Temple of Augustus**, trapped like an exotic orchid in a hothouse.

East of Plaça Sant Jaume

From the north (Gothic) side of the Ajuntament, C/de Hèrcules leads to the **Plaça Sant Just** and two palaces: **Moxió**, adorned with sgraffito, and **Palau Requesens** (Palau de la Comtessa de Palamós). The latter, housing a Gallery of Illustrious Catalans, was the grandest private address in medieval Barcelona, built in the 13th century. Here, too, is the parish church of the count-kings, **Sants Just i Pastor**, founded according to tradition by Louis the Pious in 801. It is the last church in Spain to preserve its ancient privilege of *Testament Sacramental* bestowed by Louis himself, which gives any citizen of Barcelona the right to make a will, orally, without a notary or writ, if said before the altar of Sant Feliu.

El Call: Barcelona's Jewish Quarter

In the Middle Ages, the entrance to Barcelona's ghetto (El Call, from the Hebrew *qahqal* or 'meeting place') was just to the left of the Generalitat, on modern C/Call. No one knows when the first Jews moved to Barcelona, although the Visigoths bear the ignominy of passing Spain's first anti-Semitic law, in 694, which made all Jews slaves. By the 11th century, the Call was a well-organized community-within-a-community that was also the intellectual centre of Catalonia, home to its finest schools, hospitals, translators, poets, astronomers and philosophers. It was here that the Girona-born mystic Moshe ben Nahman debated in the famous 'Disputation of Barcelona' in 1263.

In 1243, however, Jaume I had ordered that the Call be walled off, and that Christians not be allowed to enter except when goods were displayed for sale; Jews were also compelled to wear cloaks with red or yellow bands. Much of this segregation was actually to protect Jews from persecution by Reconquista fanatics; Jews expelled from other territories in Spain were made welcome here by the count-kings, who depended on the community as bankers, ambassadors and interpreters (especially to Arab courts).

El Call began to incite a dangerous amount of envy. In 1391, a group of Castilians spread rumours that the Black Death had been brought by Jews from Navarre; a mob attacked the Call, brutally wiping out most of the community. King Joan I had the instigators put to death, but could not halt the growing tide of anti-Semitism. In 1424, with the Castilians on the throne of Aragon, the Jews were expelled from the Call. In 1492, Fernando and Isabel compelled all the Jews in Sepharad (Hebrew for Spain) to convert or leave.

Over four centuries later, in 1925, Primo de Rivera granted the Sephardim around the world citizenship and protection under Spanish consulates. Not long after, Barcelona rediscovered its role as a haven, as 7,000 Jewish refugees moved into the city in the 1930s. Franco, for all his many faults, never persecuted Jews.

Picasso's *Demoiselles d'Avignon*

The 19-year-old Picasso had a studio near C/Avinyó at C/Escudellers Blancs, and he had the local ladies in mind when he painted *Les Demoiselles d'Avignon* (1907), his unfinished manifesto of Cubism. The painting was so incomprehensible even to other artists that it wasn't displayed publicly until 1937. In an interview in 1933 Picasso explained the name:

Les Demoiselles d'Avignon! How that name gets on my nerves! It was coined by Salmon [André, poet and friend]. *You know at first it was called* The Brothel of Avignon. *You know why? Avignon has always been a familiar name for me, a name connected with my life. I lived only a few steps from the Carrer d'Avinyó. There I bought my paper and watercolours. Then, as you know, Max Jacob's grandfather was a native of Avignon. We were always making jokes about this picture. One of the women was supposed to be Max's grandmother...*

On tiny C/Marlet, off C/Sant Domènec del Call, one stone remains poignantly in place, inscribed in Hebrew: 'Sacred foundation of Rabbi Samuel Hassareri, of everlasting life. Year 692.' The city's oldest synagogue, the **Sinagoga Major**, in a building dating back to Roman times, has been partially restored and opened to the public, with a delightful multilingual staff.

Sinagoga Major
t 93 317 07 90, www. calldebarcelona.org; 🚇 *Jaume I; open Mon–Fri 10.30–2.30 and 4–6, Sat and Sun 10.30–3; adm; guided tours of the Call by prior arrangement*

West of Plaça Jaume

Carrer de Ferran links the Plaça Sant Jaume to the Rambla; along it stands the little church of **Sant Jaume**, which was built over a synagogue in 1394 by a confraternity of converted Jews and dedicated to the Trinity. In 1876 it was re-dedicated to St James the Moor-slayer, and topped in 1876 with a strikingly late, if not very politically correct, relief of the same. Here, in a Parisian-style arcade called **Passatge de Crédit**, Joan Miró was born in 1893. On **C/Avinyó**, where Picasso once had a studio, several old palaces were converted into brothels around the turn of the 20th century; note the fine *esgrafiados* that embellish the houses at Nos.26 and 30.

Around the Plaça del Pi

Plaça del Pi

C/Banys Nous, extending north of C/Avinyó, follows the curve of the Roman walls and was named after its 'new' Jewish baths, new in 1160 at any rate; this and its extension, C/Palla, are chock-a-block with antiques shops. It leads to the Barri del Pi, one of the first medieval 'new towns' built outside the Roman walls; its name comes from a majestic pine that once stood in Plaça del Pi, in front of **Santa Maria del Pi**. This was founded in the 10th century and rebuilt in 1322 as a textbook example of Catalan Gothic – austere and wide, but with a rose window said to be the largest in the world. The interior was gutted during the Civil War.

The intimate squares surrounding the church, **Plaça del Pi** with its commemorative pine tree and **Plaça Sant Josep Oriol** on the side, were originally cemeteries, and are now filled with cafés.

Barri de Santa Anna

By the 12th century Barcelona was too big to fit in its Roman walls and overflowed to the north and east, an area that Jaume I enclosed in his 13th-century enceint as the Barri di Santa Anna. One landmark, at C/Montsió 3, is the **Casa Martí** (1895), the first building by Josep Puig i Cadafalch, a Modernista fantasy combining elements of Catalan and northern Gothic. Eusebi Arnau sculpted the St George and the Dragon (*see* p.34) on the corner, a motif that Puig would make his own.

Els Quatre Gats
t 93 302 41 40,
www.4gats.com;
Ⓜ *Urquinaona or*
Catalunya; open daily
10–2; adm free

The building is renowned as the home of **Els Quatre Gats** ('The Four Cats', slang for 'Just a few guys'),the bohemian taverna that once provided much of the impetus for the city's cultural life. Founded in 1897 by four former habitués of Montmartre – painters Santiago Rusinyol and Ramon Casas, puppeteer Miquel Utrillo (father of the Parisian painter Maurice Utrillo) and the eccentric Pere Romeu, who abandoned painting to devote himself to cabaret and cycling – it soon became the informal late-night meeting place for writers, artists, journalists and musicians.

The Quatre Gats published its own art review, held Avant Garde shadow-puppet shows, presented recitals, and put on exhibitions, including Picasso's very first, while Romeu ran things after a fashion, having a screaming fit if anyone touched a cobweb. Six years later, he closed the taverna to devote himself entirely to his bicycle, and the place, ironically, was taken over by Gaudí and Llimona's pious Catholic Cercle de Sant Lluc, founded in reaction to the blasphemous tomfoolery of Casas and Rusinyol. But now there's a new Quatre Gats, an expensive reproduction of the original, but minus Romeu's precious cobwebs.

Turn left at the end of C/Montsió for shop-lined **Avinguda del Portal de l'Àngel**. Its landmark is the Modernista **Catalana de Gas** at No.20 (1895), an eclectic structure by Josep Domènech i Estapà, recently and controversially converted into an outpost of an international fashion chain. Another landmark is the giant thermometer, marking Cottett, one of the city's oldest opticians.

A row of simple 2nd–4th-century AD Roman tombs in **Plaça de la Vila de Madrid** were discovered under a burned-out convent in 1957. Such tombs once lined the roads out of the city; you can see how much the ground level has risen in 1,600 years.

Ateneu Barcelonès
t 93 343 61 21,
www.ateneubcn.org;
Ⓜ *Catalunya;*
open daily 9am–11pm

At 6 C/Canuda, the **Ateneu Barcelonès** was founded in 1836 as a literary and cultural club, and occupies an 18th-century palace. It's got a good restaurant, and hosts regular exhibitions and concerts.

From here, C/Santa Anna leads to the simple Romanesque church of **Santa Anna** with its elegant double-decker Gothic cloister. Founded by the Knights Templar in the early 12th century, the church hosted the Corts held under Fernando the Catholic – the last parliament before Catalonia was tacked on to Castile.

Santa Anna
Ⓜ *Catalunya*
open daily 9–1 and
6.30–8.30, hols 10–2;
adm free

La Ribera

In 1907, the newly built Vía Laietana cut the Barri Gòtic off from La Ribera, the old maritime and business district. In the days before the building of Barceloneta, the sea washed up to what is now Avinguda Marquès de l'Argentera, and there was a constant bustle as goods were ferried to and from waiting ships.

When the Rambla was still a sewer, the Born was the throbbing heart of Barcelona, surrounded by artisans and their shops, while medieval tycoons wheeled and dealed in the Llotja, the hub of western Mediterranean commerce in the 13th and 14th centuries.

Then came the lean centuries, and then the traumatic amputation of half of La Ribera for the Ciutadella in the early 1700s. And then Barcelona spread into the Eixample and took most of La Ribera's trade with it. Today the neighbourhood has returned to fashion, a transformation that begun with the rehabilitation of Carrer Montcada, the finest medieval street in Barcelona.

Museu Picasso and Around

Museu Picasso

Museu Picasso
C/Montcada 15–23,
t 93 256 30 00, www.
museupicasso.bcn.es;
Ⓜ Jaume I; open
Tues–Sun 10–8, hols
10–3; adm exp,
free Sun 3–8

Today, the once-secret palaces along Carrer Montcada are nearly all museums or galleries, thanks to an initiative taken in 1963 to restore the loveliest of them all, the 15th-century **Palau Aguilar** (with a courtyard by Marc Safont) and four adjacent palaces, in order to house the Museu Picasso. This remains the best place in Spain to see the works of a Spaniard acclaimed as the greatest artist of the 20th century. But go early: it can get very crowded.

The core of the collection was donated in 1963 by Picasso's friend and secretary Jaume Sabartés, whom he met in Barcelona in 1899. After Sabartés' death it was augmented by Picasso himself, who, in spite of his refusal to have anything to do with Franco's Spain, had a special place in his heart for the city. The collection begins with the drawings and doodlings of an eight-year-old in Málaga, kept by his doting mother and sister Lola; Picasso was so precocious that people believed he was a reincarnated grand master. Also here is his first major academic painting, *Science and Charity*, painted in 1897 under pressure from his father to find himself a wealthy patron. Picasso spent a year in Madrid, heading daily to the Prado to study the grand masters who 'breathed down my neck' as he put it. He then spent a few months in Horta de Sant Joan (*see* p.278) where he painted assured, fluid landscapes. On his return to Barcelona, his work became more eclectic and his style more personal. After a sprinkling of works from the Blue Period (1901–1904) – the eerie *Madman* (1904) and the touching, helpless mother and child of *Desamparados* (1904) – and others of the Pink Period in Paris (1905), we skim forward to the celebrated *Harlequin* of 1917. By this time, Picasso was back in Barcelona, collaborating with Diaghilev and his Ballets Russes, and falling headlong for dancer Olga Kokhlova. It was to be his last period in Barcelona.

The collection quietly skips four decades here, and then explodes with the extraordinary series donated by Picasso to the museum. Between 1954 and 1962, he embarked on a series of interpretations of three major paintings – Delacroix's *Les Femmes d'Alger*, Manet's *Le Déjeuner sur l'Herbe* and Velázquez's exquisite *Las Meninas*. Painted in intense seclusion between 17 August and 30 December 1956, each element in *Las Meninas* was meticulously pored over and re-evaluated, and developed 'like the characters and storyline of a serial novel'. Finally come paintings from his last years near Cannes, and ceramics donated by his last wife, Jacqueline. The upper galleries contain a curious collection of etchings entitled *La Suite 156*, a surreal combination of the erotic fantasies of an old man and a personal interpretation of the history of art, with sly digs at grand masters from Raphael to Matisse, the same who used to breathe down his neck. A large collection of Picasso's prints were added to the collection in 2008; temporary exhibitions are held in the adjoining Palau Meca.

Around the Museu Picasso: Carrer Montcada

Carrer Montcada was given in 1148 by Ramon Berenguer IV to a rich merchant named Guillem Ramon de Montcada in return for financing the reconquest of Tortosa. Montcada sold lots to nine of his buddies, all 12th-century merchant tycoons, and they created a medieval Millionaires' Row. Most of their Gothic embellishments have disappeared, but lovely interior courtyards remained intact.

The presence of money and the old Roman road led to the founding of the *correus volants* – 'flying runners', the origin of the *correros*, the Spanish postal service, which is first mentioned in 1166. These early Catalan pony express riders, the *Troters*, were headquartered at the northern end of the street, by the tiny Romanesque **Capella d'en Marcús**, where they would ride in to be blessed before setting out.

Museu Barbier-Mueller d'Art Precolumbí
C/Montcada 12–14, t 93 310 45 16, www. barbier-mueller.ch; Ⓜ *Jaume I; open Tues–Fri 11–7, Sat 10–7, Sun and hols 10–3; adm (free first Sun of the month, 10–7)*

Nearly every palace on Carrer Montcada has a story. The 16th-century Gothic **Palau dels Marquesos de Llió**, now the Museu Barbier-Mueller d'Art Precolumbí was painstakingly restored in 1996 to hold this exquisite collection of art from 2000 BC–AD 1500 by the Olmecs and Mayas of Mexico, the Central Americans, the Chavín, Moche, Nazca and Inca civilizations of the Andes: gold ornaments, mummy masks, lip and nose jewellery, each item illuminated against a black background as if on stage. The sculpture is powerful stuff, often complacent and serene, sometimes vicious and frightening. One room contains rare works by the Amazonian islanders of Caviana and Marajó, who buried their dead in beautiful abstract vases.

Renovated from a Gothic original, the 17th-century **Palau Dalmases** at No.20 is the finest Baroque palace in Barcelona; don't miss the flamboyant courtyard stair, carved with the Rape of Europa, while Neptune and Amphitrite race up the waves in defiance of gravity. Part of the palace is now a café, the sumptuous and florid **Espai Barroc**. Opposite, the **Galerie Maeght** occupies the 16th-century **Palau dels Cervelló**, with four severe gargoyles guiding the rainwater away from the solarium. Near the bottom of C/Montcada, **C/Mosques**, the 'street of flies', is the narrowest in the city (40 inches wide).

Galerie Maeght
t 93 310 42 45,
www.maeght.com,
open Mon–Sat 10–7.30

Santa Maria del Mar and Around

Santa Maria del Mar

⭐ **Santa Maria del Mar**
Plaça Santa Maria,
Ⓜ *Jaume I; open daily*
10–1.30 and 4.30–8;
adm free

This, the most beautiful of all Catalan Gothic churches, occupies an ancient holy site: the first church was built in the 4th century over the tomb of Santa Eulàlia. When Jaume I conquered Mallorca in 1235, he promised a temple to Mary, Star of the Sea, but his promise remained unfulfilled until Alfons III took Sardinia. Alfons laid the first stone in 1329 and entrusted the design to sculptor Berenguer de Montagut. As Catalan maritime interests expanded, so did La Ribera's population of sailors, porters, tradesmen and merchants. Santa Maria del Mar was to be their church, and all able-bodied men in the parish donated their labour to build it, completing it in 50 years – a supersonic speed in those days, which accounts for its rare stylistic unity.

The exterior is almost startlingly simple, a great, austere mass of plain sandstone masonry. The façade, on Plaça Santa Maria, has a rose window framed by a pair of plain buttresses and twin octagonal towers. Two small 15th-century bronze figures of the builders huddle below. Yet just behind this fortress-like front waits a miracle, a sublime interior of airy spaciousness and light, ironically revealed by the Anarchists, who in 1936 started the fire that devoured all the Baroque fittings. The current lack of decoration emphasizes an absolute minimum of interior supports: the octagonal piers of the nave stand 42ft apart, a distance unsurpassed in any medieval building. Two lofty aisles, half the width of the nave, have only simple niches for chapels between the buttresses. The raised altar is set in a transcendent crescent of slender columns that transform the apse into a glade in an enchanted forest. The stained glass dates from every century; the best, from the 1400s, shows the Ascension and Last Judgement.

Around the Fossar de les Moreres

Along the southern flank of Santa Maria, a low wall and the fan-shaped **Fossar de les Moreres** (the cemetery of Mulberry Trees) marks the mass tomb of those who resisted the Bourbon troops of Felipe V in 1714. Some 3,500 bodies were brought here; all who fought on the Catalan side were buried within a now vanished ring of mulberry trees, and all who fought for the Bourbons were buried without. In 1989 the cemetery was made into a small square, with a huge sculpture bearing a torch.

On the map, Santa Maria resembles a big beetle caught in an intricate web of streets, each bearing the name of the medieval trade. In the days of mass illiteracy, shops would identify themselves by hanging out a model of their goods; all that remains now are the stone female faces you see here and there that marked the brothels. **C/Sombrerers** along the side of the church was the realm of hatters; busy **C/Argenteria** was the silversmiths' street. On **C/Dames**, ladies' street, hopeful spinsters gathered after bad storms; unmarried sailors often vowed to marry the first single woman they saw on shore if they survived.

Passeig del Born and Around

The wide Passeig del Born extends from Santa Maria's apse. Born means tournament and it was used for jousting in the Middle Ages, as well as for the Inquisition's *autos-da-fé*. It was also the place to see and be seen before the Rambles stole its thunder, but now trendy shops and bars are bringing the wandering Barcelonins back. The end of the Born is closed off by the **Mercat del Born** (1876), a striking iron structure with a patterned roof, by Josep Fontseré. In 2003, renovation work started to convert the building into a national library – when builders found the remains of streets and homes from the time when Felipe V ordered half of La Ribera demolished for the building of the Ciutadella (*see* p.98). Current plans are to install glass flooring so the remains are visible.

Plaça de Palau

The Plaça del Palau, once the site of the viceroy's palace, is a graceful 19th-century square. Its **fountain of the Catalan Spirit** is topped with a little cherub who started life naked and has been dressed and undressed according to the sensibilities of the age for the past 150 years. Its most important building, the **Llotja**, or exchange, was the secular cathedral of Catalan capitalism. Financed by a three per cent tax on imports and exports, it was built by Pere Arbei for Pere III the Ceremonious in 1380, after the navy of Peter the Cruel of Castile damaged a more modest building. Although remodelled over the years and slapped with a bland neoclassical facelift, the magnificent Gothic **Sala de**

Contractacions with its 14m high ceilings was left untouched; until Barcelona's *bourse* moved to the Passeig de Gràcia in 1996, it was the oldest continuously operating stock exchange in Europe. After 1775 it was used as a school of fine arts, the Reial Acadèmia Catalana de Belles Arts de Sant Jordi; Picasso's father taught here and Picasso attended classes until he quit out of boredom.

Opposite the Llotja, on Passeig d'Isabel II, the **Cases d'En Xifré** (1840) are two neoclassical blocks built by moneybags Josep Xifré i Casas (1777–1856), who made his pile in Cuba's slave-worked sugar plantations. On the arcades are portraits of explorers and conquistadors, and terracotta reliefs of charming *putti* in cheerfully bowdlerized allegories of Cuban trade.

The Noucentista **Estació de França**, on Avenida Marques de l'Argenteria, was erected in 1929 for the International Exhibition and built on a curve in the tracks, lending the iron structure an unusually sensuous beauty.

Opposite the station, walk up the Passeig de Picasso to see Antoni Tàpies' **Homenatge a Picasso** (1983) – a glass cube in a pool that contains household items impaled by steel bars, perpetually splashed by jets of water.

Parc de la Ciutadella

Parc de la Ciutadella
open Nov–Feb daily 10–6; Mar and Oct daily 10–7; April and Sept daily 10–8; May–Aug daily 10–9

In 1714, that bitter date in the annals of Barcelona, the besieged city fell to the troops of Felipe V after an extraordinary, heroic, 11-month resistance. Barcelona knew if it fell it would lose all its vestiges of independence, and so it did. But there was worse to come: half of La Ribera was wiped off the map to construct, at Barcelona's own expense, the 270-acre **Ciutadella**, one of the largest fortifications ever built in Europe. Before leaving, the 5,000 evicted residents were compelled to tear down their homes stone by stone, and there was never any illusion about the Ciutadella's purpose: the army of occupation kept its cannons aimed at the city.

When the progressive Catalan General Prim took power in 1869, he gave the fort to the city, designating 150 acres for a **park**, and declared that the heirs of original property owners should be compensated. A competition was held for the park's design, and the winner was Josep Fontseré, an able architect and spotter of talent – his design team included two then unknowns, Domènech i Montaner and Gaudí.

The trees Fontseré planted were just beginning to produce shade when Barcelona's buoyant mayor, Francesc de Paula Ruis i Taulet, announced that it was the chosen location for the 1888 Universal Exhibition, to be opened in a mere 11 months' time. Fontseré protested, Fontseré was fired, and the project lurched full speed ahead in spite of doomsday predictions; Barcelona in the 1880s was in the grip of another recession and the mood was glum.

Although it left Barcelona deeply in debt, the Exhibition was in fact the key event that kept Barcelona from sliding irrevocably into provincial backwaters. Like all good exhibitions, it also served as a stage for innovation – think of London and the Crystal Palace in 1851, or Paris and the dazzling ironwork of the Eiffel Tower of 1889. Barcelona in 1888 presented the world with Modernisme. It also gave the city a Dizzy Gillespie-size taste for tooting its own horn.

Zoo
*t 90 245 75 45, www.
zoobarcelona.com;
Ⓜ Ciutadella-
Vila Olímpica;
open Nov–mid Mar
daily 10–5; mid Mar,
April, May and Oct daily
10–6; June–Sept daily
10–7; adm exp*

The Ciutadella also contains Barcelona's cramped **Zoo**, which is currently being split in two; from 2010, the aquatic animals can be visited in the **Zoo Marí** (Marine Zoo) currently under construction in Diagonal Mar (*see* p.106).

Nearby is the **Plaça d'Armes**, the old parade ground and now a formal garden. The square has the only surviving buildings from the Ciutadella: the chapel, Governor's Palace and Arsenal, designed by Prosper Verboom, with trumpet-mouthed gargoyles. This was converted into a royal residence, then into an art museum, and during the Republic, with a nice sense of irony, into the seat of the Catalan Parliament.

The Parc de la Ciutadella is well used, especially at weekends, when families come to paddle in little boats in the **lake** opposite Josep Fontseré's **Cascada**. This superbly ugly pile of stone is set in a monumental stair inspired by the Palais Longchamps in Marseille, with lashings of mythological allusions: four spitting dragons, Venus emerging from her half-shell, and the Quadriga of Aurora. Gaudí, they say, arranged the boulders of the grotto. Fontseré redeems his Cascada-splashed reputation with his pretty **Umbracle**, a cast-iron greenhouse for shade plants, with a wooden lattice roof, next to Josep Amargós' iron-and-glass **Hivernacle** winter greenhouse. In between, the neo-Pompeiian building opened in 1882 as Barcelona's first public museum, the Museu de Geología (now, like the nearby Museu de Zoología, part of the

**Museu de Ciències
Naturals**
*t 93 319 68 95,
www.bcn.es/
museuciencies;
Ⓜ Arc de Triomf;
open Tues–Fri 10–6.30,
Sat–Sun 10–8; adm,
free Sun 3–8*

Museu de Ciències Naturals), which is chock full of minerals, fossils and rocks from across Spain.

Best of all the park's buildings is the great brick **Castell dels Tres Dragons,** designed by Domènech i Montaner as the Universal Exhibition's café-restaurant, although it wasn't finished in time to sell a single *pa amb tomàquet*. This was the herald of Modernisme, with its innovative use of exposed plain brick and iron, crowned with whimsical ceramic decoration. It was nicknamed the 'Castle of the Three Dragons' after a poem by Frederic Soler, although these days a herd of stuffed creatures calls it home as part of the **Museu de Ciències Naturals** (formerly the Museu de Zoología, *see* above).

Fontseré designed the broad **Passeig Lluís Companys** outside the northern gate as the park's salon, although all but one of his bronze statues of Catalan heroes were melted down under Franco to make the giant Virgin presiding over the dome of the church of

La Mercè. At the top of the promenade stands the entrance to the 1888 fair, the **Arc de Triomf** by Josep Vilaseca. With no triumph in particular to commemorate (besides getting the exhibition ready on time), Vilaseca's ensemble of mudéjar-style ceramic brickwork topped with four crowns manifests, if nothing else, the eternal Catalan longing to be different.

Museu de la Xocolata
36 C/Comerç,
t 93 268 78 78;
🚇 Ciutadella-Vila Olímpica; open Mon-Sat 10–7, Sun 10–3; adm

Around the corner, the **Museu de la Xocolata** is dedicated to its history, art and preparation of chocolate with state-of-the-art, multilingual, interactive exhibitions.

Barri Sant Pere

Palau de la Música Catalana

Palau de la Música Catalana
C/Sant Pere Més Alt,
t 90 244 28 82,
www.palaumusica.org;
🚇 Urquinaona;
guided tours in English daily at 9, 10, 11, 12, 1, 2 and 3; adm exp

There's an old joke: one Catalan starts a business, two start a corporation and three start a choral society. No one can deny that this gruff, taciturn, capitalist tribe has a musical soul, and in the 1850s Renaixença fervour an ardent Republican named Josep Anselm Clavé founded the first workers' choral groups. There were 85 of them by 1861. The most important, the **Orfeó Català**, was founded in 1891 by Clavé and Amadeu Vives, and soon became an important representative of Catalan ideals and culture in Spain.

Flushed with success, in 1904 the Orfeó gave Lluis Domènech i Montaner a brief to create a 'Temple of Catalan art, a palace to celebrate its renaissance'. The idea warmed the cockles of Domènech's nationalist heart, and he delivered in spades, sub-contracting the most accomplished artists of the day to create a Modernista garden of delights. But the Barcelonins are fickle folk. A decade after the palace won the city's prize for the best building of 1907, opinion had swung violently against it: Noucentista architects were calling for the destruction of the 'Palace of Catalan Junk'. Needless to say it survived all these insults to celebrate its glorious centenary in 2008, but some remodelling has been necessary over the years, the most recent a sympathetic restoration and extension by Oscar Tusquets. No one has really managed to fix the famously bad acoustics.

In the narrow streets, the Palau resembles a bouquet stuffed in a cupboard: the site simply wasn't big enough. The decoration on the **façade** is a rapturous allegory of Catalan music and the music Catalans loved. Busts of Wagner (a big favourite), Beethoven, Bach and Palestrina by Eusebi Arnau decorate the second floor. Miquel Blay, a disciple of Rodin, sculpted the huge corner group that projects like a figurehead on a ship, with a knight and damsel emerging from a cloud of legendary figures. Mosaics by Lluís Bru along the top of the façade show the Orfeó performing in front of the Catalan Mount Sinai, Montserrat.

The lavish **lobby** is a cleaner's worst nightmare. The ceiling is decorated with a ceramic trellis adorned with plump clusters of roses, while the banisters are encased in smoky topaz glass and surrounded with blooms and vines. The starring role goes, of course, to the **auditorium**, an epiphany of stained glass and ceramics. Domènech wanted to bring in as much light as possible, and he dematerialized the walls Gothic-style, but with modern technology and a steel frame, making this the first curtain-wall building in Spain. Rainbow-coloured sunlight streams in through Antoni Rigalt's huge stained-glass skylight, filling the jewel-like glass box. The stage set is composed of 18 unforgettable half-tile, half-3D-ceramic maidens by Eusebi Arnau, each brandishing a musical instrument before a background of *trencadís*. The proscenium is dramatically marked by flowing sculptures designed by Domènech, executed by Didac Masana and finished by Pau Gargallo: Beethoven and galloping, wild-eyed Valkyries confront Josep Clavé smiling serenely under a tree, while maidens below him act out his perennial choral hit song, *The Flowers of May*.

Sant Pere de les Puelles and Around

The Palau de la Muisca's neighbourhood grew up in the 11th century on land owned by **Sant Pere de les Puelles**, a church founded outside the Roman walls by the Visigoths, then refounded in 945 by the counts of Barcelona as a Benedictine convent. The *puelles* were the strictly cloistered young nuns, who enjoyed a great reputation for their beauty. When al-Mansur's troops burst in in 985, the women cut off their own noses, hoping to avoid a fate worse than death; in disgust the Moors chopped off the rest of their heads. The church was rebuilt in 1147, and when the nuns left in the 19th century their cloister became a prison. After a burning in the 1909 Setmana Trágica, it was given its fortress façade; after more arson in 1936, only a few columns and capitals remain (the best ones are in the MNAC museum).

For as long as anyone can remember, Barri Sant Pere was Barcelona's textile centre. In the 18th century, when the city couldn't ship enough calico to Spain's colonies, much of the medieval fabric was replaced with factories and housing for merchants and workers. Lively **C/Sant Pere Més Baix** is the district's shopping street, lined with medieval and 18th-century palaces. The **Farmacia Pedrell** at No.52, the oldest in Barcelona, dates back to 1562; in 1890 it was given a pretty Modernista facelift.

Farther south (backtrack a bit to C/Freixures) is the big neighbourhood market, the **Mercat de Santa Caterina** (1847), renovated according to plans by the late Enric Miralles, architect of the Scottish Parliament, and capped with an undulating roof of multicoloured tiles.

Sant Pere de les Puelles
Plaça de Sant Pere
Ⓜ *Arc de Triomf;*
open in theory
8.30–9.30am and
7–8.30pm

07
Barcelona | La Ribera

Seaside Barcelona

In the 13th and 14th centuries, Barcelona's dominance in the Mediterranean was such that her sailors boasted that 'not even a fish would dare to appear without the *quatre barres*', the flag of Catalonia. Endowed by nature with only a mediocre port, Barcelona's success came by way of sheer determination and mercantile savvy. The sea, however, was a strictly business proposition, leaving no room for any Venetian-style monuments or razzmatazz. The change began in 1980: with the same determination that made the mess in the first place, the Ajuntament swept the freighters and containers away into the Zona Franca, and turned Barcelona into a Mediterranean playground, bobbing with yachts instead of rubbish, buzzing with clubs, bars, restaurants and shops instead of flies.

Around the Drassanes

Museu Marítim
Avinguda de les Drassanes, t 93 342 99 20, www.mmb.cat; Ⓜ *Drassanes; museum open daily 10–8; adm;* **Santa Eulàlia** *schooner, moored at Moll de la Fusta, open for viewing May–Oct, Tues–Fri 12–7.30, Sat–Sun, 10–7; Nov–April Tues–Fri 12–5.30, Sat and Sun 1–5.30*

To begin where it all began, start in the Drassanes, the best-preserved medieval shipyards in the world, and now the **Museu Marítim**. The first Arab *darsena*, or shipyards, were enlarged and improved between 1283 and 1328, and in 1388 the Drassanes took their present form. Thirty galleys could be built in their long bays at the same time. The Spanish navy took them over in 1663, then in 1941 gave them back to the city to restore and make into a museum on Catalonia's shipfaring past. Although the architecture steals the show – the vaults are long enough to melt into shadows – the exhibits offer much to ponder. There's a display on medieval cartography when Mallorca's Jewish community had Europe's most advanced school of map-making. Displays illustrate ancient and medieval ship construction, with models (some in ivory, some in bottles, and instructions on how to get them in there); there are figureheads, seamen's chests painted with biblical warnings of women's wiles, and a copy of Jaume the Conqueror's famous *Llibro del Consolat de Mar*, medieval Europe's first maritime code. The most dramatic exhibit is a full-scale replica of *La Real*, Don Juan's flagship at Lepanto, built in 1971 in honour of the 400th anniversary of the battle. The newest addition to the museum is a beautiful old schooner in the port, the **Santa Eulàlia** (1918).

Monument a Colom
Plaça Portal de la Pau, t 93 302 52 24 Ⓜ *Drassanes; open June–Sept daily 9–8.30; Oct–May daily 10–6.30; adm*

Barcelona's original 225-tonne seaside bagatelle, the **Monument a Colom**, a 164ft cast-iron column made of melted cannons from the castle of Montjuïc and topped with a statue of Columbus, was erected at the foot of the Rambla for the 1888 Universal Exhibition. You can ascend into the crown under Columbus' feet for the big view by taking the lift up – the first one, according to Barcelona's tireless boasters, to be installed inside a column.

Columbus, Pro and Con

This Columbus is the biggest monument to the admiral anywhere in the world, and the irony of honouring the one man who led to Barcelona's decline, as Spain turned to the Atlantic and Seville took over as premier port, was not lost on the citizenry. Note that he has his back to Castile, and points not to America but towards Italy (where Barcelona's merchants wish he had stayed).

Actually the intention in 1888 was to catalanize Columbus. Since Catalan, along with Portuguese and Castilian, were among the languages the admiral wrote (rather than Italian), and because he always went to great lengths to cover up his origins, there was a nationalist faction that claimed that he was really the Catalan Joan Colom from Girona (Gerona), which could easily be confused by a slip of the pen with Genoa (Genova). Others say he was from a Jewish family in Mallorca who had fled the bigotry by emigrating to Genoa, and that when Columbus was shipwrecked in Portugal in 1476 he had the chutzpah to completely re-invent himself. Mallorca was famous for its maps, which would explain where Columbus and his brother picked up their considerable cartographic skills.

Barcelona does have some authenticated Columbus associations, all of which are celebrated in the statuary around the base of the pillar. He met Fernando and Isabel here in 1493 after his first voyage, when he received the title of Admiral of the Ocean Sea and an annual stipend that kept the wolf from the door in his later years, when the Catholic Kings reneged on all their other promises. On his second voyage he took along a Catalan priest, Bernat de Bol, who became the first bishop in the New World. Today Catalan nationalists are more likely to disclaim him altogether: a replica of the *Santa Maria* moored nearby was burned by militants in 1989, and events celebrating the anniversary in 1992 were boycotted – even the choral societies refused to sing. The biggest celebration turned out to be the statue's wedding, arranged by Catalan conceptual artist Antoni Miralda, with the Statue of Liberty.

Next to Columbus, the **Duana Nova**, or New Customs House, is a silly neo-Renaissance wedding cake by Enric Sagnier (1902). Beyond this extends the Moll de Barcelona, where I. M. Pei's huge semicircular World Trade Center spearheads Barcelona's ambition to become the Mediterranean's container port capital as well as its busiest cruise port. If you aren't on a big cruise boat, you can catch a little one, a **Golondrina** ('swallow') for a tour of the port and coast at the Moll de les Drassanes under Colombus.

Golondrina
t 93 442 31 06, www. lasgolondrinas.com

The Port Vell

The flashy redevelopment the Port Vell, or old port, is crossed by a handsome wooden bridge of high undulating arches, the **Rambla de Mar**, which rotates to let sail boats through. The old Moll's new occupants include a huge glass and chrome shopping mall called **Maremagnum** (*open Sundays as well*) and an **IMAX cinema**. The **Aquàrium** was the largest in Europe until arch-rival Valencia stole its thunder. Best here is the vast central tank, encircled by a 225ft viewing tunnel equipped with a slow human conveyor belt and serenaded by gentle New Age music; the patterns of silvery fish and sharks swimming all around are remarkably soothing.

On the landward side of the Port Vell, the Moll de la Fusta is overlooked by Mariscal's 20ft fibreglass prawn, and culminates in Roy Lichtenstein's brightly coloured *Barcelona Head* (1992). The old warehouses, the Magatzems Generals, have been reincarnated as

IMAX cinema
Moll d'Espanya, t 93 225 11 11, www.imaxportvell.com

Aquàrium
Moll d'Espanya, t 93 221 74 74, www. aquariumbcn.com; Ⓜ Drassanes; open July–Aug daily 9.30am–11pm; June and Sept daily 9.30am–9.30pm; Oct–May daily 9.30am–9pm; adm exp

Museu d'Història
de Catalunya
3 Plaça Pau Villa,
t 93 225 47 00;
www.en.mhcat.net;
Ⓜ *Barceloneta;*
open Tues and
Thurs–Sat 10–7, Wed
10–8, Sun and hols
10–2.30; adm free first
Sun of the month

the **Palau de Mar**, home to restaurants and the **Museu d'Història de Catalunya**. Designed to give an overview of Catalan history, the emphasis is on kid-friendly interactive devices, and there's a huge glass-topped relief that lets you tramp like Gulliver across Catalonia. The rooftop café is a treat with views over the port.

Around the Carrer Ample

The palm-lined **Passeig de Colom** was widened when the sea ramparts were razed – in 1882, it became the first street to get electric lighting. Two streets in from here is the **Carrer Ample**, 'wide street' – wide enough for carriages, which in the 16th century was good enough to make it the city's most aristocratic address, hosting the likes of Emperor Charles V and the kings of Hungary and Bohemia. Now better known for tapas than kings, the street ends at Barcelona's temple of letters, the **Correus** (1927), the post office designed for the 1929 Exhibition.

Basilica de
La Mercè
Plaça de La Mercè;
Ⓜ *Drassanes;*
open Mon–Sat 10–1
and 6–8.30, Sun 10–1.30
and 7–8.30; adm free

Further along is the **Basilica de La Mercè**. Our Lady of Mercy joined St Eulàlia as co-patroness of Barcelona when she appeared to Jaume the Conqueror, asking him to found an order devoted to the deliverance of Christians held by Barbary pirates. The church was built in 1267, then rebuilt to fit Counter-Reformation ideals; its concave façade was transplanted from a demolished Baroque church. The fittings are Baroque, too, and there's a fine Gothic statue of the Virgin (1361) by Pere Moragues. She saved Catalonia from a plague of locusts in 1687 and, when Barcelona was besieged in 1714, she was made commander of the army, although unfortunately the Bourbons proved to be tougher than the insects. As if to emphasize the point, her statue on the dome, destroyed in the Civil War, was recast in 1956 from melted-down bronze statues of Catalan heroes. Among the Virgin's devotees are members of FC Barcelona, who sing a hymn of thanks whenever the team wins an important match. During the third week of September, the Festa Major de la Mercè draws crowds from across Barcelona.

Barceloneta

In 1718, the destruction of 61 streets and 1,262 homes in La Ribera to build the Ciutadella left many people in makeshift shelters on the beach. The misery continued until 1753, when a French military engineer with the delicious name of Prosper Verboom designed a neighbourhood for the displaced (or at least their children) on this 25-acre triangle reclaimed from the sea. Following the most progressive planning ideas of the time, the streets of Barceloneta were laid out in a grid, with a market in the central square and long, narrow blocks of houses, permitting every room to have a window. As all houses were allowed only one upper floor, all had access to sunlight and air. Verboom's height prohibition was modified in 1837 and ignored ever since, turning the straight narrow streets into mini canyons.

Barceloneta is still vibrant, filled with great seafood restaurants, edged by the city's oldest beach. The central Plaça de la Font is the site of the **market** (rebuilt in 2007) and of a pair of original two-storey houses at Nos.30 and 32. On **Plaça de la Barceloneta**, the little 18th-century Baroque church of Sant Miquel is dedicated to Barceloneta's patron saint. The neighbourhood is something of an outdoor art museum; Mario Merz's *Crescendo Appare* (1992) along the Moll de la Barceloneta consists of the numbers of the Fibonacci series embedded under glass in the pavement. The beach is decorated with Rebecca Horn's lofty *Homage to Barceloneta* (1992), a swaying, stacked iron column which echoes the narrow old buildings of the *barri* and the famous but long-disappeared seafood shacks. In Plaça de Mar, towards the tower of the aerial cableway, is the most mysterious *A Room Where it Always Rains* (1992) by Juan Muñoz.

Nearby, the Torre de Sebastià supports the Transbordador Aeri (aerial cableway) that crosses the sea to Montjuïc, with a stop at the World Trade Center. Strung up for the 1929 fair, it offers sensational views which are well worth the vertigo.

Sant Miquel
open mornings only

⭐ *Transbordador*
Aeri
(aerial cableway)
t 93 225 27 18;
Ⓜ *Barceloneta;*
open mid Oct–Feb
daily 12–5.30; Mar–mid-
June and mid-
Sept–mid-Oct daily
10.30–7; mid-June–mid-
Sept daily 10.30–8;
adm exp

07

Barcelona | Seaside Barcelona

Vila Olímpica and Around

Until the late 1980s, the seafront between Barceloneta and the River Besos was occupied by decrepit textile factories, warehouses and train yards. Even if you could get to a beach, the water stank. The need to house 15,000 athletes for the Olympics propelled the Ajuntament in 1986 to undertake Barcelona's biggest urban-renewal project of the last century. Coastal train tracks were relocated, and 500 acres of Poblenou were expropriated and flattened to create the Parc de Mar, opening up 5km of new public beaches, and the Vila Olímpica, a district as rigidly planned as Barceloneta, but in many ways its antithesis. Each building was commissioned from a past winner of the FAD Architecture prize, and each ducked the occasion. Even the opportunity to make something interesting out of the deluxe **Hotel Arts** and the **Torre Mapfre**, at the time Spain's tallest buildings, was declined, leaving two boring boxes by the beach.

This is the one area of Barcelona clearly more friendly to cars than people, with car parks along the marina and big desolate spaces between the traffic. Needless to say, it's all fantastically popular, especially the **Port Olímpic**, a confluence of shops, restaurants, beachside cafés and clubs, topped with the enormous headless bronze *Peix (Fish)* by Frank Gehry, a glistening hunk of postmodernist bait.

Cementiri de l'Est
Ⓜ *Llacuna;*
open daily 9am–dusk

At the end of Avinguda d'Icària, the **Cementiri de l'Est** was the city's first monumental cemetery, founded in 1773 when all the old graveyards in the choked, walled town were turned into squares and building sites. It, too, is choked, with a surreal accretion of monuments to the fathers of Barcelona industry, a preview of the lavish postmortem paraphernalia in Montjuïc's Cementeri de Sud-Ouest. Madrid is proud of its sculpture of Satan in the Retiro park, but here Barcelona has something just as fey in its *Kiss of Death*. Jean Nouvel's contemporary **Parc del Poblenou**, opened in 2008, offers a leafy retreat from the bedlam of the nearby seafront.

Diagonal Mar

Further north, the Diagonal Mar district grows apace around the Fòrum. In spite of a shaky start, the area has found a second life as a weekend concert and party venue, destined only to grow. In 2012 you should be able to visit a Marine Zoo by the Parc del Fòrum, with four watery ecosystems, a waterpark, a centre dedicated to re-introducing Mediterranean marine species, and visits by snorkel to observe the creatures; a Marine Park at the mouth of the Besos is due to be completed by 2014.

El Raval

South of the Rambla, the *barri* of El Raval (Arabic for 'an area outside the walls') is the largest surviving section of the old city. Originally covered with orchards and gardens, the Raval gradually found its role as a haven for the city's rejects – its unpleasant trades, its criminals, but mostly its poor and diseased. When it was joined to the Barri Gòtic by the 14th-century walls, convents and monasteries moved in to fill up the gaps. And so it marinated quietly in its own juices until Spain's industrial revolution was born here. Soon, workers were cramming into tenements pressed up next to the factories, and by the 1850s the Raval was perhaps the unhealthiest neighbourhood in Europe. The streets towards the sea became a crowded den of misery, prostitution and crime known as the Barri Xinès – Chinatown. It owed its name to journalist Àngel Marsá, who was inspired by the lurid descriptions of Chinatowns in America, and its denizens were painted by Isidre Nonell and by the young Picasso, who used the district's poor as the subjects for his Blue Period. Much to the disgust of proper

Barcelona, the notoriety of the Barri Xinès brought thousands of tourists to peep up the city's skirts when they should be been in the Eixample, admiring its fancy dress. In recent years, the Barri Xinès has been so decaffeinated that neither Genet nor Picasso would recognize it today. Since a massive clean-up before the Olympics, old blocks of flats were restored; new ones are being built. The lower part, the old Barri Xinès, is still rough around the edges; but the upper Raval, by the gleaming Museu d'Art Contemporani, is full of arty galleries, bars and fashion stores.

Around the Barri Xinès

Palau Güell

Palau Güell
*3 C/Nou de la Rambla, **t** 93 317 39 74, www.palauguell.cat;* Ⓜ *Drassanes or Liceu; open Tues–Sat 10–2.30; under partial restoration at the time of writing, adm free*

In 1886, when everyone else of means was moving into the Eixample, the great industrialist Eusebi Güell asked his new protegé, Antoni Gaudí, to build him a new home in the Raval. The young architect finished it in 1888, at enormous cost, to coincide with the Universal Exhibition. For all the expense, the Güells spent little time here, although the house has had an interesting afterlife: in 1937 it was used by the Communists as a prison for members of the POUM, who had supported the Anarchists.

The **façade** is restrained for Gaudí, with the exception of the swirling ironwork incorporating the Catalan coat-of-arms splayed across the tympanum of the two main arches. Güell's coaches passed into an courtyard vaulted with Gaudí's signature bare-brick paràbolic arches, from where a marble-columned staircase ascends to the first floor. Columned galleries overhang the street, expanding the interior space. The **visitors' gallery** has a particularly elaborate ceiling; among the dense, Moorish designs are secret spyholes which enabled the Güells surreptitiously to overhear their guests' conversations.

At the heart of the house is the lofty **salon**, overlooked by galleries and culminating in a magical three-storey-high parabolic cupola, a honeycombed beehive pierced with silvery shafts representing a constellation topped by the moon; this was Güell's Montsalvat, the castle where the Grail was kept in Wagner's *Parsifal*. The salon has perfect acoustics and was used for concerts, and the wide upper stairway formed a convenient musicians' gallery. The richest materials were reserved for the family chapel: 16ft-panels of rare hardwoods and ivory sheathed in white tortoiseshell fold back to reveal an alcove which once held a sculpted altarpiece of tortoiseshell and wood, destroyed during the Civil War. Some furnishings survived the war by being moved elsewhere, including a huge Japanese-style fireplace, guarded by scaly wooden serpents, and the enormous dining table, recently

Catalan Bats

They're not as obvious as the dragons, but they're there, like a B-minor chord in the Catalan bestiary. If you've ever been to Mallorca, you will recall that Palma's symbol is the bat, installed there directly after its capture in 1229 by Jaume the Conqueror. Whether or not Jaume was fluent in Arabic is unknown, but his Templar counsellors were: '*bat*' in Arabic has the same root as the word associated with ruins and 'to overthrow'. But the bat was not a mere message of a *fait accompli* to his new Moorish subjects, for it had a second meaning in Arabic as well – 'seeing well only at night'. Idries Shah, the great writer on Sufis, once explained: 'Like the bat, the Sufi is asleep to "things of the day" – the familiar struggle for existence which the ordinary man finds all-important – and vigilant while others are asleep. In other words, he keeps awake the spiritual attention dormant in others. That "mankind sleeps in a nightmare of unfulfilment" is a commonplace of Sufi literature.'

For Güell, a peeker into esoteric corners, the bat was the perfect creature to watch over his house. You'll also see bats on Pere Falque's streetlamps along the Passeig de Gràcia, and on the Casa Oller on the same street. It's also the trademark of a Catalan wine exporter to Cuba named Facundo Bacardi Masós, who began to distil rum in 1862. The Bacardi company, however, claims that their bat is merely a visitor who haunted the rafters of their first distillery. Or so they say.

purchased from Güell's heirs. The upper floors contain the family's **apartments**. Above them, a narrow staircase leads out on to an amazing rippling **roof**, the best feature of the house. One of Gaudí's personal missions was to make roofs as interesting as the rest of his buildings, and here, in a space few people would actually see, he let his imagination run wild to create a forest of 20 chimney sculptures, each organic and covered in *trencadís*. In the centre, the beehive dome of the salon is contained in a spire with a row of parabolic windows, topped by a lightning rod and an eerie bat.

Around the Rambla de Raval

Just up from the Palau Güell, is the **Rambla de Raval**, completed in 2000; several blocks of dilapidated housing were demolished to make way for this wide, new, tree-lined Rambla. While it still lacks café life and the trees look a little too transplanted, the Rambla has promise, and has already become a gathering point for the local community. Fernando Botero's bronze sumo wrestler *Gat* (1981) is a favourite with the local kids.

Head down C/Sant Pau to find the landmark **Hotel España** at No. 9. In 1902–1903, Domènech i Montaner redesigned the ground floor of this hotel, and the well-preserved Modernista dining room is still decorated with a mural of sea creatures and mermaids with scuba flippers by Ramon Casas.

Sant Pau del Camp
🅜 *Paral.lel; open for visits to cloister Wed–Mon 5–8; closed Tues and public hols; adm*

At the opposite end of the street, the **Sant Pau del Camp**, or 'St Paul's in the Field', is the best of the few surviving Romanesque churches in Barcelona, and was probably founded by the son of Wilfred the Hairy, Count Guifré-Borrell (d. 911), whose tombstone is here. Subsequently destroyed in the Moorish raids in 985 and 1115, Sant Pau was rededicated in 1117. In 1528, the monastery became a Benedictine priory linked to Montserrat. Sant Pau's façade looks its age, decorated with blind arcading and archaic reliefs of the hand of God, the symbols of the Evangelists and bizarre little masks. Inside, three apses are crowned by an octagonal tower – the rest burned in the Setmana Trágica in 1909. Best of all is the tiny cloister with its paired columns and triple-lobed Moorish arches and a garden, one of old Barcelona's most magical corners.

Along Carrer de l'Hospital

Antic Hospital de la Santa Creu
C/Hospital 56,
Ⓜ *Liceu*

At the end of the Rambla de Raval, Carrer de l'Hospital is named after the **Antic Hospital de la Santa Creu**. One of the oldest hospitals in the world, it was founded in 1024 and rebuilt here in 1401, with the aim of concentrating all Barcelona's diseases in one place. In the 16th century it had 500 beds; in the 17th century there were 5,000, and in 1926, not long after Gaudí died here, it moved, after 900 years, to Domènech i Montaner's Modernista hospital near the Sagrada Família. The hospital's long vaulted halls now shelter books instead of patients: it's now the National Library of Catalonia. The former Gothic chapel now functions as a gallery,

La Capella
t 934 42 71 71;
open Tues–Sat 12–2
and 4–8, Sun 11–2;
adm free

La Capella, with exhibitions by young artists.

Just down C/Hospital from the library, the woebegone 18th-century church of **Sant Agustí,** with its knobbly stone spikes colonized by pigeons, was never finished. It does, however, hold a place in Barcelona's heart, since in 1971 it became the birthplace of the Assemblea de Catalunya, a broad-based opposition movement that called for liberty of expression and the re-establishment of the 1932 Statute of Autonomy.

Mercat de Sant Antoni
Ⓜ *Sant Antoni;*
open Mon–Sat 8–2
and 3–8, Sun 9–2 for
old books and coins

In the old days, C/Sant Antoni, off the western end of C/Hospital, led to the gate that linked Barcelona to the rest of Spain, a scene of grand entrances and royal processions now occupied by the **Mercat de Sant Antoni**. Designed in 1882 by Antoni Rovira i Trias (author of the losing plan for the Eixample), this Modernista cathedral of spuds and carrots remains one of Barcelona's most impressive iron structures, shaped like an X with four long naves extending crossways to each chamfered corner. It's currently being restored, but the stalls have been transferred to a huge tent nearby.

Museu d'Art Contemporani de Barcelona (MACBA)
Plaça dels Àngels,
t 93 412 08 10, www. macba.es; Ⓜ *Universitat;*
open winter Mon and Wed–Fri 11–7.30, Sat 10–8, Sun 10–3; summer Mon and Wed 11–8, Thurs and Fri 11– midnight, Sat 10–8, Sun 10–3; closed Tues; adm

Around the Museu d'Art Contemporani

Museu d'Art Contemporani de Barcelona

Looming over the northern Raval is the glowing white **Museu d'Art Contemporani de Barcelona or MACBA**, designed by American architect Richard Meier and completed in 1995. The building almost overwhelms the collection: all the glassed-in space in front is devoted to ramps (you can't help but wonder how the skate-boarders outside in the square would love to have a go at them).

It is a vibrant and varied gathering, nonetheless; the core includes such lights as Tàpies, Calder, Dubuffet, Barceló, Klee, Oldenburg, Rauschenberg and Christian Boltanski. Tàpies is represented by a number of pieces, among them *Pintura Ocre* (1959), and Joan Brossa has some delightful 'poem-objects'. In Perejaume's *Postaler* (1984), the artist took a tall cylindrical frame fitted with angled slotted mirrors into different landscapes and photographed it with its shimmering reflections. There are several unsettling pieces, poised between horror and laughter, including the *Training Table for Reconverted Communists* (1991) – an elongated ping-pong table with guns laid at each end instead of bats, by Francesc Torres.

The CCCB and Around

Around the corner, the former Casa de Caritat at 5 C/Montalegre first built in 1362 was remodelled over the centuries to do duty as a cloister for Franciscan nuns, seminary, hospital and, after 1802, as a workhouse for the poor. Then in 1987 the Maremagnum architects, Piñon and Viaplana, dipped it in a postmodernist solution, and it emerged as the **Centre de Cultura Contemporània de Barcelona**, or **CCCB**. The dilapidated north courtyard was replaced by a huge glass and steel block that tilts forward; the south façade was also replaced, to make way for the MACBA. The entrance is by way of the pretty 18th-century Pati de les Dones, with mosaic decoration. The CCCB hosts imaginative exhibitions with urban themes.

Nearby, in Plaça de la Universitat, Barcelona's **Universitat Central** is the heir of the Estudi d'Arts i Medicina, founded by King Martí in 1401. Planned and built between 1860 and 1873, the university was the first monumental building in the new Eixample. The architect, Elias Rogent i Amat, was a disciple of Viollet-le-Duc, and used the Romanesque idiom to evoke Catalonia's roots. The courtyard to the left of the entrance, the **Pati dels Lletres**, with its orange trees and arcades, is especially pretty. Like most totalitarians, Franco was keen to get students and their ideas out of the city centre, and in the 1950s most of the university was relocated to Pedralbes.

Centre de Cultura Contemporània de Barcelona (CCCB)
t 93 306 41 00,
www.cccb.org;
Ⓜ *Universitat;*
exhibition opening hours Tues–Sat 11–8; adm

The Eixample

Barcelona's Eixample ('ay-sham-play'), like the world's other great one-offs, came about through a rare combination of factors, in this case a blank slate to build on, and the talent, skill, quirkiness, imagination and money to make it something thoroughly unique, with Anarchist bombs providing a restless *basso continuo* in the background and Gaudí off in his corner trying to save their souls by building the Sagrada Família. And, perhaps most intangibly, it's all thoroughly Catalan. The Eixample's highlights will take half a day

The Making of the Eixample

By the early 19th century, Barcelona was going crazy, bursting in its walled straitjacket. The city fathers endlessly petitioned the government in Madrid to remove the walls, but permission was only finally granted in 1854, during one of Spain's brief interludes of liberalism. When word reached Barcelona, wild celebration filled the streets as every man, woman and child started hacking at walls.

Once the lid was off, the city in 1859 sponsored a competition for the plan of the 'extension' or Eixample. The finalists were both Catalans. The Ajuntament chose the plan of municipal architect Antoni Rovira i Trias, who proposed exciting prospects and boulevards fanning out of the Old City, respectful of its axes and origins, an organic translation between old and new.

To Barcelona's dismay, Madrid intervened and imposed the losing scheme (to this day no one knows why) by a Socialist engineer named Ildefons Cerdà, whose plan had nothing whatsoever to do with the Old City in its modular grid of uniform wide streets, with its distinct chamfered corners (*xamfrans*) to allow the new steam trams to turn more easily. Cerdà's visions were utopian: his pure abstract plan would eliminate social classes – there was no reason why one block should be better than another – and there would be gardens in the centre of each block, with light, air, and windows for all.

It's hard not to feel sorry for Cerdà, who spent his life and fortune on his vision. Few city plans have had their intentions as gleefully sabotaged. Barcelona quintupled in size over the next 50 years, but key elements of Cerdà's plan – the height and density restrictions, the parks and social services – soon went by the wayside; buildings and car parks filled in the blocks instead of gardens. Nor did Cerdà's ideas on equality make it off the blueprints. The Right Eixample (Dreta de l'Eixample), where Modernista architects created fabulous palaces for their wealthy clients, became more desirable than the Left Eixample (Esquerra de l'Eixample).

If the Barri Gòtic is Europe's largest medieval neighbourhood, the Dreta de l'Eixample (or to be more precise, the Quadrant d'Or between the Barri Gòtic, Diagonal, C/Roger de Flor and C/Muntaner) holds the greatest trove of 19th-century architecture, with over 150 listed Modernista buildings.

to see – walk straight up the Passeig de Gràcia to the Diagonal, then take the metro to the Sagrada Família. To see more requires perseverance; it's vast, and some of the buildings are a fair old trot.

The Passeig de Gràcia and the Fairest of Discords

The greatest concentration of Modernista masterpieces is along the Eixample's most elegant boulevard, the **Passeig de Gràcia**, north of the Plaça Catalunya (*see* p.82). In the late 18th century, the old road to Gràcia was the 'Elysian fields' of dance halls, theatres, beer gardens and amusements. The first trees were planted in 1827, and by 1872 it had its first horse-drawn trams. If you love architecture, though, duck into C/Casp, where at No.48 stands the **Casa Calvet** (1898), Gaudí's first apartment building – the ironwork detail, the two crosses and the decorative elements presage his future masterpieces on the Passeig de Gràcia.

The most dazzling stretch of the Passeig de Gràcia, between C/Consell de Cent and C/Aragó, is known as the '**Mançana de la Discòrdia**' – or the 'block of discord', using a pun on *mançana*, which means 'apple' and 'block'. Here, any passer-by can play the role of the Trojan Paris and award the prize to the fairest of these three wildly contrasting Modernista beauties.

Casa Lleó Morera

The first, the Casa Lleó Morera at No. 35, was built in 1864. Between 1902 and 1906, the owner let Domènech i Montaner have his way with it, and the result is his most lavish residential project, the corner crowned with an ethereal ceramic cupola, the whole frosted with decoration inside and out. For Barcelona's élite, wealth wasn't the only thing to flaunt on a façade: the family's interests, social status, business connections and hobbies were advertised as well.

As the ground floor of the Casa Lleó Morera was destined to house a photographer's studio, Arnau covered it with nymphs and reliefs relating to electricity and cameras, all sacrificed in 1943 by Loewe of Madrid, of leather goods fame, for larger shop windows.

On the second floor, however, the nymphs survived the ruthless leather-goods-mongers. A gorgeous stained-glass bay window of happy roosters in the country by Joan Rigalt provides both a glamorous screen and a voluptuous rush of colour, while the walls are covered in delightful ceramic mosaic portraits by Gaspar Homar; the furnishings he designed for the room are now in the Museu Nacional d'Art de Catalunya.

Casa Amatller

Casa Amatller
*t 93 487 72 17,
www.amatller.com;
Passeig de Gràcia;
guided tours of the
entrance, photography
studio and kitchen
Mon–Fri in English at
12 noon; adm*

Two doors down, Casa Amatller was called 'the apotheosis of decorative arts' when it was completed in 1898. Antoni Amatller i Costa, the Willy Wonka of Catalan chocolate, started the redecorating trend on the Mansana when he hired Puig i Cadafalch to give his existing house a Gothic makeover. Puig's Gothic, however, is like no one else's: the façade, decorated with ceramic plaques and discreet sgraffito, culminates in a remarkable stepped gable, richly aglitter with blue, pink and cream tiles.

The façade, in fact, is one big allegory of Amatller's life and passions, one of which was Catalan nationalism. Between the two doorways, we see St George battling the dragon; soulful figures represent painting, sculpture and music; monkeys hammer away at iron while rabbits stow the finished product, in a vignette of happy industrious workers. A bespectacled donkey engrossed in a book while his friend twiddles with a camera are references to Amatller's love of reading and his new photographic interests.

Perhaps Amatller spent too much time on his hobbies, because his wife ran off with an opera singer before the façade was finished; as a consequence, the *tribuna*, which in the best houses was used to show off the latest fashions to hoi polloi in the street, was built to one side, near the bedroom of Miss Amatller, the new lady of the house. The window decoration culminates in an almond tree, a play on the family name, with a curling letter 'A'. The same motif is found on the grand staircase, along with a stern eagle and a lovely stained-glass skylight. The original elevator still wheezes its way between floors, and the *piano nobile* retains most of its rich decoration by Eusebi Arnau and Gaspar Homar.

Casa Batlló

In stark contrast to Casa Amatller's sharp right angles is the absolutely extraordinary Casa Batlló, the block's third 'apple of discord'. This too was an older building, belonging to textile tycoon Josep Batlló, who basically wanted to outdo the Joneses next door and in 1904 commissioned Gaudí to give the house a facelift. Gaudí turned it into Barcelona's biggest allegory of St George and the Dragon, covered with a rippling blue skin of ceramic plaques and *trencadís* – the architect would stand in the middle of the Passeig de Gràcia to 'paint' the façade, directing workmen in the arrangement of the colours, which shimmer and change according to the light. Gaudí's great collaborator Josep Maria Jujol topped it with an equally sublimely coloured roof for the dragon's scaly back. The pinnacle with its bulb dome and cross is St George's lance, piercing the dragon and placed to one side to complement the symmetry of the Casa Amatller; the *trencadí*-covered chimneys are the dragon's multi-spiked tail. The first floor is the dragon's lair; the first balcony depicts the rose which grew from its blood, while the other balconies hint at the skulls and tibia in its larder.

Or so it seems. Some have seen other visions in the façade – a representation of the sea, with soft aquatic blues and greens and bubbling windows hollowed out by the waves, the balconies of delicate wrought iron like fishing nets being tossed in the air. Or is it an allegory of the Venice Carnival, with a pert Harlequin, balconies forming masks and a dappled, confetti-strewn façade?

The first-floor apartment, completely redesigned for Batlló, is just as stunning: there isn't a straight line in the whole place, and it contains what must be the most sensuous staircase in the world, based on the curve of the dragon's tail. Note the magnificent blue ceramic light-well, which imperceptibly avoids the effect of light glaring down a pit by means of colour, using dark tiles at the top, gradually introducing lighter ones until reaching white at the bottom. The back of the house is covered in a skin of multi-coloured *trencadís*, visible from an undulating terrace scattered with ceramic fountains and sculpted ponds.

Museu del Parfum
t 93 216 01 46, www. museudelperfum.com;
Ⓜ *Passeig de Gràcia*

Museums of the Eixample

Squeezed between fancy façades is the inconspicuous Regia perfume shop, with its **Museu del Parfum** devoted to the history of the perfume bottle, with everything from tiny Corinthian alabastrons from the 7th century BC to film star atomizers from the early 20th century.

Round the corner from the Mançana de la Discòrdia, the **Fundació Antoni Tàpies** occupies the headquarters built by Domènech i Montaner for his brother's publishing company (1880–85), a prototype of Modernisme, as well as an early example of the architect's love for honest Catalan brick and iron. It was Barcelona's first domestic building with an iron frame, and the elaborate brick patterns are a reference to the Moorish-influenced mudéjar work of medieval Spain. Tàpies himself loved everyday materials, which he used for the *Núvol i Cadira* (Cloud and Chair) hovering over the building like a giant steel-wool pad.

Fundació Antoni Tàpies
C/Aragó 255,
t 93 487 03 15,
www.fundacio
tapies.org;
ⓜ Passeig de Gràcia;
open Tues–Sun 10–8;
adm (library by app't)

Born in 1923 to a bourgeois family in Barcelona, Antoni Tàpies was a sickly child who relished days spent in bed, sketching and gathering a fund of images which would insinuate themselves into his later works. Like Miró, with whom he was close, he sought the extraordinary within the ordinary, while colouring much of his work with a pervasive self-referential and sometimes oblique film: graffitied walls recall those of the old Barcelona of his childhood; the recurring motifs of mirrors and wardrobes echo the images thrown back at the young invalid. These pieces, bleak and yet hauntingly spiritual, were created from found objects, scraps of paper and rags. In 1984 he set up this foundation for the study of contemporary and non-Western art; there is a selection of Tàpies' art and changing exhibitions of other people's.

Fundació Francisco Godia
C/Diputació 250,
t 93 272 31 80, www.
fundacionfgodia.org;
ⓜ Passeig de Gràcia;
open Wed–Mon
10–8; closed Tues; adm

The **Fundació Francisco Godia** occupies Enric Sagnier's beautiful Modernista **Casa Garriga Nogués**. Its founder, Paco Godia (1921–90) was a Formula 1 racing car driver, businessman and art collector with a good eye who amassed a number of treasures, beginning with the elegant 14th-century *Virgen de la Llet*, attributed to Llorenç Saragossa, court painter to Pere the Ceremonious, a brilliantly red-robed *Magdelene* by Jaume Huguet, and a choice set of medieval ceramics. Godia also liked 20th-century art, with works by Sunyer, Tàpies, Ramon Casas and Picasso (a funny *Portrait of Pere Romeu*).

Museu Egipci
C/Valencia 284,
t 93 488 01 88,
www.museuegipci.com;
ⓜ Passeig de Gràcia;
open Mon–Sat 10–8,
Sun 10–2; adm

That's not all: millionaire enthusiast Jordi Clos' excellent private collection of Egyptian art at the **Museu Egipci** (Fundació Clos) has reconstructions of tombs and a choice collection of masks, ceramics, jewellery, statuettes and mummies, including a baby crocodile that looks like a pencil and other swaddled animals, complete with X-rays.

La Pedrera (Casa Milà)

Casa Batlló created such a sensation that some even richer people, Pere Milà, a member of the Spanish parliament, and his wife from Reus, Gaudí's home town, immediately hired Gaudí to outdo himself a few blocks up the Passeig de Gràcia. Here he was given a virgin *xamfrà*, and the result, the Casa Milà (1905–10), was just what the couple ordered: the most extraordinary, singular apartment building ever built, nicknamed La Pedrera, 'the stone quarry'. As much sculpture as building, the five-storey stone façade (supported by a complex steel armature and hammered to give it the desired rough texture) undulates around the bevelled corners of the intersection like a cliff sculpted by waves of wind, pierced by windows that seem to be eroded into the stone, underlined by Jujol's fantastical balconies of forged iron seaweed spilling over the edges. The honey-coloured sea cliff culminates in a roof of cresting white sea foam – or icing. Newspaper cartoons compared the building to a gooey cake.

The interior courtyard is as striking as the façade, with its two irregular circular patios open to the sky, enclosed in winding ramps; Gaudí had wanted residents to be able to drive to their doors, but settled for Europe's first underground car park.

The ticket includes a visit to a re-created Modernista apartment, **El Pis de la Pedrera**, which is chock-full of the then-latest modern gadgets – electric lights, time-saving domestic appliances and telephones. Because Gaudí dispensed with interior load-bearing walls, no two apartments are alike. The first people to move in complained snootily that none of their furniture fitted in the swirling rooms; Santiago Rusinyol joked that residents would have to have snakes for pets, instead of cats and dogs.

Even the Casa Milà's attic is no ordinary attic, but a great wavy tunnel of catenary parabolic arches resembling the ribcage of a dragon – what the princess would have seen had not St George arrived on time. It contains the **Espai Gaudí**, offering a thorough overview of the man's work through models, photos, drawings and videos. The total effect is vertiginous, but this is the best place to get to know Bellesguard, Casa Vicens and his other inaccessible buildings, as well as the few outside Barcelona.

Steps lead up to the **roof**. Gaudí's installations have been called the precursors of Surrealism, Expressionism and Cubism, and you can wander around this beautiful if troubling garden of chimneys and ventilators shaped like bouquets of visored knights in reddish stone (baptised the *espantabruixes*, or 'witch-scarers'), who keep company with four fat globs of Cheeze Whiz holding the stair exits, coated in white *trencadís*. Perhaps the most extraordinary thing

La Pedrera (Casa Milà)
Passeig de Gràcia 92, t 90 240 09 73, http://obrasocial.caixa catalunya.es; Ⓜ *Diagonal; open Nov–Feb daily 9–6; Mar–Oct daily 9–8; adm exp (includes the apartment El Pis de La Pedrera, and the Espai Gaudí)*

'The corners will vanish, and the material will reveal itself in the wealth of its astral curves... and it will be like a vision of Paradise.'
Gaudí

about the roof is what it is missing. Gaudí saw La Pedrera as a pedestal for a 40ft-high statue of the Virgin Mary and a pair of angels, an idea the Milàs prudently vetoed after the 1909 Setmana Trágica left Barcelona smouldering in a bout of church-burnings. Gaudí was furious, left an assistant to finish the job, vowed he would never work for the bourgeoisie again, and devoted the rest of his life to trying to expiate the church-torching sins of his fellow Catalans by building the Sagrada Família.

Around La Pedrera: Other Modernista Highlights

Just beyond La Pedrera, **Avinguda Diagonal** slices across the waffle of the Eixample. If in the Mansana de la Discòrdia you gave the prize to Puig i Cadafalch, two of his principal works astonish just to the right. The **Palau Baró de Quadras** (1904), now home to the **Casa Asia** cultural centre, is his most flamboyant Gothic palace, its projecting first-floor windows covered with a Flemish Plateresque menagerie of fabulous creatures, plus George and the Dragon designed by the indefatigable Eusebi Arnau. At Nos. 416–20, Puig's massive neo-Gothic apartment block, the **Casa de les Punxes** (1903–5), or 'House of Spikes', bristles with the pointiest witch's-hat roofs ever, as needly spires rise out of its brick gables.

If, in the Mansana de la Discòrdia, you gave the apple to Lluís Domènech i Montaner, be sure to follow C/Mallorca, running to the right off the Passeig de Gràcia to see the **Casa Thomas**, C/Mallorca 291 (1898), which has the earliest examples of his decorative ceramic appliqués – strange hybrid creatures, half-carnation, half-lizard. The **Palau Montaner** at C/Mallorca 278, home of Domènech's publisher brother, was begun in 1889 by Josep Domènech i Estapà in a sober eclectic style. However, it was finished with pizzazz by Lluís, who frosted the top floor with mosaics by Gaspar Homar and showered decoration on the grand stair, with a lovely skylight by Joan Rigalt and sculptures by Eusebi Arnau – if you're wondering where the dragons are lurking, they're at the bottom of the steps. The building is now the seat of the Delegació del Govern a Catalunya – Madrid's representatives in the autonomous region.

Casa Asia
Diagonal 373; t 93 238 73 37, www.casaasia.es; Ⓜ Diagonal; open Tues–Sat 10–8, Sun 10–2

⭐ **Sagrada Família**
C/Mallorca 401, t 93 208 04 14, www.sagradafamilia.cat; Ⓜ Sagrada Família; open April–Sept daily 9–8; Oct–Mar daily 9–6; adm exp; combined adm available with Gaudí's house in the Park Güell; guided tours in English for an additional fee, May–Oct daily at 11am, 1pm, 3pm and 5pm; Nov–April at 11am and 1pm; lift extra adm

Sagrada Família

George Orwell, writing of the church burnings during the Civil War in his *Homage to Catalonia*, wondered ruefully why there was one that the arsonists spared, 'the ugliest building in the world', with spires 'shaped like hock bottles'. These 350ft bottles, of course, belong to Gaudí's great, unfinished Sagrada Família. Occupying an entire block of the Cerdà plan, the Expiatory Temple of the Holy Family is surely the most compelling, controversial and unfinished building site in the world, the symbol of Barcelona and of the scale of its extraordinary ambition.

The Building of the Sagrada Família

The church was begun on a cheap plot in 1882, the brainchild of bookdealer Josep Bocabella Verdaguer, founder of a society dedicated to St Joseph (the 'Josephines') and devoted to preserving the family values which he felt were being eroded throughout society. For the design, Bocabella hired Francesc del Villar (one of Gaudí's professors), who planned a typical neo-Gothic church. He got as far as the crypt in 1883 when disagreements led to his replacement by Gaudí – who was only 31 and had hardly built anything, but he was pious, and that was enough for Bocabella.

Gaudí finished the crypt and worked on the project off and on for the next 43 years. At first there was plenty of money, and the building survived the Setmana Trágica arson in 1909, probably because it employed 300 workers. But the Setmana Trágica gave Gaudí a new purpose: the temple would also expiate the sins of Catalonia. By then it had become Gaudí's full-fledged obsession, and in 1912, after the death of his collaborator Francesc Berenguer, he accepted no other commissions. When money ran low, he sold everything he owned for the project, and in 1925 moved into a hut on the construction site, increasingly unkempt, living on bread, water, fruit and vegetables, soliciting funds, even going door-to-door for handfuls of pesetas. People crossed the street at the sight of the mad old genius with the piercing blue gaze. Fashion had moved on, away from Modernisme and Josephine piety.

Gaudí planned three façades, dedicated to the Birth, Passion and, the main one, Glory; each would have four towers, symbolizing the twelve Apostles. Four higher towers rising over the crossing would be dedicated to the Evangelists, and in the centre a truly colossal 575ft tower would symbolize the Saviour, with a tower of the Virgin over the apse. Although it was Gothic in plan, the architect promised that it would go beyond Gothic, using the system of inclined columns and parabolic arches that he used at the Güell Crypt (see p.158). There would be no buttresses, or 'crutches', as he called them. He fussed over every detail and, when a bishop asked him why he worried about the tops of his towers, Gaudí replied: 'Your Grace, the angels will see them.'

Gaudí started on the Birth Façade and completed one tower in 1926, then absent-mindedly wandered in front of a streetcar. He died three days later in a public ward in the medieval Hospital de la Santa Creu. By 1935, his followers had completed the other three towers of the Birth Façade according to his models. But Orwell was wrong when he wrote that the Anarchists never damaged the Sagrada Família: they hated everything it represented, and in 1936 they broke into the workshops and set fire to every plan and model they found, hoping to stop further work.

According to the philosopher Ferrater i Mora, four elements define the Catalan character: *seny* (wisdom, good sense), measure, irony and *continuitat*, which means not only continuity of tradition, but also the urge to finish a job once begun. In the case of the Sagrada Família, this fourth element is proving more powerful than the other three combined. In 1954, the Josephines (who are answerable to neither the city nor the Church) raised enough money to continue the project in 'the manner of Gaudí', instructing architects to guess the master's intent from the photos of a few surviving drawings. Their work has offended purists, who believe the temple should have been left alone as a memorial to the man's unique genius; they also point out that Gaudí never even followed his own models but was forever improvising, which gave his work its unique dynamism. The Josephines, however, insist that Gaudí wished the Sagrada Família to be like the cathedrals of the Middle Ages, built over the generations – he himself estimated it would take 200 years to complete, but 'my client is not in a hurry'.

Since 1987, architect Jordi Bonet (whose father worked with Gaudí) has been in charge of the project. As interest in Gaudí grows and money pours in, the pace of building has accelerated. Whatever reservations the city once had about the project have gone by the wayside, as the Sagrada Família has proved its value as a tourist attraction – it is already the most visited site in Catalonia, with some 2.5 million annual visitors, whose tickets are the main source of funding. And whatever you think of the aesthetics, it's impossible not to admire the devil-may-care momentum the project has gathered. The Josephines hope to complete the work by the centenary of Gaudí's death, 2026. One problem is the main **Glory Façade**. Gaudí intended it to nudge into C/Mallorca, with a wide stair cascading into the next *xamfrà*, but in 1979 an apartment building was built in the way. The planned Sants–Sagrera high-speed train tunnel under the site of the Glory Façade has also been a cause for concern- and a lawsuit.

Gaudí' spersonal touch is visible on the **Birth Façade**. He based the sculpture on photographs of everyday people, using a 33-year-old worker for Christ on the Cross and a six-toed barman for a Roman soldier. He made plaster casts of plants, flowers, people and a live donkey (which survived the ordeal); if you look closely you may even see a figure of a bomb-tossing Anarchist. The new sculpture here is by the Japanese sculptor Etsuro Sotoo, who was so overwhelmed when he saw the Sagrada Família that he immediately converted to Catholicism. Gaudí finished one 394ft tower with its bright ceramic finial, and the other three were built according to his models.

Sculptor Josep Maria Subirachs, an avowed atheist born exactly nine months after Gaudí died, took on the job of the **Passion Façade** on the condition that he lived on the site and had complete artistic freedom. He proved to be sufficiently thick-skinned to survive all pleas from artists, architects and religious conservatives that he stop. He completed the facade in 1998, three years ahead of schedule, using synthetic stone of reinforced concrete with resin-bonded finishes. He decorated this with robotic sculptures, including centurions derived from the 'witch-scarers' on La Pedrera, a controversial naked Christ on the Cross, a figure of Gaudí and a magic square based on the number 33. Whereas the Birth Façade has Gaudí's unmistakable textured style, resembling primordial growth – a 'terrifying, edible beauty', as Dalí described it – Subirachs' façade is mechanical, sinister and kitsch, as purposely brutal as its subject matter. The sculptor himself has stated that it 'has nothing to do with Gaudí'. Finishing touches include the great bronze door inscribed with 8,000 letters from a page of the Gospel, four huge travertine statues of the apostles and a 25ft metal Christ, placed on a bridge between the two central towers.

For a small fee you can take the lift up the **Passion Towers**, for a vertiginous dreamlike ramble high over the city, with the option of a terrifying descent down the tightly spiralled staircase.

The **interior** is a building site. The nave, which Gaudí intended to resemble 'a forest of stone', was completed, with its 147ft flat brick vaults. On top of this stands the crane ready to construct the tower dome and four towers of the Evangelists, to be supported by vaults on the immense columns of basalt and porphyry. New technoglogy is helping architects to calculate the thrusts and build as Gaudí wanted, without buttresses, and to precision-cut each stone offsite, saving time. By 2010 the vaults of the crossing and the apse should be completed and roofed; the apse alone will be big enough to swallow the church of Santa Maria del Mar whole.

In the crypt the you can visit **Gaudí's tomb** and the **Museu de la Sagrada Familía**, with photos, diagrams, models, bits of sculpture and Gaudí's astonishing catenary model, made of chains and small sacks weighted in proportion to the arches and the load they would have to bear, which he used to build the Güell Crypt.

Around the Sagrada Família:
Hospital de la Santa Creu i Sant Pau

Avinguda Gaudí leads from the Sagrada Família to another, completed and useful, if almost as gargantuan, Modernista work: Lluís Domènech i Montaner's Hospital de la Santa Creu i Sant Pau (1902–30), covering nine blocks of the Eixample, the world's most beautiful hospital and a World Heritage site. You may have seen it before; Woody Allen used it as the language school in his *Vicky*

Hospital de la Santa Creu i Sant Pau
C/Sant Antoni Maria Claret 167,
t 93 256 25 04,
www.santpau.es;
Ⓜ *Hospital de Sant Pau; guided visits Mon–Sun in English 10.15 and 12.15; adm*

Cristina Barcelona (2008). Domènech i Montaner conceived the hospital as a garden city of 26 pavilions on a human scale, connected by underground service tunnels. The project was only a quarter built in 1911 when the money dried up, so it was decided to merge with the medieval Hospital de la Santa Creu in Raval, which provided the needed cash. Domènech worked with his son, who took over when his father died in 1923, and finished it in 1930. The grounds invite aimless wandering, becoming an alternative universe at twilight, each brick pavilion different, topped with fantastically tiled roofs and encrusted with mosaics, lavishly decorated with sculptures by Eusebi Arnau and Pau Gargallo and their workshops. Rich stained glass and elaborately wrought lamps cast strange shadows. The large administration building (1910) has the most ornate interior and views from the upper floors.

Centre de Modernisme
open daily 10–2

It now contains a **Centre de Modernisme**, with information on the Ruta del Modernisme, *see* p.138.

Along the Gran Via de les Corts Catalanes

Around the Plaça Tetuán

The Eixample's main east-west artery, Gran Via de les Corts Catalanes, has several monuments, beginning with a surprising one in Plaça Tetuán: Josep Llimona's **Monument to Dr Bartolomeu Robert**. Dr Robert became the first Catalanist mayor of Barcelona in 1899, and sanctioned the bank strike that year: Madrid had raised taxes on banks to cover its losses in the 1898 war and, rather than pay, Barcelona's banks shut down.

The **Plaça de Toros Monumental** at No.749 is the only Modernista bullring in Spain, designed in 1916 by Ignasi Mas Morell and Domènec Sugrañes Gras. Made of brick, covered with blue and white *azulejos* and *trencadís*, the arena is laced with parabolic arches and punctuated with towers supporting huge yellow, white and blue ceramic dinosaur eggs. The Beatles played here in 1965, a landmark event in Franco's regime. Its seldom-visited **Museu Taurí** has a collection of famous bulls' heads and memorabilia.

Museu Taurí
t 93 245 58 03;
Ⓜ *Monumental;*
open daily 10.30–2
and 4–7, Sun 10–1; adm

Around the Plaça de les Glòries Catalanes

Cerdà's vision of the **Plaça de les Glòries Catalanes** – where the Diagonal, Meridiana and Gran Via de les Corts Catalanes meet like the Union Jack – as the throbbing centre of Barcelona was sabotaged by its conversion into a giant elevated roundabout. Yet as improbable as it might seem, the days of grey anomie here are numbered, and the Square of Catalan Glories may even some day live up to Cerdà's vision. Its beacon is Jean Nouvel's skyline-changing, 466ft **Torre Agbar** (2005),reminiscent of Sir Norman Foster's 'Gherkin' in London, and quickly dubbed 'the Suppository' by the scatalogical Catalans; 4,500 LED luminations give it a colourful nocturnal shimmer. The hideous roundabout is destined to go underground by 2011, replaced by a great lawn, with an added subway line and regional rail station. A new public library, sports centre and cinema complex designed by Zaha Hadid, should attract some fashion action, along with the Ona building by Federico Soriano and the Centre de Disseny, by Bohigas, Martorell and Mackay, a new home for the **Disseny Hub Barcelona** (*see* p.136). For the time being the open air **Els Encants flea market** remains studiously the same on C/Dos de Maig, with plenty of desirable junk, and sneaky pickpockets, but plans are to put it in a building as well.

Els Encants
t 93 246 30 30; open Mon, Wed, Fri and Sat; auctions at 7am; stands 8.30–6

New buildings are already going up along Avinguda Meridiana. In the **Auditori** (1994) architect Rafael Moneo gave Barcelona the austere antithesis of its Palau de la Música Catalana, containing an acoustically flawless auditorium clad in Canadian maple and the **Museu de la Música** a fascinating collection of antique and exotic instruments from the 16th century onwards, including one of Adophe Sax's original saxophones. Ricardo Bofill, who has not an iota of Moneo's discretion, contributed an updated Parthenon for the **Teatre Nacional de Catalunya** (TNC) on the other side of C/Padilla. Just past Plaça de les Glòries, the 19th-century brick factory building of **Farinera del Clot** at Gran Via 837 has been tarted up as a cultural centre (*www.farinera.org*).

Museu de la Música
C/Lepant 150, t 93 256 36 50, www.bcn.cat/museumusica; ⓜ *Marina; open Mon, Wed–Sat 10–6, Sun 10–8; adm, free Sun 3–8*

Esquerra de l'Eixample and Sants

Esquerra de l'Eixample

There are far fewer sights on the Left Eixample. Modernisme fans may want to seek out **Casa Golferichs**, a Modernista Moorish medieval family townhouse (now a cultural centre), with a rare garden by the side. It was designed in 1901 by Gaudí collaborator Joan Rubió i Bellver while still in his 20s, but already demonstrating his trademark – expressive brick- and stonework, often in angular volumes (as in the wide eaves), and attention to detail. The interior was inspired by Gaudí's bishop's palace in Astorga.

Casa Golferichs
Gran Via 491, t 93 323 77 90, www.golferichs.org; ⓜ *Urgell; usually open Mon–Sat 10–2 and 5–9; adm free*

Another good one is the **Casa de Lactància** (1913) at Gran Via 475, a late-Gothic Modernista public-welfare building by Pere Falqués and Antoni de Falguerra, crowned with a relief showing an allegory of Barcelona helping the unfortunate by Eusebi Arnau. It's now a retirement home; ask to step inside to see the enchanting covered courtyard.

Just off the Diagonal, the **Casa Company**, C/Casanova 203, is a relatively simple house, built in 1911 by Puig i Cadafalch in his 'white period', when he began to turn away from his historical fantasies. Its owner, Dr Melchior Colet, made it into a small **Museu de l'Esport**, with an emphasis on Catalan endeavours. In the same area, look for the **Universitat Industrial at** C/Comte d'Urgell 173–221, built in 1895 on the site of the former Batlló ceramics factory. In 1927–31, Joan Rubió i Bellvé designed the university's **Escola del Treball**, which includes a superb entrance hall of huge parabolic arches.

Museu de l'Esport
Ⓜ *Hospital Clínic;
open Mon–Fri 10–2
and 4–8; adm free*

Sants

The Sants district, on the far left of the Eixample, grew up along the C/Creu Coberta, the old Roman road to the rest of Spain. It was home to giant textile mills in the 19th century, including Güell's **Vapor Vell** (now a public library) with its tremendous tall brick chimney, at C/Galileu 51. Sants also has Barcelona's main **train station**; the nearby **Plaça dels Països Catalans** (1981–2) was originally a traffic intersection, and the architects, Helio Piñón and Albert Viaplana, were given a difficult brief: they could not build or plant anything because of train tracks directly below. Their response was to create a minimalist playground dotted with metal pole 'trees'; unfortunately, it became the template for a dozen equally new squares around Barcelona. On the south side of the station is **Parc de l'Espanya Industrial,** named after the huge mill that once stood here. This is far more convivial, with a boating lake and *St George and the Dragon* (1985), by Andres Nagel, the largest of all dragon and Jordi sculptures in Barcelona, and the most popular with the small fry, who use it as a slide.

Montjuïc

The south end of Barcelona is closed off by the 705ft slope of Montjuïc, Barcelona's grandstand and showcase. Its name is derived either from 'Mons Jovis' – the mountain of Jove – or from the 'mountain of Jews' for the Jewish cemetery discovered by the castle. Barcelona lost its count-kings before they had a chance to lay out any palatial gardens or hunting preserves – the source of the great parks of Madrid and other European capitals. But in compensation there was Montjuïc, and for centuries it provided a place to breathe for a city suffocating inside its walls.

In 1914, the entire northern slope was beautifully landscaped by Jean-Claude Forestier and Nicolas Rubió i Tuduri, who went on to become the Johnny Appleseed of Barcelona's parks, adding a dozen new green spaces to the city. The driving force, of course, was a

Getting to and around Montjuïc

The **PM** (Parc Montjuïc) **bus**, which makes a loop around the main sights every 20mins, and **bus 61** from Espanya metro station, take in most of the park, making a loop from the Plaça Espanya past the Poble Espanyol, the Olympic stadium and the Fundació Miró to the castle.

A **funicular** to Plaça Dante from the Paral.lel metro station connects with the **Telefèric de Montjuïc** (cable car) up to the castle (*runs June–mid-Sept Mon–Fri 11.15–8, Sat–Sun 11.15–9; mid-Sept–Oct daily 11.30–2.45 and 4–7.30; Nov–May Sat and Sun only*). Check times out of season (TMB, **t** 93 318 70 74, *www.tmb.net*).

There's also an **aerial cablecar** that runs from Barceloneta to Miramar (*see* p.105) and a **tourist 'train'** (actually an open-top minibus) between Plaça d'Espanya and Miramar (*April–Sept daily 10am–11pm*).

show, although, unlike in 1888, politics and economics kept intruding, and it wasn't until 1929 that the International Exhibition was under way. It bequeathed a permanent fair to the city and provided homes for its collections. Then, in 1992, it was all dusted off and crowned with an Olympic ring.

Plaça d'Espanya and Around

Plaça d'Espanya is the big doughnut gateway to Montjuïc, with its six radiating streets and fountain in the centre. Its Moorish-style **Les Arenes**, the older of Barcelona's bullrings, is being converted by Richard Rogers into a domed shopping and leisure centre. Next to it at C/Llança 20 is a remarkable block of flats, the **Casa de la Papallona** (1912) by Josep Graner, who built five workmanlike floors then, overcome by whimsy, stuck an enormous *trencadí*-covered butterfly on top. It sets the tone for the **Parc Joan Miró** behind the bullring, featuring Miró's last major work, the *Dona i Ocell* (*Woman and Bird*), a 70ft-high bowling pin or phallus with a horned cylindrical head. Miró intended to plant a whole forest of these, but death intervened, and dwarf palms have taken their place.

CaixaForum
Avda Marquès de Comillas 6-8, **t** *93 476 86 00, http:// obrasocial.lacaixa.es/ centros/english/caixa forumbcn_en.html;* ⓜ *Espanya; open daily 10–8, Sat 10–10; adm usually free, prices vary for special events*

Also off Plaça d'Espanya, heading towards the Palau Nacional on the hill, is Puig i Cadafalch's **Fábrica Casarramona** (1911), a striking Modernista brick and iron cotton-thread mill; the two towers disguise water tanks. Used after the Civil War as a police barracks, it's been spectacularly restored by the Fundació La Caixa as the **CaixaForum** to display its ever-expanding art collection. It's a vast, glassy place with concert halls, a library, bookshop, café-restaurant and galleries.

Pabellón Mies van der Rohe
Avda Marquès de Comillas **t** *93 423 40 16, www.miesbcn.com; open daily 10–8; adm guided visits in English, Wed and Fri at 5pm (book in advance)*

Opposite, in contrast, stands the cool, elegant **Pabellón Mies van der Rohe**, designed by the famous Bauhaus architect for Germany's exhibit in the 1929 fair. Mies, a stickler for fine materials and craftsmanship (unlike many of his disciples), once said, 'I would rather be good than original,' but here he was both, although his sleek horizontal work of travertine, onyx, glass and chrome, sited over a pair of reflecting pools, went unnoticed by most fair-goers. But Barcelona's more perceptive architects were intrigued, among them Rubió i Tudurí: 'It just encloses space,' he marvelled. The original was demolished after the fair, and the present replica was reconstructed by the Ajuntament in 1986; inside, the prize exhibit is Rohe's perhaps all too familiar *Barcelona Chair*, denizen of a million waiting rooms.

Two semicircular buildings cupped around Plaça d'Espanya mark the entrance to the 1929 International Exhibition, next to twin St Mark's campaniles standing there like souvenir salt and pepper shakers from Venice. Beyond the towers, pompous palaces line up for inspection, including the twin Baroque-Moderne **Palau de Victòria Eugènia** and **Palau d'Alfons XIII**, which were built according to Puig i Cadafalch's plans after he was dismissed from the project in 1923. Further up, one of the star attractions of 1929, the **Font Màgica**, still performs aquatic ballets of colour and light to the rhythms of Tchaikovsky and Abba, while blue searchlights radiate a peacock's tail of beams from the hilltop Palau Nacional in unforgettable cheesy splendour.

Font Màgica
www.bcn.es/fonts;
runs May–Sept
Thurs–Sun and eves
before hols,
shows every half-hour
9.30pm–11.30pm,
Oct–April Fri–Sat
7pm–8.30pm, shows
every half-hour, free

Museu Nacional d'Art de Catalunya (MNAC) and Around

Museu Nacional d'Art de Catalunya (MNAC)

A sun-baked never-ending stair and outdoor escalators ascend to the shamelessly bombastic **Palau Nacional**, which survived the Exhibition when it found a new role as Catalonia's chief art museum. Gae Aulenti's arrangement of the museum in 1992 was only slightly less controversial than her Musée d'Orsay in Paris: Barcelonins grumble that it doesn't respect the architecture of the Palau Nacional (as if it deserved any respect). But the contents have enough power to mesmerize away all misgivings.

✪ **Museu Nacional d'Art de Catalunya (MNAC)**
Mirador de Palau Nacional, t 93 622 03 76, www.mnac.es; Ⓜ Espanya; open Tues–Sat 10–7, Sun 10–2.30; closed Mon exc public hols; adm exp; free first Sun of month

Romanesque Art

The Romanesque gallery contains the world's foremost collection of Romanesque murals, rescued in the 1920s from deteriorating chapels in the Pyrenees – and also from the wealthy Americans who wanted to buy them. Barcelona's Ajuntament intervened, bought many and brought them here: Catalan art would remain in Catalonia, thank you very much. Above all, the murals demonstrate just how wealthy Catalonia was in the 11th and 12th century, when over 90 per cent of business was transacted in gold. The money attracted some of the top artists of the day, who translated Byzantine iconography and illuminated Catalan Bibles into strikingly bold, expressive figures, sharply outlined and filled in with flat rich reds, greens and golds. Even in the gloom of their original settings, in the flickering candlelight of almost windowless stone churches, these saints and martyrs would stand out, staring with their riveting dark eyes, red circled cheeks, stylized stringy hair and hands that look like flippers.

One of the first, from the 12th-century Sant Joan de Boí, shows jugglers along with the *Stoning of St Stephen*, in which the hand of God descends from heaven to zap sainthood on Stephen with a laser beam. The more graceful paintings of the Pedret circle are attributed to an itinerant painter from Lombardy, whose frescoes from the Mozarabic Sant Quirze de Pedret show a familiarity with the art of Ravenna, notably in the Byzantine dress of the *Seven Foolish Virgins*. On the other hand, the artist of the strange and childlike 11th-century *Sant Miquel de Marmellar* could hardly draw a face, although like the others he struggled to depict seraphim just as the Bible described them, with six wings and 1,000 eyes. In the apse of Sant Climent de Taüll (1123), the famous *Christ in Majesty* is one of the most commanding, direct images in medieval art. Painted by an artist with a precocious sense of foreshortening and expressive line, the powerful atmosphere of watchfulness is emphasized by angels and other wide-eyed figures. Santa María de Taüll, in which the Virgin holds pride of place, has a striking *Last Judgement* with nasty scenes of hell, peacocks and a wonderful surreal David beheading a Goliath with a sausage body.

Beyond are fine sculpted capitals, a room full of polychrome Virgins, and a harrowing *Deposition* from Santa María de Taüll, in which the Christ has moveable arms and dead, staring eyes. The *Majestat Batlló* portrays the crucified Christ, not in the exquisite agony but dressed like a king, open-eyed and serene, in the beautiful blue tunic of a sultan, symbolizing the triumph over death. At the end of the Romanesque section is the ceiling of the chapterhouse of Sigena in Aragon (1200), damaged by fire in 1936 but still beautiful, its Old and New Testament figures inspired by English miniatures and Norman Sicilian mosaics.

Gothic Art

Cross into the Gothic section and the atmosphere changes at once to the decorative, courtly and elegant style of chivalry, knights, ladies and dragons. Unlike the Romanesque, this is primarily urban art, commissioned during Barcelona's heyday, and appropriately enough begins with the 13th-century murals from the Palau Caldes (now the Museu Picasso) of Jaume I's *Siege of Mallorca*, with its curious Arabic motifs in the upper section. The Second Master of Bierges' vivid *Life of St Dominic* has a great scene of a young scholar falling about with his books. Where Romanesque Virgins stare, their gracious Gothic counterparts, in wood, stone, ivory and alabaster, smile and relax. Among the are best are those by Jaume Cascalls (active 1345–79).

One room has 14th-century Florentine and Sienese paintings that came to Catalonia by way of Avignon and influenced local painters, especially brothers Pere and Jaume Serra in the new International Gothic style, as in Lluís Borrassà's *Retable de Gaurdiola* (1404). Joan Antigó, his contemporary, was a master of tender expressions, as in the beautiful *Annunciating Angel*; less tender, the Mestre d'Ail's altarpiece of SS Catherine and Barbara shows Catherine stepping on the king as if he were a worm. The masterful *Virgin of the Councillors* (1445) is the only certain surviving painting by Lluís Dalmau, who went to Bruges and then painted this for the Ajuntament's chapel. Inspired by Van Eyck, Dalmau realistically depicts the five pious city councillors in an elaborate but naturalistic Gothic setting. Although the influential Bernat Martorell is represented only by his *Retable de St Vincenç*, his great follower Jaume Huguet fills up a big room on his own. Best of all is the central panel of his triptych of a very young and serious-looking *St George and the Princess*. By the mid-15th century, Flemish realism became the rage in Barcelona, visible in Bartolomé Bermejo's memorable *Resurrection from Limbo*.

Cambó Bequest and Thyssen-Bornemisza Collection

The museum runs out of Catalans at this point. The Renaissance and Baroque galleries are devoted to two spectacular bequests. The **Cambó collection** has superb paintings by the Master of Frankfurt, Pedro Berruguete; plus Giovanni de Ser Giovanni, Sebastiano del Piombo, Giandomenico Tiepolo, Goya (a lush and luminous *Amor and Psyche*), Velázquez, Zurbarán, Quentin Metsys, Quentin de la Tour and Lucas Cranach.

The **Thyssen-Bornemisza Collection** fills Gallery 48. Although Madrid received the bulk of the Baron's collection, his Catalan beauty-queen wife made sure that 72 of his paintings settled in Barcelona. These are works by Italian masters such as Lorenzo Daddi, Lorenzo Monaco and Fra Angelico, whose sublime, ephemeral *Madonna of Humility* steals the show. Other works are by Titian, Tintoretto, Veronese, Giambattista and Giandomenico Tiepolo, Guardi, Canaletto and an excellent portrait by Velázquez of Mariana de Austria with her Habsburg face.

Modern Art

'Modern art' in this case means Catalan art from 1850 to 1920 (the city's patricians never gave a fig for collecting paintings, so local talent is all there is). The earliest works are by Marià Fortuny (1838–74): his enormous *Battle of Tetuan* (1863) honours the 500 Catalan volunteers who fought under General Prim. There are street scenes by Ramon Martí i Alsina, and rural idylls by the Olot School, especially by Joaquim Vayreda (1843–94), and bright seascapes by Joan Roig i Solé and Arcadi Mas i Fontdevila.

Then come the Modernistas. Ramon Casas' famous *Tandem Bike Self-Portrait* painted for Els Quatre Gats is here, and his remarkable, almost photographic, *Corpus Christi Procession Leaving Santa Maria del Mar* (1898). Other works are by his friend Santiago Rusinyol, who liked to shock the bourgeoisie, but more in his life than his painting. The leading sculptors – Josep Llimona, Miquel Blay and Eusebi Arnau – are represented, although Arnau left his best works scampering on buildings. There's beautiful furniture designed Gaudí and Puig, and exquisite pieces by Gaspar Homar.

Later Modernistas are shown too: Isidre Nonell, Francesc Gimeno and Joaquim Mir (see his voluptuous stained-glass screen), followed by the more classical Noucentistas: Joaquim Sunyer, Joaquim Torres-Garcia and Josep Clarà. The whimsical Pau Gargallo is here, along with the iron art by Juli González and Salvador Dalí's famous *Portrait of his Father,* one of his few works in Barcelona.

The museum also has a superb collection of drawings, and photographs going back to the early 19th century, including scenes from the Civil War by Robert Capa and Agustí Centelles.

Around the Palau Nacional

A short walk west of the Palau Nacional lies the extensive **Jardí Botànic**, the **Mirador del Llobregat** (with Josep Llimona's statue of a St George) and another survivor of the 1929 fair, the **Poble Espanyol**. Conceived as an anthology of Spanish architecture, replicas of 117 buildings and streets across the country were cunningly arranged. In 1990, when the whole tourist schtick was nodding off in its polkadot flounces, it was head-butted awake by a pair of nightclubs, the Torres de Ávila and La Terrazza, both still there, along with the Tablao de Carmen flamenco show, restaurants; arts and crafts workshops, kids' activities, and the **Fundació de Arte Contemporáneo Fran Daurel**, housing works by Miró, Picasso, Dalí and others.

Montjuïc's other attractions lie east of the Palau Nacional. Just downhill, the **Museu Etnològic** has a fascinating collection, particularly from Latin America, featuring Amazonian shrunken heads, skeleton dolls from Mexico, and a Peruvian head-deformer.

Below this, steps lead down to the oldest gardens of Montjuïc: **La Rosaleda**, which contains the **Teatre Grec**, used for the summer theatre festival; and the pretty **Jardins Laribal** with the Font del Gat ('cat fountain') and charming café.

The **Museu d'Arqueologia de Catalunya** is across from the Greek theatre. There are copies of the Catalonia's Paleolithic cave paintings of hunting and battle scenes; Bronze Age jewellery, including a magnicent headband and bracelets of beaten gold; and primitive fertility sculpture and the beautiful Carthaginian *Dama de Ibiza*. The ancient Iberians check in with vases and votives and a

Jardí Botànic
C/Doctor Font i Quer,
t *93 426 49 35, www.
jardibotanic.bcn.cat;*
Ⓜ *Espanya, then bus;
open Nov–Jan daily 10–5;
Feb, Mar and Oct daily
10–6; April, May and Sept
daily 10–7; June–Aug
daily 10–8; adm, free Sun
3–closing time*

Poble Espanyol
*Avda Marquès de
Comillas,* **t** *93 508 63 30,
www.poble-
espanyol.com;*
Ⓜ *Espanyol, then bus;
open Mon 9–8,
Tues–Thurs 9–2, Fri 9–4,
Sat 9–5, Sun 9–9; adm
exp; joint ticket with
MNAC available*

Museu Etnològic
*Psg de Santa Madrona
16–22,* **t** *93 424 68 07,
www.museuetnologic.
bcn.cat;* Ⓜ *Espanya, then
bus; open Wed and
Fri–Sat 10–2, Tues and
Thurs 1–7, Sun 10–8; adm,
free Sun 3–8*

**Museu
d'Arqueologia de
Catalunya**
*Psg de Santa Madrona
39–41,* **t** *93 424 65 77,
www.mac.es;*
Ⓜ *Poble Sec; open
Tues–Sat 9.30–7, Sun
10–2.30; adm*

07 Barcelona | Montjuïc

skull with a huge nail driven into it (evidence of posthumous rites, says the reassuring explanation). There are fine mosaics and an ivory gladiator in a wacky mask, and a reproduction of a room in Pompeii, filled with fine glass. The Visigoths left mosaic belt buckles, gold crosses studded with gems and a curious crown.

The Anella Olímpica

Estadi Olímpic Lluís Companys
Avinguda de l'Estadi;
Ⓜ *Espanya, then bus*

The Anella Olímpica, or Olympic ring, holds the principal venues of the 1992 games, including the Olympic Stadium, now the **Estadi Olímpic Lluís Companys**, a relic of the 1929 fair. Barcelona had bid to host the 1936 games here, but lost out to Hitler's Berlin; in defiance it planned a 'People's Olympics', only the party was spoiled by another fascist named Franco, whose revolt began the Civil War the day before the games were to open. The interior was rebuilt for the 1992 games, while preserving the façade and bronzes by Pau Gargallo. Barcelona memorably beat Hollywood at its own game by igniting the Olympic cauldron with a flaming

Museu Olímpic
Avda de l'Estadi 60,
t 93 292 53 79, www.
museuolimpicbcn.com;
Ⓜ *Espanya, then bus;*
open Oct–Mar Tues–Sat
10–6, Sun 10–2.30;
April–Sept Mon-Fri
10–8, Sun 10–2.30; adm

arrow. The new multi-media **Museu Olímpic** is devoted to the history of sport.

The adjacent **Palau Sant Jordi**, by Japanese architect Arata Isozaki, was the architectural marvel of the 1992 games. The enormous space-frame roof seems to hover, undulating over the surrounding portico. The Barcelonins say it resembles a sleeping dragon.

Nearby, the elegant 394ft white needle-in-a-loop, death to any passing Zeppelin, is the **Torre de Telefònica** (1991), designed by Santiago Calatrava. The mast was aligned with the earth's axis so it can also be used as a sundial after the collapse of electronic civilization; the curving base clad in *trencadís* is a nod to Gaudí.

Fundació Joan Miró

Fundació Joan Miró
Avda de l'Estadi,
t 93 443 94 70, http://
fundaciomiro-bcn.org;
Ⓜ *Paral.lel then*
funicular; open
Oct–June Tues–Sat 10–7,
Thurs 10–9.30, Sun
10–2.30; July–Sept
Tues–Sat 10–8, Thurs
10–9.30, Sun 10–2.30;
adm exp

Miró (1893–1983) wanted his native Barcelona to have his own collection of art, and in 1972 asked his friend Josep Lluís Sert to design its home. The white building, bathed in natural light, is a bookend to Sert's earlier Maeght Foundation in St-Paul-de-Vence, and in 1986 it was enlarged in the same style by Sert's collaborator, Jaume Freixa, to contain the growing collection. The core, of course, is an excellent sampling of Miró's paintings, sculptures, textile works and drawings made between 1917 and the 1970s.

Miró's early pre-Paris paintings reveal a fascination with Cézanne and the Cubists: geometric landscapes, still lifes and portraits, which glow eerily in bright, mad colours. When he moved to Paris in 1919 he joined André Breton's Surrealist movement, only to go a step beyond the other Surrealists by evolving his own playful language to express the dream reality of the creative unconscious.

'Lovers are forms that struggle, that devour each other.'
Miró

Central to all art is the tension between abstraction and representation. Miró claimed that this duality came from the *seny i rauxa* (common sense/wisdom/practicality and uncontrolled passion, *see* pp.36–7) opposition at the heart of the Catalan identity, of which he was always intensely proud. The turning point from perceptual to conceptual came in the early 1920s when he painted a series of objects, as in *Still Life I* and *Still Life II*, in a single-minded search for the extraordinary in the commonplace. By 1930, he was, on Matisse's advice, experimenting with automatic painting, allowing his hand to guide him unconsciously, drawing great motifs in black paint and filling in the colour later.

Miró was invited to contribute a painting to the Spanish Pavilion in the 1937 World's Fair in Paris, along with Picasso's *Guernica* and Alexander Calder's *Mercury Fountain*. Miró's passionate *The Reaper (Catalan Peasant in Revolt)* disappeared almost immediately after the exhibition, but Calder's lissom sculpture-fountain, dedicated to the mercury-mining towns of Almadén, has been remounted here. The red circle spiralling slowly above the fountain could have been lifted from Miró's own peculiar sign language, honed throughout his life; the circle, for example, repeatedly appears with a tall, inclined crescent shape, clearly phallic, which represented what Miró described as *'le bonheur conjugal'*. Another favourite in his vocabulary is the asterisk, recalling the merrily perverse and pervasive Catalan fascination with arseholes, either of *caganers* (*see* pp.35–6) or Barça fans, the *culés*.

Most of the works here are from Miro's final two decades. Among the most startling is the brilliant white *Solarbird* (1968), a sensuous, undulating sculpture in flight against a deep blue wall, and the funniest is the bronze *Ladder of the Evading Eye* (1971), with a staring eyeball poised at the top of a wobbling ladder. Some of his mature works are marked by a desire to isolate the language of signs and refine the colours in order to create a state of mind which would 'go beyond painting'; one of the loveliest is *The Day* (1974), a dark, inky swoop culminating in a vermilion circle. There's also a permanent collection of works made by artists honouring Miró, including Chillida's luminous *Homage to Miró* (1985).

The gardens east of the Fundació Miró, the **Jardins Mossèn Jacint Verdaguer**, are especially pretty in spring, when water trickles lazily down the stepped terraces and the flowers burst into colour. Here too is the **Jardin Joan Brossa** with musical activities for pipsqueaks.

Jardins Mossèn Jacint Verdaguer
Avda de Miramar
Ⓜ *Paral.lel then funicular; open 10am–dusk; adm free*

Castell de Montjuïc
Parc de Montjuic, t 93 329 86 13, www.bcn.cat/castelldemontjuic; funicular from Ⓜ *Paral.lel to Montjuic, then cablecar; open Tues–Sun 10–8; free*

Castell de Montjuïc

For centuries, fires would burn on the brow of Montjuïc to guide Barcelona's fishing fleet home. In 1640, during the Reapers' War, the old beacon tower was hurriedly converted into a castle in 30 days as the army of Felipe IV approached, before Barcelona was starved into submission. The rest of the castle's history is just as unhappy. After the siege of Barcelona in 1714, Bourbon troops blew up the old castle, and in 1759 rebuilt it with another that would specialize in torturing political prisoners. In 1896, after the Corpus Christi bombing, Anarchists, and anyone in Barcelona who looked like one, were herded up here to be tortured. In 1909, the Anarchist founder of Barcelona's secular Modern Schools, Francesc Ferrer, was executed here after a sham trial following the Setmana Trágica, raising a storm of protest throughout Europe. The castle functioned as a military prison until 1960. Work has begun on its transformation into a Peace Centre, which may put its demons to rest.

Next to the castle, the **Fossar de la Pedrera** is the old stone quarry where Republicans were shot and buried in a communal grave after the Civil War, marked by a memorial of 1985 and stone columns listing the known dead (an estimated 10,000 Republicans were executed in Barcelona in the first month, and 20,000 over the next two decades). One was the Catalan president Lluís Companys, who was captured by the Gestapo in Belgium in October 1940 and handed over to Franco, who had him taken here and shot. Companys' last request was to take off his shoes so that he could feel his homeland under his feet as he died.

Around the Edge of Barcelona

On the map, the ragged edges of the Eixample's grid mark its contact with older, once independent towns such as Gràcia. The Collserola foothills to the north, the Zona Alta, once held the summer retreats of the noble and rich, but the trams attracted moneyed Barcelona in the early 20th century, leaving some fine works by Gaudí, especially the sublime Park Güell. And above the rich suburbs rises the city's mountain girdle, with fun Tibidabo and the utterly delightful Collserola Park, with views down on the city that bring home Barcelona's uniquely privileged position.

Gràcia

Gràcia was a vortex for 19th-century liberals: Anarchists, feminists, vegetarians, Protestants and Republicans flourished here, formed movements, and published progressive periodicals, including one in Esperanto. In 1898 the town was annexed to Barcelona, not altogether willingly, and in the 1960s it once again became a centre of alternative left-wing ideas (as much as such things were allowed under Franco). Today Gràcia's laid-back narrow streets wander between compact squares, offering a nice contrast to the Barcelona of big art and monuments.

Gràcia begins just north of the Dia[...]
the street narrows when it meets th[...]
(1908–11), the last residential projec[...]
A right turn on to C/Goya will take [...]
Gràcia, **Plaça Rius i Taulet,** named a[...]
mayor of 1888 and dominated by t[...]
square is flanked by Gràcia's town[...]
lamps and the town's coat of arm[...]
Berenguer. At the end of C/Siracu[...]
1993 with a record-shaped plaque inscribed 'Give peace [...]

Toto, I don't
think we're
Kanso[...]

132

07

Barcelona | Around the Edge of Barcelona

Plaça del Sol is the centre of Gràcia's nightlife, despite being soullessly revamped in 1987. It is surrounded with lively bars, restaurants and cafés, with chairs and tables spilling into the square on warm summer nights. Berenguer was responsible for many of the homes around here, including the **Casa Rubina** on C/de l'Or 44, embellished with shimmering mosaics and brickwork.

Gaudí's first house, **Casa Vicens** at C/Carolines 18–24 (1883–5), was one of the first colourful buildings in Barcelona, covered with brickwork and chequerboard patterns of green and white tiles. (Senyor Vicens was a tile merchant, but even so the price of the house nearly bankrupted him.) The interior is inaccessible, although the elegant circular glass smoking room with its Moorish ceiling can be obliquely admired from outside.

The **Rambla del Prat** is Gràcia's showcase for Modernista architecture, where buildings retain fanciful façades, painted ceilings, wood-panelled staircases and elaborate ironwork. The oldest part of Gràcia is sandwiched between C/Gran de Gracia and Vía Augusta, with the lively **Mercat de la Llibertat** (1893) at the centre, capped with a wrought-iron roof.

Park Güell and Around

🌟 **Park Güell**
t 93 213 04 00
Ⓜ *Lesseps, then 10-min walk; or bus no.24 from Plaça Catalunya to the main gate; open Nov–Feb daily 10–6; Mar and Oct daily 10–7; April and Sept daily 10–8; May–Aug daily 10–9*

Perhaps the 20th century's greatest evocation of the infinite variety and magic of life, Gaudí's masterpiece occupies one of Barcelona's great balconies, 'Bald Mountain', Mont Pelat. The park, at once Surrealist – it was a major source of inspiration for Miró and Dalí – and abstract *avant la lettre*, owes its existence to Eusebi Güell, who bought two farms here in 1902 to lay out an exclusive English garden suburb (hence the English 'K' in Park).

To attract buyers Güell gave his pet architect free rein to design amenities: a grand entrance, a pair of lodges, a central market area and terraced drives. As a housing development it was a complete flop, but Güell was too rich to care. After his death in 1918, his family donated the park to the city. In 1984 Park Güell was listed as a World Heritage Site.

in
s any
more.

Dorothy in
The Wizard of Oz

In the midst of the bland, not-so-hoity-toity housing that actually was built on Bald Mountain, the Park Güell glows like a mirage. As in most of Gaudí's work, there are layers of symbolism in every aspect of the park. There's the usual Catalanism, but also, according to the Gaudí scholar Josep M. Carandell, much more: Masonry, Rosicrucianism, alchemy and all the garam masala of mysteries that fascinated the *fin de siècle* élite.

On either side of the gate are two pavilions as bright as candy, possibly inspired by a staging in 1900 of Engelbert Humperdinck's opera *Hansel and Gretel*. Both are crowned by superb sloping roofs of swirling coloured mosaics, cupolas, mushroom forms (a magic *Amanita muscaria* on the wicked witch's house) and Gaudí's signature steeple with its double cross. The porter's lodge (to the right of the entrance) is now the **Centre d'Interpretació i Acollida del Park Güell** with Gaudí-related exhibitions.

Centre d'Interpretació i Acollida del Park Güell
t 93 285 68 99;
open daily 11–3; adm

The grand stair swoops around the most jovial salamander imaginable, clinging to the fountain and covered with brightly coloured *trencadís* that symbolize fire. Above the salamander is a tripod with a stone representing the *omphalos*, navel of the universe: a reference to Delphi as the seat of wisdom. The bench above is shaped like a Greek tragic mask.

The remarkable, cavernous **Sala Hipóstila** was planned by Gaudí as a covered market. Known as the **Hall of a Hundred Columns** (actually, there are only 86 – a number that recurs in other measurements in the park), its Doric columns in their thick forest are cleverly hollow inside, allowing rainwater to run down into a vast cistern below, designed to store water for emergencies or irrigation. The shallow vaults of the ceiling look as if they were soft as marshmallow, covered with white *trencadís* and beautiful *plafonds*, representing four large suns (the four seasons), the phases of the moon and spiralling shapes, designed by Gaudí and brilliantly executed by Josep Maria Jujol.

The scalloped roof of the hall is rimmed with a snaking ceramic collage that also serves as the back of the **serpentine bench**. It is a masterpiece of three-dimensional art, a Surrealist, Cubist collage that predates Surrealism, Cubism and collages. To form the mould of the seat, Gaudí got a naked man to sit in wet plaster, while the *trencadí* design was the work of Jujol, who was so inspired that he broke up his own cupid-painted dinnerware for the project. The bench's seemingly random patterns of colour, and simple and abstract designs, offer new delights with each turn; the restorers discovered with some consternation that they had to match 21 different tones of off-white. Among the figures are crabs and symbols of the zodiac, and Catalan or Latin graffiti, inscribed in the clay and so well hidden that the words weren't discovered until the 1950s. No one knows what's going on here; some believe the words form a mystic dialogue, perhaps with the Virgin Mary, who trampled the serpent, symbolized by the bench.

Then there are Gaudí's extraordinary **porticoes and viaducts**, 3km of them, sloping in and out of the hillside. All are made of stone found on the site and fitted together to form magical, sinuous passageways with walls like curling waves and fanciful stone tree-planters with aloes growing on top. They drove Dalí crazy. None of the viaducts are alike; one has a column that resembles Carmen Miranda holding a pile of rocks on her head, called *La Bugadera* – but Carandell suspects she is really 'Sister Mason'. There is more weirdness off the path leading to the nub of the hill: a six-lobed, truncated stone tower called **the Chapel**, shaped like a Rosicrucian rose, but hermetically sealed. There are three stone crosses on the chapel, esoterically pointed on top like arrows; look towards the east and the three merge to form a single arrow.

Gaudí, a confirmed bachelor, lived for 20 years with his father and niece in the Torre Rosa. It's a rosy-pink cottage with a morel-shaped chimney covered with *trencadís* and a garden filled with flowers wrought from bits of cast-off fencing. Now the **Casa-Museu Gaudí**, it contains plans and examples of the beautiful organic furniture that Gaudí designed. Upstairs is Gaudí's simple bedroom, with a narrow bed and a framed copy of his prayer book and death mask.

Casa-Museu Gaudí
t 93 219 38 11, www. casamuseugaudi.org; open April–Sept daily 10–8; Oct–Mar daily 10–6; adm

Around the Park Güell

Up from the Park Güell, the **Parc de la Creuta del Coll** was created in 1981–7 from an abandoned quarry, with a popular palm-rimmed swimming lake with an island and beach. The de rigueur public art is here as well: a piece by Ellsworth Kelly, and Eduardo Chillida's giant gentle claw, the *Elogi de l'Aigua* ('water eulogy').

Parc de la Creuta del Coll
Mare de Déu del Coll, bus no.25, 28, 87; ⓜ *Penitents; open daily 10am–dusk; adm free*

When Barcelona boomed in the 1960s, it was at the expense of the old estates in the Collserola foothills. The **Parc del Laberint d'Horta** fortunately escaped the bulldozers. Originally occupying 133 acres (now reduced to 17), this beautiful, atmospheric park was the brainchild of the Marques de Alfarràs, a son of the Enlightenment. He designed the master plan in 1791 on the theme of Love and Disappointment and hired Italian architect Domenico Bagutti to lay out the gardens, lake, waterfalls, pavilions, statuary and a not-so-easy cypress **maze**, its centre marked by a statue of Eros. His descendants added a romantic garden and, in 1967, sold the park to the city.

Parc del Laberint d'Horta
Passeig del Vall de Hebrón, entrance by a footbridge near the Velódrom; ⓜ *Mundet; open May–Aug daily 10–9; April and Oct daily 10–8; Mar, Nov and Dec daily 10–7; Jan–Feb daily 10–6; adm*

Tibidabo

Towering just west of the city, Mount Tibidabo's name, peculiar even by Catalan standards, comes from St Matthew, who quotes Satan trying to tempt Christ while he fasted in the desert: '*Haec omnia tibi dabo si cadens adoraberis me'* ('All this I will give to you if you will fall down and worship me'). Purists might claim the incident took place in the Sinai, but a Catalan would counter, 'Just what's so tempting about a rocky desert?' Whereas the view from 1,804ft Tibidabo, encompassing all Barcelona, Montserrat, the Pyrenees and even Mallorca, is a pretty seductive offer.

The FGC Avinguda del Tibidabo will get you as far as Plaça de John F. Kennedy; the landmark here is the brightly coloured, dainty mosaic filigree Modernista tower and cupola of **La Rotonda** (1918), designed by Adolf Ruiz i Casamitjana. From here the **Tramvia Blau** ascends Avinguda Tibidabo to link up with the funicular. It passes, on the left at No.31, the **Casa Roviralta** (1913), by Joan Rubió i Bellvé, a striking mudéjar fantasy with white stucco and elaborate, corbelled, angular brickwork; the lavish interior is the Asador de Aranda restaurant, where Madonna was once famously entertained by a male stripper. Just up at No.56 is Rubió's **Casa Casacuberta** (1907), now a school.

If you have the kids in tow, you may want to get off the tram halfway up the Avinguda del Tibidabo to visit the **CosmoCaixa (Museu de la Ciència)**. The older building was designed as an asylum by Josep Domènech i Estapà in 1894, while the brand new one next to it houses enough hands-on science exhibits to keep most children entertained for at least a couple of hours.

The **Funicular del Tibidabo** (Plaça Dr Andreu, every 30mins when the Parc d'Atraccions, *see* below, is open) creaks up to the summit and its crowning glory – the huge, spiky, expiatory temple of **Sagrat Cor** built in atonement for the Setmana Trágica of 1909. A lift sweeps you up to the roof for staggering views.

Stop for a cocktail at one of the panoramic bars, best in the late afternoon on a clear day, as the lights begin to twinkle in the great city below. Tibidabo's **Parc d'Atraccions** is the oldest funfair in Spain and is still going strong, offering all the usual thrills – a wicked House of Horrors, funhouse mirrors, a harrowing aeroplane ride and one of the most panoramic Ferris-wheel rides imaginable.

A 10-minute walk south of the Parc d'Atraccions rises Norman Foster's slender and dynamic 800ft **Torre de Collserola**, a high-tech telecommunications tower built for the Olympics, 'pure sculpture', as Sir Norman himself describes it. A glass lift shoots up to the 10th-floor observation deck for giddily vertiginous views.

CosmoCaixa
*C/Teodor Roviralta 47,
t 93 212 60 50, http://
obrasocial.lacaixa.es;
bus 17, 22, 58, 73, 75, 60
and 196, or the Tramvia
Blau from FGC
Avinguda del Tibidabo;
open Tues–Sun
10–8; adm*

Parc d'Attraccions
*t 93 211 79 42, www.
tibidabo.es; open July
and Aug daily;
Sept–June weekend
afternoons only; adm*

Torre de Collserola
*t 93 211 79 42 , www.
torredecollserola.com;
open same hours as
Parc d'Attraccions*

Around Collserola

Barcelonins have been playing country squire at the foot of Collserola at least since 1400, when King Martí the Humane built a summer residence at Bellesguard. Five hundred years later, Gaudí

Torre Belleguard
C/Bellesguard 46;
best to take a taxi

was commissioned to build the **Torre Bellesguard** by its ruins (visible only from the exterior). Gaudí created a tall, neo-Gothic castle (1905), with his trademark four-armed cross at the top of the pinnacle.

It is hard to believe that bold, brassy Tibidabo forms part of one of the loveliest urban parks in Europe: made up over 16,000 acres of undulating forests, **Collserola Park**, dotted with fountains, forgotten villages, churches and old farmhouses, all seemingly a world away from the city at their feet. From the FGC Baixador de Vallvidrera you can take the funicular up to the pretty hilltop and very wealthy village of **Vallvidrera**, with lovely views over the big city. Alternatively, walk 15 minutes up to the **Park information centre**, and the nearby **Museu-Casa Verdaguer** in the charming, 18th-century Vil.la Joana, an old honey-coloured farmhouse covered with twisting wisteria. This was the home of the Miralles family, who invited the impoverished tuberculosis-stricken poet-priest Jacint Verdaguer (*see* p.223), author of the great Catalan epic poems *L'Atlàntida* (1876) and *Canigó* (1886), to spend his last weeks in the fresh air.

**Collserola Park
information
centre**
Ctra de l'Església 32,
t 93 280 35 52,
www.parccollserola.net

**Museu-Casa
Verdaguer**
t 93 204 78 05
open weekends and
hols 10–2; adm free

Sarrià and the Palau Reial de Pedralbes

Sarrià, the last independent township to be annexed to Barcelona, is slightly schizophrenic: the new part is full of smart homes, but old Sarrià hasn't changed much at all. The main street, **C/Major de Sarrià**, strings along small squares with a lazy, village atmosphere. A church has stood on **Plaça Sarrià** for more than a millennium, although the present **Sant Vicenç** dates only from the early 20th century. Just off the square is a lively, red-brick Modernista **market** (1911). Farther up, **Plaça Sant Vicenç** is surrounded by a higgledy-piggledy collection of narrow, arcaded houses, all painted different colours. Gaudíphiles won't want to miss his **Col.legi de les Teresianes** (1890), a private school built by Gaudí in 1890. Although constrained by finances, he endowed the building with elaborate wrought-iron details and defined the corners with his favourite cross-crowned steeples.

**Col.legi de les
Teresianes**
off the Via Augusta at
C/Ganduxer 85–105,
FGC Les Tres Torres;
open Sept–June Sat 11–1
by appointment only,
t 93 212 33 54

Palau Reial de Pedralbes

**Palau Reial de
Pedralbes**
Avinguda Diagonal
686; **Ⓜ** *Palau Reial*

On the south end of Sarrià, the Palau Reial de Pedralbes was a rather nice present to Alfonso XIII from Eusebi Güell's heirs to thank him for making dad a count. It became headquarters of the Republican government at the end of the Civil War; from here President Azaña and La Pasionaria joined the rest of Barcelona on 29 October 1938, tearfully cheering as the last 12,673 members of the International Brigades marched down the Diagonal towards

France and away from a hopeless cause. Franco made the palace his residence in Barcelona, and King Juan Carlos' daughter, Christina, held her wedding banquet here in 1997. One wing is filled with the **Museu de Ceràmica** with items garnered from famous ceramic centres of the Crown of Aragon – Paterna, Teruel, Manises, Barcelona – as well as from 13th-century Arab-Catalan Mallorca. The upper floor is devoted to a mixed bag of modern and contemporary ceramics, including some by Picasso and Miró.

Museu de Ceràmica / Museu de les Arts Decoratives
t 93 256 34 65, www.dhub-bcn.cat; open Tues–Sat 10–6, Sun 10–6; adm, free Sun 3–6

In the opposite wing, the **Museu de les Arts Decoratives** is set in galleries overlooking an enormous throne room and filled with tapestries, furniture and handicrafts from the Middle Ages to the present. It currently includes a fashion museum, the **Museu Tèxtil i d'Indumentària**, and the **Gabinet de les Arts Gràfiques**; in 2011, everything in this wing is slated to move into the new Disseny Hub Barcelona (DHuB) in the Plaça de les Glòries (*see* p.120).

Leafy trees shade the palace's **park**, a delicious retreat dotted with lily ponds and secret bowers laid out in 1925 by Nicolas Rubió i Tuduri. Tucked away in a tiny bamboo forest is a fountain by Gaudí, only discovered in 1983 under the ivy, in the shape of a dragon spewing water from curling jaws.

Just behind the park is a fence and gate guarded by one of Gaudí's first and most formidable ironworks, the **Pedralbes Dragon** (1884). Spanning 18ft, the dragon whips its scaly tail and roars, baring long, pointy teeth. It also incidentally guarded Eusebi Güell's own orange grove and country house, to which Gaudí contributed the exotic, Hindu-inspired, corbel-roofed gatehouse and stable now known as the **Pabellones Finca Güell** (1884–7), which were also the first to be decorated with his signature *trencadís* and Greek cross.

Pabellones Finca Güell
Avinguda Pedralbes 7, t 93 204 52 50 open Fri–Mon 10–2

Monestir de Pedralbes

Monestir de Pedralbes
Baixada del Monestir, t 93 203 92 82; www.museuhistoria. bcn.es; bus no.22 from Plaça Catalunya or FGC Reina Elisenda, then 15min walk; open Tues–Sat and hols 10–2, Sun 10–8; adm, free Sun 3–8

At the top of the Avinguda de Pedralbes, a cobbled lane leads up to the handsome Gothic Monestir de Pedralbes founded for noble ladies by Queen Elisenda, the fourth wife of Jaume II, in 1326. It is a rare time capsule of Catalan Gothic, built quickly and scarcely altered since.

The three-storey cloister with its delicate columns, garden and fountains is serene and lovely, surrounded by the Poor Clares' tiny prayer cells. The small, irregular **Capella de Sant Miquel** houses perhaps the finest Gothic fresco cycle in Catalonia, Ferrer Bassa's *Seven Joys of the Virgin* and the *Passion*, painted in 1346, two years before the Black Death killed the painter and a third of the population of Barcelona. The single-naved church contains stained glass by Mestre Gil and the lovely alabaster tomb of Queen Elisenda, sculpted in 1364 and before her death – she wasn't taking any chances on getting a good likeness.

Eleven Men with One Ball Between Them

Barça...mes que un club ('Barça...more than just a club').

First there were a few bored Englishmen getting up a game on turnip fields outside town. Then they formed clubs, as expats do: the Hispania Football Club and the Barcelona Football Club, or Barça. The Barcelonins were intrigued and began to play too, encouraged by the news from the city's hygienists that football was good therapy for the ills caused by the industrial revolution. Hispania (now Espanyol) was supported mainly by pro-Hispanic residents of Barcelona (nicknamed the *periquitos*), but Barça became linked with Catalan nationalism. Immigrants were fairly impervious to the choral societies and the Renaixença of Catalan verse, but most of them adored football, and Barça became the prime vehicle for them to identify with the Catalan cause.

Politics, as usual, was never far away, and in times of trouble matches turned into mass political rallies. In 1936 the president of the club had the misfortune to be in Castile, where he was caught and executed by Franco. When Barcelona was occupied in 1939, Franco ordered that the club be purged – saying it had been infiltrated by the Communists, Anarchists and Catalan Nationalists. Yet, in spite of a Spanish Football Federation run by Falangists, Barça won five cups in the early 1950s. They offered the best alternative to the invincible machine of Real Madrid, a club pumped full of money by the old dictator until it became the best in the world. Supporting Barça became an act of protest against the regime. It was the 'unarmed army' of the Catalans, forbidden even to speak their own language, and one of the few outlets available to express national unity.

Camp Nou and Barça

Museu del Futbol Club Barcelona
Camp Nou, entrance gate 9; t 93 496 36 00, www.fcbarcelona.cat; Collblanc; open Nov–Mar Tues–Sat 10–6.30, Sun and hols 10–2.30; April–Oct Tues–Sat 10–6.30, Sun and hols 10–2.30; closed on days of League and Champion's League matches; adm exp; guided tours of Camp Nou

Barça of course means FC Barcelona, the city's beloved football club, magnificently headquartered in Europe's largest stadium (seating 98,000) at Camp Nou, south of the Diagonal and the Zona Universitaria. Built in 1957, the money was raised by fans paying their fees up to five years in advance – a first act of architectural self-affirmation of Catalan will after the Civil War. The **Museu del Futbol Club Barcelona** is as popular as the Museu Picasso, and yet, despite the crowds, it maintains a reverent silence, akin to that in any great cathedral. Today Barça has more members than any club in the world; even Pope John Paul II, visiting in 1982, accepted membership. Queues form for the obligatory photograph with the big prizes, including the 2009 Champion's League cup.

Information and Services in Barcelona

Main Post Office
Plaça d'Antonio López, at the bottom of the Via Laietana, t 93 318 35 07. Open Mon–Sat 8am–8pm.

Medical Emergencies
Go to the nearest *hospital de la seguretat social* which have 24-hour casualty (*urgències*) departments. *See* also p.60.

Hospital Clínic, C/Villarroel 170; Hospital Clínic.

Santa Creu i Sant Pau, Avda Sant Antoni María Claret 167; Hospital de Sant Pau.

Farmàcia Clapés, La Rambla 98, t 93 301 28 43. A 24-hour pharmacy.

Lost Property Office
Ajuntament, Plaça Pi y Sunyer, t 010; Liceu. Open Mon–Fri 9–2.

Police
Barcelona has more than its share of pickpockets. If you've been robbed,

go straight to the nearest *Comisaria*. The most convenient for tourists is near La Rambla at C/Nou de la Rambla 62.

Discount Tickets

Barcelona Card: Valid for 2–5 days, this offers discounts at many major attractions, restaurants and concerts and includes unlimited use of the metro and bus. Available from tourist offices, or at *www.barcelonacard.com*.

Articketbcn (€20). A single ticket giving admission to the CCCB, MACBA, MNAC, La Pedrera, Fundació Antoni Tàpies, Fundació Joan Miró and Museu Picasso. For further information, see *www.articketbcn.org*.

Ruta del Modernisme: A self-guided tour of the Modernista highlights of Barcelona. Discount vouchers, a map and guide to the 115 finest Modernista works in Barcelona and in other *comunes* in Catalonia for €18. Available from the Centre del Modernisme booth in the main tourist office at Plaça Catalunya, and at two more Modernisme centres: Hospital de Santa Creu i Sant Pau, at C/Sant Antoni Maria Claret 167; and Güell Pavilions, Avda Pedralbes 7. Call **t** 93 317 76 52, or see *www.rutadelmodernisme.com*.

Shopping in Barcelona

Barcelona claims to have the highest ratio of shops to residents in Europe. The main central shopping areas are the **Barri Gòtic** and the **Raval** for trendy streetwear, secondhand clothes, interesting junk and antiques; and the centre of the **Eixample** (Rambla de Catalunya, Passeig de Gràcia and Avinguda Diagonal) for good-quality clothes and jewellery.

Most of the popular chains can be found along the Carrer Portaferissa and the Avinguda del Portal de l'Àngel (in the Barri Gòtic) and the Passeig de Gràcia. The Eixample is best for slick interior design shops. Serious shoppers hit Barcelona in January and July, when everything's on sale.

Design and Household Goods

Vinçon, Passeig de Gràcia 96, **t** 93 215 60 50; **M** Diagonal. Celebrated design emporium right next to La Pedrera.

(i) **Barcelona** >
Plaça Catalunya
(underground on the Corte Inglés side); open daily 9am–9pm; **t** 807 117 222, from anywhere in Spain; **t** + 34 932 853 834, from outside Spain

Ajuntament
Plaça de Sant Jaume; open Mon–Fri 9–9, Sat 10–8, Sun and hols 10–2

Airport, Terminal B, **t** 93 298 38 38; open daily 9–9

Palau Robert
Pg de Gràcia 107, **t** 932 38 80 91, www.gencat.es/probert; open Mon–Fri 10–7, Sat 10–2.30; for information on all of Catalonia

(★)Vila Viniteca >>

L'Appartement, C/Enric Granados 44, **t** 93 452 29 04, *www.lappartement.es*; **M** Diagonal. Quirky knick-knacks.

Fashion

Como Agua de Mayo, C/Argenteria 249, **t** 93 310 64 41; **M** Jaume I. Floaty dresses, and gorgeous shoes.

Mies & Felj, C/Riera Baixa 5, **t** 93 442 07 55; **M** Liceu. One of several vintage stores on this cool street.

Zara, Passeig de Gràcia 16, **t** 93 318 76 75; **M** Passeig de Gràcia. Affordable, trendy fashions for men, women and kids as well as a fabulous homeware section (Zara Home).

One-stop Shopping

El Corte Inglés, Plaça de Catalunya; **M** Catalunya. A huge department store with a good supermarket.

Maremagnum, Port Vell; **M** Drassanes. Mall with everything from fashion chain shops to some new intriguing boutiques. *Open every day of the year.*

Souvenirs and Gifts

Almacenes del Pilar, C/Boquería 43, **t** 93 317 79 84; **M** Liceu. Spanish costumes and flamenco outfits.

Fet Amb Love, Passeig del Born 2, **t** 93 319 66 42; **M** Jaume I. Scarves, bags and jewellery by local designers.

La Manual Alpargatera, C/Avinyó 7, **t** 93 301 01 72; **M** Jaume I. Traditional Catalan rope-soled shoes (espadrilles) sold here since the 1940s.

Wine and Gastronomy

Formatgería La Seu, C/ Dagueria 16 **t** 93 412 65 48; **M** Jaume I. Fine Spanish cheeses and a tasting room.

Vila Viniteca, C/Agullers 7–9, **t** 93 268 32 27; **M** Jaume I. Superb range of Catalan and Spanish wines, with a gourmet grocery section next door.

Xocoa, C/Petritxol 11–13, **t** 93 301 11 97; **M** Jaume I. For wonderful chocolates packaged in slick Barcelona style.

Where to Stay in Barcelona

Barcelona ✉ 08000

There are good places to stay all over the city, with cheaper choices clustered in and around the Barri

Gòtic and the Raval. Wherever you stay, it's essential to book in advance.

Luxury

*****Casa Fuster, Passeig de Gràcia 132, **t** 93 255 30 00, *www.hotelcasa fuster.com*; Ⓜ Diagonal. A landmark Modernista building by Domenech i Montaner, meticulously restored to become of the city's most opulent hotels, complete with a panoramic roof terrace with pool.

*****Claris, C/Pau Claris 150, **t** 93 487 62 62, *www.derbyhotels.com*; Ⓜ Urquinaona. Gives luxury a twist, blending refined modern design with a connoisseur's collection of Egyptian and Roman art. Courtesy Smart cars.

⭐ **Hotel Arts Barcelona >**

*****Hotel Arts Barcelona, C/Marina 19–21, **t** 93 221 10 00, *www.ritzcarlton. com*; Ⓜ Ciutadella-Vila Olímpica. Occupies one of the two Olympic towers of the Port Olímpic, and in a class by itself, offering stunning views of the sea and city and with a fantastic seaside pool. Superb dining and stunning spa.

*****Hotel Palace, Gran Via de les Corts Catalanes 668, **t** 93 510 11 30, *www.hotelpalacebarcelona.com*; Ⓜ Passeig de Gràcia. Formerly known as the Ritz, this remains Barcelona's classic grand hotel, as it has been since 1919; undergoing a €20 million restoration at the time of writing.

****1898, La Rambla 109, **t** 93 552 95 52, *www.hotel1898.com*; Ⓜ Liceu. The former Philippines Tobacco Company is now a designer hotel with lovingly preserved details, and a plush spa.

⭐ **Market Hotel >>**

Very Expensive

****Hotel Omm, Rosselló 265, **t** 93 454 00 00, *www.hotelomm.es*; Ⓜ Diagonal. A sleek über-cool hotel that has become a fave of the fashion pack. Open-air pool with views of La Pedrera's chimneys. Very fashionable Michelin-starred Moo restaurant, too.

****Majestic, Passeig de Gràcia 68, **t** 93 488 17 17, *www.hotelmajestic.es*; Ⓜ Passeig de Gràcia. A classic grand hotel with a pool, parking and outstanding dining. The sister hotel, **Hotel Murmuri**, is new and stylish.

****Neri, 5 C/Sant Sever, **t** 93 304 06 55, *www.hotelneri.com*; Ⓜ Jaume I. The loveliest hotel in the Gothic quarter, in

a beautifully restored palace. It has stylish co décor and an enchanting .

Expensive

****Colón, Avda de la Catedral 7, **t** 93 301 14 04, *www.hotelcolon.es*; Ⓜ Jaume I. A classic hotel in the Barri Gòtic, in a historic building with fine views of the cathedral. Parking.

***Chic & Basic Born, C/Pricesa 50, **t** 93 295 46 52, *www.chicandbasic.com*; Ⓜ Jaume I. Bright white ultra-modern hotel in a mansion with high ceilings. In the ultra-hip Born neighbourhood.

***Gaudí, C/Nou de la Rambla 12, **t** 93 317 90 32, *www.hotelgaudi.es*; Ⓜ Liceu. The newly renovated rooms are modern rather than Modernista, but there are views of the great roof of the Palau Güell (*see* pp.107–108).

Hotel 54, Passeig Joan de Borbó 54, **t** 93 225 00 54, *www.hotel54 barceloneta.com*; Ⓜ Barceloneta. A stylish, affordable place to stay by the sea, with a panoramic roof terrace.

Hostal L'Antic Espai, Gran Via 660, **t** 93 304 19 45, *www.anticespai.com*; Ⓜ Passeig de Gràcia. If you've had enough of minimalism, this delightful retreat, replete with chandeliers and antique furniture, will fit the bill.

***Jazz, C/Pelai, **t** 93 552 96 96, *www.hoteljazz.com*; Ⓜ Catalunya. Just off the Plaça de Catalunya, a sleek, ultra-modern hotel with striking black-and-white décor. Facilities include a small rooftop pool.

** Market Hotel, Passatge Sant Antoni Abad 10 (off C/Comte Borrell 68), **t** 93 325 12 05, *www.markethotel.com.es*; Ⓜ Sant Antoni. Smart little boutique hotel, close to the Modernista Sant Antoni market, in an authentic traditional neighbourhood.

Mesón Castilla, C/de Valldonzelia 5, **t 93 318 21 82, *www.mesoncastilla.com*; Ⓜ Universitat. This is tucked down a quiet side street near the Museu d'Art Contemporani. It has a delightful interior garden, and spacious, air-conditioned bedrooms furnished with antiques; parking garage.

***Nouvel Hotel, C/Santa Anna 20, **t** 93 301 82 74, *www.hotelnouvel.com*; Ⓜ Catalunya. Handy for shopping and the Rambla, in a sympathetically renovated Modernista building.

18th-century
...temporary
...oof terrace.

...riente, La Rambla 45, **t** 93 302 25
...*www.husa.es/hoteloriente*; ⓜ Liceu.
...ly refurbished, luminous rooms
...ped with wi-fi in one of the
...s oldest buildings, from 1670. A
...monastery, the cloister now
...ves as the hotel ballroom.

...ente, Rambla de Catalunya 76,
..., 59 89, *www.hcchotels.es*;
ⓜ Passeig de Gràcia. Behind a
Modernista façade, this has an air
of stolid stateliness and lots of oak
and gilt. Small, rooftop pool.

****Montecarlo**, La Rambla 124,
t 93 412 04 04, *www.montecarlobcn.
com*; ⓜ Catalunya. Plush lobby, full
of gilt and marble, and modern,
comfortable rooms. Well located right
on La Rambla, and usually well priced.

Moderate

⭐ **Banys Orientals >**

***Banys Orientals**, 37 C/Argentería,
t 93 269 84 90, *www.hotelbanys
orientals.com*; ⓜ Jaume I. Lovely
boutique-style hotel in the
fashionable Born, with small but
pretty rooms. Larger suites available in
a nearby building.

***Gran Via**, Gran Via de les Corts
Catalanes 642, **t** 93 318 19 00, *www.
hotelgranvia.com*; ⓜ Passeig de Gràcia.
This preserves a touch of 19th-century
grace, from its courtyard to its lounge
and the antique furnishings. Can
creep into the expensive category.

Hostal Jardí, Plaça de Sant Josep Oriol
1, **t** 93 301 59 00, *www.hoteljardi-
barcelona.com*; ⓜ Liceu. Very popular
budget hotel with clean, plain, air-
conditioned rooms at a slightly
inflated price.

***Paseo de Gràcia**, Passeig de
Gràcia 102, **t** 93 215 06 03, *www.
hotelpaseodegracia.es*; ⓜ Diagonal.
Reasonable for this chi-chi district.
Try for a room on the eighth floor
with Modernista details.

****Peninsular**, C/Sant Pau 34–6,
t 93 302 31 38, *www.hotelpeninsular.
net*; ⓜ Liceu. Nestled in the shell of a
convent in El Raval, with simple rooms
overlooking an inner courtyard filled
with plants.

Inexpensive

⭐ **Bonic B&B >**

Bonic B&B, C/Joseph Anselm Clavé 9,
t 62 605 34 34 (*mobile*); *www.bonic-
barcelona.com*; ⓜ Drassanes. Friendly
little guesthouse just off the Rambla

with tastefully decorated rooms and
charming hosts. Shared bathrooms.

Hs Eden, C/Balmes 55, 1st and 2nd
floors, **t** 93 452 66 20, *www.
hostaleden.net*; ⓜ Passeig de Gràcia.
A pleasant budget surprise, in an old
Eixample building, with eccentric
rooms; some have whirlpools, and
some have patios.

****Hs Gat Raval**, C/Joaquín Costa 44,
t 93 481 66 70, *www.gatrooms.com*;
ⓜ Universitat. A sleek modern *hostal*,
with small but well equipped rooms,
contemporary art and free Internet.
They also run the slightly more
upmarket **Hs Gat Xino**.

****Hs Oliva**, Passeig de Gràcia 32,
t 93 488 01 62, *www.hostaloliva.com*;
ⓜ Passeig de Gràcia. Large, airy rooms,
vintage feel and great views, this is
one of the cheapest in the street that
Gaudí made famous.

****Hs Windsor**, Rambla de Catalunya
84, **t** 93 215 11 98; ⓜ Passeig de Gràcia.
Charmingly old fashioned and chintzy.
Try to get a room with a balcony
overlooking the Rambla de Catalunya;
the rest are a bit stuffy.

La Terrassa, C/Junta de Comerç 11, **t** 93
302 51 74, *www.laterrassa-barcelona.
com*; ⓜ Liceu. Run by the same people
as the Jardí, but slightly less well
equipped and cheaper as a result.
Pretty interior patio in summer.

The Praktik, C/Diputació 325, **t** 93 467
32 87, *www.praktikhotels.com*;
ⓜ Girona. A comfortable, contemporary minimalist hotel with free
wi-fi. Nice rooftop terrace too

Youth Hostels

Albergue Kabul, Plaça Reial 17, **t** 93 318
51 90, *www.kabul.es*; ⓜ Liceu. A central
youth hostel with dorm rooms.

Centric Point, Passeig de Gràcia, **t** 93
231 20 45, *www.equity-point.com*;
ⓜ Passeig de Gràcia. The biggest and
newest of a chain of private youth
hostels throughout the city.

Eating Out in Barcelona

La Rambla and Barri Gòtic

Els Quatre Gats, C/Montsió 3, **t** 93 302
41 40 (€€€); ⓜ Catalunya. Once a
famous Modernista taverna, now

a smart, but touristy Catalan restaurant. Good-value lunch menu. *Closed Sun, 3 weeks in Aug.*

Agut, C/d'En Gignàs 16, t 93 315 17 09 (€€); ⓜ Jaume I. Warm and traditional restaurant that has been serving up succulent Catalan specialities since 1924. *Closed Sun eve, Mon, Aug.*

Agut d'Avignon, C/Trinitat 3 (just off C/Avinyó), t 93 302 60 34 (€€); ⓜ Jaume I. Classic Catalan cuisine prepared with seasonal ingredients and some imaginative twists.

Amaya, La Rambla 20–24, t 93 302 61 38 (€€); ⓜ Drassanes. Good Basque cuisine in the old-fashioned restaurant and traditional tapas at the bar. Good set lunch menu.

★ **Cafè de l'Acadèmia** >

Cafè de l'Acadèmia, C/Lledó 1, t 93 319 82 53 (€€); ⓜ Jaume I. Take in the enchanting Plaça Sant Just from the candlelit terrace. Emphasis is on Catalan cuisine, *Closed Sat and Sun.*

Pla, C/Bellafila 5 (behind the Ajuntament), t 93 412 65 52 (€€); ⓜ Jaume I. Delightful, small and chic – and serves excellent fusion cuisine. *Dinner only.*

Living, C/Capellans 9 (off Avda Portal de l'Àngel), t 93 412 31 37 (€€); ⓜ Liceu. Airy and arty, serving creative Catalan dishes, as well as snacks and coffee. Summer terrace. *Closed Sun.*

Pinotxo, Mercat de la Boqueria, t 93 317 17 31 (€€); ⓜ Liceu. Run by a real character with great home-cooked food in the hurly-burly of the market. *Closed dinner and Sun. Cash only.*

Pitarra, C/Avinyó 56, t 93 301 16 47 (€€); ⓜ Jaume I. Founded in 1890 and decorated with memorabilia devoted to the eponymous poet, this place serves authentic, traditional Catalan cuisine. *Closed Sun and Aug.*

La Ribera

Comerç 24, C/Comerç 24, t 93 319 21 02, www.comerc24.com (€€€€); ⓜ Arc de Triomf. Run by El Bulli-trained Carles Abellan, this slick joint offers miniature portions of truly spectacular food. *Closed Sun, Mon.*

★ **Passadís d'en Pep** >

Passadís d'en Pep, Pla del Palau 2, t 93 310 10 21 (€€€€); ⓜ Barceloneta. Gourmet heaven. There are no menus, but the freshest seasonal specialities (mainly seafood), accompanied by fine wines, are served. *Closed Sun.*

Set Portes, Passeig d'Isabel II 14, t 93 319 30 33 (€€€); ⓜ Barceloneta. One of the city's most famous restaurants, founded in 1836, and still popular, serving delicious rice and seafood.

Cuines de Santa Caterina, Avda Francesc Cambó 29, t 93 268 99 18 (€€); ⓜ Jaume I. Bright, restaurant in the market offering a fresh and interesting mix of traditional Mediterranean and world cuisine. There's also a tapas bar.

Euskal Etxea, Plaçeta de Montcada, t 93 310 21 85 (€€); ⓜ Jaume I. Authentic Basque cuisine in the restaurant and fabulous *pintxos* (crusty bread with elaborate toppings) at the bar. *Closed Mon and Aug.*

Senyor Parellada, C/Argenteria 37, t 93 310 50 94 (€€); ⓜ Jaume I. In a magnificent 18th-century building, this elegant restaurant serves deftly prepared Catalan classics.

Cardamón, C/Carders 31, t 93 295 50 59 (€); ⓜ Jaume I. Marble-topped tables give this friendly place a traditional feel, but the house speciality is excellent curry. *Closed Mon, Sun lunch.*

Pla de la Garsa, C/Assaonadors 13, t 93 315 24 13 (€); ⓜ Jaume I. Serves tasty tapas and traditional Catalan dishes in a dramatic vaulted stone cellar. Excellent wine list. *Dinner only.*

La Cocotte Minute, Passeig del Born 16, t 93 319 17 34 (€); ⓜ Jaume I. Colourful retro-style dining room, a trendy crowd, and a cheap weekday lunch menu. *Closed Sun dinner.*

Sandwich and Friends, Passeig del Born 27, t 93 310 07 86 (€); ⓜ Jaume I. Great for a quick lunch, with more than 50 kinds of *entrepans* served up in a colourful café-gallery with a huge Pop Art-style fresco. Popular terrace.

El Raval

Ca l'Isidre, C/Flors 12, t 93 441 11 39 (€€€€); ⓜ Paral.lel. Long a favourite of artists as well as King Juan Carlos, this serves elaborate Catalan cuisine. *Closed Sun, 2 weeks in Aug.*

Can Lluís, C/Cera 49, t 93 441 11 87 (€€); ⓜ Paral.lel. A piquant favourite of the old music hall crowd, with black-and-white photos of the old stars; try the *bacallà* (salt cod). There's also an inexpensive *menú del día*. *Closed Sun.*

Sésamo, C/Sant Antoni Abat, t 93 441 64 11 (€€); Ⓜ Sant Antoni. A hip little spot that serves inspired veggie dishes prepared with fresh, locally grown produce. Good lunchtime menu. *Closed Mon eve and Tues.*

Silenus, C/Àngels 8, t 93 302 26 80 (€€); Ⓜ Universitat. This quiet spot serves excellent fusion cuisine in a charming setting with modern art. Good set lunch menu. *Closed Sun.*

Biocenter, C/Pintor Fortuny 24, t 93 301 45 83 (€); Ⓜ Liceu. A vegetarian restaurant (and shop) with a salad bar and various hot dishes to choose from. *Closed eves Mon–Thurs and Sun.*

⭐ **Cinc Sentits >>**

Elisabets, C/Elisabets 2, t 93 317 58 26 (€); Ⓜ Liceu. Nothing much has changed here over the decades, and it remains as popular as ever for its hearty Catalan dishes. *Closed Mon.*

Pla dels Àngels, C/Ferlandina 23, t 93 329 40 47 (€); Ⓜ Universitat. Bright and modern with a terrace facing MACBA outside, this offers salads, pasta, grilled meat and fish at great prices. *Closed Sun, and Mon eve.*

Seaside

Llucanés, Plaça de la Font, t 93 224 25 25 (€€€€); Ⓜ Barceloneta. Fashionable, Michelin-star-winning restaurant stunningly set in the new Barceloneta market; superb cuisine, with lots of seafood. *Closed Sun eve, Mon.*

Antigua Casa Solé, C/Sant Carles 4, t 93 221 50 12 (€€€); Ⓜ Barceloneta. Over a century old, with pretty blue tiles, and an astonishing range of seafood. *Closed Mon and Sun evening.*

Can Majó, C/Almirall Aixada 23, t 93 221 54 55 (€€€); Ⓜ Barceloneta. Traditional place right on the beach, serving divine seafood. Try the *suquet* (fish stew with monkfish, hake and mussels). *Closed Sun eve and Mon.*

⭐ **Kaiku >**

Kaiku, Plaça del Mar 1 (off Passeig Joan de Borbó), t 93 221 90 80 (€€); Ⓜ Barceloneta. Dine on the terrace overlooking the beach at this excellent seafood restaurant. The chef's special paella (*arròs del xef*), made with smoked rice, is out of this world. *Lunch only, closed Mon.*

Ca La Nuri Platja, Passeig Marítim 55 (in front of the Hospital del Mar), t 93 221 37 75 (€€); Ⓜ Barceloneta. Right on the beachfront, this elegant fish restaurant specialises in paellas and rice dishes. *Closed eves Sun–Tues.*

The Eixample

Alkimia, C/Indústria 79, t 93 207 61 15 (€€€€); Ⓜ Sagrada Família. Exquisite, experimental cuisine by an extraordinary young chef in a chic modern setting. *Closed Sat, Sun.*

Casa Calvet, C/Casp 48, t 93 413 40 12 (€€€€); Ⓜ Passeig de Gràcia. Fine Mediterranean cuisine in an elegant mansion designed by Gaudí.

Cinc Sentits, C/Aribau 58, t 93 323 94 90 (€€€€); Ⓜ Universitat. One of the newest stars in Barcelona's firmament, the 'five senses' uses only the finest local ingredients artfully prepared to seduce the tastebuds. Recently awarded its first Michelin star. *Closed Sun, Mon.*

Drolma, in the Hotel Majestic, Passeig de Gràcia 70, t 93 496 77 10 (€€€€); Ⓜ Passeig de Gràcia. Old-fashioned luxury in what is probably Barcelona's finest restaurant where chef Fermín Puig has garnered numerous awards.

Hofmann, C/La Granada del Penedès 14–16, t 93 218 71 65 (€€€€); Ⓜ Diagonal. This highly acclaimed restaurant run by top chef Mey Hofmann offers creative haute cuisine. *Closed Sat, Sun, Easter, Aug.*

El Racó d'en Baltà, C/Aribau 125, t 93 453 10 44 (€€); FGC Provença. A colourful little restaurant with fresh Mediterranean cuisine. *Closed Mon lunch and Sun.*

Madrid/Barcelona, C/Aragó 282, t 93 215 70 27 (€€); Ⓜ Passeig de Gràcia. A popular hangout serving modern Catalan dishes, which is named for the old railway station. *Closed Sun.*

L'Olivé, C/Balmes 47, t 93 452 19 90 (€€); Ⓜ Universitat. A deservedly popular restaurant serving traditional Catalan cuisine with a modern twist. *Closed Sun eve.*

La Bodegueta, Rambla de Catalunya 98, t 93 215 48 94 (€); Ⓜ Diagonal. Join the rest of Barcelona down in this cellar for a well-priced, home-cooked lunch. *Cash only.*

Outside the Centre

Asador de Aranda, Avda Tibidabo 31, Tibidabo, **t** 93 417 01 15 (€€€€); **FGC** Avinguda Tibidabo. Award-winning Castilian cuisine in a beautiful Modernista setting. *Closed Sun eve.*

Botafumeiro, C/Gran de Gràcia 81, Gràcia, **t** 93 218 42 30 (€€€€); ⓜ Fontana. A prestigious but atmospheric Galician seafood restaurant, with a tapas bar.

Cafés and Tapas in Barcelona

Bar Jai Ca, C/Ginebra 13, **t** 93 319 50 02; ⓜ Barceloneta. Friendly neighbourhood tapas bar with a small but much coveted pavement terrace.

Bauma, C/Roger de Llúria 124, **t** 93 459 05 66; ⓜ Diagonal. An arty, glass-fronted café offering sandwiches, and more substantial fare at lunchtimes.

Bliss, Plaça Sants Just i Pastor, **t** 93 268 10 22; ⓜ Liceu. A pretty café with sofas to sink into, a good range of snacks and light meals, and a terrace on a magical Gothic square. *Closed Sun.*

Café de l'Òpera, La Rambla 74, **t** 93 317 75 85; ⓜ Liceu. An institution and the classiest place on the Rambla, this café was founded in 1929, opposite the Liceu. With a terrace, but pricey.

Cal Pep, Plaça de les Olles, **t** 93 310 79 61; ⓜ Barceloneta. A much-loved local stalwart in La Ribera; excellent tapas, and a charismatic owner. *Closed Mon lunch, Sat eve and Sun.*

Casa Alfonso, C/Roger de Llúria 6, **t** 93 301 97 83; ⓜ Urquinaona. A charmingly old-fashioned tapas bar with hanging hams. *Closed Sun.*

Cata 1.81, C/València 181, **t** 93 323 68 18; ⓜ Passeig de Gràcia. A fine selection of local wines and cavas accompanied by some extraordinary gourmet tapas. *Closed Mon and Sun.*

Cerveceria Catalunya, C/Mallorca 236, **t** 93 216 03 68; ⓜ Passeig de Gràcia. A dazzling array of tapas line the curved bar. Expect queues.

Cova Fumada, C/Baluard 56, **t** 93 221 40 61; ⓜ Barceloneta. This offers a glimpse of old Barceloneta, right down to the sawdust on the floor. *Open erratically.*

El Jardí, C/Hospital 56, no tel; ⓜ Liceu. A delightful outdoor café in the beautiful Gothic courtyard of the Antic Hospital (*see* p.109). *Closed Mon.*

Inopia, C/Tamarit 104, **t** 93 424 52 31; ⓜ Poble Sec. Owned by Ferran Adriá's brother, Albert, this is a contemporary take on a classic tapas bar. Simple, but superb, food and wines. *Closed Mon.*

La Pineda, C/del Pi 16, **t** 93 302 43 93; ⓜ Liceu. A delightful, old-fashioned delicatessen hung with hams, with just a couple of tables. *Lunch only. Closed Sun.*

Quimet & Quimet, C/Poeta Cabañas 25, **t** 93 442 31 42; ⓜ Paral.lel. This bottle-lined bodega has been going since 1914 and serves high-quality tapas and a great range of wines by the glass. *Closed Sun eve, Mon, Aug.*

El Roble, C/Riera Sant Miquel 51, **t** 93 218 73 87; ⓜ Diagonal. A bustling neighbourhood favourite, with big boards listing all the Gallego seafood tapas on offer. *Closed Sun.*

Sol Solet, Plaça del Sol, **t** 93 217 44 40; ⓜ Fontana. Pretty café with marble tables serving tasty tapas – including plenty of veggie options.

Tapaç 24, C/Diputació 269, **t** 93 488 09 77. New tapas venture run by celebrity chef Carles Abellan, with tasty titbits at prices rather more affordable than those at Comerç 24.

Entertainment and Nightlife in Barcelona

Barcelona offers world-class classical music, dance, theatre and opera, but it is in the world of cutting edge, contemporary performing arts that it really excels. The **Barcelona Festival Grec**, in summer, offers a spectacular line-up of Catalan and international performers.

Newsstands sell the weekly *Guía del Ocio* (published on Wednesday) with detailed listings of events and a short English language section. The *La Vanguardia* newspaper publishes a free supplement on Fridays, *Que Fem?*, which is packed with useful information on what's on (in Spanish and Catalan). Also see the city hall's excellent website, *www.bcn.cat*. For information on cultural events, visit

⭐ Inopia >>

⭐ Bliss >

07 | Barcelona | Eating Out and Entertainment and Nightlife the Palau de la Virreina, La Rambla 99, t 93 316 10 00; can also book tickets.

Bars and Nightclubs

Almirall, C/Joaquim Costa 33, t 93 318 99 17; ⓜ Universitat. Founded in 1860, Almirall has preserved its beautiful Modernista woodwork. Great place to start the night. *Closed Sun.*

Bar Marsella, C/Sant Pau 65, t 93 442 72 63; ⓜ Liceu. A classic, with faded mirrors, marble tables, paddle fans, and the whiff of absinthe.

Boadas, C/Tallers 1, t 93 318 88 26; ⓜ Catalunya. A famous Art Deco cocktail bar from 1933 that introduced Cuban drinks to Barcelona. *Closed Sun.*

CDLC, Passeig Marítim 32, t 93 224 04 70; ⓜ Ciutadella-Vila Olímpica. Fashionable club on the beach.

Club Fellini, La Rambla 27, t 93 272 49 80; ⓜ Drassanes. Glitzy nightclub, a little trashy, but great DJs.

La Terrazza, Avda Marqués de Comillas, no tel, *laterrrazza.com*; ⓜ Paral.lel. Glossy outdoor dance club in the Poble Espanyol.

Pop, Rock, Jazz, Blues, World Music

Antilla Barcelona, C/d'Aragó 141–3, t 93 451 21 51, *www.antillasalsa.com*; ⓜ Hospital Clínic. For salsa, live bands.

Harlem Jazz Club, C/Comtessa de Sobradiel 8, t 933 10 07 55; ⓜ Jaume I. A small club with live jazz, world music, flamenco, country and just about everything in between.

Jamboree, Plaça Reial 17, t 93 319 17 89; ⓜ Jaume I. A good club with a busy programme of live jazz and blues. After the set it becomes a club.

Razzmatazz, C/Almogávers 122, t 93 272 09 10; ⓜ Marina. Great combined nightclub and live venue which attracts big international names.

Classical Music and Opera

You can book tickets for major classical music concerts through **Telentrada** (*www.telentrada.com*, t + 34 93 326 29 46 from outside Spain, or t 90 210 12 12 within Spain) or **Servicaixa** (*www.servicaixa.com*, t + 34 93 495 39 99 from outside Spain, or t 90 233 22 11 within Spain).

L'Auditori, C/de Lepant 140, t 93 247 93 00, *www.auditori.org*; ⓜ Marina. Prestigious venue, with a wide-ranging music programme.

Gran Teatre del Liceu, La Rambla 51, t 93 485 99 00, *www.liceubarcelona.com*; ⓜ Liceu. Barcelona's lavish and romantic opera house also stages ballet and concerts.

Palau de la Música Catalana, Sant Francesc de Paula 2, t 932 95 72 00, *www.palaumusica.org*. Magnificent Modernista edifice.

Theatre and Dance

Teatre Lliure, Plaça Margarida Xirgu, t 93 228 97 47; ⓜ Espanya. This prestigious theatre showcases Catalan talent.

Teatre Nacional de Catalunya, Plaça de les Arts, t 93 306 57 00, *www.tnc.es*; ⓜ Glòries. Another top venue.

Mercat de les Flors, C/de Lleida 59, t 93 426 1875, *www.mercatflors.org*; ⓜ Poble Sec. Contemporary dance.

Cinema

For undubbed films (*V.O.– versió original*), try the following cinemas: **Filmoteca de la Generalitat**, Avda Sarrià 33, t 93 410 75 90; ⓜ Hospital Clínic.

Icaria Yelmo, C/Salvador Espriu 61, t 93 221 75 85; ⓜ Ciutadella-Vila Olímpica.

Verdi, C/Verdi 32, t 93 237 79 90; ⓜ Fontana. Also nearby Verdi Park.

Around Barcelona

As in many great cities, there's a dark secret lurking out here on the outskirts of Barcelona. While the immaculately kept centre glistens with money and taste, large parts of the hinterlands are just plain awful, not the first place you'd choose to go touring in.

But the buses and trains can easily whisk you to any of the little oases within it. Foremost among these is Montserrat, the Catalans' holy mountain, its surreal peaks sitting incongruously amidst the sprawl. Another of the oases is resolutely urban; the surprising city of Terrassa reminds us that the industrial age is part of our history and culture too. Just as surprising is the Penedès, the quiet wine region that supplies the Catalans with their bubbly cava. There are two wild national parks here too, along with some Modernista panache from Gaudí and Jujols, and the beach blanket Babylon of Sitges.

08

Don't miss

⭐ Catalonia's holy mountain
Montserrat p.155

⭐ Wild life and even wilder art
Sitges p.164

⭐ A window on the Dark Ages: the churches of Terrassa
Terrassa p.149

⭐ Modernisme and medieval art
Manresa p.153

⭐ Juanita, Spain's most famous fish
Vilanova i la Geltrú p.167

See map overleaf

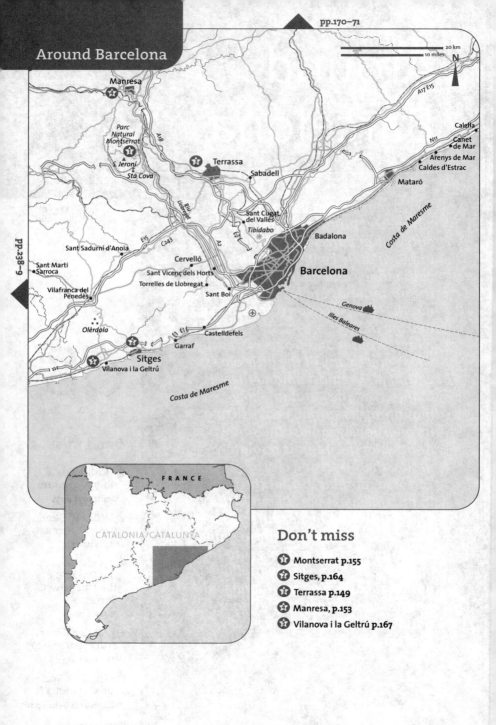

pp.170–71

20 km
10 miles

N

pp.338–9

Manresa

Parc
Natural
Montserrat

S. Jeroni
Sta Cova

Terrassa

Sabadell

Calella

Canet
de Mar

Arenys de Mar
Caldes d'Estrac

Mataró

Costa de Maresme

A17 E15

N11

A8

Riu Llobregat

Sant Cugat
del Vallès

Tibidabo

Badalona

Barcelona

E15

C243

A2

Sant Sadurní d'Anoia

Sant Martí
Sarroca

Cervelló

Sant Vicenç dels Horts

Torrelles de Llobregat

Sant Boi

Vilafranca del
Penedès

Genova

Illes Baleares

Olèrdola

Garraf

Castelldefels

Sitges

Vilanova i la Geltrú

Costa de Maresme

FRANCE

CATALONIA / CATALUNYA

Don't miss

⭐ Montserrat **p.155**

⭐ Sitges, **p.164**

⭐ Terrassa **p.149**

⭐ Manresa, **p.153**

⭐ Vilanova i la Geltrú **p.167**

Getting to and around the Costa del Maresme

Commuter **trains** (*rodalies*) depart every 30mins from Barcelona-Sants and Plaça Catalunya and stop at all the coastal towns. **Buses** for the same depart from the Estació Barcelona Nord.

The Costa del Maresme

The 72 kilometres between Barcelona and Blanes, the Costa del Maresme, may not be the most glamorous of *costas* ('*maresme*' means 'swamp') but it's a convenient stretch of weekend sand for city-dwellers, with the rail line right behind the beach. It wasn't bad until the 1960s, when most of the coast was transformed beyond recognition by a mass invasion of cement-mixers and apartment blocks.

Badalona (Roman Baetulo), with a long beach and palmy Rambla, will soon be the terminus of the L2 metro. A major industrial centre and 'the cradle of Spanish basketball', it now has one of the great ethnically mixed populations of greater Barcelona. The **Museu de Badalona** was built in 1966 over Baetulo's Roman baths to shelter the small but exquisite marble torso of the *Venus of Badalona*, along with Iberian *stelae* (stone slabs) and Roman mosaics.

In 1848 the first train in Spain chugged from Barcelona to **Mataró**, and in 1867 the town gave birth to one of brightest stars in the Modernista constellation, Josep Puig i Cadafalch, who designed the Ajuntament and several other buildings here. The hot springs at **Caldes d'Estrac** drew Barcelonins in the 19th century, and they covered the piney hills with attractive villas. One who came later was writer, poet and art critic Josep Palau, a good friend of Picasso and world-renowned expert on his work, so much so that, when art dealers asked Picasso to authenticate a piece, he would send them to Palau, saying 'Palau knows my work better than I do.' He left his private collection of Picassos (including a startling self-portrait) and other 20th-century Catalan artists to the **Fundació Palau**.

Over two miles of sand link **Caldes d'Estrac** to **Arenys de Mar**, where the **Museu d'Arenys de Mar** has a collection of every known type of lace, and rocks and minerals from around the world.

Canet del Mar, next up the coast, was a favourite spot of Domènech i Montaner, and in 1918–20 he built a house, now the **Casa Museu Lluís Domènech i Montaner**. It's all rather restrained compared to his Barcelonin flights of fancy, but is packed full of memorabilia and architectural drawings. Various guided tours start at the house, one taking in Montaner's other buildings: the **Ateneu Obrer** (1887) and pointy, ornate **Casa Roura** at Riera Sant Domènech, as well as the other Modernista villas built by the '*americanos*'.

Museu de Badalona
*Plaça de l'Assemblea de Catalunya 1, **t** 933 84 17 50; www.museubdn. es; open July and Aug Tues–Sat 11–2 and 5–8; Sept–June Tues–Sat 10–2 and 4–8, Sun 11–2; adm*

Fundació Palau
*C/Riera 54, **t** 937 91 35 93, www.fundacio palau.cat; open summer Tues–Sat 11–2 and 5–8.30, Sun 11–2; winter Tues–Sat 10.30–2 and 4–7, Sun 10.30–2; adm*

Museu d'Arenys de Mar
*C/Església 43, **t** 937 92 44 44, http://museu. arenysdemar.or; open April–Sept Tues–Sat 11– 1 and 6–8, Sun 11–1; Oct–Mar Tues–Sat 11– 1 and 2–6; Sun 11–1; adm*

Casa Museu Lluís Domènech i Montaner
*Xamfrà Rieres Buscarons i Gavarra, **t** 937 95 46 15, www.canetdemar.org. open Aug Tues–Fri 5–9; Sat 10–2 and 9–5; July and Sept Tues–Fri 5–9; Sat 10–2 and 9–5, Sun 10–2; Oct–June Tues 9–2 and 5–8, Wed–Fri 9–2, Sat 10–2, closed Sun and Mon; adm*

Where to Stay and Eat on the Costa del Maresme

There are some exceptional restaurants here, close enough for a night out from Barcelona.

Caldes d'Estrac ✉ 08393

****Castell de l'Oliver**, just inland at Sant Vicenç de Montalt, t 937 91 15 29, *www.hotelcastelldeloliver.es* (€€€€). Eight gorgeous rooms under big oak beams, with terraces and balconies in a vintage 1619 manor; pool, billiards room, and an excellent gourmet restaurant (€€€).

****Fonda Mandau**, C/Sant Josep 11, t 937 91 04 59, *www.casafonda.com* (€€–€). Six rooms in a handsome 19th-century house with a beautiful patio, and an excellent restaurant, **Can Raimón** (€€). *Restaurant closed Tues.*

Marola, Pg dels Anglesos 6, t 937 91 32 00 (€€). Simple restaurant serving all the usual seafood classics on a lovely seaside terrace.

Arenys de Mar ✉ 08350

Hispania, Carretera Real 54, t 937 91 04 57, *www.restauranthispania.com* (€€€€). One of the oldest restaurants in the area, where the King of Spain drops in to feast on Catalan country classics such as *mongetes amb coliflor i botifarra negra* (beans with cauliflower and black sausage) and mouthwatering seafood.

Portinyol, in the port, t 937 92 00 09 (€€€–€€). Grand old place by the fishing port, with light-filled dining areas and a terrace; splurge for the freshest shellfish and lobster.

Canet de Mar ✉ 08360

La Queixalada, C/Castanyer 18, t 937 94 06 20 (€). Get there early to beat the crowds at this informal place specializing in *coques* (Catalan pizza).

Restaurant del Santuari, Parc del Santuari, t 937 94 10 07 (€). Modernista restaurant designed by Puig i Cadafalch, by the Misericordia sanctuary, serving seafood and desserts featuring local strawberries.

Sant Pol de Mar ✉ 08395

Sant Pau, C/Nou 10, t 937 60 06 62, *www.ruscalleda.com* (€€€€). In a beautiful old villa of 1881 overlooking sea and gardens, chef Carme Ruscalleda creates astonishing seasonal concoctions for 35 lucky guests. Besides the constantly changing *à la carte* and tasting menus, you can choose from an array of special micro-menus – for your aperitif, cheese or dessert. *Closed three weeks in May and Nov.*

Inland from Barcelona: Sant Cugat del Vallès to Manresa

Well within day-trip distance of Barcelona, there are superb Romanesque and Visigothic churches, Modernista mansions and factories, and a mellow old monastery in Sant Cugat del Vallès.

Sant Cugat del Vallès

Just over the Collserola hills northwest of Barcelona, Sant Cugat del Vallès is a leafy commuter suburb with a handsome Modernista train station. Originally the Roman Castrum Octavianum, it has a suburb centrepiece in the **Reial Monestir de Sant Cugat**, in Plaça Octavia. Founded by Louis the Stammerer in 878, it became the most powerful Benedictine house in the county. The church was rebuilt in the Gothic style with a huge rose window and Lombard tower.

*Reial Monestir de Sant Cugat
church open daily 9–12 and 6–8*

Getting to towns inland from Barcelona

Sant Cugat is about 20 minutes from Barcelona's Plaça Catalunya on the S5 **FGC train** line. For Sabadell, take the S2. For Terrassa, the C4 line goes to the central station from Sants, and the S1 line of the FGC takes you there (Terrassa-Rambla station) from Plaça Catalunya. The C4 carries on to Manresa. Manresa is also served, via Montserrat, by the FGC train R5 from Plaça Catalunya.

Museu de Sant Cugat
t 936 75 99 51; open June–Sept Tues–Sat 10–1.30 and 3–9, Sun 10–2.30; Oct–May Tues–Sat 10–1.30 and 3–7, Sun 10–2.30; adm

The Romanesque cloister is the star of the show, with 144 capitals depicting scenes from the New and Old Testaments sculpted by the monk Arnau Cadell in the 1190s; one capital with an inscription even shows him at work in a rare moment of medieval non-anonymity. In the chapter house, the **Museu de Sant Cugat** houses another masterpiece, the golden *Retaule de Tots Sants* by Pere Serra (1375).

Sabadell

Sabadell is the bitter arch-rival of Terrassa, the Manchester to its Leeds, a sprawling city of big banks. It was making woollen cloth on a large scale by the 15th century, and, when the industrial revolution took off, the population soared from 2000 in 1800 to 200,000 today, making Sabadell Catalonia's second city.

Near the FGC train stop at La Rambla you can walk along C/de l'Indústria, passing two fine Modernista buildings by Juli Batllevell, the **Hotel Suisse** at No. 59 and the **Lluch Offices** at No.10. A bit further up, in the peaceful historic centre, the 19th-century mayor's residence is now the **Museu d'Història de Sabadell**, with changing exhibitions. Best of all is the headquarters of one of Spain's biggest banks, the **Caixa de Sabadell** (1905–1915), at C/de Gràcia 17, by Jeroni Martorell, a temple to Mammon tricked out to the gills.

Museu d'Història de Sabadell
C/Sant Antoni 13 t 93 727 85 55; open Tues–Sat 5–8, Sun 11–2

Terrassa

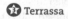 **Terrassa**

In Terrassa they told us that their city doesn't get a lot of tourists. If you've ever tried to drive there you'll find out why. The city is stuck in the most craptastic corner of all Catalonia, where a pall of smoke hangs over industrial wastelands. And even if you want to get there you might not be able; road signs to the city centre usually lie, and it's all too easy to cruise in circles looking for the city until life seems a cruel joke.

Which is a pity, because Terrassa, if you ever find it, is a pretty nice town. Catalonia's fourth-largest city was built by industry, lives for industry, and isn't ashamed to say so. They're proud of their hard work and their history, which goes back a mere million years or so. Their accomplishments are many; after Barcelona, they may have the biggest collection of Modernista architecture anywhere.

History

Recent excavations along the Vallparadís, the ravine that runs through the city, have unearthed evidence of human habitation from 800,000–1,000,000 years ago, among the oldest anywhere in Europe. Terrassa only enters history as a Roman town called Egara. By the time of the Visigoths it was an important bishopric, and they left the wonderful complex of pre-Romanesque churches that is Terrassa's great landmark today.

The Moorish occupation began in 718, and lasted for an uncertain period. There must have been trouble, for somewhere along the way old Egara became Terra Rasa – 'wasteland'. Terrassa got back on its feet by the 13th century, but it didn't make a splash until 1833 when the first steam engine in Catalonia was installed here. A minor town grew into a city, and filled up with factories. The first boom was followed by a bigger one in the 1950s. Since then the population has increased five-fold, to over 200,000.

Like Reus, Terrassa is a town where they left the old brick smokestacks standing when the textile mills and foundries of a century ago were demolished. They're quite elegant, and they make perfect symbols for the city. Terrassa today considers itself the jazz capital of Catalonia. There are no points for guessing what its politics are like: not far from the Visigothic churches you can stand on the corner of Equality Street and Human Rights Square.

Around Plaça Vella

The closest thing to a centre is the shady Plaça Vella. It has the nondescript **Catedral del Sant Esperit** (1593) which contains an excellent alabaster *Burial of Christ* (1540) by Italian-trained Martí Diez de Liatzasoloi, and an outlandish parabolic-arched chapel by Terrassa's most renowned Modernista architect, Lluís Muncunill. The cathedral's neighbour is the imposing **Torre del Palau**, the only part remaining from the castle that once occupied this square.

A block north up C/Cremat, Plaça Raval de Montserrat has the odd pseudo-medieval **Ajuntament** (1902), an early work of Muncunill; peek inside to see the grand stairwell.

The city fathers sacked Muncunill as city architect right after the Ajuntament was finished, and that, finally, gave him a chance to show he was capable of something more than eclectic pastiches. Just around the corner on C/Joan Coromines is his **Societat General d'Electricitat** (1908). It's a very modest brick building (now used as a restaurant) but an exceptional one. The architecture has less in common with Catalan Modernisme than with international trend-setters such as Louis Sullivan or Hendrik Berlage, putting it right up with the mainstream avant-garde of the time. It practically screams Modernity, a symbol of a new world full of possibility as much as the electricity once generated inside it.

Just to the west on the city's promenade, the Rambla d'Egara, is another Modernista monument, the elegant **Mercat de la Independència** (1906), where the architecture makes a perfect setting for the gorgeous produce inside.

Museum of Science and Technology

Muncunill's best-known factory in Terrassa was the big Vapor Aymerich Amat i Jover, just to the north on the Rambla d'Egara, which is now the home of the **Museu de la Ciència i de la Técnica de Catalunya** or **mNACTEC**. Industrial history is very important in Catalonia, and mNACTEC runs 22 other former industrial sites in the region, including mines, foundries, car and rail museums, a cement plant and a cork factory (most are mentioned in this book).

Museu de la Ciència i de la Técnica de Catalunya (mNACTEC)
Rambla d'Egara 270,
t 937 36 89 66; open
July and Aug Tues–Sun
10–2.30; Sept–June
Tues–Sat 10–7, Sat and
Sun 10– 2.30; adm;
***guided tours** around*
the city are offered,
including a Modernista
tour and another
devoted to the city's
remarkable chimneys,
including a climb up
the tallest chimney in
the world; book on
t 937 33 63 69

Here, the building itself is the star exhibit, a magnificent interior space under a saw-tooth roof of brick arches and glass (Muncunill's invention) that floods the building with light. The exhibits detail technology from Neolithic times onward, with working antique machinery, collections of cars, aircraft, motorcycles, and all kinds of gadgets – you can even cook snacks on their big solar reflector.

After the museum, take a detour across the Rambla for a few blocks to see Terrassa's splashiest Modernista building, the **Masia Freixa** (1907) in the Parc de Sant Jordi on C/de Volta. Muncunill originally designed it as a factory for industrialist Josep Freixa i Argemí, but Freixa liked the result so much, he had the architect turn it into a house for his family. It's quite a folly, surrounded by porticoes of parabolic arches and undulating brick domes.

West of the Centre

You have seen how Terrassa made its money; to the east, you can see how it spent it. The posh side of town contains such flashy landmarks as the **Teatre Principal** (1911) on Plaça Maragall, currently under long-overdue restoration, and Muncunill's **Gran Casino** (1920) on C/Font Vella.

Most of the bosses lived in this part of town, within walking distance of their factories, but you'd never pick out their mansions; sober, austere façades were the rule – probably sound policy when your working class was mostly Communists and Anarchists.

Casa Alegre de Sagrera
t 937 31 66 46; open
Tues–Sat 10–1 and 4–8,
Sun 10–2; adm

A typical example on C/de Font Vella is the **Casa Alegre de Sagrera**. Francesc Alegre i Roig, an *arriviste* textile magnate, married into an old-money family and turned its 18th-century home upside down, with Modernista-influenced stained glass, paintings and wrought iron. Besides the furnishings and garden, the attractions here include a room full of Chinese art, with porcelains and ivories going back to the T'ang dynasty, and another with views of old Terrassa made in the 1920s and '30s by a very talented local artist named Mateu Avallaneda.

The Three Churches

Together they're one of Spain's greatest early medieval monuments, a little Brigadoon hidden away just outside the centre of industrial Terrassa. The way in is down C/de la Creu, from near the Teatre Principal, and then over the Torrent de les Bruixes ('Witches' Creek') on a picturesque medieval bridge called the **Pont de Sant Pere**. The three churches stand in a row, on a height between two narrow ravines. It was a habit in Visigothic Spain, as in northern Italy, to sometimes build not one big metropolitan church, but an ensemble of smaller ones. Here Santa Maria was the seat of the bishop, with an adjacent episcopal palace that is now lost; Sant Miquel was for baptisms; and Sant Pere served as the parish church. This is the only such church complex in Spain to have survived in something like its original form.

A plaque in **Santa Maria** dates the consecration to 1112, though what we see is a reconstruction of a building that may go back to the 5th or 6th century. The surviving original work includes the apses and the pretty pavement of coloured stone. The apse retains some faded 10th- or 11th-century paintings, and some excellent later medieval frescoes, including a cycle of the *Life of St Thomas of Canterbury* – Thomas à Becket, always a popular saint in Spain.

In the middle stands the exquisite little **Sant Miquel**, built, like many pre-Romanesque churches, in a Greek-cross plan. Note the 'Moorish' horseshoe arch above the portal and window; this trademark feature of Islamic architecture in Spain really isn't Moorish it all, but Visigothic in origin. Inside, the columns that hold up the cupola re-use Roman capitals. Underneath is an unusual three-lobed crypt, dedicated to the truly obscure Sant Celoni.

Sant Pere, also a reconstruction of a Visigothic-era church, contains remnants of faded medieval frescoes, and a glorious 15th-century altarpiece by Jaume Huguet, tucked away on a side wall.

Church complex (Sant Maria, Sant Miquel, Sant Pere)
open Tues–Sat 10–1.30 and 4–7, Sun 11–2

Parc de Vallparadís

Right in front of the three churches, the Torrent de les Bruixes and Torrent Monner come together to form the ravine called the Torrent de Vallparadís. Old Terrassa grew up on the edge of this ravine. Cleaned up and landscaped as the 2.5km long Parc de Vallparadís, it is becoming an exciting new focal point, one that will shape the growth of the city for decades to come. The best parts of the park begin south of the Pont de Passeig. Here you can ride up and down the park on the miniature **Vallparadís Railway**. The Llac de Vallparadís is a popular swimming spot, and the city puts on a schedule of events year round.

Just across the park from the three churches on C/Salmerón is the **Museu Textil**, which exhibits fabrics and clothing from all over the world, with examples going back to earliest times.

Museu Textil
t 937 31 52 02; open Tues and Thurs 9–8, Wed and Fri 9–2, Sat and Sun 10–2; adm

Castell Cartoixa de Vallparadís
t 937 85 71 44;
open Tues–Sat 10–1.30
and 4–7, Sun 11–2; adm

Across the street is the **Castell Cartoixa de Vallparadís**, a 12th-century castle converted to a Carthusian monastery in 1344, housing a municipal museum with sculptures, ceramics and 19th-century paintings.

Manresa

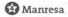 **Manresa**

Like Terrassa, Manresa is a surprisingly pleasant place to spend a day, an oasis on the edge of the Barcelona industrial belt. It's much smaller, though, with only 60,000 people; you can see open country from the top of town. Manresa blossomed in the Middle Ages, but its decline followed the rest of Catalonia's under Spanish rule. The town was sacked in the War of the Spanish Succession, and partly destroyed by Napoleon's troops in 1808, but started its comeback soon after as one of Catalonia's early industrial towns.

Col.legiata Basilica de Santa Maria

Manresa began as an Iberian village on the Puigcardener, a hill overlooking the confluence of the Cardener river and the Llobregat. Now, it holds the city's landmark: the Col.legiata Basilica de Santa Maria, or, as everybody calls it, 'La Seu'. It's a stout and worthy example of Catalan Gothic, with rows or buttresses and pinnacles that give it an alert and military air. Inside, the attraction is a wealth of 14th-century painted altarpieces that managed to escape being carted off to Barcelona's MNAC museum.

The greatest of these, Pere Serra's magical *Retaule de l'Esperit Sant* (1394) is considered this important painter's masterpiece. It tells the whole Christian story from the creation of the world to the Crucifixion, with the emphasis on the presence of the Holy Spirit in the miracles of scripture. Among the other altarpieces is the *Retaule de Sant Marc* (1346) by Arnau Bassa, a work that looks as if its author might have had a trip to Tuscany (Catalans call this period of their art 'Italogòtic'). Some bits of the original Romanesque church survive, including parts of the cloister and the lovely, unusually stylized Portal of Santa Maria, from the 13th century. More art from the city's churches can be seen at the adjacent **Museu Històric de la Seu**.

Museu Històric de la Seu
t 938 72 15 12
open Sun only
12–1.30; other days by
appointment; adm

Manresa Modernista

Like Terrassa, Manresa's first century of industry left it with a good collection of Modernista buildings, most concentrated around the central C/Sant Miquel. For an introduction, there's the charming **Farmàcia Esteve** (1912) on Plaça de l'Om. Continue down the pedestrian C/Born, past the **Sastreria Tuneu** (1906) to Plaça Sant Domènec for the **Casa Torrents** (1905), an imposing home built by Manresa's own Modernista architect, Ignasi Oms; nearby, don't miss the prettiest thing in town, a little **kiosk** (now a tourist information point) built in 1917 after a design by Puig i Cadafalch.

Modernista magic continues along the city's elegant and urbane rambla, Passeig de Pere III. First, on the right, is the **Casal Regionalista** (1918) by another local architect, Alexandre Soler i March, and then, a little further along on the left, the two finest works of Ignasi Oms: the **Casa Lluvia** (1908; just around the corner on C/Oms) and the absolutely glorious **Casino** (1906).

St Ignatius' Cave

Íñigo López de Recalde, the Basque from Guipuzcoa who would one day become St Ignatius of Loyola, founder of the Jesuit Order, found his spiritual vocation as he spent a year recovering from the wounds he suffered fighting in the Battle of Pamplona in 1521. As soon as he was well enough, he exchanged clothes with a beggar and set out on a pilgrimage to Montserrat. After that he ended up in a monastery in Manresa, where he spent a very ascetic year fasting, performing menial labour, having visions and writing his *Spiritual Exercises*, the foundation of his later missionary work.

For most of that time he was living in a cave on the edge of the city, one with a view of Montserrat. This **Santa Cova** is the seed from which an enormous complex has grown. The cave itself has become a shrine, sumptuously decorated in mosaics, alabaster reliefs and stained glass. There's also a small museum, and an audiovisual show on Ignatius' life. Perhaps the best part of the complex is the church, with a delightful rococo façade.

Below the Santa Cova is another landmark that appears on all the postcards. The camel-back, 370ft **Pont Vell** has been carrying people over the Llobregat for 700 years and it's still in good nick.

Above the Santa Cova, at C/Sant Ignasi 40, the **Museu Comarcal** has a small but choice collection: late Roman mosaics from local villas, some fine painting and altarpieces from rural churches, paintings and views of Manresa. Best perhaps are the ceramics, colourful works that were manufactured here in the 14th century.

Just northeast of Manresa, the **Monestir de Sant Benet i Sant Fruitós de Bages** was not one of Catalonia's luckier religious houses; the Moors sacked it twice and what was left burned up in a fire in 1633. It was abandoned and cannibalized until 1907, when Elisa Carbó, mother of painter Ramon Casas, converted part of the monastery into a cosy Modernista family home. In 2000, the Caixa de Manresa purchased the lot and restored the church, its enchanting cloister and Modernista rooms, and then added a hotel and restaurant (*see* opposite). It also offers tours.

The monastery overlooks the **Parc Natural de Sant Llorenç del Munt i de l'Obac** – two ranges of coastal hills and cliffs between the Llobregat and Ripoll rivers, covered in holm oaks and pines.

Santa Cova
east of La Seu on Cami de Santa Cova;
t 938 75 15 79; open summer Tues–Sat 10–1 and 4–7; winter Tues–Sat 10–1 and 3–5

Museu Comarcal
t 938 74 11 55 open Fri and Sat 10–1, 4–7, Sun 10–1; adm

Monestir de Sant Benet i Sant Fruitós de Bages
t 902 87 53 53, www.monstbenet.com, open Tues–Fri 10–2, Sat 10–3 and Sun and hols 10-5; individual or combined admission tickets for the medieval tour, the Modernista tour or the Alicia tour; it's best to ring ahead to book; tickets for all three €17

Parc Natural de Sant Llorenç del Munt i de l'Obac
Information Office, Ctra. BV-1221 from Terrassa to Navarcles, km 14.8, t 938 31 83 50; open Mon–Sat 9–2

Market Days Inland from Barcelona

Sant Cugat, Thursday; **Terrassa**, Wednesday; **Manresa**, Thursday, Saturday. There's always something going on in Manresa's Plaça Major on Saturdays: speciality food markets, concerts, flea markets or garden fairs.

Where to Stay and Eat Inland from Barcelona

Terrassa ✉ 08227

**Tàrrega, C/Tàrrega 7, t 937 36 36 40 (€€). A bit strange and modern, but comfortable, with covered parking.

El Asador, C/Valls 9, t 937 89 40 14 (€€). Rib-sticking roast meats, including suckling pig, Castilian-style, and a sweet little terrace at the back.

L'Hort de Ullastrell, C/Valls 119, just south of Plaça Vella, t 937 85 99 63 (€€). Everything's fresh and simple here: salads and grills, including wild mushrooms in season. They do a lovely inexpensive lunch menu.

La Torretta, C/Nou Sant Pau 50, near the three churches, t 937 31 47 75 (€€). If you like *botifarra*, the noble Catalan sausage and its many cousins, this is the place, with six different kinds.

La Terrassa del Museu, Rambla d'Egara, in mNACTEC, t 937 00 44 00 (€). One of the most popular new places in the city centre is actually the museum café (how often does that happen?). A terrace with a view over Muncunill's famous factory roof, and some surprising traditional Catalan recipes, like the *bacallà* with honey.

Manresa ✉ 08241

La Brasa, Ctra Santpedor 128, t 938 74 22 10 (€€). Grilled meats, but many other interesting dishes too; good-value lunch menu. *Closed Aug.*

Kapriz, C/Sant Llorenç de Brindisi 9, t 938 73 05 10 (€€). Manresa's only Russian restaurant. Borscht? Of corscht.

Sant Fruitós de Bages ✉ 08272

****Món St Benet, Camí de Sant Benet, t 938 75 94 04 *www. monstbenet.com* (€€€). Modern stylish rooms with huge private balconies overlooking the monastery and Parc Natural. Jordi Cruz, one of Catalonia's great up-and-coming chefs, has recently moved here as well and displays his considerable talents at **L'Angle**, t 672 20 86 91, *www. restaurantangle.com* (€€€€); book well in advance.

ⓘ **Sant Cugat**
Plaça Octavia,
t 934 75 99 52

ⓘ **Manresa »**
Via de Sant Ignasi 40
(Museu Comarcal)
t 938 78 40 90;
information kiosk *in*
Plaça Fius i Palà

ⓘ **Terrassa >**
Ajuntament,
Raval de Montserrat 14,
t 937 39 70 19; see
mNACTEC, p.151,
for guided tours
around the city

Montserrat, the 'Dream turned Mountain'

⭐ Montserrat

Uncanny, mystical Montserrat, the 'spiritual heart of Catalonia', is visible from just about anywhere from within the Barcelona province. Its apt name means 'serrated mountain'. This isolated, fantastical 10km massif made of jagged, pudding-stone pinnacles rises precipitously over deep gorges and shallow terraces. It is so different from the surrounding countryside, it seems that heaven itself may have dropped it there.

Geological upheavals ten million years ago left the mountain to be sculpted by the wind and rain into a hedgehog of phallic peaks with names like the 'Potato', 'Bishop's Belly', 'Salamander', and a hundred others. Its human history is just as fantastical: St Peter supposedly came here to hide an image of the Virgin carved by St Luke in a cave; in another grotto, the good knight Parsifal discovered the Holy Grail – a legend used by Wagner for his opera. In 880, not long after Christians regained the region, the statue of

Getting to and around Montserrat

From Barcelona, there's a daily **Juliá bus** to Montserrat (*departures at 9.15, return 5pm*, **t** *93 317 64 54*) leaving from Plaça dels Països Catalans by Sants station. Alternatively, take an **FGC train** (line R5) from the station under the Plaça d'Espanya, with daily departures every hour starting at 8.36am with the last train out at 3.36pm. Get off either at the station Aeri de Montserrat for the *telèferic* (cableway, *departs around every 15mins*) or at the next stop for the *cremallera* (rack-and-pinion railway, *runs at least every hour from 8am; at peak times it's much more frequent, usually about 20mins*). They sell combination tickets that include museum admission (€14) or admission plus lunch (€29). Both offer free parking at the base.

If you're coming from Barcelona you can buy your combined tickets for the metro, train and *cremallera* at any station, or you can choose from two **all-inclusive tickets**: one called the **TransMontserrat** (€20.90), which includes metro, train, cable car, Sant Joan funicular and an audiovisual show; and one called the **Tot Montserrat** (€34.40), which includes metro, train, cable car and Sant Joan funicular, but also entrance to the museum and lunch at the self-service café. Trains return to Barcelona hourly 11.35am–6.35pm.

If you choose the *cremallera*, you might take a few minutes to look at the little **museum** in the original station dedicated to the train's history. The first railway replaced the horse-drawn coaches that took 3½ hours to get to the top. It began service in 1892 and closed in 1957, and it had a colourful history. For more information, call the FGC on **t** 93 237 71 56, *www.fgc.net*.

the Virgin (hidden by someone before the advance of the Moors) was discovered on Montserrat and, as is so often the case in Christian legend, it stubbornly refused to budge beyond a certain spot. Count Wilfred the Hairy built a chapel to house it, and in 976 this was given to the Benedictines of Ripoll. Throughout the Middle Ages it was a magnet for pilgrims. Independent and incredibly wealthy, Montserrat was favoured by Charles V (the old hypocrite visited nine times), and his son Felipe II rebuilt the church. During the Peninsular War, Catalan guerrillas fortified it as a base, and in reprisal the French looted and sacked the monastery.

As the Catalan Renaixença gathered steam, Montserrat became its symbol. In 1918, the first Bible in Catalan was printed here, and Verdaguer, Gaudí and Pau Casals were all fervent devotees of the Virgin. Under Franco, Montserrat was the only church permitted to celebrate Mass in Catalan, and couples flocked here to be married in their own language. Even today Montserrat evokes the same image for Spaniards as Niagara Falls for Americans; it's a traditional honeymoon destination, to receive the blessing of the Moreneta ('the little brown one'), as the Virgin is affectionately called, before undertaking the supreme adventure of marriage.

The monastery can hardly compete with the fabulous surroundings; after a lovely ride, the *cremallera* and *telefèric* leave you in a somewhat grim and businesslike square of grey stone buildings. On the lower level are the enormous gift shops and the **Museu de Montserrat** with two sections of gifts donated by the faithful: Old Masters, including an El Greco and a Caravaggio, a room of orthodox icons, and archaeological finds from Greece, Palestine, Mesopotamia and Egypt. The modern section houses 19th-century paintings, especially by Catalans of the Renaixença movement, notably Santiago Rusinyol. There's a Picasso too, a 1959 work called the *Sardana of Peace*.

Museu de Montserrat
open daily 10–3; adm

Basilica
*open daily 8–10.30
and 12–6.30,
no visits during mass*

**Escolanía
boys' choir**
*virrolei and salve
Mon–Fri at 1pm, Sun
12pm; vespers
Sun–Thurs at 6.45pm,
except in July*

Behind the chilly façade of the **Basilica**, there's a beautiful courtyard decorated in green *esgrafiat* work. Felipe's Basilica lost most of its sumptuous furnishings to Napoleon's men, but the enthroned Virgin of Montserrat still presides over the high altar; the strange statue with a faraway look dates from the 12th century, though it is believed to be a copy, coloured black to imitate the original idol. Pilgrims still come to worship her in droves on 27 April and 8 September. The **Escolanía boys' choir**, founded in the 13th century – the oldest music school in Europe – still performs a *virrolei* and *salve* at lunchtime; and throw in a motet at vespers.

Best of all, though, are the walks around the mountain. An easy walk called *Els Degotalls* takes in a wonderful view of the Pyrenees. A funicular descends from Pla Santa Creu (*10–1 and 3.20–7, every 20mins*) to the **Santa Cova**, where a 17th-century chapel marks the exact finding place of the Moreneta; another (*10–7, every 20mins*) will take you up to the **Hermitage of Sant Joan**, from where you can take a spectacular walk in just over an hour up to the **Hermitage of Sant Jeroni** – traditionally the one given to the youngest and most spry hermit. From the hermitage a short path rises to the highest peak in the range (4,110ft), offering a bird's-eye view of the holy mountain and across to the Pyrenees.

Heinrich Himmler Comes to Montserrat

These days, everyone's looking for the Holy Grail again (especially those poor souls who haven't yet found out that *The Da Vinci Code* was based on a literary hoax). Is the Grail a chalice, a dish or a stone? And is it somewhere in Glastonbury, or Rennes-le-Chateau, or Valencia, or in the Cloisters Museum?

Why not here in Catalonia? In truth, people have been asking that question for centuries. A recurring stream of mystical thought and legend associates the Grail and the Grail castle with the eastern Pyrenees. The German knight and poet Wolfram von Eschenbach, whose *Parzifal*, written in about 1198, is the most complete and most provocative account of the Grail legend, gives the name of the Grail castle as Munsalvaesche, which sounds like 'Montsalvat', an old name for Montserrat. Eschenbach's work inspired Wagner's opera *Parsifal*, which turned a great medieval epic into treacly pudding, but did a lot to renew interest in Grail matters. Interestingly, *Parsifal* had its first authorized performance outside Bayreuth at the Liceu in Barcelona.

Thanks perhaps to Wagner, the Nazis were obsessed with this aspect of the Grail story. In the 1930s Grail addict and future SS officer Otto Rahn poked all over the French Pyrenees for ruined castles or secret caverns where the Grail might be hiding. Under the occupation the Nazis were at it again. In 1940, while Hitler was having his famous conference with Franco on the French-Spanish border at Hendaye, a certain Heinrich Himmler checked into the Ritz in Barcelona. Next day, he paid a call on Montserrat. The abbot, aware of Himmler's attacks against the Church, wouldn't see him, but referred him to the only monk who spoke a little German. He apparently told the Nazi big-shot that he didn't know anything about any Grails, and Himmler had to go back to Berlin empty-handed. The story took a new twist with a recent book by a Canadian professor named Joseph Goering. In *The Virgin and the Grail*, Goering notes that 'grail' is an old Catalan word for a kind of serving dish, and he claims that Catalan art in the 12th century provides the first artistic representations of the Grail. In particular, he cites the frescoes of Sant Climent de Taüll (*see* p.322); here, under the famous image of *Christ Pantocrator*, the Virgin stands holding something with radiating lines emanating from it that looks rather like a bowl of hot soup, but might indeed be a Holy Grail. All of which leaves Grail-hunters back where Grail-hunters are always left – at square one.

Coves de Salnitre
t 937 77 90 76; open Sat, Sun and hols 10–1, 4.30–6.30; adm

Down on the southern slopes of the magic mountain, at **Collbató**, you can visit the **Coves de Salnitre**, a beautiful stalactite cave that reminds all the Catalans of Gaudí, and is just about worth the 244 steps you'll have to climb to get in.

Down the River Llobregat: South of Montserrat

From Manresa all the way down to the sea, the Llobregat is a hard-working river. From the *cremallera* train up to Montserrat, you might have noticed the new factories popping up even around the skirts of Catalonia's holy mountain. The towns that follow the river along its way may be decidedly lacking in charm, but then, somebody has to do the work that keeps the world turning, no?

Colonia Sedó (mNACTEC)
t 937 89 22 44; open Sat 10–2; weekdays by appointment; adm

South of Montserrat, Esparreguera can only offer a branch of Terrassa's mNACTEC; the **Colonia Sedó** was a 19th-century model industrial village built around a cotton mill. Here, mNACTEC wants to show off the industrial organization, the advanced water power system that ran the mill, and a crazy corkscrew smokestack, a masterpiece of brickwork.

After that the motorways start to converge, and the valley is almost completely built up. **Martorell** is where they make Seats, among many other things, but long before that the town was famous for its great **Pont del Diable** (it's always the devil's bridge, though this one has a chapel right in the middle). It crosses the Llobregat with a single lofty arch of 122ft, one of the biggest built in the Middle Ages.

The Colonia Güell and Gaudí's Crypt

Labour and class disputes in Barcelona led magnate Eusebi Güell to consider a little adventure in paternalism in 1890. He closed his Barcelona textile mill, fired all his anarchist workers, and set off for a new start in what was then open country (from the A2, take the exit for Sant Vicenç des Horts and follow the signs). Located just outside the city at Santa Coloma de Cervelló, the Colonia Güell was planned as a pseudo worker's co-operative (Güell was still boss) around a cotton goods mill, with houses, a store, a school and other buildings for the workers designed by Gaudí's assistants, Francesc Berenguer and Joan Rubió Bellver. Almost all of it survives, as a peaceful and rather dreamlike neighborhood set around a little square with the company shops, the Ateneu, or cultural centre, and a statue of Joan Güell, Eusebi's father and founder of the dynasty.

The original chapel on the estate was found to be too small, and in 1898 Güell asked Gaudí to design a larger church, set apart in a grove of trees. The sketches for this look like a cross between Coney

Getting to and around South of Montserrat

For the **Colonia Güell**, Oliveras buses from Pla Espanya will take you as far as the Ciutat Cooperativa; the nearest train station (FGC) is Molí Nou; by car, if you can find your way to the Sant Vicenç dels Horts exit of the A2, it's signposted from there. **Catalunya en Miniatura** is easiest reached by car (just off the A2, exit 3) or the FGC train from the Plaça Espanya to Sant Vicenç dels Horts, followed by a 1½km walk.

Crypt
*open daily 10–3,
except during masses,
Sun and hols at 11 and 1*

Island and the Emerald City of Oz, but, once Güell died in 1918, funds for the church dried up, and only the **crypt** was completed. Yet of all Gaudí's works, this magical, primordial avant-garde grotto is the most innovative – a marvel of virtuosity and engineering. It has no right angles and no straight lines; all the pillars bend at weird expressionist angles. Many critics consider it Gaudí's greatest work. It contains no religious painting or sculpture; the spirituality in it is expressed in architecture alone.

Gaudí employed some of his mathematical magic here, as in the parabolic arches, but he also had something else modern architects don't have: Catalan bricklayers. There is no steel reinforcing anything, anywhere: the whole thing is made of rough-hewn stone and brick, primitive textures brightened with stained glass and *trencadí* collages. Robert Hughes' description of Gaudí's architecture as a 'womb with a view' fits it to a T.

Jujol and Sant Joan Despí

While you're out here, bumming around in the miasmic suburbs looking for Modernista treasures, you can find two more just over the Llobregat in the little industrial community of **Sant Joan Despí**. Gaudí's disciple Josep Maria Jujol came here in 1913 to build a house for his aunt, and the result was the **Torre de la Creu** at Passeig de Canalies 12 by the RENFE train station. Locals call it the Torre dels Ous, the 'Egg Tower'; the building is a composition of six cylindrical towers topped by egg-shaped domes. It all seems symmetrical, but, when you look closely, it never is.

Casa Negre
*t 936 35 27 27
open Tues–Sat 5.30–8,
Sun 10–2; adm*

Jujol came back from his work in Tarragona and the Alt Camp to complete a few more projects here, all within walking distance. The **Casa Negre** (1915–30) on Plaça Catalunya has a delightful curvy façade decorated in *esgrafiat* work, with a bay window in the shape of a rococo-era coach stuck incongruously in the centre. There's some beautiful decorative work inside; don't miss the quirky, spectacular chapel. You can see four more from Jujol on nearby C/Jacint Verdaguer, including three houses in a row: the **Torre Jujol** (1932), **Torre Serra-Xaus** (1921) and **Can Rovira** (1926), and the interior decoration of the church of **Sant Joan Baptista** (1943).

**Catalunya en
Miniatura**
*t 936 89 09 60;
open daily 10–6;
Mar–Sept 10–7, July and
Aug 10–8; adm exp*

In **Torrelles de Llobregat**, **Catalunya en Miniatura** is the biggest folly of its kind in Europe, and your chance to ride a miniature train and see the best monuments of Catalunya from the perspective of a Gulliver. Naturally, there's a special section devoted to Gaudí.

Market Days around Montserrat

ⓘ **Collbató**
Plaça de l'Era,
t 937 77 90 76

Collbató, *Mercat de la Tradició*: food, crafts and antiques, 3rd Sun of month.

Where to Stay and Eat around Montserrat

ⓘ **Montserrat >**
Plaça de la Creu,
t 938 77 77 77

Montserrat ✉ 08691

To get a feel for Montserrat, stay overnight, but be prepared: it can get quite cold even in summer. The monks operate two hotels:

***Abat Cisneros**, t 938 77 77 01 (€€€–€€). A honeymooners' special. Prices depend on whether you want breakfast, full or half board.

****Hs El Monestir**, t 938 77 77 01 (€€). Cheaper, with simpler rooms. *Open April to Oct.*

Monistrol de Montserrat
✉ 08691

The alternative to monkish hospitality is staying down in this village on the C55, a few minutes' walk from the *cremallera*. Monistrol has a small collection of rooms, restaurants and cafes; it's a good idea to book well in advance.

****P Guilleumes**, C/Guilleumes 3, t 938 28 40 65, www.guilleumes.com (€). Rooms with a view of Montserrat, not from it. An excellent budget hostal, with a very good restaurant: the €15 lunch menu can't be beaten.

****P La Barca**, Ctra Manresa, t 938 35 02 59 (€). Another very good, inexpensive *pensió*; a little noisier since it's on the main road. La Barca's restaurant (€€–€) is a tad more upmarket, and popular with the locals for seafood.

Alt Penedès, the Kingdom of *Cava*

Wine and the Penedès have always gone together. According to archaeologists, vines have been growing in the shadow of Montserrat for at least 2,500 years, and the region's fortunes have risen or fallen with the grapes ever since. In the 18th century they were selling Penedès wine to the British and the Dutch. When it went out of fashion there, they turned it into brandy and shipped it to Latin America. That went like a bomb until phylloxera wiped out the vines in the late 1880s. But when it was time to replant on American rootstock, the winemakers realized they were just in time to cash in on the new fashion for sparkling wines, and the Penedès made its new *cava* a worthy competitor to champagne.

Vilafranca del Penedès

Some wine regions have a lush and idyllic air; this isn't one of them. It's small and intense, with a definite air of agribusiness about it (the power lines running through it don't help either). The big town is sun-baked Vilafranca del Penedès, known throughout Catalonia not only for wine, but *castellers*; here they build their human towers ten storeys high.

Vilafranca's parish church of **Santa Maria** (1285) was one of the first Gothic buildings in Catalonia; ask at the tourist office and they'll get you in to climb the bell tower for a view of the town. Across Plaça Jaume from the church, a medieval palace and adjacent building have been restored to house the **Vinseum**,

Vinseum
t 938 90 05 82;
open Tues–Sat 10–2
and 4–7, Sun 10–2; adm

Getting to and around the Alt Penedès

Nothing could be easier than hopping out from Barcelona to Sant Sadurní or Vilafranca for a day's wine excursion in the Penedès. You can reach both by the R4 **train**. In Sant Sadurní, the Freixenet cellars are right by the station, and in both towns many of the others are right in town, not in the country.

Spain's first museum dedicated to wine, founded in 1944. Today it includes a bit of everything else too, with collections of art, natural history, and ceramics thrown in.

North of Vilafranca, the village of **Sant Martí Sarroca** grew up around a 10th-century castle called La Roca and the adjacent church of **Santa Maria**, a building with a fine Romanesque choir and a 1421 painted altarpiece attributed to Jaume Cabrera.

La Roca
church and castle open summer daily 10–2 and 4–8; winter daily 10–2 and 3–6; adm

Further west, the next scenic road down towards the coast passes the impressive Castell de Castellet, long a hot spot on the Moorish-Christian border; parts of it date to the 10th century. Recently restored by a corporate foundation, it's open for visits.

Castell de Castellet
t 902 43 04 62; guided tours Sat and Sun 10–2

South of Vilafranca, on a height overlooking the road to Sitges, **Olèrdola** was the big town in this region until the late Middle Ages. Lost in a forest of pines and palmettos, there isn't much left of it now, outside of the Conjunt Històric, maintained by the Barcelona Archaeological Museum; traces go back to the Iberians and the Neolithic era, and the ruins of a medieval church.

Conjunt Històric
t 938 90 14 20; open mid-Mar–mid-Oct 10–2 and 3–6; mid-Oct–mid-Mar Tues–Fri 10–2 and 3–6, Sat and Sun 10–4; adm

Sant Sadurní d'Anoia

Sant Sadurní d'Anoia produces 90 per cent of all Catalonia's *cava*. The giant producers Codorníu and Freixenet have their enormous operations on the outskirts, but many of the other 80 or so smaller cellars are right in the town.

Sant Sadurní is where wine and Modernisme come together. As they rebuilt their business after the phylloxera crisis, the wine barons hired some of Catalonia's top architects, including Puig i Cadafalch, to build their homes and cellars. Outside of the Codorníu winery (see p.162), none is particularly special in itself, but the tourist office offers guided tours of the 'Ruta Modernista' that includes a visit to Codorníu.

If you're ever up in the hills north of Sant Sadurní, have a look at the **Pont Nou** at Sant Pere Riudebittles. This is the arcade of an aqueduct, 82ft high and 262ft long, built not by the Romans but the medieval Catalans (restored in 1721 after an earthquake). Why was such a huge work erected in an isolated rural setting? The answer is another secret from Catalonia's remarkable industrial past. Back in the 13th century, all that water was powering paper mills. The remains of some of these can be seen in and around the village, along with one impressive water wheel.

Cava

'*Cava*', as you might have guessed, simply means a cellar. In the old days the better Catalan wines, those that were laid down, were called '*cava*' wines, and somehow through the years that came to be the name given to Catalonia's beloved bubbly.

And beloved it is. Catalans don't save the *cava* for New Year's, but drink it as an aperitif, or an everyday tipple at the bar after work. We have seen bottles of *cava* emptied and left on door sills in back alleys. It is still *de rigueur* for celebrations, though, and sometimes it can be a symbol of Catalan nationalism. On the memorable night in 1975 when Franco died, they drained every last bottle in Barcelona.

The great European festival of fizz really got its start in the decadent, over-the-top Paris of the 19th century, when champagne first became synonymous with high times. In 1872, an aristocratic old Penedès vintner named Josep Raventòs made a visit to Champagne to see how it was done, and decided to try it at home.

That was the origin of *cava*, and the first great *cava* house, Codorníu. 'Champagne Catalan', as it was called before denomination laws came in, was a hit, and other producers soon followed. Today, it's usually made from macabeo (viura), xarel·lo and parellada grapes; since the 1980s chardonnay has also become popular. There are also various varieties of rosé *cava*. The process is almost exactly the same as for champagne. At first the wine is almost colourless; some yeast is added for further fermentation, and the wine is bottled and given a metal cap like a beer bottle's. This second fermentation is when the carbon dioxide that makes the bubbles is formed, in an aging process that can last from nine months to four years.

Then comes the tricky bit, the *remuage*, or riddling. For a period, the bottles are tilted downwards and carefully rotated a fraction each day, to make the yeast settle out. Then they quickly freeze the necks where the sediment has collected; when the cap is removed, the pressure pops the frozen lees out. A little extra *cava* from the same vintage (the *licor d'expedició*), with a carefully measured content of sugar, is added to govern the flavour. And then, in goes the cork.

Penedès doesn't just make *cava*; Catalonia's biggest wine region produces still red and whites, some of great distinction, but nevertheless *cava* is its fame and its prosperity. Wine-lovers who come for a visit may be a little disappointed; don't expect the kind of convivial wine tourism you can enjoy in other parts of Spain, or France and Italy. It's a little too close to the big city for that. Almost everywhere, you're expected to ring ahead for a reservation, and pay for admission; in the bigger estates a visit can be little more than a promotional film followed by a perfunctory tour and tasting.

In Sant Sadurní, the *cava* capital, a trip to **Codorníu** (*Avda Jaume Codorníu, t 938 91 33 42*) is definitely worthwhile, as much for the wine as for the remarkable Modernista complex of buildings (1915) designed by Puig i Cadafalch, with a museum and over a million square feet of cellars. Although it has become a multinational concern, Codorníu is still run by the Raventós family; its great rival **Freixenet** (*Avda Joan Sala 2; t 93 891 70 96*), which has been making it only since 1914, is even bigger and much more corporate in spirit. Their advertising over the decades has made them almost as much of a consumer icon as Coca-Cola or Guinness.

Among the others, **Antonio Mascaró** (*C/Casal 9, Vilafranca del Penedès, t 938 90 16 28*) also produces still wines and brandies. **Albet i Noya** made the first organic *cava* for the Danish market in 1972, and they have gone all-organic since (*Can Vendrell, Sant Pau l'Ordal, t 938 99 48 12*). **Ludens** has another Modernista cellar (*at Masia Grabuac, Font-Rubí, t 938 97 81 29*).

Jean León, who went to America as a stowaway and eventually founded the famous Hollywood restaurant La Scala in partnership with James Dean, gave it up in the 1960s to make prize-winning wines in Penedès. His modern estate makes for one of the more interesting visits (*at Torrelavit, 7km north of Sant Sadurní, t 938 99 55 12*). Jean León is now owned by **Torres**, another global wine giant that began in Vilafranca with an '*americano*' who came back from Cuba in 1870 to start his wine empire here. Torres' huge estate outside Vilafranca can be visited too (*www.torres.es*), though you'll want to get well sloshed before you go. There's an automated train trip through the vineyards and cellars, and a 'multimedia experience with vineyard aromas'. *Oy!*

Market Days in the Alt Penedès

Vilafranca del Penedès, Saturday; **Sant Sadurní**, Thursday and Saturday; **Sant Pere de Riudebitlles**, Tuesday.

Where to Stay and Eat in the Alt Penedès

Vilafranca del Penedès ✉ 43400

****Hotel Domo**, C/Francesc Macià 4, t 938 17 24 26, www.domohotel.com (€€€). Right in the centre of town, this agreeable hotel has all kinds of extras including Jacuzzi and sauna.

Masgranell, Ctra Moja-Daltmar km 1, at Moja, just south of Vilafranca, t 938 98 10 01, www.masgranell.com (€€). Definitely one of the few real finds in this area: 15 sharp, modern rooms in a beautifully converted *masia* among the vineyards, and a fine restaurant (€€€–€€) with some refined cooking and a huge list of local wines. Nature pool, Jacuzzi and wi-fi.

Cal Ton, C/Casal 8, t 938 90 37 41 (€€€). Local cuisine paired with an excellent wine list (of course).

Sant Sadurní d'Anoia ✉ 08770
****Sant Sadurní**, C/Sant Antoní 99, t 938 91 43 35, www.hss.com.es (€). Immaculate small hotel in the centre.
****Sol i Vi**, Ctra Vilafranca, t 938 99 32 04, www.solivi.com (€€). Country inn 4km west of Sant Sadurní; big pool, and a restaurant that shines with roast and grilled meats (€€€–€€).

ⓘ **Vilafranca del Penedès >**
C/de la Cort 14, t 938 18 12 54

ⓘ **Sant Sadurní d'Anoia >>**
t 938 91 31 88

Sitges and the Costa de Garraf

When Barcelonins want to sprawl on a beach they usually head south to the Garraf. This little patch of rugged mountains gives Barcelona some unspoiled green space on its doorstep, and it pushes right down to the coast, keeping it from being as frantic and overbuilt as the strip north of the city.

Altogether, it's a coast thoroughly tamed to the ends of the metropolis; the commuter trains make it practically a Barcelona suburb. There are two big beach towns: sophisticated Sitges, very much a petal of the Fiery Rose of Anarchism that fluttered down to the sea; and the more workaday Vilanova i la Geltrú.

Castelldefels and the Parc Natural de Garraf

South of Barcelona, the coastline is taken up for over 20km by the airport and industry. The main highway hits the coast at Castelldefels, a big Barcelona suburb with a hugely popular, 5km-long, Blue Flag-certified, wi-fi-equipped stretch of sand. A dozen old watchtowers survive, relics from the 16th century when Turkish pirates were a constant menace. Castelldefels' council prides itself as a patron of the arts, and there's enough modern sculpture in its parks and roundabouts to fill a scrapyard. The town church, **Santa Maria**, is a right peculiar Modernista-neo-Romanesque-Byzantine work of 1903 with some paintings inside to match, supplied with a slight touch of Dalí by the Argentine-Catalan artist Josep Serrasanta. Casteldefells hosted many of the canoeing events in the 1992 Olympics, and you can take a turn in a boat or try other sports at the **Canal Olímpic**.

Getting to and around Sitges and the Costa Garraf

R2 commuter **trains** from Barcelona's Estació de Sants and Plaça Catalunya depart every 20mins for Castelldefels (the Castelldefels-Platja station is a minute from the beach), Garraf and Sitges (30 mins from Barcelona) and Vilanova i la Geltrú.

You're certainly welcome in Sitges, but your **car** isn't. They already have far too many; street parking can be nearly impossible and the rates in the city-run car parks are extortionate.

After Castelldefels, the coast and its nearly empty hinterland are enclosed in the **Parc Natural de Garraf**. It's a dry, spare wilderness, kept empty by rugged terrain, but there's just enough water for pine forests and vines. There are no roads through the park, although hiking and bicycling paths have been laid out; you'll find park information centres in Sitges and all the surrounding villages. Inland, at **Olivella**, one of the old *masies*, called **Palau Novella**, has become Spain's first Tibetan Buddhist monastery; they have a museum of Tibetan art and welcome visitors.

Palau Novella
t 902 50 33 53,
www.sakyapa.org

The coast south of Castelldefels is a busy place, squeezed under the Garraf peaks; there is a pretty sandy beach, lined with miniature, whitewashed, wooden beach cabins at the fishing port of **Garraf**, and several smaller and less crowded ones along the way. Garraf has another attraction, the **Bodegas Güell** (1895–1900) designed by Gaudí and Francesc Berenguer. Eusebi Güell had envisaged a hunting lodge here. Before it was finished, the plan got twisted around, and the hunting lodge turned into a winery with a gatekeeper's house. The result is as jaw-dropping as anything of Gaudí's; it's now a restaurant (*see* p.167).

Sitges

 Sitges

Wedged between the Garraf massif and a lovely long crescent of sand, Sitges has been Barcelona's favourite resort ever since the Modernistas flocked here at the turn of the century, led by painter and writer Santiago Rusinyol (1861–1931). Rusinyol, the son of a textile tycoon, was a Catalan original, a proto-Dalí in life if not in his art. His bohemian lifestyle and his Sitges *Festes Modernistes* and art exhibitions brought a little of Belle Epoque Paris to Catalonia.

The little fishing village of Sitges would never be the same again. Even when the artistic buzz faded, it remained a devoted party town. Its wild carnival was the only one in Spain that Franco was never able to completely suppress. Today, the trains from Barcelona's Sants station run every 20 minutes, and Sitges is essentially a Barcelona-on-the-beach in flip-flops and a silly straw hat. It attracts a big international crowd besides. In summer, and for special events like the carnival and the film festival in October, you can barely squeeze in.

Sitges was probably a discreet gay rendezvous for decades before the post-Franco liberalization brought things out into the open. Today it's arguably one of the pinkest little nipples on the globe. There are not only gay bars and clubs, but gay beaches, gay hotels, even a gay laundry. Though there have been occasional dust-ups, as in 2006 when a right-wing council unleashed the undercover cops, it all works out nicely. There is no gay ghetto: Sitges is an utterly cosmopolitan, artsy resort with an interesting mix of folks from all over. It helps that Sitges possesses two little museums, neighbours on a back street behind the church, that you won't soon forget.

Cau Ferrat

Sitges' picture-postcard view is the one framing its pretty parish church, **Sant Bartolomeu i Santa Tecla**, on a terrace overlooking the beach. They only open it for masses; Sitges is that kind of town.

The most picturesque corner is the few narrow streets directly behind the church, calm and lovely and well-whitewashed, with some whimsical notices and painted *azulejo* tiles stuck here and there. C/Fonollar is the heart of it, and home to the two museums. First is the **Cau Ferrat**, in a pair of old fisherman's cottages joined together and magnified to a celestial folly by Santiago Rusinyol.

Only in Spain! (or as the Catalans would say, Only in Catalonia!) There's more than a touch of madness in Rusinyol's hideaway. The house itself may be the star of the show, with its electric blue-painted walls and acres of *azulejos* and enormous inglenook fireplace. The upstairs is a sort of great medieval hall, where Rusinyol would put on performances and exhibitions for his famous *Festes Modernistes* from 1892 to 1899. Naturally, there's plenty of painting everywhere, by Rusinyol and many others, including an early Picasso (*La Cursa de Braus*) and two luminous El Grecos, of the Magdalene and St Peter. Rusinyol got these cheap in Madrid, and when he brought them back he hired a band and led them in a parade through the streets. Rusinyol was an avid collector of many things, and this great curiosity shop displays them all. Antique locks, keys and door-knockers were evidently closest to his heart, but there's a wonderful collection of glass work from the earliest times – the 8th century BC – up through the Romans to the artists of Venice and Bohemia.

Museu Maricel

Right next door is the Museu Maricel, built by the Chicagoan Charles Deering, heir to the International Harvester tractor fortune, and a man who made nearly as much an impact on Sitges as Rusinyol. With its big sea-view windows, this house would rate a visit even if it were empty. As it is, the city has stuffed it with more than 3,000 works of art collected by Jesús Pérez-Rosales. Who was

Cau Ferrat
t 938 94 03 64;
open June–Sept Tues–Sat 9.30–2 and 4–7, Sun 10–3; Oct–May Sat 9.30–2 and 3.30–6.30, Sun 10–3; adm

Museu Maricel
t 938 94 03 64;
open June–Sept Tues–Sat 9.30–2 and 4–7, Sun 10–3; Oct–May Tues–Sat 9.30–2 and 3.30–6.30, Sun 10–3; adm

08

Around Barcelona | Sitges and the Costa de Garraf

Jesús Pérez-Rosales? The town gynaecologist; business must have been very, very good.

And he had a good eye. Some of the works come uncomfortably close to the kitsch barrier (lots of Bouguereau-style naked ladies invariably described as 'allegories'), and that perhaps has kept the collection from getting the attention it deserves. There are few big names here, but a lot that is first-rate. There is an exceptional room of 13th–15th-century Catalan painting and sculpture, notably a *Crucifixion* by the Aragonese Tomás Giner, court painter to King Fernando El Católico. The allegories don't stop. The best, perhaps, is the *Miracle of Saint Genevieve*, an entire room painted in weirdly compelling *chiaroscuro* by Josep Maria Sert depicting the famous Battle of the Marne in 1914. Upstairs, there is loads of aristocratic clutter. If you've never seen a writing desk in the shape of Paris's City Hall before, here's your chance.

Across the street, Deering restored an unused hospital for his main residence, the **Palau Maricel**. It's a gorgeous building, especially the courtyard inside, but right now the town is restoring it again. Ask the tourist office if you can get in and have a look.

Another museum, the **Museu Romàntic Can Llopis** in the centre of town, conjures up the elegance of the 19th century and its love of gadgets – not to be missed by music-box fans. There's also a huge doll collection, some dating back to the 17th century.

Museu Romàntic Can Llopis
C/Sant Gaudenci 1
t 938 94 29 69; open June–Sept Tues–Sat 9.30–2 and 4–7, Sun 10–3; Oct–May Tues–Sat 9.30–2 and 3.30–6.30, Sun 10–3; adm

Vilanova i la Geltrú

If Sitges is too exciting, or too expensive, and you still want to have a good time on the beach, hop on the bus and slide over to Vilanova i la Geltrú, just 9km down the coast. This unusual three-headed town is many things, but exciting is not really one of them. La Geltrú is the original village. They say that in the Middle Ages the barons who ran it were so rough on La Geltrú's people that many of them moved to some land close by that he didn't control. Their new settlement, Vilanova, soon outstripped the mother village; the third head appeared only a century ago, when a resort strip grew up around the fishing port and nearby beaches.

Vilanova is mad for museums. In the busy centre, near the RENFE station on Avda Victor Balaguer, the **Museu Victor Balaguer** commemorates its founder, a 19th-century poet-politician, the 'Troubadour of Montserrat' who won the first Jocs Florals (*see* p.35). In an impressive Beaux-Arts building, the collection is mostly Catalan painting, with works by Rusinyol and Casas.

Just to the east, by the rail station on Plaça Maristany, the **Museu del Ferrocarril** has tons of memorabilia and what they claim is the biggest collection of steam engines in Europe, set in the old workshops.

Museu Victor Balaguer
t 938 15 42 02; open winter Tues, Wed, Fri and Sat 10–2 and 4–7, Thurs 10–2 and 6–9, Sun 10–2; summer Tues, Wed, Fri and Sat 10–2 and 4.30–7.30, Thurs eve 10–2 and 6–9, Sun 10–2; adm

Museu del Ferrocarril
t 938 15 84 91; www. museudelferrocarril.org open Tues–Fri 10.30–2.30, Sat 10.30–2.30 and 4–6.30; adm

Museu de Curiositats Marineres Roig Toqués
C/Alexandre de Cabanyes 2, t 938 154 263; open Tues–Sat 12–2 and 5–8; adm

A long, shady Rambla Principal connects workaday Vilanova with the seafront *Barri Marítim*. The beaches are as good as Sitges', though the scene is much calmer, even in summer, and everything's noticeably cheaper. Beyond doubt, the main reason for visiting Vilanova is the **Museu de Curiositats Marineres Roig Toqués**. Francesc Roig Toqués, a former boat-builder and fisherman, is responsible for this delightful collection of briny bric-a-brac, including ship's figureheads, models and everything else you can imagine – or not. Undoubtedly the biggest attraction here is

😊 **Juanita the carp**

Juanita the carp. She's a very small, goldfish-sort-of-carp, but Mr Roig has taught her to eat from a spoon and drink from a wine *porró*, among other tricks which have earned her a host of fans. You can join them any time except in winter, when she's hibernating.

Museu de Mar
t 938 15 04 02; open Tues–Sat 10–1.30 and 5–8.30, Sun 10–1.30; adm

At the eastern end of the strip, the very picturesque old **Sant Cristòfol lighthouse** is now home to the **Museu de Mar**, a more conventional hoard of clutter with no talented carp at all. There's a serious fishing port here, one of the biggest on Spain's Mediterranean coast, and you can see the auctions going on most days when the boats come in.

Market Days on the Costa de Garraf

Sitges, Thursday; **Vilanova i la Geltrú**, Saturday.

ⓘ **Castelldefels**
C/Pintor Serrasanta 4, t 936 35 27 27

Where to Stay and Eat on the Costa de Garraf

Garraf ✉ 08870

⭐ **Garraf >**

**Garraf, Platja de Garraf, t 936 32 00 07, *www.hotelgarraf.com* (€€–€) Literally on the beach, one of the prettiest in the region. A basic but delightful hotel (if the occasional passing train doesn't bother you). Rooms with a sea view are a little extra but worth it.

Gaudí Garraf, on the main C31, t 936 32 01 80, *www.gaudigarraf.com* (€€€). Surprisingly good restaurant in a Gaudí landmark. Refined cooking with a slight Italian touch; an interesting range of carpaccios, lots of seafood and some creative desserts.

ⓘ **Sitges >**
C/Sínia Morera, t 938 94 42 51

Sitges ✉ 08870

⭐ **El Xalet >>**

Sitges isn't for the staid nor the economy-minded, nor for those without a reservation. Things calm down considerably in the off season,

when many hotels close down, but even then, be sure to call in advance.

****Subur Maritim, Pg Maritim, t 938 94 15 50, *www.hotelsuburmaritim.com* (€€€€–€€€; *see site for discounts*). One of the better four-star options, with big pool, wi-fi and free bikes; most rooms have sea-view balconies.

***La Santa María, Pg de la Ribera 52, t 938 94 09 99, *www.lasantamaria. com* (€€€). Seafront hotel with bright, prettily furnished rooms and a little sun terrace with geraniums. Downstairs is a popular restaurant (€€€–€€) with a terrace. *Closed 20 Dec–end Jan.*

**Romàntic, C/Sant Isidre 33, t 938 94 83 75 (€€€). Three atmospheric 19th-century villas which are particularly popular with gay couples. All rooms are beautifully furnished with antiques. *Closed Nov–Mar.*

***Parrots, C/Joan Tarrida, t 938 94 13 50, *www.parrots-sitges.com* (€€; € *in low season*). The brightly painted centre of gay life in Sitges, with a terrace bar, restaurant and sauna.

**El Xalet, Isla de Cuba 33–5, t 938 11 00 70 (€€€–€€). Small hotel near the station in one of the prettiest Modernista houses in Sitges.

**Madison Bahia, C/Parelladas 27, t 938 94 00 12, *www.hotelmadison*

bahia.com (€€€–€€). Recently spruced up and very comfortable, this is conveniently close to the beach and the centre.

P Termes, Passatge Termes 9, t 938 94 23 43, www.hostaltermes.com (€€–€). Rooms are a bit of a tight squeeze, but otherwise good for this expensive town, with a roof terrace.

*P Parellades, C/Parellades 11, t 938 94 08 01 (€). Simple, friendly pensió with a small terrace and large rooms.

Mare Nostrum, Pg de la Ribera 60, t 938 94 33 93 (€€€). For imaginatively prepared fish and crustaceans (try the fresh cod steamed in cava). There's a decent wine list, a pretty seaside backdrop to your dinner, and a good set lunch menu.

★ El Velero >

El Velero, Pg de la Ribera 38, t 938 94 20 51 (€€€). On the seafront: good fresh seafood changing with the seasons and an excellent menú de degustació. Closed Sun.

El Celler Vell, C/Sant Bonaventura 21, t 938 11 19 61 (€€). In the former cellars of the Museu Romàntic, where they used to make malvasia wines, a nice spot for grills and seafood. There is an exceptional and inexpensive lunch menu. Closed Jan.

Izarra, C/Major 22, t 938 94 73 70 (€€). A Basque bar with pintxos all day, also a restaurant with good seafood: hake in green sauce, and bacallà from the people who do it best.

El Racó de la Carreta, C/de la Carreta, t 93894 78 36 (€€–€). The old town centre, away from the beaches, is the place to go for lunch. This one does duck confits and maigrets – but not quite like in France.

El Castell, C/de la Carreta, t 938 94 33 49 (€€–€). Nothing special, but a very good, inexpensive midday menu.

Eguzki, C/Sant Pau (€). Popular in the evenings, this bar has good Basque pintxos to go with local wines.

ⓘ **Vilanova i la Geltrú** >>
Passeig Carme (on the marina), t 938 15 45 17

★ Ceferino >

Vilanova i la Geltrú ✉ 08800

***Ceferino, Pg Ribas Roges 2, t 938 15 89 31, www.hotelceferino.com (€€; €€€ in July and Aug). Vilanova's best, a swanky beachfront hotel. They will arrange activities, or take you on a guided tour of the coastline on their sailboat.

**Ricard, Pg Marítim 88, t 938 15 99 57 (€). A comfortable hotel right on the beach. Closed mid-Dec–mid-Jan.

**Solvi 70, Pg Ribes Roges, t 938 15 70 02 (€). Another good one, family-run, bright and cheerful and very well-kept. Closed Oct, early Nov.

La Cucanya, in Racó de Santa Llúcia, just west of Vilanova on the coast, t 938 15 19 34 (€€€). A solid local favourite with an Italian touch: seasonal menus with some orgasmic seafood, but also more simple pizza and pasta. Closed first two weeks Nov.

L'Oganqüit, C/Llibertat 128, t 938 15 63 62 (€€–€). A little duck, a little seafood, but this place made its reputation with a list of thoroughly exotic pizzas and salads

Les Finestres, C/Ferrer i Vidal, t 938 15 62 36 (€€). Near the beach, on a back street off the Rambla, fine seafood at reasonable rates; good-value lunch menu. Closed 2nd half Sept.

Beaches, Bars, Golf and Hedonism in Sitges

Sitges has sixteen good sandy beaches with all the facilities. Eight of these line the town centre's seafront, including the **Platja de la Bassa Rodona**, the current gay muscle beach. In town, the action is centred on bar-lined C/Marqués de Montroig–C/Primer de Maig, popularly known as 'Sin Street'. This is the home of **Parrots**, a combination gay hotel, restaurant, sauna and bar that is a centre for people-watching (see p.167).

Currently, two of the most popular clubs are **Mediterraneo** and **Bourbon's**, both on C/Sant Bonaventura. Among the gay bars and clubs, there's the big and noisy **XXL** on C/Joan Tarrida, **Organic** and the **Bears' Bar** on C/Bonaire, the **Man Bar** on C/Sant Bonaventura. For more info, see www.gaysitges.com.

The big warehouse-style open-air disco, for gays and straights, is **l'Atlantida**, out west by the golf course on Ctra de Golf. **Pachá** on Pg San Diego is the posey Sitges club that turned itself into an international chain. **Bar Voramar**, on Sant Sebastià beach, has occasional jazz concerts.

Girona

Girona is one jammy province. In many ways it's the California of Spain – the wealthiest province per capita, and one containing more than its share of good things. Its seafront is the spectacular Costa Brava, while the snow-capped winter and summer playground of the Pyrenees beckons on the horizon. Cork forests and olive groves decorate the coastal mountains; orchards and farms prosper in the rich volcanic soil. Girona itself is one of Spain's most atmospheric medieval cities, while the honest traveller is constantly waylaid by Neolithic dolmens, Iberian oppida, Greek and Roman relics, medieval villages, Romanesque churches and Gothic castles.

The Modernistas were here, too, if somewhat few and far between, but so was a certain Salvador Dalí, who left behind Spain's second most popular museum (after Madrid's Prado) in Figueres, as well as his residences in Portlligat and Púbol – duly promoted as the 'Dalí Triangle'.

09

Don't miss

⭐ Delicious Cadaqués
Cadaqués p.191

⭐ An evocative, medieval city
Girona p.203

⭐ The beaches of Cap de Begur
Cap de Begur p.180

⭐ Dalí's madcap Teatre Museu
Figueres p.197

⭐ Bucolic, volcanic charms
La Garrotxa p.215

See map overleaf

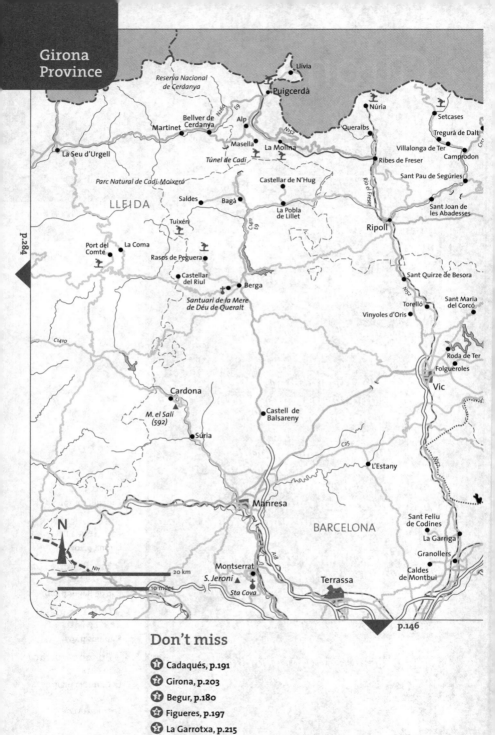

Llívia

Reserva Nacional
de Cerdanya

Puigcerdà

Núria

Setcases

Bellver de
Cerdanya

Martinet

Alp

Tregurà de Dalt

Queralbs

Villalonga de Ter

Masella

La Molina

Camprodon

La Seu d'Urgell

Túnel de Cadí

Ribes de Freser

Sant Pau de Segúries

Parc Natural de Cadí-Moixeró

Castellar de N'Hug

LLEIDA

Saldes

Bagà

Sant Joan de
les Abadesses

La Pobla
de Lillet

Tuixén

Ripoll

Port del
Comte

La Coma

Sant Quirze de Besora

Rasos de Peguera

Sant Maria
del Corcó

Castellar
del Riul

Berga

Torelló

Vinyoles d'Oris

Santuari de la Mere
de Déu de Queralt

Roda de Ter

Folgueroles

Vic

Cardona

M. el Salí
(592)

Castell de
Balsareny

Súria

L'Estany

N

Manresa

BARCELONA

Sant Feliu
de Codines

La Garriga

Granollers

20 km

Montserrat

Caldes
de Montbui

S. Jeroni

Sta Cova

Terrassa

10 miles

p.146

Don't miss

p.284

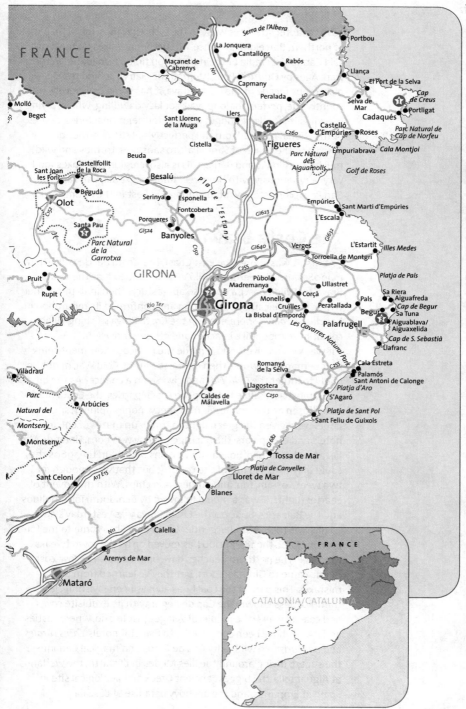

This chapter stretches west to the Llobregat river, taking in part of northern Barcelona province. Altogether it makes up most of 'Old Catalonia', cradle of the new nation first consolidated in the Dark Ages by Guifré el Pilos (Wilfred the Hairy). Behind the glamorous façade of the Costa Brava, it has some truly lovely countryside, perfect for long walks or lazy dawdling, while staying in exquisite hotels or budget B&Bs in former monasteries, castles or traditional *masies*. From the perfectly salted anchovies of L'Escala to the beans of Santa Pau, to sausages, truffles and wild mushrooms in Vic and Berga, this is also a region that takes food very, very seriously, with three restaurants (El Bulli, Can Fabes and Can Roca) consistently rated among the best in the entire world.

The Costa Brava

At first it was simply the East Coast, the 'Costa del Llevant'. Then in 1908, journalist Ferran Agulló Vidal described it as the 'Costa Brava' (or Wild Coast), a name so apt it stuck. Then in 1949 another writer, Rose Macauley, came along and confirmed its reputation in her classic *Fabled Shore*, evoking the Costa Brava's fishing villages, cobalt bays, moon-like beaches and otherworldly light.

It was well received. And it made the Franco government think that perhaps the world, then immersed in the Cold War, might be ready to forget the Civil War and give Spain a chance? As the bit of Spain most accessible to European coach parties, the Costa Brava was chosen as the first foreign currency money-spinner; speculators were given the green light to throw up mazes of cheap hotels and cheap bars: the package holiday was born. Lloret de Mar became the 'abroad' holiday for millions of Brits. In the 1960s they could only take £50 out of the country, but that was enough for two weeks of sun, fun, and burgers and chips. With the advent of charter flights, it was a model followed by Benidorm, Torremolinos and the Balearics. By 2000 the Costa Brava was yesterday's news.

That was then. A kinder, gentler Costa Brava has come to the fore. Even in Lloret, the 18–30 club has moved on as the town tweaks its image. The northern beaches have opened up since low-cost flights came to Girona airport, but they've learned from past mistakes. This part of the coast has always been ravishing, less trampled, less known: the Cap de Begur with its exquisite coves and coastal walks; the medieval villages just inland, where castles and *masies* have been converted into five-star hotels, *cases rurales* and *agriturismes*; wild, salty Cap de Creus and magical Cadaqués; the superb diving around the Illes Medes in L'Estartit, the wetlands at Aiguamolls, the biggest ancient Greek archaeological site in Spain at Empúries, and the anchovy paradise of L'Escala.

Getting to the Costa Brava

Trains from Barcelona frequently stop at Blanes and Lloret de Mar. **SARFA buses** (*t 902 30 20 25, www. sarfa.es*) serve the Costa Brava from Girona and Barcelona's Estació del Nord; many resorts are served by direct buses from Girona airport as well (*see* p.204).

SARFA (*t 932 65 11 58 or t 932 65 12 09*) run direct buses from Barcelona to Roses and Cadaqués. Portbou and Llançà are most easily reached by trains to France.

Blanes to Palamós

Blanes

With a long beach and fishing fleet, Blanes is where it all begins. Uniquely, it's bookended by lush botanical gardens. To the south, by the pretty cove of **Sant Francesc**, German botantist Karl Faust planted the beautiful ten acre **Jardí Botànic Mar i Murtra** on the hill of Sant Joan, with some 3,000 species, including a unique selection of *androcymbium* (related to lilies) and century-old *araucarias* next to his villa, the very embodiment of the old Costa Brava élite. On the north end of Blanes, thousands of cacti, prickly pears and aloes grace the **Jardí Botànic Pinya de Rosa**, planted in 1954 by Fernando Riviere de Caralt, a civil engineer.

Lloret de Mar

Ask any Catalan, and they'll say the best way to see Lloret de Mar is from a fast car speeding down the highway. The town has 200 hotels, cheek-to-jowl with theme parks, go karts, bars, burger stands, flashing noises and glaring lights and a casino to rake up any loose change, all radiating from a long beach set in lush cliffs.

Once the Roman Loryma, Lloret in the 18th and 19th centuries was so poor that thousands sailed away to seek a better life in the Caribbean. At least some made it big (there's a poignant plaque on the seafront, remembering those who didn't) and returned as *americanos* to build villas and flaunt their wealth. One of a handful of surviving villas on the waterfront now houses the **Museu del Mar**, dedicated to seaworthy things, with models, figureheads, films and interactive displays.

Nearby, a cat-mad Russian couple have set up the oddball **Cat's House**, offering three floors of feline art and kitsch going back to the 18th century. In the attractive pre-mass-tourism village centre, Lloret's pretty **church** is also worth a look, with its party-coloured tiled dome and Modernista chapels.

There are great views from the landmark 10th–11th-century watchtower, the **Torre Sant Joan**, or from the dreamy **Jardí Santa Clothilde**, set on a cliff on the southern edge of Lloret, rising on a hill above a tidal wave of new apartment blocks. The gardens were designed in 1919 by young Nicolau Rubió i Tuduri, who was inspired by the Renaissance gardens of Rome and Florence with terraces of

Jardí Botànic Mar i Murtra
Pg Carles Faust, t 972 33 08 26, www.jbotanic marimurtra.org; open June–Sept daily 9–8; April, May and Oct daily 9–6; Nov–Mar daily 10–5; adm

Jardí Botànic Pinya de Rosa
Platja de Santa Cristina, t 972 35 52 90; open daily 9–6; adm

Museu del Mar
Pg Camprodon i Arrieta 1–2; open June–Sept Mon–Sat 9–8, Sun 10–1 and 4–7; Mar–May and Oct–Nov Mon–Sat 9–1 and 4–7, Sun 10–1 and 4–7; Dec–Feb Mon–Sat 9–1.30 and 3.30–6, Sun 10–3; adm

Cat's House
C/Sant Albert 10 (near Hotel Marsol), t 972 36 62 66, www.catsmuseum. com; open Mon–Sat 10–1.30 and 5–8; adm

Torre Sant Joan
t 972 35 20 64; open Sat and Sun 11–6, or at 4.30 Tues–Sun via the little tourist train; adm

Jardí Santa Clothilde
open Tues–Sun 10–5, guided tours Sat and Sun at 10:30; adm

fountains, statues and towering cypresses descending languidly towards the sea.

Tossa de Mar

A pretty drive up the coast from Lloret, Tossa de Mar was 'discovered' back in the 1920s by the first foreign visitors to the Costa Brava, but it has maintained considerably more charm. Roman Turissa shows its pedigree in the foundations and simple mosaic floors of the 1st-century BC **Villa Roma Els Ametller**, tucked up behind the tourist office; its gate is usually open.

The picturesque old town or **Vila Vella**, tumbles over the cape – a maze of alleys, stone and whitewashed houses, embraced by a 12th-century walls and seven towers overlooking Tossa's wide swath of beach. In its heart, the **Museu Municipal** has finds from the Roman villa, as well as a somewhat motley collection of paintings by artists who stayed in Tossa. One was Marc Chagall, who spent the entire summer of 1934 here; the museum's *El Violinista Celeste* is his only painting in Spain.

Inspired by the Chagallian presence, Tossa has more than its share of public art, including, along the Passeig Marítim, Spain's only statue to Joan Salvador Gavina (aka Jonathan Livingston Seagull), and a bronze, life-sized (but still petite) Ava Gardner gazing out from the Vila Vella's walls. The beautiful Ava fell in love with the Costa Brava while filming 1951's *Pandora and the Flying Dutchman*. According to rumours, she fell in love with a bullfighter too – rumours that brought the jealous Frank Sinatra flying over.

At its highest point the Vila Vella had a castle, but this was knocked down for a lighthouse in the 19th century; the current **Far de Tossa** (1917) has displays on lighthouses, and the lives of their keepers, from around the Mediterranean.

Inland from Tossa: Llagostera and Caldes de Málavella

From Tossa, the GI681 to Girona climbs dramatically over the granite **Cadiretes Massif** to the Selva plain (*selva* means 'jungle') where the farming town of **Llagostera** just happened to produce one of the most successful poster and advertising designers in Paris in the 1920s and '30s. Emili Vilà i Gorgoll (1887–1967) may not be a household name, but you can fill in all the gaps in your knowledge at his house, now the **Museu Emili Vilà**, with some 300 works by the master, including portraits of movie stars, dating from his days in Hollywood, as well as small works by Modigliani, Toulouse-Lautrec and Picasso.

Although the volcanoes in the Garrotxa (*see* pp.215–17) draw most of the attention, there was plenty of volcanic activity in these parts 30 million years ago as well. Their warmth lingers in the springs at **Caldes de Malavella**; used by the ancient Romans, they

Museu Municipal
Plaça Roig y Soler,
t *972 34 07 09;*
open winter Tues–Sat
10–2 and 4–6, Sun
10–3; longer hours in
summer; adm

Far de Tossa
Plaça del Far,
t *972 34 01 08; open*
winter Tues–Sun 10–6,
longer hours in
summer; adm

Museu Emili Vilà
C/Sant Pere 25/27,
t *972 830 253, www.*
fundacioemilivila.com;
open Mon–Sat
11–1 and 4–6

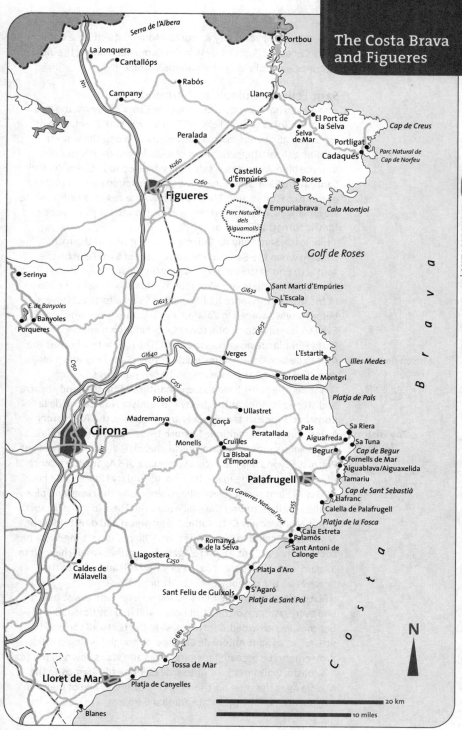

Serra de l'Albera

Portbou

La Jonquera

Cantallóps

Rabós

Campany

Llança

El Port de
la Selva

Cap de Creus

Peralada

Selva
de Mar

Portlligat

Cadaqués

Parc Natural de
Cap de Norfeu

Castelló
d'Empúries

Roses

Figueres

Parc Natural
dels
Aiguamolls

Empuriabrava

Cala Montjoi

Golf de Roses

Serinya

E. de Banyoles

Banyoles

Sant Martí d'Empúries

L'Escala

Porqueres

L'Estartit

Illes Medes

Verges

Torroella de Montgrí

Platja de Pals

Púbol

Ullastret

Madremanya

Corçà

Pals

Sa Riera

Girona

Monells

Peratallada

Aiguafreda

Sa Tuna

Cruïlles

Begur

Cap de Begur

La Bisbal
d'Emporda

Fornells de Mar

Aiguablava/Aiguaxelida

Tamariu

Palafrugell

Cap de Sant Sebastià

Les Gavarres Natural Park

Llafranc

Calella de Palafrugell

Platja de la Fosca

Romanyá
de la Selva

Cala Estreta

Palamós

Llagostera

Sant Antoni de
Calonge

Caldes de
Málavella

Platja d'Aro

S'Agaró

Sant Feliu de Guíxols

Platja de Sant Pol

Tossa de Mar

Lloret de Mar

Platja de Canyelles

Blanes

C o s t a

B r a v a

N

20 km

10 miles

now gurgle up in a snazzy, colourful Modernista spa, the Catalan Vichy. Geologists know it best for its **Camp dels Ninots**, the 'field of figurines' – chunks of opal in curious shapes.

Sant Feliu de Guíxols and Around

If you still have any doubts about the Costa's bravura, the 23km road from Tossa to Sant Feliu de Guíxols will cure them, with its legendary 365 bends, dotted with *miradors* along the way for admiring the vertiginous views of musclebound cliffs tumbling into the blue. After 7km, a side road winds up to the 19th-century **Santuari de Sant Grau**, where the vistas inspired Ferrán Agulló to give the coast its name. There are a few chances for a swim on the way, involving descents on tiny winding roads; keep an eye peeled for the turnoff at Rosamar.

Like Tossa, **Sant Feliu de Guíxols** was a big shot in the 10th century, when the Benedictine **Monastery of Sant Feliu** on the southern end of the modern town was one of the wealthiest in Catalonia. The huge complex, rebuilt after a sacking by the Moors in the 9th century, once had a moat and seven fortified towers before it was savaged in Catalonia's 1835 church-burning spree. Even so, its surviving walls, towers, Gothic church and Mozarabic Porta Ferrada are an impressive sight. The monastery houses the **Museu de la Vila** with items made of cork (Sant Feliu was a major exporter) as well as glasswork, and a few paintings.

Museu de la Vila
Plaça del Monestir,
t 972 82 15 75;
open Tues–Sat 10–1
and 5–8, Sun 10–1

Wander the palm-lined **Passeig Marítim**, lining the sandy beach, and stop for a drink at the pretty Modernista **Nou Casino de la Constància**. Or visit the old dolls and tin cars in the **Toy History Museum**, featuring antique Spanish toys and fun model trains.

Toy History Museum
Rambla Antoni Vidal
48–52, t 972 82 22 49;
open July–Sept daily
10–1 and 5–9; Oct–June
Tues–Fri 10–1 and 4–7;
Sat 10–1 and 4–8,
Sun 10–2; adm

Sant Feliu's more intimate, prettier beach is 2½km north at **Sant Pol**. Just beyond lies the exclusive enclave of **S'Agaró**, the brainchild of José Ensesa. In the 1920s, his now-legendary Noucentista hotel La Gavinia and surrounding villas overlooking the coves and pines rivalled Antibes among the Hollywood set. Then, in 1959, Elizabeth Taylor, Montgomery Clift, Katherine Hepburn and director Joseph Mankiewicz came to film Tennessee Williams' unsettling *Suddenly Last Summer* at Sant Pol and S'Agaró. In summer, when the road to S'Agaró is blocked, park at Sant Pol (or try to!) and walk to the beaches on the magnificent seaside promenade.

Platja d'Aro is Lloret de Mar's younger sister, with a vast beach and even vaster assortment of hotels and holiday flats. Other beaches, less crowded, dot the coast to the north all the way to the litte resort of **Sant Antoni de Calonge**, although parking is often problematic; be prepared for long walks and stairs down to the sea.

A coastal walk links Sant Antoni de Calonge to **Palamós**, in the Middle Ages the chief port serving Girona. It was one of many on the coast sacked by the pirate admiral Barbarossa in 1543, which led to a rapid decline; Palamós recovered as a cork-exporting port, only to suffer grave damage and the loss of hundreds of houses in the Civil War. Today it's the most important commercial fishing port on the Costa Brava, specializing in prawns. The **Platja de la Fosca** is safe for the smallest child and the **Cala Estreta**, a double cove divided by a sand bar, is as pretty as a picture. Palamós also has an award-winning museum dedicated to fishing, the **Museu de la Pesca**: ask them about tours of the unloading of the fleet and the fish auction.

Inland, lie Platja Aro's medieval village 'descendants'. The most atmospheric is **Romanyà de la Selva**, built around the 10th-century church of Sant Martí, up in the heart of **Les Gavarres Natural Park**, the source of all that cork. To the east of Romanyà stands one of Catalonia's largest dolmens, the **Cova d'en Daina** (2700 BC), surrounded by a granite cromlech of smaller stones.

Museu de la Pesca
Plaça dels Països Catalans, t 972 60 12 44, www.museudelapesca. org; open 15 June–15 Sept daily 11–9; 16 Sept–14 June Tues–Sat 10–1.30 and 3–7, Sun 10–2 and 4–7, closed Mon; adm

⭐ Diana >>

Where to Stay and Eat from Blanes to Palamós

Blanes ✉ 17300

Can Tarranc, Ctra Blanes a Toderà s/n, t 937 64 20 37 (€€). Very traditional Catalan dishes (potatoes stuffed with *brandade* of cod) served up in a pretty 18th-century *masia* set amid gardens and a pool, 3km outside Blanes.

Can Flores II, Esplanada del Port, t 972 33 16 33 (€). Very popular, big, brightly lit seafood restaurant overlooking the old port.

Lloret de Mar ✉ 17310

If you want to stay here, it's best to book a package.

El Trull, Cala Canyelles, 2km from Lloret, t 972 36 49 28, www.eltrull.com (€€€). This restaurant has been going strong for over 40 years, serving excellent, ultra-fresh seafood and variations on Catalan 'surf and turf' (pigeon with chestnuts and cod for the daring), home-made ice creams, in a pretty garden setting.

Mas Vell, C/Sant Roc 3, near the bullring, t 972 36 82 20 (€€). Rustic atmosphere: good value seafood which you can sample *al fresco*.

Tossa de Mar ✉ 17320

*****Mar Menuda**, Av. Mar Menuda s/n, t 972 34 10 00, www.hotelmarmenuda. com (€€€). Right on the beachfront, with a pool and Jacuzzi, and a smart restaurant.

****Diana**, Plaça d'Espanya 6, t 972 34 18 86, www.diana-hotel.com (€€€). Delightful old villa with a pretty courtyard backing onto the seaside promenade. Inside there's an original Gaudí fireplace, Modernista frescoes and plenty of light from the glass roof. Reserve in advance. *Closed mid-Nov–Mar.*

****Capri**, Pg del Mar 17, t 972 34 03 58, www.hotelcapritossa.com (€€). Perfect location on the seafront with a pleasant terrace. *Closed Nov–April.*

***Cap d'Or**, Pg de la Vila Villa 1, t 972 34 00 81, www.hotelcapdor.com (€€). Eleven cosy rooms in a former family home by the sea, just under the walls with free wi-fi; the closest parking, however, is 10 minutes away.

***Canaima**, Avda La Palma, 24A, t 972 34 09 95, www.hotelcanaima.com (€€–€). A genial choice in town, 500m from the beach, with crisp, white-painted en-suite rooms.

La Cuina de San Simon, C/Portal 24, t 972 34 12 69 (€€€€). You'll need to book to get one of the handful of tables at this cosy gourmet temple, situated in a house built in 1714. Don't hesistate: splash out on the six-course *menú degustació*.

Bahía, Pg del Mar 19, t 972 34 03 22 (€€). Since 1953, the place for good seafood and *sopa de mero* (fish soup with grouper).

Es Molí, C/Tarull 5, **t** 972 34 14 14 (€€). Well-rounded menu with outdoor dining on a gorgeous patio in summer and around the fireplace in the winter.

Berlín, C/Sant Antoní 8, **t** 972 34 02 18 (€). It's been there for over 40 years, tucked away and serving big hearty helpings when you need no fuss meat, fish and potatoes. *Closed late Nov–late April.*

Caldes de Malavella ✉ 17455

*****Meliá Golf Vichy Catalán, Ctra N-II km 701, **t** 972 18 10 20, *www.meliagolfvichycatalan.com* (€€€€). New, curvaceous designer resort hotel with all trimmings; set amid gardens, swimming pools and golf courses.

Sant Feliu de Guíxols ✉ 17220

***Eden Roc, 1km north of Sant Feliu, **t** 972 32 01 00, *www.caproig.com* (€€€; *half board required in high season*). Modern resort hotel in a gorgeous location on a little peninsula, with every imaginable amenity.

 La Malcontenta >>

***Plaça, Plaça Mercat 22, **t** 972 32 51 55, *www.hotelplaza.org* (€€€–€€). In the centre, just 100m from the beach, pleasant lodgings. *Open year-round.*

Can Toni, C/Sant Martirià 29, **t** 972 32 10 26 (€€). Reliable family-run restaurant, with traditional favourites.

S'Agaró ✉ 17853

*****Hostal de la Gavina, Plaça Rosaleda s/n, **t** 972 32 11 00, *www.lagavina.com* (€€€€€). Since 1932, the legendary Costa Brava hotel of the stars – everyone from Liz Taylor to U2 has stayed here. Sumptuous whitewashed villa on the beach, filled with antiques and surrounded by lush gardens, with a solarium, spa, gym, tennis, and an 18-hole golf course nearby. The restaurant (€€€€) is one of the finest in Catalonia, with a gorgeous terrace. *Closed 13 Oct–Easter.*

Platja d'Aro ✉ 17250

****Big Rock, Barri de Fenals 5, **t** 972 81 80 12 (€€€€). This stately 18th-century *masia* on a hill (get there by way of Avda Juli Gerreta from the centre) has five rooms, but is best known up and down the coast for its inventive seafood.

****Park Hotel San Jorge, Ctra Palamós s/n, **t** 972 65 23 11, *www.parkhotelsanjorge.com* (€€€€–€€€). Set on a cliff over a beautiful sandy cove, a superb renovation of a hotel from the 1950s with a swimming pool and spa. Book on line for bargains. Its restaurant **La Cala** (€€€) is equally lovely.

Planamar, Pg del Mar 82, **t 972 81 71 77, *www.planamar.com* (€€€–€€). Central, beachfront hotel; with a pool and gym. *Closed mid-Oct–Mar.*

***Els Pins, C/Verge del Carme 34, **t** 97281 72 19, *www.hotelelspins.com* (€€). Family run modern hotel with a small pool and terrace, just 25m from the beach.

Romanyà de la Selva ✉ 17246

Can Roquet, Plaça de l'Església, **t** 972 83 30 81, *www.canroquet.com* (€€€). Run by two artists from Belgium, set in a 19th-century *masia* in the village centre. Lovely food, and views.

Palamós ✉ 17230

*****La Malcontenta, Paratge de Torre Mirona, Platja de Castell 12, **t** 972 31 23 30, *www.lamalcontentahotel.com* (€€€€–€€€). Wonderful 19th-century mansion opened as a hotel in 2005. Peaceful, set in elegant grounds with a lovely pool.

***Sant Joan, Avda de la Llibertat 79, **t** 972 31 42 08, *www.hotelsantjoan.com* (€€€). Peaceful rooms in an 18th-century *masia*, set in a spacious garden with a pool, just a 10-minute walk to the beach. The breakfast buffet is an added bonus.

***Trias, Pg del Mar 7, **t** 972 60 18 00, *www.hoteltrias.com* (€€€). Recently refurbished, century-old hotel by the sea (Truman Capote stayed here), but a short stroll from the middle of town. There's a pool and one of Palamós' best restaurants, famous for its rice served with fresh crab (*cranc*).

Nauta, Av. 11 de Setembre 44, **t 972 31 48 33, *www.hotelnauta.com* (€). A trim, well-kept bargain choice, a block from the sea.

La Gamba, Plaça Sant Pere 1, **t** 972 31 46 33, *www.lagambapalamos.com* (€€€–€€). For 40 years the Cuadrat family has put smiles on diners' faces with the freshest lobster.

The Heart of the Costa Brava

The ancient Greeks had exquisite taste, and chose the stunning site of Empúries for their most important settlement in Spain. It has since evolved into Baix and Alt (Lower and Upper) Empordà, home to the Costa Brava's most scenic beaches, coves and landscapes, littered with handsome medieval towns and castles that recall the days of the Counts of Empordà, a feisty bunch of feudal lords set up to safegaurd the lands conquered from the Moors. For centuries their history would be one of bloody politics. The Count Kings of Barcelona finally put an end to it in 1402, when the last of the local dynasties died off. In the intervening 600 years the counts of Empordà built so many castles that some linguists think the name Catalonia derives from Castle-onia.

Palafrugell

In medieval times, the deliciously named Palau Frugell (or Palace of Fruits) sheltered Norman raiders and pirates within its walls. Today old Palafrugell is a web of narrow, curiously anonymous streets converging on busy central Plaça Nova. It has a couple of claims to fame: as the birthplace of Catalonia's best known journalist, Josep Pla (1897–1981), and home to Spain's one and only cork museum, the **Museu del Suro**. In the late 18th century, as the market for champagne took off, so did the demand for quality cork – and the surrounding Gavarres and L'Ardenya hills had some of the best.

Museu del Suro
C/de la Tarongeta 30,
t 972 30 78 25,
www.museudelsuro.cat;
open 15 June–15 Sept
daily 10–2 and 4–9;
16 Sept–14 June
Tues–Sat 5–8, Sun and
hols 10.30–1.30; tours in
English on Tues
at 5pm; adm

Palafrugell became a major manufacturer: the money was excellent compared to wages in Barcelona's mills, and far more certain than fishing. Most of the work was done by hand, while factory readers read aloud to pass the time. It wasn't long before the newly educated cork-workers were founding literary athenaeums and *casinos* (clubs) where they could meet, read and discuss the issues of the day. Most cork factories closed down with the First World War but one, owned by an American firm, lingered on until 1970. The factory building itself is now the **Fundació Vila Casas en Can Mario**, dedicated to contemporary sculpture, with both a permanent collection and temporary exhibitions.

Fundació Vila Casas en Can Mario
Plaça Can Mario 7,
t 972 30 62 46, www.
fundaciovilacasas.org;
open 15 June–Sept
Wed–Mon 5–9.30,
Oct–14 June Sat 11–2
and 4.30–8,
Sun 11–2; adm

Palafrugell's beaches are some of the most beguiling along the Costa Brava, at their best in September, when the water's still warm but the crowds have cleared off and parking isn't a nightmare (all the beaches are served by Sarfa buses from Palafrugell's new station). The largest of these, at the end of an incongruous highway, is **Calella de Palafrugell**, an archetypal whitewashed fishing village tucked under Cap Roig, with a few of the traditional fishing smacks called *mallorquinas* bobbing in the bay.

Habaneres and Cremat

In summer Calella de Palafrugell lilts to Catalan-Cuban sea shanties called *habaneres*. The songs grew out of a cultural give-and-take that began in early colonial times, when Europe's *contradansa* (a fast-paced folk dance) was introduced to the New World; the Cubans added their own Caribbean beat and in the 19th-century the songs, accompanied by guitar and accordian, were brought back to Catalonia by returning emigrés and sailors. The first *habanera* score, *El amor en el baile*, was published in 1842; and the first worldwide hit, *La Paloma* by Basque composer Sebastián Yradier, came out in 1855. Yradier's other classic, *El Arreglito*, was borrowed by George Bizet's for *l'Amour est un oiseau rebelle*. Today in Catalonia over a hundred groups play *habaneres*. In 1967, the *Amics dels Habaneres* in Calella de Palafrugell started a festival that today draws some 30,000 fans in late June or early July. And the perfect traditional drink on a cool evening sitting by the sea? *Cremat*, a potent shot of burnt rum, flavoured with cinnamon, lemon and coffee beans. Be warned; it's an acquired taste.

Cap de Sant Sebastià and Cap de Begur

⭐ Cap de Begur   Cliffs pirouette to the sea between a series of gently shelving strands and lapis lazuli coves, while parasol pines cling to every ledge: these two capes are among the crown jewels of the Costa Brava. You can drive or bus down to most of the beaches, but walking along the shore is far more beautiful, while kayaking (*see* below) around the coast can get you to many places inaccessible by land. The **GR92 path**, blazed by watch towers from Calella de Palafrugell, meanders north to sheltered **Llafranc**, with a silvery crescent of sand and smart hotels and restaurants; this was probably Roman Cypsela, and in 1950 they say you could still find bits of wall, mosaic, pottery and coins lying around.

From Llafranc's church the path continues to the Cap de Sant Sebastià (site of the Can Mina dels Torrents dolmen) and up 161 steps to the **Far de Sant Sebastià**, a lighthouse built in 1857; the reward for using up all your puff is a truly magnificent vista. Then continue north to **Tamariu** beach, enveloped in fragrant pines. Next come **Aiguaxelida** and **Aiguablava**, with the Costa Brava's *parador* on the promontory hidden in the trees above. The beach at **Sa Tuna** has a whitewashed fishing village for a backdrop; **Sa Riera** is another Blue Flag beauty. **Begur**, on the hill above, is a pleasant hilly village gathered under a 10th-century fortress, built to shelter shore-dwellers from Norman raiders.

Medieval Villages Just Inland

Medieval villages dot the slopes of the **Gavarres** mountains and the fertile plain between Begur and Girona, where zoning laws have helped to preserve the countryside from the worst of the sprawl. The striking walled ensemble of **Pals** was almost destroyed in the Civil War but has since been meticulously rebuilt to become a honeypot for coach tours. Sand dunes back the 6km-long **Platja de Pals**, framed by a great tree-topped chunk of rock and much frequented by German families.

Historically the most important town in the area was **La Bisbal d'Empordà**, a market town first recorded in 901. Its attractive Romanesque castle, built by the Bishop of Girona ('Bisbal' comes from Bisbe, or 'bishop'), now houses the Baix Empordà historical archive. You don't have to be in town long to notice that it makes pots; the ceramics trade dates from the 17th century and a long street of shops does a brisk trade. La Bisbal can also boast of Catalonia's top *sardana* dance band, the *Cobla Principal de la Bisbal*, founded in 1888 and now the Generalitat's official *cobla*. Nearby are two churches to seek out: Mozarabic **Sant Julià de Boada** with horseshoe arches, off the road to **Pals**, and the lovely Romanesque Sant Esteve at Canapost on the road to **Peratallada**.

Northeast of La Bisbal, where the Gavarres mountains begin to rise, stands **Peratallada**. Its name means 'cut rock' – an accurate description, with its deep moat, Romanesque-Gothic castle and tangle of lanes carved in the rock. Just north, medieval **Ullastret** is near the even older Iberian settlement of **Ullastret**, where, in the 5th century BC, the Indiket tribe built their most important hilltop settlement in Catalonia, defended by enormous walls. Inside are the remains of houses, reservoirs, canals, and a main square. Lead plaques discovered here are among the most important records of Iberian scripts (and incidentally helped to disprove the theory that the Basque language descended from Iberian). Finds from the site are in a museum in a 14th-century hermitage.

Northwest of La Bisbal, there are more pretty villages: **Corçà** (if a tad over-restored); **Cruïlles** with a striking 11th- to 12th-century donjon; atmospheric **Monells**, and walled **Madremanya**, with attractive townhouses. From here you can drive up to the **Convent de la Mare de Déu dels Àngels** (1,600ft), jam-packed with picnickers at weekends, who come for strolls and to take in the stupendous views. Dalí and Gala were secretly wed here in 1958.

Not long after Dalí met Gala in 1929, he promised her a palace. It took him until 1969, but he finally kept his word, purchasing and restoring the ruined 11th-century castle in **Púbol**, off the C66 towards Girona. Their rule was that Dalí could only enter if she invited him, which she very seldom did, preferring to entertain scores of young lovers. In 1980, as she became increasingly senile, Gala accidently mixed up Dalí's medicine and badly poisoned him, so he could no longer physically paint. When she died two years later, King Juan Carlos, who always had a soft spot for Dalí, made the 78-year-old artist the Marquis of Púbol. He moved into the castle, but, two years later, after being burned in a mysterious fire, he moved back to Figueres, where he spent the rest of his life.

Opened to the public since 1996, the **Gala Dalí Castle** offers up Gala's throne room (after her death Dalí liked to sit on the throne

Ullastret
t 972 17 90 58;, open June–Sept Tues–Sun 10–8; Oct–May Tues–Sun 10–2 and 4–6; adm

Gala Dalí Castle
t 972 48 86 55 www.salvador-dali.org; open 15 June–15 Sept daily 10–8; 16 Mar– 14 June and 16 Sept–Oct Tues–Sun 10–6; Nov and Dec Tues–Sun 10–5; adm

for interviews) and plenty of kooky Daliesque details, portraits, drawings and sculptures, Gala's *haute couture* frocks, and a pool watched over by statues of Wagner.

Torroella de Montgrí and L'Estartit

Once a royal town like Pals, **Torroella de Montgrí** is easy to spot from a distance, thanks to its enormous castle on the Montgrí massif. This was begun in 1294 by Jaume II as an outpost to keep tabs on the Counts of Empordà, and as their quarrel was settled before the castle was completed, he left it a great hollow shell.

Torroella, rather surprisingly, was once Girona's port. In 1178, a band of Moors sailed up and massacred the monks in a nearby monastery. Not long after, the Counts of Empordà, to spite the count-kings, diverted the course of the River Ter so successfully that the port silted up completely. Most of Torroella's magnificent walls were demolished in the 19th century. Yet the town itself still wears its head high: laid out by royal planners in a grid, it has a Renaissance tower and gates, an arcaded Plaça de la Vila, and Sant Genis, a big 14th-century Gothic church. There's an Augustinian monastery with a beautiful Tuscan Renaissance-style cloister unique in Catalonia, which now serves as a viola school. In the heart of the old town, a Renaissance mansion houses the new **Museu de la Mediterrània** with interactive displays and artefacts on both local history and human settlements in the wider Mediterranean. Another palace from Torroella's glory days, the 15th-century Palau Solterra is the home of the extensive Catalan photography collection of the **Vila Casas Foundation**.

Torroella's seaside extension **L'Estartit** has a 5km sandy beach. Yet it's claim to fame is among divers, who come to pester the sea creatures around the seven little picturesquely lopsided **Illes Medes**, floating a mile off the coast. In the bad old days pirates used them as a base, and in the 15th century a fort was built on the largest, Meda Gran, though it eventually fell into the sea. The surrounding waters, full of caves, crags and shipwrecks going back to ancient times, were designated a nature reserve since 1990, are among the richest in marine life in the western Mediterranean-providing a full larder for the estimated 14,000 yellow-legged gulls, shags and cormorants who make up the islands' population. If you're not a diver, there are glass-bottom boat cruises, snorkelling and sea kayak tours.

Just west, **Verges** attracts crowds on Holy Thursday nights, when men don luminous skeleton costumes and cardboard skulls to scamper about to the booming drums in a 'Dança de la Mort', their Hallowe'en caperings a reminder of the Black Death.

Museu de la Mediterrània
C/ Ulla 31, t 972 75 51 80; www.museudela mediterrania.org; open July and Aug Mon–Sat 10–2 and 6–9, Sun 10–2; Sept–June Mon and Wed–Sat 10–2 and 5–8, Sun 10–2, closed Tues; adm

Vila Casas Foundation
C/Església 10, t 972 76 19 76, www.fundacio vilacasas.org; open 15 June–Sept Wed–Mon 5–9.30; Oct–9 Dec and Feb–14 June Sat 11–2 and 4.30–8.30, Sun 11–2; closed 10 Dec–Jan; adm

Market Days in the Heart of the Costa Brava

Palafrugell, Tuesday and Saturday fruit and veg, Sunday big food market; **Begur**, Wednesday food and clothes street market; **Pals**, Tuesday at the Pavelló Poliesportiu, Saturday second-hand market in Plaça de Catalunya; **La Bisbal**, Friday Street market; **Torroella de Montgrí**, Monday in Carrer de l'Ullà; **L'Estartit**; Thursday on Avinguda de Roma.

① Palafrugell >>
Plaça de l'Església,
t 972 61 18 20

Sports and Activities in the Heart of the Costa Brava

Diving and Snorkelling

Poseidon Nimrod Diving, Platja Port Pelegri s/n, Calella de Palafrugell, t 972 61 53 45, *www.divecalella.de.*

Snorkel, Llafranc, t 972 30 27 16, *www.snorkel.net.*

Barracuda, Llafranc, t 666 32 39 74, *www.barracudallafranc.com.*

Xaloc, L'Estartit, t 972 75 20 71, *www.xalocdive.com.*

La Sirena, L'Estartit, t 972 75 09 54, *www.la-sirena.net.* Also offers family snorkelling tours around the Medes islets.

Kayaking

Kayaking Costa Brava, C/Enric Serra 42, t 972 77 38 06, *www.kayakingcostabrava.com.* Offers fantastic three-hour sea-kayaking tours of the *calas*, caves and cliffs of Cap Begur, starting at Tamariu, from May to mid-Oct.

★ Sant Roc >>

Walking

The **GR92 coastal path** is one of the most enchanting walks in the entire Mediterranean; the tourist office has maps. If you're lazy, start in Begur and walk downhill to Llafranc.

Golf, Riding, Hot Air Balloons

Golf Platja de Pals, t 972 66 77 39, *www.golfplatjadepals.com.* One of the top ten courses in Spain.

Cavalls de Forallac, Santa Susanna de Peralta (near Peratallada), t 972 63 42 65. Horse-riding stables.

Globus Empordà, in La Bisbal, t 972 64 15 50, *www.aventuraemporda.net.* Rides over the countryside in a hot air balloon.

Where to Stay and Eat in the Heart of the Costa Brava

In seafood restaurants, look for local classics such as *garoines* (sea urchins' eggs), *suquet de peix* (a sumptuous fish stew) and *arròs negre* (rice cooked in cuttlefish ink).

Palafrugell ✉ 17200

*****Fonda** L'Estrella, C/de les Quatre Cases 13, near Plaça Nova, t 972 30 00 05, *hostalestrella@gmail.com* (€). Modest rooms around a quiet courtyard. *Closed Oct–Easter.*

La Xicra, C/Estret 17, t 972 30 56 30, *www.restaurantlaxicra.com* (€€€). Creative, regional cuisine right in the centre of town, with the emphasis on seafood.

La Casona, Paratge la Sauleda 4, t 972 30 36 61 (€€). Good food at moderate prices; try the *arròs negre.*

Mas Olivier, Avda Espanya, t 972 30 10 41. (€€–€). Restaurant with a pretty garden; excellent, good-value duck and other dishes.

Calella de Palafrugell ✉ 17210

*******Sant Roc**, Plaça Atlàntic 2, t 972 61 42 50, *www.santroc.com* (€€€). Opened in 1955, a pleasantly 'lived-in', family-run hotel surrounded by gardens and a gorgeous terrace overlooking the bay. Very popular, so book ahead. Prices jump in August, when half board is mandatory. *Closed Nov–Mar.*

*******La Torre**, Pg La Torre 26-28, t 972 61 46 03, *www.latorre.cat* (€€€–€€). Superbly set on a little peninsula near Canadell beach, a ship-shape modern hotel immersed in woods.

Casa Dos Torres, C/Chopitea 59, t 972 61 70 19, *www.casadostorres.com* (€€). Delightful Scottish-owned B&B with a pool. Five nights' minimum in summer.

*****Hs del Plancton**, C/Codina 16, t 972 61 50 81 (€). Small, basic – but spotless and good value.

Taverna La Bella Lola, Plaça de Sant Pere 4, t 972 61 52 79, *www.taverna labellalola.com* (€€). A typical Catalan place, but great for listening to *habaneres* and drinking *cremat* year round. *Closed Nov.*

⭐ Tragamar >

Tragamar, Platja del Canadell, t 972 61 51 89 (€€). Just your perfect, reasonably priced seaside restaurant – lovely prawns and mussels and the freshest of fish.

Llafranc ✉ 17210

⭐ El Far >

****El Far**, t 972 30 16 39, *www.elfar. net* (€€€€€–€€€€). A stunner; converted from an 18th-century inn and set amid the pines high over the sea. Just nine delicious colour-soaked rooms, a beautiful patio, and fine restaurant. The only thing that might disturb the peace are wedding parties.

***Llevant**, C/Francesc de Blanes 5, t 972 30 03 66, *www.hotel-llevant. com* (€€€€–€€€). Right on the beach, this elegant hotel was established in the 1930s. It's small and smart, with a good restaurant – try for the rooms with terraces at the front with panoramic views.

***Llafranch**, Pg Cypsela 16, t 972 30 02 08, *www.hllafranch.com* (€€€). Recently spruced up star-studded old favourite from 1958, where Sophia Loren, Liz Taylor and Rock Hudson once hung out; one of the original owners, nicknamed 'the Gypsy', threw legendary parties. Lovely beach terrace and good restaurant serving old family recipes from cocktails to desserts.

***Terramar**, Pg Cipsela 1, t 972 30 02 00, *www.hterramar.com* (€€€–€€). Right on the seafront in 1934 and recently remodelled (there are several family rooms); the restaurant (€€€) serves excellent local dishes such as *arròs a la cassola*, the rice speciality of Palafrugell. *Closed mid-Oct–Mar.*

Casamar, C/del Nero 3, t 972 30 01 04, *www.hotelcasamar.net* (€). A 2min walk from the beach, family-run hotel with small rooms but gorgeous food in the restaurant (€€). Book well in advance. *Closed Jan–mid Mar.*

Tamariu ✉ 17210

***Hostalillo**, C/Bellavista 22, t 972 62 02 28, *www.hotelhostalillo.com* (€€€€).

White, modern hotel set on the cliffs above the beach, with a lovely, geranium-filled terrace. *Closed mid-Oct–mid April.*

***Tamariu**, Pg del Mar, t 972 62 00 31, *www.tamariu.com* (€€€–€€€). Excellent little family run hotel, right on the seafront. There's a good restaurant, too (€€€).

Begur ✉ 17225

****Parador Costa Brava**, Aiguablava, t 972 62 21 62, *www.parador.es* (€€€€€). A modern white box, magnificently located on the cliffs surrounded by pines, boasting one of the finest views in Spain; each room faces the sea with a balcony. Pool and beach just below, and the wonderful **Mar i Vent** bar, with its exquisite seafood (€€€€). *Open all year.*

****Aigua Blava**, Playa de Fornells, t 972 62 45 62, *www.aiguablava.com* (€€€€€). Set in a charming villa on different levels, more family-orientated than the *parador*, with its pool, tennis, and volleyball. The restaurant (€€€€) with local specialities and especially good fish, is excellent. *Closed Nov–mid Mar.*

El Convent, Ctra del Racó 2, t 972 62 30 91, *www.hotelconventbegur.com* (€€€€–€€€). In a quiet setting, a minute below Begur, a 17th-century convent set amid ancient terraces and Mediterranean forest. Rooms are prettily furnished if small. There are massage cabins, a sauna, and electric bicycles to make it easy to get up those hills from the beach. *Closed Jan and Feb.*

***Aigua Clara**, C/Sant Miquel 2, t 972 62 32 86, *www.aiguaclara.com* (€€€). Luminous, characterful rooms, with a smattering of antiques and old fixtures in a pretty white mansion built in 1866.

***Bliss Begur**, San Josep 3, t 972 62 45 40, *www.blissbegurhotel.com* (€€€). Small, stylish Italian-run hotel a short walk from the centre, plus an excellent Italian restaurant, **Primo Piatto** (€€€).

Hs Sa Tuna, Platja Sa Tuna, t 972 62 21 98, *www.hostalsatuna.com* (€€€). Five delightful beachside rooms, and an excellent restaurant (€€€–€€) serving wonderful seafood and *arròs negre*.

Mas Comangou, C/Ramon Llull 1, t 972 62 32 10, *www.mascomangau.com* (€€€). Classic rooms with beamed ceilings in a 19th-century stone *masia* on the outskirts of town and a lovely terrace and restaurant.

Rosa, C/Forga i Puig 6, t 972 62 30 15, *www.fondacaner.com* (€€). Pretty, friendly hotel in the centre, serving delicious breakfasts; the staff are happy to arrange bike hire and give ideas for walks around town. The hotel's stone-vaulted restaurant, **Fonda Caner (€€€) offers hearty Catalan dishes that are out of this world (open to non-guests, and be sure to book). *Closed Nov–Mar.*

⭐ Hostal Sa Rascassa >

Hostal Sa Rascassa, Aiguafreda, t 972 62 28 45, *www.hostalsarascassa.com* (€€). Beautifully isolated by the sea, five lovely, award-winning rooms and delicious grilled fish by candlelight. Wednesday is music night.

Rostei, C/Concepció Pi, t 972 62 27 04 (€€€). Seasonal menu with a strong emphasis on local fish, grilled vegetables and mushrooms in the autumn, and a good choice of dessert classics. The wine list includes those grown by the Rostei family on their estate. Be sure to book, and ask for a table in the garden. *Open eves only 15 June–15 Sept, closed Mon; rest of the year open Fri and Sat eve, and Sat and Sun lunch.*

Sa Rascassa, Aiguafreda, t 972 62 28 45 (€€). Delicious grilled fish and tasty pasta dishes served on a terrace right on the sea.

ⓘ Pals >
C/Hospital 22,
t 972 63 73 80

Pals ✉ 17256

*****Mas de Torrent, Alfueras de Torrent s/n, 4km from Pals at Torrent, t 902 55 03 21, *www.mastorrent.com* (€€€€€). One of the best hotels in Spain – superb Relais & Chateaux hotel set in an 18th-century country house with stylish rooms furnished with antiques, plus 20 secluded bungalows and a pool set in extensive gardens, plus a gastonomic restaurant, spa, hammam and more.

⭐ La Plaça >>

Font de Sabruixa, Puig Vermell s/n, t 972 637 111 (€). In the woods, just back from the beach – very simple, but legendary for its succulent meats grilled over charcoal.

El Pedró, t 972 63 69 83, *www. elpedropals.com* (€€). Satisfying home-style dishes in one of the oldest restaurants in Pals; try the local rice and old-fashioned desserts. *Closed Sun eve, and Thurs out of season.*

Peratallada ✉ 17113

Mas Rabiol, 3km from Peratallada in Sant Climent de Peralta, t 619 78 21 05, *www.masrabiol.com*. (€€€–€€). Handsome 16th-century stone *masia* with seven rooms, set in five hectares of gardens, with a pool and pretty views.

El Cal del Papibou, C/Major 10, t 972 63 40 18, *www.hotelelcau.net* (€€–€). Eight cosy and quiet rooms in a medieval house in the centre. Good meals.

La Bisbal de Empordà ✉ 17115

****Castello d'Empordà, t 972 64 62 54, *www.castelldemporda.com* (€€€€–€€€). In the 1970s, Dalí tried to buy Gala this castle, built in 1301 and once owned by a captain who sailed with Columbus. Where Dalí failed, current owners Albert Diks and Margo Vereijken succeeded, and have created a stunning hotel in a gorgeous Mediterranean setting. Rooms have great views, whether you stay in the castle or in the garden annexe by the heated pool. There's also a fine restaurant (€€€).

Monells ✉ 17121

****Arcs de Monells, C/Vilanova 1, t 972 63 03 04, *www.hotelarcsmonells. com* (€€€€). A medieval hamlet around a castle converted into a serene and beautiful hotel, featuring arches and stone vaults, with a modern addition deftly tacked on; the restaurant (€€€) is a destination in its own right.

Madremanya ✉ 17462

****La Plaça, C/Sant Esteve 17, t 972 49 04 87, *www.restaurantlaplaca.com*. (€€€). Dine under the stone vaults of a 14th-century country house or in the pretty garden; this was Lance Armstrong's favourite restaurant while he was training for the Tour de France; delicious nine-course tasting menu. They also have stylish rooms and suites (€€€€).

(i) **Torroella de Montgrí >**
Can Quintana,
C/ Ulla 31, t 972 75 51 80

(i) **L'Estartit**
Pg Marítim 47,
t 972 75 19 10

Torroella de Montgrí ✉ 17257

****Molí del Mig**, Camí Moní del Mig s/n, t 972 75 53 96, www.molidelmig.com (€€€). A combination of a 15th-century mill and a contemporary, eco-friendly structure set on seven hectares of land, with a swimming pool, library museum, and dedicated facilities for cyclists, including local bike hire.

L'Estartit ✉ 17258

***Panorama**, Av. de Grécia 5, t 972 75 10 92, www.hotelpanoramaestartit.com (€€€). Good place to bring the whole family without breaking the bank: nicely located on the beach, with a pool and garden. *Open all year.*
***Flamingo**, C/de l'Església 112, t 972 75 09 27, www.hotelflamingo.info (€€–€). Friendly, good-value hotel near the beach, with a pool; diving and golf offers available. *Closed Nov–Mar.*

The Gulf of Roses

Museu de l'Anxova de la Sal
Av. Francesc Macià 1,
t 972 77 68 15,
http://anxova-sal.cat,
open July–mid Sept
Tues–Fri 10–1.30 and
5–8, Sat 11–1 and 6–8,
Sun 10–1; mid-
Sept–June Tues–Fri
10–1.30, Sat 11–1 and
5–7, Sun 11–1; adm

The Gulf of Roses may be the name on the map, but foodies know this as the southern reaches of the Anchovy Coast, which extends north to Collioure in France: the waters here are cooler than elsewhere in the Mediterranean and rich in the plankton the anchovies love. Founded in the 16th century by fishermen, **L'Escala** has several shops near the port sell nothing but anchovies caught by its fleet of traditional *tranynas* – and they're the world's finest, as any Catalan will tell you. You can study in depth at the **Museu de l'Anxova de la Sal**. The locals are also proud of their Sardana; statues of complete *sardana* band play silently right in front of the town beach.

Ancient Empúries

Empúries
t 972 77 02 08,
open June–Sept daily
10–8; Oct–May daily
10–6; adm

The excavations of Spain's most important ancient Greek city of **Empúries** lie within the sound of the waves just north of **L'Escala**, in a peaceful garden setting dotted with parasol pines It wasn't always so peaceful. Around 600 BC, Greeks from Phocaea set up a trading counter here that they called Emporion, or 'market', on its little isthmus where an indigenous Iron Age settlement had exisited since the 9th century BC. It traded with the Phoenicians, Etruscans and Greeks. When a second wave of Greek colonists settled a new site, a bit further south, the first settlement became known as Palaiapolis (the 'old city'). In 218 BC, during the Second Punic War, Scipio captured Emporion in the first Roman action in Iberia; a Roman military camp set up in 195 BC and the new Emporion evolved into a city ten times the size of the Greek one. Under Augustus the whole became the Municipium Emporiae. Pirate attacks beginning in the 3rd century and made it less desirable. The Visigoths showed up to build a few churches, but it was completely abandoned not long after.

Excavations began in 1908, and archaeologists reckon only 25 per cent of the site has been revealed. Behind the mighty walls of the

Yes, with Anchovies!

Anchovies are key to Catalan cuisine, but don't mistake them for the grey slivers of salt that show up on our pizzas: the Catalan version is rosy-coloured, firmer and meatier. There are over a hundred species, but only one, the European anchovy – *Engraulis encrasicolus* or *seitó* – is commercially viable, sturdy enough to not be damaged in the nets.

Anchovy season runs from May to October, and traditionally they are bagged by night using a lamp that mimics the full moon the little fishies love. Once unloaded in port, they are immediately beheaded and gutted , and layered with sea salt in large barrels and kept in cool rooms to ripen for at least three months – the art of the master-salter is to know exactly for how long. Afterwards the anchovies are cleaned in fresh water, manually deboned, laid out to dry overnight and packed in jars, tubs or cans and filled with sunflower oil. Shops in L'Escala also sell them the way many Catalans prefer, whole and packed in salt, so they do the cleaning themselves.

Although family anchovy-salting factories survive in L'Escala and Collioure, they are worried: since the 1980s, the catch in the Mediterreanean (which connoisseurs prefer to the more common Atlantic anchovy) has declined, owing to warmer summer temperatures and the use of huge French ships that use nets so fine that they sweep up the baby fish before they have a chance to reproduce. Most of the anchovies you see in supermarkets these days come from Morocco and are cured with cost-cutting methods – so you may do a double-take at the prices in L'Escala's anchovy shops. But great Catalan chefs will use no other.

Ampurias to-day is a place inexpressibly moving in its beauty and desolation... you may wander through the city among the ghosts of Greek traders, Iberian vendors [and] Roman gentlemen.

Rose Macauley,
Fabled Shore

Greek 'New Town' or Neapolis lie the foundations of sanctuaries to Asklepios, god of healing and the Egyptian god Serapis. There's an agora and stoa, the centre of any Greek city, cisterns, houses (with a few mosaics) a forge, and a workshop from the 1st century BC used for salting anchovies, converted by the Romans into a factory for making their beloved fermented fish sauce, or garum. A garden and road separates the Greek Neapolis from the Roman town. Only a fraction of the latter has been uncovered: two grand houses with fine mosaics, the forum, temples, part of a wall and gate, apartment houses, shops and an amphitheatre. The site's museum has as its prize a life-sized, 3rd-century BC statue of Asklepios with his snake, but there are other treasures as well: an unusual altar from the 2nd century BC painted with a cock and a pair of snakes, remains of a Roman catapult, and beautiful intricate mosaics – of fish, a partridge taking jewels out of a basket, and the Sacrifice of Iphigenia.

While Neapolis was abandoned, Palaiapolis evolved into the charming village of **Sant Martí d'Empúries**. This was important enough in the 8th century to become the capital of the county of Empúries, although in the 11th century even that relocated to **Castelló d'Empúries** (*see* overleaf), and the place has managed to stay out of history ever since. A seaside promenade links Sant Martí to L'Escala; along it you can see the huge stone jetty built by the Greeks just before the arrival of the Romans. There are beaches and dunes here, well known among local wind-surfers, all the way to the little port resort of **Sant Pere Pescador**. **Sant Miquel de Fluvià**, just inland, has a fine Romanesque church of 1066.

Parc Natural dels Aiguamolls and Castelló d'Empúries

North of L'Escala, the Ter, Fluvià and Muga rivers once flowed into ancient lakes. These were drained in the 18th and 19th century to create farmland and pastures, leaving only a strip of coastal wetland,which in 1983 was protected as the 478-hectare Parc Natural dels Aiguamolls.

Migratory birds adore it; a network of walking and bike paths make it easy to spot the ospreys, storks, flamingos, great bitterns and purple herons among the 324 species here. The wetlands were only protected after a chunk was turned into **Empuriabrava**, the 'biggest marina town in Europe' where residents park their boats in their backyards.

If you want nightlife, Empuriabrava delivers, especially in summer with its massive clubs (Pachá, Viva) at the entrance; but year-round (especially at weekends) you'll find a lively strip of bars and clubs known as **Los Arcos**, just in from the beach.

Empuriabrava is the offspring of venerable **Castelló d'Empúries**, a handsome medieval town that once served as the port and seat of the Counts of Empúries, occupying its own little island. In the 6th century the Visigoths built a church at the highest point in town; it was destroyed by the Moors and rebuilt in 888 by Wilfred the Hairy. From the 11th to the 13th centuries, the Counts of Empúries, hoping to get their own bishop, rebuilt Wilfred's church the size of a cathedral. The scheme failed to nab a prelate, but the church of **Santa Maria** still impresses with a lavish marble portal, covered with statues of the saints and alabaster windows. One chapel holds the alabaster Gothic altarpiece by Vicenç Borràs (1435), while the Capella de la Mare de Deu dels Dolors of 1777 is an over-the-top gold and white confection; other bits are in the Museu Parroquial in the sacristy

The count's palace is now the Ajuntament, and there's also a once densely populated **Call** (Jewish quarter), in a network of little streets; remains of the **New Synagogue** can still be seen on C/Peixateries Velles. The Eco-Museu Farinera is in an flour mill, where you can learn all about mid-19th-century technology. You can even visit the clink, the Museu Cúria Presó of 1336, complete with prisoners' grafitti. Down by the free car park, a picturesque **cloister** has a public wash-house in the centre.

Roses

Domino stacks of high rises sprawling over the coastal hills and along the long sandy beach are what's coming up in Roses. Named after the Greek island of Rhodes, home of the traders who founded it on a low hill in 776 BC, Roses grew into an important Hellenistic,

Parc Natural dels Aiguamolls
Visitors' Centre El Cortalet, Sant Pere Pescador–Castelló d'Empúries road (GIV-6216, km 13), t 972 45 42 22, www.parcsde catalunya.net; open April–Sept 9.30–2 and 4.30–7; Oct–Mar 9.30–2 and 3.30–6

Museu Parroquial
t 972 15 80 19, open Mon–Sat 10–1 and 4–6, Sun 11–12, 1–2 and 3–7; adm

Eco-Museu Farinera
C/Sant Francesc 5–7, t 972 25 05 12, www.ecomuseu-farinera.org, open mid June–mid Sept Tues–Sun 10–2 and 5–8; mid-Sept–mid-June Tues–Fri 10-1, Sat 10–1 and 4–7, Sun 10.30–1.30; adm

Museu Cúria Presó
Plaça Jaume I, t 972 15 62 33; open July–mid-Sept 9–9; mid-Sept–June Mon–Sat 10–2 and 4–6, Sun 10–2; adm

'The Dalí of the Kitchen'

This was *Gourmet* magazine's name for Ferran Adrià, and it's true in many ways: like Dalí, Adrià is a Catalan artist unique in his field, wildly imaginative and wise in the management of his image, praised to the heavens, but not without controversy. And one can't help but think Dalí would have been delighted by dishes such as deep-fried rabbit's ears or yin-yang of chickpea water. There's even a surreal touch to the restaurant's name: *bulli* was the breed of bulldog favoured by the wife of a German doctor who set up a mini golf course at Montjoi in 1961. It closed three years later, but the name stayed on when a restaurant took over the site. In 1983, Ferran Adrià arrived to do his work experience at El Bulli; today he's co-owner and widely recognized as the world's best and most influential chef and perhaps the most passionate.

His fiercest critic, of course, is Catalan: the region's first Michelin three-star chef, Santi Santamaria at Can Fabes (*see* p.228) caused a stir in 2008 when he accused Adrià of culinary unnatural acts – that the additives and gelling agents used to make his foams, airs and infusions were 'a public health issue'. Adrià countered that his dishes never have more than .01 per cent of any additive, and that all are EU-approved and commonly used in other foods like ice-creams.

Where Adrià differs from Dalí is his lack of megalomania. Money doesn't tempt him. Even though El Bulli receives two million requests for reservations each year for a mere 8,000 places, he opens for dinner only six months of the year. Adrià says working only half the year helps him maintain his enthusiasm (unlike many famous chefs, he's still very hands-on in the kitchen). He devotes the other six months to travelling and experimenting with new dishes in his Barcelona laboratory. He takes his role as missionary for a new culinary form of art very seriously: among young chefs a stint in El Bulli's kitchen is as coveted as a reservation. Some dishes are so novel that they come with instructions on how to eat them. 'At El Bulli, we created a language that was not known by anyone,' as Adrià explains.

Just like surrealism.

Ciutadella de Roses
*t 972 15 14 66,
www.rosesfhn.org;
July–Aug Tues–Sun
10–9; June and Sept
Tues–Sun 10–8;
Oct–May Tues–Sun
10–2, closed Mon; adm*

Roman, Visigothic and medieval settlement, especially after the port at Castelló d'Empúries silted up. Ruins of old Roses and the medieval church of Santa María all lie within the embrace of the vast, brooding star-shaped **Ciutadella de Roses** built in 1543 by Emperor Charles V, after Barbarossa decimated the town; it also houses a museum on Roses' history.

One of the sweet things about Roses is a 23km-long footpath, the Camí de Ronda that follows the shore from the new yacht marina along the port to the old tuna-fishers' cove of **L'Almadrava**, past the pretty *calas* of the wild **Punta Falconera**. One of the prettiest beaches to aim for is **Cala Rostella**, one of the few with any shade (park on top and walk down the path); another is **Cala Murta**, where swimsuits are optional. Beyond **Cala Montjoi** and the world famous El Bulli restaurant (*see* box, above, and p.190), you'll find a couple of other lovely coves before the road gives up at **Cala Jóncols**.

Roses was popular in Neolithic times, too: the town has set up a **megalithic route** towards Punta Flaconera. The funeral chamber of the **Casa Cremada** has two menhirs (4th–3rd millennia BC), slightly predating three large dolmens: the **Creu d'en Cobertella,** claimed the largest in Catalonia, topped by a four-ton slab; the **Llit de la Generala** and the **Cap de l'Home**.

Market Days in the Gulf of Roses

L'Escala, Tuesday and Thursday for fruit and vegetables, Saturday on the Passeig Maritim; **Roses**, Saturday.

Where to Stay and Eat in the Gulf of Roses

(i) L'Escala >
Plaça de Les Escoles 1,
t 972 77 06 03

(i) Roses >>
Avinguda de
Rhode 101,
t 972 25 73 31

(i) Castelló
d'Empúries >
Plaça Jaume I s/n,
t 972 15 62 33

(★) El Bulli >>

L'Escala ✉ 17130

***Nieves-Mar**, Pg Marítim 8, **t** 972 77 03 00, *www.nievesmar.com* (€€). Big, modern white hotel, with tennis, children's activities, and a seawater pool. Rooms have recently been renovated. *Closed Nov–Mar*. The hotel restaurant, **Ca la Neus** (€€€), is one of the very best in town.

****Hs el Roser**, C/Església 7, **t** 972 77 02 19, *www.elroserhotel.com* (€). Old-fashioned hotel in the historic centre. The same family also run a great seafood restaurant specializing in prawns, **El Roser 2**, Pg Lluís Albert 1, **t** 972 77 02 19 (€€).

Sant Martí d'Empúries ✉ 17130

***Riomar**, **t** 972 77 03 62, *www.riomarhotel.com* (€€€–€€). On the beach, peaceful family-orientated hotel, vintage 1969, but updated since, with a pool and restaurant. *Closed Nov–Mar*.

Can Roura, C/Major 10, **t** 972 77 33 80, *www.canroura.com* (€€). Restaurant opened in 1958 and still serving good Mediterranean Catalan dishes (plenty of fish, duck breast in port) in an old Catalan farmhouse. They also have a few basic rooms (€€).

Castelló d'Empúries ✉ 17486

****De la Moneda**, Plaça de la Moneda 8–10, **t** 972 15 86 02, *www.hoteldelamoneda.com* (€€€–€€). In a 17th-century palace in the Jewish quarter, 11 rooms all painted in rich yellows, blues and reds. There's a pool, and some rooms have Jacuzzis. *Closed Jan–mid Mar*.

***Canet**, Plaça Joc de la Pilota, **t** 972 25 03 40, *www.hotelcanet.com* (€€–€). Owned by the same people as the Moneda. Cheaper rooms in the centre, and a reputed restaurant; guests can use the pool and other facilities at the Moneda.

Palau Macelli, C/Carboner, **t** 972 250 567, *www.girsoft.com/macelli* (€). In the centre, a B&B in a palace built in 1666, with a charming courtyard, marble stairway and back garden; quirky old-fashioned rooms furnished with antiques.

Portal de la Gallarda, C/Pere Estany 14, **t** 972 25 01 52 (€). Reliable grilled meats and salads, just behind the church by the 11th-century fortified gate to the city; pretty garden and terrace. *Closed Tues out of season, Dec and Jan*.

Roses ✉ 17840

*****Terraza**, Av de Rhode 32, **t** 972 25 61 54, *www.hotelterraza.com* (€€€€). Classic resort hotel with a pool and spa; free parking.

*****Almadraba Park**, Platja de Almadraba, **t** 972 25 65 50, *www.almadrabapark.com* (€€€€–€€€). The sleekest choice, founded by the Mercader family (owners of the Hotel Empordá in Figueres). Plush, air-conditioned rooms, with amenities including a fine, award-winning restaurant (open to non-residents, €€€€), heated pool, sauna and tennis courts. *Closed Nov–April*.

***Cala Jóncols**, 12km north of Roses in Cala Jóncòls, **t** 972 19 90 28, *www.calajoncols.com* (€€€). White, fresh rooms deliciously isolated on the beach amid gardens and olive groves, with a pool and a diving club, canoes to hire for exploring the coast, and good restaurant; kids welcome.

***Nautilus**, Av. Nautilus 17, 150m from the beach, **t** 972 25 62 62, *www.hotelnautilus.net* (€€€–€€). A surprisingly good bargain, with lots of facilities including a pool.

***Hs del Sol**, **t** 972 25 60 37 (€). Unpretentious family run hotel, low on creature comforts but filled with art; try to get a room in back, on the beach.

****Puig Rom**, Plaça Levant 1, **t** 972 25 67 16 (€). Six en-suite rooms, good value for the central location.

El Bulli, Cala Montjoi, 6km from Roses, **t** 972 15 04 57, *www.elbulli.com* (€€€€). At the world's most famous

⭐ **Rafa >>**

restaurant overlooking a lovely bay, dinner is an unforgettable 32-course tasting menu and costs around €300. *Open mid-June–Dec Wed–Sat, eves only.* Book by sending an e-mail (*bulli@elbulli.com*) with four dates by October 14; responses are sent in November. If you don't bag a table, you can trying ringing to see if there's been a cancellation.

Cal Campaner, C/Mossen Carles Feliu 23, t 972 25 69 54 (€€). Tiny, hard to find, informal, and serving nothing but deliciously prepared seafood

Rafa, C/Sant Sebastià 56, t 972 254 003 (€€). This is famous as Adrià's favourite restaurant – or at least that's what Rafa told Anthony Bourdain. There's no menu, only the day's catch (often including anchovies) personally chosen by Rafa, then perfectly grilled. If he doesn't like the day's fish, he won't open.

Cap de Creus: Cadaqués to Portbou

On the map it protrudes from the coast like a nipple on a frosty day, and up close Cap de Creus is just as fascinating. Its fabric is 450-million-year-old rock, shattered and upended when the Iberian peninsula collided with Europe to form the Pyrenees, then scoured and eroded into strange shapes by the *tramuntana* wind that blows so fiercely. Joan Maragell famously called Empordà the 'palace of winds'. Terraces laboriously carved over the ages are now abandoned: the phylloxera epidemic in the 1880s killed the vines, a devastating frost in 1956 killed the olives, and wildfires over the past couple of decades have left the rock prey to the elements. Dalí spent much of his life amid this 'grandiose geological delirium'; its brilliant light, coves and weirdly-shaped rocks appear repeatedly in his paintings. In spite of all the disasters, the Cap de Creus is a nature reserve, boasting the largest stretch of undeveloped coast in Spain, a priveleged home to rare flora and fauna on land and in the surrounding seas.

Cadaqués

⭐ Cadaqués

They call it the 'Saint-Tropez of Spain', and in many ways this jewel of the Costa Brava fits the bill. Cadaqués is just as hard to reach, at the end of long, tortuous roads over the Cap de Creus, and although it lacks St-Trop's big sandy beaches it boasts similar arty-celebrity credentials: not only Dalí and Lorca, but Picasso, Matisse, Man Ray, Max Ernst, Chagall, Marcel Duchamp, Albert Einstein, Walt Disney, Mick Jagger and a gaggle of film stars and millionaires have spent time here.

And it's easy to see why: with its whitewashed houses and cobbled streets clustered around a giant white mother ship of a church and a bijou fishing port, Cadaqués is the most beautiful town on the coast. There's no room for high-rise buildings or even cars (if you have one, it's easiest to leave it in the pay-and-display car park by the bus station). But although the young, the wealthy and the hip converge here, it's not posey like St-Tropez, but laid-back, like a Greek island.

Museu de Cadaqués
C/Narcis Montuiol 15,
t 972 25 88 77,
www.cadaques.org;
open Sat–Thurs 10–1.30
and 4–8, closed Fri; adm

The village's illustrious arty history gets a nod at the **Museu de Cadaqués**, with rotating exhibits that often relate in some way to the surrealist maestro. For older art, visit the outsized **Església de Santa María**, built after the original version was burned to the ground by Barbarossa in 1543. It has a show-stopping Baroque altarpiece sculpted and painted by Jacint Moretó and Pere Costa, and a chapel by Dalí. Cadaqués loves music as much as art.In August it hosts one of Spain's oldest and most prestigious music festivals. It has a legendary jazz club, **L'Hostal**, on the seafront where Dalí spent many an evening.

...Her fishermen sleep dreamless on the sand.

On the high sea a rose is their compass.

The horizon, virgin of wounded handkerchiefs,

links the great crystals of fish and moon...

Federico Garcia Lorca,
'Ode to Salvador Dalí'

As a child, Salvador Dalí spent holidays with his grandparents in Cadaqués, and In the 1920s he brought along his university friends, Lorca (who had a crush on him) and Luis Buñuel. Dalí was one of the first painters to take a keen interest in film, and he collaborated with Buñuel on his two Surrealist classics, *Un Chien Andalou (1929)* and *L'Âge d'or* (1930). Lorca, an Andalucian, took umbrage at *Un Chien Andalou* (rightly or wrongly believing that the title was an insult directed at him) and broke off his friendship with the pair. *L'Âge d'or* (originally titled *The icy water of egotistical calculation*) opens with scenes filmed on Cap de Creus with a cast of locals, and it too caused umbrage – and a riot – when it opened in Paris.

The Casa-Museu Salvador Dalí

Casa-Museu Salvador Dalí
guided tours for up to
eight people at a time
by advance reservation
only, at www.salvador-
dali.org or t 972 25 10 15;
open 15 Mar–14 June
and 16 Sept–6 Jan
Tues–Sun 10.30–6;
15 June–15 Sept
9.30–9; closed 7 Jan–14
Mar; adm exp; free
parking nearby; pick up
tickets 30mins before
your reservation time

In 1929, the surrealist French poet Paul Éluard and his Russian wife Gala came to visit Dalí in Cadaqués. Gala was 11 years older than Dalí, but he was smitten, much to the disapproval of his father. Dalí senior booted him out; Dalí junior defiantly bought a fisherman's cottage in Portlligat just down the coast. It was the first of four shacks the artist purchased and strung together.

Although exhibitionists in public, Dalí and Gala were intensely private at home. Once past the clutch of eggs on the roof and jewellery-encrusted stuffed polar bear at the entrance, his home turns out to be surprisingly restrained, a cosy labyrinth, filled with dried bouquets of immortelles gathered by Gala, who shared Dalí's obsession with immortality. A mirror was placed so that Dalí could be the very first person in Spain to see the sun rise each morning, without getting out of bed. He always painted while sitting down, so invented a giant easel on pulleys that slid into the floor below, allowing him to work on large canvases from his armchair.

For Gala he built an acoustically wonderful egg-shaped boudoir, which she filled with objects from Russia; the doors of her dressing room are covered with newspaper clippings about the couple. There are no guest rooms, but visitors were admitted to the

Every morning upon awakening, I experience a supreme pleasure: that of being Salvador Dalí

Dalí

charming patio, where olive trees grow in giant tea cups, and where Dalí the voyeur could observe them through peep holes. The long phallic swimming pool is watched over by the Michelin Man.

The one major exception to Dalí's no-guest rule was the beautiful multilingual and possibly transexual model, singer and disco queen Amanda Lear, whom the artist met in a Paris club in 1965. Lear became Dalí's last muse, and, according to many, his greatest creation. He introduced her to art; she introduced him to the Beatles and the Rolling Stones. Most biographers claim that Dalí in his last years fell into the hands of corrupt advisors who forced him to sign countless forgeries and as many as 35,000 blank sheets of paper for future lithographs (others say he just wanted to make money, and signed them on his own). When his manager, the late 'Captain' John Moore, was arrested in 1999 for altering Dalí's *Double Image of Gala* (1969), police found 10,000 fake Dalí lithographs in his house in Cadaqués.

In 1970, Kirk Douglas visited Dalí during the shooting of *The Light at the Edge of the World*, a thriller filmed on the Cap de Creus. Dalí, according to Douglas, talked of erect penises and tried to snare him in a threesome before Douglas managed to escape. The lighthouse built for the film – and the real one – are a 10km drive from Cadaqués, on a road passing many sandy coves. The wild, rocky tip of the cape is the easternmost point of Spain, the throne room of the 'palace of winds'. The views are superb, and, this being Catalonia, there's a good restaurant, too (*see* p.196).

High Overhead: Sant Pere de Rodes

In her 1986 autobiography, *My Life with Dalí*, Amanda Lear describes how she and Dalí rode donkeys up to the vertiginous **Monastery of Sant Pere de Rodes** to enquire whether or not they should be married. Perhaps ancient inhabitants did as well, when a Roman temple of Venus Urania stood here; in ancient times this was Cape Aphrodision, until St Helen, on her way back from the Holy Land in the 4th century, Christianized the temple of love and left it a piece of the Holy Cross.

Monastery of Sant Pere de Rodes

t 972 38 75 59; open June–Sept Tues–Sun 10–7.40; Oct–May Tues–Sun 10–5; adm; there's a small fee to park under the church of Santa Elena, a five-minute walk from the monastery

Jump ahead to 610, when enemies were at the gates of Rome. In a panic, Pope Boniface IV entrusted three monks with the Church's holiest relics – the head and right arm of St Peter – and told them to get out of town. The monks brought the relics to Cap de Creus, hid them in a safe place and returned to Rome, only to find the threat had passed. The pope sent them back to retrieve the relics, but the monks had hid them only too well, and rather than return and face a furious pope, they founded a monstery on the site of the ex-temple. In 979, Pope Benedict VII issued a bill saying that if a pilgrim physically couldn't make it to Rome, a trip to Sant Pere was just as good, thus beginning the monastery's heyday.

In 1022 it was rebuilt in the new Romanesque style. By 1100 only Santiago de Compostela was a more popular pilgrimage destination in the western Mediterranean. The monks had estates throughout the Empordà; they carved terraces in the ancient rock and made the best wine in Catalonia. The great Master of Cabestany laboured for years in the cloister, carving capitals that were said to be the finest anywhere.

In 1348, the Black Death struck, leaving only 30 monks; in 1409, King Martí the Humanist, who had just gobbled up Empordà, took advantage of a temporary lack of abbots and took control. Luxury and immorality began to creep in. Abbots stopped living in the monastery. In 1708, French mercenaries under the Duc de Noailles pillaged its art and treasure, and destroyed what they could not carry, including the sculptures by the Master of Cabestany.

The monks abandoned Sant Pere altogether by 1798 (which casts doubt on Amanda Lear's story, but never mind). Doors, windows and other bits were carted away. The picturesque ruin is said to have inspired Umberto Eco's novel *The Name of the Rose*, but in 1998 Sant Pere suffered a final ignominy at the hands of restorers. All the original bits, outside of a couple of capitals and fragments of wall paintings, are now in museums. Even so, the location is breaktaking: the 89ft-high belltower and little crypt, and lofty main body of the church are original, although the rest feels like a confusion of floors, stairs, cloisters and walkways.

You can often see partridges scampering along the winding road from Sant Pere de Rodes to **El Port de la Selva**, where fishing boats bob among the pleasure craft. **Platja Gran** just south of town is the busiest beach, but, if it's windy, follow the shore road north to the more sheltered pebble cove of **Tamariu**. Far fewer visitors make it up to the handsome fortified nucleus of **Selva de Mar**; there's a lovely path to an old watermill.

Llançà

At the frontier with France, the coast is no less *brava*. Llançà, the biggest town, was built a couple of kilometres inland to protect it from pirates, and conveniently concentrates its monuments in the Plaça Major: there's a 14th-century **Torre de la Plaça**, with exhibits on the town's history, and a 15th-century **episcopal palace**, and the **Arbre de la Llibertat** – a Liberty Tree planted in 1870, during the heady days when the Catalan general Joan Prim was seeking a constitutionally minded king for Spain.

Here too is the **Museu de l'Aquarel.la**, featuring a nice array of watercolours mainly by local painter Josep Martínez Lozano. At 4.30pm locals gather to see what the fishermen have brought into **Llançà Port**, the little harbour set on either side of the wild **El Castellar** headland, offering grandstand views of the town and

Looking for a democratic monarch in Europe is like trying to find an atheist in heaven
General Prim

Museu de l'Aquarel.la
t 972 12 14 70, www. mda.cat; open 15 June– 15 Sept Tues–Fri 7–9pm; 16 Sept–Oct and Dec–14 June Sat, Sun and hols 11–1 and 6–8; closed Nov

15

the Pyrenees. The best beaches are 2km north, **Platja Grifeu** and
the sandy curve of **Platja Borró**, and tiny coves further along.

Portbou: the End of the Line

Hemmed in by the final toss of the jumbly rock-dice of the Albera
mountains at the tail end of the Pyrenees, Portbou is only 3km
from Roussillon in France. For centuries it was a perfect smugglers'
port, shelted from the *tramuntana* wind; towards the end of the
Spanish Civil War, it was one of the few ports that the Republicans
could still use to bring in goods.

Portbou sounds vaguely ghostly, and its can still send shivers
down the spine of certain travellers. Spain made her national rail
gauge wider than France's to keep the French from invading by
train. Built in 1929, Portbou's cavernous station used to entail long
queues for passport inspections and customs and hefting bags
across the tracks. In 1995, the Schengen Accord threw 500 officials
out of work. Portbou (pop. 1500) isn't quite a ghost town, but off
season it can seem like it.

Poet Stephen Spender was here during the Civil War in 1936, but
the place reserved its biggest nightmare for a visitor who arrived
by foot: philospher and culture critic Walter Benjamin, associate of
Theodor Adorno, Max Horkheimer, and Herbert Marcuse at the
Frankfurt School for Social Research.

> *It is a more arduous task to honour the memory of the anonymous than that of the famous. Historical construction is consecrated to the memory of those who have no name.*
>
> Walter Benjamin

09 **Girona Province** | The Costa Brava

The Death of Walter Benjamin

With the rise of the Nazis in the 1930s, Adorno and Horkheimer had relocated to New York and
encouraged Benjamin to follow. Fatally he didn't, and lingered in Paris, lonely and impoverished,
convinced that he needed the Bibliothèque Nationale for his research.

Benjamin had initially hoped that Communism would act as a potent weapon again Fascism but,
like many intellectuals, he was abruptly disabused by the Hitler-Stalin pact. In early 1940 he
channelled his fury into *Ober den Begriff der Geschichte* (*Theses on the Philosophy of History*), a bleak,
searing critique of Marxism. He left the manuscript with his friend Hannah Arendt and fled from Paris
to Lourdes the day before the Nazis arrived. August Horkheimer managed to organize a provisional US
passport and Spanish transit visa for him via the American consulate in Marseille. Benjamin hoped to
reach Lisbon and fly to New York and, on 25 September 1940, he and two companions walked from
Banyols-sur-Mer to Portbou. Benjamin was only 48, but he was a heavy smoker and had a bad heart.
He was carrying his last work in a briefcase. No one knew what was inside, though he told everyone it
was very important and to be saved it all costs. At Portbou, the Spanish frontier guards gave Benjamin
the heartbreaking news that the rules of the game had been changed the day before: he now needed
a French exit visa and would have to be deported back to France. Seeing he was unwell, the police
allowed him to spend the night in the Hotel de Francia (formerly at C/del Mar 5). The next day
Benjamin was found dead in his bed. He is known to have had morphine on him, and it was assumed
that the terror of being deported had led him to take his own life, although the death certificate gives
the cause of death as a brain haemorrhage. Henny Gurland, the woman travelling with him (and
future wife of Erich Fromm), claimed Benjamin had given her two suicide notes for Adorno which she
later destroyed. She and her son were allowed to go on to Lisbon the next day. Conspiracy theories
have been woven.

There was enough money in the dead man's pocket to pay for a niche in Portbou's Catholic cemetery
for five years. His bones were removed in the 1940s and placed in the communal ossuary, although you

can see a plaque on the cemetery wall, put up after Franco's death with a quote from the *Theses on the Philosophy of History*: 'There is no document of civilisation which is not at the same time a document of barbarism'. And the manuscript in Benjamin's briefcase? It was given to a fellow refugee who lost it on the train to Madrid.

Benjamin is remembered, along with all the other 20th-century refugees who passed to and fro through Portbou, with an unsettling monument called *Passagen*, by Israeli sculptor Dani Karavan. A rusty metal chute of claustrophic stairs descends from the cemetery to the sea, blocked by a plate of glass, evoking Benjamin's last surviving if unfinished work, the *Passagen-Werk* (the Arcades Project, published in 1982).

Where to Stay and Eat in Cap de Creus

(i) **Cadaqués >**
C/Cotxe 2,
t 972 25 83 15

★ **Cap de Creus >>**

★ **Blaumar >**

Cadaqués ✉ 17488

***Rocamar**, C/Dr. Bartomeus s/n, t 972 25 81 50, www.rocamar.com (€€€€–€€€€). On a hill overlooking Cadaqués' port and a quiet beach, the village's biggest hotel has spacious rooms, two pools and a tennis court.

***Playa Sol**, Platja Pianc 3, t 972 25 81 00 (€€€€–€€€). On the beach, overlooking the bay. Big rooms sleeping up to four, many with balconies over either the sea or garden and pool at the back. *Closed mid-Dec–mid-Feb.*

***Llané Petit**, Dr Bartoneus 37, t 972 25 10 20, www.llanepetit.com (€€€). Smallish, modern and very comfortable hotel with a garden, pool and a garage on a little beach. *Closed Jan 8–Feb.*

Port Lligat, Platja de Portlligat, t 972 25 81 62, www.port-lligat.net (€€€–€€). Long established, next to Dalí's house, with fine views over the bay and a children's playground, pool and Jacuzzi.

Blaumar, C/Massa d'Or 21, t 972 15 90 41, www.hotelblaumar.com (€€). Lovely peaceful hotel with airy rooms, 10-minute walk to the centre, with a small pool, parking and bike rental available. *Closed mid Nov–mid Mar.*

*Hostalet de Cadaqués**, C/Miquel Rosset 13, t 972 25 82 06, www.hostaletcadaques.com (€€–€). Opened in 2008 in the centre of the village, eight trim en-suite doubles aimed at the young who go to bed late.

*Hs Ubaldo**, C/Unió 13, t 972 25 81 25, www.hotelubaldo.com (€€–€). In the heart of old Cadaqués – simple, white, and friendly.

*P Vehi**, C/Església 5, t 972 25 84 70 (€). The cheapest place to stay; four little rooms with bathrooms down the hall, a few minutes from the beach.

Casa Nun, Plaça de Portixó 6, t 972 25 88 56 (€€). Home cooking with pizzazz in a pretty setting – the rabbit is especially delicious.

La Galiota, C/Narcis Monturiol 9, t 972 25 81 87 (€€). Serves a mix of Catalan and French favourites. *Closed mid-Sept to mid-June.*

La Sirena, C/d'Es Call s/n, t 972 25 89 74 (€€). Famous for perfectly grilled and beautifully fresh fish.

Cap de Creus, Cap de Creus, t 972 19 90 05, www.cbrava.com/restcap.uk.htm (€). Just 100m from the lighthouse, it's worth booking ahead to get tables with views. There's a very eclectic menu – which even includes a vindaloo curry.

Casa Anita, C/Miguel Roset, t 972 25 84 71, www.casa-anita.com (€). In business for over forty years, the legendary family run restaurant has doodles by Picasso and Dalí. Delicious freshly fried fish and seafood *a la planxa* (grilled).

El Port de la Selva ✉ 17489

***Porto Cristo**, C/Major 59, t 972 38 70 62, www.hotelportocristo.com (€€€). The prettiest hotel in town, in an old manor house dating from 1864 and completely refurbished in 2007, with four different types of rooms; the smarter ones have their own jacuzzi.

*Fonda Felip**, Plaça Camp de l'Obra 15, 2km up in Selva de Mar, t 972 38 72 71 (€). The only place to stay in the village, sweet and peaceful. There's a restaurant specializing in *arròs de cabra de mar*, which sounds like 'sea goat' but turns out to be spider crab.

(i) Llançà >
Av. Europa 37,
t 972 38 01 81

(i) Portbou >>
Pg Lluís Companys
s/n, t 972 12 51 61

*Hs Sol i Sombre, C/Nou 8–10, t 972 38 70 60 (€). In the village centre a stone's throw from the sea, with en-suite rooms and some even cheaper with bathrooms down the hall.

Llançà ✉ 17490
**Grifeu, Ctra. de Portbou s/n, t 972 38 00 50, www.hotelgrifeu.com (€€€–€€). Overlooking the beach, rather pink on the outside,but rooms are immaculately white. Half board required in season. Closed Nov–Easter.
**La Goleta, C/Pintor Tarruella 22, t 972 38 01 25, www.hotellagoleta.com (€€). Seaside hotel with comfy rooms

decorated with with a smattering of antiques.
**Hs La Florida, C/Floridablanca 23–25, t 972 12 01 61, www.costabrava nord.com/hotelflorida (€€). In the old part of town, tidy and a bit old-fashioned. Adjacent car park; open summer only.
*Hs Miramar, Pg Marítim 7, t 972 38 01 32 (€). Typical hostal on the beach.

Portbou ✉ 17497
**Pension Costa Blava, C/Cervere 20-25, t 972 39 03 86 (€). Nicest in town, but only open June-Sept.

Figueres

The only difference between me and the surrealists is that I am a surrealist.

Dalí

As the birthplace of Dalí, Figueres (originally Roman Juncaria on the Via Augusta) could claim to be the world capital of Surrealism. It could have made his museum into a major tourist factory. Think of all the mileage Memphis gets out of Elvis. But Figueres doesn't do anything of the sort. Instead it has fun being a kind of anti-Girona; in contrast to the medieval, romantic city of dark alleys, Figueres is youthful and a bit nutty from having its brain-box battered by the *tramuntana*, which blows 60 days of the year.

Teatre-Museu Dalí

⭐ Teatre-Museu Dalí
Plaça Gala-Salvador Dalí 5, t 972 67 75 00, www.salvador-dali.org; open July–Sept 9–8; Mar–June and Oct 9.30–6; Nov–Feb 10.30–6; closed Mon from Oct–May; adm exp; in Aug you can also visit at night from 10pm to 1am and sip a glass of cava; book in advance on the website

Forget the Vatican: this is 'the spiritual centre of Europe' according to Dalí, who opened this museum in 1974 in a merry reconstruction of Figueres' municipal theatre, which had been badly damaged in the Civil War. The building itself is a Surrealist work of art. Its landmark **Galatea Tower** wears a garland of eggs and is covered in a meticulously tidy pattern of ceramic turds. St Peter's in Rome is topped by statues of halo-ed saints; here they beckon with loaves of bread on their heads.

Expect surprises at every turn – and allow at least three hours to see it all. Giant figures of Dalí and Gala rocket to the heavens on the *trompe l'œil* ceiling; Dalí's 1948 installation *Cadillac* has a system to sprinkle its snail-covered mannequin occupants. In a more serious vein, it also houses some of Dalí's most iconic paintings: the early light-filled *Port Alguer* (1924), *The Spectrum of Sex Appeal* (1932), *Soft Self-Portrait with Fried Bacon* (1941), *Poetry from America, the Cosmic Athletes* (1943), *The Bread Basket* (1945), and *Atomic Leda* (1949), and larger works, such as the wonderful *Face of Mae West Which Can Be Used as an Apartment*, plus Dalí's collection of works by other artists. The old wizard lived his final years in an apartment in the Torre Galatea, at the side of

Getting to and around Figueres

All **trains** from Barcelona to France stop in Figueres, which is the centre of the bus network to the upper Costa Brava. SARFA buses (*t 902 30 20 35, www.sarfa.com*) run regularly from Figueres to Roses and Cadaqués.

his collaborator Antoni Pixot, now the museum director. After his death, Dalí was embalmed in a fluid guaranteed to keep his body intact for two centuries, and buried – controversial to the bitter end – under the glass dome in the museum, not far from the toilets.

Dalí-Joies
t 972 67 75 00; open July–Sept daily 9–8; Mar–June and Oct daily 9.30–6; Nov–Feb daily 10.30–6; adm

Dalí began designing gold and precious gems back in 1941. An annexe to the museum, Dalí-Joies, contains 39 exquisite pieces.

Opposite the museum, the tall, startling clean-looking Gothic church of **Sant Pere** was built by King Pere the Ceremonious in 1378, but much reconstructed after being pillaged and burnt by anarchists and bombarded by Franco in the Civil War. In its day it witnessed a royal wedding: in 1701, King Philip V married Maria Louisa of Savoy here. It later witnessed the baptism, first communion and funeral of Dalí.

Along La Rambla

Little survives of medieval Figueres, but a short walk down from the museum you'll come to the town's handsome Rambla, built over a foul-smelling stream in 1832 and lined with towering plane trees. Monuments honour the city's famous sons: Dalí's face is reflected in a funhouse mirror of a bright lipstick-like tube, and an elaborate Noucentista memorial by Enric Casanovas honours Narcís Monturiol i Estarriol (1819– 85), who invented the first, partially working combustion-powered submarines. The fascinating **Museu dels Joguets** houses some 4,000 toys, including some once played with by Lorca, Miró and Dalí, plus an impressive collection of *caganers*. Some mostly unexceptional Catalan painting, plus archaeological and historical items (ceramics from ancient Empuriès, Roman glass, capitals and more from Sant Pere de Rodes) fill the halls of the **Museu Empordà**.

Museu dels Joguets
La Rambla and C/Sant Pere 1, t 972 50 45 85, www.mjc.cat; open June–Sept daily 10–7, Sun and hols 11–6; Oct–May Tues–Sat 10–6, Sun and hols 11–2; adm

Museu Empordà
Rambla 2, t 972 50 23 05; www.museuemporda.org; open Tues–Sat 11–7, Sun and hols 11–2; adm

There are several Modernista buildings in Figueres: one of the prettiest is the **Teatre Jardí**, one street back from La Rambla, in Plaça Josep Pla.

Castell Sant Ferran
Pujada del Castell, t 972 50 60 94; guided visits 10.30–2 and 4–6; Holy Week and July– mid-Sept 10.30–8; Nov–Feb 10.30–2; adm; longer visit includes a boat visit to the cisterns

Castell Sant Ferran

On a hill above the Dalí museum sprawls the jumbo pentagonal **Castell Sant Ferran**. Although the Treaty of the Pyrenees established the frontier with France at Pertús in 1659, King Fernando VI still didn't entirely trust the French and ordered the construction of this fort in 1753. The story goes that his courtiers once found the king in his gardens in Madrid, staring towards the

Dalí

'The difference between me and a madman is that I am not mad.'

It's a shame that this outrageous megalomaniac, so obsessed with immortality, didn't live forever. Salvador Felipe Jacinto Dalí i Domènech was born in Figueres on May 11, 1904 at Carrer Monturiol 10, the son of a well-to-do notary. One might say even his conception and birth were surreal: he was born almost exactly nine months after the death of his two-year-old brother, who was also named Salvador, which left him convinced that he was his brother's reincarnation. His precocious talent for art was encouraged by his father's best friend, artist Raymond Pixot, the father of Dalí's collaborator. Not long after Dalí's mother's died in 1921, he was admitted to the Academia San Fernando in Madrid. He wrote in his diary of the time: *'The world will admire me. Perhaps I'll be despised and misunderstood, but I'll be a great genius, I'm certain of it.'*

Gifted with an impeccable technique, endlessly creative, and capable of painting in any style he put his hand to, Dalí became the most famous of the Surrealists while still in his 20s, when he painted his first 'hand-painted dream photographs' of melting watches and human bodies fitted with sets of spilling drawers. During the Civil War he offered to go to Barcelona and run a Department for the Irrational Organization of Daily Life (only to be told: thanks anyway, it already exists). He and Gala would later move to the United States, living there full-time from 1940 to 1948.

If other Surrealists drew their inspiration from the irrational well of the unconscious, Dalí claimed his came from 'critical paranoia' – a carefully cultivated delusion, a conscious suspension of rational thought, a way of art and life. Part of his paranoia came from his fear of madness – his grandfather, reportedly driven mad by the wind, committed suicide. Some have argued that the public bluster, provocation and showmanship was only a screen that allowed Dalí the space back in Portlligat to investigate his personal obsessions and anguish (he was apparently impotent) with remarkable candour. When not at work, he went about offending everyone, not worrying that the art world considered him a publicity-mongering, money-grubbing buffoon (André Breton, the 'pope' of Surrealism, famously excommunicated him). Essentially apolitical, he was the one Catalan artist to get along with Franco, but on the whole Spain's conservatives didn't like him much. Like a gadfly, he broke art taboos right and left – cheerfully painting religious kitsch (all the while arguing that Jesus Christ was made of cheese), 'selling out' by doing some very funny television commercials, designing the logo for *Chupa Chups* lollipops; he may even have been behind forgeries of his own work (*see* p.193). As a posthumous insult to Catalonia, he left everything to the Spanish state. Although with this museum, the house at Portlligat, and the castle at Púbol, the arty anchors of Costa Brava's rejuvenation, Catalonia didn't do too badly.

northeast; when asked what he was looking at, he replied that, given the money he was spending, he reckoned he should be able to see the fort from Madrid! It didn't even keep the French out – Napoleon's armies grabbed it twice. During the Civil War, it served for a week in 1939 as the last bastion of the Spanish Republican government, when for a brief while Figueres was the capital of Republican Spain. It is Europe's second-largest fort, and set to become the new home of Barcelona's Military Museum.

Around Figueres: Into the Alt Empordà

The country around Figueres is pure Mediterranean, an idyll of vines, cork oaks, cypresses and olives, and astonishingly unspoiled –

99 per cent of people driving to Spain barrel down the motorway
and never get off. Signs on rutted tracks lead up to dolmens, which
are exceptionally plentiful, as are *bodegas* where city-slickers come
to stock up on wine. Quite a few foreigners have fixed up farms
and houses in the nearly abandoned villages of the Serra de
l'Albera, giving them a fresh lease on life. The Serra itself is a Nature
Reserve – based in Figueres, you can easily spend a day or two
exploring.

Peralada

Peralada was in 1270 the birthplace of the medieval chronicler
Ramon Muntaner. Muntaner joined the Almogàvers, a feared and
ruthless band of mercenaries who dressed in animal skins and
fought under the command of former German-Italian Knight
Templar Roger de Flor in 1302, stirring up all kinds of trouble in
Sicily and the Eastern Mediterranean. Muntaner survived to retire
and record his *Crònica*, one of the main sources of Catalan
medieval history. He would have known Peralada's 13th-century
Dominican monastery, of which only the cloister survives.

The village's main focus, however, is the 16th-century **Castell de
Peralada** of the Rocabertí family, former counts of Empordà, with
its two round crenellated fairytale towers smothered in ivy. It
houses a **casino** and hosts a major music festival in July and
August. Nearby, the former Carmelite convent contains the
Castell de Peralada Museum which includes a library famous for a
thousand editions of *Don Quixote*, an atmospheric wine museum,
and a museum of glass, with enamels and delicate pretty pieces
going back to Roman times. The castle is also a leading maker of
DO Empordà wines and excellent *cavas* and offers a variety of
tastings and tours.

Serra de l'Albera

The Serra de l'Albera is one of the last native habitats for the
Hermann's tortoise; north of Peralada in Garriguella, you can visit
the **Centre de Reproducció de Tortugues de l'Albera** and learn all
about them. The area also has an important concentration of
dolmens – **Espollo** even has a dolmen fountain, as well as the
Albera Nature Reserve's **Centre d'Informació** where you can learn
the locations of two dozen other megaliths around the village and
nearby Sant Climent Sescebes. Sant Climent also has something
you don't see every day: a falconry school (**Escola de la Falconeria**).

The landmark at **Rabós**, further up the GI603, is an impressive
fortified church, but an even more impressive one waits futher up
the road, in the wild dolmen-dotted **Serra de la Mala Veïna**, the
fortified **Monestir de Sant Quirze de Colera**, consecrated in 935 and
renovated in 1123, and currently undergoing another very slow

Castell de Peralada
to book wine tastings
and wine tours, t 972 53
80 11, www.
castilloperalada.com

Casino
t 972 53 81 25, www.
casino-peralada.com

Castell de Peralada Museum
Plaça del Carme s/n,
t 972 53 81 25,
www.museucastell
peralada.com,
hour-long guided visits
daily July and Aug on
the hour 10–12 and 4–8;
Sept–June Tues–Sat
10–12 and 4.30–6.30,
Sun 10–12; adm

Centre de Reproducció de Tortugues de l'Albera
t 972 55 22 45, www.
tortugues.cat; open
summer daily 10–6;
winter Tues–Sun 10–1
and 3–5, closed
Nov–mid Mar; adm

Centre d'Informació
Rectoria Vella,
C/Amadeu Sudrià 3,
t 972 54 50 79; open
weekends only in winter

Escola de la Falconeria
Mas Ullastre, t 639 68
52 92, www.freewebs.
com/falconeria

renovation. The Benedictines here once held extensive estates and vineyards in Empordà and Roussillon; the basilica has three naves and barrel vaulting with traces of frescoes, and stands next to the 11th-century abbot's house and scant remains of the cloister. There's a restaurant in the former stables.

Pretty little **Capmany** to the west is a wine centre, with another important group of dolmens. It's close to the bustling frontier town of **La Jonquera**, the last motorway stop in Spain, as busy these days as Portbou is empty, brimful of car parks, restaurants and petrol stations. As it's illegal for big rigs to circulate on Sundays in France, it becomes a huge festival of trucks every weekend. A side road, however, leads up to another world altogether: the medieval village of **Cantallóps** and the romantic **Castell de Requesens** rising high above a lush green cork forest on the French border. The first castle was built on the site by the Empordà counts in the 9th century, and, a thousand years later, the Count of Peralada rebuilt it as a summer retreat; it suffered decades of depredations as a Guardia Civil barracks, but is fascinating nonetheless, even in its funky state.

Castell de Requesens
open 15 July–10 Sept daily 11–7; 11 Sept–14 July Sat, Sun and hols only 11–6; adm

Northwest of Figueres

There isn't much shaking these days in **Llers**, just northwest of Figueres, but that wasn't always the case; although flattened by the Nazi Condor Legion during the Civil War, the village still has the raggedly jumbled ruins of one of Catalonia's most notorious castles, belonging in the 1170s to Count Guifré Estruc – who may well have been the world's oldest vampire. The story goes that he set out to convert the last local pagans to Christianity, only to earn himself their curses instead. And, unlike the outcome one expects in pious stories, this time the bad guys won; Count Estruc returned home to Llers, terrorizing the locals, sucking their blood and raping their women and fathering monsters. In the end, an old nun courageously went into the cemetery, dug up his body and drove a stake into his heart.

These days Llers prefers to promote its cherries, and holds a festival in early June dedicated to its sweet red beauties; **Terrades**, 6km west, boasts 100,000 cherry trees. There's a 14th-century castle, partially converted into a *masia* just south at **Vilarig**, while **Cistella** has a medieval core. The artificial lake, the **Pantà de Boadella**, has rarely been full in recent years, but it enjoys a beautiful setting, and the surrounding villages are favourite weekend destinations. The old walled town of **Sant Llorenç de la Muga** has a very picturesque fortified 14th-century bridge, and **Maçanet de Cabrenys,** set in cork oak forests, boasts a striking menhir, the Pedra Dreta, on the edge of town.

Market Days in and around Figueres

Figueres, Tuesday, Thursday and Saturday in the Plaça del Gra. Big antiques market, *Mercat del Bracaner*, on the Rambla on the third Saturday of each month.

Sports and Activities in and around Figueres

⭐ El Molí >>

Golf

Club de Golf Perelada, Rocabertí s/n, t 972 53 82 87, *www.golfperalada.com*.

Where to Stay and Eat in and around Figueres

ⓘ Figueres >
Plaça del Sol,
t 972 50 31 55

Figueres ✉ 17600

Figueres is famous for its cuisine, and all of its best restaurants are in hotels.
*****Durán**, C/Lasauca 5, t 972 50 12 50, *www.hotelduran.com* (€€€). Right on the Rambla since 1855, the Duran offers cosy modern rooms, wi-fi and parking. Dalí, who loved good food, often held court in the hotel's renowned restaurant (€€€); try the *sarsuela amb llagosta* (fish stew with lobster).
*****Empordà**, 3km north on Ctra N11, Km763, t 972 50 05 62, *www. hotelemporda.com* (€€€). A mythic place, overlooking pretty countryside on the road to France. Founded in 1961 by Josep Mercader, the great pioneer in the revival of gourmet Catalan cuisine, the hotel has had a recent facelift, and the restaurant, now in the hands of Jaume Subiros and Josep's sons, remains one of the best, acclaimed for its imaginative adaptations of regional specialities. Game dishes are a speciality, as are Mercader's original broad bean and mint salad and *taps de Cadaqués* – an incendiary rum cake (*menú degustació*, €€€).

⭐ Mas Pau >
****Mas Pau, just west of Figueres in Avinyonet de Puigventós, t 972 546 154, *www.maspau.com* (€€€). On the road to Besalú, just outside Figueres, a beautiful 16th-century stone farm-

house housing a well-known **restaurant** now run by Toni Gerez and Xavier Sagristà from El Bullí. The rooms are cushy, and there's a pool in the garden. *Closed Jan– mid Mar.*
*****Travé**, Ctra Olot, s/n (along the N260, southwest of the centre), t 972 50 06 16, *www.hoteltrave.com* (€€€). In walking distance of the centre, comfortable, with a pool, good breakfast, and free parking. Family rooms available.
*****El Molí**, Ctra Pont de Molins a les Escaules (just north of Figueres), t 972 52 92 71, *www.hotelelmoli.es* (€€€–€€). Rooms filled with heirloom furniture in a 17th-century water mill on the River Muga, which gurgles a lullaby for peaceful slumbers. Good traditional Catalan **restaurant** too, under the stone vaults (€€€).
*****Pirineos**, Avda Salvador Dalí 68, t 972 50 03 12, *www.hotelpirineos pelegri.com* (€€). Spacious, recently renovated rooms with satellite TV, 500m from the Dalí museum. Popular with tour groups.
*****Plaza Inn**, C/Pujada del Castell 14, t 972 51 45 40, *www.plazainn.es* (€€). Opened in 2004, a stone's throw from the Dalí museum, a friendly arty retreat; delicious breakfast.
****Hs La Barretina**, C/Lasauca 13, t 972 67 64 12, *www.hostallabarretina.com* (€). Up-to-date, cosy rooms and restaurant, just off La Rambla. *Closed Nov.*
*España, C/La Jonquera 26, t 972 50 08 69 (€). Basic rooms in the pedestrian centre north of La Rambla, a short walk from the Dalí museum.

Peralada ✉ 17491

*******Golf Peralada**, t 972 53 88 30, *www.golfperalada.com* (€€€€). Luxurious rooms overlooking the golf course and the Albera nature reserve, complete with a spa for beauty treatments using wine and grape by products and the posh **Masia Peralada** (€€€€) restaurant favoured by Catalan bigwigs, with good rice dishes and 'olive oil and salt tastings'. Check their website for special offers.
*****Hs de la Font**, Baixada de la Font 15–19, t 972 53 85 07, *www.hostaldela*

font.com.es (€€). Comfortable little hotel with 12 rooms, occupying a former convent and its pretty cloister.
Ca la Maria, 6km north in the centre of Mollet de Peralada, **t** 972 56 33 82 (€€). Since 1960, one of the most popular restaurants in the Alt Empordà, set in an 18th-century cellar and serving big helpings of rabbit, kid, duck and pork dishes.

Garriguella ✉ 17780

***Hotel de La Plaça**, Plaça de l'Església 2, **t** 972 53 18 07, *www.hotel garriguella. com* (€€€–€€). Stylish hotel offering a choice of snug wood-panelled rooms, a pool with a counter current, and a restaurant (€€€) run by chef Sebastian Lobel who used to cook for the prime minister of France.
Can Garriga, C/Figueres, 3, **t** 972 53 01 84, *www.cangarriga.net* (€€). Peaceful little B&B in a traditional stone house; three antique-filled bedrooms; owners cook up big breakfasts and at other times allow guests access to the kitchen.

Cantallops ✉ 17708

****Can Xiquet**, **t** 972 55 44 55, *www. canxiquet.com* (€€€€). Comfortable hotel and excellent restaurant and gorgeous views from the rooms, a wide range of activities: outdoor pool, gym, excursions in the Albera nature reserve, cooking courses and tastings, and much more.

Terrades ✉ 17731

La Fornal dels Ferrers, C/Major 31, **t** 972 56 90 95, *www.lafornal.com*

(€€€). The antique-filled 18th-century 'Smithy's Smith' offers four romantic rooms and a lovely restaurant (€€) with a garden, and a special cherry menu in season.

Cistella ✉ 17741

Carles Antoner, Plaça Major 2, **t** 972 54 71 58 (€€). Small, rustic, creative Catalan cuisine based on the daily market in the heart of a medieval village.

Maçanet de Cabrenys ✉ 17720

Hs la Central, Antiga Carretera de Darnius, **t** 972 53 50 53, *www. hlacentral.com* (€€). A pretty Modernista chalet with stylish rooms redone in 2008. The setting is gorgeous, on a rushing stream feeding the reservoir; offers spa treatments, and hires out boats, bikes, fishing tackle, and plenty of suggestions for excursions. The restaurant (€€) has lots of seafood on the menu and lovely views.

Orriols ✉ 17468

*****L' Odissea de l'Empordá**, C/del Castell 6, 18km south of Figueres (Exit 5 off the A-7), **t** 972 55 17 18, *www.odissea-emporda.com* (€€€€€–€€€€). Five suites in a 17th-18th century castle filled with paintings and designer furniture; the delicacies in the restaurant (€€€) are prepared by Antonio Ferrer – one of the favourite chefs of the late Barcelonin novelist Manuel Vázquez Montalbán.

Girona

 Girona

Girona is a serious, secretive and fascinating city, with an historical palette as varied as its much-photographed, ochre-hued houses hanging over the River Onyar. The medieval streets of the Barri Vell have been lovingly neglected, leaving intact an evocative neighbourhood of vaulted passageways, winding steps and tiny squares, crowned by a cathedral unique in Europe. It has a small but excellent collection of museums, including one devoted to what was one of the most important Jewish quarters in Spain. The intellectual torch is now held by the university – although students grumble that Girona has the worst nightlife in Spain.

Getting to and around Girona

By Air and Getting from the Airport

Girona Costa Brava **airport** (*t 972 18 67 08*), 12km south of the city, receives numerous international flights on Ryanair. **Shuttle buses** (*t 902 361 550, www.sagales.com*) from the airport run to Girona and Barcelona (around 70mins). Sarfa **buses** (*t 902 302 025, www.sarfa.es*) service the Costa Brava. Another option, if you book at least 24 hours in advance, is Shuttle Direct (*www.shuttledirect.com*) which will take you directly to your accommodation.
Airlines: Ryanair, **t** 807 22 02 20; Spanair, **t** 902 13 14 15; Transavia, **t** 807 07 50 22.

By Bus, Train and Taxi

Girona's **bus** (**t** 972 21 23 19) and **train** stations (**t** 902 24 02 02) are side-by-side on Plaça d'Espanya. All trains between France and Barcelona stop here, as well as the Costa Brava Express to Tarragona, Lleida, Zaragoza and Madrid.
Taxis: t 972 22 23 23 or **t** 972 22 10 20.

By Car/Parking

Finding legal street parking is next to impossible, so use the **underground garages** in the new town (there's one in Plaça de Jaume Vincens i Vives by the Pont de Sant Feliu) and walk over the bridge into the medieval core. **Hire a car** at the airport where all the usual companies have counters, or in town at Marius, Ctra. Santa Eugènia 11, **t** 972 22 09 06, *www.mariusrentacar.com*, or Cabeza, C/Barcelona 30, **t** 972 21 82 08.

Oh, stop moaning and hop on a bike, Girona would say. The city is one of Europe's cycling capitals, surrounded by 700 miles of mountain bike trails, 'Vías Verdes' converted from extinct rail lines, and a network of relatively empty, often stunning mountain roads.

Girona 'The Immortal'

As a city, Girona was inevitable: there just had to be a city on this hill, at the confluence of four rivers, midway between the Pyrenees and the Mediterranean. The Iberians were here first, followed by the Romans who founded Gerunda on the Rome-to-Hispania Via Augusta. St James, they say, preached here, and the see was founded in 247. Goths and Franks invaded, the walls were improved, and by the 5th century it was the seat of a bishop. The Visigoths held it briefly, followed by the Moors. In 778 Charlemagne took it back, and made it the seat of a county in the Hispanic Marches. The first Jews in the city were recorded in 890. The 12th century was a golden period, when Girona grew so quickly that it expanded onto the left bank of the Onyar river.

It was contested throughout history. Its nickname, 'City of a Thousand Sieges', is a slight exaggeration; the real number is 25, but, by May 1809, when 18,000 French troops appeared at the gate for the third time in two years, it must have seemed like a thousand. The French controlled the rest of Catalonia by then, but Napoleon knew that as long as Spain controlled Girona, his army was in danger of being cut off.

Girona was not particularly well defended. The medieval walls around the old town had not been improved, and the local garrison

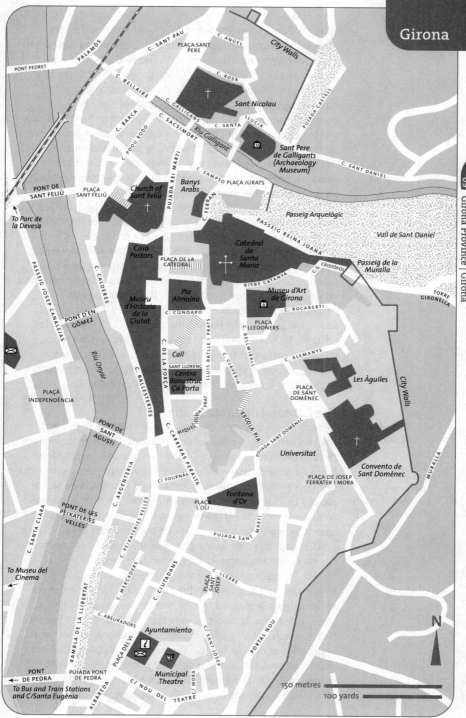

City Walls

C. SANT PAU
PLAÇA SANT
PERE
C. ANGEL
C. ROSA
PALAMÓS
PONT PEDRET
C. BELLAIRE
C. GALLIGANS
Sant Nicolau
C. SACSIMORT
C. BARCA
C. POUU RODO
C. SANTA
Riu Galligant
LLUCIA
PUJADA CASTELL
Sant Pere
de Galligants
(Archaeology
Museum)
C. SANT DANIEL
C. SAMPSO PLAÇA JURATS
PONT DE
SANT FELIÚ
PLAÇA
SANT FELIÚ
Church of
Sant Feliú
Banys
Arabs
C. FERRAN
Passeig Arqueològic
Vall de Sant Daniel
To Parc de
la Devesa
PUJADA REI MARTI
PASSEIG REINA JOANA
Casa
Pastors
PLAÇA DE LA
CATEDRAL
Catedral
de
Santa
Maria
Passeig de la
Muralla
TORRE
GIRONELLA
C. CALDERES
PONT D'EN
GÓMEZ
PASSEIG JOSEP CANALEJAS
Museu
d'Història
de la
Ciutat
Pia
Almoina
BISBE CATANYA
C. CRISTÓFOL
Museu d'Art
de Girona
C. ROCABERTI
Riu Onyar
C. CÚNDARO
C. DE LA FORÇA
Call
SANT LLORENÇ
Centra
Bonastruc
Ça Porta
LLUIS BATLLE I PRATS
PLAÇA
LLEDONERS
C. BELLMIRALL
City Walls
C. BALLESTERIES
C. CLAVERIA
C. ALEMANYS
Les Àguiles
PLAÇA
INDEPENDÈNCIA
PONT DE
SANT
AGUSTI
C. DE LA PALMA I PLANT
PLAÇA
DE SANT
DOMÈNEC
MURALLA
Universitat
PUJADA SANT DOMÈNEC
Convento de
Sant Domènec
C. CARRERAS PERALTA
C. ARGENTERIA
C/ FOURNÁS
PLAÇA DE JOSEP
FERRATER I MORA
PONT DE LES
PEIXATERIES
VELLES
Fontana
d'Or
PLAÇA
L'OLI
C. PEIXATERIES VELLES
C. SANT MARTI
C. SANTA CLARA
PUJADA SANT MARTI
To Museu del
Cinema
C. MERCADERS
C. LLEBRE
PLAÇA
SANT
JOSEP
RAMBLA DE LA LLIBERTAT
C. CIUTADANS
C. ABEURADORS
PORTAL NOU
Ayuntamiento
C/ MORA
C. SANT JOSEP
PONT
DE PEDRA
PUJADA PONT
DE PEDRA
PLAÇA DEL VI
Municipal
Theatre
C/ NOU DEL
TEATRE
N
To Bus and Train Stations
and C/Santa Eugènia
ALBAREDA
150 metres
100 yards

numbered only 5,700 Spanish regulars and 1,100 local troops. However, the surrounding hills were well fortified and Girona had a brilliant commander in Mariano Álvarez de Castro. The French fired some 20,000 shells and 60,000 cannon balls into the city, brought in reinforcements, and finally, in August, managed to capture the strategic castle of Montjuïc above the city. They thought Álvarez would soon surrender; instead, he built barricades and trenches inside the city and the fight, now urban warfare, continued into December. Supplies were exhausted, and after a last daredevil sortie Álvarez was so exhausted and ill that he handed over command and received his last rites. Two days later, on 12 December, the town capitulated.

It is estimated that in all 10,000 people, soldiers and civilians, had died inside Girona; the French lost some 13,000 men during the eight months of the siege, including many to disease. Yet even though the French won the battle, they lost the war: the terrible sieges of Girona and Zaragoza succeeded in pinning down, delaying and demoralizing the French. 'Immortal' Girona became a rallying cry for Spanish resistance for the rest of the war.

During the Civil War, Nationalists bombarded it from air, anarchists pillaged and burned the churches, and thousands of refugees tramped through on the way to France. In the 1960s, things began to pick up again: the city expanded into 'Greater Girona', devouring and incorporating satellite towns in its path; by the 1980s it was the wealthiest city per capita in Spain.

The Catedral de Santa Maria

Catedral de Santa Maria
Plaça de la Catedral, t 972 214 426,www. catedraldegirona.org; open April–Oct daily 10–8; Nov–Mar daily 10–7; adm includes an audioguide; free on Sunday

Few cathedrals enjoy such a stupendous setting, high over the city and visible from miles around. Navigate the intimate lanes of the **Barri Vell** until you reach Girona's version of Rome's Spanish Steps – a majestic 18th-century stairway, with 90 steps waiting to test your piety. The cathedral's remarkable, nearly square façade pierced by its great rose window dates from the 18th century as well. The three tiers of figures are mostly replicas: the only ones spared by sentimental anarchists are the allegories of Faith, Hope and Charity. Only one planned bell tower was ever built, topped by Girona's guardian angel – a bronze weather vane.

Yet the cathedral surpasses the grandeur of its stairs with its single nave, 72ft across – a width surpassed only by St Peter's in Rome. Originally planned by architect Pere Sacoma as a typical three-aisled church, work began in 1347 – just in time for the Black Death, which not only killed some 1,000 Gironans, but set off a long period of decline. In 1404, the new master builder, Guillem Bofill took over, and, as the apse was completed, he devised a money-saving improvement: to replace Sacoma's planned three naves with a single great nave. His proposal was so radical that in

1416 the bishop of Girona summoned all the leading architects of Catalonia to a council to solicit their opinions as to whether or not such a cathedral would actually stand. It did, and does, a survivor of so many sieges, now threatened by something the builders never dreamed of: numelites, minute fossils of worms in the city's limestone. Whole blocks of stone have had to be replaced.

The colossal Gothic vault soars 75ft above the floor, supported by its interior buttresses; the poet Joan Maragall called it the 'canopy of heaven'. Look out for a host of other details: the 11th-century alabaster high altar; a 14th-century masterpiece of silverwork, surmounted by an equally remarkable silver-plated canopy; the 11th-century **'Throne of Charlemagne'**; the beautiful 14th-century alabaster tomb of Countess Ermessenda by Guillem de Morell; the exceedingly strange painting of the *Last Supper* by Perris de la Roca (1560), where St John seems to have been replaced by a woman, tucked under Christ's arm, with what looks like Mount Canigou in the background. The trapezoidal double-colonnaded **Romanesque cloister**, built in the 12th century, is unique, and has exquisitely carved capitals, sculpted with a mix of the sacred and secular.

The cathedral boasts an exceptional treasury, starring the 11th-century **Tapestry of Creation**, which, along with the Bayeux Tapestry, is the best surviving 1,000-year-old work in textile in the west. It records a magical view of Genesis, with the Creator surrounded by sea monsters, wind-bags, the seasons, and Eve popping out of Adam's side, and much more. Equally precious is the **Código del Beatus**, an illuminated commentary on the Apocalypse from 974, one of the most beautiful books ever made with its richly coloured and fantastically imagined Mozarabic miniatures by the monk Emeterio and the nun Eude (one of the first recorded women artists). The small coffer of Caliph Hisham II, a Moorish work from the 10th century, is one of the finest in Spain.

Around the Cathedral

More medieval delights await right next to the cathedral in the former Episcopal Palace, now the **Museu d'Art de Girona**. Exhibits include a remarkable beam, the 'Biga de Cruïlles' dated 1200, carved and painted with funny-faced monks lined up like a chorus line; a unique 16th-century glazier's table, used by the cathedral's stained glass-makers; a beautiful 15th-century catalogue of martyrs from Bohemia; a 10th-century portable altar from Sant Pere de Rodes and a *Calvary* by Mestre Bartomeu (13th-century), with a serenely smiling Christ with a face like Shiva, ready to dance off the Cross. There are a pair of exceptional 15th-century altarpieces: the retable of Púbol by Gothic master Bernat Martorell, and one from Sant Miquel de Cruïlles by Lluís Borrassà. Upstairs, there are rooms of

Museu d'Art de Girona
Pujada de la Catedral, t 972 20 38 34, www. museuart.com; open Mar–Sept Tues–Sat 10–7, Sun 10–2; Oct–Feb Tues–Sat 10–6, Sun 10–2; closed Mon; adm

09

Girona Province | Girona

19th- and 20th-century Catalan paintings, with a selection of landscapes by Joachim Vayreda and others of the Olot school.

Back down the 90 steps, turn left and pass through the Portal de Sobreportes and its two round towers. The huge stones of their bases pre-date even the Romans, and there's a niche hollowed out on top for a statue of 'Our Lady of Good Death' invoked by the unfortunates led through the gate on their way to execution.

To the left, the 13th–17th-century church of **Sant Feliu** stands at the summit of its own smaller flight of stairs. Like the cathedral, it only received one of its two planned towers – a stone filigree one that had its point knocked off by a streak of lightning. The church stands over an early Christian cemetery, where the city's first bishop and patron Saint Narcís 'of the Flies' suffered martyrdom in 307. He is honoured in an 18th-century chapel, where a painting illustrates the origins of his unusual sobriquet: during the siege of 1285, when French invaders broke open his tomb, an angry swarm of monster flies emerged and bit the soldiers to death. It was a lesson the French never forgot in the their subsequent 24 sieges of Girona – whatever they did, they didn't mess with Narcis – but Girona never forgot the saint's big moment, and you can still buy chocolate *mosques de Girona* – (flies) in the local pastry shops.

Set inside Sant Feliú's presbytery walls are two Roman and six Palaeochristian sarcophagi with fine carvings: one shows a vigorous lion hunt, another Pluto carrying away Persephone into the depths of hell. There's a replica of Girona's most famous statue, the 12th-century **Leonessa**, in Plaça Sant Feliu, whose bottom needs to be kissed if you're considering a move here.

Turning right after the Portal de Sobreportas, a door in a wall leads to the 12th-century Banys Àrabs, the best preserved public baths in Catalonia, built by Morisco craftsmen, its beautiful tiled pool illuminated within by an elegant, eight-sided oculus on slender Roman columns. It functioned into the 16th century.

Across the Galligants river from the baths stand two attractive 12th-century churches: tiny **Sant Nicolau** with its three apses, and the elegant **Monestir de Sant Pere Galligants**, with a striking tower and a beautiful little Romanesque cloister, its capitals sculpted with plants, animals and scenes from the childhood of Christ. It now houses the Museu d'Arqueologia with Neolithic, Iberian, Greek and Roman finds. The Passeig Arqueològic offers a stroll along the Galligants amid medieval walls, towers, springs and gardens to the pretty Vall de Sant Daniel, where Countess Ermessenda (who helped finance the building of the cathedral) founded a convent in the 11th century. Here the lofty 11th-century **Torre de Carlemagne** is one of several access points to the delightful Passeig de la Muralla, a narrow walkway along the city

No pot ser veí de Girona/qui no faci un petó al cul de la lleona

(You can't reside in Girona/Until you've kissed the lioness's arse).
Local saying in Girona

Banys Àrabs
*C/Ferran el Católic;
t 972 21 32 62; www.
banysarabs.org; open
April–Sept Tues–Sat
10–7, Sun 10–2; Oct–Mar
Tues–Sun 10–2; adm*

**Museu
d'Arqueologia**
*t 972 20 26 32; open
Tues–Sat 10.30–1.30 and
4–6, Sun 10–2; adm*

**Passeig
Arqueològic**
open daily 10–8

Passeig de la Muralla
open daylight hours

ramparts once reserved for patrolling soldiers, which allows you stroll among the rooftops and towers of the Barri Vell.

Museu d'Historia
de la Ciutat
*C/Força 27,
t 972 222 229, www.
ajuntament.gi/
museu_ciutat; open
Tues–Sat 10–2 and 5–7,
Sun and hols 10–2; adm*

From Plaça de la Catedral, Carrer de la Força leads to the **Museu d'Historia de la Ciutat**, occupying a 15th-century townhouse that was later converted into a Capuchin convent; exhibits cover everything from prehistoric pots to Roman milestones and a lively mosaic of a chariot race (300 AD), to paintings of the 1809 Siege and relics of the Civil War and Franco years. Other highlights include the Tarlà, a puppet version of a local man who during the Black Death, when the city was quarantined and the children were going crazy, went out and entertained them with mad dances on a beam suspended over the street.

Girona's Jews and El Call

Carrer de la Força also defined the western border of Girona's Call. At its height, in the 1200s, this intricate little ghetto counted some 1,000 souls and the most important school of Jewish mysticism in the west.

As in Barcelona and Tarragona, Girona's Call came under the direct authority of the crown, enjoying autonomy from the municipal council, the Jurats. The count-kings regarded the Jewish communities as a national resource and favoured them, but they also made use of these enclaves to meddle in city affairs. This created no end of tensions over the years; the Jurats, egged on by a fanatical clergy and jealous debtors, isolated Girona's Call into an almost windowless ghetto with only one entrance. During Easter people would gather to throw stones on it from the heights of the cathedral. During the persecutions of 1391, many Jews were killed; after a century of decline and restrictions culminating in the expulsions of 1492, the Call was built over; locals forgot it existed.

In the 1970s, when people began to return their attention to the Barri Vell, a local restaurateur bought up some of the buildings here, excavated the old stones and streets and discovered the *yeshiva* (learning centre) and had the Star of David laid on the patio. In 1987, the local authorities purchased the property, and made it into the **Centra Bonastruc Ça Porta**. The centre's **Museu d'Història dels Jueus** charts the history of the Jews in Catalonia and houses an important collection of funerary stones. The **Institut d'Estudis Nahmànides** is dedicated to medieval Jewish studies.

Centra Bonastruc
Ça Porta
*C/Força 8, t 972 21
67 61, www.ajuntament.
gi; open June–Oct
Mon–Sat 10–8, Sun and
hols 10–3; Nov–May
Mon–Sat 10–6, Sun and
hols 10–3; adm; Segway
tours, 'Jewish Girona
on wheels', Fri pm in
summer: book ahead
on t 972 21 81 44*

From the Call, follow C/de la Força and C/Peralita south to one of Girona's most photographed corners, the Pujada de Sant Domènec, a little poem of urban design where the beautiful Renaissance **Casa dels Agullanas** arches gracefully over the bifurcating steps; the elaborate façade atop the right hand stair belongs to the 16th-century church **Sant Martí**. Above Sant Martí, the 14th-century Dominican convent is now used by university students, replacing the militant friars who were proud to be known as the *Domini canes*, the 'hounds of the Lord'.

I would rather play 'Chiquita Banana' and have my swimming pool than play Bach and starve.

Xavier Cugat

Further south, just off Plaça del l'Oli, in little C/del Sac, a star marks the house where, on 1 January 1900 **Rumba King Xavier Cugat** was born. His family moved to Havana five years later, and he attained fame and fortune in America while conducting his band with a baton in one hand and holding a chihuahua in the other. When Cugat died in 1990, he was brought home and buried in Girona. Carrer dels Ciutadans, south of Plaça del l'Oli, was the fancy address of stately mansions: one, the enormous Romanesque-Gothic **Fontana d'Or**, has a lovely garden courtyard usually open to the public. At the end of C/dels Ciutadans stands Girona's **Ajuntament** in handsome, arcaded **Plaça del Vi**, the former wine market, along with the 19th-century **Municipal Theatre**, where two Catalan *gegants* stand vigil, waiting for a holiday, when they're allowed to sally forth and menace the children.

Most of the action, however, is concentrated in Girona's favourite street, the delightful porticoed **Rambla de la Llibertat** that runs parallel to the Onyar river, lined with bars and boutiques.

Reflections in the Onyar and the Left Bank

The Riu Onyar divides medieval Girona from its newer quarters on the left bank. In 1876, the Gustave Eiffel firm built the most striking of the footbridges that lace the city together, the **Pont de les Peixateries Velles** ('bridge of the old fishmongers') which even looks a bit like a fishnet in iron. It's a favourite for a view of the houses in a dozen shades of ochre built up directly over the Onyar as if it were a Venetian canal. It wasn't always this way: the houses long served as an outer defensive wall to the river's moat. After the last siege people began to open windows, galleries and balconies in the walls, and in the 1980s local architects fixed them up and painted the façades with an Italian flair. The Onyar's fat carp glide under the nattering ducks, while the reflections lead to jokes about exactly which Narcissus is the city's patron – the saintly one 'of the flies' or the one in love with his own beauty.

Even the Middle Ages the city had begun to expand to the left bank, the Barri Mercadal. In 1855, Girona demolished an Augustine monastery to create the handsome arcaded **Plaça de l'Independència**, a favourite place for people-watching, with a monument dedicated to the defenders of 1809 in the centre. Carrer Santa Clara is the main street here, lined with shops; two streets south of Plaça de l'Indepència, C/Obra leads to the **Museu del Cinema (Tomàs Mallol Collection)**. Filmmaker Tomàs Mallol not only collected equipment and memorabilia from the early days of cinema, but also the mirrors, shadow puppets, magic lanterns and other items used to illustrate stories, pre-celluloid.

Museu del Cinema (Tomàs Mallol Collection)
C/Sèquia 1, t 972 41 27 77, www.museudel cinema.org; open May–Sept Tues–Sun 10–8; Oct–April Tues–Fri 10–6, Sat 10–8, Sun 11–1; closed Mon; adm

The *barri* has a handful of buildings designed by Rafael Masó (1880–1935), Girona's only Modernista architect. His masterpiece, the recently restored **Farinera Teixidor**, at C/de Santa Eugénia 42, behind the train station, has a curving roof and pinnacle clad in white ceramics to resemble the flour that was originally milled here. He also designed the **Casa de la Punxa** opposite, named after its pinnacle that wears a jaunty green ceramic wizard's hat.

Girona's favourite green space, the **Parc de la Devesa**, extends along the banks of the Ter, where you can often see cormorants diving in the water. The park, with its neatly ordered grove of 2,500 plane trees, is a delicious retreat on a hot day; in summer it fills up with bars and restaurants, where there's often something musical or theatrical happening.

Market Days in Girona

Girona, Tuesday and Saturday, food and clothes at Parc de La Devesa. On Saturday, crafts on the Pont de Pedra and C/Santa Clara.

Sports in Girona

Cicloturisme i Medi Ambient, C/Impressors Oliva 4, Local A, Girona, t 972 22 10 47, *www.cicloturisme.com*. Cycling holidays in the area – whether you want to pedal with the family for a day, or scale mountain passes for a week or more.

Golf Girona, north at Santa Julià de Ramis, t 972 17 16 41, *www.golfgirona. com*. The most convenient course for the city.

⊛ Històric »

Where to Stay in Girona

ⓘ Girona ›
Rambla de la Llibertat 1, t 972 22 65 75

Girona ✉ 17000

Mas Ferran, Cami de la Bruguera s/n, t 972 4 28 8 90, *www.masferran.com* (€€€€). Handsome stone *masia* in a peaceful rural setting, where you can combine sightseeing with health treatments, a pool, gym and tennis.

****Carlemany**, Plaça Miquel Santaló 1, t 972 21 12 12, *www.carlemany.es* (€€€). Just a few minutes from the Barri Vell in the heart of the city, and recently renovated: elegant, comfortable, immaculate rooms and service, and one of Girona's best restaurants, **El Patí Verd** (€€€).

****Ciutat de Girona**, C/Nord 2, t 972 483 038, *www.hotel-ciutatdegirona. com* (€€€). Stylishly modern, luminous grey, red and white rooms with all mod cons near the Plaça de l'Independència. The hotel's equally stylish restaurant, **Blanc**, t 972 41 56 37, (€€) is popular for its Mediterranean cuisine.

***Costabella**, Avda de França 61, t 972 20 25 24, *www.hotelcostabella. com* (€€€). Functional, modern hotel with pool to the north of the city.

****Històric**, C/Bellmirall 4a, t 972 22 35 83, *www.hotelhistoric.com* (€€). Lovely famil-run hotel close to the Cathedral (and its bells – be warned), in a palimpsest of Girona's early history, with walls dating back to the 3rd to the 9th century; six beautiful rooms, a gorgeous suite and self-catering apartments.

***Peninsular**, C/Nou 3, t 972 20 38 00, *www.novarahotels.com* (€€). One of Girona's oldest hotels, with bright, modern rooms, just five minutes from the centre off Avda Sant Francesc.

***Bellmirall**, C/Bellmirall 3, t 972 20 40 09, *www.grn.es/bellmirall* (€). A diminutive charmer in a 14th-century building near the cathedral.

Condal, C/Joan Maragall 10, t 972 20 44 62, *www.hotelcondalgirona.com* (€). In the new part of town near the train station, family-run and recently renovated, with comfortable, modern rooms. Parking available.

Margarit, C/Ultònia 1, t 972 20 10 66, *www.hotelmargarit.com* (€). A classic no-frills, but very tidy, family run hotel by the river, all rooms en-suite.

*Pensió Viladomat, C/Ciutadans 5, **t** 972 20 31 76 (€). Popular, slightly quirky, good-value *hostal* in the historic centre.

Youth Hotel Cerveri de Girona, C/Ciutadans 9, **t** 972 21 80 03, *www.reaj.com* (€). Girona's youth hostel has a perfect location in the old town, with a kitchen and laundry.

Eating Out in Girona

★ **El Celler de Can Roca** >

★ **La Penyora** >>

El Celler de Can Roca, C/Can Sunyer, just west in Taialà, **t** 972 22 21 57, *www.cellercanroca.com* (€€€€). Founded in 1929 in a nondescript suburb by the grandparents of the current owners, Girona's most famous restaurant is run by the charming, highly skilled and unpretentious Roca brothers: Joan (head chef), Josep (sommelier) and Jordi (pastry chef) who pioneered the Roner system of cooking *sous-vide*. The contemporary dining room looks out over young maples, and a list of wines so vast that it comes to the table on wheels. Elegant takes on classic Catalan dishes are 'inspired by emotions, childhood memories, scents and the Catalan landscape'.

Albereda, C/Albereda 7, **t** 972 22 60 02, *www.restaurantalbereda.com* (€€€). Next to the Ajuntament, a pretty vaulted dining room, serving creative food based on the market. It's famous for its carpaccios. Tasting menu €60.

Cal Ros, C/Cort Reial 9, **t** 972 21 91 76, *www.calros-restaurant.com* (€€€). Since the 1920s, at the north end of Plaça de la Llibertat, Cal Ros has featured traditional classics updated to lighter, modern tastes: rice casseroles, goose with turnips, stews, roast chicken and seasonal dishes.

Massana, C/Bonasatruc de Porta 10, **t** 972 21 38 20, *www.restaurant massana.com* (€€€). Elegant contemporary dining room to match the elegant, beautifully presented cuisine of Pere Massana.

Boira, Plaça de l'Independència 18, **t** 972 22 29 33 (€€). Contemporary bar and tapas downstairs, restaurant upstairs serving tasty regional dishes

and good value menus. Big *al fresco* terrace on the square and views over the Onyar from the dining room.

Bronsoms, Av Sant Francesc 7, **t** 972 21 24 93 (€€). Intimate setting in an 1890s residence, with daily changing market-based menus and a famous *arròs negre*.

Can Barris, Crta de l'Aeroport a Cassà, km 242 (exit 8 off the A7) at Camplong, near the airport, **t** 972 46 10 05 (€€). Set in a massive car park, it hardly looks promising, but this a local institution, where happy families come to slurp up industrial quantities of *cargols* – little snails in a rich, tomato sauce.

La Penyora, C/Nou del Teatre 3, **t** 972 21 89 48 (€€). As recommended by the locals, with superbly prepared classics such as red peppers stuffed with salt cod and other delights, in an old-worldy setting.

Le Bistrot, Pujada Sant Domènec, **t** 972 21 88 03 (€). Good-value option for pizzas and set menus with a French touch in the Call; the duck dishes are particularly good.

Casa Marieta, Plaça Independència 5, **t** 972 20 10 16, *www.casamarieta.com* (€). Girona's oldest restaurant; generous helpings and hearty fare such as *botifarra amb mongetes* (pork sausage with white beans).

El Museu del Vi, C/Cort Reial 4, **t** 972 21 34 85, *www.elmuseu.com* (€). The 'wine museum' is popular with students, with a good choice of tapas too.

El Pou del Call, C/de la Força 14, **t** 972 22 37 74 (€). Another much loved local haunt serving reasonably priced Catalan dishes and filling stews.

Bars and Nightlife in Girona

Girona's not totally dead after dark. In summer, there's often music in the Parc de la Devesa. Clubs are concentrated on **C/Pedret**, north of the Barri Vell.

Llibreria 22, C/Hortes 22, **t** 972 22 14 30, *www.llibreria22.net*. A bookshop by day, trendy bar by night.

Local & Bar Platea, C/Jeroni Real de Fontclara 4, near Plaça Indepència, t 972 22 72 88, *www.localplatea.com*. An old theatre, sleekly refurbished, with frequent live jazz and blues concerts, stand up comedians (in Catalan) and dancing to the DJs Friday and Saturday nights.

La Sala del Cel, C/Pedret 118, t 972 21 46 64, *www.myspace.com/lasaladelcel*. Giant techno disco from the 1990s and still going strong, with famous DJs, two dance floors, and a pool. It draws clubbers from southern France and Barcelona.

Northwest of Girona: La Garrotxa

Gironans are fortunate in their choice of weekend destinations: if they don't fancy a Costa Brava beach, or Barcelona, or the Pyrenees, they can make a short hop just northwest of the city to the arcadian landscapes of the Pla de l'Estany and La Garrotxa, dotted with some 30 well-preserved volcanic cones that last flipped their lids some 11,500 years ago. People come to walk around the craters, or fly over them in balloons and eat in the excellent restaurants.

Banyoles and El Pla de l'Estany

No one thinks of lakes when they think of Catalonia, but there's a pretty one 17km northwest of Girona, the Estany de Banyoles. It's not big, covering only a square kilometre, but it's unique, located at the confluence of two subterranean rivers flowing down from the Alt Garrotxa. Over the millennia the rushing water ate at the karstic crust above and caused it to collapse, forming the lake. For years, it slumbered peacefully, a favourite of carp fishermen, until it was chosen as the site for rowing events during the 1992 Olympics, and developments sprang up along its shores – but nothing too drastic. There are bikes, row boats, and canoes to hire.

Banyoles

Before there was the town of Banyoles, there was the Benedictine **Monestir de Sant Esteve**, founded in 812 at the end of C/Nou; if it's open (a rare event: ask at the tourist office) you can admire a beautiful Gothic altarpiece of 1437 by Joan Artigo and a cloister with tombs of medieval abbots. The parish church in the centre, the 13th-century **Santa Maria dels Turers**, is one of the first examples of Catalan Gothic, with good stained-glass windows.

The vortex of daily life is the lovely porticoed 13th-century Plaça Major. There are two museums to visit: the **Museu Darder d'Història Natural** honours adopted son Francesc d'Assís Darder i Llimona, the first zoo-keeper in Barcelona, who came to Banyoles in 1910 to fish, and introduced new species into the lake. His taxidermic skills are on display, but what was once the most

Museu Darder d'Història Natural
Plaça dels Estudis 2, t 972 57 44 67, www. museusdebanyoles.cat, open July and Aug Tues–Sat 10.30–1.30 and 4–7.30, Sun 10.30–2; Sept–June Tues–Sat 10.30–1.30 and 4–6.30, Sun 10.30–2; adm

Getting to and around La Garrotxa

Teisa **buses** from Girona (t *972 20 02 75, www.teisa-bus.com*) run roughly every 30mins to Banyoles, Besalú and Olot. Teisa also run the local bus, el Transversal, every hour between Castellfollit de la Roca, Sant Joan les Fonts and Olot.

famous exhibit is missing: the 'Negre de Banyoles', a bushman mummified by French taxidermists in the 1830s and acquired by the museum in 1916, who became something of Banyoles' mascot. No one said a word about it until 1991, when a local politician of Haitian origin wrote to the mayor of Banyoles, asking him to remove it. Locals protested. African nations threatened to boycott the Olympics. Even Kofi Annan got involved before El Negre was removed and sent off to Botswana for a decent burial.

Museu Arqueològic Comarcal
Plaça de la Font 11, t 972 57 23 610, open July and Aug Tues–Sat 11–1.30 and 4–8, Sun 10.30–2; Sept–June Tues–Sat 10.30–1.30 and 4–6.30, Sun 10.30–2; adm

No whiff of scandal has tarnished the **Museu Arqueològic Comarcal** housed in the old Gothic almshouse. Banyoles, it turns out, has been populated since the cows came home – there's a copy of the unique and famous (in Palaeontological circles at any rate) 80,000-year-old Neanderthal **Jaw of Banyoles**, found in 1887 by the chemist Pere Alsius i Torrent, one of Catalonia's pioneer prehistorians. There are finds from the Paleolithic caves at Serinyà, Roman artefacts from the Vila Romana de Vilauba, and Iberian and Visigothic finds from Porqueres.

Parc Neolític de la Draga
t 972 57 23 61, tours Sat at 12 and 6pm, Sun at 12; adm

The only Neolithic lake settlement in Iberia was discovered here in 1990: the **Parc Neolític de la Draga** dates back to 5000 BC – older than most of the similar settlements in the Alps and northern Italy.

Pla de l'Estany

The area around the lake, the triangle formed by Besalú, Figueres and Girona, is known Pla de l'Estany, a gently rolling region of farms, *masies*, second homes and Romanesque churches. In **Porqueres**, across the lake from Banyoles, don't miss the beautiful church of **Santa Maria** (1182), with a barrel-vaulted roof, an intriguing frieze of symbols, heads and animals in medallions arched over the door, exquisitely carved capitals, and triumphal arch. Just west of Porqueres, off the GI524 to Sant Miquel de Campmajor, are the striking landscapes of **Etunes**, giant slabs of limestone cracked into massive fissures by earthquakes, and the

Can Ginebreda Forest
t 972 58 25 38, www.canginebreda.com

Can Ginebreda Forest, where since 1972, sculptor Xicu Cabanyes has created an unusual erotic sculpture garden and restaurant, a vortex of counter-culture life in the Garrotxa.

You can spend a couple of peaceful hours exploring the other churches and villages of the Pla de l'Estany: **Esponellà**, **Crespià**, **Orfes**, **Galliners**, **Vilavenut** (with ruins of a Roman villa) and **Fontcoberta**. Or explore where the owner of Banyoles' famous jawbone might have resided, in Serinyà's **Parc de les Coves**

Parc de les Coves Prehistòriques
on the Banyoles-Besalú road, t *972 59 33 10; open mid-July–mid-Sept daily 11–7; mid-Sept–Mar Tues–Fri 10–4, Sat 11–5, Sun 10–3; April–mid-July Tues–Fri 10–4, Sat and Sun 10–6; adm; joint adm possible with the Banyoles museums*

Prehistòriques with its Neanderthal cave shelters and the lovely cave Reclau Viver.

Besalú and its Dog-legged Bridge

Set at the confluence of the Fluviá and Capellada rivers, the walled town of Besalú is irresistible, one of Catalonia's purest, most dreamlike medieval ensembles. First a Roman and Visigothic settlement, it had its glory days as a little feudal capital; Louis le Debonair captured it from the Moors in 800. Wilfred the Hairy freed it from the control of Girona, and, from the year 1000, Besalú (pop. 800) was the seat of the County of Cerdanya-Besalú, thanks to its most famous count, Bernat Tallaferro (990–1020) who fought the Moors in Cordoba and earned the favour of the pope. In the year of 1111, it was all inherited by the County of Barcelona.

After that, time stood still in Besalú. Its pride and joy is a remarkable 11th-century dog-legged fortified bridge, made of eight irregular arches with a tax-collecting tower at the bend, last rebuilt after it was damaged in the Civil War. The town itself is a medieval stage set, but to have a peek behind the facades, you'll need to join

Besalú guided tours
ring them weekdays t *972 591 150, from 10–2 and 4–7, or check www.besalu.cat for hours; in July and Aug they also do tours by torchlight at 11pm, book ahead*

one of the tourist office's guided tours. There are two churches from Besalú's 11th century heyday: the large **Monestir de Sant Pere**, finished by Bernat Tallaferro and decorated by a pair of stone lions triumphant over evil, and **Sant Vicenç** (1018), its entrance prettily decorated with floral motifs. There's an 11th-century hospital, and the **Casa Cornellà** furnished with antique tools and furnishings.

Like Girona, Besalú had an important **Call**, centred around C/Comte Tallaferro and C/Rocafort. In 1964, a 12th-century **Miqvé** (a ritual Jewish bathhouse) was discovered next to the ruins of the synagogue when a local dry cleaner tried to dig a well; as the last Jews left Besalú in 1436 they had sealed and hidden the entrance. It's the only one ever found in Spain.

Olot and the Parc Natural de la Zona Volcànica de La Garrotxa

⭐ **La Garrotxa**

Museu Comarcal de la Garrotxa
C/Hospici 8, t *972 27 11 66, www.mnac.cat; open July–Sept Tues–Sat 11–2 and 4–7, Sun 11–2; Oct–June Tues–Sat 10–1 and 3–6; closed Mon; adm; combined ticket available with the Museu dels Volcans and the Can Trincheria*

After an earthquake in 1427, the Garrotxa's bustling capital **Olot** was rebuilt in an attractive Renaissance grid around a bijou Plaça Major. But it was Olot's outskirts, the dappled beech and oak forests and lush volcanic cones illuminated by a diaphanous light, that drew Catalan landscape painters, beginning in the late 18th century and leading to the founding of the Escola de Belles Arts d'Olot, now housed in the beautiful Renaissance **Claustres del Carme** just east of the Plaça Major. Some of their paintings are in the Museu Comarcal de la Garrotxa.

Located in the massive stone building of the former Hospice, it displays one of Ramon Casas' most famous paintings, *The Charges* (of the Guardia Civil routing a crowd of strikers in Barcelona), sculpture by Josep Clarà and Miquel Blay, and a collection of *Cigarillos París* posters. The large parish church of **Sant Esteve** has a couple of Baroque altarpieces, and an El Greco in its parish museum. Nearby, the Can Trincheria has its original furnishings, typical of an 18th-century bourgeois family, as well as a remarkable, enormous *pessebre* (Christmas crib), made by the house's obsessive owner and his servant.

Parish museum
visits by appointment only, t 972 26 04 74

Can Trincheria
C/Sant Rafel 29, t 972 27 27 77; open Mon–Fri 10–2 and 5–7, Sat 11–2 and 5–7, Sun 11–2; adm

In the 19th century, swells from Barcelona followed the artists to Olot and built a handful of Modernista mansions; two of the best are **El Drac** (now a bookshop) opposite Sant Esteve, by Alfred Paluzie (1901) and the **Casa Solà Morales** (1915), a pretty confection by Domènech i Montaner on the Passeig d'en Blay, covered with lavish floral designs and a pair of caryatids by Eusebi Arnau.

Four dormant volcanoes surround Olot; only 500m north of the centre you can walk up to the **Volcà Montsacopa**, with a hermitage on top and fine views over Olot. On the south edge of town, amid the beautiful old oaks and botanical gardens of Parc Nou, the Modernista Torre Castanys now houses the Museu Casal dels Volcans with volcanic audiovisuals, an earthquake simulator to rattle you, and a Natural Park Information centre.

Museu Casal dels Volcans
Av. Santa Coloma, t 972 26 67 62; open July–Sept Tues–Sat 10–2 and 4–7, Sun 10– 2; Oct–June Tues–Fri 10–2 and 3–6, Sat 10–2 and 4–7, Sun 10–2; adm

Five km north of Olot, **Sant Joan les Font** offers two lovely walks: one along a stretch of the ancient Roman Via Annia, or Via de Capsacosta, passing several Romanesque chapels; the second, a two-hour circuit (No. 16) beginning in the Plaça Major and passing curious basalt columns left by the volcanic flows. Sant Joan's 12th-14th century Castell Estada Juvinyà has displays on local history. A favourite subject for painters, **Castellfollit de la Roca** is just east, built on an startling 131ft basalt escarpment over the river Fluvià; its medieval buildings and narrow streets are paved with the dark volcanic rock.

Castell Estada Juvinyà
t 972 29 05 91, open Sat and Sun 10–1 and 5–8

South of Olot off the road to Santa Pau, the **D'en Jordà Nature Reserve** is a huge beech forest growing on ancient lava flow. Next is **Santa Pau**, a little charmer with a 13th-century castle, medieval lanes and arcaded square, the Fira dels Bous, scene of the old cattle market. There are lovely views from the walls, and restaurants and shops cooking or selling its famous *fesols de Santa Pau*, or white beans.

The surroundings offer lovely walks, including a steep hike up to the Garrotxa's largest crater, the verdant **Volcà Santa Margarida**, 1,148ft across, with a 13th-century chapel in its former crater. Another, the Volcà del Croscat, has a neat slice quarried out of its side, as if it were a giant chocolate cake.

Another dozen walking trails surround medieval **Sant Feliu de Pallerols** further south, a handsome town with medieval bridges and mills. Just to the northeast, little **Els Hostalets d'en Bas** has an extremely photogenic street, **Carrer Teixeda**, lined with houses with old wooden balconies.

Markets in La Garrotxa

Banyoles, Wednesday (since the 11th century) in the Plaça Major; **Besalú**, Tuesday; **Olot**, Monday.

Activities in La Garrotxa

Olot lies in the centre of two beautiful **bike paths**: the Girona–Olot Via Verde del Carrilet and Ripoll–Olot Via Verde del Ferro (start in Ripoll if you want to go downhill). For more information see *www.viesverdes.org*. Hire a bike at Centre Logístic del Bici Carril, at the Antiga Estació in Les Preses, **t** 972 69 20 23, *http:// atma.garrotxa.net*

Vol de Coloms, Santa Pau, **t** 972 68 02 55 or **t** 972 68 10 01, *www. voldecoloms.cat*. Hot air balloon-rides over the craters.

Can Genassa Riding Club, Maià de Montcal, **t** 667 35 17 11, *www. cangenassa.com*. Horse riding.

Where to Stay and Eat in La Garrotxa

A number of restaurants specialize in 'volcanic cuisine' based on ingredients from La Garrotxa's rich soil: endives, Santa Pau beans (*fesols*), potatoes, turnips, onions, truffles, and chestnuts, along with snails, pork and wild boar.

Banyoles ✉ 17820

****Ca l'Arpa**, Pg Industria 5, **t** 972 57 23 53 (€€€). Opened in 2008 to rave reviews and a Michelin star. Stylish unfussy rooms in a handsome 19th-century home and first-rate contemporary cuisine in the restaurant (€€€).

****Mirallac**, Pg Darder 50, **t** 972 57 10 45, *www.hotelmirallac.com* (€€€–€€). Lake views and large, airy rooms make this small hotel, built in the 1960s, a

good base. It's surprisingly inexpensive considering the facilities on offer, which include a pool.

****Hs L'Ast**, Pg Dalmau 63, **t** 972 57 04 14, *www.hotelast.com* (€€). Near the lake, with a pool and wi-fi.

***Can Xabanet**, C/Carmen 27, **t** 972 57 02 52 (€). Near the lake as well: less expensive but equally pleasant, and with a very good restaurant. *Due to reopen after major restoration in late 2009.*

***Fonda Comas**, C/Canal 19, **t** 972 57 01 27 (€). Down-to-earth little *pensió*.

La Masia, Porqueres, **t** 972 57 00 05, *www.restaurantlamasia.es* (€€€). Since 1957, and serving ever tastier dishes; try the ravioli of smoked salmon and foie gras. **Can Roca**, C/Carles Fortuny, Esponellà (10km north of Banyoles), **t** 972 59 70 12 (€€). Favourite for traditional cuisine; try the *canelones* filled with game.

Quatre Estacions, Pg de la Farga s/n, **t** 972 57 33 00 (€€). Traditional cuisine based on whatever is in season. Try the mouthwatering seafood *croquetas* and finish up with a local liqueur. *Closed Sun eve and Mon.*

Besalú ✉ 17850

Mas Salvanera, Mas Salvanera s/n, Beuda (8km from Besalú) **t** 972 59 09 75, *www.salvanera.com* (€€€). Utterly charming 17th-century stone farmhouse set into the hillside, with eight pretty rooms (named after signs of the zodiac) stunning views, a beautiful garden and pool.

*****Sant Ferriol**, 2km south of Besalú, **t** 972 59 05 32, *www.santferriol.com* (€€€). Peaceful woodland setting for a plush little hotel, with a spa for pampering and the area's top restaurant.

****Comte Tallaferro**, C/Ganganell 2, **t** 972 59 16 09, *www.grupcalparent. com* (€€€–€€). In a 16th-century building in the old centre, recently

ⓘ **Besalú »**
Plaça de la Llibertat 1, t 972 59 12 40 daily guided tours of the town in English

★ **Mas Salvanera »**

ⓘ **Banyoles »**
Pg Indústria 25, t 972 57 55 73

★ **Ca l'Arpa »**

09 Girona Province | Northwest of Girona: La Garrotxa

09

Girona Province | Into the Catalan Heartland

smartened up with light-filled rooms and suites.

La Fustana, 5km east of Besalú in Maià de Moncat, t 972 59 04 79, *www.lafustana.com* (€€€–€€). Brand new, very eco-friendly, contemporary rural hotel; very reasonably-priced, tasty dinners as well.

★**Els Jardins de la Martana** >

★★Els Jardins de la Martana, C/Pont 2, t 972 59 00 09, *www.lamartana.com* (€€). A charming hotel in a garden villa. Ten handsome rooms overlook the famous bridge and there's a pretty tiled breakfast room with enormous windows, and a library with a fireplace for snuggling.

★Marià, Plaça Llibertat 7, t 972 59 01 06 (€). Pleasant little *pensió* overlooking the attractive central square.

★Siqués, Av. Lluís Companys 6–8, t 972 59 01 10, *www.grupcalparent.com* (€). Old-fashioned, traditional stone guesthouse at the entrance to the town with a pool and a popular local restaurant (€€) serving Catalan classics.

Pont Vell, C/del Pont Vell 24, t 972 59 10 27 (€€). In a pretty stone house, serving traditional and market Catalan cuisine.

ⓘ **Olot** >
C/Hospici 8,
t 972 26 01 41

ⓘ **Santa Pau** >>
Can Vayreda,
t 972 68 03 47

Olot ✉ 17800

Les Cols, Carretera de la Canya, t 972 26 92 09, *www.lescols.com* (€€€€). This beautifully restored 13th-century house is the ancestral home of award winning chef Fina Puigdevall, whose market-fresh, imaginative cuisine elevates the finest Garrotxa ingredients to new heights. There are also five stunning rooms (€€€€€) in cubic glass pavilions (designed by the Olot-based studio RCR) that strive to get as close to nature as possible; showers resemble waterfalls, the baths, similar to a Japanese *onsen*, are akin to lying in a mountain stream,

and as you lie in bed stars twinkle over your head.

★★★La Perla d'Olot, Ctra. La Deu 9, t 972 26 23 26, *www.laperlahotels.com* (€€). Friendly modern hotel with rooms and apartments for families, gardens and a children's play area.

★★★Borell, C/Nònet Escubós 8, t 972 27 61 61, *www.hotelborrell.com* (€€–€). Good, small, sleekly designed hotel in the centre of Olot.

Can Guix, C/de les Mulleras 3, t 972 26 10 40 (€). Popular restaurant for its heaping portions of traditional dishes at low prices.

Pension La Vila, Plaça Major, t 972 26 98 07 (€). Quirky little *pensió*, en-suites with bathrooms out on the former balconies.

Hs Sant Bernat, C/de les Feixes, t 972 26 19 19; *www.hostalsantbernat.com* (€€). Well-signposted up a hill. Fill up on the 'farmer's breakfast': Santa Pau beans with the local sausage.

La Deu, Ctra La Deu, t 972 26 10 04 (€€–€). Restaurant and founding member of the 'volcanic cuisine' group, specializing in the good things of the earth.

Hs Els Ossos, on the road to Olot, t 972 26 61 34 (€). A popular famous restaurant in a *masia* with a vine-covered terrace, famous for its succulent grilled meats (*carn a la brasa*).

Santa Pau ✉ 17800

★★★Cal Sastre, C/Cases Noves 1, t 972 68 00 49, *www.calsastre.com* (€€€). Delightful small hotel in the centre; each room is filled with antiques, including beautifully hand-painted bedsteads. There's a charming restaurant at Placet dels Balls 6, t 972 68 04 21 (€€€), well known for its preparation of Santa Pau's beans. You can even get them in dessert with the *menú de degustació*.

Into the Catalan Heartland

In the 9th century, the river valleys and small mountain ranges north of Barcelona were Count Guifré el Pilos' front lines; by the time of his death Catalonia extended as far west as the Llobregat. The Hairy One founded and lavishly endowed three important

Getting to and around the Catalan Heartland

Vic is the last station on Renfe's Cercania 3 **train** line (**t** *902 24 02 02*) from Barcelona Sants: as well as on the Barcelona-Vic-Ripoll-Ribes de Freser rail line; **Sagalés buses** (**t** *902 13 00 14, www.sagales.com*) from Barcelona's Plaça Catalunya go (not always directly) to most of the Vic region. **Teisa buses**, *www.teisa-bus.com*, link Vic and Girona, and Sant Joan de les Abbesses with Olot and Ripoll.

There's no regular public transport to Setcases and Vallter 2000, although you could book a ski package in Barcelona (check the Sagalés website, above).

The **rack railway** (*la cremallera, see* p.227) from Ribes to Núria runs five times daily, connecting with the train from Barcelona; save money by purchasing a package with RENFE (*see www.valldenuria.cat*).

monasteries to anchor his claim – at Vic, Ripoll and Sant Joan de les Abadesses – which helped immensely in getting the power of the literate on his side. Montseny, Barcelona's bucolic playground, is just beyond the collar of sprawl, and the dramatic Collsacabra peaks east of Vic are great places for walks and dotted with striking, if sometimes twee, medieval villages.

Parc Natural del Montseny

The highest of Catalonia's pre-coastal mountains, the massif of Montseny – 'Mount Signal' (5,600ft) – earned its name from the times when travellers used the mountains to orientate themselves and judge distances. Only 55km from Barcelona, Montseny is a deep green oasis of peaks and valleys, high plains and abrupt cliffs, springs and rivers, majestic beech, oak and fir forests, a collage of landscapes and climates ranging from Mediterranean to subalpine, home to over 200 vertebrates of all kinds.

Natural Park Office
Ctra. de Sant Celoni–Turó de l'Home, km 10.8, Fogars de Montclús, t 938 47 51 02; open daily 9–2 and 3–4

The main gateways to the Parc Natural del Montseny lie off the AP 7 (exit 11), and at **Sant Celoni**, a town synonymous with Can Fabes, Catalonia's first Michelin three-star restaurant (*see* p.228); Sant Celoni also has the grandest sgrafittoed façade in the region, on the church of **Sant Martí** (1703).

Fortificació Ibèrica del Turó del Montgròs
guided visits only through the Centre d'Informació in El Brull, t 938 84 06 92, Jan and Feb at noon; Mar–June and Nov–Dec 11am and 1pm; July–Oct at 11am, 1pm and 4pm; adm

From here the road (BV5114) ascends to Santa Fé near the summit of Montseny's highest peak, Turó del Home, reached by a 1½-hour path. The reward is a view over most of Catalonia across to the Pyrenees; an easier 2½-hour green-marked path goes through the forest around a reservoir. A second route just to the west, the BV5301, follows the Tordera river into the mountains, where you can pick up information at the **Natural Park Office** at **Fogars de Montclús**. The village of **Montseny** is further up, in a lovely setting, with the remains of the 13th-century monastery of Sant Marçal. Nearby **El Brull** has the mighty walls of the 5th-century BC **Fortificació Ibèrica del Turó del Montgròs**.

Centre Cultural Europeu de la Natura
C/Migdia 1, t 938 84 80 35; open Tues–Sat 11–1.30 and 3.30–6, Sun 10–1.30

Viladrau, an old spa town on the northern edge of the park, is another exceptional area for walks; its **Centre Cultural Europeu de la Natura** has interactive features on all aspects of Montseny.

Arbúcies to the east is set in a lush valley bubbling with springs. In its picturesque streets are the Plaça de la Vila, shaded by a huge plane tree planted to celebrate the first short-lived Spanish Republic (1873), and a Modernista building, the sgrafittoed Granja Royal on C/Francesc Camprodon. The **Museu Etnològic del Montseny La Gabella** covers the inhabitants and customs of Montsény. A film recounts local legends– many places have 'witch' (*bruixa*) in their name, recalling the benighted years of 1617 and 1627, when 22 local women were sent to the gallows, accused of causing the violent storms that destroyed the local crops.

Museu Etnològic
del Montseny
La Gabella
*C/Major 6, t 972 86
09 08; open Tues–Sat
11–2 and 5–8, Sun 11–2*

The nearby 13th–14th-century **Castell de Montsoriu** is one of the finest surviving Catalan Gothic castles, and has huge views over the valley, and there are several Romanesque churches for the keen to seek out.

Granollers to Vic

The C17 runs just to the west of the Montseny Natural Park, skirting **Granollers**, Catalonia's breadbasket and most important agricultural market town; its Thursday market, first recorded in 1040, is still going strong. The city's iconic Renaissance **Gran Porxada** (1586) grain market is in its handsome square, next to the pink neo-Gothic **Ajuntament** (1904) designed by Simó Cordomí; other good buildings are the Gothic **Casa del Condestable** in C/Sant Roc and the **Hospital de Sant Domènec**, now used as a public library. The **Museu de Granollers** has archaeological finds, medieval paintings and sculpture, bridal chests, glass and ceramics.

Museu de
Granollers
*C/Anselm Clavé,
40–42, t 938 70 66 47,
www.museugranollers.
org; open April–Nov
Tues–Sun 6–9pm, Tues
also 11.30–1.30;
Nov–Mar Tues–Fri
5.30–8.30, Tues also
11.30–1.30, Sat
and Sun 6–9pm*

If you aren't in any hurry to get to Vic, there are some tempting detours off the highway. To the west of Granollers, **Caldes de Montbui** has steaming hot springs that made it a popular resort in Roman times and again in the 1890s; a bevy of Modernista villas mark its second heyday. **Thermalia** in Plaça de la Font de Sant Lleó doubles as a tourist office and museum housing the still-usable Roman baths, historical artefacts, and sculpture.

Thermalia
*t 938 65 41 40;
open Tues–Sat 11–2
and 5–8, Sun 11–2*

Sant Miquel de Fai
*t 938 65 80 08, www.
santmiqueldelfai.cat,
open Tues–Fri 10–5,
Sat 10–6, Sun 10–6;
adm exp; special
Sagalés bus service from
Barcelona on Sun*

La Garriga north of Granoller is another spa town, site of the glamorous **Balneari Blancafort** (1876) where many leading figures of the Renaixença came to ease their aches and pains. Nearby C/dels Banys has several lovely Modernista buildings, but the best, four townhouses built around 1910 by Manuel Joaquim Raspal, are concentrated in a block known as the Illa Raspall. There's a fine Gothic retable in the Església de la Doma; the hermitage of Santa Maria del Camí dates from the 10th century and contains the tomb of Xixilona, daughter of Wilfred the Hairy.

West of La Garriga, a narrow road climbs from **Sant Feliu de Codines** to one of Catalonia's beauty spots, **Sant Miquel de Fai**.

In 997 the Counts of Barcelona donated the spot to a pious lord named Gombau to build a little monastery. A Gothic priory was added. But it's the setting, surrounded by cliffs and grottoes, waterfalls and lakes, that brings the weekend day-trippers and wedding parties.

Vic

Midway between Barcelona and the Pyrenees, Vic is a lively little university city. Originally Ausa, the capital of the Ausetani Iberians, it survived into Visigothic times, only to be destroyed in 826 when it rebelled against the Franks. In 878, Wilfred the Hairy, hoping to repopulate the area, refounded the town on the site of an old suburb, Vicus Ausonae, now capital of the *comarca* of Osona. Wilfred's scholarly great grandson Oliba (c. 971–1046), was the Count of Berga, but renounced worldly things to become abbot of Ripoll and Cuixà (in Roussillon) in 1008, and then bishop of Vic in 1018. Oliba was one of the most important churchmen in his day: besides fostering learning at Ripoll (*see* p.224), he promoted the movement of Peace and Truce of God, setting aside certain days when no one could quarrel; his assemblies of Peace and Truce would eventually evolve into the Catalan Corts.

Vic's first markets took place in Oliba's day in the vast **Plaça Major**, encompassed by an attractive mix of Baroque and Modernista buildings, all with porticoes. One is the **Ajuntament**, housing a collection of works by Josep Sert (*see* below), including fragments from the first cathedral murals. The medieval core occupies a hilly triangle just behind: on the highest point, in **Plaça del Pare Xifré**, the *cella* of a 2nd-century AD Roman temple survives as part of the 11th-century Palau Montcada.

Bishop Oliba's aluminum statue stands in front of the **cathedral** he reconstructed. In 1781 Vic saw fit to knock it all down (except for the bell tower and crypt) and replace it with a massive neoclassical pile. In the early 20th century, the bishops, perhaps feeling a bit guilty, led the campaign to restore Catalan monasteries and use Catalan in sermons, and hired Josep María Sert (1874–1945) to cover the interior of the cathedral with golden chiaroscuro **murals**, the largest series in the world, a job Sert completed in 1929. He went on to decorate Barcelona's Ajuntament and New York's Rockefeller Center but then received the devastating news that the cathedral was set on fire in 1936, and the murals were irreparably damaged. Yet, in what must be a world record of some kind, the no-longer-young Sert returned, and reapplied an acre or so of gold leaf before his death in 1945. Robert Hughes called him 'the Tiepolo of the dictatorship', but, whatever his politics, his heroic murals are

Ajuntament
Plaça Major 1, ring ahead to visit,
t 938 89 54 14

astonishing, turbulent, painted with a personal iconography that often seems to have little to do with religion.

The Romanesque **crypt** and **treasury** contain works which managed to escape the restoration and the flames: the painted alabaster retable (1427) on the lives of Mary and St Peter by Pere Oller, a beautiful gold processional cross of 1397 by Joan Carbonell, and a chain made from the melted gold recovered from Sert's original murals.

Museu Episcopal de Vic

Plaça Bisbe Oliba 3, t 938 86 93 60, www. museuepiscopalvic.com; open April–Sept Tues– Sat 10–7, Sun 10–2; Oct–Mar Tues–Fri 10–1 and 3–6, Sat 10–7, Sun 10–2; adm

In 2002 a spacious new home was constructed for the fabulous **Museu Episcopal de Vic** which dates back to 1811. A local and Egyptian archaeological collection and a lapidary collection formerly kept in the Roman temple are downstairs; upstairs is a horde of Catalan medieval art second only to Barcelona's. Works include a marvellous array of 12th-century altar frontals, a famous stylized wooden *Descent from the Cross* from Erill la Vall, *majestats* and polychrome Virgins from glamorous Madonnas to stodgy matrons; surreal Gothic drawings of the *Last Supper* from La Seu d'Urgell, a baldachin from the Ribes Valley, beautiful paintings by Jaume Huguet, Pere Serra, Ferrer Bassa, Jaume Ferrer, Lluís Borrassà, Ramon de Mur and sweet works by Joan Guascó and his son Perot of the local Vic school.

Museu de l'Art de la Pell

C/Arquebisbe Alemany 5, t 938 83 32 79; open Tues–Sat 11–2 and 5–8, Sun 11– 2; adm

Sala Sert

C/de l'Historiador Ramon d'Abadal i de Vinyals 5, t 938 89 54 14; open Mon–Fri 9–1 and 4–6

The wide, languid curl of Vic's Ramblas follows the old city walls. Well signposted, off the Rambla del Carme, a former convent houses the **Museu de l'Art de la Pell** with a thousand objects all made of leather assembled by local tanner Andreu Colomer Munmany, including gilt leather altar frontals, bags, armchairs, saddles, masks, and shadow theatre puppets. The **Sala Sert** in the Edifici el Sucre has Sert's paintings on the *Wedding of Camacho*, the same that grew into murals in the dining room of New York's Waldorf Astoria.

Around Vic: The Osona and Collsacabra Natural Park

Once you get past the sprawl, the Osona region has its share of wild forests, picture-postcard villages and country houses. A big lure is the food: Vic is famous for its pork sausages and *charcuterie*, truffles and wild mushrooms.

Monestir de Santa Maria de l'Estany

Plaça del Monestir, t 938 30 30 00: ring ahead

If you're keen on the Romanesque, there's a treat in remote little **Estany** southwest of Vic; take the Manresa road to exit 164, and follow the signs. The **Monestir de Santa Maria de l'Estany** was founded in 1080 by Augustian canons and rebuilt in the 12th and 13th century; the church is handsome but the best bits are the 72 capitals in the luminous cloister, sculpted by several different hands with animals, biblical scenes (the *Slaughter*

The Catalan Homer: Jacint Verdaguer

Like many a bright younger son from peasant backgrounds, Verdaguer was enrolled in a seminary where he could get a good education – in this case, Vic, where he was a mediocre student and angered his teachers by writing secular poetry. But his poetry was very good. In 1866, his *Ode to Rafael Casanovas*, on the Barcelonin hero of the 1714 siege, won a prize in the Jocs Florals, Barcelona's poetry competition. The poem not only impressed the judges with its refreshingly direct, vivid use of the Catalan language, but Verdaguer impressed them as well, a handsome young peasant in his rough clothes and *barretina*, the red Phrygian cap. Both the man and his art seemed to perfectly embody the spirit of the new national Renaixença.

But Verdaguer also took the priesthood seriously, and at the age of 25 he was ordained and served as a country priest at Vinyoles north of Vic. In 1874 he became ill, and when the doctor recommended a sea voyage he took a job as a ship's chaplain sailing back and forth from Cádiz to Havana. During his journeys he wrote what has become the best-loved poem in the Catalan language, *L'Emigrant*, and an epic *L'Atlàntida*, recounting how the submersion of Atlantis created the Atlantic ocean separating Spain and Latin America, and how the Spanish discovery of America reunited the two lands.

It was the beginning of a meteoric rise to fame. *L'Atlàntida* won first prize at the Jocs Florals. The poet was declared a '*Mestre en Gai Saber*'. He went to Rome to meet the pope to discuss the poem, and travelled widely and luxuriously, writing among other works the *Ode to Barcelona* and, in 1885, a second epic, *Canigó*, about the mythic origins of Catalonia in a Pyrenean monastery, earning him the title of 'Poet of Catalonia' and the 'Catalan Homer'. His delight in nature and deep love for Catalonia, combined with an extraordinary gift for imagery have kept him on his pedestal, even if other aspects of his poetry, its sentimentality and religious fervour, may not at first glance appeal to modern tastes.

Casa Museu Verdaguer
C/Major 7, t 938 12 21 57, www. verdaguer.cat; open April–Nov Tues–Sun 10–1.30, Sat and Sun 10–1.30 and 5–7; Dec–Mar Tues–Sat 10–1.30, Sun 10–1.30 and 5–7; adm

Sant Pere de Casserres
t 937 44 71 18, www. santperedecasserres. com; open mid-June–mid-Sept Tues–Sun 10–7; mid-Sept–Feb Tues–Sun 11–5.30; Mar–mid-June Tues–Sun 10–5.30, closed last two weeks in Jan; adm

Museu Arqueològic de l'Esquerda
C/Bac 6, t 93 854 02 71, www.lesquerda.com; open June–Oct Wed and Fri 11–1, Sat 6–8; Nov–May Wed and Fri 11–1, Sat 5–7

of the Innocents), hunting scenes, floral subjects, mermaids and elephants.

The main attraction is to the east of Vic: the villages and stunning landscapes along the Ter, its reservoirs and craggy Collsacabra mountains. First to the east, however, is **Folgueroles**, birthplace of Jacint 'Mossèn Cinto' Verdaguer in 1845. The Casa Museu Verdaguer not only has memorabilia but is also the seat of the Verdaguer foundation and can direct you other sites around town related to the poet.

Northeast of Folgueroles, the Counts of Osona founded the Benedictine monastery of **Sant Pere de Casserres** in 1005. King Philip II later gave it to the Jesuits: there's a massive basilica and a little cloister, with well-worn capitals that were felled in an earthquake and recently repaired.

On the northwest bank of the Sau Reservoir, **Roda de Ter** was long a hotbed of banditry; when Catalonia's market for mercenaries collapsed in the 16th century with its decline in the Mediterranean, banditry was one of the few career options left for the unemployed. (In *Don Quixote*, there's a passage where Sancho Panza remarks that they must be near Barcelona, because the trees are full of hanged bandits.) Roda's predecessor, the Ausetani Iberian-medieval town of **L'Esquerda**, is gradually being excavated, and finds are housed in the Museu Arqueològic de l'Esquerda.

Further east lies the medieval village of **Santa Maria del Corcó**, where a road winds up into the Collsacabra to **Tavertet**; here, a clutch of 17th- and 18th-century houses and the Romanesque church of **Sant Cristòfol** are dwarfed by the remarkable sinuous 700ft-cliff the village stands on, high over the Ter Valley.

Back along the road to Olot, amid more splendid Collsacabra crags and cliffs, are a pair of picturesque villages from the same era with oddly anagrammatic names: **Pruit**, with a fine collection of *masies*, and **Rupit**, famous for its wooden 'hanging bridge' rebuilt in the 1990s, but packed with tourists at weekends.

Ripoll 'the Cradle of Catalonia'

Santa Maria de Ripoll
t 972 70 42 03; open April–Sept 10–1 and 3–7; Oct–Mar daily 10–1 and 3–6; adm

Mallards quack merrily at the confluence of the Ter and Freser rivers in the centre of Ripoll, but the rest of the town just seems to shuffle along. In 589, the Visigothic king Recaredo founded the first church here after converting from Arianism to Catholic orthodoxy, and in 888 Count Guifré el Pilos (the Hairy One, again) and his wife Guinedell refounded it as the Benedictine monastery of Santa Maria de Ripoll. As first Count of Barcelona, Guifré designated it as the pantheon of his dynasty (a role later taken over by Poblet, *see* p.263). In the 11th century, its scholarly abbot Oliba directed the monks in the Scriptorium to translate Arabic manuscripts into Latin, making it one of the great diffusers of learning in the West, filling Ripoll's vast library with classical texts. Oliba rebuilt the church in 1032, and in the next century Santa Maria reached its apogee; Count Bernat II of Besalú funded the great west portal, and Ripoll's scriptorium produced the *Gesta Comitum Barcinonensium* (Deeds of the Counts of Barcelona). The *Gesta* was medieval Catalonia's foundation myth, complete with some fact-adjusting justifications for its independence from France as well as explaining how Guifré got his name: 'he had hair in places where other men did not'.

The roof of Oliba's church collapsed in the earthquake of 1428, but it suffered an even worse fate in the 1820s when it was rebuilt in a neoclassical idea of what a basilica should look like, although the monks got little joy from it; a decade later, the monastery was suppressed and set alight. In the 1880s, in the first wave of Catalan nationalism, it was soullessly restored.

Today an enormous Catalan flag flaps over the tower. Light filters into the cold, pious grey spaces through alabaster windows, while banners designed by Puig i Cadafalch hang in the nave. In the left transept, you can pay your respects to the modern (1985) **tomb of Guifré el Pilós**, whose bones were discovered in the cloister. The cloying mosaic altarpiece was a gift from Pope Leo XIII.

There are however, two compelling reasons for visiting Ripoll: the **alabaster portal**, one of the greatest works of Romanesque sculpture in Spain, weathered and damaged over the years but now glassed in to protect it from the elements. In over a hundred individual scenes, it is a great 'Bible in stone' with the Pantocrator on top that encompasses much of scripture, the tales told with vigor, verve and imagination, with the Zodiac, Labours of the Months, and some monsters thrown in for good measure.

The **cloister** (1171–1205) is the second reason, its paired columns crowned by delightful medieval bestiary of dragons, dogs, monsters, mermaids, pigs and musicians – everything, in fact, except scenes from scripture.

Across the Riu Ter, the former Municipal Hospital now houses the Ripoll *comarca*'s archives and a display on the **Scriptorium** with fascimiles of some of the masterpieces made by the monks (fortunately, the abbot had sent all of its treasures to the archives in Barcelona before the monastery was wrecked in the 1830s).

Iron was key to Old Catalonia's fortunes, and the **Palau Forge**, until it closed down in 1978, was a rare surviving 17th-century foundry famous for its nails (Ripoll once produced most of Spain's supply), firearms and railings. A system of ponds and channels from the River Freser supplied the hydraulic power behind the forge's mighty drop hammers; it was so noisy that most of the workers were deaf by the time they retired.

Balancing all of Ripoll's piety and industry are the legends of wicked Count Arnau, who was said to have sold his soul to the devil. He lived in **Gombrèn** up in the mountains to the west, where the **Museu de Comte Arnau** has finds from the **Castell de Mataplana**, the count's supposed residence.

A few kilometres further on is the wonderfully scenic 9th-century **Santuari de Montgrony**, reached by steep steps that the dastardly Count Arnau is said to have ordered his unhappy serfs to carve out of the rock before cheating them of their pay.

Scriptorium
Raval de l'Hospital s/n, t 690 69 28 16; open July–mid-Sept Tues–Sat 10–1.30 and 4–7, Sun 10–1.30; mid-Sept–June Sat and Sun 10–1.30 and 4–6.30

Palau Forge
Pg de la Farga Catalana, t 972 70 23 51, www.mnactec.com; guided tours offered by the tourist office

Museu de Comte Arnau
Casal de Cultura, C/Carbasse; open by appointment, t 972 73 03 00, or seek out Senyora Angelina at C/de la Plaça 1

Sant Joan de les Abadesses

East of Ripoll, you can drive or walk the **Ruta de Ferro** (a paved path though the pretty countryside, replacing the old rail line) to Sant Joan de les Abadesses on the River Ter, a medieval town planned on a tidy grid in the 13th century around a bijou Plaça Major. It is named for the **Monastery of Sant Joan de les Abadesses** founded by Guifré el Pilós in 878 for his daughter Emma, the first abbess. In 1017, the abbess and her nuns were given the boot due to the machinations of Bishop Oliba and Count Bernat Tallaferro of Besalú, who went to Pope Benedict VII and claimed that the convent was full of 'parricides and whores of Venus'. Monks moved in, and it came under the control of Besalú.

Monastery of Sant Joan de les Abadesses
t 972 72 23 53; open July–Aug daily 10–7; Mar–June and Sept–Oct daily 10–2 and 4–7; Nov–Mar Mon–Fri 10–2, Sat and Sun 10–2 and 4–6; adm

The complex was mostly rebuilt in the 12th century, and again after the 1428 earthquake brought down the roof. It was spared rebuilding and remains atmospherically dark, austere and mysterious, an aura heightened by the very unusual but moving 13th-century wooden Deposition, known as the *Santissime Misteri* but nicknamed *Las Bruixas* – the witches – for the stiff weirdness of its wooden figures. Apparently a communion wafer survived for seven centuries wedged in the forehead of the figure of Christ.

The museum has a good collection of art dating back to the 11th century, including richly decorated gold and silverware, rock crystal crucifixes, fabrics, sculptures and paintings. The handsome abbot's palace next to the church houses the tourist office. The fountain in nearby Plaça de l'Abadessa Emma was a gift from Mexico, thanking local composer Jaume Nunó, who composed the Mexican national anthem. There's a second church to seek out, where the locals went: the 12th-century **Església de Sant Pol**, which is worth a look for its tympanum sculpted with Christ, SS Peter and Paul.

The **Pont Vell** over the Ter dates from 1140; it was destroyed in the last fight in the Civil War in February 1939 and rebuilt in 1970.

Camprodon and its Valleys

Continuing up the Riu Ter, the water becomes cleaner, the scenery grander. **Sant Pau de Segúries** is proud of a picturesque stretch of ancient Roman road, and has a bike path along the old rail line to **Camprodon**. With the trains, Camprodon became a favourite summer resort in the 19th century, promoted by Dr Bartolomeu Robert who set up the first summer camp. Today, it's a pretty, if rather worn mountain town with houses overhanging the river.

Camprodon's medieval roots show in its Romanesque monastery **Sant Pere**, founded in the 10th century by Guifré II, grandson of the Hairy one, and in its stone bridges, especially the 12th-century **Pont Nou**. Its most famous son was the composer Isaac Albéniz (1860–1909), whose bust presides in front of the parish church of Santa Maria and whose memory is evoked in the mid-July to mid-August Albèniz Music Festival; there's also a **Museu Isaac Albéñiz** with memorabilia donated by descendants. As a composer he was inspired by traditional Spanish tunes: his famous 'Leyenda' from the *Suite Espanõla* was used in The Doors' 'Spanish Caravan' and played at Nicolas Sarkozy's inauguration, in honour of his then-wife Cécilia, Albéñiz's great-granddaughter.

Museu Isaac Albéñiz
C/Sant Roc 22,
t 972 74 11 66; open Wed–Mon 11–2 and 4–7, closed Tues; adm

Northwest of Camprodon the road climbs to **Villalonga, Tregurà de Dalt** and **Setcases**, where many of the old stone houses are now holiday homes, and then to the **Valter 2000 ski station**. The **Ulldeter refuge** is a pretty 30-minute walk up on the GR11 from the car park. The original refuge, another hour up, was the first one on the Iberian peninsula, but was ruined in an avalanche. Just above the ruin, a path leads to the source of the Riu Ter.

Northeast of Camprodon, you can follow the Ritort up to **Molló.** Its striking Romanesque church, **Santa Cecilia**, has an ornate portal decorated with animal modillons and the Seven Deadly Sins. In 1936 Republicans took down its bells to make ammunition, and banged on them for three days trying to break them into pieces, driving everyone mad until a villager finally told them to fill them first with sand. Up towards the French border are the soft green meadows of **Prats de Molló.**

Alternatively, follow the road towards the Garrotxa by way of **Rocabruna**, with its ruined castle, and the medieval village of **Beget** with its 12th-century tower and Romanesque church **Sant Cristòfol**, the only one in the area the Republicans didn't ransack. Inside, it still has a superb 12th-century *Majestat* sculpted from a 7ft piece of wood, a Romanesque font, and a Gothic alabaster altarpiece, made by the sculptors at Sant Joan de les Abadesses.

Sant Cristòfol
ring the Camprodon valley tourist office
t 972 74 09 36, or try the keyholder, Senyora Maria Vila Sauquet, who lives opposite

09 Girona Province | Into the Catalan Heartland

Ribes de Freser and Núria

Up the River Freser from Ripoll, Ribes de Freser is a rather refreshing, ordinary market town where most people stop only for the extraordinarily vertiginous journey up to the top of the Pyrenees by the *cremallera*. This private rack-and-pinion railway, built in 1931, rises over 1,000m in 12.5km, stopping by way of the attractive grey stone village of **Queralbs** with a very pretty marble porch on its 10th-century church. Beyond are dramatic canyons of the Núria and many tunnels before the *cremallera* emerges in the **Vall de Núria** (4,166ft), a beautiful, lofty, bowl-shaped valley with a rather grim sanctuary, rebuilt in the 1880s and 1950s. It houses the 11th-century Virgin *La Mare de Déu de Núria*, reputedly carved by St Gil, the patron of local shepherds.

Cremallera
t 972 73 20 20,
www.valldenuria.com

Apparently there was once a menhir in the valley that infertile women would hike up to and rub against, in the hopes of becoming pregnant; today couples more decorously pray before the cross, put their heads in the sacred pot and ring the bell. It apparently works quite often, and, if they have a girl, parents are likely to name her Núria. The Virgin is officially the patronness of winter sport, and fittingly, Núria has a **ski station**, while in summer there are lovely walks that skirt the edges of precipitous chasms; the most popular is the 2½-hour walk down to Queralbs on the GR11. Elsewhere in the valley, the big news is the twinned ski resorts of **La Molina and Masella.**

Market Days in the Catalan Heartland

Vic, Tuesdays and Saturdays; **Ripoll**, Saturday; **Camprodon**, Sunday; **Ribes de Freser**, Saturday.

Skiing in the Catalan Heartland

Vallter 2000, Setcases, **t** 972 13 60 57, *www.vallter2000.com*. This is set in a cirque reaching 8865ft; it has 12 runs, seven lifts and night illumination and a new snow park for the kids.

Núria, **t** 972 73 20 20, *www.valldenuria .cat*. This has 10 pistes – a couple over 4km long – and two teleskis, plus a wide range of activities for children, including a huge tobaggan run.

La Molina, near Plandas, **t** 972 89 20 31, *www.lamolina.com*. This is the oldest ski resort in Spain (1909) although it only got its first lifts in 1942. It has fairly wide runs, a 5km-long cross-country course, a five jump ramps. The Alp 2500 lift links it to nearby **Masella t** 972 14 40 00, *www.masella.com*; a day's combined ticket gives access to 96 runs of all degrees of difficulty. Winter buses link it to Puigcerdà.

Where to Stay and Eat in the Catalan Heartland

Sant Celoni ✉ 08470

★★★★**Can Fabes**, C/Sant Joan 6, **t** 938 67 28 51, *www.canfabes.com* (€€€€). Santi Santimaria was born here in 1957, and his quest to bridge the region's tradition with modernity made him the first Catalan three-star Michelin chef in 1994. Santimaria's kitchen at Can Fabes sources only the best local ingredients. There's also the less formal **Espai-Coch** for set price lunches and, for patrons, an ultra-modern hotel, **t** 938 67 28 51 (€€€€).

Montseny ✉ 08460

Can Barrina, Ctra Palautordera km 12.7, **t** 938 47 30 65, *www.canbarrina.com* (€€€). Peaceful rooms in a *masia* built in 1620, surrounded by forests; there's a pool and an excellent restaurant (€€€) serving game and mushroom dishes.

Husa Monestir de Sant Marçal, Ctra GIV between Viladrau and Santa Fe, **t** 938 47 30 43, *www.hotelhusa santmarcal.com* (€€€–€€). Charming rooms of character, with lots of exposed stone, and a good restaurant (€€€) in a restored Romanesque monastery in a lush mountain pass. Wonderful service gives it an edge over others in the region. A favourite for weddings.

Viladrau ✉ 17406

Xalet Coromina, Ctra de Vic 4, **t** 938 84 92 64, *www.xaletcoromina.com* (€€€). In the centre of the Parc Natural del Montseny, eight snug rooms in an ivy covered mansion, set in a little garden with lovely mountain views. The **Salvador Casaseca** restaurant (€€€) features imaginative cuisine.

Can Celestino, C/Sant Hilari 18, Espinelves, **t** 938 84 92 85 (€). Famous far and wide for its tasty home cooking and the set menu – 11 courses for €11, including wine. Next door is a bakery that makes excellent *coques* (pizza).

Seva ✉ 08553

★★★★**El Montanyà Resort and Spa**, Avda Montseny, **t** 938 84 06 06, *www.elmontanya.com* (€€€–€€). Woodsy rooms attached to a spa (*open to the public*) with all the kit to make you relaxed, beautiful and fit. There is also a sports centre with paintball, quads, archery, tennis, etc.

Vic ✉ 08500

★★★★**Parador de Vic-Sau**, **t** 938 12 23 23, *www.paradores-spain.com* (€€€). Some 14km from Vic on C/de Roda de Tera: charming idealization of a Catalan *masia*, or country house, in a pine grove and overlooking the Sau reservoir.

★★★**Can Pamplona**, Eix Onze de Setembre 10, **t** 938 83 31 12, *www. canpamplona.com* (€€). Modern hotel in Vic's new quarters (on the other side of the tracks) with easy parking; rates include a decent buffet breakfast.

⭐ **Husa Monestir de Sant Marçal** ≫

⭐ **Can Fabes** ›

ⓘ **Vic** ≫
C/de la Ciutat 4,
t 938 86 20 91

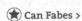

(i) **Ripoll >>**
*Plaça de l'Abat Oliba
s/n,* **t** *972 70 23 51*

Mas La Miranda, Camí Antic de Muntanyola, 8km from Vic in Sentfores, **t** 630 93 65 47, *www.maslamiranda.com* (€€–€). A *casa rural* in an old stone farmhouse set in a peaceful garden with a pool and comfy hammocks.

Hs Osona, C/del Remei,3, **t** 938 83 28 45 (€). Your basic *pensió*, located south of the centre, by a bridge just off Crta de la Guixa.

Cardona 7, C/Cardona 7 **t** 938 86 38 15 (€€). Vic's best-known chef is Jordi Parramón; this chic, tapas-style restaurant is set in an attractive old town house.

La Taula, Plaça Don Miquel de Clariana 4, **t** 938 86 32 29 (€). Classic, old-fashioned restaurant in the heart of Vic serving traditional local dishes.

Sant Julià de Vilatorta ✉ 08504

Mas Albereda, Avda Sant Llorenç 68, **t** 938 12 28 52, *www.masalbereda.com* (€€€€). Comfortable digs in a historic house in a garden setting with a pool.

Ca la Manyana, Avda Verge de Montserrat 38, **t** 938 12 24 94, *www.calamanyana.com* (€€). Homey welcome in the rooms and one of the best-known restaurants in Osona (€€€), with a wide choice of dishes with truffles and wild mushrooms. *Closed Jan, and 2 weeks in Sept.*

Collsacabra ✉ 08569

Hs Can Nogué, C/del Mig 2, Tavertet, **t 938 56 52 51, *www.hostalcannogue.com* (€€). Cosy rooms in an old stone *masia* and succulent grilled meats served on the terrace; be sure to book in summer.

Hs Estrella, Plaça Bisbe Font,Rupit, **t 938 52 20 05, *www.hostalestrella.com* (€€). Cosy rooms in an old stone mountain house. The restaurant (€€) serves a wide selection of meats.

Cabrerès Hostal, C/Major 26, Cantonigròs, **t** 938 56 50 22, *www.cabrereshostal.com* (€€). New in the village centre, with eight double rooms and bike hire for exploring the remarkable Collsacabra.

(i) **Sant Joan de les Abadesses >>**
C/Palau Abadia,
t *972 72 05 99*

(★) **Ca l'Ignasi>**

Ca l'Ignasi, C/Major 4, Cantonigròs, **t** 938 52 51 24, *www.calignasi.com* (€€€). Simply spectacular creative mountain cuisine by Ignasi Camps.

Open for lunch Tues–Sun, dinner Fri and Sat only.

Ripoll ✉ 17500

***Solana de Ter, about 2km outside town on the Barcelona road, **t** 972 70 10 62, *www.solanadelter.com* (€€). A resort unto itself, with rooms, a campsite, tennis courts, a pool and children's playground in a park-like setting.

** Hs del Ripollès, Plaça Nova 11, **t** 972 70 02 15, *www.elripolles.com/hostaldelripolles* (€€). Decent, though slightly over-priced, *hostal* with a restaurant and café-bar downstairs.

Reccapolis, Ctra Sant Joan 68, **t** 972 70 21 06 (€€€). Ripoll's best restaurant is 2.5km from the centre, in a handsome mansion; lots of lovely mushroom dishes in season, and creative combinations of fruits, nuts and meats. Go for the scallops sautéed with onion and peach marmalade, or candied suckling pig in ginger and honey.

Gombrèn ✉ 17531

*Fonda Xesc, Plaça del Roser 1, **t** 972 73 04 04, *www.fondaxesc.com* (€€). Friendly, stone-built, old-fashioned *fonda* founded in 1730, in a tranquil village; it's well worth visiting for the excellent restaurant (€€€–€€).

Santuari de Montgrony, up next to the sanctuary, **t** 972 19 80 22, *www.montgrony.net* (€€). Peaceful, 11-room stone *hostal* amid the rocks under the sanctuary, restored in 2001, with stunning views and an excellent restaurant.

Sant Joan de les Abadesses ✉ 17860

*Can Janpere, C/Mestre Andreu 3, **t** 972 72 00 77 (€). En-suite rooms and a decent restaurant (€) with good-value set menus.

Casa Rudes, C/Major 10, **t** 972 72 01 15 (€€–€). A village institution for over a century. The food is good rather than great – try the venison.

La Teuleria, Ctra. Camprodon km 1,5 **t** 972 72 05 07 (€€€–€€). In a strikingly modern stone building with views over the mountains, serving delicious market-based cuisine and seafood – try the marinated salmon.

ⓘ Camprodon >
Plaça d'Espanya,
t *972 74 00 10*

Camprodon ✉ 17867

***Calitxo**, El Serrat s/n, **t** 972 74 03 86, Molló, *www.hotelcalitxo.com* (€€€–€€). A dozen cosy rooms with balconies in a big chalet, with lovely views into the Pyrenees: it has a good restaurant (€€) and an outdoor pool in the garden.

***Camprodon**, Plaça Dr Robert, **t** 972 74 00 13, *www.hotelcamprodon.com* (€€, *higher on weekends*). Central, pink Modernista classic from 1916, with pleasant gardens and a pool.

***Maristany**, Pg Maristany 20, **t** 972 13 00 78 (€€). Ten lovely rooms in a typical mansion along the town's prettiest street with a pool.

Hs Forn, **t 972 74 12 30, Beget (€€). Four comfortable en-suite doubles in a 16th-century inn. Restaurant with a beautiful terrace overlooking the river.

*San Roc, Plaça Carm 4, **t** 972 74 01 19, *www.hotelsantroc.info* (€). Family hotel in the centre, warm and friendly.

Can Po, Ctra Beget s/n, **t** 972 74 10 45, Rocabruna (€€). Probably the best restaurant in the area, serving a mix of traditional and creative dishes.

El Pont 9, Camí de la Cerdanya 1, **t** 972 74 05 21 (€€). Bright dining room with fine views over the Romanesque bridge and tasty market cuisine, with plenty of duck and fruit combos.

ⓘ Ribes de
Freser >
Plaça Ajuntament 3,
t *972 72 77 28*

Ribes de Freser ✉ 17534

****Resguard des Vents**, Camí de Ventaiola, **t** 972 72 88 66,

www.hotelresguard.com (€€€). Peaceful hotel with 17 big rooms and a spa, lounges with open fires and traditional mountain dishes served in the restaurant.

Prats, C/Sant Quintin 3, **t** 972 72 70 01, *www.hotel-prats.cat* (€€€). It means 'meadows' in Catalan, and it's a comfy little family-run inn, at the bottom end of this price category.

***Els Caçadors**, C/Balandrau 24, **t** 972 72 70 01, *www.hotelsderibes.com* (€€). Since 1919, a central, comfortable hotel (they also have seven cheaper rooms) but best known for its excellent restaurant (€€), that specializes in tasty dishes using mountain ingredients. *Closed Nov.*

*Catalunya, C/Sant Quintí 37, **t** 972 72 70 17, *www.catalunyaparkhotels.com* (€, *slightly higher on weekends and hols*). Pretty, recently renovated rooms near the train station, with access to the pool and garden in its pricier sister hotel, **Catalunya Park**, nearby.

Núria ✉ 17534

***Vall de Núria**, Estació de Montaña Vell de Nuria, **t** 972 73 20 30, *www.valldenuria.com* (€€€–€€). Set in the grim-looking sanctuary, but with nicely furnished rooms and a decent restaurant (€€) serving mountain meals.

Pic de l'Àliga, **t** 972 73 20 48 (€). The youth hostel enjoys a spectacular setting right at the top of the ski-centre's cable car.

Into the Pyrenees

The two Catalonias, Old (lands conquered under Wilfred the Hairy in the 9th century) and New (conquered in the 12th century) are generally divided by the Llobregat river. From Barcelona, the C16-E9, which follows the valley by way of Manresa and through the Cadí tunnel, is the fastest route to the Cerdanya and Andorra. If you're a slow traveller, however, take the panoramic detour northwest of Manresa on the C55 towards Cardona (*see* p.308) to see **Súria**, a handsome fortified town under its castle that controlled the Cardener river and protected Cardona's salt route. The scenic if narrow BP4313 will return you to the Llobregat at another important fortification, the 14th-century pentagonal **Castell de Balsareny**, crowned with tidy crenellations.

Getting around the Pyrenees

There are five **buses** daily from Barcelona to Manresa, Berga and La Pobla de Lillet, and one a day to Castellar de N'Hug with Alsina Graells (*t 938 21 04 85 or t932 65 65 92*) which go on to Androrra and Llivia. The Manel Mir Vila bus company (*t 972 70 30 12*) also runs services from Ripoll to La Pobla de Lillet.

Berga and the Sierra del Cadí

Berga, at the base of the Sierra del Cadí (the southern confines of the vast mountain plan of the Cerdanya) has a pleasant if unremarkable historic centre. But what it lacks in monuments it more than makes up for with an extraordinary festival, **La Patum**.

Two churches, just outside of Berga stand out. A narrow road from the Plaça de Guernica leads eastwards to the Romanesque **Sant Quirze de Pedret** (there's a car park by the pretty bridge). Although its famous artworks are now in the National Museum of Catalan Art in Barcelona (MNAC, *see* p.124) and in Solsona, a restoration in 1995 uncovered some fascinating murals which date back to around 1100.

Sant Quirze de Pedret
t 608 22 86 37,
open Sat, Sun and hols
11–2, also 5–7 in
July–Sept at other times
ring ahead to make
an appointment

Just west of Berga, the 18th-century **Santuari de La Mare de Déu de Queralt**, the 'Balcony of Catalonia', is balanced on a narrow mountain ridge (a funicular makes the trip up from the car park daily except Mon, or there are steps if you have sufficient puff). Inside, its rather unusual 14th-century figure of *Virgin and Child* has a swallow resting on the Virgin's hand and a weasel underneath her foot. Of late Queralt has been promoted as the end of an eight-day walk, the **Camí dels Bons Homes**, from Montsegur, retracing the steps of the Cathars who fled this way from France. The same road, the BV4142, heads north to the **Rasos de Peguera ski station**.

Camí dels Bons Homes
Consell Regulador del
Camí dels Bon Homes,
C/Pujada a Palau 7,
t 938 24 48 61, Bagà,
www.camidelsbons
homes.com

Into the Serra del Cadí

To the northwest, the scenic B400 follows the southern edge of the stunning, unspoiled Serra del Cadí, a chain that includes one of Catalonia's biggest national symbols, the iconic 8192ft, twin-

---

Berga's La Patum

La Patum takes place from Wednesday night to the Sunday of Corpus Christi in late May or June; it was declared a Masterpiece of the Oral and Intangible Heritage of Humanity by UNESCO in 2005. La Patum grew out of medieval plays on the battle between good and evil; they feature ancient songs, processions, dances, and mock battles, surrounded by swirling crowds of people dancing and singing along. There's the crowned *L'Àliga* (The Eagle); Turks and *Cavallets* (Little Horses), a battle of Maces, Giants and Dwarves. A relative newcomer to La Patum, the *La Guita Xica* is a long-necked fire-spewing dragon, a good protective spirit that evolved from a demonic mule.

The climax of La Patum is one of the great displays of Catalan *rauxa*: the wild dance of the *'Plens'* features masked men covered partly in green foliage with Roman candles sticking out of their heads like antennae: lights in the square are turned off while they are lit, streaming golden sparks while fireworks blast just overhead.

peaked **Pedraforca** ('pitchfork stone,'supposedly the devil's own fork, or some say his cloven hoof), a favourite challenge of trekkers and daring rock-climbers who ascend its sheer walls; it's so popular that the mountain has its own **information centre** in **Saldes.**

In **Gósol**, to the west, Picasso and his lover Fernande Olivier stayed in the only inn for three months in 1906. The artist (who by then was living in Paris and deep in his Blue Period) painted villagers and landscapes, seeking his pagan Mediterranean roots – just before he invented Cubism. There are copies of paintings from his Gósol period in the Ajuntament's **Museu Municipal de Gósol**.

Tuixén, further west, is famous for its *trementinaires* – literally the 'turpentiners' – women who gathered medicinal mountain herbs, and who travelled across Catalonia for several months at a time. There's a **Museu de les Trementinaires** along the road to La Seu d'Urgell, and a **Jardí Botànic de les Trementinaires** planted with the herbs they grew.

More grand scenery awaits to the east up the Llobregat. At Guardiola de Berguedà turn east to pretty **La Pobla de Lillet** ('field of lilies') with a pair of medieval bridges and a statue of Eusebi Güell, the area's great benefactor (see below). A life-sized 12th-century *Majestat* holds pride of place in the parish church, transferred here from the Romanesque **Monestir de Santa Maria de Lillet**, 2km from the centre and next to a curious round chapel dedicated to St Miquel.

There are numerous springs in the area; and, along the River Llobregat and the little train line that once linked La Pobla de Lillet to the Clot de Moro (*see* below) there's a surprise: Gaudí's lush **Jardines de Can Artigas**, designed for his patron Güell's industrialist friend Joan Artigas. Gaudí drew out plans and sent two workers from the Park Güell to oversee the project, but the gardens fell into disrepair when the nearby Artigas factory was burned in the Civil War. In 1994 they were restored. As in the Park Güell, the emphasis was on local stone, in sinuous walls and terraces and bridges and fountains; statues of the symbols of the four Evangelists figure prominently. Gaudí also designed the **Xalet Catllaràs** in 1901 (it's in the meadows beyond the **Santuari de Falgars**, reachable only by a four-wheel drive) for workers in the local coal mines.

Up the road towards Castellar de N'Hug is another Modernista work: the remarkable **El Clot del Moro** (1904), a cement factory designed by Rafael Guastavino. Built for Eusebi Güell, it was the first in Catalonia to produce Portland cement and it functioned until 1975; it's now the **Museu del Ciment Asland**. Some believe that the fairy tale chalet of the manager was by Gaudí as well. **Castellar de N'Hug** itself, with its cobbled streets and rural houses, is a popular resort; Catalans love to visit the never-failing **Fonts de Llobregat**, the source of Barcelona's river, which gushes from the

Centre d'Informació Massíf del Pedraforca
t 938 25 80 46

Museu Municipal de Gósol
Plaça Major 1, t 973 37 00 55, generally open office hours

Museu de les Trementinaires
Plaça Serra del Cadí 1, t 973 37 00 30, www.trementin aires.org; open mid-July–Aug and Christmas and Easter holidays daily 10–2 and 5–8; rest of year Sat 10–2 and 5–8, Sun 10–2

Jardines de Can Artigas
t 938 23 61 46, open July–Sept daily 10–7; Oct–June Tues–Fri by appt, Sat, Sun and hols 10–5; adm

Museu del Ciment Asland
t 938 25 70 37, open Sat and Sun 10–3, weekdays by appt; adm

rocks in a waterfall. The village's 12th-century church of **Sant Vicenç de Rus,** has kept some of its original mural paintings; another good one is south in **Sant Jaume de Frontanyà,** proud to be the smallest municipality in Catalonia (pop.31)

Back on the main C16 to Puigcerdà, little **Bagà** was the home to the ancient Pinós family of barons. The pretty porticoed Plaça Galceran de Pinós recalls a knight who was rescued from a Moorish prison in Almería by the miraculous intervention of a silver Byzantine cross. It was reputedly brought over from the First Crusade and is now kept in the handsome Transitional church of **Sant Esteban** (1339). In the medieval Palau de Pinós, the **Centre Medieval i dels Càtars** has several rooms dedicated to local history and the link with the Cathars.

Bagà is one of the access points of the **Parc Natural Cadí-Moixeró,** the biggest nature reserve in Catalonia. Made up of densely forested limestone mountains, it has Spain's greatest population of chamoix and offers some serious trekking for experienced walkers and paths for mountain bikes. Pick up maps and information at Bagà's **Centre de Documentació del Parc.**

Centre Medieval i dels Càtars
t 938 24 48 62, ring ahead to make sure it's open, generally daily in July and Aug, weekends the rest of the year

Centre de Documentació del Parc
C/de la Vinya 1, t 938 24 41 51, mediambient. gencat.net

Skiing in the Pyrenees

Rasos de Peguera, t 938 21 13 08, www.ajberga.cat Only 125km from Barcelona, near Berga in Castellar del Riu-Montmajor. It has 14 runs, two cross-country trails and five lifts. It's a small resort with no difficult runs, making it good for families, first-timers, and one-day skiers.

Tuixent-Lavansa, t 973 37 00 30, Tuixent, *www.tuixent-lavansa.com*. 30km of cross-country ski circuits in the Serra del Cadí.

Where to Stay and Eat in the Pyrenees

ⓘ **Berga** ›
C/Àngels 7, t 938 21 13 84

Berga ✉ 08600

Estel, Ctra. Sant Fruitós 39, **t 938 21 34 63, *www.hotelestel.com* (€). Basic modern hotel, with wi-fi and easy parking nearby.

Queralt, Plaça de la Creu 4, **t 938 21 06 11 (€). In the centre of Berga's action; trim and equipped with wi-fi.

*Cal Nen, Drecera de Queralt, **t** 938 21 00 27, *www.calnen.com* (€). A pleasant rooms with a garden terrace and parking.

La Cabana, just north of Berga on the C1411 (the old road to Ribes), **t** 938 21 04 70, *www.lacabanaberga.com* (€€). One of the best for tasty seasonal cuisine prepared to traditional recipes.

Sala, Pg de la Pau 27, **t** 938 21 11 85 (€€). Reliably good meals prepared to local recipes especially if you come in mushroom and game season.

La Pobla de Lillet ✉ 08696

Hs Santuari de Falgars, 7km from La Pobla, Ctra Santuari de Falgars s/n, **t** 937 44 10 95, *www.falgars.com* (€€). Utterly peaceful setting isolated in the mountains; eight simple double rooms and a restaurant in a 17th-century *hostal*, at the bottom of this price category. *Closed Jan–mid-Mar.*

*Fonda Cerdanya, Plaça del Fort 5, **t** 938 23 62 41, *www.fondacerdanya. com* (€). In the centre, basic but tidy rooms in the village's oldest inn.

Castellar de N'Hug ✉ 08696

HS Les Fonts, BV-4031, Km8, **t 938 25 70 89, *www.hostallesfonts.com* (€€). Just 800m from the river source, this is a good bet for families, with cosy rooms and an indoor pool and solarium, playground, ping-pong, etc.

ⓘ Bagà >
C/de la Vinya 1,
t 938 24 41 51

★ Moli del
Caso >>

Hs La Muntanya, Plaça Major 4, t 938
25 70 65, *www.hostallamuntanya.cat*
(€). A warm welcome and pleasant
rooms, and hearty traditional
escudellas – all sorts of meats and veg
simmered in a earthenware pot – in
the restaurant (€).

Bagà ✉ 08695
Molí del Caso, Barri Terradellas 10,
t 938 24 40 76, *www.molidelcaso.es*
(€€) A 19th-century mill converted
into an eco-sound, five-room B&B,
with an organic veg garden and
master chef owner. Cooking lessons.

Puigcerdà and the Cerdanya

The lofty plateau-valley of the Cerdanya covers 419 square miles
of the bed of a prehistoric lake. Once all part of Catalonia, it was
divided equally between Spain and France by the Treaty of the
Pyrenees in 1659, Spain getting the valley of the Segre. Guifré el
Pilos' third son Miron was count of Cerdanya, and his descendants
remained players in the stew of Old Catalan politics until the line
died out in 1117 and it passed to the count of Barcelona.

Although it produces potatoes and pears (it gets more sun than
anywhere in the Pyrenees) tourism is the Cerdanya's main money-
spinner: alpine and cross country skiing, snow-shoeing and
dog-sledding, riding and hiking, golf and balloon rides, trekking
and mountain biking are all on offer. Yet it's hardly crowded: this is
one of the least densely populated areas in Europe. Catalan is
lingua franca on both sides of the frontier, although an even older
language is behind the Cerdanya's bizarre place names such as Er,
Pi, Ro, Ix, and Ur.

The one urban patch is **Puigcerdà** right on the border with France.
The town has been the capital of the Cerdanya ever since it was
founded in 1117; now a bustling resort town ringed in by holiday
apartments, it had considerably more character before it was badly
bombed in the Civil War. Somehow the bombs missed its
landmark, the lofty 13th-century octagonal bell tower, while
destroying the rest of the church of Santa Maria. Nearby in Plaça
dels Herois is one of the town's most striking buildings, the eclectic
pink **Casino Ceretà**, home to Puigcerdà's cultural society. Around
the corner in Passeig 10 d'Abril, the Dominican monastery church
of **Sant Domènec** has frescoes from 1362, showing brutes dealing
the saint a splitting headache.

The town's lake, **Estany de Puigcerdà**, is a feat of medieval
engineering from 1260, bringing water by aqueduct to irrigate local
farms and provide ice. In the 19th century, when the rail line was
extended to town, wealthy Barcelonins built summer houses
overlooking the water. The romantic 19th-century **Parc Schierbeck**
around the lake was the work of Danish consul German
Schierbeck, who was fond of the place.

Getting to and around the Cerdanya

Puigcerdà is linked to Barcelona by **trains** eight times a day, and with La-Tour-Carol in France, where you can make connections for Toulouse or catch *Le Petit Train Jaune* de Cerdagne to Villefranche-de-Confluent, with links to Perpignan.

Teisa **buses, t** 972 20 48 68, link Puigcerdà to Girona, Llívia, Ribes de Freser, Ripoll, Sant Joan de les Abadesses and Olot.

In the Treaty of the Pyrenees Spain gave France 33 villages of Upper Cerdanya – but not the 'towns'. Hence the anomaly of **Llívia** (pop. 900), an islet located 6km from Puigcerdà inside France. An Iberian oppidum called Kerr, later Julia Libyca on the Roman highway Strata Ceretana, Llivia was the ancient ('and logical', it sniffs) capital of the Cerdanya. Visitors come for pizza (*see* p.236) and its little medieval core, home to **Farmacia Esteva**. Dating from 1415, this pharmacy is said to be the oldest in Europe – and owned by the Esteva family from 1660 to 1926. It was purchased by the government of Girona in 1965 on condition that it always remains in Llívia. The medicines are stored not in cabinets, but ornate shrines, veritable retables of drugs – all now part of the eclectic **Museu Municipal.**

Up a small road northwest of Puigcerdà, **Guils de Cerdanya** has a popular cross-country ski resort. Other sights are west of Puigcerdà off the N260 which follows the Riu Segre across a giant meadow. This was also one of the roads to Santiago de Compostela; at **Bolvir** the little church of **El Remei** has displays on the pilgrims. Just after Ger you can turn up the winding road to **Meranges**, a small stone hamlet famous for carving clogs. You can see how they did it at the **Museu de l'Esclop**. It's also the base for the popular walk to the small Malniu lakes, legendary rendezvous for witches in the 16th and 17th centuries. Down in the valley, **Bellver de Cerdanya** is surrounded by a bevy of tiny hamlets. The 10th-century Santa Eugènia in **Nerellà** keeps its bells in the startling 'Leaning Tower of the Cerdanya'.

Towards Le Seu d'Urgell, the road south of **Martinet** you can visit a relic of the bad old days – part of Franco's secret defences across the Pyrenees, consisting of two thousand bunkers thrown up in the 1940s in case the Allies were angry enough to invade. The Cerdanya was considered particularly vulnerable and had the greatest concentration: you can explore some at the **Parc dels Búnquers.**

On a lighter or at least more musical, note, tiny **Arsèguel** might tempt you to stop with its **Museu de l'Acordió** with a collection of accordions from the Pyrenees. La Seu d'Urgell (*see* p.311) waits at the end of the road.

Museu Municipal
t 972 89 63 13; closed for restoration at the time of writing, but due to reopen soon

Museu de l'Esclop
ring the Ajuntament, t 972 88 00 54

Parc dels Búnquers
Ctra. LV-4055, Partage de Cabiscol, t 648 14 10 70, www.bunquers martinet.com; guided tours July and Aug mid-Sept Tues–Sun 10–2 and 4–7; May and June Sat 10–2 and 4–7, Sun 10–2.30; Mar, April, Oct, Nov and Dec Sat Sun and hols 10.30–2.30; closed Jan, Feb; adm

Museu de l'Acordió
t 620 61 08 79, www. museudelacordio.cat, ring ahead to visit

(i) **Llívia >>**
C/dels Forns 10,
t 972 89 60 11

(i) **Puigcerdà >**
C/Querol 1 (in the
Ajuntament)
t 972 88 05 42

(★) **Torre del
Remei >**

(★) **Pizzeria
Taller >>**

Sports and Activities in the Cerdanya

Guils Fontanera, Guils de Cerdanya, t 972 197 047, *www.guils.com*. Cross-country ski resort, often site of the Spanish National Championships. 45km of tracks.

Lles de Cerdanya, t 973 29 30 49, Lles, www.lles.net. Cross country skiing and snow-shoeing.

Aransa, Arànser, t 973 29 30 51, *www.aransaski.com*. Cross-country skiing.

Golf Sant Marc, 1km from Puigcerdà, t 972 88 34 11, *www.golfpuigcerda.com*. 18 holes.

Where to Stay and Eat in the Cerdanya

Puigcerdà ✉ 17520

****Hospes Villa Paulita, Avda Pons i Gasch 15, t 972 88 46 22, *www.hospes. com* (€€€€€). Stylish boutique hotel in an old mansion (and an annexe) in a garden, with a fancy spa and a gourmet restaurant with lovely views over the lake.

****Torre del Remei, Camí Reial s/n, 4km outside town in Bolvir, t 972 14 01 82, *www.torredelremei.com* (€€€€€). For a real treat, head for this stunning Modernista palace with extensive gardens, a pool, a large, elegant terrace and plenty of activities including golf, hiking and skiing close by. The restaurant (€€€€), easily the finest in the region, serves refined Cerdanyan cuisine.

**Del Lago, Av. Dr Piguillem 7, t 972 88 10 00, *www.hotellago.com* (€€€). Near the bottom of this price category, with old-fashioned charm and a new indoor/outdoor pool and spa.

***Avet Blau, Plaça Santa María 14, t 972 88 25 52 (€€€–€€). Small and charming; just six rooms, so book in advance.

***Del Prado, Ctra de Llívia s/n, t 972 88 04 00, *www.hoteldelprado.cat* (€€€–€€). Delightful, chalet-style hotel with a pool, and an excellent restaurant (€€€).

Cal Marrufes, E-17529 in Age just east of Puigcerdà, t 972 14 11 74, *www. calmarrufes.com* (€€). Rooms in an old farmhouse, beautifully restored.

El Pati de la Tieta, Ctra dels Ferrers 20, t 972 88 01 56 (€€). They're not afraid to try unusual ingredients like kangaroo here, and they do them well.

La Vila, C/Alfonsol 34, t 972 14 08 04 (€€). Warm, rustic ambience, and the local favourite for creative cuisine.

Llívia ✉ 17527

***Bernat de So, C/d'en Calvera, t 972 14 62 06, *www.hotelbernatdeso.com* (€€€). In one of the oldest properties in Llívia, comfy design, friendly owners and a pool. *Closed Oct–May.*

Hs Rusó, Pujada de l'Església 2, t 972 14 62 64, *www.portalcerdanya.com/ hostalruso* (€). Cosy rooms in an old stone building with a courtyard in the historic centre.

La Formatgeria de Llívia, Pla de Rho, C/Gorguja s/n, t 972 14 62 79, *www.laformatgeria.com* (€€€). Stylish glass dining room with views and wonderful fondues, raclettes and other cheesy (and non-cheesy) dishes in this cheese factory, along with excellent wines.

Pizzeria Taller, C/Frederic Bernade 7, t 972 14 62 19, *www.fabian-martin.com* (€). The headquarters of Fabian Martin, former boxer, famous for his excellent and highly unusual pizzas with wildflowers or edible gold (it's in the balsamic vinegar), and also for his pizza acrobatic skills.

Meranges ✉ 17539

**Can Borrell, C/Retorn 3, t 972 88 00 33, *www.canborrell.com* (€€). Peaceful rooms in an old stone farmhouse far from the hurly-burly, with an excellent creative restaurant, with dishes based on local ingredients.

Tarragona Province

Everyone knows Girona and the Costa Brava. Now it's time to come to terms with the other side of Barcelona. Once the northern coast had made the touristic big time, this one had to have a name too, and Spain's indefatigable tourist bureaucracy eventually came up with 'Costa Daurada'.

Don't expect the 'Golden Coast' to be an endless sandy tourist trap; in fact there are only a few small patches of overbuilt beaches, and these are close to the big city, Tarragona. The tourist promoters should have left it alone. Tarragona and its province have enough character and interest; they don't really need a contrived nickname. The coast isn't even the major attraction: there's a wonderful diversity of landscapes here, a little bit of everything packed into a small space.

10

Don't miss

⭐ **Mighty Roman ruins**
Tarragona p.240

⭐ **Modernista masterpieces**
La Ruta Jujol p.257

⭐ **A Gothic jewel in a gorgeous setting**
Poblet p.263

⭐ **Top-shelf wine**
El Priorat p.266

⭐ **Picasso's hideaway**
Horta de Sant Joan p.278

See map overleaf

Tarragona Province

LLEIDA

Mequinenza

Prades

Cornudella

Escaladei · Siurana

Riba-Roja

Flix

Gratallops

Bellmunt de Priorato · Falset

TARRAGONA

Corbera d'Ebre

Coll de Moro (481 m)

Móra la Nova

Pratdip

Gandesa

El Pinell de Brai

Miravet

Miami Platja

Benifallet

Les Coves

Horta de St Joan

El Perelló

L'Ametlla de Mar

Valderrobres

L'Ampolla

Tortosa

Delta de L'Ebre

Deltebre

Amposta

Parc Natural de l'Ebre

Sant Carles de la Rápita

Ulldecona

Port dels Alfacs

Alcanar

Don't miss

- Tarragona **p.240**
- La Ruta Jujol **p.257**
- Poblet **p.263**
- El Priorat **p.266**
- Horta de Sant Joan **p.278**

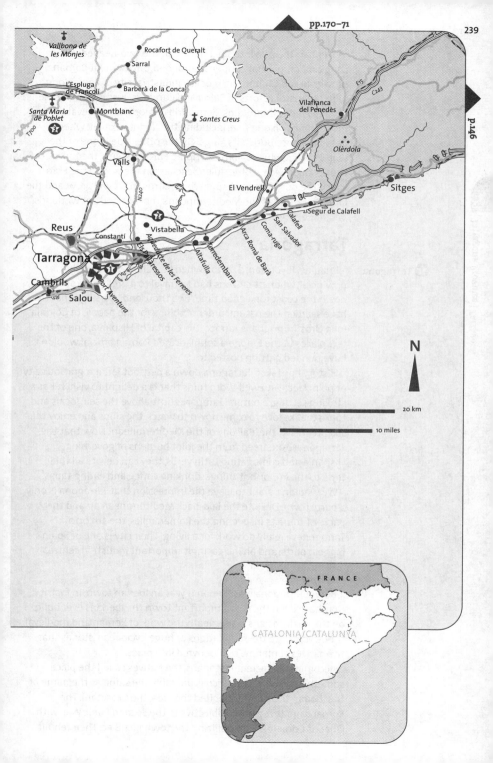

Vallbona de
les Monjes

Rocafort de Queralt

Sarral

L'Espluga
de Francolí

Barberà de la Conca

Santa Maria
de Poblet

Montblanc

Santes Creus

Vilafranca
del Penedès

Olèrdola

Valls

El Vendrell

Sitges

Calafell

Segur de Calafell

Reus

Vistabella

San Salvador

Coma-ruga

Constantí

Arc Roma de Barà

Tarragona

Altafulla

Torredembarra

Aqüeducte de les Ferreres

Els Escipions

Cambrils

Port Aventura

Salou

N

20 km

10 miles

FRANCE

CATALONIA/CATALUNYA

Over half the province's people live in the two-headed urban conglomeration that contains Tarragona, once a great Roman provincial capital, and the modern industrial city of Reus, along with the major resorts of Salou and Cambrils. Just inland are the rugged Prades mountains, with a trio of glorious medieval monasteries on one side, including the famous Poblet, where Catalonia once buried its kings. On the other side is one of the world's great wine regions, El Priorat. Further south, the tail end of the Costa provides some quiet beaches, on the way to the Ebro valley, the northernmost spot where citrus fruits will grow, and the Ebro Delta, one of the Mediterranean's most important wetlands.

Tarragona

 Tarragona

Imagine, if you can, a period when Barcelona was merely provincial, when its citizens had to travel to a great metropolis down the coast for a good time. Two thousand years ago that must have seemed the natural order of things for the people of Colonia Iulia Urbs Triumphalis Tarraco, the capital of Hispania, one of the few places in the Empire a sophisticated Roman official wouldn't have minded getting posted to.

History has taken Tarragona down a peg, but left it a gracious city of palm trees and well-worn ruins that is a delight to visit. It has a striking setting, a natural rampart 200ft above the sea; locals and tourists alike love to come down to watch the ships and enjoy the sea breezes at the 'Balcony of the Mediterranean'. Now that the Tarragonese are freed from the joint burdens of governing Hispania and conjugating Latin verbs, they can devote all their time to the important things: drinking coffee and eating tapas.

We wouldn't want to leave the impression that Tarragona is only a party town. Despite the laid-back Mediterranean air and the packs of tourists inspecting the Roman relics, the 261,000 Tarragonese really do work for a living. Their city is one of Spain's biggest ports, and an increasingly important industrial centre.

History

Before Tarragona was Roman it was an Iberian town; in fact, it may have been the most important town the Iberians ever built; on the fortifications, underneath the work of Roman and medieval times, you'll see the foundations of huge 'cyclopean' stones that the natives somehow manoeuvred into place.

According to ancient historians, the natives called the place something like 'Kesse', which is probably the same as the name of the Iberian tribe that inhabited the area, the Cessetani. The Romans made it a prime objective in the Second Punic War, with Gnaeus Cornelius Scipio seizing the town in 218 BC. Their rebuilt

Getting to and around Tarragona

By Air

Tarragona is served by Reus airport, only 12km away (*see* p.255).

By Train

Tarragona is linked frequently to Barcelona, Lleida, Zaragoza and Valencia by rail several times a day. The **RENFE station** is just below the Balcó del Mediterrani. The new high-speed AVE trains can take you to Lleida (31mins) or Madrid (2½ hrs); the AVE station, called **Tarragona Camp**, is out in the country north of town (off the N240 near Peñafort) and connected to the main station by buses.

By Bus

The new **Estació de Autobuses** (*t 977 22 91 26*) is at Plaça Imperial Tàrraco, the big circle on the western edge of the Eixample. The bus is the easiest way to get to Barcelona; there are connections for all other major Spanish cities, and of course regular buses run to Salou, Cambrils, Port Aventura, Reus, and other towns in the province.

---

and resettled version, now called Tarraco, was soon filled with immigrants from Italy and the Greek east. It would be the base for the long and difficult Roman conquest of Spain and the capital of the vast province of Hispania Citerior. Tarraco was the most elegant city on the Iberian peninsula; the poets Martial and Pliny praised its superb climate, fertile fields and delicious wines, and Augustus relaxed here after his 26 BC campaign in the north of Spain. By the 2nd century AD it had 30,000 inhabitants.

A Christian community existed from an early date; a local legend has it that St Paul preached in Tarraco. The Visigoths made it one of Spain's leading bishoprics in the 5th century; St Hermenegild, a Visigoth prince who converted to Catholicism, led the city in a revolt against the Arian heresies of his father King Leovigild, who had him martyred. By then Tarraco was only a shadow of its former self. Fires, invasions and the silting up of its harbour whittled the population down, and those who remained gradually moved up into the old Roman citadel, within the safety of its impressive walls. As home to an archbishop, it continued to be a seat of authority, and important churches were built, all now vanished.

With the coming of Moorish rule after 713, the city lost its political *raison d'être* and almost disappeared. A much-reduced Tarragona – probably little more than a village – is said to have been almost entirely Jewish. Its second chance came after it was taken by Ramon Berenguer III in 1118. The count gave it to the Archbishop of Barcelona, who in turn handed it over to a Norman mercenary named Robert Bordet. Norman rule only lasted until 1171, but it laid the foundation for the city's revival. They began the 'King's castle' and the new cathedral.

Tarragona got a city government of its own in 1336. After playing a full part in Catalonia's imperial adventure in the Middle Ages, the city once again declined into a backwater under Spanish rule.

Tarragona was besieged in the War of the Spanish Succession, and twice in the Napoleonic Wars, including a particularly brutal siege at the hands of the French in 1811: after the French forced their way in, they butchered 2,000 of the townspeople.

Now, a modern city has spread far beyond the hilltop walled enclosure, building one of the most spacious and urbane *eixamples* (extensions) of any Catalan city. The economy has been growing apace, thanks to its port, which ships out the products of industries in the suburbs as well as the majority of Catalonia's agricultural exports. There is a new university, and tourism has been important too; greater Tarragona, counting its twin city Reus, now has a population of nearly half a million.

Usually, it isn't hard to tell how a Roman city looked, even when a modern one is piled on top of it; its bones are still warm – a neat grid of streets, though maybe worn and kinked a bit over the centuries – and there's often a square where the old forum used to be. Tarragona is different, and, if you mean to wander around town looking at the widely scattered Roman remains, you'll have to know the layout to make sense of it. The plans and reconstructions in the Archaeological Museum (*see* p.244), or the great model (*maqueta*) of the city in Plaça del Pallol (*see* p.247), will help.

The ancient Tarragonese must have taken their horse racing pretty seriously, because the track was set in the very centre of town: the circus filled all the space between the Rambla Vella and Carrer Ferrers. The north side of Plaça del Font was roughly the line of the *spina*, the centre strip of the race course, lined with monuments, statues and perhaps an obelisk or two.

Tarraco's circus overlooked an equally imposing amphitheatre. In the Roman Empire, only cities in the west had amphitheatres. The Greek east wasn't so impressed with staged combats and mass slaughters of exotic animals (or occasionally people), but colonials like the Celts, North Africans and Iberians lapped it up.

Tarragona's Casca Vieja, now the colourful old town, probably had very little population at all in Roman times. Its mighty walls were built to shield an administrative city, the seat of the provincial government. All that space held nothing but soldiers and bureaucrats, working in offices set around two huge forums.

On the other side of the circus lay the real, workaday city, in the area bisected by the delightful Rambla Nova today. Everything here went to seed in the Dark Ages, as the surviving Tarragonese took shelter inside the administrative city's stronger walls, and this area remained open country until the 19th century. Now, ancient foundations lie under blingy skyscraper apartments, and remains of its Praetorium and Forum are kept up as little parks.

Of course, the great Roman roads that connected the cities were part of the same unified style of urbanism. If you leave Tarragona

PLAÇA DELS PESCADORS

MOLL DE PESCADORS

C SANT PERE

El *Serrallo*

To Salou, Centcelles

To Valencia/Reus

Palaeochristian Necropolis

AVINGUDA RAMÓN Y CAJAL

AVINGUDA DE ROMA

AVINGUDA IMPERIAL TARRACO

AVINGUDA PRESIDENT COMPANYS

PLAÇA D'ANDORRA

AVINGUDA IMPERIAL TARRACO

To Lleida, AVE station, the Aqueduct and Capus Secselades

Bus Station

RAMBLA NOVA

Museu del Port

Ferry Terminal

MOLL DE COSTA

MOLL DE LEVANT

Port Esportiu

Bull ring

AVINGUDA RAMÓN Y CAJAL

AVINGUDA PRAT DE LA RIBA

C CAPUTXINS

Municipal Forum

C GASÒMETRE

C SOLER

PLAÇA CORSINI

Mercat Central

RAMBLA NOVA

Information Office

Passeig Arqueològic

PORTAL DEL ROSER

Camp de Mart

Cathedral

PLAÇA DE LA SEU

Roman Theatre

C APODACA

C UNIÓ

C IXART

C ASSALT

Maqueta Tarraco Romana

Casa Castellarnau

VIA DE L'IMPERI ROMÀ

C MAJOR

C CAVALLERS

C MERCERIA

Hospital de Santa Tecla

C LES COQUES

C SANT LLORENÇ

C OROSI

PLAÇA DE LA FÒRUM

C POMPEU FABRA

Estació FFCC

C SANT FRANCESC

C AUGUST

C SANT AGUSTÍ

RAMBLA NOVA

RAMBLA VELLA

Ajuntament

PLAÇA DE LA FONT

Information Office

Museu d'Art Modern

Museu Arqueològic

Praetorium

Roman Circus

C TRINQUET VELL

C D'ENRAJOLAT

PASSEIG DE SANT ANTONI

C CABAT

platja del Miracle

PASSEIG DE LES PALMERES

Balcó del Mediterrani

Roman Amphitheatre

VIA AUGUSTA

To Barcelona

Mediterranean Sea

N

200 metres
200 yards

along the coast to the north, the main N340 follows the Roman Via Augusta. Romans used the roads outside their cities as a setting for important tombs and monuments, as along Rome's famous Appian Way. On the Via Augusta you'll see a triumphal arch, and the Tomb of the Scipios, the brothers who inaugurated the conquest of Spain for Rome. No Roman town would be complete without an aqueduct, and Tarragona has one of the grandest survivors, the Pont del Diable out in the woods 7km north of town (*see* p.249), and worth the trouble it takes to find it.

Old Tarragona

The 'Balcony of the Mediterranean'

As in Barcelona, Tarragona's main promenades are called *rambles*: the Rambla Vella and the parallel Rambla Nova, both decorated with Modernista buildings. Both begin at the **Balcó del Mediterrani**, its famous 320ft-high belvedere overlooking Tarragona's port and beautiful beaches. Looking the other way, punctuating the end of the Rambla Nova, is a wonderfully cinematic statue of King Pere III's great admiral-privateer Roger de Llúria, the man who conquered Sicily for the crown of Aragon.

The Balcó, with its fountains and palm trees and panoramic views, is the gathering place of the Tarragonese, especially on Sunday morning. Down below, besides the sea and the port, you can see the ruins of the Roman amphitheatre (*see* below, p.248)

Just behind the Balcó, north of the Rambla Vella, you can climb over the remains of the southern curve of the **Roman Circus**, with the vaulting that held up some of the banks of seats. Far as they were from the finish line, these weren't the cheap seats. If it worked like Rome's Circus Maximus, seats weren't numbered, so it would have been first come first served. Domitian, that most sporting of emperors, built the circus in the 1st century AD.

Praetorium
*open summer
Tues–Sat 9–8, Sun 10–3;
winter Tues–Sat 9–7,
Sun 10–3; adm*

Adjoining the circus is the 1st-century BC **Praetorium** popularly called the 'Castle of Pilate'. (Tarragona perversely liked to claim Pontius Pilate as a favourite son.) It's really a medieval palace built over a Roman one; it hosted Augustus and Hadrian, and later the Kings of Aragon. The French destroyed much of it in the siege of 1811, but one defence tower survives. Underground passages lead into the restored remains of the circus.

Museu Arqueològic
*t 977 23 62 09, www.
mnat.es; open June–Sept
Tues–Sat 9.30–8.30,
Sun 10–2; Oct–May
Tues–Sat 10–1.30 and
3.30–7, Sun 10–2; adm*

The Archaeological Museum

Next to the Praetorium, the **Museu Arqueològic** has an exceptional collection of everything Roman. There's a quorum of statues of emperors and togaed local worthies (the heads are largely missing; as elsewhere in the empire, cities would often knock them off when an emperor died and replace them with the visage of the new man). Some rare mural paintings from the interiors of houses have been moved here, including a lively hunting scene, and plenty of mosaics, including one lovely fountain with mosaics of fish at the bottom of the basin, designed to be seen through the water.

Another mosaic shows nearly every variety of seafood available in Tarragona's waters in precise detail. Besides making us hungry for lunch, it also serves as a prelude to the many rooms of everyday objects: candlesticks, cosmetics and jewellery, lamps, and lots of kitchen equipment. These help make old Tarraco come alive, even if you can't puzzle out the Catalan explanations.

There's some genuine art here too: a chubby, charming baby Hercules with his club, or a remarkable giant marble medallion bearing the image of Zeus Ammon with his ram's horns. There's nothing in Tarragona that would look out of place in Rome itself. Artists and architects in Gaul developed their own unique variations on the classical styles, but Hispania was so completely a colony that its art often betrays a wish to out-Italy Italy.

In the back streets around the museum, you can see what remains of Tarragona's Jewish quarter, in the narrow arched lanes around Pla Àngels, where the synagogue once stood. Around the corner is a small **Museu d'Art Modern**, on C/Santa Anna. Beyond this is the Plaça del Forum and a tiny fraction of the remains of the tremendous Roman **Provincial Forum**, headquarters of the government. This gives on to the 14th-century arcaded C/Merceria; where it meets C/Major, the fine 17th-century **Casa Consistorial** has been restored as a museum and information office (*see* p.250).

Museu d'Art Modern
t 977 23 50 32;
open Tues–Fri 10–8,
Sat 10–3, Sun 11–2

The Cathedral

Cathedral of Santa Tecla
open Mon–Sat 10–5,
but check with the
tourist office; adm;
entrance through
cloisters except for
during services

A stairway from C/Major ascends to Tarragona's tremendous cathedral of Santa Tecla, a masterpiece of the Transitional style, begun in the 12th century and completed in the 15th. The cathedral complex almost exactly covers the spot once occupied by the upper square of the Provincial Forum, with the governor's offices and a temple to the deified emperors – a religious and political continuity of over 2,000 years. The principal façade, though incomplete, presents a very French-Norman air, with a magnificent rose window and fine 13th-century statues.

Inside, more than the other great Catalan cathedrals, Tarragona has preserved its mystical gloom – which makes it difficult to see the magnificent wood and alabaster *Retaule de Santa Tecla* in the Capilla Mayor, a 1430 work by Pere Johan honouring Tarragona's patron saint. In the predella the details become increasingly minute and include tiny spiders and butterflies, as fine as filigree. Santa Tecla was a girl from Konya, Turkey who was converted by St Paul and followed him for a long time thereafter, dressed as a boy. Her legendary story consists largely of fighting off cads and miraculously escaping tortures, as you can see on the retable.

To the right of the altar stands a starkly realistic tomb effigy of Archbishop Joan d'Aragó, made by a 14th-century Italian artist. There's a *mudéjar* sacristy from the same era, a 16th-century organ and the 14th-century Gothic **Chapel of Santa Maria dels Sastres** (of the tailors), a profession wealthy enough here to have endowed the cathedral's finest chapel.

The enormous cloister is decorated with 12th-century sculpture that alone would make the trip to Tarragona worthwhile. Moorish influences are evident in the geometric panels that fill the spaces below the arches. The scenes over the door are especially robust and, among the fanciful capitals, don't miss the one just to the right as you enter, depicting two scenes from the medieval fable of the clever cat who feigns death to outsmart the cautious mice hiding in the rafters. Note also the *mihrab*, the little niche in the wall orientated towards Mecca. What's this doing in a Christian cloister? If they know, the Tarragonese aren't saying.

Museu Diocesano
*t 977 24 41 84;
same hours and adm
as the cathedral*

The **Museu Diocesano** is just off the cloister, with an archaeological collection and some fine Gothic painting and sculpture from parish churches. Among the highlights are a Roman sarcophagus, a carved Arab archway, and a 15th-century tapestry.

Just across C/Coques from the cathedral complex stands the **Hospital de Santa Tecla**, a rare and remarkable example of a workaday medieval building. It has a charming Romanesque arcade over the pavement, and the well-worn air of a building that has seen it all over its 800 years.

Casa Castellarnau and the Passeig Arqueològic

Head back down the C/Major, turn left on to aristocratic C/Cavallers. At No.14, the Gothic **Casa Castellarnau**, home of a once-powerful local family (Emperor Charles V slept here), is slowly on its way to becoming the **Museu d'Història de Tarragona**. In the meantime, this fine mansion wavers between the historical museum it is to become, and the old aristocratic curiosity shop it has always been. It's fun, with rooms arranged around a gorgeous, intimate courtyard. The archaeological section includes a perfectly serviceable pair of Roman dice, and some lead plumbing with the manufacturer's name stamped on it. There's a reconstructed kitchen in *azulejos* you'd die for, a crazy wooden intarsia copy of Rembrandt's *Syndics of the Cloth Hall*, 19th-century wall paintings of the Tarragona countryside, the biggest chandelier in town, and lots of portraits of people we probably wouldn't enjoy knowing.

Casa Castellarnau
*t 977 24 22 20; open
summer Tues–Sat 9–9,
Sun 9–2; winter
Tues–Sat 9–7,
Sun 10–2; adm*

Near the end of C/Cavallers is the picturesque Plaça del Pallol, where Gothic buildings were built over the western end of the huge Provincial Forum. One of these now holds exhibits on Roman

10 Tarragona Province | Tarragona

Maqueta de la Tàrraco Romana
open summer Tues–Sat 9–9, Sun 9–2; winter Tues–Sat 9–7, Sun 10–2; adm

Passeig Arqueològic
open summer Tues–Sat 9–9, Sun 9–2; winter Tues–Sat 9–7, Sun 10–2; adm

Tarragona, and the impressive **Maqueta de la Tàrraco Romana**, a complete architectural model of the ancient city.

From here, we pass through the walls at the Portal del Roser, one of the six city gates. On the surrounding lower stones, note the double axes and Iberian letters carved into the cyclopean blocks. Outside this gate begins the **Passeig Arqueològic**, where through a manicured garden between the ancient and Baroque-era walls you can get the best view of the old works – rugged Iberian blocks at their base, tidy Roman stone added by the Scipios on top, surrounded by walls put up by the English during the War of the Spanish Succession. The best part is near the **Minerva Tower**, where a bronze statue of Augustus, donated by Mussolini just before the Civil War, looks on authoritatively.

Lower Tarragona: Plaça de la Font

Situated between old Tarragona and new, the Plaça de la Font is the closest thing this city has to a centre, home of the Ajuntament and ringed with bars and restaurants; all of Tarragona comes down in the evening (and it's pretty lively the rest of the day too). The buildings on the southern side of this square are built over the vaults of the Roman circus; you'll find plenty of other bits of the circus sticking out from the houses on the surrounding streets.

The **Ajuntament**, which once was a Dominican monastery, conceals a real surprise within, one that fills a courtyard. Lluís Domènech i Montaner was called on in 1906 to create a bit of colossal, over-the-top *Modernisme* for the **Tomb of Jaume I**. This is a great canopy over a marble ship, encrusted with glittering mosaics and meant to carry heavenward the remains of the greatest of the Catalan count-kings. Jaume, unfortunately, isn't in it. He was buried at the monastery of Poblet (*see* pp.263–4) and, when the place was sacked and looted in 1835, grave-robbers left him lying in pieces on the floor. A priest gathered up the remains, which eventually found their way to Tarragona cathedral. Franco moved them back to Poblet in 1952, and now Domènech's grand tomb sits empty, waiting for some new count-king to fill it.

The Eixample

From Plaça de la Font, head south across the Rambla Vella and enter modern Tarragona, a sharp, elegant district full of high-rise apartments, and a touch of Modernista architecture here and there. The Rambla Nova is the main drag, connecting the Balcony of the Mediterranean with the grandiose Plaça Imperial Tàrraco.

Among the Modernista monuments on the Rambla are Bernardí Martorell's massive brick **Theresian Convent** at C/Assalt (1922), and three early works by Tarragona's own Modernista architect Josep

Maria Pujol: the **Teatre Metropol** (1908), **Casa Bofarull** (1920) at C/Sant Agustí, and the **Casa Aleu** (1927) at C/Ixart.

From the Casa Aleu, cross over the Rambla and head south on C/Cañellas for more Pujol. There's a grand and glorious **Mercat Central** (1919) and, across Plaça Corsini, the striking **Casa Porta Mercadé**. A block further south, behind the main post office, you will see the columns and foundations of Roman Tarraco's porticoed **Municipal Forum**; the excavated section includes a basilica, possibly used as law courts, a bit of a temple and some adjacent streets and buildings. Carry on another two streets, to C/Caputxins, for the scanty remains of the **Roman Theatre**, which was built into the hillside overlooking the port.

Municipal Forum
open summer Tues–Sat 9–9, Sun 9–3; winter Tues–Sat 9–7, Sun 10–3; adm

At the western edge of the Eixample, on the banks of the Francolí River at Avda Ramon i Cajal, the city's gargantuan, garish new shopping mall, **Park Central**, makes a noisy neighbour for the **Palaeochristian Necropolis**. This was unearthed during the construction of a tobacco factory – that huge hulk now standing forlorn and empty behind the excavations. After the burial of the bishop St Fructuosus, martyred in 259, this area became a place of pilgrimage and a popular spot for burials. As the city dwindled, the cemeteries became overgrown and forgotten. The necropolis is the richest yet discovered in Spain, producing funerary monuments and mosaics, from the pagan Romans to the Visigoths.

Palaeochristian Museum
t 977 25 22 86; open June–Sept Mon–Sat 10–1.30 and 4–8, Sun 10–2; Oct–May Mon–Sat 9.30–1.30 and 3–6, Sun 10–2; adm

Two interesting crypts remain *in situ*, while the best artefacts are in the adjacent **Palaeochristian Museum**. Note the strange Lions' Sarcophagus, an 4th-century ivory doll, and the mosaic of Optimus. When Park Central was going up, the builders found that the Necropolis stretched out onto the site. After some negotiations and excavations this part is now, weirdly enough, on display in the shopping mall's basement car park.

Beaches, the Port and El Serallo

You've already seen everything down under the cliffs, in the panoramic view from the Balcony of the Mediterranean. The city's mile-long beach, the **Platja del Miracle**, is parallelled by the main rail line for Barcelona (if you need a beach, there's a good one that's usually less crowded at Arabassada, 1.5km to the north).

Roman Amphitheatre
t 977 24 25 79; open summer Tues–Sat 9–9, Sun 9–3; winter Tues–Sat 9–7, Sun 10–3; adm

Behind the railway and just under the Balcony stands the 2nd-century AD **Roman Amphitheatre**. By the standards of Rome's Colosseum it's a midget, but with seating for 14,000 bloodthirsty provincials this is still an impressive civic ornament. St Fructuosus, along with his deacons Augurius and Eulogius, were burned here in 259, and a 5th-century bishop built a basilica in their honour right over the ruins, on the exact spot of their execution. That church fell into a Dark Age ruin, and the medieval one that replaced it, the 12th-century **Santa Maria del Miracle**, hasn't fared too well either.

On the other side of the train station sprawls Tarragona's bustling port, where, under the gaze of a stately neoclassical clocktower, container cargo ships jostle for space with Catalonia's biggest fishing fleet, car ferries for the Balearic Islands, and some startlingly opulent yachts.

At the end of the port area you'll come to Tarragona's venerable fishermen's quarter, **El Serrallo**. It's a dense urban neighbourhood now, and a bit of a disappointment when the crumbling, picturesque fishermen's houses turn out to be council blocks from the 1950s, but there are plenty of good spots along the quay for seafood and tapas, as well as ships' chandlers and antiques shops. There are ship models and maritime paraphernalia to inspect at the **Museu del Port de Tarragona**, or you can take a cruise around the harbour with a fish dinner on the *Tarragona Blau*, which leaves from the Serallo end of the port.

Museu del Port de Tarragona
t 977 25 94 42; open summer daily 10–2 and 5–8; winter daily 10–2 and 4–7; adm

Tarragona Blau
t 619 81 96 76

The Roman Environs of Tarragona

The Aqueduct

Pont del Diable
always open, on the N240 to Lleida, 4km from Tarragona

The aqueduct at Segovia may be bigger, but Tarragona's **Aqüeducte de les Ferreres** (better known locally as the **Pont del Diable**), certainly makes an impression. This graceful golden beauty, one of three Tarraco built, supplied the city with water from the Francolí River. Note that this is a divided highway, and you can only get to the aqueduct from the lanes headed outwards from Tarragona. It's signposted with a little brown sign near the toll booth for the Barcelona motorway; blink and you'll miss it)

The effect is heightened by the aqueduct's isolated position, lost in the woods outside the city. From the car park, pass through the crumbling ornate gate – this land used to be the private park of a wealthy family, and the gardens are slowly being rehabilitated. Follow the path for about five minutes and it will appear.

The aqueduct bridge, 85ft high and 817 ft long, may have been the biggest expense in the builders' budget, but the real art of the Roman engineers lies in the things you can't see. Consider that this aqueduct begins 25km away, and that the channel that carries the water, most of it just underground, has to keep a constant slope of precisely 0.04 per cent. Bridges are necessary only when the aqueduct has to cross a valley or ravine. This one, lovely as it is, also provides a lesson in plain, no-nonsense Roman engineering, rather like one of the great Victorian-era railroad viaducts. With a tape, you could see how every measurement in it works out to a simple multiple or fraction of a Roman foot (about 30cm).

Villa de Centcelles

Villa de
Centcelles
open June–Sept
Tues–Sat 10–1.30 and
4–8, Sun 10–2; Oct–May
10–1.30 and 3–5.30;
Sun 10–2; adm

After all these Roman marvels, Tarragona saves perhaps the best for last: the Villa de Centcelles is six kilometres from Tarragona (take the Valencia road from Plaça Imperial Tàrraco). In the 4th century, when the Roman world was falling apart, the wealthy had largely given up on the decayed cities, and they spent most of their time in great private villas, home to the very small number of noble families that had come to own nearly everything in Roman society.

Relatively little of this one has yet been excavated; the fascinating bit is a mighty domed chamber that survived thanks to its conversion into a church in early medieval times. From the outside, it's only a plain and unassuming stone building. Once within, you're looking up at a 35ft dome – the biggest (and only) ancient dome surviving in Spain, built in the same ingenious double-dome architecture as the Pantheon in Rome.

The dome was built as a mausoleum, entirely covered with some of the most important mosaics of early Christendom. Only fragments remain, but enough to create a magical world in tawny-coloured stone and glass tesserae. As is common in the earliest Christian art, classical and scriptural images co-exist side by side. Down at the bottom are hunting scenes; above, scenes from both Testaments, including Noah's Ark and Daniel in the lions' den; for some of these, the versions here are the oldest known representations in mosaic. These are accompanied by allegories of the Four Seasons, interspersed with what were probably ceremonial scenes from the Imperial court, now mostly lost.

In the hunting scene, note the dominant, centrally placed figure with portrait features. He's the boss, the scholars say – the man for whom this mausoleum was built. But who was he? One intriguing possibility is that he is no less than Emperor Constans I, son of Constantine the Great, who was assassinated just over the Pyrenees at Elne in 350 AD. That's still a matter of dispute, but in Centcelles we have one of few examples anywhere outside Rome of the beginnings of official Christian art and iconography.

Tourist Information in Tarragona

Ask tourist offices about the **Tarragona Card**, sold here and in hotels. It comes in 1-, 2- and 3-day versions, and gives free admission to most sights, plus other discounts.

Just about everything you need to know about the city is on their excellent and comprehensive website *www.tarragonaturisme.cat*.

(i) Tarragona >
municipal tourist info
C/Mayor 39,
t 977 25 07 95
provincial tourist info
C/Fortuny 4,
t 977 23 34 15
information booths
Passeig Arqueològic and
Plaça Imperial Tàrraco

Market Day in Tarragona

Tarragona, Thursday, Friday

Where to Stay in Tarragona

Tarragona ✉ 43000

****Imperial Tarraco, Pg Les Palmeres s/n, t 977 23 30 40, *www.hotelhusa imperialtarraco.com* (€€€). Tarragona's finest, a bit of Miami Beach modern, beautifully sited on the Balcó del Mediterrani and handy for the old town; with a pool.

(★) La Grava > ****La Grava**, C/Pareteta 6, El Morell, 10km from Tarragona, t 977 84 25 55, www.lagrava.com (€€€). A new, family-run boutique hotel in this old village inn, planned around one of the area's most innovative restaurants (see below). In a stylish townhouse, with pool, terrace, and top breakfasts.

***Lauria**, Rambla Nova 20, t 977 23 67 12, www.hlauria.es (€€). Charming, classic, central hotel with a pool.

*El Callejón**, Vía Augusta 141, t 977 23 63 80 (€€). One of several well-priced but very basic hostales along this street, near the old town.

*Plaça de la Font**, Plaça de la Font 26, t 977 24 61 34, www.hotelpdelafont. com (€€). A little more expensive than the others here, but with bright rooms, the nicest of which have balconies on the square.

Forum, Plaça de la Font 37, t 977 21 13 33 (€). Pleasant pensió, offering decent rooms (most with en-suites) right in the centre of the action.

Noria, Plaça de la Font 53, t 977 23 87 17 (€). Long-established.

Eating Out in Tarragona

Plaça de la Font is definitely the place to go for a drink, people-watching, tapas, or a modest meal. Or you could spend the evening in the tapas bars facing the port. L'Ancora is a good one, with a wide choice, and the Taverna del Mar will do you a paella with lobster for €18.

(★) La Grava > La Grava, C/Pareteta 6, El Morell, 10km from Tarragona, t 977 84 06 18, www.lagrava.com (€€€€). The raison d'être of the hotel listed above, one **(★) Leman >>** of the most talked-about new restaurants in Catalonia. Try duck with sweet-and-sour onions or rabbit stewed with chocolate and quince. Enormous wine list. The €45 menú degustació is a bargain. Closed Sun.

Estació Marítim, Moll de Costa, t 977 23 21 00 (€€€). In the new port building, this may be the place for your seafood splurge. Closed Sun.

Sol Ric, Vía Augusta 227, t 977 23 20 32 (€€€). One of the best-known places in town, a short walk north from the Balcó, this specializes in both simple and elaborate seafood. Great wine list, and you can dine outside in summer. Closed Sun eve and Mon.

Degvsta, Cavallers 6, t 977 25 24 28 (€€€–€€). Modern Catalan cuisine in a Modernista town house. Closed Sun, Mon and Tues eves.

Milonga Argentina C/Les Coques, t 977 22 90 54 (€€€–€€). An unassuming place where you can get real Argentine beef and home-made pasta dishes. Closed Sun, Mon nights.

Barquet, C/Gasómetro 16, t 977 24 00 23 (€€). This is a good seafood restaurant near the Roman Theatre offering very well priced set menus. Closed Mon eve and Sun.

Cal Brut, C/Sant Pere 14, t 977 21 04 05 (€€). Two streets back from the port, this atmospheric restaurant has been serving up seafood since 1914.

Club Nàutic, Port Esportiu, t 977 24 00 68 (€€). One of the better known and more inspired restaurants of the district, with imaginatively cooked seafood and views over the busy port.

Les Coques, C/Sant Llorenç 15, t 977 22 83 00 (€€). A top-rated, long-established restaurant, in a new location by the cathedral. Closed Sun.

La Puda, Moll de Pescadors 25, t 977 21 15 11 (€€). An institution on the waterfront. Go for the €18.50 seafood menu. Closed Sun night and in winter.

Tecla 60, C/l'Abat, t 977 22 07 49 (€€). This one offers something a little different: a Catalan version of southern France's confit de canard. Closed Sun, plus Mon eve.

Les Voltes, C/Trinquet Vell 12, t 977 23 06 51 (€€). Dine under the arches of the Roman circus. Closed Sun, Mon, and all of July and Aug.

Leman, Rambla Nova 27, t 977 23 42 33 (€). A café and pâtisserie serving delicious ice creams, fresh pastries, and now with a restaurant, especially good for seafood at reasonable prices.

Bufet el Tiberi, C/Martí d'Ardenya 5, t 977 23 54 03 (€). A pleasant, popular neighbourhood local serving hefty portions of traditional favourites. Closed Sun eve, Mon.

The Costa Daurada
East from Tarragona

You may have had your fill of ruins in Tarragona, but the Romans aren't done with you yet. Along the coast, the ancient Via Augusta is now the N340 for Barcelona. Along its way it passes three other Roman monuments. At the 6km mark stands the impressive 30ft **Torre de los Escipiones**, once fancied to be a funerary monument to the two famous Scipio brothers, Publius and Gnaeus, who died fighting the Carthaginians in 212 BC; the two figures in relief represent a popular military deity, the Anatolian god Attis. At eight kilometres a tall, strange monolith marks the centre of a Roman stone quarry, the **Cántara del Médol**. At 20 kilometres the **Arco de Barà**, a triumphal arch, spans the ancient road, erected for some forgotten victory in the 1st century BC.

Altafulla and the Castell de Tamarit

If only the Romans could see their Via Augusta now. All their monuments on the N340 are pretty much lost in the boiling traffic. This stretch of coast, part suburb of Tarragona and part resort strip, has been intensively developed, and the last empty spaces are rapidly filling with *urbanizaciónes* and villa subdivisions. Charming it ain't, though the beaches are splendid. One oasis amidst it all is **Altafulla**, with a lovely, well-restored walled centre and a small fishing port. The remains of another wealthy Roman villa, with some of its mosaics and other art, have been found here in the **Villa de Els Munts**, which was first excavated in the 16th century.

Villa de Els Munts
*open June–Sept
Mon–Sat 10–1.30 and
4–8, Sun 10–2; Oct–May
Mon–Sat 10–1.30
and 3–5.30; adm*

The landmark on this part of the coast is the **Castell de Tamarit**, restored by Charles Deering before he moved on to Sitges (*see* pp.165–6). Once this castle housed a fabulous hoard of art, but Deering eventually sent it all back home to Chicago. There isn't a lot to see now, though guided tours are offered.

Castell de Tamarit
*t 977 44 91 61
ring for guided tours*

Calafell and around

Neighboring **Torredembara** and **Coma-Ruga** are even bigger and more intense than Altafulla. So is **Calafell**. This village which consists of an old centre and a beach strip on opposite sides of the motorway, has a famously haunted castle, the **Castell del Calafell**, that attracted so many goblins, witches and storms that the the locals built a *comunidor* inside it (a magical, four-sided shrine or building, open to the four winds). You'll see these all over Catalonia. Not all of them are ancient; this one dates from the 18th century.

Castell de Calafell
*t 977 69 46 83
open Mar–Sept daily
11–2; Oct–Feb Sat and
Sun only 11–2; adm*

Iberian town
*currently closed to
visitors; though it may
reopen soon when the
museum they're
building is finished*

Calafell also has a recently excavated **Iberian town**.

El Vendrell

Near Calafell, the busy town of El Vendrell seems to exist largely to honour its famous son, the great cellist Pau Casals. There's a statue in the central Plaça Nova, a year-long schedule of concerts in the **Auditori Pau Casals**, his **Casa Natal** (birthplace) at C/Santa Anna 2 and the house near the beach on Avda Palfuriana where he lived 1909–39, now the **Museu Pau Casals**. Casals, born in 1876, was an international star by 1899. A fervent Republican, he left Spain at the end of the Civil War and vowed never to return until democracy was restored. He died in 1973, two years before Franco.

El Vendrell has no end of strange little museums: the **Museu Deu**, dedicated to art, bric-a-brac and oriental rugs; a small **Museu Arqueològic**, and one for the sculptor **Apelles Fenosa**, a friend of Picasso. Why not skip them all and head straight for **Aqualeon Safari**, where there are waterslides, a double-decker bus tour through a safari park, and a zoo with racoons, prairie dogs, meerkats, emus, boa constrictors and their friends?

Casa Natal Pau Casals
*t 977 68 42 76,
www.paucasals.org;
open Tues–Fri 10–2 and
4–6, Sat 10–2 and 4–7,
Sun 10–2; adm*

Museu Pau Casals
*same hours as the
birthplace*

Aqualeon Safari
*www.aqualeon.es;
open 13 June–13 Sept
daily 10–7; adm €21
adults, €16 children 4–12*

10 Tarragona Province | The Costa Daurada East from Tarragona

Market Days on the Costa Daurada

Torredembara, Tuesday; **El Vendrell**, Friday.

⭐ **Da Giorgio >>**

ⓘ **Altafulla**
*C/Marques de
Tamarit,
t 977 65 14 26*

ⓘ **Torredembarra >**
*Avda Nostra Senyora
de Montserrat 28,
t 977 64 45 80*

ⓘ **El Vendrell >>**
*C/Dr. Robert,
t 977 66 02 92*

Where to Stay and Eat on the Costa Daurada

People around here are crazy for *xató*, the traditional Catalan sauce made with almonds and hazelnuts, garlic, maybe tomatoes and...well, every village has its own prized recipe. It's usually served with a salad of endives, tuna and anchovies, and restaurants are measured by how well they do it.

Torredembarra ✉ 43830

***Morros**, C/Pérez Galdós 15, t 977 64 02 25, www.morros.es (€€–€). Excellent bargain for a beach hotel. *Open all year.*

Morros, Pg Rafel de Campelans, 42, t 977 64 00 61 (€€€). A branch of the same family that runs the hotel has a fine restaurant too; good seafood and rice dishes.

Calafell ✉ 43820

***Kursaal**, Avda San Joan de Deú 119, t 977 69 23 00, www.hotelkursaal.org

(€€). Modern, beachfront hotel with broadband connection and a good restaurant run by a kindly family. *Closed 15 Oct–3 Mar.*

***Salomé**, C/Monturiol, t 977 69 01 00 (€). Well-equipped hotel near the beach. Some rooms with balconies.

Da Giorgio, C/Guimerá 4, t 977 69 11 59 (€€€, *less for pizza*). One of the best Italian restaurants in Catalonia. They grow a lot of their own produce and produce their own olive oil. Outside tables. Leave room so as to finish with their ice cream made with fresh mascarpone cheese and strawberries. *Closed Mon.*

L'Estany, C/Mercé Rodoreda, Calafell-Platge, t 977 69 26 50 (€€). Nice seafood (and much more, also *xató*) at a good price.

El Vendrell ✉ 43700

***Hs Patricia**, Ctra de Valls, t 977 66 11 63 (€). Not by the beach, but good value for a short stay. *Open all year.*

El Molí de Cal Tof, Avda Santa Oliva 2, t 977 66 26 51 (€€€–€€). A local favourite for decades, which is as good for grilled meats as for seafood. Famous for winter-time *calçotadas*. *Closed Mon.*

Reus

It was a strange fate that cast Reus and Tarragona together as twin cities, the two centres of one sprawling conurbation, like a fried egg with two yolks. The yolks must have come from different roosters; they couldn't have less in common. Tarragona with its palms and Roman columns and seafood tapas seems a world away from modern, glossy hard-working Reus, a town that didn't get going until Tarragona had already been rebuilt twice. In Tarragona, they come for the ruins and museums. In Reus, they go shopping.

Reus's history won't take long to tell. There seems to have been a village on the site in Roman times, but Reus as Reus only appears in the wake of the Reconquista: a Norman named Roberto de Aguiló founded the town in 1150. The archbishops of Tarragona gave it the right to hold a trade fair, and Reus grew rapidly. From the 1600s it fell victim to a really horrible run of bad luck: the plague hit it 15 times in that century, and three more in the next. That was accompanied by economic decline, and political troubles. The city came under rough French occupations in 1640 and again in 1723.

Reus's fortunes picked up with the rest of Catalonia when Madrid permitted the American trade to reopen in 1778. Almost at once, this led to an industrial boom in the town; Reus was soon sending its textiles all over the world, a little Catalan Manchester that grew to be the second-largest city after Barcelona. While the creative juices were flowing and money was plentiful, Reus contributed two of the central figures of the Catalan cultural renaissance: the painter Mariano Fortuny, and the architect Antoní Gaudí. Reus's collection of Modernista buildings is one of the main reasons for visiting the city today, and to commemorate their most famous son they've just cleared one the most prominent corners of the old centre and dropped down the shiny, startling Gaudí Centre on it. There aren't a lot of other sights, but Reus is a bright, urbane, attractive city; with a population that has recently passed 100,000. It's worth a day when you're in the neighbourhood.

Plaça Mercadal and the Gaudí Centre

Gaudí Centre
t 902 36 02 00;
www.gaudicentre.com;
open summer Mon–Sat
10–8, Sun 10–2; winter
Mon–Sat 10–2 and 4–8,
Sun 10–2; adm

This elegant pedestrian square was the centre of medieval Reus. The market may be gone, but you can still have a look at one of Reus's finest Modernista buildings, the richly ornate 1902 **Casa Navàs** of Lluís Domènech de Montaner. It offers all the contrast in the world to the new boy on the square, the gleaming new **Gaudí Centre**. The architecture doesn't look entirely right here, with its black louvres and stainless steel trim – more of a high-tech radio than a building. But don't be afraid, push right in. A lot of cleverness went into this museum; not only does it entertain, but it

Getting to Reus

Reus **airport** serves Reus (3km), Tarragona (13km), and the Costa Daurada. It has become quite a busy place in the last few years, as the low-cost airlines have moved in. Currently it connects with a number of UK and Irish destinations, as well as Madrid, Palma and other Spanish cities.

A **taxi** into Reus should cost about €16, to Tarragona or Salou €20. If you're going to Reus, the no.50 **bus** only costs €1.10 and takes you right to the bus station in the centre. It runs about once every hour. Less frequently, there are also buses for Tarragona, Salou and Cambrils, and to Barcelona. These generally (but not always!) coincide with flights. For Reus **bus** info, **t** 977 77 06 98.

teaches us non-specialists a lot about the mathematical tricks and brilliant emulation of nature that made Gaudí so special.

The ground floor contains the city's **tourist office** (where you can get the brochure to do the Modernista tour later) and a rather posh music shop, besides the entrance. Once you get inside, the atmosphere is less Gaudí and more Flash Gordon. Sliding doors open and close mysteriously and lights constantly blink on and off. Do take the audio headphones; they're almost indispensable.

Exhibits include models of the pinnacles of the Sagrada Família, and contraptions that demonstrate some of Gaudí's fascinating solutions to engineering problems, using working models to explain the natural ventilation system of Casa Batlló and the water storage system that is the secret purpose of the Park Güell. Another model explains the ingenious upside-down system of hanging chains that Gaudí used to work out the advanced mathematics of his 'catenary' vaults and arches.

'Nature, who is always my teacher...'

In the Gaudí Centre, they'll show you a model of the pinnacles of the Sagrada Família, along with a photo of the little *crespinell*, a pretty flowering succulent that is common in the meadows of Catalonia. The *crespinell* gave the architect the idea for the pinnacles' shape.

Gaudí wasn't the first architect to spend a lot of time looking at flowers. Back in medieval Paris, the carved decoration for Nôtre-Dame and the Sainte Chapelle was provided respectively by two of France's most common spring flowers, the celandine and the lowly buttercup. To Gaudí, as to the medievals, the columns in a cathedral recalled the trees in a forest. A constant attention to the forms of nature was something that he and the builders of the Middle Ages had in common. In his case, it could lead to extremes (and usually did). Gaudí's devotion to nature was also one of things that made him so hard for his contemporaries to understand. As the principal of the School of Architecture in Barcelona had reflected when Gaudí graduated in 1878, he didn't know if he was giving a degree to a genius or a madman.

One of the most enduring lessons he learnt was that nature does not like straight lines, and in architecture the straight line is always the easiest solution. So Gaudí, quite alone, went off in the opposite direction. Nature's forms, along with his profound knowledge of mathematics, taught him to make parabolic and hyperbolic arches, and virtuoso tricks like the breathtaking convex vaulting used in the Colonia Güell crypt. Studying forms in nature and in mathematics, one puzzle often seems to lead to another, deeper one, and the same is true with Gaudí, who left scores of little mysteries in his works for others to ponder. Gaudí's deep religious faith is the other big difference between his architecture and everyone else's. It required that every work, large or small, sacred or secular, be designed as praise for the Creator. To the Great Perfectionist, this devotion had to be extended to the tiniest detail in everything. No short cuts. Not ever.

The exhibit that really fills out the picture of this endlessly fascinating character, though, is the reproduction of Gaudí's dusty, cluttered workshop, stuffed full of books, drawings and natural models. The Sagrada Família and every excruciatingly planned and executed detail in it were made for the glory of God – so were his apartment buildings, though their inhabitants probably never dreamed it. Here, in contrast, are the table and chair Gaudí built for himself, knocked together out of scraps from the work sites.

Around Reus

Ask the average inhabitant of this end of Catalonia what Reus is famous for, and chances are they won't mention Modernista architecture or even Gaudí, but shopping. There's plenty of swank and glitter in the shops here, especially on **Carrer Monterols**, the pedestrianized shopping street that runs northwards to the lovely and shady **Plaça de Prim**, a bustling square decorated by a ferocious equestrian statue of another local hero, General Joan Prim i Prats, a successful general in Morocco and later a major figure in Spanish politics. If you have a chance while you're in Reus, take in an opera or a concert at the 1882 **Teatro Fortuny**, a monument to Reus's golden years and one of the most lavish opera houses in all Spain.

Museu d'Arqueologia
Raval de Santa Anna 59, t 977 01 06 60; open Tues–Sat 10–2 and 5–8, Sun 11–2; joint adm

Museu d'Art i Història
Plaça de la Llibertat t 977 01 06 60; open Tues–Sat 10–2 and 5–8, Sun 11–2; joint adm

Reus has two more museums: a small Museu d'Arqueologia at Raval de Santa Anna 59, and a Museu d'Art i Història on Plaça de la Llibertat. There isn't much here yet, though there are plans to expand the collection, but upstairs you can see a good helping of Catalan art, including several works of Reus's own artist, Mariano Fortuny.

You might take the time to follow the tourist office's **Ruta del Modernisme** and see all the Modernista buildings in town, but don't expect anything as spectacular as in Barcelona. If there's only time for a few, **Carrer Sant Joan**, leading westwards from Plaça de Prim, is the showcase street. Among a number of buildings here are two by Domènech i Montaner, the **Casa Gasull** and **Casa Rull**.

Reus's biggest Modernista treasure, however, lies just outside town, signposted off the CN420 for Falset. The **Institut Pere Mata** was a highly progressive and modern psychiatric hospital when it was completed in 1912, one that covers over 40 acres. For architect Domènech i Montaner, it was practice for one of his greatest works, the even bigger Hospital de Sant Pau in Barcelona. Here, the decoration is more restrained, but the Arab-influenced details and wealth of stained glass and blue and white *azulejos* make it one of the most beautiful hospitals you'll ever see. Ask about the tours organized by the Reus tourist office.

Market Day in Reus

Reus, Monday, Thursday.

Where to Stay and Eat in Reus

(i) Reus ›
*Gaudí Centre,
Plaça del Mercadal 3
t 977 01 06 70*

Reus ✉ 43200

***Hotel Gaudí**, C/Arabal Robuster 49, t 977 34 55 45, *www.hotelgaudireus. com* (€€). Centrally located and newly refurbished, with large, bright, modern rooms.

**P Santa Teresa, C/Santa Teresa 1, t 977 31 62 97, *www.hostalsantateresa. com* (€). Good cheap accommodation near the centre is rare here; this rambling old building is the best. *Closed in winter.*

(★) Viena ››

*Olle, Passeig del Prim 45, t 977 31 10 90 (€). A bit out from the centre, but there's a pleasant garden.

Piano Piano, C/Santa Anna 11 t 977 34 34 83 (€€€–€€). In a warm and charming room in the historic centre of Reus, serving a careful cuisine based on Argentine beef and fresh Mediterranean seafood. *Closed Sun.*

La Glorieta del Castell, Plaça del Castell, t 977 34 08 26 (€€). Reus's most celebrated restaurant, spread over three floors with rustic decoration. Typical Catalan cuisine and an excellent set lunch menu. *Closed Mon night, Sun.*

Pizzeria-Ristorante Trastevere, Avda Riera d'Aragon, just south of the medieval centre, t 977 77 13 90 (€€). Italian is popular in Reus; here you can get a pizza solidly *all'italiana*, or home-made pasta with a wide choice of sauces.

Triant, Plaça Catalunya 7, t 977 34 22 40 (€€–€). A modest place, but good cooking on a *menú del dia* that often includes grilled fish.

Viena, C/ Llovera 48 and Plaça del Prim 4 (€). Right in the heart of the shopping district, two bars with Catalonia's most famous sandwiches which attract rave reviews (the roast beef is particularly good, along with the chicken and veggie wraps).

La Cerveseria, C/Vallroquetes 4 (€). Is Reus up to date? How many Spanish towns have a micro-brewery? Tasty home brew and tapas here.

North of Tarragona

Tarragona has always owed some of its prosperity to the fertile plain that surrounds it, the Camp de Tarragona. This is down-to-earth farming country, rich in Catalan folk traditions, but here too, surprisingly, are two of the greatest works of Modernista architecture outside Barcelona.

At its northern edge, the Camp climbs up to the *comarca* called the Conca de Barbera; here you can see some beautiful country-side, and one of the province's biggest attractions, the 'Cistercian Triangle' of opulent medieval monasteries, as well as the walled medieval city of Montblanc. To the west, there's a very small patch of very big mountains, the Muntanyas de Prades, which slope down to the serious wine country of El Priorat.

La Ruta Jujol: Vistabella to Montferri

(🚗) La Ruta Jujol

You saw some of the early and minor work of Josep Maria Jujol in Tarragona's Eixample. North from the city, in a string of out-of-the-way villages, you'll find the buildings that, along with his Barcelona

Getting around north of Tarragona

The five **trains** a day between Lleida and Tarragona/Barcelona stop at L'Espluga de Francolí, Montblanc and Valls.

There are several **buses** a day running between Lleida and Tarragona which stop at Valls, L'Espluga de Francol, and Montblanc. Other destinations are served by provincial buses out of Tarragona; the tourist offices have timetables.

collaborations with Gaudí, established Jujol's name among the greatest of Modernista architects.

Heading up into the plain called the Camp de Tarragona, just off the N240 beyond Tarragona's Roman aqueduct, the first stop is **Els Pallaressos**, where Jujols' family lived. It has several buildings he remodelled early in his career, and also the wonderful and outlandish **Casa Bofarull** (1914–31).

Further north, near La Secuita lies the hamlet of **Vistabella**. Here Jujol designed a church that many consider to be his masterpiece, **El Sagrat Cor** (1918–23). It was done on a shoestring; Vistabella at the time counted only 128 inhabitants, and they spent a lot of time collecting stones from their fields to make this church possible. Still, despite a tiny construction budget, the final effect is stunning, a complex play of interlaced geometric forms that seems almost Islamic in inspiration, under a *cupola* made of parabolic ('catenary') arches topped with a needle-sharp belltower. Jujol was a painter too, and he did some of the lovely decoration inside; this is still being restored, after Anarchists set it on fire in the Civil War.

Further north, across the valley of the little River Gaiá, you'll see what seems to be a fairy-tale castle atop a distant hill. This is the 'little Sagrada Família', the **Santuari de Montserrat**, located just north of the village of Montferri. Begun in 1921, funds ran out five years later and the church was completed only in the 1990s. Working for Gaudí, Jujol had contributed much of the design and decoration in the Park Güell, and it shows in this exquisite, playful building. Like El Sagrat Cor, the Santuari was designed for a small village with a very limited budget, and everything in it is made of the simplest materials. But if the materials are plain,the geometry in the design is as mind-spinningly complex as a Bach fugue. The bulbous parabolic vaults around the central tower were meant to recall the mountain pinnacles of Montserrat. Inside, an octagon of parabolic arches holds everything up.

Santuari de Montserrat
usually closed; if you want to see the interior, ring t 686 76 32 39

Valls: *Castells* and Spring Onions

The capital of the Alt Camp *comarca* is a modern, busy place. It hasn't much to attract the visitor, but it is the homeland of two of the great Catalan fetishes, symbols of the national identity. One is

Calçotada: a Rite of Winter

There's El Bulli, there's Casa Fabes, but for a genuine Catalan soul feast there's nothing like heading outdoors, donning a bib and slurping grilled spring onions, or, as they're properly known, *calçots de Valls*, a protected brand in Catalonia since the 1990s.

The Spaniards like their onions – they grow more than any country in Western Europe and they eat the most as well, demolishing on the average of seven kilos annually per capita. But *calçots* are something special, barbequed on vine cuttings until charred and black on the outside, but tender and sweet inside and served to diners who strip off the sooty outer layers (a messy business, necessitating bibs) and drench them in a sauce made from toasted almonds and locally grown hazelnuts, roast tomatoes, roast garlic, local olive oil, red pepper, salt and parsley. Then the *calçot* is suspended over the mouth, white side down, and dropped in. In the old days, the traditional meal included artichoke omelettes, fruit and coffee; today it's plenty of bread, grilled sausages and lamb chops. The season extends from later January to early spring; the biggest *Calçotada* festival, in Valls, takes place in late January, when mountains of *calçots* are served to 30,000 happy slurpers. You'll get your chance too; plenty of restaurants in the province have *calçots* on the menu for starters.

the humble *calçot* (*see* above). The other is the *castell*. Valls was the birthplace of the fine art of building human towers, and it is still famous throughout Catalonia for the daring and skill of its *castellers*, who are honoured by a monument in the town centre, a 45ft obelisk decorated with scenes of some of the more famous *castells* made here. Valls has three *casteller* clubs, including the celebrated Colla Xiquets de Valls. The best times to see them are the festivals of Sant Joan on June 24, and Santa Úrsula on the third Sunday in October.

Valls' **Call**, the Jewish quarter, is still reached via its medieval arch and still well preserved; also worth a look are the Gothic **Sant Joan Baptista** and the **Chapel des Roser**, with a 17th-century portrayal in *azulejos* of the Battle of Lepanto, the great 1571 sea fight in which the Spaniards and their allies finally stopped the tide of Ottoman Turkish expansion in the Mediterranean. The **Museu de Valls** on Passatge dels Caputxins has archaeological finds and a large collection of Catalan painting.

Museu de Valls
*t 977 60 66 54;
open Tues–Sat 11–2 and
5–8, Sun 5–8; adm*

The Cistercian Route

Santes Creus

The first of the region's three great monasteries (*see* p.260) is **Santes Creus**, just north of the village of Aiguamúrcia. This one isn't nearly as crowded as Poblet in summer, and, since there are no monks in residence, you get to see everything. More importantly, perhaps, you aren't obliged to tag along on a guided tour. Instead, you'll get a flashy, prize-winning audiovisual show.

Santes Creus was founded in 1158, devastated with the dissolution of the monasteries in 1835, and has been carefully restored since. The monastery reached the height of its influence

Santes Creus
*t 977 60 66 54; open
mid-Mar–mid-Sept
Tues–Sun 10–1.30 and
3–7; mid-Sept–mid-Mar
Tues–Sun 10–1.30 and
3–5.30; joint adm with
Poblet and Vallbona*

The Cistercian Empire

Strategically located between Tarragona and Lleida, at the centre of the 'New Catalonia' conquered from the Moors, stand three huge and magnificent Cistercian monasteries, the most impressive in all of Spain. They are: Santes Creus, east of Valls; Poblet, in the mountains to the west; and Vallbona de les Monges, built for women, further north towards Tàrrega.

As the Catalans, Aragonese, Templars and their allies reclaimed this distant outpost of al-Andalus in the mid-12th century, the monks of the Cistercian order were marching right behind them. Never believe for a minute that anything that happened in the Middle Ages was just a feudal muddle. This expansion of medieval Christendom was a highly planned operation, one that mobilized men and women from all over Europe. Conquering a country requires a lot of blood and treasure. The Cistercians, among others, were here not only to Christianize the conquest, but to make it pay.

And that, above all the other monastic orders, is where the Cistercians excelled. This order, founded only in 1098, was then in the midst of a wave of expansion that contemporaries found almost miraculous. The Cistercians' great leader, St Bernard of Clairvaux (d. 1153), had built it into a model of intelligence and efficiency while shoring up Christian theology and earning himself sainthood and status as a Doctor of the Church. (On the other hand, Bernard was a damn rotter who persecuted Peter Abelard and free scholarship, burned books, promoted attacks against the Cathars and anyone else he saw as heretical, and generally made life miserable for people he suspected might be having a good time.)

The Cistercians began as an attempt to restore the original, strict monastic rule of St Benedict. When Bernard's Cistercians weren't praying, they were working, and – here's the new twist – when they stopped working they were dreaming up ways to work more effectively. Cistercians pioneered improved methods in agriculture and husbandry. They built trading networks that stretched across Europe. Where there were swamps, they drained them; where there was ore, they mined it and smelted it. They were behind many of the technological innovations that made the Middle Ages such an economic boom time, notably the use of water power, which they employed to run big workshops that are seen as the precursors of the modern factory system.

It's a little mystery why the three big Cistercian installations in Catalonia should have been placed so close together. But it would be a mistake to think of them as purely local institutions. Each held lands and farms and workshops spread across the kingdom of Aragon and beyond. Royal patronage was important to all three from the start, as evidenced by the Aragonese kings buried inside. When you visit one of these Cistercian houses, remember that this was a branch of an international conglomerate, closely bound to the centres of political and economic power.

Cistercians didn't care much for poetry or art, but they had a terrible weakness for architecture. Even in Bernard's day, they made sure they picked the best available architects and workmen for the new monasteries they were building across Europe. At the same time, the ethos of austerity that lay at the heart of everything Cistercian required a whole new aesthetic. The classic Cistercian abbey church is Gothic at its grandest – the order and the Gothic style were practically born together – but without the elaborate decoration of a city cathedral; the fantastical figurative ornaments that so enlivened the capitals and portals of the Romanesque was strictly forbidden. Abbey church façades are often nothing more than an unadorned portal underneath plain lancet windows, with sometimes a small rose window on top; it was architectural Protestantism, four centuries before the Reformation.

The three churches here have little in common with the stout, quirky Catalan Gothic of Barcelona; just as the Order was an international movement, its architecture was a mature international style, which took its inspiration from France. To compensate for the lack of frills, Cistercians insisted on sheer perfection in conception and proportions. And they usually got it; their churches are acclaimed as some of the most elegant productions of the Middle Ages.

In truth, Cistercian austerity fades proportionately with time, and with distance from the order's home at Cîteaux, in Burgundy. In each of the three monasteries here you can see how the original stern and solid Romanesque gave way to delicate Gothic soon after building had commenced. The gorgeous rib-vaulting and window traceries of Catalonia's three houses would be the envy of any metropolitan cathedral.

in the 14th century, when its abbots were friends and counsellors to kings, though in this respect it was gradually eclipsed by Poblet. In 1317, after the dissolution of the Templars, the Abbot of Santes Creus was permitted to start the Order of Manresa, which was similar in purpose and organization, and took in many former Templars as members.

The church, begun in the 1170s and completed in 1221, has an especially austere façade, with crenellations that give it a military look that is carried on inside, down a nave lined with plain, massive pillars. There is no pretence of austerity at all, though, in the big Baroque retable or in the royal tombs, which include those of Jaume II, Blanche of Anjou and Pere III, along with the great admiral Roger de Llúria. Perhaps the best part of Santes Creus is the lovely **cloister** (1313–41), in which the Cistercian prohibition of figurative decoration was somehow suspended to allow some charming carvings on the capitals, the work of an Englishman whose name has come down as Reinart Funoll.

Montblanc

From Santes Creus to Poblet, you'll pass into the *comarca* called the Conca de Barbera, an agricultural region known for its DO Conca de Barbera wine. The '*conca*' is a broad natural basin, running roughly from Barbera to Tarres, that creates some striking scenery as you descend into it from the surrounding hills. The *comarca*'s capital is Montblanc, an attractive walled town with an air of distinction; in the late Middle Ages it was the seat of a dukedom, and the Catalan Corts (parliament) sat here four times. They'll tell you that Saint George, or rather Sant Jordi, killed his dragon here – he's the patron of Catalonia as well as England. A plaque marks the spot at the Porta de Sant Jordi. and the feat is re-enacted every April during Montblanc's Medieval Festival.

The 14th-century walls, which survive almost completely intact, along with their 34 towers, are still impressive today. Outside them, a little 12th-century bridge survives too, in a neglected part of town over the River Francolí. On the Raval de Santa Anna, have a peek inside the medieval **Hospital de Santa Magdalena**, now the town archives, for its charming little courtyard and fountain.

The **Carrer Major**, the main street of the old town, used to be covered with medieval arches. Side streets to the right lead to the picturesque town centre: the **Plaça Major** with the town hall, and the adjacent **Plaça Santa Maria**, a picture-postcard setting for the Catalan Gothic parish church **Santa Maria** and its elegant Baroque portal, which replaced an original destroyed in the Reaper's War.

Museu Comarcal
t 977 86 03 49,
www.mccb.es;
open Tues–Sat 10–2
and 4–7, Sun 10–2; adm

Across from the church, the 14th-century Casal dels Josa is now the main building of the **Museu Comarcal**, with local archaeo-logical finds, art and crafts; ask here for admittance to the

10
Tarragona Province | North of Tarragona

museum's other facilities, including a collection of nativity scenes, a museum of natural history, works of art donated by the sculptor Frederic Marès, and a working water-powered grain mill. Behind the church, the **Centre d'Interpretación d'Art Rupestre** is dedicated to the scores of prehistoric painted caves that have been discovered in this part of Catalonia. None is currently open to visitors, but here you can see reproductions of some striking art.

Centre d'Interpretación d'Art Rupestre
open Tues–Sat 10–2 and 4.30–7.30, Sun 10–2; adm

Back on Carrer Major is the ruggedly primitive 12th-century church of **Sant Miquel**. It's hard to believe that the Catalan parliament met here twice. The streets behind, around Carrer dels Jeues, were once the Jewish district. Carrying on down Carrer Major through the western city gate, you'll come to the ruined **Monastery of Sant Francesc**, with a large 14th-century church that until recently was used as a winemaker's warehouse. Nowadays the wine is kept in a 1922 César Martinell Cooperativa outside the walls on C/Santa Tecla. The Montblanc area grows many Conca de Barbera and other wines, but the co-operative here is mostly known for *cava*, named Pont Vell after the medieval bridge.

North of Montblanc in the Conca, Sarral is a village known for centuries for mining and working alabaster. It has reproduced a 1917 workshop, with demonstrations of how it was done: the **Museu d'Alabastre**. There are 16 more modern workshops in the village, and they turn out some quite artistic works.

Museu d'Alabastre
t 977 89 01 58; open Tues–Sat 11–1 and 4–7, Sun 10–2; adm

L'Espluga de Francolí

Just west of Montblanc, on the way to Poblet, **L'Espluga de Francolí** gets its name from the enormous cave (or spelunca) that lies underneath its centre, called the **Cova Museu de la Font Major**. The town carried that name for centuries without knowing why; the cave was only rediscovered in 1853. Though an impressive two and a half miles in length, this isn't a pretty stalactite cave, but Espluga tries to make up for that with a merciless guided tour and a ton of information on its geological formation and archaeological finds; that's why it is a *'cova museu'*. You can book in advance for their *'visita d'aventura'*: real cave-exploring complete with headlamps and wet suits, on a tour through the less accessible parts of the cave that includes a subterranean lake used by the ancients for religious rituals.

Cova Museu de la Font Major
t 977 87 12 20; open July and Aug daily 10.30–1.30 and 4.30–7.30; Sept–June Tues–Sun 10.30–1.30 and 4–6; adm

Espluga has other attractions: the 12th-century Gothic **Sant Miquel Arcàngel**, a town library that once was a hospital of the Knights Hospitallers, and a **Museu de la Vida Rural** on C/Canós. Catalonia has plenty of museums about farming life in the old days, but this is perhaps the most interesting, a serious attempt to present the history of the region through the articles of everyday life. The collection is arranged in an elegant old mansion that belonged to Lluís Carulla, a name to reckon with in these parts.

Museu de la Vida Rural
t 977 87 05 76, www. museuvidarural.com; open Tues–Sat 10–2 and 4–6.30, Sun 10.30–2; adm; closed for expansion till late 2009

Espluga's great benefactor was also the founder of a remarkable institution called the **Casal d'Espluga**. You can't miss its big complex of buildings on the edge of town—behind the picnic ground with the house shaped like a gigantic barrel. It's a very Catalan idea, dating from the Franco years, when Carulla began it to help keep Catalan language and culture alive. That remains its purpose today, and it acts a kind of social and cultural club for all the people of the town. There are gardens and meeting halls, a theatre company, a literary circle, a newspaper and radio station, sports clubs and courses; you can learn anything from quilting to judo here. Maybe every town should have one (the Casal also includes a hotel and restaurant; *see* p.265).

Poblet

🔁 **Poblet**

Santa Maria de Poblet
*t 977 87 00 89,
www.poblet.cat; open
summer Tues–Sat
10–12.45 and 3–6, Sun
10–12.30 and 3–5.30;
winter Tues–Sat
10–12.45 and 3–5.30,
Sun 10–12.30 and
3–5.30; joint adm with
Santes Creus and
Vallbona; admission by
guided tour in various
languages, or ask for
the explanation card
in English*

From L'Espluga de Francolí, it's only 5km to the famous Cistercian monastery of **Santa Maria de Poblet**, founded by Ramon Berenguer IV in 1151 to commemorate the end of the Reconquista in Catalunya. For centuries Poblet was its most powerful and privileged monastery, and it shows. Architecturally, it is the richest of the three Cistercian sisters, and the view through the traceries of its golden tower takes in blue mountains, behind gorgeous rolling hills covered in vines. This is a house built for gentlemen.

That, of course, is exactly what most of the monks were. Even before Pere III made the monastery a pantheon for the kings of Aragon, Poblet was already the Catalan aristocratic retreat *par excellence*, even possessing a royal palace for visiting kings. Openly dissipated and corrupt in later years, Poblet was so despised that, when the monks were suspected of harbouring Carlist sympathies at the time of the dissolution in 1835, the locals found an excuse to avenge centuries of maltreatment. In their fury they wrenched apart the buildings and torched its famous library. The ruins of Poblet stood overgrown with wildflowers until the 1940s, when a band of Italian Cistercians reclaimed it and restored it beautifully.

At the ceremonial entrance, the **Porta Daurada**, stands a little Plateresque jewel, the freestanding **Capilla de Sant Jordi**, built in 1442 by King Alfons V (better known to us as Alfonso the Magnanimous) in thanks for his conquest of the Kingdom of Naples. The Porta Daurada was completed in 1493, to commemorate a visit of Fernando and Isabel, and it bears the arms of newly united Aragon and Castile over the arch.

The gate leads to the **Plaça Major**, with the 13th-century **Capella de Santa Caterina**, one of the oldest parts of the complex. The façade of the church and the rest of the monastery is enclosed behind yet another wall, the **Porta Reial**, dripping with Baroque decoration. The church, although begun almost when Poblet was founded, took another two centuries to be completed, with plenty of modifications in style along the way. At the end of the heavy Romanesque nave stands a glistening Renaissance altarpiece, carved in alabaster by the Valencian sculptor Damián Forment.

Poblet was known as 'Catalunya's Escorial' for its many **tombs of the kings of Aragon**, on both sides of the high altar, which were wonderfully restored by sculptor Frederic Marès. Among the many are Alfons I el Batallador (d. 1134) and Jaume I 'the Conqueror' (d. 1276), who finally made it back here in 1952 after his long posthumous exile in Tarragona (*see* p.247). When he came back he had two skulls, and they're still trying to figure out which one's really his. The exquisite effigy is carved wearing a simple monk's habit; Jaume asked to become a Cistercian of Poblet just before he died.

Outside is a richly sculpted **cloister**, with a lovely fountain in a little pavilion at its centre that could be an image from a medieval illumination. The guided tour will lead you on to the huge vaulted wine cellar; the fine Gothic chapterhouse; the dormitory; the refectory and kitchen, a museum, and the 1397 **Palace of King Martí l'Humà** (Martin the Humanist); the kings came to Poblet so often, eventually they built themselves a proper home here. This handsome building now houses a small **museum**, with some charming carved medieval wooden sculpture, architectural fragments, paintings and ceramics.

Vallbona de les Monjes

Vallbona, Vallbona, the third member of the Cistercian trio lies 30km up in
de les Monjes the hills, just over the border in Lleida province. It was built for
t 973 33 02 66, nuns, and located far away from anything else so they wouldn't be
www.vallbona.com; distracted. Nevertheless, a village eventually grew up around the
open summer Tues–Sat convent. In 1573, the Church decided to ban convents for women in
10.30–1.30 and isolated places, and Vallbona languished. Like Poblet, it has been
4.30–6.45, Sun 12–1.30; restored and repopulated only in this century.
winter Tues–Sat
10.30–1.30 and 4.30–6; The architecture differs little from Poblet and Santes Creus: four-
joint adm with Poblet square Cistercian Romanesque laid on with a frosting of delicate
and Santes Creus Gothic, bits and pieces of everything else, most of it unfinished, all
topped with a lovely octagonal Gothic tower. The church has a few royal tombs, including those of Violant of Hungary, the wife of Jaume I, and their daughter Sança. In a chapel on the right, note the beautiful Gothic statue of the *Mare de Déu del Cor* (Our Lady of the Choir) by Guillem Seguer, a sculptor from Montblanc.

This Virgin Mary is one of many at Vallbona. Another fine one, by an unknown artist, can be seen in the chapterhouse, the *Mare de Déu del Claustre*. There are so many other noble tombs on the floor in the church and chapterhouse that Vallbona has been called a 'museum of Catalan heraldry'. The cloister dates from the 12th–15th centuries.

(i) **L'Espluga del Francolí >>**
Plaça de Mil.lenari 1,
t 977 87 12 20

(i) **Santes Creus**
Plaça Sant Bernat,
t 977 63 81 41

(i) **Valls >**
C/de la Cort 61,
t 977 61 25 30

(i) **Poblet >>**
Passeig Abat Conill 9
(in the nearby village of
Vimbodí de Poblet)
t 977 87 12 47

(i) **Montblanc >**
inside church of Sant
Françesc, just outside
the walls, t 977 86 17 33;
adjacent parking is a
convenient place to
leave your beast since
there's almost no
parking in the town

(★) **Masia de la Font de l'Oca >>**

Market Days North of Tarragona

Valls, Wednesday, first Saturday of each month; **Montblanc**, Friday; **Barberà**, Thursday; L'**Espluga de Francolí**, Monday, Friday; **Poblet** (Vimbodí), Wednesday.

Where to Stay and Eat North of Tarragona

Valls ✉ 43800

***Fèlix**, just off the N240, t 977 60 90 90, *www.felixhotel.net* (€€€). Hotel set in pretty gardens, with a pool and tennis courts, and spacious rooms in the main building or in bungalows; a favourite for weddings and *calçotadas* (see p.259) in the lovely restaurant.

***Class**, Pg President Tarradella, t 977 60 80 90, *www.hotelclassvalls. com* (€€). On Catalonia's 'Cistercian Route', a very pleasant business hotel that prides itself on its energy-efficiency; wi-fi-equipped rooms offer excellent value for money; great restaurant, too.

Montblanc ✉ 43400

**Hotel Coll de Lilla, Ctra Nacional 240, t 977 86 01 24 (€€€). On the road to Valls, near Lilla: a hotel in a spectacular setting with 12 pretty rooms and a good restaurant (€€) specializing in game dishes and, from Dec–Mar, *calçotada* with lamb.

*Ducal, C/Francesc Macià 11, t 977 86 00 25 (€€). Cosy rooms with bath.

*Hs Fonda Bohèmia Riuot, C/Pietá 23, t 977 86 05 07, *www.tinet.org/~rdomingo* (€). Good basic rooms, also apartments.

Fonda dels Angels, Plaça dels Angels, t 977 86 01 73 (€). Basic rooms and a very popular restaurant (€€–€).

El Call de Montblanc, C/Sant Josep 15, t 977 86 01 20 (€€€–€€). Best in town for seafood; with a Basque touch.

El Cairat, C/Nou 3, t 977 83 04 81 (€€). Wonderful home cooking, including home-made pasta. Friendly owners.

Molí del Mallol, Muralla Santa Anna, t 977 86 05 91 (€€). Refined cooking in an old mill by the town walls. Snails are the house speciality.

L'Espluga de Francolí ✉ 43400

**Hostal del Senglar, Plaça Montserrat Canals 1, t 977 87 04 11, *www. hostaldelsenglar.com* (€€). Part of the Casal (see p.263) so it's a village institution. Very simple, almost spartan, rooms but well kept, with a garden. The restaurant (€€) is where everybody goes in L'Espluga, and serves stewed boar and other game.

Casa Nostra, C/Sant Miquel, t 977 87 94 77 (€€–€). A pleasant surprise, this modest little hole-in-the-wall serves excellent home cooking, such as *escudella* or roast rabbit.

L'Ocell Francolí, Pg Cañellas t 977 87 12 16, *www.ocellfrancoli.com* (€). Immaculate small inn with a good restaurant (€€–€).

Casa Pairal Espasa, C/Font Major, t 977 87 09 51, *http://personales.ya. com/espasa/casarural* (€). Family-run; five pleasant rooms in an old house on the edge of town; kitchen facilities.

Poblet ✉ 43440

The gorgeous countryside around Poblet makes it a great place to stop over, or rest up for a few days. Some exceptional **accommodation** can be found in the hamlet of **Les Masies**, a ten-minute walk from the monastery.

***Masia de la Font de l'Oca**, Les Masies, t 639 32 80 70, *www. ocamasia.com* (€€€). An exquisite 18th-century manor set in extensive wooded grounds. Unpretentious and welcoming; rooms furnished with antiques. Riding, biking, archery and other activities.

**Fonell, Plaça Ramon Berenguer IV, t 977 87 03 33, *www.hostalfonoll.com* (€€€–€€). You might think the only place by the monastery (literally right outside the gate) would be a tourist trap, but no. The Fonell family has run this place for 150 years now. Pleasant rooms, with garden, and a good restaurant (€€€–€€) with an outside terrace.

***Monestir Les Masies**, Les Masies, t 977 87 00 58, *www.hotelmonestir. com* (€€). A long-time favourite, an 1860-country house surrounded by an elegant garden shaded by rows of tall plane trees.

The Prades Mountains and El Priorat

Between Poblet and Reus, there's a patch on the road maps where all the roads are lined with green for scenery. It looks enticing on the map, but you'll find that these mountains, however green, can be downright unreasonable.

Entering this pocket massif is an adventure from any direction, like storming a castle; the most spectacular of the roads leading in, perhaps, is the one from Reus through Vilaplana: a hundred hairpin turns taking you up almost 3,500ft straight up, with breathtaking views over the sea. The mountains have become a popular spot for hiking, cycling, rock-climbing (at the abandoned village of La Mussara) and other activities. The biggest village up there is **Prades**, called 'La Vila Vermella' from the striking red colour of the local stone, used in the medieval walls and many of the buildings. In the centre of the pretty, arcaded Plaça Major stands the odd, spherical Fountain of Prades from the 1500s. The source of the fountain is unknown, but it has never in known memory run dry.

Siurana, on the road to Cornudell, is a romantic spot, with its Arab castle perched atop a cliff known as 'the Balcony of El Priorat', ancient stone-built houses, and a primitive 12th-century church with an unusual and finely carved portal down by the river gorge. The castle was the Moors' last stronghold in Catalonia, where they held out until 1153. Siurana lies on the edge of the Priorat wine region, but this village has recently achieved its very own DO status, for its high-quality and intensely fruity olive oil. It's easy to see how the Moors held on so long; Siurana hangs over 2,000ft in the air. Down below, you can go kayaking on the reservoir, the **Embassement de Siurana**.

El Priorat

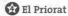 El Priorat

A monastery, a land, a wine – it's all tied together. The sum of them make up everything you need to know about this little region, scarcely 50km wide. The Prior was the man who held the keys to the Charterhouse of Scala Dei, which owned just about everything here. The wine his monks learned to make is still the Priorat's very identity, and has become one of Catalonia's finest.

El Priorat's growers had been winning medals back in the 1880s and 90s, before the phylloxera hit. For decades afterwards, there wasn't much ambition left, and much of the old knowledge and techniques were lost. Things began to change radically in the 1970s and '80s. As in so many other ways in those fizzy post-Franco years, the Catalans were waking up in a hurry. A new generation of vintners rebuilt the medieval terraces, planted new stock, and hit the books, trying to recapture the old Carthusian magic. They did

Catalan Quintessence: El Priorat and Montsant Wines

El Priorat wines are complex blends, often using five or more different varieties of grape. *Garnacha* (grenache) was the original, and *cariñena* (carignan) the first new variety to be planted after the phylloxera decimated the original vines after 1900. Now, besides these, cabernet sauvignon and syrah are also common.

The newly famous names of El Priorat are mostly small, artisanal operations, many only ten hectares or less. Getting great wine out of stony soil, in a climate that tends to extremes, is an art. They baby their low-yielding vines, and then they hand-pick the grapes. Lately, some big interests have been moving in, planting large vineyards on the higher slopes; there's concern that these might eventually lower the Priorat's reputation.

Many of the best-known producers are around the village of **Gratallops**, where the Priorat wine revolution began. These include **Clos Mogador**, **Clos Erasmus** and the current superstar of El Priorat, **Álvaro Palacios**, whose l'Ermita wine has won top prizes all over the world (some of their other labels, such as Les Terrasses, are a little more affordable). **Costers del Siurana**, one of the most renowned estates (makers of Clos de l'Obac), has opened a restaurant for lunch and wine-tastings (*t 977 83 90 36*).

In addition to Priorat, this little corner of Catalonia also produces DO Montsant wines, red and white, in a doughnut-shaped area that neatly surrounds the very small kingdom of El Priorat. Montsant, made by about forty producers, uses the same grapes; the difference is in the soil. This too is an up-and-coming denomination; though the DO was granted only in 2002, some Montsant labels are already getting rave reviews and commanding high prices – still, they are still considered one of the best values in Spain. The co-operative **Celler Capçanes** (*t 977 17 83 19*) in the village of that name makes a variety of wines including Flor de Primavera, which they modestly suggest might be the best kosher wine in the world. The co-operative offers tastings and tours on weekends, excursions around the area and even **air tours**.

their work so well that nowadays the best El Priorats are counted among the finest wines in the world.

It all began when the monks arrived from Provence in the 12th century, bringing the first grenache grapes with them. Long before chartreuse was invented, even before their Baroque-era slide into high-living decadence, Carthusians knew a thing or two about drink. It started innocently enough, with the order's vocation in medicine and pharmacy. One medieval Carthusian scholar wrote of alcohol as the fifth element, the quintessence, and sovereign against any imbalance in the body's humours.

No one knows how they ended up in El Priorat, but we might suspect that someone tipped them off, that some wine-bibbing monkish scout sent a note to the Charterhouse saying that here, in these obscure hills lately reclaimed from the Moors, was the perfect soil for wine. What makes it special, they say, is the slate bedrock, which pushes up a layer of chips on the surface to keep the roots moist while it gives the soil an extra helping of useful minerals. Catalan vintners call this stony soil *llicorella*, and the stuff it produces can be drunk young, or put away for amazingly long periods – up to 50 years, it has been claimed. It also makes El Priorat one of the world's most potent wines – some labels go up to 24 per cent.

Falset, the modern capital of El Priorat, is an attractive village with a castle and an ensemble of medieval and Renaissance buildings around its arcaded *plaça*. Like so many villages of western Catalonia, it has a lovely Modernista **Bodega Cooperativa** by César Martinell (1888–1973). Martinell was one of the great architects of Catalonia's golden age. He studied with Gaudí, and worked with him on the Sagrada Família, but the gods of architecture had a most peculiar destiny reserved for him. Martinell ended up spending much of his life designing wine *bodegas* – over 40 of them, mostly in the villages of Tarragona province. That was the hand he was dealt, and, like the true artist he was, he made them the most beautiful, most functional wine *bodegas* ever built. Architectural historians and wine-makers note how cleverly and efficiently he arranged the interior spaces, but, for us non-specialists, the striking thing will be the soaring parabolic arches he learned from Gaudí, built in brick with an ingenious system of supporting columns.

Once you're out of Falset and onto the back roads, you'll see just how peculiar a place El Priorat really is. Those back roads are narrow, and they tend to meander about as if they've had a little too much El Priorat wine. Here and there outcrops of the metamorphic slate stick up between the vineyards, and sometimes the striations are as twisty as the roads. Villages perch high in the air, and if you manage to get inside them there's no place to park.

What do you do in the Priorat besides drink? Choices are limited. Hiking is becoming increasingly popular, and there is a movement to clear and mark the area's ancient pathways. Or you might drive over to **Bellmunt de Priorato** and its **Museu de les Mines**, where they'll take you down for guided tours of the nine miles of tunnels where they once mined lead. Or go to **Gratallops** and take a ride on the world's shortest **tramway** – 10 metres long. Built from bits of old Barcelona trams by a private collector, it really doesn't go anywhere, and it doesn't care.

There isn't a lot left of the old charterhouse, **Scala Dei** in the village of **Escaladei**. After the dissolution of Spain's monasteries in 1835 it was abandoned and eventually fell into ruin. The local people were delighted to be rid of the monks, along with their rents and tithes, and they helped themselves to most of the stones. The monastery got its name, the story goes, when a shepherd had a vision of a stairway with angels ascending to heaven. Scala Dei was the first Carthusian establishment in Spain, and the head of all those that followed. It's worth a visit for the stunning, isolated setting under the Montsant cliffs. Lone arches still stand, along with part of the church façade, to give an idea of what sumptuous digs this once must have been. One of the original Carthusian cells has been recreated for visitors.

Museu de les Mines
t 977 83 05 78; open July–15 Sept Tues–Sat 11–1 and 5–7, Sun 11–1.30; 16 Sept–June Sat and Sun 11–1.30; adm

Tramway
open usually at weekends 5–7pm

Scala Dei
open June–Sept Tues–Sun 10–1 and 4–7; Oct–May Tues–Sun 10–1 and 3–5; adm

Market Days in the Prades Mountains and El Priorat

Prades, Tuesday, Saturday; **Alcover**, Tuesday; **Falset**, Tuesday; **Ulldemolins**, Tuesday, Thursday.

Where to Stay and Eat in the Prades Mountains and El Priorat

Prades ✉ 43664

*Espasa, C/Sant Roc, **t** 977 86 80 23 (€). Most people come up to these mountains as a day trip, so this is the only hotel in town; simple but good.

La Botiga, Plaça Major, **t** 977 86 83 21 (€€). Under the arches of the Plaça Major, a fine restaurant serving hearty mountain favourites: stews, snails, duck, and rabbit with chestnuts.

Alcover ✉ 43460

Mas la Torre, **t** 977 26 92 71 (€€). Way up in the hills east of Prades, near the hamlet of Mont-Ral, four gracious rooms on a working farm.

Falset ✉ 43740

***Sport, C/Miquel Barceló 6, **t** 977 83 00 78, *www.hostalsport.com* (€€). Built in the 1920s and recently remodeled; attractive rooms and a restaurant.

Fonda Nacional, Av. Catalonia 8, **t** 977 83 01 57 (€). Excellent value, with a

decent restaurant; all of the rooms have shared bathrooms.

El Celler d'Aspic, C/Miquel Barceló, **t** 977 83 12 46 (€€€). Set in Martinell's co-operative building, a restaurant with style and quality to match the wines. The menus offer some seafood, and unusual local cheeses.

Quinoa, C/Miquel Barceló, **t** 977 83 04 31 (€€). Next to the Celler d'Aspic, and a more economical choice. Tasty rice and seafood, plus some exotic and vegetarian dishes.

Bellmunt de Priorat ✉ 43738

Economat de les Mines, C/Clos, **t** 977 83 09 96 (€€). Set in the mine's old company store, with great views over the village below.

Gratallops ✉ 43737

Cal Llop, C/de Dalt 21, **t** 977 83 95 02, *www.cal-llop.com* (€€€). A swanky new boutique hotel at the heart of the village. This is Catalonia, and the emphasis is on high design.

La Cassola, on the T710 towards Falset, **t** 977 26 21 46 (€€). Right at the heart of the wine country, an elegant but laid-back restaurant with some unusual dishes (rabbit with snails!).

Porrera ✉ 43739

La Cooperativa, Carrer Unió, **t** 977 82 83 78 (€€). A delightful restaurant that has recently opened in the village's wine co-operative. Surprising dishes from cod to curries, and plenty of wine from the vines you see out the window.

El Celler d'Aspic >>

ⓘ **Prades >**
Plaça Major 2,
t 977 86 83 02

ⓘ **Escaladei**
Ctra de la Cartoixa,
t 977 86 83 02

ⓘ **Falset >**
C/Sant Marcel 2,
t 977 83 11 50

La Cooperativa >>

The Costa Daurada South from Tarragona

Spain's 'Golden Coast' continues on past Tarragona out towards the delta of the Ebro. While its beaches are often long and even gold-coloured, they lack that most elusive quality, charm. This side (at least once you get past Cambrils) isn't nearly as intense as the other side of Tarragona. The scenery is siesta-sleepy, and the resorts attract old folks enjoying the sun and tranquillity, and families with young children who require nothing more than good castle-building sand, shallow sea, and their peers for a perfect holiday (most of the visitors are Spanish and French).

Getting to and around the Costa Daurada south from Tarragona

Both Salou and Cambrils have **train** connections with Tarragona and Barcelona along the coastal route, as well as frequent **bus** connections.

Salou is a major bus node; the station on Passeig Jaume I serves several different lines, with connections not only to Reus airport and other local destinations but to cities throughout Spain and beyond.

In summer, everyone in Salou gets around by the *trenet*, or tourist road-train, known to the large community of jaded ex-pats as the 'Wally Wagon'. It operates three routes, which will get you all over Salou and to adjacent Port Aventura.

Port Aventura, the Biggest Theme Park in the Med

Port Aventura
t 0800 9665 40, www.portaventura. co.uk; open year-round, but closed at periods subject to change; check website for up-to-date information and opening times; tickets available online; crrent one-day admission €42 for adults, €33.50 children, discounts for multi-day tickets and night tickets (7pm to midnight)

Beginning from Tarragona, the first few steps aren't so promising. The first attraction is a Mordor-like skyline of smokestacks and petroleum towers at the enormous industrial area at **Vila Seca**. Just inland, is **Port Aventura**, the Catalan answer to Eurodisney, with a watery annexe called Caribe Aquatic Park. The park is divided into five zones, connected by boats and Mickey-Mousey steam trains. In the Mediterranean Zone there's an ever-so-charming fishing village, though if you step on a boat you're likely to end up in China. In this zone, they'll bundle you on an ultra-modern, ultra-speedy rollercoaster called the Dragon Khan that looks as if it was designed by Santiago Calatrava on crack, with a little help from Dr Seuss.

Climb back on the boat or the steam train and the hallucinations multiply. You can cruise under the Polynesian seas with a friendly talking dolphin to guide you, or experience a simulated buffalo stampede in the Wild West. Best of all perhaps is the Mexico Zone, which seems to be based on some brooding Aztec ritual of human sacrifice, possibly yours. Here, after the Templo del Fuego fun fair, you will be invited to the indigenous ceremony of the Plumed Serpent, which (surprise!) involves being whirled at indecent speeds around the Sacred Totem Pole.

Each zone contains a playground, restaurants, shows, boat rides and souvenir shops, all tarted up to some stereotype from the prevailing theme. It's enough to make any normal mom and dad gag, but Port Aventura redeems itself with the pure kitsch hilarity of it all. Some of the shows aren't bad either: come after dark in July or August when the sweaty crowds are at their sweatiest and crowdiest to see such trippy after-dark spectaculars as the 'Fiestaventura' and the 'Aquamusic', in the Mediterranean zone.

Salou and Cambrils

After Port Aventura and the promontory of Cap Salou, you're at the southern end of the Tarragona-Reus conurbation, specifically in the tastefully landscaped roundabouts of **Salou**, the biggest and brashest package-tour ghetto on the Costa Daurada. You wouldn't guess it, but there is an old settlement here. Jaume the Conqueror sailed off from Salou in 1229 to do some conquering, in this case the island of Mallorca. He wouldn't know the place today. Turn a corner, and behind a long wall of plate glass windows a thousand English and Scandinavian ladies are playing bingo. Around the next bend, another seafront palace opens to vistas of waltzing blue-rinse battalions.

Salou is a family kind of place; it is an agreeable and civilized city by the sea, though the air of a tourist bubble is unmistakable. A city it undeniably is, with a bit of old town, built around a 1530s blockhouse called the **Torre Vella**, which now houses a small **museum of enamelwork** from around the world. Beyond that is a huge modern Eixample, a long and attractive beachfront promenade named for King Jaume, a market district with a busy weekly street market on Via Roma, and a lovely fountain with an impressive colour and light show called the **Font Lluminosa**, designed by Carles Buigas, the mad genius who created Barcelona's Font Magica.

Everyone in **Cambrils** will tell you that Cambrils is a much nicer resort: less frenetic, smaller, more convivial. That's about half true, Cambrils is an old fishing village (with one of Catalonia's biggest fleets) that luck has made into an overspill suburb of Salou. Its old town has another old defense tower, a lot of very good fish restaurants, a mile or two of *urbanizaciones* (housing estates), and another endless beach beyond the old fishing harbour.

The **Museu d'Història** on Via Augusta is built in an old water mill, recently restored and grinding flour once again. There's a small archaeological collection in this location, but this ambitious little museum is really spread all over Cambrils. They'll direct you to the other sites; the **Torre de l'Hermita**, a medieval watchtower with exhibits on medieval Cambrils, the **Torre del Port** in the centre of the waterfront, and an **Agricultural Museum**, all with the same hours and joint admission. The Marques de Marianao, from a local family that had most of its interests in Cuba, built Cambrils' other attraction, the **Parc Sama** in 1882. This is a large botanical garden, designed to recapture some of the beauty of the Caribbean island that was then the jewel in Spain's empire. Some of the plants, though, come from as far afield as Brazil and Australia; highlights include parterres of palms, cypresses and orange trees and a two-acre lake studded with fantasy islands.

About 15km inland from Cambrils is the pretty village of **Riudecanyes**, where the seven medieval streets were named after the seven days of the week. The only reason for coming up here though is the the fortified hilltop **Monestir de Sant Miquel d'Escornalbou** with a 12th-century church, a collection of prints and ceramics that belonged to the last owner, and a lovely belvedere with views down to the sea.

Torre Vella museum of enamelwork
open by appointment,
t 977 38 32 35

Museu d'Història
open June–Aug
Tues–Sat 11–2 and 6–9,
Sun 11–2; Sept–May Sat
11–2 and 5–8, Sun 11–2;
adm; ring t 977 97
45 28 for mill
demonstration times

Parc Sama
open daily when it's
not raining, from 10 to
about sunset; adm

Monestir de Sant Miquel d'Escornalbou
t 977 83 40 07; open
summer Tues–Sun 10–1
and 4–7.30; winter
Tues–Sun 10–1.30
and 3–5.30; adm

10

Tarragona Province | The Costa Daurada South from Tarragona

Back on the coast, heading south, the next town tried to drum up some notoriety by dubbing itself 'Miami Beach': **Miami Platja**. Despite its name, you couldn't ask for a more anonymous, innocuous resort; Interpol will never find you here. Something worse might: up in the hills above Miami you can visit **Pratdip**, and learn about the *dips*, spectral vampire dogs that used to terrorize the countryside, sucking the blood from their human and animal victims. There's one figured on the village coat of arms, and some more on a retable in the church. In some versions of the legend they are hellacious uncanny beasts with glowing eyes, in others they seem more like border collies gone radically wrong. You'll always know one if you see it; they're black and white, with one lame front leg.

L'Ametlla del Mar

After Miami Beach is a long, empty stretch of coast, ending in a modest little charmer at the end of the Costa Daurada, **L'Ametlla del Mar**. Like Cambrils, this is a working fishing village. Unlike Cambrils, it's still small and peaceful, and not yet overbuilt. People come for the tranquillity, and to tour around the attractive shoreline on foot or by boat. There is no big beach of the kind that has attracted so much development to other parts of the Costa, but maybe something better: about two dozen little coves with small, clean beaches on them. Finding some of them will require some exploring, but the tourist office (*see* p.273) will give you a good map.

Ametlla goes back only to the 1770s when some families of fishermen from Valencia settled, bringing new life to a stretch of coast that had become abandoned due to marauders and malaria. Down by the fishing port there is a pair of modest hotels, and tapas are never in short supply. Up by the main coastal road, the N340, the Museu de Ceràmica has traditional pottery from all over Spain and beyond.

Museu de
Ceràmica
*t 977 48 68 10; open
summer Mon–Fri 10–2
and 4–8; winter Sun
10–2; adm*

Market Days
South of Tarragona

Cambrils, Wednesday; **Mont-Roig del Camp**, Friday; **Vandellós**, Monday; **Ametlla de Mar**, Monday.

Where to Stay and Eat
South of Tarragona

This is package tour country, jam-packed with two- and three-star establishments, all relatively new and all pretty much alike. You don't want to be here in the summer madness, especially in Salou or Cambrils, but the rest of the year – and most hotels do stay open – either of these towns can be an pleasant stopover. You should get a discount in the off season in the more expensive places.

Salou ✉ 43840

***San Diego**, C/Penedès 23, t 977 38 07 16 (€€€–€€). Typical package hotel, but a good one, especially if you have kids; playground and pool.

***Caspel, C/Alfons V 9, **t** 977 38 02 07, *www.hotel-caspel.com* (€€). One of the best-value hotels on the Costa Daurada; central and near the beach. Excellent facilities include a pool.

*Niza, C/Barcelona 23, **t** 977 38 13 91 (€). A short walk to the beach, with simple, cheap accommodation near the train station.

*El Recó, C/Vaporet 8, Platge de Racó, **t** 977 37 02 16 (€). By the beach in the quieter part of town, Cap de Salou.

Arena, Passeig Jaume I, **t** 977 38 40 00, *www.arenarestaurant.com* (€€€). Very refined cooking, with innovative starters with a French touch (come here if you like goat's cheese); serves a great black rice paella. The Arena has one 'surprise day' each month (look on their website) which might involve wine-tastings, a special dish or even cooking lessons.

Portofino, Passeig Jaume I, **t** 977 38 07 10 (€€). Italian pasta and pizzas.

Terramar, C/Espigó del Moll, **t** 977 38 31 24 (€€). Tasty seafood and tapas at reasonable prices.

Cambrils ✉ 43850

Cambrils is known around Catalonia for its restaurants, and standards are high. *Bon profit!*

****Mónica, C/Galceran Marquet 1, **t** 977 79 36 78 *www.hotelmonica.com* (€€€€–€€€). Centrally located and luxurious. with a garden, pool and spa; rates range from good-bargain standard rooms to suites with solarium. Your bike is very welcome; this hotel is popular with pro-bicycle racers for training and there's a bike mechanic on call.

***Rovira, Avda Diputació 6, **t** 977 36 09 00, *www.hotelrovira.com* (€€€–€€). A decent beach choice, with a pool and a good seafood restaurant (€€€).

Can Solé, C/Ramon Llull 19, **t 977 36 17 68 (€). A few blocks from the beach and the restaurant strip. Friendly, talkative folks.

*Miramar, Passeig Miramar 30, **t** 977 36 00 63 (€). They've been around a long time, and, besides cheap rooms

on the beachfront, they run a fine restaurant (€€), still one of the best places for an honest seafood dinner on the waterfront.

Can Bosch, Rambla Jaume I 19, **t** 977 36 00 19 (€€€). Another culinary landmark in the region, in a central and elegant location. Creative cooking and a big wine list; for a memorable splurge there's a €65 *menú degustació*.

Casa Gatell, Pg Miramar 26, **t** 977 36 00 57 (€€€). One of the Michelin-starred seafood restaurants run by the Gatell dynasty of chefs. This one has a wonderful terrace on the port and is famous for its Catalan version of *bouillabaisse*, and for a seafood sampler called *entremesos* Gatell.

Fragata, C/Mont-Roig 9, **t** 977 36 00 23 (€€€–€€). Very tasty *bacallà* and some surprising dishes, plus a good inexpensive *menú*.

Méson La Barbacoa, C/Balears 34, **t** 977 79 48 01 (€€). If you ever get tired of fish, try this place for Catalan *charcuterie* and barbecued meats.

Miami Platja ✉ 43892

****Pino Alto, Urb Pino Alto, **t** 977 81 10 00, *www.hotelpinoalto.com* (€€€–€€). Well-designed complex with a hotel and apartments; plenty of facilities: two pools, gym, sauna, hydromassage, squash court; good bargain off season.

L'Ametlla del Mar ✉ 43860

L'Alguer, C/Mar 20, **t 977 49 33 72 (€€–€). Clean and modern, up on the hill above the port; ask for a room with a sea view.

*Hotel del Port, C/Major 11, **t** 977 45 70 43 (€€–€). Another good choice, with rooms overlooking the port.

Café Xavier, C/Major 17, **t** 977 49 36 49 (€€). Part of the Hotel del Port. Excellent value for seafood: fresh fish, *calamars a la romana*, black rice. Outside tables; if you stay in L'Ametlla you might end up coming every day.

There are plenty of other places for seafood and tapas around the fishing port on C/Major. **La Cova** and **La Nau** also have outside tables.

(★) **Arena** >

(i) **Miami Platja** >>
Plaça Tarragona,
t *977 81 09 78*

(i) **Cambrils** >
Pg de les Palmares,
t *902 15 47 41*

(i) **L'Ametlla del Mar** >>
Plaça Jaume I,
t *977 35 01 02,*
www.ametlla delmar.org

(★) **Miramar** >

The Ebro Delta

It's time to introduce the Ebro (Ebre in Catalan), Spain's most voluminous river if not quite its longest. The Ebro starts far to the west in the Cantabrian mountains. The Romans called it Iberus Flumen, and from that we get the name of Iberia. Until the Romans pushed the Carthaginians out of Spain in the Second Punic War, this river was the Roman-Carthaginian border. It became a border again for a while in 1938 – between Nationalist and Republican Spain, and the long struggle over its course made for the biggest battle of the Civil War (see p.281).

The Ebro isn't much good for navigation; Spain's dry climate makes it too shallow in summer. But fisherman love it; some of the biggest catfish and carp in Europe live in the Catalan and Aragonese stretches of the river. There may be some big changes; all this water in a thirsty country isn't likely to be left flowing out to sea forever. Under former Prime Minister Aznar, the Spanish and Catalan regional governments cooked up something called the National Water Plan (PNH), which proposed damming the Ebro and diverting some of its waters to the city of Barcelona, and some to Spain's parched but fertile southeast for agriculture. Spain's environmentalists counter-attacked fiercely, pointing out that removing too much of the river's water could have catastrophic effects on the delta, with its unique flora and fauna, its agriculture and fishing. Right now the PNH is on the shelf, but the anti-dam groups are keeping a close eye on the politicians just in case.

As deltas go, the Ebro's isn't very old. Back in Roman times the town of Amposta was a busy port; now it's marooned some 30km upstream. Ironically, the natural wetlands the environmentalists are struggling to save are themselves the product of a man-made ecological disaster. A thousand years ago, the vast Iberian plateau was almost entirely under trees, and it was said that a squirrel could travel from Extremadura to the Pyrenees without touching the ground. Deforestation began during the Reconquista as Castile, Leon and Aragon were settled by a burgeoning Christian population. Then, during the mad, violent scramble for booty and power that Spain still calls its 'Golden Age', in the 16th–18th centuries, enormous areas were cleared for land speculation, to make money to replenish the eternal deficits of kings and princes.

This deforestation created the wasted, empty landscapes we see all over central Spain today, and much of the Iberian plateau's best topsoil ended up in a mushrooming Ebro delta, where it now grows rice for Spain's paellas. A century ago this delta was a desolation cursed by malaria; today, over 60 per cent of it is under rice paddies, dotted with new villages that look a little rough, but prosperous and happy.

Oddly enough, the delta is currently shrinking. Upstream dams and a lower rate of soil erosion mean that the sea is washing it away faster than the Ebro can rebuild it. If there is any serious rise in the level of the Mediterranean, half of the delta could be underwater in another century.

Meanwhile, the paddies and rice-processing plants occupy the centre of the delta; everything around the edges is devoted to the waterfowl – some 300 species of them – and the tourists who come to see them. Since the 1980s, the fringes of the delta have been protected as the Parc Natural del Delta de l'Ebre.

The park's headquarters and information office lies at the entrance to the village of **Deltebre**, right in the middle of the delta. This includes an Ecomuseu with an interesting little aquarium and exhibits on the delta's flora and fauna, on its traditional life and work, and on the ecological issues related to its upkeep and survival. Deltebre itself, the delta's little capital, is a new raw sort of place, with the only accommodation around. It spreads along the river, and, since there are no bridges, if you want to get across you'll have to avail yourself of the services of one of the three *trasbordadores*, little private ferries that can take two or three cars across at a time. On this same stretch of the river are places to rent boats and bicycles, as well as cruise boats that will take you for a couple of hours, or half-day tours, around the delta and its lagoons.

Among the places of interest in the park is the **Estany de l'Encanyissada**, a lagoon and major bird area with bike paths, and a park information office in the Casa de la Fusta. This is the place to visit if you mean to do any serious bird-watching; there are exhibits on many of the species that call the delta home. The **Punta de la Banya** is a small island near Encanyissada, connected to the southern tip of the delta by a sand spit, part of a string of beaches that line the delta's southern edge. There are more beaches on the northern side, notably at **Punta del Fangar**, where sunny summer days sometimes produce mirages over the water. The next lagoon east, **El Canal Vell**, is where you're most likely to see flamingos.

The coastal road (N340) here marks the landward boundary of the delta; following it, you'll pass through a string of villages that marked the shoreline before the delta was born. At the northern end of the delta, **L'Ampolla** is a fishing village that has grown into a fair-sized town, famous for oysters (the ones grown here are Japanese oysters, *casostrea gigas*, and pretty tasty too). There's nothing picturesque about L'Ampolla, and it won't trouble you with sightseeing, but it's a good place for a seafood dinner, or an afternoon on the beach. Like L'Ametlla, L'Ampolla has lots of little beaches and coves around its strip of coast.

In the hills above L'Ampolla, **El Perelló** has some **Roman remains**, including a long surviving stretch of the Via Augusta, and also a

Ecomuseu
t 977 48 96 79; open Mon–Sat 10–2 and 3–6, Sun 10–2

El Perelló Roman remains
usually not open to the public, but ring the tourist office, t 977 49 10 21, to see if they can get you in

painted cave called Cabrafeixet, decorated with hunting scenes similar to those at Ulldecona (*see* below). **Amposta** was a port in ancient times; now it's a lively and noisy place with a little suspension bridge over the Ebro built in 1918 and a small archaeological museum.

Sant Carles de la Rápita, at the southern end of the delta, is splendidly located on Europe's largest natural harbour, the Port dels Alfacs. In 1780 Charles III wanted to take advantage of nature's gift and make this a great seaport, to replace marooned Amposta as a port and bring some economic life to the area. Little came of it, but today Sant Carles is a busy resort in summer, popular with Barcelonins though of no special charm, except around the old fishing port, where boats are still made the old-fashioned way.

Catalonia's Southern Tip

Continuing south on the coastal road, we'll take you as far as **Alcanar**, the southernmost town in Catalonia. Alcanar has a beach, and above the road north to Ulldecona you'll see a bowl-shaped hill crowned with what was the ancient town of **La Moleta del Remei**. Occupied in the 7th–2nd centuries BC, La Moleta belonged to the Iberian tribe called the Ilercavons.

La Moleta del Remei
open July–Sept Sat–Sun 5–8; Oct–June Sun 11–2; to book a guided tour ring
t 977 73 76 39

Up in the hills, across the motorway from Alcanar, **Ulldecona**, a well-kept little town with a castle begun by the Moors, a bit of a medieval centre with a Catalan Gothic church, and a few Modernista buildings, including three by César Martinell. Today, though, Ulldecona is best known for its cave art, discovered only in 1975. This consists of thirteen **caves** in the Godall hills north of town, of which only one can be visited right now, by guided tours arranged through the tourist office (*see* p.277). They're not nearly as old as the famous paleolithic cave art in Cantabria or southwest France – only *c.* 8,000 years. Neither are they as artistically sophisticated. Still, they are vigorous, colourful works, mostly hunting scenes with deer and other animals along with stick-figure representations of hunters, some with bows.

Tourist Information and Services in the Ebro Delta

ⓘ **Amposta**
Avda Sant Jaume I,
t 977 70 34 53

ⓘ **L'Ampolla**
Plaça González Isla,
t 977 46 00 18

There is an information office for the **Parc Natural** at C/Dr. Marti Buera 22, Deltebre, **t** 977 48 96 79. The **Deltarium**, on the T340 between Deltebre and the river's mouth, **t** 977 48 10 30, is an educational park with typical animals and exhibits. There's a café, restaurant, and shop and they also conduct tours, and rent bikes.

Market Days in the Ebro Delta

Deltebre, Saturday; **L'Ampolla**, Wednesday; **El Perelló**, Saturday; **Amposta**, Tuesday; **Sant Carles de la Ràpita**, Saturday; Ulldecona, Friday.

Where to Stay and Eat in the Ebro Delta

Deltebre ✉ 43580

****Delta**, Avda del Canal, t 977 48 00 46, www.deltahotel.es (€€). A nice hotel in an unlikely setting; extensive grounds with a lagoon on the edge of town. There's a pool, and maybe the best restaurant around (€€).

***Rull**, Avda Esportiva 155, t 977 48 77 28, www.hotelrull.com (€€). Plain but very comfortable modern hotel outside Deltebre, with a pool and restaurant (€€).

El Faro, Avda Goles Ebre 257, t 977 48 02 29 (€). A simple and unpretentious hotel-restaurant on Deltebre's main street.

Nuri, Riumar, t 977 48 01 28 (€€). At the end of the road east from Deltebre, this is a fine restaurant in a converted barn.

Olmos, t 977 48 05 48 (€€–€). Olmos will fill you up with river eels in a happy, laid-back bar-restaurant with outside tables.

Sant Carles de la Ràpita ✉ 43540

****Miami Mar**, Passeig Marítim 18, t 977 74 58 59, www.miamicanpons.com (€€€€–€€€). Right on the beach, with a pool, and spacious rooms with balconies. A family establishment that grew out of a great restaurant, **Can Pons** (€€€).

****P Agusti**, C/Pilar 23, t 977 74 04 27 (€). First-rate bargain *hostal* in the town centre; also rents studios and apartments. Roof garden and parking.

***Juanito Platja**, Pg Marítim s/n, t 977 74 04 62, www.juanitoplatja.com (€). Delightful, simple beach hotel run by a friendly family; restaurant (€€€–€€).

Can Vicent, C/Carmen 28, t 977 74 16 13 (€€€–€€). A convivial seafood palace right on the port.

Casa Ramón, C/Arsenal, t 977 74 23 58 (€€€–€€). Reasonably priced seafood and a good wine list. Also inexpensive rooms, and they arrange Delta tours.

Ulldecona ✉ 43550

Bon Lloc, Ctra de Vinaròs, t 977 57 30 16, www.hotelbonlloc.es (€). A small and gracious country inn with a pool and an excellent restaurant: good farm cooking and local wines.

El Rajolar, Ctra La Sénia, t 977 57 31 70, www.elrajolar.com (€€). Nice rooms with a pool and garden,and a restaurant (€€) that specializes in grills and barbecued meats and fish.

Les Moles, Ctra La Sénia, t 977 57 32 24 (€€€–€€). The area's prize-winning restaurant, with unusual seafood pasta dishes. Good value lunch menu or splurge for the €52 tasting menu.

Les Cases d'Alcanar ✉ 43569

Racó del Port, Pg Marítim, t 977 73 70 50 (€€). Les Cases is a little fishing village just outside Alcanar. Here by the port is an unpretentious seafood spot with some good cooking.

Deltebre Plaça Vint de Maig, t 977 48 70 67

Ulldecona t 977 57 33 94

Bon Lloc

Sant Carles de la Ràpita Plaça Carles III 13, t 977 74 46 24

Tortosa and Around

If you want to bet on the future of Tortosa, there are some glorious, empty Modernista buildings here you could get for a song. But betting on Tortosa is problematic. It's a grim old town, weathered into a uniform shade of dingy brown. No one seems to like it much. The Catalans regard it as somehow peculiar, and the natives call themselves Tortosans rather than Catalans. Publius Cornelius Scipio (father of Scipio Africanus), after wrecking the place in 215 BC in the Punic Wars, refounded it and gave it the new name Dertusa, 'city of stones'.

Tortosa knew some good days as the capital of a Moorish *taifa*, and it must have enjoyed some prosperity under the Christians too, as evidenced by its impressive Gothic cathedral. Medieval

Tortosa had a large and sophisticated Jewish community and an important Templar commandery. Little has been heard from it since. The town suffered greatly in the Civil War, when the Battle of the Ebro was raging nearby, and today much of the historic centre is still a ruin, half abandoned and half immigrant slum. They're finally getting around to fixing it up now. It's about time.

The best thing about Tortosa is its **market**, an early Modernista work (1884) covering an entire block along the Ebro. From here, look up and you can see **La Suda**, the dramatic citadel that was a Roman-Iberian acropolis, an Arab palace and a Templar castle before getting blown to smithereens in 1938. After the war the government picked up the pieces and reassembled them as a *parador* (*see* p.282). Look out over the river, and you'll see a bizarre rusty column covered with inscrutable figures; this is the *Monument to the Battle of the Ebro*, built under Franco.

Underneath La Suda, you might have noticed a hulking stone mass with bushes growing out the top. This is the **cathedral**, one of Catalonia's largest. The incredible, crumbling façade, mostly from the 18th century, can't decide whether it wants to be neoclassical or perhaps Mexican Baroque. Beyond it, though, there's a fine Gothic interior with a beautiful apse, a pretty cloister with a fountain at its centre, and some fine chapels, especially that of the city's patroness, Nostra Senyora de la Santa Cinta. With luck the cathedral will be open by the time you read this; big chunks have been falling off it, and major repairs are under way.

Further up, near La Suda on the Costa del Castell, Tortosa's back streets hide a Renaissance jewel, the **Reials Col.legis**, founded by Emperor Charles V himself in 1544. One of the two buildings, the College of Sant Jaume, has a glorious arcaded courtyard. Nearby, the church of **Sant Doménec** houses the small archaeological collection of the **Museu Municipal**.

Museu Municipal
*open Mon–Sat
11–2; adm*

Horta de Sant Joan and Benifallet

South of Tortosa, the Ebro valley is lush and green, lined with gardens and even orange groves. North of the city, though, it climbs into some dramatic scenery, rugged, forested mountains where human habitations are few and far between. There aren't any bridges for 30km north of the city. If you take the west bank, roads leading up into the hills will try to entice you into the **Parque Natural dels Ports** (Puertos de Beseit in Castillian), set around the slopes of 4,747ft Mount Caro on the borders of Catalonia, Aragon and Valencia. The park isn't well developed for tourism – there aren't even any roads through, which makes it ideal for serious hikers and for the Spanish mountain goat, which thrives in great numbers. For an introduction, at **Horta de Sant Joan** (just north of Xerta) there's an **Ecomuseu** and visitors' centre.

✪ **Horta de Sant Joan**

Ecomuseu
*open Tues–Fri and Sun
11–1.30, Sat 5–7.30*

Horta, a little labyrinth of rugged stone streets, is an attractive, typically Catalan village. The Templars once ruled here too, and they began the interesting **Convent de Sant Salvador** 2km outside town, with a church and cloister still in good shape. Horta's current fame, though, is that it briefly served as the home of Pablo Picasso, in 1898 and again in 1909. Of course, every place where Picasso spent more than half an hour has tried to make a cottage industry out of it, but the artist does seem to have been greatly influenced by this village and its rural life. 'Everything I know I learned in Horta,' he is recorded as saying. The paintings of the village he finished here on his second trip are landmarks in the development of cubism. You can learn about them at the **Centre Picasso**.

If you take the east bank of the Ebro north from Tortosa, you'll pass **Tivanys**. Here another Iberian settlement can be inspected on the hills above the modern village. Further on comes **Benifallet** and the **Coves de Benifallet**. There are a number of caves here, including the Cova de Cullas, with some Neolithic-era paintings, but the main atraction is two beautiful stalactite caves, the Cova Meravelles and the Cova del Dos.

Centre Picasso
t 977 43 53 30, www.centrepicasso.cat; open summer Tues–Fri and Sun 11–2, Sat 5–8; winter Tues–Sun 11–1.30; adm

Coves de Benifallet
open summer daily 10–2 and 4–7.30; winter Fri–Sun 10–2 and 4–6.30; adm

Gandesa

Like everything else in this part of the Ebro valley, Gandesa was once Templar property. That's about the whole of its history, save for a few terrible months in 1938 when this village of 2,600 was in the world's headlines every day, as the focal point of the Battle of the Ebro, the climactic battle of the Spanish Civil War.

As the main objective of the last great Republican offensive, Gandesa took a lot of blows, and it had to be almost completely rebuilt. A number of relics do remain though, from what must have been a rather genteel past. The church of **L'Assumpció** is a dull 18th-century building, but it retains a fascinating portal from its medieval predecessor, decorated with minute, precise carvings of scenes and figures that have had the Romanesque experts guessing for a long time. Next to it stands a Renaissance town hall, the **Casa de la Vila**, and nearby is the modest Templar commandery, the **Palacio del Castellà**, for centuries the local jail.

Gandesa is a wine centre, home of the Terra Alta denomination, which includes a number of wines made mostly from macabeo and *garnacha* (grenache) grapes. Gandesa's **Bodega Cooperativa**, built in 1919, is one of the first and most spectacular of the many designed by Cesár Martinell, with soaring brick parabolic arches and 'Catalan' vaulting, ideas that the architect developed here.

Most visitors to Gandesa, though, are interested in the war, and they get all they can use at CEBE, the **Centre d'Estudis de la Batalla de l'Ebre** on Avda Catalunya. Exhibits include arms and relics from the battle, posters, and even a reconstruction of a Republican

Bodega Cooperativa
t 977 420 017, www.coopgandesa.com

Centre d'Estudis de la Batalla de l'Ebre
t 977 420 760, www.tinet.org/~cebe; open Mon–Fri 10–2 and 4–8, Sat 10.30–2 and 4–8, Sun 10.30–2; adm

trench. Military historians say one of the reasons the Republic lost was its leaders' inability to understand modern warfare. While the Germans and Italians were teaching Franco how to fight with air power and armoured *blitzkrieg*, the Republicans were still fighting First World War-style, with trench lines and murderous frontal infantry assaults.

The high-water mark of the Republican advance was a line roughly from Xerta to Gandesa and on to Fayón. Almost all of the fighting took place between that line and the Ebro – not a very large space for 36,500 men to die in. After the war Franco's government did nothing to clean up the battlefield, or give the Republican soldiers who died there a decent burial. Even today, big storms still wash bones out from the hill slopes. Much of the area was wasteland for decades, and now it draws a strange breed of war-tourists, armed with metal detectors, hunting for relics.

Near the modern village of **Corbera d'Ebre**, northeast of Gandesa, you can visit the ruins of old Corbera (the '*poble vell*') up in the hills, abandoned after Nationalist artillery and the German Condor Legion blasted it to bits. It's an eerie place, looking pretty much as it did when the villagers left it.

Coll de Moro, where Franco made his headquarters during the battle, has yet another Iberian village under excavation. **El Pinell de Brai**, on the way to Benifallet, is a wine town, with another, less grandiose **co-operative building** by Martinell, adorned with an frieze of *azulejos* depicting the grape harvest and drunken hunters by jovial Xavier Nogués.

Miravet

We have been mentioning the Templars all through this section, and you can see what's left of their headquarters at the **Castle of Miravet**. When the order helped Ramon Berenguer IV seize the lower Ebro from the Moors in the 1150s, the king granted them vast lands that they would hold for the next century and a half. They rebuilt the Moorish castle here to oversee it all. After the order was outlawed, Miravet became one of the last Templar redoubts, falling in 1308 after a year-long siege. Luxurious as it must have been in its heyday, there's little to see inside but the fine view over the parapets. In the deathly silence that hangs over the place you can explore the Templars' Romanesque chapel, with a spiral stair to the tower, the dormitory and refectory – although, curiously, no one has ever found a trace of a chimney or kitchen. The upper patio is called the Patio de la Sang; here, in 1308, the last Templars of Miravet were beheaded.

Miravet village, spilling down from the castle to the river, is an interesting place, with its ancient steps and alleyways, its artisan potters who recreate Moorish designs, and a ferry across the Ebro.

Castle of Miravet
t 977 40 73 68; open June–Sept daily 10–1 and 4–7.30; Oct–May Tues–Sun 10–1.30 and 3–5.30; adm

Hell on the Ebro

All the vines and olives have been been carefully replanted, and all the blasted tanks and trucks long ago hauled off for scrap. It's almost impossible to tell that 70 years ago these hills witnessed the biggest battle of the Spanish Civil War.

By the summer of 1938, Republican Spain was in dire straits. Franco's Nationalists had taken the Basque lands, and pushed their way to the coast south of the Ebro, cutting the area controlled by the legitimate government in two. The Republican leadership in Valencia, largely in the hands of the Communists, decided on one big roll of the dice. They would give General Juan Modesto the best divisions the Republic had left, and make one big push to drive Franco from the Mediterranean, reunite the two Republican zones, and perhaps change the course of the war.

It began 15 minutes after midnight on Sant Jaume's Day, 25 July 1938, when Republican volunteers swam across the river and established beachheads on a broad front that extended from Amposta all the way to Mequinenza, near Lleida. At first the Loyalists advanced, in a slow and bloody fashion. Massive bombardments from the German Condor Legion eventually slowed them down. The Germans blew up all the bridges over the river, and Franco, who commanded the front personally, ordered all the dams upstream to release water, which raised the river level and made repairing the bridges more difficult.

Gandesa was the first objective of the attack, but the Republicans never quite made it even this far. The Nationalists began their counter-offensive on 1 August, as soon as the ever-cautious Franco could get enough reinforcements in place. This part of the Republican front was under the command of a bitter Communist apparatchik with little military experience, Enrique Lister, who gave an order that anyone who attempted to retreat would be shot. The battles would last for 116 days. Though the Republicans had lost the initiative and would never regain it, they had no choice but to hold on; for his part, Franco saw his chance to break the Loyalist army once and for all. Slowly through August, September, October, the front inched back towards the Ebro. On one single day near the climax, 30 October, 17,000 tons of shells and bombs fell on the Serra de Cavalls east of Gandesa.

The Battle of the Ebro was the last stand of the International Brigades, the young idealists who had come from all over the world to fight fascism in Spain. The government in Madrid cynically tossed them all into the front lines, where they bore the brunt of the casualties, and then, when little was left of the Brigades, Prime Minister Negrín announced their dissolution before the League of Nations, in a vain attempt to convince Britain and France to do something to force Franco to reciprocate, by getting rid of his German and Italian helpers.

The last broken Loyalist forces crossed back over the Ebro at Flix on 18 November (with them was war correspondent Ernest Hemingway). It had all been for nothing. The Nationalists lost only 23,000 men in total casualties, the Republicans 70,000. Their army was finished as a fighting force and, though the war dragged on for another four months, now there was no longer any doubt of the outcome. In January 1939 Franco's men would march into Barcelona.

The Battle of the Ebro is the kind of thing that most Spaniards are happy to forget, but it came back at them in February 2008, when 88-year-old Faustino Olivera of Barbastro, in Aragon, asked his doctor to remove what he thought was an old cyst in his shoulder that had begun to give him pain. It turned out to be the last bullet of the Spanish Republic still on the job. Olivera, a Nationalist conscript, took the shot while defending a position on the Ebro and somehow carried it with him unawares for 70 years.

Not many intrepid visitors press any further up the Ebro valley. Past **Riba-Roja** the working stretch of the Ebro begins, with a string of dams and reservoirs that get some use for water sports and fishing. Here we're already on the border with the region of Aragon, and the landscapes are looking sparser and stranger, on the edge of the weird little salt and gypsum desert called **Los Monegros** that stretches all the way to Zaragoza.

Tourist Information and Services in and around Tortosa

Ask the tourist office in Horta Sant Joan about the **Vía Verde**, a 24km trail for hikers, bikers and horses that has been created from an abandoned rail line through some pretty countryside between Arnés and Pinell de Brai.

There are information centres for the **Parque Natural dels Ports**, open year-round, at Roquetes, just across the river from Tortosa, at Alfara de Carles, and Horta de Sant Joan, **t** 977 50 40 12.

(i) **Horta de San Joan >>**
Plaça de Catalunya,
t 977 43 56 00

(i) **Benifallet**
Avda Lluís Companys 3,
t 977 46 22 49

(i) **Gandesa >>**
Avda Catalunya,
t 977 42 09 10

(i) **Tortosa >**
Parque Municipal,
t 977 44 25 67

(★) **Rosa Pinyol >**

Market Days in and around Tortosa

Tortosa, Saturday; **Benissanet**, Sunday; **Horta de Sant Joan**, Wednesday, Friday; **Gandesa**, Tuesday, **El Pinell de Brai**, Thursday; **Corbera d'Ebre**, Monday; **Móra d'Ebre**, Friday; **Móra la Nova**, Wednesday; **Miravet**, Saturday; **Flix**, Wednesday, Thursday; **Riba-Roja**, Monday, Friday; **Ascó**, Friday

Where to Stay and Eat in and around Tortosa

Tortosa ✉ 43500

****Parador Nacional Castell de la Suda**, **t** 977 44 44 58 (€€€). It may be the only reason people come to Tortosa (and the King of Saudi Arabia's been here). Considering the destruction in 1938 the restorers did a terrific job: the palatial rooms have tremendous views, and there are gardens and a pool. Restaurant (€€€). **Rosa Pinyol**, C/Hernán Cortés 17, **t** 977 50 02 01 (€€€–€€). Tortosa is a great town for restaurants, and this one is considered by many as the best. Innovative cooking, lots of wild mushrooms in season and a memorable seafood ravioli. An impressive wine list, too.

****Hs Virginia**, Avda Generalitat 139, **t** 977 44 41 86, *www.hotelvirginia.net* (€). Definitely a bright spot in this town; simple, modern and welcoming.

El Paiolet, Rambla Felip Pedrell 56, **t** 977 44 66 53 (€€). In the centre by the bridge, an elegant room and a clever young chef named Clara Segarra who is making a name for herself. A €14 menu you can get excited about.

Sidreria Amets, Pg Moreira 13, **t** 977 44 66 99 (€€–€). Over the river by the Parque Municipál, an institution in Tortosa with real Basque cooking, plus a bar and cafeteria with great *pintxos* and tapas, and plenty of cider everywhere.

Horta de Sant Joan ✉ 43596

****Hs Casa Barceló**, Avda Generalitat, **t** 977 43 53 53, *www.casabarcelo.com* (€). Much like its neighbour, the Miralles, and also with a very good restaurant (€€).

***Miralles**, Avda Generalitat 21, **t** 977 43 51 1 4, *www.hotelmiralles.com* (€). Good, simple rooms with views over the village Picasso painted and the lovely countryside, and a fine restaurant (€€) where the speciality is *crestó* – mountain goat in *escabeche* (not poached from the park; they raise their own!).

Gandesa ✉ 43780

Piqué, Avda Catalunya 68, **t** 977 42 00 68, *www.hotelpique.com* (€). Gandesa doesn't get many visitors, and there's nothing special here, but this is a good, honest inexpensive hotel and restaurant.

Can Manolo, Avda Germandad 28, **t** 977 42 11 77 (€€) Grilled chops and local wines, no problem.

Miravet ✉ 43540

*****Mas de Taniet**, at Benissanet, **t** 977 40 76 04, *www.mastaniet.com* (€€). Eight simple rooms in a restored country house; pool and restaurant.

Molí de Xim, C/Major, **t** 977 40 77 58 (€€–€). One of the best places to eat in the area, in a restored old olive oil mill.

La Ponderosa, C/Palau, **t** 609 23 78 09, (€). Charmingly furnished, family-owned traditional house in the village, with a few rooms and kitchen facilities.

Lleida Province

How exciting is it? Not the right question, really. This western end of Catalonia is decidedly lacking in coastal corniches and spectacular seafood, Modernista palaces and Surrealists. Its one great age of art was 800 years ago, and most of that has been carted off to the museums of Barcelona and New York.

So why come? For starters, there's the surprising city of Lleida, with its hilltop cathedral, one of the forgotten treasures of Spain. Lleida and its plain full of orchards lie at one end, the High Pyrenees with ski resorts and mountain scenery at the other. And in between are some delightful places you've probably never heard of.

11

Don't miss

1 Spain's loveliest cloister
La Seu, Lleida **p.288**

2 A most gracious small town
Solsona **p.305**

3 A spectacular cliff walk
Congost de Mont-Rebei **p.303**

4 Great Romanesque art
Vall de Boí, **p.319**, and Vall d'Aran **p.324**

See map overleaf

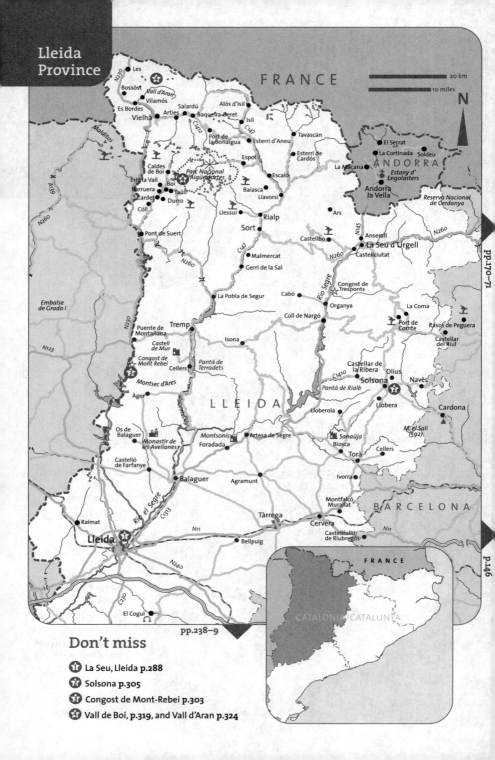

Lleida Province

FRANCE

Les
Bossòst
Vall d'Aran
Vilamós
Es Bordes
Salardú
Vielha
Arties
Alós d'Isil
Baqueira-Beret
Isil
Maladeta
Port de
la Bonaigua
Esterri d'Aneu
Tavascán
Espot
Esterri de
Cardós
La Maçana
ANDORRA
Caldes
de Boi
Parc Nacional
Aigüestortes
Escaló
El Serrat
La Cortinada
Soldeu
Erill la Vall
Boi
Estany d'
Engolàsters
Barruera
Taüll
Baiasca
Cardet
Durro
Llavorsí
Andorra
la Vella
Cóll
Llessui
Reserva Nacional
de Cerdanya
Pont de Suert
Rialp
Sort
Ars
Castellbo
Anserall
La Seu d'Urgell
Malmercat
Castellciutat
Gerri de la Sal
Rio Segre
Congost de
Tresponts
Embalse
de Grado I
La Pobla de Segur
Cabó
Organya
La Coma
Coll de Nargó
Port de
Comte
Rasos de Peguera
Tremp
Isona
Castellar
del Riul
Puente de
Montañana
Castell
de Mur
Pantà de
Terradets
Castellar de
la Ribera
Olius
Congost de
Mont-Rebei
Cellers
Solsona
Navès
Montsec d'Ares
Pantà de Rialb
Llobera
Àger
Cardona
LLEIDA
Lloberola
M. el Salí
(592)
Os de
Balaguer
Sanaüja
Monastir de
les Avellanes
Montsonis
Foradada
Artesa de Segre
Biosca
Cellers
Castelló
de Farfanye
Torà
Ivorra
Balaguer
Agramunt
Montfalcó
Murallat
BARCELONA
Raimat
Rio el Segre
Tàrrega
Cervera
Lleida
Bellpuig
Castellfollit
de Riubregos
El Cogul
pp.238-9

20 km
10 miles
N

FRANCE

CATALONIA/CATALUNYA

pp.170-71
p.146

Don't miss

1 La Seu, Lleida **p.288**

2 Solsona **p.305**

3 Congost de Mont-Rebei **p.303**

4 Vall de Boí, **p.319**, and Vall d'Aran **p.324**

In between Lleida and the High Pyrenees are sweet and lovely towns like Solsona, Cervera and Balaguer, the remote and very medieval never-never land of the Llobregós, and pre-Pyrenean massifs like Montsec that are very attractive places for hiking and outdoor sports.

Prices are low, the food's good and the people friendly. It's a low-key province, without a lot of crowds and bustle and hustle, and a perfect spot for a kind of understated, informal tourism that many people find very enjoyable. Instead of frantic sightseeing, it offers a place to relax a bit and get to know a little rustic corner and its people and traditions well. If you have time to spend and an eye for detail, you'll discover it is a rich region indeed.

Lleida

When you first come to Lleida (Lérida in Castilian), you might not think much of it at all. First you pass through miles of orchards, then the busy outskirts full of warehouses stacked with crates of fruit, a reminder that Lleida has always made its living from apples, peaches and pears. When you get inside the city, it seems a hopeless jumble of big boulevards that don't lead anywhere and all look the same. But persevere; hidden down by the river is a fine old historic centre with lots to see and do. The place grows on you. After taking some hard knocks from history Lleida is on its way back again, slowly and carefully, and once you get to know it you'll find it a lively and quite likeable town.

History

Barcelona is the capital of Catalonia on the sea, and Lleida on the land.

Chronicler Ramon Muntaner, 1325

Lleida lies along the river Segre in the midst of Catalonia's most extensive plain. It begins with the *Ilergetes*, the Iberian tribe that occupied the plain. About 425 BC, they decided to found a capital for themselves on the height over the Segre called the Roca Sobirana. Its name was *Iltirta*.

Two centuries later, after the Second Punic War, the bosses up in the citadel were Roman, and they called their refounded city Ilerda. Ilerda consisted of a fortified governmental forum similar to Tarragona's, up where the Seu is now, and a small grid of streets on the slopes to the west and south, with another forum near the bridge over the Segre, roughly where the Pont Vell stands today. The city became famous in the Roman world when Julius Caesar defeated Pompey's generals here in 49 BC.

Ilerda fell to the Visigoths in the 5th century, and to the Moors in AD 719. Little is known about it in these periods, but the Reconquista and the settling of 'New Catalonia' gave the city a chance to make a brilliant comeback. After Ramon Berenguer IV

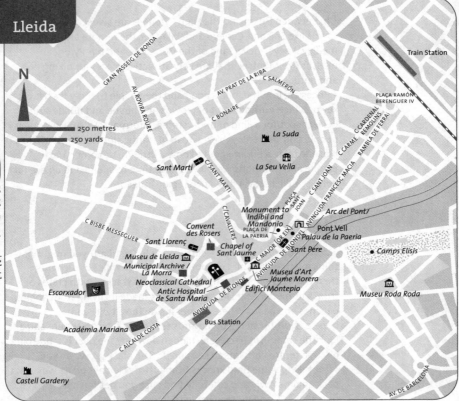

Map labels:

Train Station

PLAÇA RAMÓN BERENGUER IV

GRAN PASSEIG DE RONDA

AV. ROVIRA ROURE

AV. PRAT DE LA RIBA

C SALMERÓN

C BONAIRE

N

250 metres
250 yards

La Suda

Sant Marti

La Seu Vella

C SANT MARTI

C/CAVALLERS

C CARME REMOLINS

C CARDENAL REMOLINS

RAMBLA DE FERAI

C SANT JOAN

AVINGUDA FRANCESC MACIA

PLAÇA SANT JOAN

Arc del Pont/

Monument to Indibil and Mandonio

C BISBE MESSEGUER

Convent des Rosers

Sant Llorenç

PLAÇA DE LA PAERIA

Pont Vell

Palau de la Paeria

Chapel of Sant Jaume

C MAJOR (OEIX)

AVINGUDA DE BLONDE

Sant Pére

Museu de Lleida

Municipal Archive / La Morra

Museu d'Art Jaume Morera

Camps Elisis

Neoclassical Cathedral

Antic Hospital de Santa Maria

Edifici Montepio

Escorxador

AVINGUDA DE BLONDE

Museu Roda Roda

Académia Mariana

C. ALCALDE COSTA

Bus Station

Castell Gardeny

AV. DE BARCELONA

took it in 1148, the three powers behind the Catalan Reconquista – the landowning nobles, the Templars and the Church – each played their part in assuring that Lleida would be New Catalonia's metropolis. The cathedral was begun in 1203; the city got the right to self-government in 1264, and in 1300 the Estudi General became the first university in the Kingdom of Aragon.

For centuries Lleida was indeed the 'capital on the land', the most important Catalan city after Barcelona. Its downfall came in the 18th century, during the Wars of the Spanish Succession. As a fervently anti-Bourbon stronghold the city was bound to suffer, but the victorious King Philip was determined to make a special example of it. The university was closed and moved to Cervera, while the king razed the entire area around La Seu Vella to build a new fortress to keep watch on the Lleidans.

Further indignities came in the Spanish Civil War, when Lleida was repeatedly bombed by the Nationalists. Today, after languishing for decades, the city's economy is thriving again. Traditionally Lleida was a place where fruit from the plain was

Getting to and around Lleida

By Air

The **Aeroport de Lleida-Alguaire** is expected to open in late 2009 and provide a major boost for the region's economy.

By Train

Lleida is on the main line from Barcelona to Manresa, Zaragoza and Madrid. Some trains also stop at Bellpuig and Cervera. Another line, somewhat less frequent, connects Lleida with Reus and Tarragona. The glorious 19th-century RENFE station is Lleida-Pirineus on Avda Francesca Macià at the end of the Rambla Ferran. **RENFE info**: *t 902 240 202; www.renfe.es*.

Besides RENFE, there is also the **FGC** (*t 93 205 15 15, www.fgc.cat*) which runs a narrow-gauge line from Lleida-Pirineus up towards Montsec, the **Tren dels Llacs**, *see p.301*.

By Bus

The big bus station is on the Avda Blondel by the river, which is handy for the town centre. You can get just about anywhere by bus: there are eight a day to Barcelona, half of them express (a little over 2hrs). There are also regular connections to Valencia, Huesca, Zaragoza and many other towns.

By Car

Parking in Lleida is as horrible as in any Spanish city. One tip for finding a space is to head up to the Seu and the streets around it, where you can usually find a place, and then take the walkway and lift down to Plaça Sant Joan.

shipped throughout Spain and Europe. Now, that has turned into an important food-processing industry. A restored university helps keep Lleida a bustling place; the population has reached 120,000, including immigrants from over a hundred countries.

La Seu Vella

La Seu Vella
t 973 023 06 53; open Jan–April Tues–Sun 11–1 and 3–5.30; May–Sept Tues–Sat 10–7.30, Sun 10–3; Oct–Dec Tues–Sat 10–5.30, Sun 10–3; adm; walk or take a taxi, or city bus no.12 from the bus station or Rambla d'Aragó (Mon–Sat), or take the elevator and walkway up from Plaça Sant Joan

As in many Catalan towns, Lleida's hill is a sort of acropolis that has witnessed a remarkable historical continuity as a religious and political centre since Iberian times. After the Bourbons destroyed the area in the early 18th century (*see* p.288), however, Lleida became a very different city indeed; and a confusing one. Now, what once was the centre is largely dead space of parks and quiet residential streets, leaving Lleida a sort of doughnut-shaped city where the action isn't in the middle, but everywhere around it. Up on top, **La Seu Vella** stands battered and more than a little forlorn, stuck in the middle of a grim fortress.

Which is a shame. Tremendous in scale, with lots of panache, this is one of the great monuments of Spain. After the Iberians and Romans, the Moors built a castle from which to rule the little kingdom that appeared after the fall of the Caliphate, and a mosque that occupied the site where the Seu is now. A church, probably converted from the old mosque, existed here from the Christian conquest, but the Seu as we see it now was not begun until 1203; it may have been conceived as a personal monument to Jaume the Conqueror. Although consecrated in 1278, the Seu was not completed until 1431, when the last stones of the **belltower** were hoisted into place.

This majestic 230ft tower forms Lleida's landmark skyline, with the help of the church's huge octagonal cupola and the smaller tower intriguingly called the 'tower of exorcisms'. Soon after the belltower was completed, it acquired its famous occupants, two venerable ladies who have been watching over the city's fortunes now for almost 600 years. These are **Silvestra** and **Mónica**, the bells, which respectively strike the hours and quarter-hours. Mónica's a little cracked, but she's still on the job; the two were joined in the 20th century by five modern bells.

The entrance to the complex is through the **Porta del Lleó** (1826), a monumental gate in the walls festooned with the arms of the Seu's Bourbon nemeses. Disaster came for Lleida and for the Seu with the Wars of the Spanish Succession. The troops of the Bourbon claimant, Philip V, took the city in 1707, and as in Barcelona, the new king ordered a fortress built to overawe the Lleidans. The height on which the Seu and the old Moorish castle stood was the logical place; the works must have destroyed the city's oldest neighborhoods and monuments. The Seu itself narrowly escaped; Philip had ordered it razed, but somehow it never happened, and it would be used first as a barracks, later as a powder magazine and a barber shop. Its return to the church, and the beginnings of the restorations, date only to 1949.

You'll have to nearly circumnavigate the vast bulk of the church to get in, passing first the **Baluard de la Reina**, with views over the city. The church has no less than four portals, of which the southern **Porta de l'Anunciata** is the oldest, and the only place in the Seu where some fragments of the mosque that preceeded it survive. The northern **Porta de Sant Berenguer** is also Romanesque in style, while the other two are impressively decorated with the sculptural work of the 'School of Lleida', including the grand main **Porta dels Apóstols** which leads into the cloister, and the **Porta dels Fillols** ('of the children') on the south.

Considering its sad history, there isn't much left inside: original alabaster windows, bits of once-impressive 13th–4th-century frescoes in the apse and some of the chapels, and fragments of tombs of the Montcada, the medieval clan from Barcelona who were powerful here, and helped build the Seu to hold their family pantheon.

The Cloister

⭐ La Seu cloister

The **cloister** was built for the cathedral chapter, and your first thought on entering it might be, where do I sign up? This is the most spectacular cloister in Spain, perhaps anywhere, and the

Lleidans also claim it as the biggest. It occupies the site of the old mosque courtyard. The unusual plan, with a campanile separated by an open courtyard from the church, is Moorish in origin; the Great Mosque in Córdoba is laid out the same way.

The cloister was built in the 14th century, when famous Catalan sculptors such as Guillem Seguer and Jaume Cascalls were in charge of the works. Its glory is the 17 enormous and beautiful **Gothic windows**. No two are alike. Note the delightful carved decoration on the capitals, some of the finest work of the Lleida school; much of it is modern restorations, after the damage sustained while the cloister was part of a barracks. Best of all, there's a feature almost no other cloister has. On one side, called the **mirador**, the windows open out to splendid views over Lleida. It's a perfect medieval fantasy setting; you could sit here all day.

Up above the church to the north stand the ruins of **La Suda**, the Roman-Moorish-Catalan castle that suffered a lot over the centuries, most recently in the Napoleonic Wars and the Spanish Civil War. It's an utter ruin, though the Lleidans are slowly trying to restore it.

Down the Eix

Today, the centre of the action is the long main street, which changes its name several times (C/Cardenal Remolins, C/Carme, C/Sant Joan, C/Major) as it passes from the train station underneath the Seu, paralleling the river. People in Lleida call the whole thing the **Eix**, or 'axis' (pronounced 'aysh' rhyming with 'day-shh'). It's a great street, closed to traffic for its entire length and lined with shops and palaces and Modernista monuments.

Starting from the station, the first square is busy **Plaça Sant Joan**, with the big, clumsy church of the same name. This was the site of the Roman-era Forum, and the main temple stood where Sant Joan is now. The big stairway off to the right leads up to a **lift** to the Seu.

The next square, **Plaça de la Paeria**, announces itself, with a bit of Catalan whimsy, 'the most beautiful street sign in the world', painted in 1931 to cover a blank wall adjoining Lleida's town hall, the **Palau de la Paeria**. This is a word unique to Lleida and some of the towns in its province. *Paeria*, the city government, and the title of the mayor, *paer*, come from the Latin *patiarii*, 'men of peace', and they have kept these titles since Jaume I granted self-government in 1264. The building was begun in the 13th century as a private residence and, though much restored since, it is one of the notable surviving works of medieval Catalan secular architecture.

Parts of the Paeria can be visited, including the **chapel**, which has a glorious gilded retable by Jaume Ferrer (1451), the *Verge dels Paers*, showing the Virgin Mary and archangels Michael and Gabriel

Palau de la Paeria
open Mon–Sat 11–2 and 5–8, Sun 11–2; adm

receiving four of Lleida's mayors. The **Municipal Archive** has two of the city's treasures on display, the *Carta Pobla*, the original charter of the city's settlement, and the *Llibre dels Usatges*, the famous 14th-century charter of Catalan rights. Downstairs, the old dungeon, **La Morra**, has some interesting graffiti from prisoners who sat here awaiting their executions. On the front of the building, note the little plaque commemorating the first six-storey *castell* (human tower, *see* p.259) in Lleida, made here on 6 April 2008. The *castellers* always rate a plaque when they perform a really good one; you'll see them all over Catalonia.

Back behind the Paeria, the 15th-century **Arc del Pont** is the only part of the city wall left standing. Near it is the **Monument to Indíbil and Mandonio**, two chiefs of the Iberians who fought the Romans during the Second Punic Wars. Rome in those days won its victories through clever diplomacy nearly as often as on the battlefield. These two handsome dupes let the Romans trick them into giving up their alliance with Carthage. Once the legions had polished off the Carthaginians, it was Indíbil and Mandonio's turn; they both fell in Rome's final victory in 205 BC.

Here on the riverfront, on the right is the **Avinguda de Blondel,** the riverfront promenade with some of Lleida's best Modernista buildings, and also, most conspicuously, the **Edifici Montepio**, the city's modest ten-storey skyscraper. Spaniards in general have been mad for skyscrapers since the 1920s, and even if they never got very tall, they certainly had style. This one now belongs to La Caixa, Catalonia's giant savings bank, and they put on some interesting art exhibitions in their gallery just behind the tower. In the oppposite direction begins Lleida's shady **Rambles** (Avinguda Francesc Macia and Rambla de Ferran).

There's more art a little further down, in a flashy 1920s building that houses the **Museu d'Art Moderna Jaume Morera**, with a collection of mostly obscure Catalan painters of the 19th and 20th centuries.

Museu d'Art Moderna Jaume Morera
t 973 70 04 19; open Tues–Sat 11–2 and 5–8, Sun 11–2; adm

Back on the Eix, the next sight is the church of **Sant Pere**, with a pretty Churrigueresque portal. Americans from the Golden State might want to drop in and pay their respects at the tomb of Gaspar de Portolà, first governor of California. A little further down, the 14th-century Gothic chapel of **Sant Jaume** marks the spot where according to local legend the apostle James (Santiago) had to stop on his way from the Holy Land to Santiago de Compostela when he got a really nasty thorn in his toe; angels came down from heaven to pull it out for him.

Off to the right, Carrer dels Cavallers leads up into the oldest neighbourhoods of Lleida, passing the 18th-century **Convent des Rosers**. Continue down the Eix and you'll meet the graceless hulk

Antic Hospital de Santa Maria
open summer Tues–Fri 10–2 and 6–8, Sat 11–2 and 7–9, Sun 11–2; winter Tues–Fri 10–2 and 5.30–8.30, Sat 12–2 and 5.30–8.30, Sun 10–2; adm

of an 18th-century neoclassical **cathedral** that Lleida built to replace the ruined Seu.

Just across the Eix, the **Antic Hospital de Santa Maria** was built in the 15th century to consolidate the city's hospitals. Now it has a small archaeological collection and holds special exhibitions, but it's worth a look any time for the gorgeous arcaded **courtyard** with its sweeping staircase, one of the glories of medieval Catalan architecture.

Museu de Lleida

Museu de Lleida
t 973 28 30 75; open May–Sept Tues–Sat 10–2 and 4–8, Sun 10–2; Oct–April Tues–Sat 10–2 and 4–7, Sun 10–2; adm

Behind the cathedral, you can find your way through some of the oldest streets in Lleida to its newest museum, opened only in 2007 to assemble collections that had been spread around town.

There's a little bit of everything here, from the beginnings of Lleida and its province up to the Renaissance. From the Paleolithic, there are reproductions of some of the many cave paintings in the area, followed by Neolithic finds, and fine Roman mosaics. The Middle Ages are represented by some fascinating art. A reconstructed ensemble of altar furnishings from various churches gives an unexpected idea of how the interior of a Romanesque church looked in its time – like a classical Greek temple, it's more wild and colourful than you might have expected. Also here are the famous Àger chessmen, one of the oldest sets ever found in Europe.

Also from the Middle Ages are works of the 'School of Lleida', the sculptors who worked on the Seu, and a wealth of painting gathered from churches and monasteries around the province.

The Àger Chessmen

Just how did princes and barons while away those dreary Dark Age Sunday afternoons? From the 9th century on, at least, the cleverer ones were playing the new game that was sweeping Europe – chess. Chess had already come to the Islamic world through Persia, and made its way to Europe through Byzantium, through Spain, and up the Volga, brought to Russia and Scandinavia by Viking traders from the Middle East. Judging from the number of surviving sets, Spain is where it caught on the strongest. Many, like the one here, were probably made in Egypt, where rock crystal carving was an established trade.

Typically for Islamic chessmen, the pieces are simple and abstract: the king is represented by his throne, the rook by a bit of crenellation. Note the piece with the slightly hooked top. That would be the bishop, except there weren't any bishops yet, or queens either. In medieval chess, there was only a slow-moving minister to keep the king company and defend him, and instead of a speedy and slyly oblique bishop you'd be stuck with a clumsy, diagonal-hopping *alfil*, or elephant, who also stayed close to the king. Like real medieval warfare, medieval chess put the emphasis on defence.

Ever wonder how things end up in museums? These little lumps of crystal have a story to tell. They belonged to none other that that doughty knight of the Reconquista, Mir de Tost (*see* p.302); 96 chessmen are mentioned in his will. The Monastery of Àger got them and, when that closed in 1857, a few of them went to the bishops of Lleida. They kept them in the episcopal bedroom until one finally donated them to this museum. All the best ones spent a long time in the parish church of Àger, which auctioned them off in 1907. Later on they would be picked up by the Emir of Kuwait, and looted by the Iraqis in 1991. At last report, the Emir has somehow managed to get them back.

The altarpieces by the late 14th-century Bartolomeo de Robió and his workshop stand out, vigorous, naturalistic works similar to the new painting that was happening then in Florence. Among the others, don't miss the wonderful scene of the medievals at dinner, from the refectory of the Seu.

Behind the museum, the church of **Sant Llorenç** looks like a smaller version of the Seu, and it is, begun about the same time by the same builders and sculptors. The lovely octagonal belltower has been recently restored and, inside, Sant Llorenç is one of the rare Catalan churches that still has most of its original artwork, including two fine retables by Jaume Cascalls. For centuries after the Conquest of 1149 this part of town was known as the **Moreria** for its surviving Moorish population, which somehow managed to remain until the 1600s; ironically enough, it has become home to many North Africans once again.

A little further into the neighborhood, on C/Sant Martí, there's the city's **market**, and beyond that the rough and rugged church of **Sant Martí**, which should give an idea of how the Catalans were building in the first generations of the Reconquista. For centuries this was the chapel of Lleida's university.

Outside the Centre

Most Lleidans live in their modern and busy streets outside the centre, though there isn't a lot to see there. The **Escorxador**, not far from the Museum on C/Lluís Companys, was originally a slaughterhouse by Lleida's best-known Modernista architect, Francesc de Paula Morera i Gatell; recently it has been restored as a theatre. Just around the corner to the south, on C/Acadèmia is the **Acadèmia Mariana**. Monumental religious art may have been dead in 1870 but no one told the Catalans, hence this colossal tribute to the Virgin Mary, combining frescoes, stained glass, Greek marble and some wonderful wrought iron work in a frothy, kitsch extravaganza.

Acadèmia Mariana
t 973 26 61 61; open daily 10–1 and 5–8

Across the Riu Segre, just over the Pont Vell from the city centre, Lleida, like Paris, has its own Elysian Fields. The **Camps Elisis** is a gracious park with avenues of plane trees. At at its eastern end, it merges into the **Fira de Lleida**, the home of the city's annual trade exhibition, which retains a number of pretty pavilions from the period 1880–1920, including the Café Chalet and a Modernista building that was once an aquarium. Across from the park on C/Santa Cecilia, the **Museu Roda Roda** has a collection of antique cars, including some luscious pre-war luxury models: a 1925 Rolls-Royce Phantom and something that in its day was even classier than a Roller, a Hispano-Suiza, made in Barcelona.

Museu Roda Roda
t 973 21 19 92; open Tues–Sat 11–2 and 5–8, Sun 11–2; adm

Castell Gardeny
t 973 27 19 42;
open summer Tues–Sat
10–1.30 and 3.30–7.30,
Sun 10–2; winter
Tues–Sat 10–1.30
and 3.30–6

Finally, on a hill overlooking the city from just outside the ring road (Gran Passeig de Ronda) on the southwest, the **Castell Gardeny** was one of the Templars' major installations in Catalonia, along with Miravet (*see* p.280). The Templars built their castle, really a small fortified commandery, almost as soon as Lleida was taken from the Moors. They weren't really worried about the Moors coming back. A Templar commandery handled loads of cash from the rents and profits on its far-flung lands, and a building like this was fortified to protect it. After the War of the Spanish Succession, Philip V turned it into a modern artillery-proof fortress, with a low wall around the original Templar building.

Though the city promotes this as one of the major sights, it's little more than a graffiti-covered ruin, though with some nice views over Lleida. In the chapel, you'll note a very faded *Viva España!* on the wall over the place where the altar once stood. That's a giveaway that either Falangists or the army once roosted here, the sort of weird echo from the Civil War that is becoming increasingly rare in Spain. Here it was the army, and as you leave the castle you'll see the vandalized barracks where Franco had once installed them to keep watch over the Lleidans.

Outside Lleida

Everyone knows that the restaurants of **Raïmat** are famous for rabbit. It's their speciality dish, and also a little joke. When villagers started growing wine grapes around 1914, so many bunnies appeared that they ate all the vine shoots, so making a casserole out of them was the only sensible solution. Raïmat today produces a variety of wines, including some well-regarded reds, made from cabernet sauvignon, shiraz or tempranillo; you can visit the

Codorníu *bodega*
on the Lleida road,
t 973 72 40 00

bodega, run by Codorníu, on the Lleida road. The older part of the *bodega* was built in 1918 by the Modernista Joan Rubió i Bellver; it was the first reinforced concrete building in Spain.

South of Lleida, in the *comarca* called **Les Garrigues**, there are millions of olive trees but not much else, though the countryside becomes increasingly pretty as it climbs up towards Montsant and El Priorat (*see* pp.266–9). At **El Cogul**, you can visit some cave

Roca dels Moros
open summer
Tues–Sat 10–1.30 and
4–7.30, Sun 10–1.30;
winter Tues–Sat 10–1.30
and 3–5.30, Sun
10–1.30; adm

paintings at the **Roca dels Moros**. Some of the paintings are 9,000 years old, some much more recent (accompanied by Iberic and Latin graffiti); ther subjects are much like the other caves further south: various animals, hunters and elegant ladies in their long skirts.

At **Arbeca**, you can see the ruins of a castle that once belonged to the Dukes of Cardona, and an pre-Iberian village, **Els Vilars**, consisting of a circle of houses built around a well, one of the few such villages not sited on a defensible height.

(i) **Lleida >**
C/Major 31,
t 902 25 00 50;
*there is also a **booth***
in front of the
train station

⭐ **Forn del Nastasi >>**

Tourist Information and Services in Lleida

The city **tourist office** offers discounts, deals, and a number of guided tours, including a night-time tour of *'Lleida secreta'*; the info is on their website: *www.turisme.paeria.es.*

Market Days in Lleida

Lleida, Thursday, Saturday. There's also an **antiques and flea market** Sunday mornings in the Rambla de Ferran, near the train station.

Where to Stay in Lleida

Why are hotels in this town so breathtakingly cheap? Nobody seems to know. Just enjoy it; stay an extra day. Information and reservation for all hotels and *hostales* in Lleida and its province can be arranged through the tourist office's new website, *www.hostelerialleida.com.*

Lleida ✉ 25007

****NH Hotel Pirineos, Gran Pg de Ronda 63, t 973 27 31 99, *www.nh-hotels.com* (€€). Modern, extremely comfortable hotel on the edge of the town, with a good, international-Catalan restaurant (€€€–€€).

***Condes de Urgel, Avda de Barcelona 21, t 973 20 23 00, *www.hcondes.com* (€€–€). Lleida will look a lot better when they demolish this gruesome pile. Meanwhile, you get a rather posh businessman's hotel at two-star prices.

**Hotel Ramon Berenguer IV, Plaça Ramon Berenguer IV 3, t 973 23 73 45 (€). Large, well-equipped hotel with some old-fashioned charm, right across from the train station: pleasant rooms at very reasonable prices.

**Hotel Principal, Plaça de la Paeria 7, t 973 23 08 00, *www.hotelprincipal.net* (€). Another large, modern hotel with good facilities; next to the City Hall.

*Goya, Alcalde Costa 9, t 973 26 67 88 (€). Reasonable hotel with 17 rooms.

*Mundial, Plaça Sant Joan 4, t 973 24 27 00 (€). Old-fashioned and well-kept, this is a real time-capsule, occupying the upper floors of a remarkable Modernista building. Mostly remodelled inside, unfortunately, but the rooms have broadband, and there's parking and a café.

Jardins del Segrià, Partida Cunillàs 82, t 973 231 137, *www.jardinsdelsegria.com* (€). This large complex on the outskirts of Lleida is a good cheap option if you're travelling with the family, or in a larger group. It's set in huge gardens, with play areas for kids, and an outdoor barbecue area with a stack of wood if you want to cook up some of the local lamb. A wide range of rooms are available, sleeping from 2 to 6, with or without en-suite facilities.

Eating Out in Lleida

There is a collection of bars around **Carrer Humbert Torres**, a little pedestrianized street off Avda Prat de la Riba that is a great place to go for a drink and tapas in the evening. Places include **Font de les Bruixes** and **Zeke** with outside tables; **Cañas y Tapas** is especially good for seafood tapas done Andalucian style.

Forn del Nastasi, C/Salmerón 10, t 973 23 45 10 (€€€). One of Catalonia's best restaurants, with an extensive menu including very good seafood, charcoal grills, and house specialities. It's been so successful that they've opened up another one nearby, the **Nou Forn del Nastasi**, Avda de l' Alcade Rovira Roure 87, t 973 22 37 28 (€€€). *Both closed first fortnight in Aug.*

Sheyton, Avda Prat de la Riba 39, t 973 23 81 97 (€€€). Elegant, classic restaurant with English ambience and, fortunately, Catalan cooking. Delicious local dishes, especially the *bacallà*; exceptional desserts.

Celler del Roser, C/Cavallers 15, t 973 23 90 70 (€€€–€€). An institution in the historic centre, set in a 17th-century cellar. Long famous for snails, also *bacallà* and dishes with wild mushrooms.

Xalet Suis, Avda de l'Alcade Rovira Roure 9, t 973 23 55 67 (€€). Popular for its great fondues; as well as the classics, you can try a seafood fondue.

Julivert, Avda Francesc Macia 15, **t** 973 25 48 34 (€€–€). On the Rambla, a small and unpretentious place. Perfect for a light lunch after sightseeing

Casa Lluís, Plaça de Ramon Berenguer IV 8, **t** 973 24 00 26 (€€–€). A friendly, budget choice near the train station.

Ducal, Avda Prat de la Riba 49 (€). Good inexpensive menus and tapas.

La Huerta, Avda Tortosa 9, **t** 973 24 24 13 (€). Next to the market just below La Seu Vella, this very popular spot specializes in grills and seafood.

Nightlife in Lleida

For **nightlife**, look south, along Carrer Bonaire, and to the west, on Avinguda d'Alcalde Rovira Roure. Younger folks also frequent the collection of bars and cafés along **Carrer Bisbe Messeguer**, off the Rambla d'Aragó behind the big University building. Thursday night tends to be the biggest night for going out, as most students return to their home towns and villages at weekends.

East of Lleida

Bellpuig and Tàrrega

Heading towards Barcelona on the A2, the great high road of Spain, there won't be much to detain you. Do stop at **Bellpuig**, though, for an apple (like fine wines they have a *denominació de qualitat*) and for an amazing small dose of the Renaissance in a very unlikely place. Barely fitting within this village's humble church of **Sant Nicolau** is the **Tomb of Ramon Folch de Cardona**, admiral of Spain and viceroy of Naples.

Everyone in the day believed that Folch was a natural son of King Fernando El Católico. Whether or not he was a literal bastard, he certainly fitted the term in every other respect. Fernando gave him Naples to rule in 1505, and Folch made himself one of the most hated men in Italy. After introducing the Inquisition to Naples, he went on a long series of campaigns across the peninsula, distinguishing himself mostly by the grisly sack of Prato in Tuscany (1512), in which thousands were massacred.

His tomb was designed and sculpted by Giovanni Meriano da Nola, a student of Benedetto da Maiano and the most renowned sculptor of his time in Naples, where most of his works are. This tomb, a few tons' worth of the finest Carrera marble, was originally installed in a Neapolitan church; it wasn't exactly welcome there, and was finally shipped over to Bellpuig, where Folch was born.

Meriano gave the bastard his money's worth: marble angels and mythological graces compete to shower his effigy with crowns and laurel. Note Folch's crossed legs, a convention in art that shows that the deceased was a crusader. Folch did lead a campaign in North Africa, capturing towns in Algeria, which also explains the stirring relief scenes of sea battles with galleys and the freeing of Christian captives. Almost every inch of the tomb is covered in finely sculpted, intricate detail, with lots of surprises hidden among the decoration. Children can see if they can spot the crocodiles.

Beyond Bellpuig lies **Tàrrega**, the second city of Lleida province. It's a cheerful (by Catalan standards) and forward-looking place, though there's not much to see beyond the **Museu Comarcal de l'Urgell**, with an archaeological collection and works of local artists.

Museu Comarcal de l'Urgell
C/Major 11, t 973 31 29 60, www.museu tarrega.com; open Sat 12–2 and 6–9, Sun 12–2; adm

South of Tàrrega, the little village of **Verdú** is built around an unusual **castle**, converted first into a palace and then into a mill, still with its medieval tower sticking out of the top. The Gothic hall and other parts are currently under restoration. Verdú is also a ceramics town, known for its black-glazed pottery, but the real attraction here is the **Museu de Joguets i Automats**, the lifetime's obsession of a private collector with a good eye for everything fond and silly: three floors of toys from all over the world in a strikingly restored building on the Plaça Major.

Museu de Joguets i Automats
t 973 34 70 49; open summer 10–2 and 5–8, Sat 11–2, 4.30–8, Sun 11–2; winter Tues– Fri 10–2 and 4–8; adm

And beyond Verdú, **Vallbona de les Monges,** one of the three famous, magnificent Cistercian monasteries of Catalonia, lies just to the south (*see* p.264).

Cervera

There is nothing in Cervera's early history to suggest that it would end up one of the loveliest and most distinctive towns in Catalonia. It followed the usual trajectory: hilltop Iberian settlement, followed by Romans, Visigoths, Moors and Aragonese. Its only mention in the history books would have been the conference where Aragonese and Castilian diplomats ironed out the terms of Fernando and Isabel's marriage.

But Cervera got one lucky break. In the War of the Spanish Succession it was one of the very few towns in Catalonia that picked the winning side. Its loyalty to the Bourbons was rewarded when Philip V shut down the universities of Lleida and Barcelona and combined them in a new, state-controlled university here. It may have been a disaster for Catalan culture, but it helped keep Cervera prosperous for another century and a half in which most of the other towns of Catalonia were going to pot. It's still prosperous and happy, but being cute does mean it's increasingly popular among the 'second home' set.

Modern Cervera is a sizeable new town with some industry, and the old medieval centre hangs from it like a pendant towards the south, giving it the air of a village surrounded by open country; the main road through town, the N11, actually passes underneath in a tunnel. Old and new towns meet at the **Universitat**, a handsome building that covers an entire block. Completed in 1740, in a style that is neoclassical with a touch of rococo and an outlandish giant iron crown on top, its plan is something of a throwback, a great rectangle with courtyards and a chapel (called the Paraninfo) at the centre, rather like the royal palace of El Escorial. The lower floor, around the stone arcades of the courtyards, housed the lecture halls and offices, while students lived in dormitories upstairs.

Showing his accustomed reverence for culture, Franco bombed the Universitat in the Civil War, and then turned it into a prison for dissidents. The university was moved to Barcelona in 1841, and the city is still hard pressed to fill this hulk; parts are still under restoration, and the rest houses archives, a library and offices.

Around the back, along Passeig Jaume Balmes there is a **belvedere** with views over the countryside. Look down and you'll see something altogether charming, the 'Parc Municipal Infantil de Trafic', a park with a little grid of streets with traffic signs where kids learn the rules of the road.

Down the Carrer Major

Continuing south into the medieval centre, Cervera's monuments line up along the Carrer Major, beginning with the **Museu Comarcal**, former home of the wealthy Duran i Sampere family. On the ground floor is the tourist office, and behind that a small museum which houses a collection of art from local churches, including a fine retable by Pere Girard. There are also some quaint and interesting relics from the old university, including silly lampshade hats that the professors had to wear, and an 18th-century voting machine used by the faculty to vote among themselves for positions. Upstairs, the rooms of the Duran i Sampere family have been restored to show how such a household lived in the 19th century.

Further down, Carrer Major passes the 12th-century **Hospital de Sant Joan de Jerusalem**, with the Maltese cross on the façade giving it away as the property of the Knights Hospitallers. Have a look down some of Cervera's ancient narrow side streets, really nothing more than alleys with vaulting grown over them. Some, like the **Carrer de les Bruixes** (Witches' Street), have buildings that go back to the 1200s. There's a whole world underneath Cervera too; you may have noticed the little windows of thick glass placed on the pavement of the Carrer Major, to let some light into the network of cellars and storehouses that lie beneath the buildings.

Carrer Major ends with the peaceful and lovely **Plaça Major,** surrounded by arcades. The centrepiece here is the town hall, like Lleida's called the **Paeria**. This elegant building, completed in 1688, incorporates earlier structures, including a 13th-century Gothic chapel, but the best part is outside: the whimsical oversized figures on the **corbels** holding up the balconies. From the left, the

Museu Comarcal
t 973 53 39 17; open June–Sept Tues–Sat 10.30–2 and 5–7, Sun 10.30–2; Oct–May Tues–Thurs 10.30–2, Fri–Sat 10.30–2 and 5–7, Sun 10.30–2; adm

first group are allegories of the senses; next come caricatures of the town merchants; and, finally, prisoners in the town jail.

Parròquia de Santa Maria and the Castle

Directly behind the Paeria stands the **Parròquia de Santa Maria**, a jewel of a Gothic church begun in the 14th century and squeezed artfully into an oddly shaped site. Many of the architectural elements, including the octagonal belltower, show the influence of the Seu in Lleida; inside, it's wonderfully light and airy, with a wide nave and delicate rib vaulting. Over the main altar is a stately Baroque baldachin, covering the medieval image of the *Madonna del Coll de les Savines*, patroness of Cervera. The Anarchists wrecked most everything else inside during the Civil War, but in this case they spared the Madonna. Also surviving is some original stained glass and a pair of 14th-century tombs.

Beyond Santa Maria we're at the tip of medieval Cervera, with a ruined, perfectly square **castle**, and the Gothic church and **monastery of Sant Domènec**. From here you can take a little walk into the countryside to see a little curiosity, the plain, round church of **Sant Pere le Gros** (1079), thought to have served as a funerary chapel or a pilgrim initiatory temple. But round chapels are always a bit of a mystery. This is one of only two in all Catalonia.

The area around the castle is a good place to have a look at Cervera's **medieval walls**, which survive almost intact in parts. Once they ran around the university, and down the length of what is now the modern main street. Now the most picturesque bits are this stretch, and the eastern side along C/Pere el Cerimoniós. From the latter, you can see across the ravine to the rock called **Les Forques**, marked with a cross, where executions would take place.

In the newer neighbourhood of Cervera, near the rail station, stands a tower that looks like it might have been dropped down from Mars. Not Mars, in fact, but César Martinell. Although 1919 was a busy year for the architect, he found time to design this fantastical tower for the town's agricultural co-operative. Some Cerverans call it **La Farinera** and some call it **El Sindicat**.

Around Cervera: The Segarra

Cervera is the capital of the *comarca* called the Segarra. It's hard-scrabble country, dotted with seldom-visited medieval hamlets, each one with a miniature castle that has been falling down since the 11th century. Before that, this was frontier country between the Christians and Moors, and that era left the Segarra with more castles than any part of Catalonia. Count Ermengol IV of Urgell took over the territory once and for all in the 1060s. Since then, outside of skirmishes in the War of the Spanish Succession or the Carlist Wars, the castles have had nothing to do.

One place that really does deserve a visit is **Montfalcó Murallat**, northeast of Cervera near Oluges. It's nothing more than a simple church and a handful of houses that have grown up inside a rough and ready castle, but no place evokes the old frontier days better. In the 11th century, a lot of people lived just like this. **Montfalcó** is packed so tightly that it seems like a single building with a little maze of passages running through it and a tiny *plaça* or two. Lately people have been moving in and fixing it up, and there is a restaurant and a couple of bars in summer.

Montfalcó Murallat *guided tours of the village can be arranged through the tourist office in nearby Sant Ramon,* **t** *973 52 42 91*

Torà and the Llobregós

If you really mean to go chasing down curiosities in the Segarra, by all means take yourself off to **Torà**, on the furthest extremes of the *comarca*, for a look at the **Tower of Vallferosa**. Vallferosa, in a pretty green setting, is a hamlet outside Torà that was largely abandoned after the Civil War. Its conical tower, over 100ft tall, is a startling sight, even more so when you consider it was begun about the year 970. This is the true monument of the Reconquista, conjuring up as no other relic can the age when the first uncouth Catalans came storming down from the hills. Round defensive towers were commonly built to help defend newly conquered lands from the Moors. This is the biggest, built in stages over two centuries. The entrance was on the second floor; when attacked, they would just pull up the ladder.

Torà itself is a thoroughly charming village, full of steps and arcaded alleys and fountains and lovely old houses. There's a medieval bridge and an aqueduct, and a 400-year-old communal oven that has become a **Museu del Pa** (bread museum). The surrounding **Llobregós valley** is an excellent spot for a walking holiday. There's a lot to see in the surrounding countryside, including plenty of Neolithic dolmens, including Catalonia's biggest, at **Llanera**, just north of Torà.

Museu del Pa *call* **t** *973 47 32 53 to visit*

There are a few more round towers like the one at Vallferosa; the most impressive are at **Castellfollit de Riubregós** and **Ivorra**. There's a rather magical ruined castle at **Sanaüja**, north of Biosca, along with an impressive medieval bridge. Among the many rustic Romanesque churches in the area, the best are at **Castellfollit de Riubregós** and **Cellers**, east of Torà, with some wonderfully primitive carved decoration in the crypt.

Finally, in Ivorra's Baroque church you can also see the **reliquary of Sant Dubte**, the 'holy doubt'. The story goes that back in the 1030s someone said that he didn't believe the eucharist was really the body of Christ, and it conveniently started bleeding for him.

Where to Stay and Eat East of Lleida

(i) **Cervera** >
C/Major,
t 973 53 13 03

(i) **Bellpuig**
Convent de
Sant Bartolemeu,
t 973 32 02 92

Cervera ✉ 25200

**La Savina, C/Horts 2, t 973 53 13 93, www.mailxxi.com/hostallasavina (€€). It doesn't look like much from the outside, but this is a rather charming, lovingly decorated *hostal* in open country just below the medieval centre. It has a swimming pool, too.

*Bonavista, Avda Catalunya 14, t 973 50 00 27 (€). Centrally located, posh and pleasant for the price. *Closed first two weeks in August.*

Les Forques, Avda Catalunya 4, t 973 53 00 52 (€€). Modest, but good cooking. Snails and seafood top the bill.

L'Antic Forn, Plaça Major 18, t 973 53 31 52 (€€–€). An atmospheric old hole-in-the-wall in the historic centre, for grills and *bacallà*.

Montfalcó ✉ 25215

Montfalcó, t 973 53 17 55 (€€€–€€). In the tiny village square, a seasonal restaurant that specializes in grills, including ostrich steaks. *Closed three weeks in Oct.*

Guissona ✉ 25600

Cal Mines, C/Santa Margarida 6, t 973 55 16 59 (€€). Right in the village centre, an unpretentious bar-restaurant serving pork, snails, duck magret and all the Catalan favourites.

Torà ✉ 25750

Hostal Jaumet, Ctra Barcelona-Andorra, t 973 47 30 77, www.hostal jaumet.com (€€–€). A modern building (the old one burned down), but the same family has been running the place since 1890. The restaurant (€€) is an institution known far and wide. If you want some real Catalan soul food, ask for the *ofegat de la Segarra*, with parts of the pig you don't want to know about.

North of Lleida: Balaguer to Tremp

Balaguer

At first glance it seems strangely familiar: on one side of the river there's a neat, straight row of big modern apartment buildings, on the other a venerable old town, with a great church inside a castle looming over it. It's no mistake; Balaguer is a baby Lleida in every way. And, for a town of 15,000 that no one outside Catalonia has ever heard of, Balaguer is a pleasant surprise.

Balaguer is mentioned in Roman records, but it didn't become a thriving town until the time of the Moors. Madinat Balagi, according to the 11th-century historian al-Himyari, was a beautiful city surrounded by orchards and gardens, made wealthy by farming, linen cloth and gold panned from the River Segre. The city fell to Count Ermengol V of Urgell in 1105, with a particularly brutal sacking and the flight of most of its Muslim population. Ermengol made it Urgell's new capital, but revival did not really come until the early 1300s, when prosperity returned and the churches and bridges were built. Balaguer's happiness would be brief; the city shared the fortune of the last Count of Urgell, Jaume II el Dissortat (the Unlucky), who pressed his claim to the Aragonese crown in 1410. Jaume lost a string of battles to the succesful claimant

Getting around north of Lleida

Catalonia's regional rail line, the FGC, operates a line called the 'Train of the Lakes' (*Tren dels Llacs*) which runs up the valley of the Noguera Pallaresa through Montsec. It starts in Lleida, and passes through Balaguer, Sant Llorenç de Montgai, Àger, Cellers, Guardia de Tremp, Palau de la Noguera, Tremp and La Pobla de Segur. It's a very scenic trip and popular with tourists in summer, when there are usually three trains a day in either direction (*information t 932 05 15 15, www.trendelsllacs.cat*).

Fernando of Antequera, abdicated in 1413, and spent the rest of his life in prison.

Around Plaça Mercadal

The place to size up Balaguer is from the foot of the **Pont Nou**, the busy main bridge over the Segre. The *pont* is *nou* because the old one got blown up in the Civil War; in the closing days Balaguer was the first big Catalan town to fall, and the gateway for Franco's final march on Barcelona. Over on the modern side, this bridge leads to the tree-lined *rambla*, the **Passeig de l'Estació**, with all the businesses and posh shops.

Looking down at the Segre, you'll probably see some of the ducks and geese that have made the riverbank their home since the city recently turned it into a park. Looking up, there's what appears to be an enormous fortress on the heights above the town, particularly impressive at night when it is illuminated. This is really only part of the **town walls**, begun by the Moors and rebuilt by the counts of Urgell.

Walk north a block, and you'll come to the **Plaça Mercadal**, surrounded by arcades and shaded by well-clipped plane trees. This absolutely lovely square hides a dark secret. Before 1492 this was the densely packed Jewish ghetto. After the Jews were expelled, the buildings were all levelled and the ground made into a new marketplace. On the corner house coming from the bridge, note the plaque marking the birthplace of Gaspar de Portolà, the first governor of California (*see* p.290).

Museu Comarcal de la Noguera
t 973. 44 51 94;
open Mon–Sat 11–2 and 6.30–8.30, Sun 11–2; adm

Two streets south of the Plaça, the new **Museu Comarcal de la Noguera** will give you a thorough grounding on Balaguer's history. The church with the octagonal belltower that hangs so fetchingly above the Plaça Mercadal is **Santa Maria**, and you'll have to climb up Balaguer's oldest (and poorest) streets to get there. Santa Maria is a testament to Balaguer's up-and-down medieval history; this ambitious project was begun in 1351 but took over 200 years to finish. The result is a little Gothic and a little Renaissance. The interior has a clean, modern look to it; its chapels have exhibits on religious art through the centuries.

Santa Maria
open Sat and Sun 10.30–2; July–mid-Sept Tues–Fri 10.30–2 and 5–7, Sat and Sun 10.30–2; adm

On the opposite bank of the Segre, near the **Pont Sant Miquel**, is the attractive Gothic church and cloister of **Sant Domènec**. From

11

Lleida Province | North of Lleida: Balaguer to Tremp

here you can look up to another set of church-and-castle on a commanding height. The church is the **Santuari de Sant Crist**; the building goes back to the Middle Ages, but most of what you see now is from 1912. Once this was a very popular pilgrimage church, for a miraculous statue of Christ said to be the work of Nicodemus, companion of Joseph of Arimathea. The legend said that angels guided his hand, and the image represented the true face of the Saviour. Before it was destroyed in the Civil War, killjoy scholars unfortunately dated it to the 14th century. Of the reconstruction you see now, only a foot survives from the original.

Montsec

From the north side, at least, it's one ugly mountain, a long grey mound that looks like a gargantuan bag of cement left out in the rain. The southern silhouette's a little more comely, weathered away into a long skyline of steep cliffs. The whole thing is almost 30 miles long, east to west. Throughout history, it has never been much more than a lumpish obstacle, blocking everyone's way on valley paths between the Pyrenees and the southern plains.

Like Montserrat, Montsec has probably contributed something to teaching surrealism to the Catalans, and it does have its good points. There are hidden defiles and ravines along its length that are popular with hikers, and rough slopes that provide the perfect drafts for hang-gliders. People here hope to attract more of them; there aren't many opportunities for young people to make a living. And, as in many parts of the Pyrenean foothills, the population has dropped dramatically in recent decades.

Montsec is divided in two by the Noguera Pallaresa river. The larger, western part, bordering on Aragon, is called **Montsec d'Ares.** If you come up this way from Balaguer on the scenic C12, you'll pass the **Monestir de les Avellanes**, with a Romanesque cloister and a Gothic church that once held the tombs of the Counts of Urgell. These, unfortunately, were spirited away by the minions of the Rockefellers long ago, after the monastery fell into ruin, and you'll have to go to the Cloisters Museum in New York to see them. Les Avellanes is now restored, and makes an interesting place to pass the night (*see* p.304).

Right at the foot of Montsec is **Àger**, a centre for paragliding and kayaking. Àger was once an important place, thanks to its most famous resident, Arnau Mir de Tost. Arnau, born *c.*1000, was one of the protagonists of the Catalan Reconquista. This knight of Urgell made Montsec his personal frontier, and by the time he died he had conquered much of it and earned himself no less than 30 castles. Historians have called him the 'Catalan El Cid.'

Arnau was responsible for completing the somewhat ruined and fascinating **Col.legiata de Sant Pere**. This Catalan backwater church has suffered like the others, with some fine frescoes moved long ago to Barcelona. Still, as an example of the earliest rugged Catalan Romanesque, it has charm. Àger's better days have further witnesses in the parish church of **Sant Vicenç**, where the baptismal font is a 3rd-century Roman sarcophagus decorated with marine mythological scenes, and a stretch of **Roman road** that survives in almost passable shape.

The **Pas de Terradets** marks the boundary between the Montsec d'Ares and the eastern part, the **Montsec de Rúbies**. The Noguera Pallaresa river cuts a dramatic gorge here and, upstream from that, a grey Franco-era dam holds back an artificial lake with a lovely mountain backdrop, the **Pantà de Terradets**, now a popular spot for boating and water sports near the village of **Cellers**.

Up on the slopes of Montsec to the west is the recently restored **Castell de Mur**. Though small, it's a remarkable sight, a narrow, triangular castle with a tall curtain wall built around a 10th-century cylindrical defence tower, like those of the Llobregós. Altogether, it looks a little like a steamboat, and a little like a steam iron. There's a church nearby, the **Col.legiata de Mur**, built at the end of the 11th century, with a small cloister. The church apse once held a wonderful fresco of Christ Pantocrator with the four Evangelists. The Americans got this one too; now it's in Boston, but an accurate reproduction has recently been put in place.

Col.legiata de Mur
guided tours of both castle and church Sat and Sun 11, 12 and 1; July–mid-Sept also Mon–Sat eves, 5, 6 and 7pm; adm

Congost de Mont-Rebei

The best part of Montsec is also unfortunately the hardest to see, nothing less than the most isolated spot in all of Catalonia. And it is utterly spectacular. The **Congost de Mont-Rebei**, the long gorge of the Noguera Ribagorciana river that divides Catalonia from Aragon, has cliffs that tower over 1,500ft, in places where the river itself is only 20ft wide. You'll have to be an experienced climber to get all the way through it. Back in the 1920s the government created a path through, but later on this was chopped short when part of the gorge was flooded for the Canelles dam.

The tourist office in Tremp (*see* p.305) can offer information about the gorge and the other hiking routes in the area. The **Remei path**, 4km in length, starts at **Puente de Montañana** at the end of a scenic back road 26km west of Tremp. Don't come if you suffer at all from vertigo: in some stretches this narrow path is thoroughly terrifying, hanging 600 feet in the air on a nearly vertical cliff, with no guard rails. If you can stand it, though, it's quite an experience, and you'll be sharing it with the bats and vultures that nest in the rock face as well as royal eagles and rare lammergeiers. Down in the river there's an abundance of otters.

Tremp and the Conca Delià

The 5,000 souls in **Tremp** make it the only town of any size in this region. Outside of that there's not a lot to say about it, just a sleepy little town with a miniature medieval centre and some surviving towers from the wall that once went around it.

East of Tremp is a broad, green basin between the mountains called the **Conca Delià**. The centre is the village of **Isona**, once the Roman town of Aeso. Isona was a little more important then, and ruins from Roman times can still be seen in and around the village – but it was really a swinging place 67 million years ago, at the end of the Cretacious period. Dinosaur fans won't want to miss the Museu de la Conca Delià. Among the many Cretaceous finds in the area is an entirely new species, an unlovely, fat-tailed brute named *Pararhabdodon isonensis* in honour of the village. One floor of the museum is devoted to dino eggs, dino footprints and dino everything else.

Museu de la Conca Delià
open July–mid-Sept daily 11–2 and 5–7; mid-Sept–June Thurs–Sat 11–2 and 5–7, Sun 11–2; adm

Market Days North of Lleida

Balaguer, Saturday; **Tremp**, Monday; **Pobla de Segur**, Wednesday; **Isona**, Saturday; **Artesa de Segre**, Sunday; **Ponts**, Monday.

Where to Stay and Eat North of Lleida

(i) **Balaguer** >
Plaça Mercadal 1, in the town hall, t 973 44 66 06

(★) **Monestir de les Avellanes** >>

(i) **Àger**
Plaça Major 1, t 973 45 50 96

(i) **Isona**
Plaça Assumció, t 973 66 50 62

Balaguer ✉ 25600

**Balaguer, C/la Banqueta 7, *www.hotelbalaguer.com* (€). Rooms overlook the river; a good bargain for a mid-range sort of hotel.

**P Urgell, Avda Urgell 25, t 973 45 06 29 (€). Good budget rooms on the new side of town.

Cal Xirricló, C/Dr Fleming 53, t 973 44 50 11 (€€€). A local favourite for over 50 years; some interesting starters and tasty seafood.

Cal Morell, Pg. de 'Estació 18, t 973 44 80 09 (€€€–€€). Josep Morell is a famous chef in Catalonia and a writer of popular cookbooks. His cooking is traditional, with a twist, as in his signature snails *a la llauna*. Worth a small splurge for the *menu degustació*.

Font Blanca, C/Molí del Comte 13, Balaguer, t 973 45 09 27 (€€). Long-established classic in the centre of town, with solid home cooking featuring Catalan dishes prepared with seasonal ingredients.

Ni Hao, 18 Avda Urgell (€€–€). Exactly what you came to Balaguer for – very tasty sushi and teppanyaki grilled at your table by German-speaking Chinese guys.

Les Avellanes ✉ 25612

Monestir de les Avellanes, Carretera C12, t 973 43 80 06, *www.monestirdelesavellanes.com* (€). This lovely medieval monastery is available for everything from spiritual retreats to business conferences. The friendly Marist fathers, who've been here since 1912, are frankly in the hospitality business; that's how they keep up the buildings. The air-conditioned rooms, though simple, are anything but ascetic. Full- or half-board is available.

Cellers ✉ 25631

***Terradets, on the C13, t 973 65 11 20, *www.hotelterradets.cat* (€€€–€€). Right on the lake in the quiet countryside. Most rooms have balconies; ask for one on the lake side. Pool, internet connection, a good restaurant (€€€–€€), and activities.

Tremp >
Plaça de la Creu 1,
t 973 65 00 05

Guardia de Tremp (Guardia de Noguera) ✉ 25632
La Rectoria, t 973 65 00 42, *www.hotel-larectoria.com* (€€–€). Nice rooms in an old stone rectory, located in this village in the hills up above the

lake. Terrace with a view, and a decent **restaurant** serving Catalan classics.
Casa Perdiu, C/del Mig 5, **t** 973 65 05 25, *www.casaperdiu.com* (€). Rooms in a simple village house, which are very cheap.

Solsona, the Solsonès and Cardona

Solsona

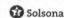 **Solsona**

In a part of Catalonia where the economy has been difficult for a long time, the exquisite town of Solsona is thriving. it used to be known for making gloves and lace. Now, every August it runs a chamber music festival and academy for students from all over the world. Solsona takes carnival very seriously, putting on one of the best in Spain, and it's even prouder of its *gegants*.

Solsona has always been here; archaeological finds go back beyond 3000 BC. The Iberians called it Xelsa, the Romans Setelsis. After some Dark Age troubles, Wilfred the Hairy helped re-establish the city; Catalonia's founder died in a battle nearby. Solsona prospered in the Middle Ages, as its merchants made a reputation throughout Spain and beyond. One of the town's barons even seized a foreign conquest, the town of Alghero in Sardinia (until recently, some of the old folks there still spoke Catalan).

The 16th and 17th centuries were very good to Solsona. The town became a city, and the seat of a bishop. It gained a university (later consolidated with Cervera's) and contributed one of the great painters of Spain's golden age, Francisco Ribalta. The 18th century was good too. Solsona thrived by manufacturing knives, gloves and lace, while most of Catalonia was floundering.

The modern era, however, brought nothing but trouble. First Napoleon's army burned the cathedral. The First Carlist War brought even worse damages. The pope took away the episcopal see in 1851, just while the city's old manufactures were losing out to the new industrial firms in Barcelona. Solsona has come through the troubles in style. It is one of the most refined and urbane towns you'll find in Catalonia, or anywhere. The people of Solsona know it's special, but they aren't very helpful in explaining why. Ask them about it and they'll just smile.

Plaça de Palau and the Comarcal Museum

Most likely you'll come into town on the bridge over the little Riera de Solsona. After the bridge was built, the gate called the **Portal del Pont** was constructed as the new monumental entrance

Getting to and around Solsona, the Solsonès and Cardona

The nearest **train** station for Solsona or Cardona is Manresa (*see* p.153), so it is more convenient to arrive by **bus**. Alsina Graells (**t** *973 271 470, www.alsinagraells.com*), and Eix Bus (**t** *973 271 470*), operate most services in the area, including several a day from Barcelona, Lleida and Manresa.

Pou de Gel
guided tours summer Sat and Sun, 12, 6 and 7; winter Sat and Sun, 12, 6.30 and 7.30; adm

to the city (1805). Just outside it, a small pavilion has been built over the **Pou de Gel**. There must be a hundred of these in the towns of Catalonia – ice wells, where ice from the Pyrenees could be packed in the winter and kept all through the summer. This one was made in the 1680s.

From here, Carrer Sant Miquel leads into the heart of the city, to the 15th century cathedral fountain, and the **cathedral**. This is a Romanesque building, completed in 1070, but it has suffered much over the centuries; the fragments on the exterior show that it must have been quite impressive in its day. To see the best thing about it you'll have to go around the back – a gorgeous Modernista dome in dark blue and yellow tiles over the cambril, or Lady chapel. This was built to house Solsona's beloved icon, the *Mare de Déu del Claustre*, an exceptional 12th-century image with a faraway gaze and stylized draperies that give away its origins in southwest France; the artist's name was Gilbert of Toulouse.

Museu Diocesà i Comarcal
t 973 48 21 01, http://museu.bisbat solsona.cat; open May–Sept Tues–Sat 10–1 and 4.30–7, Sun 10–2; Oct–April Tues–Sat 10–1 and 4–6, Sun 10–2; adm

A block to the north is the lovely **Plaça de Palau**, with a wonderful fountain decorated with begonias and ivy. The former episcopal palace is now the **Museu Diocesà i Comarcal**. Except in summer when the tourists are about, it's usually dead quiet inside, but this little museum has an astounding hoard of medieval art, most of it frescoes taken here for preservation from village churches.

Before you see these, though, there's the equally astounding **Col.lecció de Sal**, sculptures made from chunks of salt from nearby Cardona. It's an old tradition in these parts; unknown madmen have contributed fantasy Gothic temples, a salty bust of a princess, and best of all, life-like sausages and slices of cantaloupe.

The medieval collection starts with fragments: original doors, a small portal carved with a not-very-Christian dragon, and some charming cartoonish painted wood icons of the Madonna. Next come perhaps the museum's star exhibits, rare pre-Romanesque paintings from **Sant Quirze de Podret** (11th century): some utterly exotic subjects framed by Moorish arches, and an *Angel of the Apocalypse* you won't forget.

After that there are some exceptional 12th-century frescoes from Sant Vicenç de Rus, and a collection of items arranged to make a complete Romanesque altar ensemble that makes it easy to imagine how early medieval churches really looked in their day. There are several altarpieces from the 14th century, including a great *Last Supper* by Jaume Ferrer.

Around the Historic Centre

Adjacent to the Plaça de Palau is the arcaded **Plaça Major**; just around the corner on C/Sant Josep de Calassanç, Solsona celebrates its ancient craft industry with a small knife museum, the **Museu Ganivet**. Carrer de Castell leads up to the northern part of town, to the stately Renaissance **Ajuntament**.

Museu Ganivet
t 973 48 21 01; open
Tues–Sat 10–2 and 5–7,
Sun 10–2; adm

A block south of the Ajuntament, **Plaça Sant Joan** has another pretty fountain, topped with a small chapel. Here you can also see the **Torre de les Hores**, the centre of the action each year at carnival. Solsonans are sardonically called 'donkey-killers' in Catalonia. The old story goes that a farmer once dragged his hungry donkey up to the top of the steeple to eat the grass that was growing out of the cornice. They used to re-enact it every year, but now, for sanity's sake, they use an effigy.

It's a delight to wander around the serene, immaculate back streets of old Solsona. Besides Plaça Sant Joan, you'll come across other squares, **Plaça Sant Roc** and **Plaça de Sant Pere**, landscaped into attractive gardens. The other surviving town gates, **Portal de Llobera** and **Portal de Castell**, lie at the northern edge of town.

The *castell*, just outside the old walls, was demolished long ago, leaving a large park called the **Camp de Serra**. Just beyond this is the Solsona's Modernista monument, the **Hotel Sant Roc** (1929), designed by Ignasi Oms and Bernardí Martorell in a fairytale sort of Modernisme that seems to fit the mood of Solsona perfectly.

Around Solsona: The Solsonès

On a road map, the area around Solsona looks thoroughly empty, as if it were some rugged mountainous wasteland. It's not quite true. The Solsonès lies just inside the boundaries of 'old Catalonia', the part never conquered by the Moors. Like the Llobregós just to the south, this was a part of the country where medieval feudalism never took root very strongly. So more farmers owned their own land and, instead of living in villages, they had their own homes, or *masies*, scattered around the country.

From almost anywhere in Solsona, you can see **Castellvell**, perched jauntily on a steep hill to the west like a cap that's just a little too small. Once it was bigger. This castle was a stronghold of the Counts of Cardona, long the big shots in this part of Catalonia. Later owners took away most of the stone to build Solsona's walls, but today it serves as a private residence.

Further west, the area around **Castellar de la Ribera** was a busy spot in Neolithic times. There are collections of dolmens and a menhir or two south of the village at the **Necròpolis de Clot** and the **Necròpolis de Llor**. There are more dolmens south of Solsona around Llobera, along with a marker for the **geographical centre** of Catalonia, near Pinós, and the rural **Santuari del Miracle**, built in the 15th century after an apparition of the Virgin Mary.

Just outside Solsona to the east, **Olius** has an interesting Romanesque church, **Sant Esteve**, with a crypt, as well as a real oddity, the only entirely **Modernista cemetery**, designed in 1916 by Bernardí Martorell. Built simply, mostly from rough stone, the construction still shows Gaudíesque steeples and parabolic arches. Further east, there are a number of plain Romanesque churches around **Navès** and further north along the Riu d'Ora. They have some rustic charm; the best perhaps is **Sant Pere de Graudescales**, at the northern end of the river in the Vall de Lord. This is a long east–west tranverse valley, and, if you're coming from the south, it's about here that you really feel you're in the Pyrenees (and the highest peaks are always on the horizon to remind you). The valley won't trouble you with sightseeing, but the scenery is grand. Just west, is the ski station of Port del Comte.

Port del Comte
www.portdelcomte.net

Cardona

They won't soon be running out of salt in Cardona. They've been mining the stuff since before the Romans came, for at least 3,500 years in fact, and there's still well over a cubic kilometre left, neatly piled up in a place just outside town called, straightforwardly enough, the Muntanya de Sal. In the 8th century, the owner of the land was Louis of Aquitaine, and he began Cardona's famous castle to protect his lucrative property. As for the town itself, Cardona is one of the few in this country to have a birthday, celebrated each year on 23 April. On that date, in 986, Count Borrell II issued its *Carta de Poblament*, one of the first such charters given.

Throughout the Middle Ages, Cardona was the headquarters of one of wealthiest noble families of Spain. The Osonas were Counts of Cardona (later Viscounts, later Dukes) and owners of 21 other castles, literally hundreds of villages and a score of towns. It is estimated that they owned 6 per cent of everything in medieval Catalonia. You can go a long way on salt. The town that grew up around their castle became wealthy too, as capital from salt went to build thriving mercantile houses and businesses.

Nothing lasts forever, and despite its inexhaustible resource Cardona was already declining in the 1650s when the Osonas packed up and moved to a more modern lifestyle in Barcelona. Their castle stayed behind to distinguish itself in the War of the Spanish Succession, when it was the last redoubt in Catalonia to fall to the Bourbons. It kept Napoleon's men out in 1806, too.

You wouldn't guess Cardona was a town of salt-miners. Like Solsona, it is a lovely place, with a dignified air to it. And like

Solsona it has a lovely square at its centre, **Plaça de la Fira**.
Underneath the arches on the edge is the **Centre Cardona
Medieval**. Here you can see exhibits and an audiovisual show on
the town's historic centre. Also on the *plaça* is the church of
Cardona's medieval merchants, the **Sant Miquel**.

**Centre Cardona
Medieval**
*t 902 40 04 75;
open Sat 10–2 and
4–8, Sun 11–3; weekdays
by appointment; adm*

Castell de Cardona

Castell de Cardona
*t 938 68 41 69; open
June–Sept daily 10–1
and 3–6; Oct–May daily
10–1 and 3–5; adm*

Cardona's real landmark is its **castle**, which stands out like a
beacon above the surrounding hills, visible for miles around. Part of
the castle is a *parador* (*see* p.310); the rest is open for visits. In form,
it's everything that Hollywood would expect of a castle, and more
than a few films have been shot here (notably Orson Welles' great
but seldom-seen *Chimes at Midnight*). If it seems gloomy from a
distance, it's only the colour of the local stone. There was already
some kind of a fortress here in 798, when Louis the Pious, son of
Charlemagne, occupied it. Much of what you see now was begun
c. 986, possibly by Wilfred the Hairy himself. One feature gives
away its early date, the **Torre de la Minyona**, a round defence tower
like those in the frontier settlements of the Llobregós.

The real surprise is that this castle contains not just a simple
chapel but a nearly cathedral-sized church, one of the important
works of the early Catalan Romanesque. The **Col.legiata de Sant
Vicenç**, consecrated in 1040, says a lot about the ethos of the
frontier. It was built to impress, in its size and muscular strength
but also in its militant austerity. Outside of the Lombard arcading
on the exterior and the eight-sided cupola (one of the first of this
Catalan tradition) there is hardly a bit of decoration inside or out.
The majestic nave once had frescoes, but the surviving fragments
of these are now in Barcelona's MNAC museum. An unusual
feature is the raised altar, with steps down to the crypt
underneath, a plan often seen in central Italian churches.

A World of Salt

Over the centuries Cardona did everything with its salt but make
it into a tourist attraction, and now they've managed that too. The
village centre has a couple of shops where you can take home a
salt sculpture curio. The **Museu de la Sal Josep Arnau** on Plaça
Santa Eulàlia is a family-run tribute to one of the most devoted
mad artists; if you've never seen a perfectly life-like plate of eggs
and sausages carved in salt before, this is the place to find them.

**Parc Cultural de la
Muntanya de Sal**
*t 938 69 24 75; open
Tues Fri 10–3, descents
into the mine at 10.30
and 1.30, Sat and Sun
10–2 and 3–6, tours
every half-hour; adm*

For something a little more didactic, come to the **Parc Cultural de
la Muntanya de Sal**, right in the working mine area, and you'll learn
everything about the history of salt and salt-mining, and then
they'll take you down into the underground part of the mines,
through salt galleries hung with salt stalactites and stalagmites –
as impressive as a good limestone cave.

ⓘ **Solsona >**
Ctra Bassella,
t 973 48 23 10

ⓘ **Sant Llorenç de Morunys >>**
Ctra Berga,
t 973 49 21 81

ⓘ **Cardona >>**
Avda del Rastrillo,
t 938 69 27 98

Market Days in Solsona, the Solsonès and Cardona

Solsona, Tuesday, Saturday;
Sant Llorenç de Morunys, Sunday;
Cardona, Sunday.

Where to Stay and Eat in Solsona, the Solsonès and Cardona

Solsona ✉ 25280

***Sant Roc**, Plaça Sant Roc, t 973 48 40 08, *www.hotelsantroc.com* (€€€). Martorell's Modernista monument still shines in all its glory – at least from the outside. Inside, sadly, it's been remodelled to death. Quite blingy, with a Jacuzzi-spa and a pretentious restaurant.

***La Freixera**, C/Sant Llorenç 46, t 973 48 42 62, *www.lafreixera.com* (€€€–€€). Right in the centre, a B&B in a 14th-century building with five varying modern and spacious rooms.

****Crisami**, C55 towards Cardona, t 973 48 04 13 (€). A modest but superior establishment. The rooms are fine, but come for the restaurant (€€). The menu may feature only simple favourites like a beef *estofat*, but someone back in the kitchen really knows how to cook.

Mare de la Font, Ctra de Bassella, t 973 48 01 52 (€€). Just outside town in a park setting, a long-time local favourite that concentrates on all the things Catalans like best: snails, *bacallà*, rabbit, stews and of course a *crema catalana* for dessert.

La Criolla, C/Castell 9 (€). A great bar for tapas and Basque-style *pintxos*.

Castellar de la Ribera ✉ 25280

Alberg Ceuró, Parròquia de Sant Julià de Ceuró, t 678 33 92 25, *www.ceuro. net* (€). This was the rectory attached to an isolated Romanesque church, set high on a hill with great views. The Alberg operates more like a *hostal* than a hotel, but there are basic rooms for two or more. They also offer meals and can arrange activities and tours of the area.

Lladurs ✉ 25283

****Casa Angrill**, Montpol, t 973 29 90 96, *www.casangrill.com* (€€–€). A restored *masia* in the countryside north of Solsona, with six rooms and a decent restaurant.

Clariana de Cardaner ✉ 25290

****Can Puig**, Ctra de Manresa, t 973 48 24 10 (€€€–€€). In a village on the road from Solsona to Cardener. It isn't much to look at, but this family-run hotel tries hard to please, with its pool, tennis and a restaurant (€€).

Sant Llorenç de Morunys ✉ 25282

****Monegal**, at Guixers, 5km east, t 973 49 23 69, *www.monegal.com* (€€). A rather sophisticated establishment for the Vall de Lord, a modern place near a lake, with an ambitious restaurant (€€€–€€). The hotel helps with any sort of outdoor activity, and in season they also arrange exhibitions and concerts.

Torre del Baró, Ctra de la Coma, t 973 49 26 36, *www.latorredelbaro.com* (€). Modest but nice, in a restored *masia*; they'll help organize cross-country skiing and other activities.

La Coma ✉ 25284

***Fonts del Cardener**, Ctra de Tuixent, t 973 49 23 77, *www.hotelfontsdel cardener.com* (€€–€). Twelve km from the ski slopes, but good in summer too; in a lovely setting with a pool, tennis and terrace with a view; also a restaurant (€€).

Cardona ✉ 08261

*****Parador Nacional Duques de Cardona**, Castell de Cardona, t 938 69 12 75, *www.parador.es* (€€€€–€€, *depending on room, season, special deals; consult the website*). Set in a stunning location high over the town, in part of the castle founded in 789 by Louis the Pious. The charming restaurant in a vaulted cellar offers well-prepared Catalan grills and roasts. The rooms are furnished with Catalan antiques; some have great views. Gym and sauna.

****P Cal Borrasca**, C/Escorxador, t 938 69 27 30 (€). Simple rooms on a quiet back street in the centre.

The High Pyrenees

When the Bourbon Philip V ascended to the Spanish throne, his grandfather Louis XIV haughtily declared (according to Voltaire): '*Il n'y a plus de Pyrenées!*' History, of course, proved him sadly deluded, although these great mountains have, of late, suffered a good deal of mental erosion as Spain takes its place as an equal partner in Europe. Yet the difference between the French and Spanish Pyrenees is striking. The former are rugged, and often forbidding, and even at the beginning of May there can be a blinding whiteout of snow, while, to the south, green valleys bask in the sun; the mountains are gentler, their aspect more benign.

Think in terms of valleys. That is the natural unit of geography here. As they get closer to the mountains, the two big river valleys, the Noguera and the Segre, split off like the branches on a tree. The easternmost, the Vall de Segre, takes you to La Seu d'Urgell with its famous cathedral, and then to the odd little mountaintop hypermarket called Andorra. The Noguera Pallaresa branch splits off into many smaller ones, each with a personality of its own: the Vall de Cardós, well known to Nordic skiers, and the Vall d'Àneu and Vall d'Asil, charming and remote, where the old traditional life of the Pyreneees still hangs on. Further west there's the Vall d'Aran, a little bit of Gascon France that got away, and the Vall de Boí, with its world-famous Romanesque churches.

In fact there are lovely medieval churches everywhere in these valleys, a testament to their greatest period of prosperity. Not much has happened here since; lately, almost all of these valleys have seen dramatic drops in population, as young people scarper off for opportunities they can't get at home. That leaves the place pretty much to the hikers and skiers, the eagles and the lizards. Like so many other corners of Europe's mountains, this one is trying to make a future for itself in nature tourism.

It has a lot to offer. Outside of Andorra, prices can be delightfully inexpensive, and the scenery is wonderful in and around the two big parks, the Reserva Nacional de Alt Pallars-Arán (comprising the tops of the Pyrenees along the French border), and the Parc Nacional d'Aigüestortes, a gorgeous region of forests and mountain lakes.

La Seu d'Urgell

La Seu, the 'See' of the mighty bishops of Urgell, once played as big a role in Catalan history as Barcelona itself. Those days are long gone, but La Seu is still the biggest town in the Catalan Pyrenees (pop. 11,000) and an urbane and agreeable base for seeing the

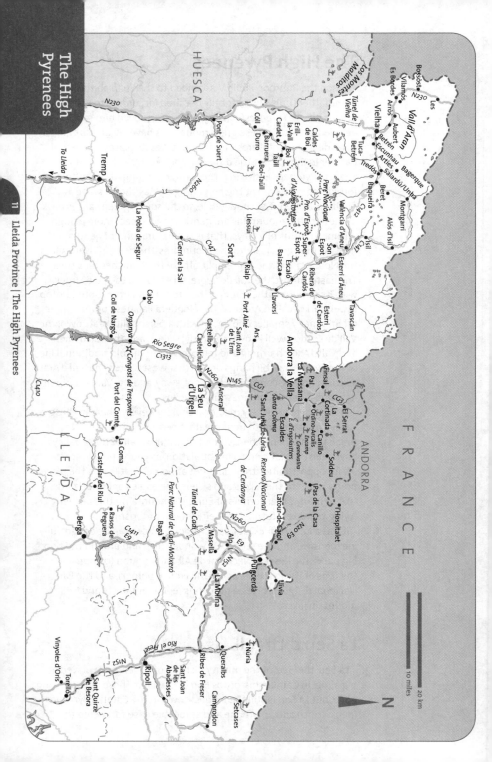

HUESCA

N230

To Lleida

Tremp

La Pobla de Segur

Pont de Suert

Coll Durro

Barruera

Cardet

Erill-
la-Vall

Boí

Taüll

Boí-Taüll

Caldes
de Boí

N260

C147

Llessui

Sort

Gerri de la Sal

Rialp

Port Ainé

Ars

Castelbò

Castellciutat

La Seu
d'Urgell

N260

N145

Gabó

Coll de Nargó

Organyà

Congost de Tresponts

Río Segre

C1313

C1410

Port del Comte

La Coma

Castellar del Riu

Berga

Rasos de
Peguera

C1411
E9

Bagà

Parc Natural de Cadí-Moixeró

Túnel de Cadí

Masella

La Molina

Llívia

Puigcerdà

N152

Alp

E9

N260

de Cerdanya

Reserva Nacional

N152

Vinyoles d'Orís

Torelló

Sant Quirzè
de Besora

Ripoll

Río el Freser

Sant Joan
de les Abadesses

Ribes de Freser

Queralbs

Núria

Campdron

Setcases

Parc Nacional

Pto. d'Espot

d'Aigüestortes

Espot

Super-
Espot

Son

Baiasca

Escaló

Valencia d'Àneu

Esterri d'Àneu

Isil

Alós d'Isil

C147

Beret

Baqueira

Montgarri

C142

Tredòs

Salardú/Unha

Artíes

Garòs

Escunhau

Betrén

Tuca-
Betrén

Vielha

Túnel de
Vielha

Los Montes
Malditos

Bossòst

Vilamòs

Es Bordes

Arró

Aubèrt

N230

Les

Vall d'Aran

Bagergue

Ribera de
Cardós

Esterri
de Cardós

Llavorsí

Tavascán

Sant Joan
de l'Erm

Andorra la Vella

La Massana

Arinsal

Pal

La
Cortinada

Ordino-Arcalis

El Serat

Canillo

Soldeu

Sant Julià de Lòria

Santa Coloma

E. d'Engolasters

Encamp

Grandvalira

Escaldes

Pas de la Casa

Latour-de-Carol

l'Hospitalet

N20

CG1

CG3

ANDORRA

FRANCE

N

20 km

10 miles

Getting to and around the High Pyrenees

La Seu d'Urgell is currently building an **airport**, largely financed by nearby Andorra, which has always wanted one but has no room to build it. If all goes well the first flights could arrive in 2010.

There is no **train** service up here, and you shouldn't expect even the **buses** to be much help in the mountains. The main roads will usually have only one or two a day, as from Lleida up the Noguera Ribagorça valley to Pont de Suert and Vielha, or Lleida up the C26 to Solsona and Seu d'Urgell, or from Barcelona up through Solsona to La Seu and Andorra. And where there are buses to the villages, they'll usually be timed to get kids to school and back.

Cerdanya (see p.234), the Serra del Cadí (see p.231) and the rest of this stretch of the mountains.

La Seu existed in Roman times, and seems to have been doing well even while the rest of the Roman world was falling apart. The first cathedral here was begun in the early 6th century. In 793 Arab armies destroyed the town, but thanks to the intervention of Charlemagne it was soon on the up again. From here, the bishops' wealth and power increased steadily, alongside that of the Counts of Urgell. They got along fine; in fact through much of the Middle Ages the two positions were usually held by the same family.

La Seu d' Urgell became the power centre from which Christian armies set off to chip away at the boundaries of al-Andalus. Its success however, was to be its bad luck. The conquest of 'New Catalonia' had tripled the size of the county, and in 1105 the Counts moved their capital down to the plains, to Lleida. La Seu has been the back-of-beyond ever since – though its bishops till get to be co-princes of Andorra.

The Cathedral

Cathedral

*t 973 35 32 42;
cathedral and Museu
Diocesà open summer
Mon–Sat 10–1 and 4–7,
Sun 10–1; winter
Mon–Fri 12–1 and 4–6,
Sat and Sun 11–1; adm,
combined ticket*

La Seu d' Urgell's glory days have left it a tremendous Romanesque cathedral, one of the greatest in Spain. Old as it is, it is at least the third church to occupy the site. The first was from Carolingian times; next, St Ermengol, one of the great medieval bishops, began a reconstruction in 1010. Finally came the work you see today, begun in 1184 in the Lombard Romanesque style.

On the façade, the sculptural decoration is concentrated on a narrow band at the centre; lacking a square to show it off, the designers had to create an imposing view down a narrow street, much as it appears today. The decoration is fanciful enough, with pairs of lions, a pentangle, a mermaid and much more.

The builders put more effort into the back than the front, a peculiarity the cathedral shares with many others that were going up at the time, such as Toulouse, Tours or Santiago de Compostela. Like these, the highlight is a beautiful colonnade of twinned columns running around the apse.

The first sight of the interior will be a surprise, heightened by the incense and piped-in music. The peculiar little façade gives no idea how big and imposing the cathedral really is. Dark and strong and tall, it has the air of a real national shrine, built before Catalonia was even really a nation. The **cloister**, rough and strange even by mountain Romanesque standards, has some vigorous sculpture on its dark granite capitals, including some beasts that look a lot like the winged monkeys from Oz.

From the cloister there is an entrance to the **Museu Diocesà**, one of the great hoards of medieval Catalan art. The prize exhibit used to be a brilliantly coloured, outlandishly stylized copy of one of Spain's greatest illuminated books, Beatus de Liébana's 10th-century *Apocalypse*. Unfortunately, someone stole it a few years back, but there is still some excellent painting, including a fine altarpiece by Pere Serra and an entire set of 12th-century frescoes from Baltarga where everyone looks terribly sad.

There are plenty of retables and other wood carvings from the MIddle Ages through the Renaissance and Baroque, including a whole room of *Mares de Déu* from village churches. It's a little depressing to see all these once-beloved icons taken away from the villages where they were worshipped for centuries and lined up here in a museum; one wonders what they all talk about when the lights are out and the tourists have gone home. St Ermengol, the bishop who built the cathedral, gets a completely over-the-top gold and silver sarcophagus from 1755.

There isn't much else in La Seu, although a walk around the old arcaded streets of the centre is fun. Just around the corner from the cathedral on C/Major, you can see the old 16th-century **grain measures** built into the walls. The medieval centre meets the newer side of town at **Passeig Joan Brudieu**, a rather gorgeous *rambla* lined with a superb avenue of plane trees – they look like the ones Van Gogh painted in Arles.

At the western edge of town, there's the pretty **Parc de la Valira** along a stream. Walk over here to see the little **cloister**, a copy of the cathedral cloister designed by Catalan writer Lluís Racionero, a La Seu native; the capitals on the cloister's columns, instead of saints and angels, have the faces of 20th-century celebrities, from Stalin and Hitler to Picasso, Groucho Marx and Marilyn Monroe.

Parc Olímpic del Segre
t 973 36 00 92

On the other side of town, along the Segre, the **Parc Olímpic del Segre** was the venue of the Olympic canoeing and kayaking events in 1992. If you ever wanted to try out something non-fatal and non-embarrassing on a real Olympic course, here's your chance. There is a white-water run, rafting, hydrospeeds, leisurely cruise boats, and they rent bikes too.

Just south, the ruined 18th-century **fort** at **Castellciutat** stands on a height, built over the original Iberian and Roman settlements of La Seu. More fine scenery waits further south, through the **Congost de Tresponts** (also called 'de Organya') a narrow, 1,968ft walled gorge formed by the river Segre, now dammed into a long lake. An excursion into the hills west of Organya is especially popular with bicyclists: ask the tourist office for a map of the 'Ruta de las Dolmenes'. It takes in seven dolmens, along with a couple of early medieval churches and a medieval aqueduct, all strung along the road to Cabó. Up at the end there's a pretty mountain plain called the Prat Muntaner, and woods full of mushroom-hunters.

Further south, Coll de Nargó on the Segre has one of the most interesting, and oldest, Romanesque parish churches in the area. The builders of the 10th-century Sant Climent apparently weren't too convinced of their ability to make a belltower; it's so much thicker at the bottom, it looks like it's melting.

There's more noteworthy Romanesque in the villages north of La Seu. Just outside town at Anserall, the imposing remains of Sant Serni de Tavernoles mark what was an important monastic church begun in Saint Ermengol's day. Further north, at Ars near the Andorra border, the 11th-century Sant Martí has a charming circular campanile.

Market Day
La Seu d'Urgell

La Seu d'Urgell, Tuesday and Saturday.

Where to Stay and Eat La Seu d'Urgell and Around

(i) La Seu d'Urgell >
Passeig Joan Brundieu
t 902 15 47 15

Avda Valls de Andorra,
t 973 35 15 11

(★) Andria >

La Seu d'Urgell ⊠ 25000

***Parador Nacional de la Seu d'Urgell, C/Sant Domènec 6, t 973 35 20 00, www.parador.es (€€€). Situated in what's left of the old quarter: built around a Renaissance cloister filled with plants, this has a heated pool, modern and comfortable rooms with air-conditioning, and a restaurant (€€€–€€) that puts a refined twist on traditional mountain dishes.

***Andria, Pg Brudieu 24, t 973 35 03 00, www.hotelandria.com (€€€–€€). Small and central, with a pretty courtyard; comfortable rooms with bath. The restaurant (€€€–€€) is excellent, with bits of truffle and foie gras and wild mushrooms everywhere. They raise their own chickens.

**Nice, Avda Pau Claris 4, t 973 35 21 00, www.hotelnice.net (€€). Functional but pleasant hotel with helpful staff.

*Habitaciones Europa, Avda Valira 5, t 973 35 18 56 (€). Don't be misled by the lacklustre name: bed down cheaply in one of 10 perfectly good, clean rooms.

Cal Pacho, C/de la Font 11, t 973 35 27 19 (€€–€). A long-time local favourite for roasts and grills. Lunch only except Fri and Sat.

Blau Arts Café, Passatge del Quartier (€). A fine little convivial hole-in-the-wall for an interesting lunch; maybe the only place in Catalonia where you can get that Tuscan favourite, spelt soup.

Castellciutat ⊠ 25710

****El Castell, Ctra Puigcerdá, t 973 35 00 00, www.hotelelcastell.com (€€€€€–€€€€). Just outside La Seu d'Urgell, an elegant modern building of wood and stone, underneath the ruins of the old castle at the entrance to the town. There's a pool with a spectacular view, sumptuously decorated rooms, and a beauty and wellness spa where they whisper of exotic pamperings involving fruits and chocolate. Two resolutely trendy restaurants share one of Catalonia's best wine cellars (€€€€ and €€€); you can try such delights as black ravioli flavoured with cuttlefish ink and stuffed with lobster.

*Hotel La Glorieta, Camí de la Seu, t 972 35 10 45 (€€). Set on the road up to Castellciutat, with views over the Segre Valley and a pool.

Calvinyà ✉ 25798

⭐ Cal Serni >

Cal Serni, t 973 35 28 09, *www.calserni. com* (€). In a tiny village just north of La Seu, this old house is a nearly self-sufficient working farm that does everything the old-fashioned way. The Troguet family has six lovely rooms

with bath, and you might want to take half- or full-board to enjoy their wonderful home cooking (they use their own produce as much as possible). Part of the house is preserved as a museum of country life in the old days, and the Troguets encourage visitors to learn about how they do things, from gathering mushrooms to making preserves; it's an experience.

West of La Seu d'Urgell: The Vall de Noguera-Pallaresa

Centre d'Interpretació Turística del Pallars Sobirà
t 973 62 10 02; open summer Mon–Sat 9–8.30, Sun 10–1, Fri also 4–7; winter Mon–Sat 9–3,

From La Seu, the only way to get over to the next valley west, the Vall de Noguera-Pallaresa, is over the twisty but beautiful N260. This road leaves you in **Sort**, capital of Catalonia's biggest and emptiest *comarca*, the Pallars Sobirà. Sort means 'luck' in Catalan, and the town is famous as a place to buy lottery tickets. Sort's fortune hasn't left it a lot to offer visitors outside of a ruined castle, but the Centre d'Interpretació Turística del Pallars Sobirà is waiting there to give you a head start on understanding the life and culture of the valley and its sights.

South of Sort, the very picturesque village of **Gerri de la Sal** has the Romanesque monastery church of Santa Maria and something you've never seen before: **salt pans** that aren't on the seashore. A salty source fills them up, just as it has done for at least 1200 years.

North of Sort is **Rialp**, a growing tourist centre for mountain activities. From here a road to the left leads up to a cluster of villages in the **Vall de Llessui**. **Llessui**, at the top of the valley, has become something of a legend for its ski station, abandoned since 1987 along with its shops, lifts and hotel-restaurant. It's an eerie place to visit, and there are some reports of jaded thrill-seekers sneaking up in winter for some 'retro ski'. Llessuí now seeks to draw

Ecomuseu dels Pastors
open summer Tues–Sun 9–1 and 3.30–7

on its traditional life with the Ecomuseu dels Pastors, where you can learn everything about shepherding, ancient and modern. On the other side of the valley there's a ski station at **Port Ainé**.

The next village up the valley, **Llavorsí** attracts sporty tourists. At Llavorsí, the Noguera-Pallaresa valley and the **Vall de Cardós** split off. This is a beautiful, heavily forested 20km dead-end, though if you had a mule and a couple of days to spare you could make it over to France or Andorra on the old smugglers' trails. At **Esterri de Cardós** the church of **Sant Pau i Sant Pere** has a wonderful apse painting of *Christ Pantocrator* (a copy, but still worth seeing).

The Vall de Cardós road ends at **Tavascán**, where there's a little ski station, but this area is more popular with cross-country skiers, snowboarders and hikers. From here you can reach a number of mountain lakes, including the **Estany de Certescans**, the biggest in the Pyrenees. One of the most remarkable things about Tavascán is the **Complex Hidràulic del Alt Cardós**, an enormous hydro-electric plant built in caverns under the mountains, begun in 1958.

Complex Hidràulic del Alt Cardós
tours April–Aug; book at the tourist office
t 973 62 30 79

Vall d'Àneu and Vall d'Isil

The northernmost stretch of the Noguera-Pallaresa is called the **Vall d'Àneu**. This valley is almost as well-endowed with Romanesque art as the famous Vall de Boí, a tribute to the relative wealth and sophistication of these remote mountain villages at the dawning of the Middle Ages. Many of the churches are ruined or altered, and the medieval paintings survive only in fragments, but these monuments are often in lovely settings and worth a detour. North of Sort, beyond Llavorsí, there are two good ones above the C13 valley road. To the east, there's the church of Santa Maria at **Ribera de Cardós**; on the other side, at **Baiasca**, there's Sant Serni with a spectacular, if fragmentary, Christ Pantocrator painted in the apse.

Escaló, with its old stone houses and wooden balconies, is one of the most attractive villages in this part of the Pyrenees. The 12th-century Benedictine monastery of **Sant Pere de Burgal** is currently under restoration. To the north, the artificial lake at **Mollera d'Escalarre** has already become a favoured spot for cormorants and other waterfowl, as well as kayakers and fishermen.

Esterri d'Àneu is the valley's biggest village. Esterri, like many of the place names in these parts, is a Basque word, meaning 'stone wall'. Long before there was such a thing as Catalans, the Basques occupied almost all of the Pyrenees. Esterri has a 12th-century bridge, the Romanesque Santa Maria with a fascinating carved font inside, and the **Ecomuseu de les Valls d'Àneu**, dedicated to researching and explaining facets of traditional life in the Pyrenees. Its main sight is the **Casa Gassia**, an 18th-century farmhouse restored and furnished to something like its original appearance, but the Ecomuseu tries to be a kind of open-air museum that takes in other sites, offering tours of each. These include a Romanesque church and *comunidor* at **Son**, the monastery at **Escaló**, as well as a hydroelectric power station and a water-powered sawmill.

Ecomuseu de les Valls d'Àneu
t 973 62 64 36;
open summer daily 10–2 and 5–8; adm

One road from the Vall d'Àneu leads up to the Parc Nacional d'Aigüestortes; the paved part ends at **Espot**. Many people visit the park from the other side, in the Vall de Boí, but Espot too has an entrance, with an information centre, the **Casa del Parc Nacional**.

Casa del Parc Nacional
t 973 62 40 36; open daily 9–2 and 3.30–6

Up above the village there is a small, inexpensive ski station, **Super-Espot**. It's a popular place, attractive and forested, with 23 runs .

After Esterri, you have a choice of heading into the Vall d'Aran (*see* below), or straight north into the mountains, along the short but scenic **Vall d'Isil**. At the main village, **Isil**, the lovely church of **Sant Joan** turns its Romanesque apse on the bank of a rushing stream. Although it may only have about 50 inhabitants, Isil is famous throughout Catalonia for its summer solstice festival – the feast of Sant Joan – called *Les Falles*. Solstice bonfires were once common all over the Pyrenees; long discouraged by both church and state in Spain, they remain an annual event on the French side of the mountains, around the Catalan holy mountain Canigou. Here in Isil, in the old days the boys of the town would bring pine logs down from the mountains a month ahead, and be rewarded by the girls with a rose and a pitcher of wine for each.

The Vall d'Àneu and the paved road go only as far north as **Alós d'Isil**, surrounded by towering mountains up by the French border. It has another of those wonderful high-arched medieval bridges, and a church of **Sant Lliser** with some remarkable survivals from the original 12th-century building, a sculpted portal and three fonts inside.

Skiing West of La Seu d'Urgell

Sant Joan de l'Erm, t 973 29 80 15; *www.santjoandelerm.com*, 20km west of La Seu d'Urgell at Montferrer Castellbo, concentrates on cross-country (Nordic) skiing with some very pretty courses.

Port-Ainé, t 973 62 03 25, *www.port-aine.com*. Up in the hills above Rialp, a newer and increasingly popular area, with nine lifts and 44km of trails.

Tavascan, t 973 62 30 79, *www.tavascan.net*. Up at the northern end of the Vall de Cardós, this is a Nordic ski area with a new ski school and only one lift.

Super Espot, t 973 62 40 48, *www.espotesqui.net*. Near Aigüestortes National Park, offers 32 pistes (five black and 11 red), 14 lifts, and modest lodgings in the town of Espot; to book accommodation, *see* the website.

ⓘ **Sort >>**
Avda Comtes de Pallars, t 973 62 10 02

ⓘ **Tavascán >**
Ctra Vall de Cardós, t 973 62 22 17

Market Days West of La Seu d'Urgell

Sort, Tuesday; **Esterri d'Aneu**, Sunday.

Where to Stay and Eat West of La Seu d Urgell

Sort ✉ 25560

***Pessets II, C/Diputació, **t** 973 62 00 00, *www.hotelpessets.com* (€€). Modern and comfortable, with a pool, garden and tennis and a popular restaurant. *Closed Nov.*

Les Brases, Avda Generalitat 27, **t 973 62 10 71, *www.lesbrases.com* (€). A solid if somewhat austere establishment, with a restaurant (€€–€) serving grilled meats and fish, as well as pizzas.

Fogony, Avda Generalitat 45, **t** 973 62 12 25 (€€). One of the most interesting restaurants in this part of the mountains; try the lamb slow-cooked for a whole day (*espatlla de xai*).

Rialp ✉ 25594

***Condes del Pillars**, Avda Flora Cadena 2, **t** 973 62 03 50, *www.hoteldelpillars.com* (€€€–€€), Sprawling complex in a pretty setting with indoor and outdoor pools, gym, gardens and activities for children.

Escaló ✉ 25596

Castellarnau, Avda Burgal 1, **t** 973 62 20 63, *www.hotelcastellarnau.com* (€€). A gracious and comfortable modern hotel in this pretty village, with a shady garden and terrace by the river. Amenities include pool, golf practice pitch and green, gym and sauna, and a good restaurant too (€€).

Espot ✉ 25597

***Saurat**, C/Sant Martí, **t** 973 62 41 62, *www.hotelsaurat.com* (€€€–€€). The poshest of the village's hotels, with a popular restaurant.

***Hotel Roca Blanca**, C/Església s/n, **t** 973 62 41 56 (€€). A modern hotel, built of traditional stone and wood in classic mountain style, this is an excellent choice. The interior is elegant and stylish, with spacious and well-equipped rooms, and it offers all kinds of amenities including a Japanese-style area with outdoor Jacuzzi, plus a small sauna and gym. A host of activities is available, from skiing in winter to hiking or white-water rafting in summer. The staff are utterly delightful.

****Roya**, C/Sant Maurici 1, **t** 973 62 40 40 (€€–€). Modest, in a scenic location with a good, reasonable restaurant. *Closed Nov.*

*La Palmira, C/Marineta s/n, **t** 973 62 40 72 (€). The economy choice, with just seven small rooms.

****Or Blanc**, Ctra Barrader, **t** 973 62 40 13, www. *superespot2000.com* (€). The bizarre modern architecture may make you laugh, cry, or both, but this still offers quite a good bargain in a lovely setting. Basically a ski hotel, at the foot of the Super Espot lifts, but staff will point you towards rafting, riding and just about every other activity imaginable. There's a pool and gardens, and a decent restaurant. *Closed mid-Sept–Nov.*

Esterri d'Aneu ✉ 25580

*Els Puis, C/Dr. Morelló 13, **t** 973 62 61 60 (€). Six nice rooms with broadband connection, but the best part is a fine restaurant (€€) where you'll find dishes outside the usual Catalan mountain favourites.

****P Vall d'Aneu**, C/Major 46, **t** 973 62 60 97, *www.hostalvalldaneu.com* (€). An old building with some character, rooms with broadband, and a restaurant (€€) that serves grilled trout or pheasant or boar stew. They'll be happy to set you up for riding, rafting and other activities.

Sorpe ✉ 25587

Els Avets, Port de la Bonaigua, **t** 973 62 63 55, *www.elsavets.com* (€€€). A classy place, in splendid isolation up near the Port de la Bonaigua, the pass into the Vall d'Aran. Very comfortable rooms, a restaurant (€€–€€€), heated pool, all activities arranged, and a free shuttle to the ski station at Beret-Baqueira.

ⓘ Llavorsí
Ctra Vall de Cardós,
t 973 6222 17

ⓘ Esterri d'Aneu >>
C/Major 40
t 973 6263 45

ⓘ Espot >
Casa del Parc Nacional,
t 973 62 40 36

★ Hotel Roca Blanca >>

☆ Vall de Boí

The Vall de Boí

The **Alta Ribagorça** is one of the smallest and emptiest *comarcas* of Catalonia. Its main road isn't even in it; the N230 runs up the Noguera Ribagorçana Valley, the boundary between Catalonia and Aragon, and most of the time it's on the Aragonese side.

Most of this *comarca* is the **Vall de Boí**. Since it made UNESCO's World Heritage list two decades ago, this valley has become a popular spot; people from all over the world come to see the remote villages whose 12th-century Romanesque churches provided so many of the masterpieces in Barcelona's Museu

Practical Information for the Churches of the Vall de Boí

The **Centre del Romanic de la Vall de Boí** in Erill la Vall has an information office (*Camí del Batalló 5, Erill la Vall*, **t** *973 69 67 15, www.centreromanic.com*) which provides information on guided tours (currently held in Catalan and Spanish only), and sells admission tickets (which are also available directly from the churches). A single joint admission ticket pays for entrance to all the churches; those that are still in use as parish churches are free. **Opening hours** are as follows:

Sant Clement de Taüll, Sant Joan de Boí, Sant Eulàlia d'Erill, Sant Feliu de Barruera and the Nativitat de Durro: *open daily 10–2 and 4–7; around Easter and late June–late Sept until 10pm.*
Santa Maria de Taüll: *open year-round, daily 10–8.*
Santa Maria de Cardet: *open July–late Sept daily 10–8.*
L'Assumpció de Cóll: *open July–late Sept Wed 6–8pm.*
Sant Quirc de Durro: *open July–late Sept Thurs 6–8pm.*

Nacional d'Art de Catalunya (or MNAC). Recently the exteriors of these slate-roofed churches and their stout square campaniles with storeys of mullioned windows (a style imported from Lombardy) have been restored, with replicas of their frescoes, offering a chance to see what they were meant to look like *in situ*.

The gateway into the Vall de Boí, and the only place of any size in the Alta Ribagorça, is **Pont de Suert**, a laid-back, well-worn, attractive old town with houses over stone porticoes and a little park along the riverfront. The best thing about Pont de Suert is probably its parish church, the **Església de la Asunció**, built in 1955 in a kind of interplanetary Modernista style, with an egg-shaped baptistry, painted bright green, and an equally peculiar detached belltower. It's beautiful in its way. At least, the locals think so; in the shops you can buy a model of it inside a snow globe.

The church was built by the electric company ENHER, which had brought so many new people to town with its dam-building that the old one was no longer big enough. This church, called the **Esgésia Vell**, now holds a museum of art from other local churches, the Col·lecció d'Art Sacre de la Ribagorça, including some good medieval carvings and Baroque retables.

Col·lecció d'Art Sacre de la Ribagorça
to visit, call ahead:
t *973 69 00 05*

The turning for the Vall de Boí lies just north of Pont de Suert, at **Castello del Tor**, where a pretty medieval stone bridge helps sets the mood. The churches are opened for visitors by the **Centre del Romanic de la Vall de Boí**, which has an information office in **Erill la Vall** (*see* box, above).

Interestingly, there is no evidence that anyone ever lived in this valley before the Dark Ages, when Christians fled here to escape the Moorish invasions and settled down. Plenty of other Pyrenean valleys have Romanesque churches, but these are a bit special. The story goes that a Count of Erill was one of the leaders of a great raid against al-Andalus in the 11th century, and he used the booty he brought back from Córdoba to finance the churches. The isolation and obscurity of the valley in later centuries helped ensure they would survive.

The valley is lovely and green. The villages, built of the same dark granite as the churches, have a solemn dignity to them. The sites are scattered across the valley; but it would be easy to see all of them in a day. The only thing to slow you down would be herds of cattle on the road – the Vall de Boí has far more cows than people.

The first two churches are minor ones: **L'Assumpció**, just outside the village of **Cóll**, has a portal with carved capitals. **Santa Maria**, a few kilometres further on in **Cardet**, is much the same. Next, **Barruera**, which is the biggest village in the valley, has **Sant Feliu**, much tampered with over the centuries, with only two apses and aisles where once there were three. In all of these, you can see the basic elements of the Lombard style: the basilican form with rounded apses and a square belltower, blind arcading (those decorative arches around the cornices). The Lombard builders of northern Italy had established this style two centuries before the churches here were built, and their architects and masons spread it all over western Europe.

Up in the hills above Barruera, a short detour takes you to the first of the great Boí churches, all of which were built at about the same time, at the beginning of the 12th century. **La Nativitat**, in the village of **Durro**, has a portal with carved capitals and another Lombard trademark, a tall belltower with more blind arcading and pairs or triplets of narrow windows, often arranged so that the fenestration gets wider with each succeeding story. Unfortunately all the interior decoration was lost centuries ago. Just outside Durro is the small, plain hermitage of **Sant Quirc**.

Back in the valley, **Santa Eulàlia** in **Erill la Vall** has an even taller and more graceful campanile, as well as a side porch supported by arches. Inside, placed unusually on a beam under the arch above the altar, is a sculpted wood group of the *Descent from the Cross*, a copy of the original that was carted off to Barcelona.

The murals of the next church, **Sant Joan** in **Boí**, are in Barcelona too, but recently they have been replaced with a complete set of copies, spectacularly colourful and alive – just as the originals undoubtedly were when they were new. The main subject is the 'Revelations', though the artists used it as an excuse to throw in the whole medieval bestiary, including their best guesses as to what an elephant, a panther and a camel might look like. Another scene shows the stoning of St. Stephen, while the last, one the scholars can't really explain, portrays what appear to be entertainers juggling swords. By the portal, note the medieval sgraffito of a battle scene.

They've saved the best for last; the climax of this trip requires climbing up to the village of **Taüll**, in a beautiful setting high above the valley. Taüll is becoming a little resort, and it's gratifying to see how the new villas and apartments, built of the same stone, fit in with the medieval village. Not many places get these simple things right. Taüll has two churches, and the records say they were consecrated on two successive days in December 1123.

Santa Maria, the parish church, has lost all its paintings to Barcelona save only a scene of the Epiphany with Mary, Jesus and the three kings. On the edge of the village, **Sant Climent** is the largest and finest of the churches, with the loftiest and most elegant belltower of them all. Inside, the building is completely dominated by the *Christ in Majesty* on the apse, surrounded by the four Evangelists, a painting that has become the most famous image of Catalan medieval art. Nothing could capture the essential Romanesque better than this Christ, with his courtly yet otherworldly expression and nervously perfect folded draperies. As one critic put it, the Master of Taüll *'further stylized what was already stylized...he made the Byzantine model even more Byzantine'*. Underneath Jesus, next to the window, note the figure of the Virgin Mary; according to one recent book, that dish she's holding is the first artistic representation of the Holy Grail (*see* p.157).

Up above Taüll, the newish ski station called **Boí-Taüll** is the busiest place in the valley in winter. Back down in the valley, if you follow it to its northern end you'll be in the old thermal spa of **Caldes de Boí**, the end of the paved road and the western entrance to the Aigüestortes park.

Parc Nacional de Aigüestortes

For beautiful mountain settings without the tax-free merchandise, this stretch of the Pyrenees can offer nothing better than the **Parc Nacional de Aigüestortes i Estany de Sant Maurici**, created in 1955 and encompassing 230 square kilometres of forests, meadows, lakes and jagged snow-capped peaks, including the pristine **Sierra dels Encantats** ('the enchanted mountains') and Comoloformo, at 10,000ft the highest mountain in the park. As the name implies (*aigüestortes* means 'crooked streams') there is water everywhere; covering one sixth of the park's area.

Few places in the Pyrenees can match the jigsaw puzzle scenery of the **Lake of Sant Maurici,** completely encircled by trees and mountains. The environs have several well-marked trails of varying difficulty. Especially pretty and none too difficult is the hike from Espot to the refuge in the Encantats, with views over the lake.

Boí is the major gateway into the park from the western side, as **Espot** with its hotels is from the east; information booths at the entrances have information on trails, refuges (*book well in advance*) and half- and full-day excursions into the park with an experienced guide. Private vehicles aren't allowed beyond the car parks at the two entrances.

Tourist Information in the Vall de Boí

For information on the **National Park of Aigüestortes**, visit the Casal del Parque in Boí, t 973 69 61 89. As well as maps, suggestions for hikes, and information on the wide range of activities available, they also arrange the 4x4 trips to the start of the main walking trails (no cars are allowed within the park's limits). The main general tourist information office for the Vall de Boí is in **Barruera**, on the main road.

Skiing in the Vall de Boí

Boí-Taüll, t 902 40 66 40, *www.boitaullresort.com*. A small, pretty resort overlooking the Boí valley, with 41 runs (including eight black and 19 red) and a range of accommodation in all price categories. For info and to book accommodation, *see* website.

Market Days in the Vall de Boí

Pont de Suert, Friday.

Where to Stay and Eat in the Vall de Boí

Pont de Suert ✉ 25520

**Can Mestre, Plaça Major, t 973 69 03 06, *www.hotelmestre.com* (€€–€). Rooms with balconies covered with flowers, on a tiny, peaceful square.

Barruera ✉ 25527

**Hs Noray, on the main road, the L500, t 973 69 40 21 (€). Cheap and cheerful; simple rooms with breakfast.
La Llebreta, on the main road, the L500, t 973 69 40 42 (€€). No, *sopa de rossinyol* ain't nightingale soup (*rossinyols* are also wild mushrooms, rather like girolles). But it's very nice, and you'll find rabbit stuffed with pine nuts and other unusual dishes on the surprising menus here.

(i) Barruera >
Passeig Sant Feliu,
t 973 69 40 00

(i) Pont de Suert >
Avda Victoriano Munoz
22, t 973 69 06 40

(★) El Xalet de Taüll >>

Boí ✉ 25528

****Balneario Manantial, Caldes de Boí, t 973 69 62 10, *www.caldesdeboi.com* (€€€€–€€ *depending on season; check their website*). An imposing spa centre, with a dramatic location, pool and gardens and every imaginable treatment.

***Caldes, Caldes de Boí, t 973 69 62 20, *www.caldesdeboi.com* (€€€–€€). Huge, 17th-century stone hospital converted into a pleasant hotel with spacious rooms. Under joint management with the Manantial.

*Hs Pascual, Pont de Boí, t 973 69 60 14 (€). By the bridge below the village, this is the best budget option if you have a car. There's a warm welcome, and the restaurant serves decent food. *Open all year.*

*Beneria, Plaça Treio, t 973 69 60 30 (€). Fairly pleasant, with basic rooms and one of Boí's few restaurants, with simple but filling meals. *Open all year.*
La Cabana, Ctra de Taüll s/n, t 973 69 62 13 (€). Succulent grilled meats and local mountain dishes.

Taüll ✉ 25528

***Boí-Taüll Resort, Pla de l'Ermita s/n, t 973 69 60 00, *www.boitaullresort.es* (€€€–€€). Really an all-inclusive complex: seven hotels and apartment buildings, six restaurants in a variety of styles and prices. Plenty of sports facilites including a spa and a pool.

**El Xalet de Taüll, C/El Como 5, t 973 69 60 95, *www.elxaletdetaull.com* (€€€–€€). An attractive hotel of wood and stone, perfectly located in the heart of the old village. All rooms have beautiful views, but some look out towards the lofty belltowers of the celebrated churches.

**Hostal Rural Santa Maria, C/Cap del Riu, t 973 69 61 70, *www.taull.com* (€€€–€€). Much like the above; a modern place, but thoroughly lovely.

**La Coma, C/Únic s/n, t 973 69 61 47 (€). Attractive, welcoming little *pensió* at the entrance to the village with a good restaurant offering game and other regional specialities; it's very popular with locals.

The Vall d'Aran

North of the park and the Vall de Boí, the western and eastern Pyrenean massifs join in a rugged embrace, enfolding the verdant **Vall d'Aran**. Once almost inaccessible, it was first linked by road with the outside world in 1932. Today, it has become one of the most popular winter playgrounds of the Pyrenees.

A little twist in the Pyrenees guaranteed this valley a destiny apart. The chain runs in a die-straight line everywhere else, but here we have the 9,449ft **Pic de Mauberme** to the north, and the huge massif called **Maladeta** (11,181ft) to the south. The Vall d'Aran, caught in between, is the only place in Catalonia where the waters run down to the Atlantic. By nature it is orientated towards the north, to France. Many inhabitants still speak Aranés, a dialect not of Catalan or Spanish, but of Gascon (since 1990, Aranés has been an official language on a level with Catalan and Spanish).

Over the centuries, no country in Europe was more skilled than France at nibbling away bits of its neighbours' land. So it's a wonder that this bit got away. In fact, the Aranese cut a deal with the Kingdom of Aragon as far back as 1174 to preserve their liberties and keep the greedy king of France out. Thanks to its isolation, for most of its history the valley was in practice independent, like Andorra. Napoleon annexed it to France, but after his fall it became officially part of Spain once again.

Nowadays, thanks to that N230 road, and the new Vielha tunnel that connects it with Lleida, the valley is one of the main routes between France and Spain, and it has become a big winter resort. Some of the villages are nearly a mile high, and the temperature passes below zero centigrade half the days of the year.

Vielha

Vielha, the little village that turned into a town thanks to tourism, has made the transition as gracefully as could be expected. If it has a little more traffic and cute shops than is good for it, at least the development and architecture has been tasteful and fits in well with the tiny old village centre. which is only a few streets of distinctive Aran-style stone houses, with their stepped gables, dormers, slate roofs, and carved wooden balconies.

Vielha has been the principal village of the Mijaran ('mid-Aran'), and really of the valley as a whole, almost forever. Jaume the Conqueror stopped here on his campaigns and granted the Vall d'Aran its royal privileges. The town lies on a pretty little stream called the Garona, which eventually becomes the mighty Garonne that flows through Toulouse and Bordeaux.

The centre gathers under the shadow of the impressive Romanesque-Gothic church of **Sant Miquel** and its octagonal tower. The portal has a wonderful confusion of angels, saints musicians and warriors around its Gothic arches, and inside is a dashing 12th-century Christ de Mijaran that originally belonged to Vielha's other church, nearby **Santa Maria**, which was wrecked by retreating Republican soldiers in 1938. The **Musèu dera Val d'Aran**, in an 18th-century mansion at C/Major 26, has a collection that ranges from archaeological finds to medieval art from the valley's churches to exhibits on rural life.

Musèu dera Val d'Aran
t 973 64 18 15; open mid-June–mid-Sept Tues–Sat 10–1 and 5–8, Sun 10–1; mid-Sept–mid-June Tues–Fri 5–8, Sat 10–1 and 5–7, un 10–1; adm

From Vielha to France

North of Vielha, the N230 that leads to France runs right beside the Garona. Along the way, there are several good opportunities for jaunts up to some of the highest accessible parts of the Pyrenees, running through beautiful forests of fir and black pine. At **Arròs** a road will take you up towards **Pic de Mauberme**; the paved road runs out a few kilometres short of a pretty waterfall, the Sauth deth Pish. On foot, or even in a car, you can detour for some spectacular scenery in the opposite direction; south of the N230 at either **Aubert** or **Es Bordes**, a road leads high up the slopes of **Aneto**, the highest peak of the Maladeta massif, where there is another glacier-fed waterfall, called Uelhs deth Joèu.

At **Vilamós**, there is a branch of the **Muséu dera Val d'Aran**, the **Ecomuséu Çò de Joanchiquet**, which is a rustic house with gardens and outbuildings, furnished to show what life was like for the Aranese a century ago (and it looks to have been pretty cosy). The last villages along the road before France, **Les** and **Bossòst**, both have plenty of supermarkets for the French to stock up on booze, smokes and petrol before they get home. Bossòst's church of **Santa Maria** has a wonderful portal of Christ and the Evangelists that looks as if it was carved by a local boy who had never seen another church but decided to give it a go.

Ecomusèu Çò de Joanchiquet
open Tues–Sun 11–2; adm

East of Vielha

The Vall d'Aran has a good dozen Romanesque churches. None possess anything like the painting and lofty Lombard campaniles of the Vall de Boí, but many have interesting features, usually the sort of vigorous naive art seen on the portal at Bossòst. **Betrén's** church of **Sant Esteve** (or Sant Sernilh in Aranés) has a portal similar to that of Vielha's. In nearby **Escunhau**, Sant Peír has a portal as good as the one in Bossòst, with strange carved capitals.

Arties has two churches, **Sant Joan**, now used as a space for art exhibitions, and the plain **Nostra Senyora de Arties**. Arties is the second tourist centre after Vielha. The village once belonged to the

Templars, who left a ruined castle, and the village centre has some fine old buildings, one of which has become a *parador*.

Next comes the attractive village of **Salardú**, traditionally, the chief village of the upper Aran, and a key fortified place in the Middle Ages. The 13th-century church of **Sant Andreu** is covered with fanciful carvings on the capitals and modillons. Rare for a simple church in the mountains, the interior has almost a complete scheme of Renaissance frescoes; there is also a fine early Romanesque painted wood crucifix called the *Majestat de Salardú*. From here, it's a short hike to another church, **Santa Eulàlia** in the village of **Unha**, the only church in the valley to retain some vestiges of its medieval painting inside. Up above Salardú, little **Tredòs** has yet another church, with a set of Renaissance frescoes similar to those of Salardú.

There are some popular spots for walking in this area: north of Salardú and Unha you can go up through the isolated village of **Bagueregue**, and from there up to the nearly abandoned village of **Montgarri** or up to the slopes of **Pic de Mauberme**. Southwards, another paths lead up to **Bany Tredòs** or along the **Arriu de Ruda**; both lead to the mountain lakes in the Aigüestortes park.

This is almost the end of the valley; further east there's nothing but the lovely road over the pass, the **Port de la Bonaigua** to the Vall d'Aneu. But for most of the valley's tourists this is the most important part. Up above the valley road is the swanky ski station **Baqueira-Beret**, a favourite with the Spanish royal family.

Market Day in the Val d'Aran

Vielha, Thurs; **Bossòst**, Wednesday.

Skiing in the Val d'Aran

Baqueira-Beret, for info call **t** 973 63 90 10; to book accommodation call **t** 973 36 90 00, or in Barcelona, **t** 932 05 82 92, *www.baqueira.es*. A clutch of rather ugly ski apartments east of Vielha, one of Spain's most modern and complete installations. There are five hotels on the site, which can be booked through the website. It overlooks the Vall d'Aran and boasts 53 pistes (four black and 20 red), 33 lifts and 104 km of runs, two slalom courses, and a helicopter service to the peaks for new thrills. It's also the most expensive of the area's resorts

(€42 a day for adults, while most of the others are about €32).

Where to Stay and Eat in the Val d'Aran

The Vall d'Aran, as you might expect, has its own unique slant on mountain cooking, with a little touch of south-west France thrown in, in the form of foie gras and duck *magrets*. They're very proud of the local *charcuterie*, and there are some favourite dishes you'll find wherever you go: grilled trout, stewed boar and rabbit, and most notably *olla aranesa*, the valley's massive traditional stew with pork, chicken, sausage, beans and vegetables.

Vielha ✉ 25530

****Parador de Vall d'Arán**, Ctra de Túnel s/n, on N230 tunnel road, **t** 973 64 01 00, *www.parador.es* (€€€). The building, modern and eccentric with a panoramic circular sitting room, is prettily situated on a wooded slope; it has a pool and a good restaurant with Aranese specialities.

⭐ **Casa Irene >>**

***Fonfreda**, Pso Libertad 18, t 973 64 04 86, *www.hotelfonfreda.com* (€€). Central, family-run hotel with superb mountain views and welcoming staff.

Delavall, Eth Pas d'Arro 40, t 973 64 02 00 (€€). Near the centre of town: well priced for the good facilities which include a pool.

Casa Vicenta, C/Reiau 7, t 973 64 08 19 (€). Charming little *pensió*; rooms without bath are cheaper.

*Busquets**, C/Major 9, t 973 54 02 38 (€). Tiny four-room lodging house.

Era Mola, C/Marrec 4, t 973 64 24 19 (€€). Romantic, cosy little restaurant, serving highly praised Aranese specialities; try the delicious wild mushrooms in season. *Closed May–15 July and 25 Sept–Nov.*

Neguri, C/Pas d'Arro 14, t 973 64 02 11 (€€). Basque cooking with some good seafood, which is rare in these parts. Also a tapas bar.

ⓘ **Salardú >>**
C/Travessa de Balmes 2, t 973 64 51 97

ⓘ **Les >**
Avda Sant Jaume 39, t 973 64 73 03

Les ✉ 25540

*Talabart**, C/Banys 1, t 973 64 80 11, *www.hoteltalabart.com* (€€–€). Modest but amiable establishment that has been around forever, with a garden and a very good restaurant (€€) for Aranese trout, snails, stews and such. *Closed Nov.*

ⓘ **Bossòst**
C/Eduard Aunós, t 973 62 20 08

Escunhau ✉ 25539

***Casa Estampa**, C/Sortaus 9, t 973 64 00 48, *www.hotelcasaestampa.com* (€€€–€€). This has 18 comfortable rooms; the surprising amenities include an indoor pool, solarium, gym and a Jacuzzi with a view. It also boasts a good restaurant.

Casa Turnay, Plaça Major, t 973 64 02 92 (€€). In this village just east of Vielha, a long-established local favourite for *olla aranesa*. Save room for the excellent desserts.

⭐ **Garos Ostau >>**

ⓘ **Arties >**
C/dera Mola, t 699 96 90 44

Arties ✉ 25598

****Parador Don Gaspar de Portolá**, Ctra de Baqueira, t 973 64 08 01,

www.parador.es (€€€). In Arties (near Salardú): part modern, part in a restored 18th-century mansion inone of the more charming corners of the Vall d'Aran and close to the skiing at Baqueira-Beret. Garden, pool, gym and sauna.

***Casa Irene**, C/Major 3, t 973 64 43 64, *www.hotelcasairene.com* (€€€€–€€€). This has 22 beautifully furnished rooms in a park-like setting. Extremely pleasant and especially cosy in the winter, with its fireplaces and very fine restaurant, featuring *recherché* dishes such as duck with truffles, lobster and garlic *confit*, boar with chocolate sauce. The king of Spain drops in here from time to time when he's skiing in Baqueria-Beret.

Montarto, C/Baqueira 2, t 973 64 80 03 (€). A simple, honest budget choice in this upscale village. *Open all year.*

Sidrería Iñaki, C/Baqueira. Basque *pintxos* and cider on a terrace with a view.

Salardú ✉ 25598

***Banhs de Tredòs**, Tredòs, t 973 25 30 03, *www.banhsdetredos.com* (€€€) A classic small spa hotel, in a beautiful isolated setting up in the mountains above Salardú. Besides the hot sulphurous waters good for whatever ails you, there is a pool and a restaurant.

Mont Rumies, Plaça Major 1, t 973 64 58 20 (€€). Small and simple but welcoming hotel in the village centre.

Casa Rufus, Gessa, 2km west of Salardú, t 973 64 52 46 (€€). A friendly place with strictly Aranese cooking, often including venison and other game dishes, as well as *bacallà*.

Garòs ✉ 25539

Garòs Ostau, Carrer Cal 3, Garòs, t 973 64 23 78 (€€). An old stone house with a pretty courtyard has been converted into a charming little inn. It's located in a tiny village, just 5km from the glitzy slopes of Baqueira-Beret. Rustic, antique-furnished rooms, and a bright breakfast room offering spellbinding views A car is essential.

328

Andorra

It's a sleazy little paradise, Andorra. Take a slow ride down the single, eternally congested road that runs through the little principality. It's packed tight for nearly all of its length with boutiques, shopping centres, four-star hotels, nightclubs, billboards for Swiss watches and perfumes, and tyre shops.

Tyre shops? At last count Andorra gets over eleven million visitors a year, and over 90 per cent of them are day-trippers. Andorra is open for business, and its business is duty-free. Decades ago, the Andorrans decided that a good living from skiing and tourism and selling postage stamps wasn't good enough. They wanted more.

Only a third of the population is native Andorran. Like Dubai or Qatar, the natives long ago started importing 'guest workers', mostly French, Italian and Portuguese, to do all the dirty work for them. Today the natives' biggest fear, besides the diseases that come with high living, is that the emigrants will take over – or at least organize themselves. Until recently there were no trade unions here, and there's still no right to strike. The government's own website brags that 'legislation is adapted to companies' needs'. Women didn't get the right to vote here until 1970.

Today, the Andorrans have found a way to exploit every single possibility open to a grasping, sweaty-palmed pipsqueak principality. Duty-free was only the beginning. They also run tax havens, offshore investment, dodgy banking and car registration schemes. Give them a ring and they'll ship you a container-load of generic Viagra at a very attractive price.

The latest angle has been a speculative boom in Andorran real estate, stoked by overbuilding. They've turned their lovely corner of the Pyrenees into a single garish supermarket. It's a worthy competitor for Europe's other Ruritanian craphole, San Marino, which, if you've never been, is the first country in the world to be entirely paved over with factory outlet car parks.

History

The **Principat de les Valles de Andorra**, as it is officially known, is an independent historical oddity in the manner of Grand Fenwick and the Marx Brothers' Fredonia, a Catalan-speaking island of mountains measuring 468 square kilometres that has managed to steer clear of the French and Spanish since its foundation by Charlemagne. Its name is apparently a legacy of the Moors, derived from the Arabic *Al-gandûra* – 'the wanton woman' – although unfortunately the story behind the name has been forgotten.

Andorra has two 'co-princes', the president of France (as the heir of the Count of Foix) and the bishop of La Seu d'Urgell. According to an agreement spelled out in 1278, in odd-numbered years the

Getting to and around Andorra

By Air

There's a small airport near La Seu d'Urgell, 23km from Andorra la Vella, used mostly by ski charters. This is currently being expanded into an international airport, which may be ready for flights in 2010, *see* p.313.

By Train and Bus

Andorra la Vella is connected by regular **buses** to La Seu d'Urgell, and from there to Barcelona and Lleida. If you're coming from France, **SNCF trains** on the Toulouse–Perpignan–Barcelona line (*www.sncf.com*) get as close as L'Hospitalet, with bus connections the rest of the way. Other buses to Andorra depart from Toulouse and Ax-les-Thermes every morning. From Perpignan you can catch the Villefranche train, which links up with the narrow-gauge **Petit Train Jaune** ('little yellow train') which passes through some awesome mountain scenery on its way to La-Tour-de-Carol, where a Pujol Huguet bus meets it to go to Andorra, through the Port d'Envalira, at 7,895ft the highest pass in the Pyrenees range.

By Car

Unless you know the old smugglers' trails, coming from Spain is straightforward – there's only one way, the N145 from La Seu d'Urgell. The same is true for France, though a new tunnel allows you to bypass the endless hairpin turns of the old N20. The real problem can be border backups, for customs or whatever other reason they do it. These are unpredictable, and of indeterminate length.

Driving in Andorra is unpleasant. The roads are good and kept clear, but the traffic is terrible in the built-up areas and parking is often impossible. Out in the country all the beautiful narrow roads were designed for mountain goats.

Note that under the recent changes in legislation day-trippers will be OK with the customs man with 300 cigarettes or 75 cigars; 1.5 litres of hooch, 3.5 litres of drink under 22 degrees of alcohol and 5 litres of wine; other agricultural goods up to €300 and non-agricultural goods up to €900. That goes for France and Spain (and Britain too).

French co-prince is sent 1,920 francs in tribute, while in even-numbered years the Spanish co-prince receives 900 pesetas, 12 chickens, six hams and 12 cheeses. Napoleon thought it was quaint and left it alone, he said, as a living museum of feudalism.

The Andorrans were always most adamant about preserving their local privileges, which they maintained through the Consell de la Terra, founded in 1419, one of Europe's oldest continuous parliaments. They also claim to be the only people in the world who have avoided warfare for 800 years, though they do have an army, which enlists every able-bodied man in the country who owns a gun. They are all officers, every one, and if it pleases them they may show up whenever the Principat needs an honour guard.

The peace was threatened twice in the last century. First came an Andorra-style civil war in 1934, when a political faction got a White Russian count to proclaim himself King Boris I. Boris soon declared war on the bishop at La Seu – a war the bishop ended after two weeks by sending four Guardia Civils, who drove King Boris to Barcelona and put him on a boat. Then, in 1939, the Andorrans realized to their horror that, since no one had remembered to invite them to the peace conference at Versailles in 1918, they were still technically at war with Germany. A rapid treaty with Hitler soon sorted that out, and the Germans largely left them alone while they occupied France. Until the 1940s Andorra remained isolated from the world, relying on dairy farming, tobacco-growing, printing stamps for collectors, and more than a little smuggling. Then this peaceful Ruritania began to change after the war with a popular new sport called skiing.

And then came the great revelation: why bother smuggling when you can get the consumer to come to you? For many Andorrans, it was simply too much of a good thing. Their traditional society, already swamped by emigrants, all but disappeared under a wave of day-trippers, passing through to purchase duty-free petrol, electronics, booze and smokes, imported tax-free by Philip Morris and Reynolds, who ran the native tobacco-growers out of business. In 1993, Andorra even gave up feudalism and got a constitution – although the co-princes still get their cash and cheese.

In the summer and peak ski seasons, you'd rather be anywhere else than here. It's not especially charming the rest of the year either. As the home page of the national tourist website puts it: 'Welcome to the Land of Shopping'. There's a good side to it – breathtaking scenery, green meadows and azure lakes; minute hamlets clustered below Romanesque churches, with stone houses drying tobacco on their south walls – but it's becoming increasingly harder to find.

Andorra la Vella

Andorra la Vella ('Europe's Highest Capital') and the former villages of **Les Escaldes-Engordany** have melded into a vast, boiling cauldron of conspicuous consumption. Worth a visit, however, are the oldest parts of the capital, with the 12th-century Romanesque churches of **Sant Esteve** and **Sant Andrieu**. Andorra has a wealth of Romanesque churches, but they're hardly ever open.

Andorra's capital is the old stone Casa de les Valles, on Carrer de les Valles, the seat of the Counsell de la Terra since 1580. It's home to the famous Cabinet of the Seven Keys, containing Andorra's most precious documents and accessible only when representatives from each of the country's seven parishes are present. You can visit the main hall and the kitchen. The latter is where the parish meetings used to take place; the councillors would walk long distances in the cold to come here, and then would warm up by the stove and eat at the table, discussing parish business. There is also a dovecote, a fountain, ornamental gardens and a monument by Pujol.

One of the nicest things you can do in Andorra la Vella is look down on it. Two marked and landscaped paths, lit on summer nights, will take you up to the mountains above the city: the **Rec del Solà** on the sunny side of the valley, starting from C/Sant

Romanesque churches
open only before and after masses, and in July and August; to see them at other times, ring t 376 82 71 17

Casa de les Valles
Carrer de les Valles, t 376 82 91 29; open June–Oct Mon–Sat 9.30–1 and 3–7, Sun 10–2; Nov–May closed Sun; note that it is closed to visitors when sessions are under way

Skiing in Andorra

They say that skiing in Andorra began in 1924 with the postman of Soldeu, who had to travel over the pass to France every week to pick up the mail, and sent off for a pair of skis so he could do it in winter. Today Andorra is the biggest ski resort in the Pyrenees. With abundant snow from December to April, combined with clear, sunny skies, it is a skier's heaven.

The scene has changed a lot over the last few years. In the past, Andorra's low prices made it extremely popular, so much so that some of the resorts, notably Pas de la Casa, acquired the same reputation as certain Greek islands as they filled up with curry-and-chips parlours and all-male bars with the Premiership on big-screen TV. Lately, the ski-operators have been been putting big money into improving their facilities in an effort to move upmarket, and the six areas of the past have consolidated into two mega-resorts. For more information, see *www.skiandorra.ad*, and check the websites of the two ski stations listed below, which will tell you what special deals they have on at the moment in conjuction with local hotels.

High season, when everywhere is extra-busy, includes the following religious holidays (dates are approximate): 4–10 Dec, 23–7 Jan, 3 Feb–4 Mar, 12–16 April and weekends.

Grandvalira occupies the eastern valleys running through Encamp, Canillo, El Tarter, Soldeu and Pas de la Casa; *t 376 80 10 74, www.grandvalira.com*. You'll never be lonely; this is the biggest ski station in the Pyrenees, with 67 lifts that can carry 100,700 skiers an hour up to the 110 runs, covering 193km. Altogether, the complex covers a sizeable part of Andorra.

Vallnord occupies the area just north of Andorra la Vella, from La Massana to Pal Arinsal and Ordino-Arcalis; *t 376 73 70 17, www.vallnord.com*. It has 63km of slopes and 31 lifts of every sort. Among its three stations, Ordino-Arcalis, 17km from town, 4km from El Serrat, is perhaps the most dramatically beautiful and the best place to ski, with 27 runs and 14 lifts.

Note that Andorra's high altitude and even terrain make it especially good for ski trekking; overnight accommodation is available in refuges around its rim.

Ermengol, and the **Rec de l'Obac**, on the shady side, starting from Avda Tarragona.

Around Andorra

Just south of the capital you can see one of the best Romanesque churches, the 11th-century **Santa Coloma**, with a unique, round belltower and Visigothic arches, and some 12th-century frescoes inside. A winding road from **Escaldes** (or the *telecabina* from Encamp to the north) ascends to the isolated 11th-century chapel of **Sant Miquel d'Engolasters**. Its fine frescoes, now in Barcelona, have been replaced by copies, and its three-storey **campanile** totally dwarfs the church. Beyond the chapel lies a forest and the pretty **Estany d'Engolasters** ('lake swallow-stars') where, according to tradition, all the stars in the universe will one day fall. It's a good place for walking or fishing.

Sant Miquel d'Engolasters
call t 376 84 41 44 to arrange a visit

Exploring the hidden corners of old Andorra can be difficult if you don't have a car to zigzag up the narrow mountain roads. Buses ply the two main roads through Andorra every couple of hours towards **El Serrat**, and more frequently towards **Soldeu**. **La Cortinada**, en route to Soldeu, makes for a good tranquil base, with only a few hotels, excellent scenery, and some of Andorra's oldest houses. In a 1967 restoration of its parish church, **Sant Martí**, some of the Romanesque frescoes were uncovered.

On the way to La Cortinada from the capital, at **La Massana**, you can see what Andorra did for a living when it was still an honest country. Before the Industrial Revolution made small-scale projects unprofitable, Andorra in fact made iron, just as Catalans had been doing since the Middle Ages. The **Farga Rossell Centre d'Interpretació del Ferro** will show you how they did it, with an demonstration of the 19th-century forge machinery.

Also in La Massana, the **Centre d'Interpretació Andorra Romanica** has exhibits, art and architectural models to teach you everything about Andorra's Romanesque heritage.

El Serrat is more touristy but worth a visit in the summer for the gorgeous panorama of snow-clad peaks from the **Abarstar de Arcalís** (via the ski resort). Another branch of the road from El Serrat leads to the three stunning mountain lakes of **Tristaina** in Andorra's loveliest and least developed northwestern corner, also the site of its finest ski centre, **Ordino-Arcalís**. In Ordino town is the **Areny-Plandolit Museum**, the ancestral home of a long-line of local nobility, arranged over three floors; the oldest part of the building dates from 1613.

Another destination reached by bus (on the Soldeu road) is **Meritxell**, the holy shrine of Andorra. Here stands an old Romanesque church,nothing more than a shell since a devastating fire in 1972, and next to it a new sanctuary designed in 1976 by Barcelona's faded superstar architect Ricardo Bofill. The lovely 12th-century church of **Sant Joan de Caselles** is located on a hillside on the north edge of **Canillo**, its interior adorned with a Gothic retablo, a painted wooden ceiling, and Romanesque paintings; the tower has fine mullioned windows in the Lombard style.

Farga Rossell Centre d'Interpretació del Ferro
t 376 83 58 52; open Tues–Sat 9.30–7.30, Sun 10–2

Centre d'Interpretació Andorra Romanica
t 376 83 95 55; open June–Sept Tues–Sat 9.30–1.30, 3–6.30, Sun 10–2

Areny-Plandolit Museum
t 376 83 69 08; open Tues–Sat 9.30–1.30 and 3–6.30, Sun 10–2; adm

Telephones in Andorra

To ring an Andorran number from abroad (including Catalonia), dial 00, and then the prefix 376 and the number.

Where to Stay in Andorra

Andorra la Vella ✉ AD500

Andorra now has some 270 hotels, the vast majority of them spanking new. They can all be full much of the year. If you get stuck, try the Association of Hoteliers, *www.uha.ad*.

*****Plaza**, Maria Pla 19, **t** 376 87 94 44, *www.hotels. andorra.com* (€€€€€–€€€€) Ultra-contemporary, elegant and classy, if right in the centre of the hubbub. The **La Cucula restaurant** has a decent set menu (€€€), but it doesn't come cheap.

****Andorra Park**, C/de les Canals 24, **t** 376 87 77 77, *www.hotansa.com* (€€€€€–€€€€). A charming palace set in a park with a beautiful rock-cut pool, croquet lawn, driving range and tennis court. Its restaurant (€€€) is

★ Andorra Park »

ⓘ **Andorra la Vella** >
C/Dr Vilanova, **t** 376 82 02 14
Plaça de la Rotonda, **t** 376 82 71 17

one of the best in Andorra, with fresh pasta dishes and excellent Spanish and Chilean wines.

****Roc Blanc, Pla de Co-Príinceps 5, Escaldes, **t** 376 87 14 00, 902 93 04 00, *www.rocblanc.com* (€€€€, *but check their website for special deals*). In terms of glamour, this takes the cake, with a five-storey atrium lobby and a glass lift, sauna and a thermal spa with a number of treatment programmes. The hotel's two restaurants, **El Pi** and **El Entrecôt** (€€€), feature a very good selection of French, Spanish and Catalan dishes.

***Pyrenees, Avda Príncep Benlloch 20, **t** 376 87 98 79, *www.hotelpyrenees. com* (€€). A fine old establishment with some surprising amenities, including a rooftop pool and tennis.

***Pitiusa, C/d'Emprivat 4, **t** 376 86 18 16, *www.hotelpitiusa.ad* (€€–€). This is modern and quiet, a good bargain on the edge of town.

Valmar, Avda Meritxell 97, **t 376 82 16 67, *www.hotelvalmar.com* (€). Clean and simple.

Marfany, Avda Carlemany 99, Escaldes, **t 376 82 59 57 (€). Long-established and comfortable; the rooms have either baths or just showers.

*Hs Del Sol, Plaça Guillemó 3, **t** 376 82 37 01 (€). One of numerous cheaper alternatives outside the centre.

Eating Out in Andorra

Andorra La Vella

Molí dels Fanals, C/Dr Vilanova 9, **t** 376 82 13 81 (€€€). Best known for its Andorran mountain cuisine, such as onion soup, pig's trotters and mushroom dishes; in an old mill with a garden terrace.

La Bohême, Avda Meritxell 1, 3rd floor, **t** 376 88 00 01 (€€). The best restaurants in Andorra tend to be French; this serves fine fish and fowl dishes.

Versailles, Cap. del Carrer 1, **t** 376 82 13 31 (€€). Roast boar, apple pie and traditional French food.

Elsewhere in Andorra

La Borda de l'Avi, on the Arinsal road, La Massana, **t** 376 83 51 54 (€€€–€€). Andorran favourites roasted over a wood fire, as well as fresh fish, foie gras, duck or snails.

La Guingueta, on the Rabassa road, Sant Julià de Lòria, **t** 376 84 49 64 (€€€–€€). A rustic French restaurant offering dishes such as roast pigeon with foie gras and charcoal-grilled sea bass with cured ham.

Topic, on the main road in Ordino, **t** 376 73 61 02 (€€). Serves an astounding selection of 60 varieties of Belgian beer and a selection of fondues and pizza alongside a traditional menu.

Catalan Glossary

ajuntament city hall

azulejos (Spanish) painted glazed tiles used in Moorish and *mudéjar* work and later architecture. *Note: the Catalan word rajoles is also used, but is a more general term for tiles.*

banys baths

barri quarter, neighbourhood

cala cove

caldes hot springs

call the Jewish quarter of a town

camí path

ca, can house, like the French *chez*

cangost a canyon

carrer street

cartoixa 'charterhouse', a monastery of the Carthusian order

casino a social club for a town's wealthy elite

castrum Roman military camp, or a new town founded on the same grid plan.

cobla sardana band

col.legiata a 'collegiate' church, an important church that is not a cathedral, ruled by a college of canons

comarca one of the counties into which modern Catalonia is divided

communidor a small shrine of pagan origins to ward off storms, with a roof over four columns open to the four winds

conca a broad basin surrounded by mountains, as the Conca de Barbéra

Corts the Catalan parliament

cremallera rack-and-pinion railroad

església church

esgrafiat sgraffito work, designs etched in stucco on a building façade

espai space

estany lake

eixample extension, or the modern district of a town.

far lighthouse

Generalitat autonomous government of Catalonia

jardí garden

mas/masia a substantial farmhouse, usually of stone

Modernisme the Catalan manner of Art Nouveau, not to be confused with the 'Modernism' of 20th-century international architecture.

mudéjar (Spanish) Moorish-influenced architecture in Chistian Spain between the 12th and 16th centuries

nou new

oppidum a (usually) hilltop settlement or trading base of the Iberians or Celts

paeria in Lleida and other towns, the city government and the building it occupies.

palau a palace

pantà reservoir

parróquia a parish church

pla plain, flat area

platja beach

pou de glaç an ice well, a feature of many old Catalan towns

pujada slope, hill

Renaixença the 19th century Catalan cultural reawakening

rambla a boulevard with a broad central pedestrian strip, Catalonia's great contribution to urban design

rauxa exuberance, madness (the opposite of *seny, see* below)

retaule retable, carved or painted altarpiece

riu river

seny reason, prudence a special Catalan virtue, according to the Catalans

seu ('see' or 'seat' of a bishop) cathedral

suda or *zuda* the Moorish palace that was the seat of government, usually on a height above a town

trencadís pieces of broken tile used for decoration on Modernista buildings

vell old

xemeneia a factory chimney, smokestack

Language

The official languages of Catalonia are Catalan and Spanish (in the Vall d'Aran, Aranes also enjoys official status). Although virtually everyone speaks both Spanish and Catalan, most people prefer to express themselves in Catalan. This is also the language used in schools, universities, and by local government. Even a simple *bon dia* or *adéu* – will be enormously appreciated by locals.

For **food and drink** vocabulary, *see* pp.43–4.

Useful Words and Phrases

Greetings and Farewells

hello *hola*
Pleased to meet you *Molt de gust*
How are you? *Com estàs? (informal)*
Com està? (formal)
good morning *bon dia*
good afternoon *bona tarda*
good evening/night *bona nit*
goodbye *adéu*
see you later *fins després*
see you soon *fins aviat*

Common Expressions

please *si us plau*
thank you (very much) *(moltes) gràcies*
you're welcome *de res*
What is your name? *Com et dius?*
open *obert*
closed *tancat*
entrance *entrada*
exit *sortida*
Do you speak English? *Parla anglés?*
I don't understand *No ho entenc*
How do you say that in Catalan? *Com es diu això en català?*
where is...? *on és...?*
when? *quan?*
where? *on?*

yesterday *ahir*
today *avui*
tomorrow *demà*
How much is it? *Quant val? Quin preu té?*
I would like... *Vull...*
toilet *els serveis/el lavabo*
good *bo (bona)*
bad *dolent(a)*
big *gran*
small *petit(a)*
expensive *car(a)*
cheap *barat(a)*
more *més*
less *menys*
with *amb*
without *sense*

Getting Around

airport *aeroport*
train/metro station *estació de tren/metro*
bus stop *parada d'autobús*
a (return) ticket *un bitllet (d'anada i tornada)*
At what time...? *A quina hora...?*
How can I get to...? *Per anar a...?*
What time does it leave/arrive? *A quina hora surt (arriba)?*
left *esquerra*
right *dreta*
straight on *tot recte*
towards *cap a*
corner *cantonada*

Accommodation

Do you have a room? *Té alguna habitació?*
... for one person *...per a una persona*
....with 2 beds *...amb dos llits*
...with a double bed *... amb llit per a dues persones*
...with a shower/bath *... amb dutxa/bany*
...for one night/one week *... per una nit/una setmana*

Numbers

0 *zero*
1 *un, una*
2 *dos, dues*
3 *tres*
4 *quatre*
5 *cinc*
6 *sis*
7 *set*
8 *vuit*
9 *nou*
10 *deu*
20 *vint;*
30 *trenta*
40 *quaranta*
50 *cinquanta*
60 *seixanta*
70 *setanta*
80 *vuitanta*
90 *noranta*
100 *cent*
1000 *mil*

Days of the Week

Monday *dilluns*
Tuesday *dimarts*
Wednesday *dimecres*
Thursday *dijous*
Friday *divendres*
Saturday *dissabte*
Sunday *diumenge*

Months of the Year

January *gener*
February *febrer*
March *març*
April *abril*
May *maig*
June *juny*
July *juliol*
August *agost*
September *setembre*
October *octobre*
November *novembre*
December *desembre*

Further Reading

Adrià, Ferran, with Juli Soler and Albert Adrià, *A Day at El Bulli* (Phaidon 2008). Monumental, incredibly detailed tome that takes the reader through every moment.

Andrews, Colman, *Catalan Cuisine: Europe's Last Great Culinary Secret* (Grub Street, 1988). The classic that introduced Catalan cuisine to the English-speaking world; excellent recipes as well.

Burns, Jimmy, *Barça: A People's Passion*, (Bloomsbury, 2000). The history of FC Barcelona, and what it has meant to Catalonia for over a century.

Eaude, Michael, *Catalonia: A Cultural History* (Signal Books, 2007). A clear-eyed look at Catalonia and its dealings with the past.

Hughes, Robert, *Barcelona* (Harvill, 1992). Simply one of the best biographies of a city ever written.

Falcones, Ildefonso, *The Cathedral of the Sea* (Black Swan, 2009). Adventure yarn set in 14th-century Barcelona, describing the construction of Santa Maria del Mar. Enjoyable, if formulaic, with some interesting insights into life in the medieval city.

Lear, Amanda, *My Life with Dalí* (Beaufort Books, 1986). Fascinating insights into the life of Salvador and Gala; sadly currently out of print.

Macauley, Rose, *Fabled Shore: From the Pyrenees to Portugal* (Oxford University Press, 1987). Originally published in 1949, one of the books that lured visitors to Spain after the Civil War; lovely evocations of pre-mass-tourism Costa Brava.

Martorell, Joannot, *Tirant lo Blanc*, trans. by David Rosenthal (John Hopkins 1996). The medieval Catalan classic; Don Quixote's favourite book.

Montalbán, Manuel Vázquez, *An Olympic Death* (Serpent's Tail, 2008). One of the best in the brilliant, offbeat detective series featuring Montalbán's acerbic, food-obsessed detective Pepe Carvalho.

Payne, John, *Catalonia: Portrait of a Nation* (Century, 1991). A personal look at the country by a long-time resident.

Perucho, Joan, *Natural History* (Alfred Knopf, 1988). Charming novel set in 19th-century Catalonia, with vampires.

Puppo, Ronald (translator), *Selected Poems of Jacint Verdaguer: A Bilingual Edition* (University of Chicago Press, 2007).

Ruiz Zafón, Carlos *The Shadow of the Wind* (Phoenix, 2005). Best-selling novel set in Barcelona during the 20th century.

Terry, Arthur, *A Companion to Catalan Literature* (Tamesis Books, 2003). Weighty, academic tome, which nonetheless manages to offer a thoroughly absorbing overview of Catalan literature from the medieval period to the present.

Xavier Hernàndez, Francesc, *History of Catalonia* (Rafael Delmau, 2007). A good outline history, available in Catalan bookshops.

Index

Main page references are in **bold**. Page references to maps are in *italics*.

1st edition published 2010 by

CADOGAN GUIDES USA
An imprint of Interlink Publishing Group, Inc
46 Crosby Street, Northampton, Massachusetts 01060
www.interlinkbooks.com
www.cadoganguidesusa.com

Text copyright © Dana Facaros and Michael Pauls 2010
Copyright © New Holland Publishers (UK) Ltd, 2010

Cover and photo essay photographs: front cover © Picture Contact/Alamy; back cover © PCL Travel
Photo essay photographs: p.1, p.3 (top and bottom), p.6 (top), p.10 (left), p.12 (top), p.14 (top), p.15 (bottom)
all © iStockphoto; p.5 © 2009 Jupiterimages (UK) Ltd; p.12 (top) © Pep Roig/Amy; p. 14 (top) © StockShot/Alamy.
Maps © Cadogan Guides, drawn by Maidenhead Cartographic Services Ltd
Cover design: Jason Hopper
Photo essay design: Sarah Gardner
Editors: Suzanne Wales and Mary-Ann Gallagher
Proofreading: Edward Houston Morris
Indexing: Sally Davies

Printed in Italy by Legoprint
Library of Congress Cataloging-in-Publication Data available

ISBN: 978-1-56656-768-8

The author and publishers have made every effort to ensure the accuracy of the information in this book at the time of going to press. However, they cannot accept any responsibility for any loss, injury or inconvenience resulting from the use of information contained in this guide.

Please help us to keep this guide up to date. Although we have done our best to ensure that the information in this guide is correct at the time of going to press, laws and regulations are constantly changing and standards and prices fluctuate. We would be delighted to receive any comments concerning existing entries or omissions.

To request our complete full-color catalog, please call us toll free at 1-800-238-LINK, visit our website at www.interlinkbooks.com, or send us an e-mail: info@interlinkbooks.com

Catalonia touring atlas

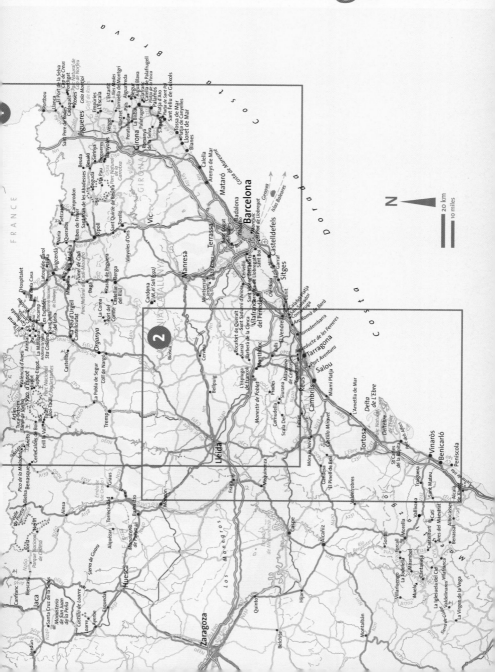

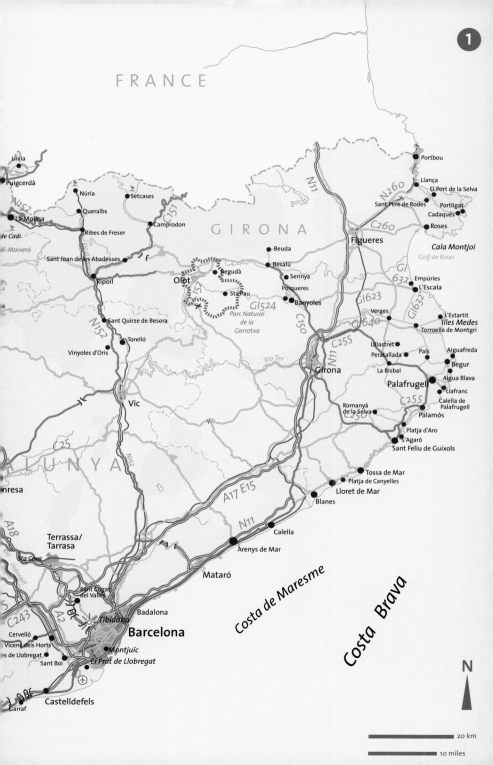

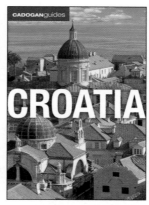

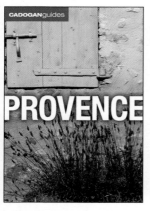

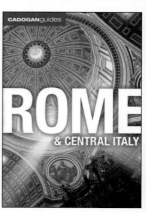

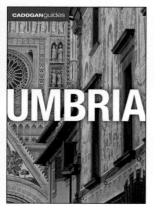

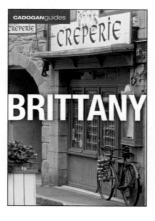

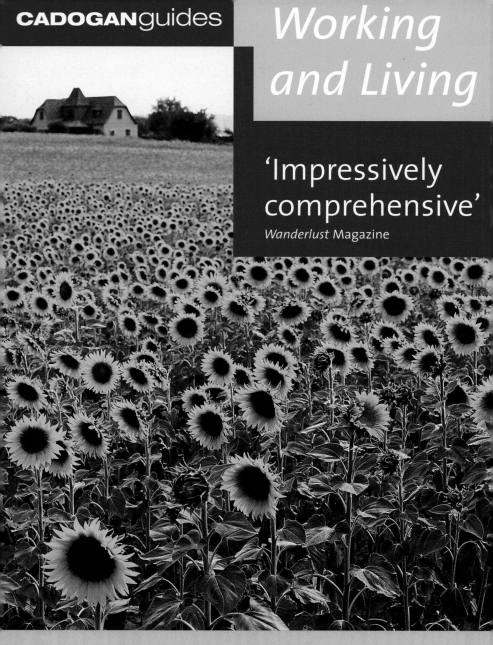

CADOGANguides

Working and Living

'Impressively
comprehensive'
Wanderlust Magazine

Working and Living Australia • *Working and Living* Canada • *Working and Living* France • *Working and Living* Italy • *Working and Living* New Zealand • *Working and Living* Spain • *Working and Living* USA

RENFE Catalonia medium-distance train map

Barcelona commuter train map

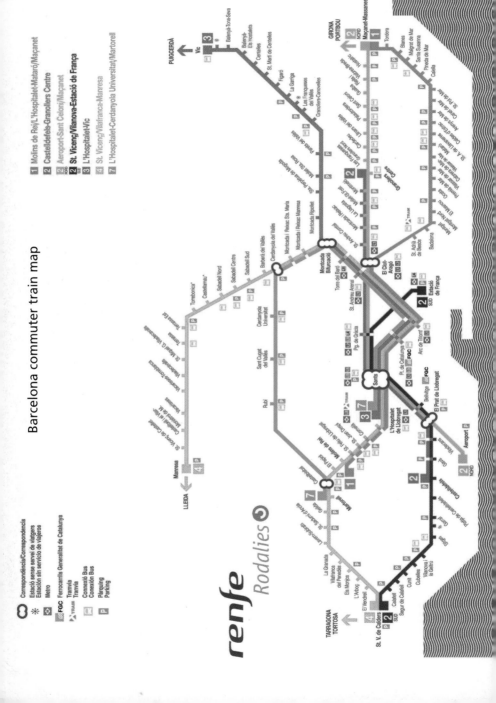